FREDERICK THE GREAT.

Frontispiece—Carlyle, Vol. Two.

THE WORKS

OF

THOMAS CARLYLE

(*COMPLETE*)

HISTORY

OF

FRIEDRICH THE SECOND

CALLED

FREDERICK THE GREAT

ILLUSTRATED

Volume Two

NEW YORK
PETER **F**ENELON **C**OLLIER, **P**UBLISHER
1897

LIST OF ILLUSTRATIONS.

VOLUME TWO.

CONTENTS

BOOK VII.—(*Continued.*)

FEARFUL SHIPWRECK OF THE DOUBLE-MARRIAGE PROJECT.

FEBRUARY–NOVEMBER, 1730.

BOOK VIII.

CROWN-PRINCE RETRIEVED: LIFE AT CUSTRIN.

NOVEMBER, 1730–FEBRUARY, 1732.

(iii)

CONTENTS.

BOOK IX.

LAST STAGE OF FRIEDRICH'S APPRENTICESHIP: LIFE IN RUPPIN. 1732–1736.

BOOK X.

AT REINSBERG, 1736–1740.

CONTENTS.

BOOK XI.

FRIEDRICH TAKES THE REINS IN HAND. 1740.

BOOK XII.

FIRST SILESIAN WAR, AWAKENING A GENERAL EUROPEAN ONE, BEGINS. 1740–1741.

FREDERICK THE GREAT.

BOOK VII.

(*CONTINUED.*)

FEARFUL SHIPWRECK OF THE DOUBLE-MARRIAGE PROJECT.

FEBRUARY–NOVEMBER, 1730.

CHAPTER III.

CAMP OF RADEWITZ.

THE Camp of Mühlberg, called more properly the Camp of Radewitz, towards which Friedrich Wilhelm, with English Hotham and many dignitaries are now gone, was one of the sublimest scenic military exhibitions in the history of the world; leaving all manner of imitation tournaments, modern "tin-tournaments," out of sight; and perhaps equalling the Field of the Cloth of Gold, or Barbarossa's Mainz Tournament in ancient times. It lasted for a month, regardless of expense, — June month of the year 1730; — and from far and wide the idle of mankind ran, by the thousand, to see it. Shall the thing be abolished utterly, — as perhaps were proper, had not our Crown-Prince been there, with eyes very open to it, and yet with thoughts very shut; — or shall some flying trace of the big Zero be given? Riddling or screening certain cart-loads of heavy old German printed rubbish,[2] to omit the Hotham

---

[2] Chiefly the terrible compilation called *Helden- Staats- und Lebens-Geschichte des, &c. Friedrichs des Andern* (History Heroical, Political and Biographical of Friedrich the Second), Frankfurt and Leipzig, 1758–1760, vol, i. first *half*, pp. 171–210. There are ten thick and thin half-volumes, and perhaps more. One of the most hideous imbroglios ever published under the name of Book, — without vestige of Index, and on paper that has no margin and cannot stand ink, — yet with many curious articles stuffed blindly into the awful belly of it, like jewels into a rag-sack, or into *ten* rag-sacks all in one; with far more authenticity than you could expect in such case. Let us call it, for brevity, *Helden-Geschichte*, in future references.

Despatches, we obtained the following shovelful of authentic
particulars, perhaps not quite insupportable to existing mankind.

The exact size of the Camp of Radewitz I nowhere find
measured; but to judge on the map,[1] it must have covered,
with its appendages, some ten or twelve square miles of ground.
All on the Elbe, right bank of the Elbe; Town of Mühlberg,
chief Town of the District, lying some ten miles northwest;
then, not much beyond it, Torgau; and then famed Wittenberg, all on the northwest, farther down the River: and on
the other side, Meissen with its Potteries not far to the southeast of you, up the River, on the Dresden hand. Nay perhaps
many of my readers have seen the place, and not known, in
their touring expeditions; which are now blinder than ever,
and done by steam, without even eyesight, not to say intelligence. Precisely where the railway from Leipzig to Dresden
crosses the Elbe, — there, if you happen to have daylight, is a
flat, rather clayey country, dirty-greenish, as if depastured
partly by geese; with a big full River Elbe sweeping through
it, banks barish for a mile or two; River itself swift, sleek
and of flint-color; not unpleasant to behold, thus far on its
journey from the Bohemian Giant-Mountains seaward : precisely there, when you have crossed the Bridge, is the south-
most corner of August the Strong's Encampment, — vanished
now like the last flock of geese that soiled and nibbled these
localities; — and, without knowing it, you are actually upon
memorable ground.

Actually, we may well say; apart from August and his fooleries. For here also it was, on the ground now under your
eye, that Kurfürst Johann Friedrich the Magnanimous, having
been surprised the day before at public worship in the above-
mentioned Town of Mühlberg, and completely beaten by Kaiser
Karl the Fifth and his Spaniards and Duke of Alba, did, on
Monday 25th April, 1547, ride forth as Prisoner to meet the
said Kaiser; and had the worst reception from him, poor man.
"Take pity on me, O God! This is what it is come to?"

[1] At p. 214.

the magnanimous beaten Kurfürst was heard murmuring as he
rode. At sight of the Kaiser, he dismounted, pulled off his iron-
plated gloves, knelt, and was for humbly taking the Kaiser's
hand, to kiss it. Kaiser would not; Kaiser looked thunderous tornado on him, with hands rigidly in the vertical direction.
The magnanimous Kurfürst arose therefore; doffed his hat:
" Great-mightiest (*grossmächtigster*) all-gracious Kaiser, I am
your Majesty's prisoner," said he, confining himself to the historical. "I *am* Kaiser now, then?" answered the sullen Tornado, with a black brow and hanging under-jaw. — "I request
my imprisonment may be prince-like," said the poor Prince.
"It shall be as your deserts have been!" — "I am in your
power; you will do your pleasure on me," answered the
other; — and was led away, to hard durance and peril of life
for five years to come; his Cousin Moritz having expertly
jockeyed his Electoral dignities and territories from him in
the interim; [1] — as was told above, long since.

Expert Cousin Moritz: in virtue of which same Moritz, or
rather perhaps in *vice* of him, August the Strong is even now
Elector of Saxony; Papist, Pseudo-Papist Apostate King of
Poland, and Non-plus-ultra of "gluttonous Royal Flunkies;"
doomed to do these fooleries on God's Earth for a time. For
the sins of the fathers are visited upon the children, — in ways
little dreamt of by the flunky judgment, — to the sixth generation and farther. Truly enough this is memorable ground,
little as King August thinks of it; little as the idle tourists
think, or the depasturing geese, who happen to be there.

The ten square miles have been industriously prepared for
many months past; shaved, swept by the best engineer
science: every village of it thoroughly cleaned, at least; the
villages all let lodgings at a Californian rate; in one village,
Moritz by name, [2] is the slaughter-house, killing oxen night
and day; and the bakehouse, with 160 mealy bakers who never
rest: in another village, Ströhme, is the playhouse of the
region; in another, Glaubitz, the post-office: nothing could

---

[1] De Wette, *Kurzgefasste Lebensgeschichte der Herzoge zu Sachsen* (Weimar,
1770), pp. 1, 33, 73.
[2] Map at page 214.

excel the arrangements; much superior, I should judge, to those for the Siege of Troy, and other world-great enterprises. Worthy really of admiration, had the business *not* been zero. Foreign Courts, European Diplomacy at large, wondered much what cunning scheme lay hidden here. No scheme at all, nor purpose on the part of poor August; only that of amusing himself, and astonishing the flunkies of Creation, — regardless of expense. Three temporary Bridges, three besides the regular ferry of the country, cross the Elbe; for the high officers, dames, damosels and lordships of degree, and thousandfold spectators, lodge on both sides of the Elbe: three Bridges, one of pontoons, one of wood-rafts, one of barrels; immensely long, made for the occasion. The whole Saxon Army, 30,000 horse and foot with their artillery, all in beautiful brand-new uniforms and equipments, lies beautifully encamped in tents and wooden huts, near by Zeithayn, its rear to the Elbe; this is the "*Armee Lager* (Camp of the Army)" in our old Rubbish Books. Northward of which, — with the Heath of Görisch still well beyond, and bluish to you, in the farther North, — rises, on favorable ground, a high "Pavilion" elaborately built, elaborately painted and gilded, with balcony stages round it; from which the whole ground, and everything done in it, is surveyable to spectators of rank.

Eastward again, or from the Pavilion southeastward, at the right flank of the Army, where again rises a kind of Height, hard by Radewitz, favorable for survey, — there, built of sublime silk tents, or solid well-painted carpentry, the general color of which is bright green, with gilt knobs and gilt gratings all about, is the "*Haupt-Lager*," Head-quarters, Main *Lager*, Heart of all the *Lagers*; where his Prussian Majesty, and his Polish ditto, with their respective suites, are lodged. Kinglike wholly, in extensive green palaces ready gilt and furnished; such drawing-rooms, such bedrooms, "with floors of dyed wicker-work;" the gilt mirrors, pictures, musical clocks; not even the fine bathing-tubs for his Prussian Majesty have been forgotten. Never did man or flunky see the like. Such immense successful apparatus, without and within; no end of military valetaille, chiefly "janizaries," in Turk

costume ; improvised flower-gardens even, and walks of yellow
sand, — the whole Hill of Radewitz made into a flower-garden
in that way.   Nay, in the Army *Lager* too, many of the
Captains have made little improvised flower-gardens in that
Camp of theirs, up and down.   For other Captains not of a
poetical turn, there are billiards, coffee-houses, and plenty of
excellent beer and other liquor.   But the mountains of cavalry
hay, that stand guarded by patrols in the rearward places, and
the granaries of cavalry oats, are not to be told.   Eastward,
from their open porticos and precincts, with imitation " janizaries " pacing silent lower down, the Two Majesties oversee
the Army, at discretion ; can survey all things, — even while
dining, which they do daily, like very kings ! Fritz is lodged
there ; has a magnificent bed : poor young fellow, he alone
now makes the business of any meaning to us.   He is curious
enough to see the phenomena, military and other ; but oppressed with black care : " My Amelia is not here, and the
tyrant Father is — tyrannous with his rattan : ye gods ! "

  We could insist much on the notable people that were
there ; for the Lists of them are given.   Many high Lordships ; some of whom will meet us again.   Weissenfels,
Wilhelmina's unfavored lover, how busy is he, commanding
gallantly (in the terrific Sham-Battle) against Wackerbarth ;
General Wackerbarth, whose house we saw burnt on a Dresden
visit, not so long ago.   Old Leopold of Anhalt-Dessau is there,
the Old Dessauer ; with four of his Princes ; instructed in
soldiering, left without other instruction ; without even writing, unless they can pick it up for themselves.   Likely young
fellows too, with a good stroke of work in them, of battle in
them, when called for.   Young Anspach, lately wedded, comes,
in what state he can, poor youth ; lodges with the Prussian
Majesty his Father-in-law ; should keep rather quiet, his
share of wisdom being small.   Seckendorf with his Grumkow,
they also are here, in the train of Friedrich Wilhelm.   Grumkow shoves the bottle with their Polish and Prussian Majesties : in jolly hours, things go very high there.   I observe
they call King August *" le Patron,"* the Captain, or " Patroon ; " a fine jollity dwelling in that Man of Sin.   Or does

the reader notice Holstein-Beck, Prussian Major-General ; Prince of Holstein-Beck; a solid dull man; capable of liquor, among other things : not wiser than he should be ; sold all his Apanage or Princeship, for example, and bought plate with it, wherefore they call him ever since "Holstein-*Vais-selle* (Holstein *Plate*)" instead of Holstein-Beck.[1] His next Brother, here likewise I should think, being Major-General in the Saxon service, is still more foolish. He, poor soul, is just about to marry the Orzelska ; incomparable Princess known to us, who had been her Father's mistress : — marriage, as was natural, went asunder again (1733) after a couple of years. — But mark especially that middle-aged heavy gentleman, Prince of Anhalt-Zerbst, Prussian Commandant of Stettin. Not over rich (would not even be rich if he came to be reigning Duke, as he will do) ; attentive at his post in those parts, ever since the Siege-of-Stralsund time; has done his orders, fortified Stettin to perfection ; solid, heavy taciturn man : — of whom there is nothing notable but this only, That last year his Wife brought him a little Daughter, Catharine the name of her. His Wife is a foolish restless dame, highborn and penniless; let her nurse well this little Catharine : little Catharine will become abundantly distinguished in a thirty years hence; Empress of all the Russias, that little girl ; the Fates have so appointed it, mocking the prophecies of men ! Here too is our poor unmentionable Duke of Mecklenburg : poor soul, he has left his quarrels with the Ritterschaft for a week or two, and is here breathing the air of the Elbe Heaths. His wild Russian Wife, wild Peter's niece and more, we are relieved to know is dead ; for her ways and Peter's have been very strange ! To this unmentionable Duke of Mecklenburg she has left one Daughter, a Princess Elizabeth-Catherine, who will be called Princess *Anne*, one day : whose fortunes in the world may turn out to be tragical. Potential heiress of all the Russias, that little Elizabeth or Anne. Heiress by her wily aunt, Anne of Courland, — Anne with the swollen cheek, whom Moritz, capable of many things, and of being *Maréchal de Saxe* by and by, could not manage to fall in love with

---

[1] Büsching's *Beiträge*, iv. 109.

there; and who has now just quitted Courland, and become Czarina: [1]— if Aunt Anne with the big cheek should die childless, as is likely, this little Niece were Heiress. *Was thut's,* What matter! —

In the train of King August are likewise splendors of a sort, if we had time for them. Dukes of Sachsen-Gotha, Dukes of Meiningen, most of the Dukes that put Sachsen to their name; — Sachsen-Weimar for one; who is Grandfather of Goethe's Friend, if not otherwise distinguished. The Lubomirskis, Czartoryskis, and others of Polish breed, shall be considered as foreign to us, and go unnoticed. Nor are high Dames wanting, as we see: vast flights of airy bright-hued womankind, Crown-Princess at the head of them, who lodges in Tiefenau with her Crown-Prince, — and though plain-looking, and not of the sweetest temper, is a very high Lady indeed. Niece of the present Kaiser Karl, Daughter of the late Kaiser, Joseph of blessed memory; — for which reason August never yet will sign the Pragmatic Sanction, his Crown-Prince having hereby rights of his own in opposition thereto. She is young; to her is Tiefenau, northward, on the edge of the Görisch Heath, probably the choicest mansion in these circuits, given up: also she is Lady of "the Bucentaur," frigate equal to Cleopatra's galley in a manner; and commands, so to speak, by land and water. Supreme Lady, she, of this sublime world-foolery regardless of expense: so has the gallantry of August ordered it. Our Friedrich and she will meet again, on occasions not like this! — What the other Princesses and Countesses, present on this occasion, were to Crown-Prince Friedrich, except a general flower-bed of human nature, — ask not; nor even whether the Orzelska was so much as here! The Orzelska will be married, some two months hence,[2] to a Holstein-Beck; not to Holstein *Plate,* but to his Brother the unfortunate Saxon Major-General: a man surely not of nice tastes in regard to marriage; — and I would recommend him to keep his light Wife at home on such occasions. They parted, as

[1] Peter II., her Cousin-german, died January, 1730 (Mannstein's *Russia*).
[2] 10th August, 1730 (Sir T. Robinson: Despatch from Dresden; in State Paper Office).

we said, in a year or two, mutually indignant; and the Orzelska went to Avignon, to Venice and else-whither, and settled into Catholic devotion in cheap countries of agreeable
climate.[1]

Crown-Prince Friedrich, doubtless, looking at this flower-bed
of human nature, and the reward of happy daring paid by
Beauty, has vivid images of Princess Amelia and her Vice-
regency of Hanover; bright Princess and Vice-regency, divided
from him by bottomless gulfs, which need such a swim as that
of Leander across the material Hellespont was but a trifle
to! — In which of the villages Hotham and Dickens lodged,
I did not learn or inquire; nor are their copious Despatches,
chronicling these sublime phenomena from day to day for
behoof of St. James's, other than entirely inane to us at this
time. But one thing we do learn from them: Our Crown-
Prince, escaping the paternal vigilance, was secretly in consultation with Dickens, or with Hotham through Dickens;
and this in the most tragic humor on his side. In such efful-
gences of luxury and scenic grandeur, how sad an attendant
is Black Care, — nay foul misusage, not to be borne by human
nature! Accurate Professor Ranke has read somewhere, —
does not comfortably say where, nor comfortably give the
least date, — this passage, or what authorizes him to write
it. "In that Pleasure-Camp of Mühlberg, where the eyes of
so many strangers were directed to him, the Crown-Prince was
treated like a disobedient boy, and one time even with strokes
(*körperlich misshandelt*), to make him feel he was only considered as such. The enraged King, who never weighed the consequences of his words, added mockery to his manual outrage.
He said, 'Had I been treated so by my Father, I would have
blown my brains out: but this fellow has no honor, he takes
all that comes!'"[2] *Einmal körperlich misshandelt*: why did
not the Professor give us time, occasion, circumstances, and
name of some eye-witness? For the fact, which stands reported in the like fashion in all manner of Histories, we shall
otherwise find to be abundantly certain; and it produced con-

[1] See Pöllnitz (*Memoirs*, &c.), whoever is curious about her.
[2] Ranke, *Neun Bücher Preussischer Geschichte* (Berlin, 1847), i. 297.

spicuous definite results. It is, as it were, the one fact still
worth human remembrance in this expensive Radewitz and
its fooleries; and is itself left in that vague inert state, —
irremediable at present.

Beaten like a slave; while lodged, while figuring about, like
a royal highness, in this sumptuous manner! It appears
clearly the poor Prince did hereupon, in spite of his word
given to Wilhelmina, make up his mind to run. Ingenious
Ranke, forgetting again to date, knows from the Archives,
that Friedrich went shortly afterwards to call on Graf von
Hoym, one day. Speaking to Graf von Hoym, who is Saxon
First-Minister, and Factotum of the arrangements here, he
took occasion cursorily to ask, Could not a glimpse of Leipzig,
among all these fine things, be had? Order for horses to or
at Leipzig, for "a couple of officers" (Lieutenant Keith and
self), — quietly, without fuss of passes and the like, Herr
Graf? — The Herr Graf glances into it with eyes which have
a twinkle in them: *Schwerlich*, Royal Highness. They are
very strict about passes. Do not try it, Royal Highness![1]
And Friedrich did desist, in that direction, poor youth; but
tried it the more in others. Very busy, in deep secrecy, corresponding with Lieutenant Katte at Berlin, consulting tragically with Captain Guy Dickens here. — Whether any hint or
whisper came to the Prussian Majesty from Graf von Hoym?
Lieutenant Keith was, shortly after, sent to Wesel to mind
his soldiering there, far down the Rhine Country in the Garrison of Wesel;[2] better there than colleaguing with a Fritz,
and suggesting to him idle truancies or worse.

With Katte at Berlin the desperate Prince has concocted
another scheme of Flight, this Hoym one being impossible;
scheme executable by Katte and him, were this Radewitz once
over. And as for his consultations with Guy Dickens, the
result of them is: Captain Dickens, on the 16th of June, with

[1] Ranke, ib.; Förster, i. 365, and more especially iii. 4 (Seckendorf's Narrative there).

[2] Wilhelmina told us lately (suprà, p. 149), Keith *had* been sent to Wesel;
but she has misdated as usual.

eyes brisk enough, and lips well shut, sets out from Radewitz express for London.   This is what I read as abstract of *Hotham's Despatch*, 16th June, 1730, which Dickens is to deliver with all caution at St. James's: "Crown-Prince has communicated to Dickens his plan of escape; 'could no longer bear the outrages of his Father.' Is to attend his Father to Anspach shortly (*Journey to the Reich*, of which we shall hear anon), and they are to take a turn to Stuttgard: which latter is not very far from Strasburg on the French side of the Rhine.   To Strasburg he will make his escape; stay six weeks or a couple of months (that his Mother be not suspected); and will then proceed to England.   Hopes England will take such measures as to save his Sister from ruin." These are his fixed resolutions: what will England do in such abstruse case? — Captain Dickens speeds silently with his Despatch; will find Lord Harrington, not Townshend any more;[1] will copiously open his lips to Harrington on matters Prussian.   A brisk military man, in the prime of his years; who might do as Prussian Envoy himself, if nothing great were going on?   Harrington's final response will take some deliberating.

Hotham, meanwhile, resumes his report, as we too must do, of the Scenic Exhibitions; — and, we can well fancy, is getting weary of it; wishing to be home rather, "as his business here seems ended."[2]   One day he mentions a rumor (inane high rumors being prevalent in such a place); "rumor circulated here, to which I do not give the slightest credit, that the Prince-Royal of Prussia is to have one of the Archduchesses," perhaps Maria Theresa herself! Which might indeed have saved immensities of trouble to the whole world, as well as to the Pair in question, and have made a very different History for Germany and the rest of us.   Fancy it! But for many reasons, change of religion, had there been no other, it was an impossible notion.   "May be," thinks Hotham, "that the Court of Vienna throws out this bait to continue the

[1] Resigned 15th May, 1730: Despatch to Hotham, as farewell, of that date.

[2] Preceding Despatch (of 16th June).

King's delusion," — or a snuffle from Seckendorf, without the
Court, may have given it currency in so inane an element as
Radewitz.

Of the terrific Sham-Battles, conducted by Weissenfels on
one side and Wackerbarth on the other; of the charges of
cavalry, play of artillery, threatening to end in a very doomsday, round the Pavilion and the Ladies and the Royalties
assembled on the balconies there (who always go to dinner
safe, when victory has declared itself), I shall say nothing. Nor of that supreme " attack on the intrenchments : "
blowing-up of the very Bridges ; cavalry posted in the woods ;
host doing its very uttermost against host, with unheard-of
expenditure of gunpowder and learned manœuvre ; in which
" the Fleet " (of shallops on the Elbe, rigged mostly in silk)
took part, and the Bucentaur with all its cannon. Words fail
on such occasions. I will mention only that assiduous King
August had arranged everything like the King of Playhouse-
Managers ; was seen, early in the morning, " driving his own
curricle " all about, in vigilant supervision and inspection ;
crossed the Tub-bridge, or perhaps the Float-bridge (not yet
blown up), " in a *Wurstwagen ;* " giving himself (what proved
well founded) the assurance of success for this great day ; —
and finally that, on the morrow, there occurred an illumination and display of fire-works, the like of which is probably
still a desideratum.

For the Bucentaur and Fleet were all hung with colored
lamplets ; Head-quarters (*Haupt-Lager*) and Army-*Lager* ditto
ditto ; gleaming upwards with their golden light into the
silver of the Summer Twilight : — and all this is still nothing
to the scene there is across the Elbe, on our southeast corner.
You behold that Palace of the Genii ; wings, turrets, main-
body, battlements : it is " a gigantic wooden frame, on which
two hundred carpenters have been busy for above six months,"
ever since Christmas last. Two hundred carpenters ; and how
many painters I cannot say : but they have smeared " six thousand yards of linen canvas ; " which is now nailed up ; hung
with lamps, begirt with fire-works, no end of rocket-serpents,
catherine-wheels ; with cannon and field-music, near and far,

to correspond; — and is now (evening of the 24th June, 1730) shining to men and gods. Pinnacles, turrets, tablatures, tipt

with various fires and emblems, all is there: symbolic Painting, six hundred yards of it, glowing with inner light, and legible to the very owls! Arms now piled useless; Pax, with her Appurtenances; Mars resting (in that canvas) on trophies of laurel honorably won: and there is an Inscription, done in lamplets, every letter taller than a man, were you close upon

it, " *Sic fulta manebit* (Thus supported it will stand)," — the *it* being either *Pax* (Peace) or *Domus* (the Genii-Palace itself), as your weak judgment may lead you to interpret delicate allusions. Every letter bigger than a man: it may be read almost at Wittenberg, I should think; flaming as *pica* written on the sky, from the steeple-tops there. *Thus supported it will stand;* and pious mortals murmur, "Hope so, I am sure!" — And the cannons fire, almost without ceasing; and the field-music, guided by telegraphs, bursts over all the scene, at due moments; and the catherine-wheels fly hissing; and the Bucentaur and silk Brigantines glide about like living flambeaus; — and in fact you must fancy such a sight. King August, tired to the bone, and seeing all successful, retired about midnight. Friedrich Wilhelm stood till the finale; Saxon Crown-Prince and he, "in a window of the highest house in Promnitz;" our young Fritz and the Margraf of Anspach, they also, in a neighboring window,[1] stood till the finale: two in the morning, when the very Sun was not far from rising.

Or is not the ultimate closing day perhaps still notabler; a day of universal eating? Debauchee King August had a

[1] 24th–25th June: *Helden-Geschichte* (above spoken of), i. 200

touch of genuine human good-humor in him; poor devil, and
had the best of stomachs. Eighty oxen, fat as Christmas,
were slain and roasted, subsidiary viands I do not count; that
all the world might have one good dinner. The soldiers,
divided into proper sections, had cut trenches, raised flat
mounds, laid planks; and so, by trenching and planking, had
made at once table and seat, wood well secured on turf. At
the end of every table rose a triglyph, two strong wooden
posts with lintel; on the lintel stood spiked the ox's head, ox's
hide hanging beneath it as drapery: and on the two sides of
the two posts hung free the four roasted quarters of said ox;
from which the common man joyfully helped himself. Three
measures of beer he had, and two of wine; — which, unless
the measures were miraculously small, we may take to be
abundance. Thus they, in two long rows, 30,000 of them by
the tale, dine joyfully *sub dio*. The two Majesties and two
Crown-Princes rode through the ranks, as dinner went on:
"King of Prussia forever!" and caps into the air; — at length
they retire to their own *Haupt-quartier*, where, themselves
dining, they can still see the soldiers dine, or at least drink
their three measures and two. Dine, yea dine abundantly:
let all mortals have one good dinner! —

Royal dinner is not yet done when a new miracle appears on
the field: the largest Cake ever baked by the Sons of Adam.
Drawn into the Head-quarter about an hour ago, on a wooden
frame with tent over it, by a team of eight horses; tent cur-
taining it, guarded by Cadets; now the tent is struck and off;
— saw mortals ever the like? It is fourteen ells (*kleine
Ellen*) long, by six broad; and at the centre half an ell thick.
Baked by machinery; how otherwise could peel or roller act
on such a Cake? There are five thousand eggs in it; thirty-
six bushels (Berlin measure) of sound flour; one tun of milk,
one tun of yeast, one ditto of butter; crackers, gingerbread-
nuts, for fillet or trimming, run all round. Plainly the Prince
of Cakes! A Carpenter with gigantic knife, handle of it resting on his shoulder, — Head of the Board of Works, giving
word of command,— enters the Cake by incision; cuts it up
by plan, by successive signal from the Board of Works.

What high person would not keep for himself, to say nothing
of eating, some fraction of such a Nonpareil ?   There is cut
and come again for all.   Carpenter advances, by main trench
and by side trenches, steadily to word of command.

I mention, as another trait of the poor devil of an August,
full of good-humor after all, That he and his Royalties and big
Lordships having dined, he gave the still groaning table with
all its dishes, to be scrambled for by "the janizaries." Janizaries, Imitation-Turk valetaille ; who speedily made clearance,
— many a bit of precious Meissen porcelain going far down in
society by that means.

Royal dinner done, the Colonel and Officers of every regiment, ranked in high order, with weapons drawn, preceded by
their respective bands of music, came marching up the Hill to
pay their particular respects to the Majesty of Prussia.   Majesty of Prussia promised them his favor, everlasting, as requested; drank a glass of wine to each party (steady, your
Majesty !), who all responded by glasses of wine, and threw
the glasses aloft with shouts.   Sixty pieces of artillery speaking the while, and the bands of music breathing their sweetest;
— till it was done, and his Majesty still steady on his feet.
He could stand a great deal of wine.

And now — ?   Well, the Cake is not done, many cubic
yards of cake are still left, and the very corporals can do no
more : let the Army scramble !   Army whipt it away in no
time.   And now, alas now — the time *is* come for parting.
It is ended; all things end.   Not for about an hour could
the *Herrschaften* (Lordships and minor Sovereignties) fairly
tear themselves away, under wailing music, and with the due
emotion.

The Prussian Royalties, and select few, took boat down the
River, on the morrow; towards Lichtenburg Hunting-Palace,
for one day's slaughtering of game.   They slaughtered there
about one thousand living creatures, all driven into heaps for
them, — "six hundred of red game" (of the stag species),
"four hundred black," or of the boar ditto.   They left all
these creatures dead; dined immensely ; then did go, sorrowfully sated; Crown-Prince Friedrich in his own carriage in the

rear; Papa in his, preceding by a few minutes; all the wood horns, or French horns, wailing sad adieu;— and hurried towards Berlin through the ambrosial night.[1]

And so it is all ended. And August the Strong — what shall we say of August? History must admit that he attains the maximum in several things. Maximum of physical strength; can break horse-shoes, nay half-crowns with finger and thumb. Maximum of sumptuosity; really a polite creature; no man of his means so regardless of expense. Maximum of Bastards, three hundred and fifty-four of them; probably no mortal ever exceeded that quantity. Lastly, he has baked the biggest Bannock on record; Cake with 5,000 eggs in it, and a tun of butter. These things History must concede to him. Poor devil, he was full of good-humor too, and had the best of stomachs. His amputated great-toe does not mend: out upon it, the world itself is all so amputated, and not like mending! August the Strong, dilapidated at fifty-three, is fast verging towards a less expensive country: and in three years hence will be lodged gratis, and need no cook or flunky of either sex.

"This Camp of Radewitz," says Smelfungus, one of my Antecessors, finishing his long narrative of it, "this Camp is Nothing; and after all this expense of King August's and mine, it flies away like a dream. But alas, were the Congresses of Cambrai and Soissons, was the life-long diplomacy of Kaiser Karl, or the History of torpid moribund Europe in those days, much of a Something? The Pragmatic Sanction, with all its protocolling, has fled, like the temporary Playhouse of King August erected there in the village of Ströhme. Much talk, noise and imaginary interest about both; but both literally have become zero, *were* always zero. As well talk about the one as the other." — Then why not *silence* about both, my Friend Smelfungus? He answers: "That truly is the thing to be aimed at;— and if we *had* once got our own out of both, let both be consumed with fire, and remain a handful of inarticulate black ashes forevermore." Heavens, will I, of all men, object!

[1] 28th June, 1730: *Helden-Geschichte*, i. 205.

Smelfungus says elsewhere : —

" The moral to be derived, perhaps the chief moral visible
at present, from all this Section of melancholy History is:
Modern Diplomacy is nothing; mind well your own affairs,
leave those of your neighbors well alone.   The Pragmatic
Sanction, breaking Fritz's, Friedrich Wilhelm's, Sophie's, Wilhelmina's, English Amelia's and I know not how many private
hearts, and distracting with vain terrors and hopes the general
soul of Europe for five-and-twenty years, fell at once into dust
and vapor, and went wholly towards limbo on the storm-winds,
doing nothing for or against any mortal.   Friedrich Wilhelm's
80,000 well-drilled troops remained very actual with their fire-
locks and iron ramrods, and did a thing or two, there being
a Captain over them.   Friedrich Wilhelm's Directorium, well-
drilled Prussian Downing Street, every man steady at his duty,
and no wind to be wasted where silence was better, did likewise very authentically remain, — and still remains.   Nothing
of genuine and human that Friedrich Wilhelm did but remained and remains an inheritance, not the smallest item of
it lost or losable ; — and the rude foolish Boor-King (singular
enough !) is found to be the only one that has gained by the
game." —

CHAPTER IV.

EXCELLENCY HOTHAM QUITS BERLIN IN HASTE.

WHILE the Camp at Radewitz is dissolving itself in this
manner, in the last days of June, Captain Guy Dickens, the
oracles at Windsor having given him their response as to
Prince Friedrich's wild project, is getting under way for Berlin
again, — whither also Hotham has returned, to wait for Dickens's arrival, and directly thereupon come home.   Dickens is
henceforth to do the British Diplomacy here, any Diplomacy
there can well be ; Dickens once installed, Hotham will, right
gladly, wash his hands of this Negotiation, which he considers

to be as good as dead for a longish while past. First, however, he has one unexpected adventure to go through in Berlin; of most unexpected celebrity in the world: this once succinctly set forth, History will dismiss him to the shades of private life.

Guy Dickens, arriving we can guess about the 8th or 9th of July, brings two important Documents with him to Berlin. *First*, the English Response (in the shape of "Instructions" to himself, which may be ostensible in the proper quarter) in regard to the Crown-Prince's project of flight into England. Response which is no other than might have been expected in the circumstances: "Britannic Majesty sorry extremely for the Crown-Prince's situation; ready to do anything in reason to alleviate it. Better wait, however: Prussian Majesty will surely perhaps relent a little: then also the affairs of Europe are in a ticklish state. Better wait. As to that of taking temporary refuge in France, Britannic Majesty thinks that will require a mature deliberation (*mûre délibération*). Not even time now for inquiry of the French Court how they would take it; which his Britannic Majesty thinks an indispensable preliminary," — and so terminates. The meaning, we perceive, is in sum: "Hm, you won't, surely? Don't; at least Don't yet!" But Dryasdust, and any readers who have patience, can here take the Original Paper; which is written in French (or French of Stratford at the Bow), probably that the Crown-Prince, if needful, might himself read it, one of these days: —

"Monsieur Guy Dickens pourrait donner au Prince les assurances les plus fortes de la compassion que le Roi a du triste état où il se trouve, et du désir sincère de Sa Majesté de concourir par tout ce qui dépendra d'elle à l'en tirer. M. Guy Dickens pourrait lui communiquer en même tems les Instructions données à Monsieur Hotham [*our Answer to the Outrageous propositions, which amounts to nothing, and may be spared the reader*], et lui marquer qu'on avait lieu d'espérer que Sa Majesté Prussienne ne refuserait pas au moins de s'expliquer un peu plus en détail qu'elle n'a fait jusqu'ici. Qu'en attendant les suites que cette négociation pourrait avoir, Sa Majesté était d'avis que le Prince ferait bien de différer un peu l'exécution de son dessein connu : Que la situation où les affaires de l'Europe se trouvaient dans ce moment critique ne paraissait pas propre à l'exécution d'un dessein de cette nature : Que pour ce qui est de l'intention où le Prince a témoigné être, de se retirer en France, Sa Majesté croit qu'elle demande une mûre délibération, et que le peu de tems qui reste ne promet pas même qu'on puisse s'informer de ce que la Cour de France pourrait penser là-dessus ; dont Sa Majesté trouvait cependant absolument nécessaire de l'assurer, avant de pouvoir conseiller à un Prince qui lui est si cher de se retirer en ce pays là." [1]

This is Document *First ;* of no concernment to Hotham at this stage ; but only to us and our Crown-Prince. Document *Second* would at one time have much interested Hotham : it is no other than a Grumkow Original seized at St. Mary Axe, such as Hotham once solicited, "strong enough to break Grumkow's back." Hotham now scarcely hopes it will be "strong enough." No matter ; he presents it as bidden. On introducing Dickens as successor, Monday, 10th July, he puts the Document into his Prussian Majesty's hand : and — the result was most unexpected ! Here is Hotham's Despatch to Lord Harrington ; which it will be our briefest method to give, with some minimum of needful explanation intercalated here and there : —

" *To the Lord Harrington* (from Sir Charles Hotham).

"Berlin, 30th June (11th July), 1730.

" My Lord, — Though the conduct of his Prussian Majesty has been such, for some time past, that one ought to be surprised at nothing he does, — it is nevertheless with great concern that I now have to acquaint your Lordship with an extravagancy of his which happened yesterday," Monday, 10th July, 1730.

" The King of Prussia had appointed me to be with him

[1] Prussian Despatches, vol. xli. : No date or signature ; bound up along with Harrington's Despatch, " Windsor, 20th June [1st July] 1730," — on the morrow of which day we may fancy Captain Dickens took the road for Berlin again, — where we auspiciously see him on Monday, 10th July, probably a night or two after his arrival.

about noon, with Captain Guy Dickens [who has just returned
from England, on what secret message your Lordship knows !].
— We both attended his Prussian Majesty, and I presented
Captain Guy Dickens to him, who delivered his credentials :
after which the King talked to us a quarter of an hour about
indifferent matters. Seeing him in a very good humor, I took
that opportunity of telling him, ' That as General Grumkow
had denied his having held a Secret Correspondence with
Reichenbach, or having written the Letters I had some time
ago delivered to his Majesty, I was now ordered by the King
my Master to put into his hands an Original Letter of General
Grumkow ' " —

— Where is that Original Letter ? ask some minute readers.
Minute readers, the *ipsissimum corpus* of it is lost to mankind.
Official Copy of it lies safe here in the State-Paper Office
(Prussian Despatches, volume xli. ; without date of its own,
but *near* a Despatch dated 20th June, 1730) ; has, adjoined to
it, an Autograph jotting by George Second to the effect, "Yes,
send it," and also some preliminary scribbles by Newcastle, to
the like purport. No date of its own, we say, though, by internal evidence and light of *Fassmann*,[1] it is conclusively datable "Berlin, 20th May," if anybody cared to date it. The
Letter mentions lightly that "pretended discovery [the St.-
Mary-Axe one, laid on the table of Tobacco-Parliament, 6th
May or soon after], innocent trifles all *I* wrote ; hope you
burnt them, nevertheless, according to promise : yours to me I
did burn as they came, and will defy the Devil to produce ; "
brags of his Majesty's fine spirits ; — and is, Jotting and all,
as insignificant a Letter as any other portion of the "Rookery
Colloquy," though its fate was a little more distinguished.
Prussian Dryasdust is expected to give it in *Fac-simile*, one
day, — surely no British Under-Secretary will exercise an
unwise discretion, and forbid him that small pleasure ! —

"which was an undeniable proof of all the rest, and could not
but convince his Prussian Majesty of the truth of them." —
Well ?

[1] p. 404

"He took the Letter from me, cast his eye upon it; and seeing it to be Grumkow's hand, said to me with all the anger imaginable [fancy the thunder-burst!], '*Messieurs, j'ai eu assez de ces choses là;*' threw the Letter upon the ground, and immediately turning his back went out of the room, and shut the door upon us,"

— probably with a slam! And that is the naked truth concerning this celebrated Intercepted Letter. Majesty answered explosively, — his poor heart being in a burdened and grieved condition, not unlike growing a haunted one, — "I have had enough of that stuff before!" pitched the new specimen away, and stormily whirled out with a slam of the door. That he stamped with his foot, is guessable. That he "lifted his foot as if to kick the Honorable English Excellency,"[1] which the English Excellency never could have stood, but must have died on the spot, — of this, though several Books have copied it from Wilhelmina, there is no vestige of evidence: and the case is bad enough without this.

"Your Lordship will easily imagine that Captain Guy Dickens and I were not a little astonished at this most extraordinary behavior. I took up the Letter he had thrown upon the floor [*ipsissimum corpus* of it lost to mankind, last seen going into Hotham's pocket in this manner]; and returning home, immediately wrote one to his Prussian Majesty, of which a copy is here enclosed." — Let us read that essential Piece: sound substance, in very stiff indifferent French of Stratford, — which may as well be made English at once : —

"*To his Majesty the King of Prussia.*"

"SIRE, — It is with the liveliest grief that I find myself under the necessity, — after what has passed to-day at the audience I had of your Majesty, where I neither did nor said anything in regard to that Letter of Monsieur Grumkow's or to putting it into your Majesty's hands, that was not by my

[1] Wilhelmina, i. 228.

Master's order, — it is, I say, Sire, with the liveliest grief
that I am obliged to inform your Majesty of the necessity
there lies on me to despatch a Courier to London to apprise
the King my Master of an incident so surprising as the one
that has just happened. For which reason I beg (*supplie*)
your Majesty will be pleased to cause the necessary Orders
for Post-horses to be furnished me, not only for the said Courier, but also for myself, — since, after what has just happened,
it is not proper for me to prolong my stay here (*faire un plus
long séjour ici*).

"I have the honor to be, your Majesty's, &c. &c. &c.

"CHARLES HOTHAM."

"About two hours afterwards, General Borck came to me;
and told me He was in the utmost affliction for what had happened; and beseeched me to have a little patience, and that
he hoped means would be found to make up the matter
to me. Afterwards he communicated to me, by word of
mouth, the Answer the King of Prussia had given to the
last Orders I had received by Captain Guy Dickens," —
Orders, "Come home immediately," to which the "Answer"
is conceivable.

"I told him that, after the treatment I had received at
noon, and the affront put upon the King my Master's character, I could no longer receive nor charge myself with anything
that came from his Prussian Majesty. That as to what related to me personally, it was very easily made up; but having
done nothing but in obedience to the King my Master's orders,
it belonged to him only to judge what satisfaction was due for
the indignity offered to his character. Wherefore I did not
look upon myself as authorized to listen to any expedients till
I knew his Majesty's pleasure upon the matter.

"In the evening, General Borck wrote a Letter to Captain
Guy Dickens and two to me, the Copies of which are enclosed,"
— fear not, reader! "The purport of them was to desire That
I would take no farther notice of what had happened, and
that the King of Prussia desired I would come and dine with
him next day." — Engaged otherwise, your Majesty, next day!

"The Answer to these Letters I also enclose to your Lord-ship," — reader not to be troubled with it. "I excused myself from dining with the King of Prussia, not thinking myself at liberty to appear any more at Court till I received his Majes-ty's," my own King's, "commands, and told General Borck that I looked upon myself as indispensably obliged to acquaint the King my Master with everything that had passed, it being to no purpose to think of concealing it, since the thing was already become public, and would soon be known in all the Courts of Europe.

"This, my Lord, is the true state of this unaccountable accident. You will see, by General Borck's Letter, that the King of Prussia, being now returned to his senses, is him-self convinced of the extravagancy of this proceeding; and was very desirous of having it concealed; — which was impos-sible; for the whole Town knew it an hour after it had hap-pened.

"As to my own part, I am not a little concerned at this unfortunate incident. As it was impossible to foresee this fit of madness in the King of Prussia, there was no guarding against it : and after it had happened, I thought I could do no less than resent it in the manner I have done, — without pros-tituting the character with which the King has been pleased to honor me. I hope, however, this affair will be attended with no ill consequences : for the King of Prussia himself is at present so ashamed of his behavior, that he says, He will order Count Degenfeld [Graf von Degenfeld, going at a leisurely pace to remove *Nosti* from his perch among you] [1] to hasten his journey to England, with orders to endeavor to make up the affair immediately.

"As I had already received the King's Orders, by Captain Guy Dickens, To return home forthwith, I thought, after what had happened, the sooner I left this place the better; and the rather because it might be proper I should make a report of it to his Majesty. I shall therefore set out a few hours after this Messenger; and will make all the expedition possible.

[1] Suprà, p. 197.

"The King of Prussia sets out for Anspach on Saturday next," — 11th July is Tuesday, Saturday next will be 15th July, which proves correct.[1] "I am, with the utmost respect, My Lord, Your Lordship's most obedient and most humble servant, CHARLES HOTHAM." [2]

No sooner was the door slammed to than his Majesty began to repent. At sight of the demand for Post-horses, he repented bitterly; sent Borck to ask Hotham to dinner, with what success we have seen. Sent Borck to negotiate, to correspond, to consult with Dickens, to do his utmost in pacifying Hotham. All which Correspondence exists, but is not worth giving. Borck's remonstrances are in rugged soldier-like style, full of earnestness and friendliness. Do not wreck, upon trifles, a noble interest we have in common; King is jealous about foreign interference with his Ministers, but meant nothing; I tell you it is nothing! — Hotham is polite, good-tempered; but remains inflexible: With myself, on my own score, it were soon settled, or is already settled; but with the King my Master, — no expedient but post-horses! The Diplomatist world of Berlin is in a fuss; Queen Sophie and "the Minister of Denmark," with other friendly Ministers, how busy! "All day," this day and the next, "they spent in comings and goings"[3] advising Hotham to relent: Hotham could not relent. The Crown-Prince himself writes, urged by a message from his Mother; Crown-Prince sends Katte off from Potsdam with this Billet[4] (if this be a correct copy to translate from)

To His Excellency Monsieur the Chevalier Hotham.

"POTSDAM, 11th July, 1730.

"MONSIEUR, — Having learned by M. de Leuvener," the Danish Minister, a judicious well-affected man, "what the King my Father's ultimate intentions are, I cannot doubt but

[1] Fassmann, p. 410.
[2] State-Paper Office : Prussian Despatches, vol. xli.
[3] Wilhelmina, i. 229, 230.   [4] Ib. i. 230.

you will yield to his desires.   Think, Monsieur, that my happiness and my Sister's depend on the resolution you shall take, and that your answer will mean the union or the disunion forever of the two Houses! I flatter myself that it will be favorable, and that you will yield to my entreaties. I never shall forget such a service, but recognize it all my life by the most perfect esteem," with which I now am, *Tout à vous,*   " FRÉDÉRIC."

This Billet Katte delivers: but to this also Hotham remains inexorable; polite, hopeful even: No harm will come; Degenfeld will go, I myself will help when at home; but for the present, no resource but post-horses! Which they at last yield him, the very post-horses ready to weep.

And so Hotham, spirited judicious English gentleman, rolls off homewards,[1] a few hours after his Courier, — and retires honorably into the shades of private life, steady there thenceforth. He has not been successful in Berlin: surely his Negotiation is now *out* in all manner of senses! Long ago (to use our former ignoble figure) he had "laid down the bellows, though there was still smoke traceable:" but now, by this Grumkow Letter, he has, as it were, struck the *poker* through the business; and that dangerous manœuvre, not proving successful, has been fatal and final! Queen Sophie and certain others may still flatter themselves; but it is evident the Negotiation is at last complete. What may lie in flight to England and rash desperate measures, which Queen Sophie trembles to think of, we do not know: but by regular negotiation this thing can never be.

It is darkly apprehended the Crown-Prince still meditates Flight; the maternal heart and Wilhelmina's are grieved to see Lieutenant Katte so much in his confidence — could wish him a wiser councillor in such predicaments and emergencies! Katte is greatly flattered by the Prince's confidence; even brags of it in society, with his foolish loose tongue. Poor youth, he is of dissolute ways; has plenty of "unwise intel-

[1] "Wednesday," 12th (Dickens).

lect," little of the "wise" kind; and is still under the years of discretion. Towards Wilhelmina there is traceable in him something, — something as of almost loving a bright particular star, or of thrice-privately worshipping it for his own behoof. And Wilhelmina, during the late Radewitz time, when Mamma "gave four Apartments (or Royal Soirées) weekly," was severe upon him, and inaccessible in these Court Soirées. A rash young fool; carries a loose tongue : — still worse, has a Miniature, recognizable as Wilhelmina; and would not give it up, either for the Queen's Majesty or me ! — " Thousand and thousand pardons, High Ladies both; my loose tongue shall be locked : but these two Miniatures, the Prince and Princess Royal, I copied them from two the Prince had lent me and has got back, ask me not for these ; — never, oh, I cannot ever ! " — Upon which Wilhelmina had to take a high attitude, and pass him speechless in the Soirées. The foolish fellow : — and yet one is not heartily angry either; only reserved in the Soirées ; and anxious about one's Brother in such hands.

Friedrich Wilhelm repents much that Hotham explosion; is heard saying that he will not again treat in person with any Envoy from foreign parts, being of too hot temper, but will leave his Ministers to do it.[1] To Queen Sophie he says coldly, " Wilhelmina's marriage, then, is off; an end to *it*. Abbess of Herford [good Protestant refuge for unprovided Females of Quality, which is in our gift], let her be Abbess there ; " — and writes to the then extant Abbess to make Wilhelmina "Coadjutress," or Heir-Apparent to that Chief-Nunship ! Nay what is still more mortifying, my Brother says, "On the whole, I had better, had not I ? " The cruel Brother; but indeed the desperate ! — for things are mounting to a pitch in this Household.

Queen Sophie's thoughts, — they are not yet of surrender ; that they will never be, while a breath of life is left to Queen Sophie and her Project : we may fancy Queen Sophie's mood. Nor can his Majesty be in a sweet temper; his vexations lately have been many. First, England is now off, not off-

---

[1] Dickens's Despatch, Berlin, 22d July (N.S.), 1730.

and-on as formerly : that comfortable possibility, hanging
always in one's thoughts, is fairly gone ; and now we have
nothing but the Kaiser to depend on for Jülich and Berg, and
the other elements of our salvation in this world! Then the
St.-Mary-Axe discoveries, harassing shadows of suspicion that
will rise from them, and the unseemly Hotham catastrophe
and one's own blame in it; Womankind and Household still
virtually rebellious, and all things going awry ; Majesty is in
the worst humor; — bullies and outrages his poor Crown-
Prince almost worse than ever.   There have been rattan-
showers, hideous to think of, descending this very week [1] on
the fine head, and far into the high heart of a Royal Young
Man ; who cannot, in the name of manhood, endure, and must
not, in the name of sonhood, resist, and vainly calls to all the
gods to teach him *what* he shall do in this intolerable inextricable state of matters.

Fate and these two Black-Artists have driven Friedrich
Wilhelm nearly mad ; and he, in turn, is driving everybody so.
He more than suspects Friedrich of an intention to fly ; which
is horrible to Friedrich Wilhelm : and yet he bullies him occasionally, as a spiritless wretch, for bearing such treatment.
" Cannot you renounce the Heir-Apparentship, then; your
little Brother is a fine youth.   Give it up ; and go, unmolested,
to the — in fact to the Devil: Cannot you ? " — " If your Majesty, against the honor of my Mother, declare that I am not
your eldest son : Yes, so; not otherwise, ever ! " modestly but
steadily persists the young man, whenever this expedient
is proposed to him, — as perhaps it already sometimes is.
Whereat the desperate Father can only snort indignantly
futile.   A case growing nearly desperate.   Desperate, yes, on
all hands : unless one had the " high mast " above alluded to,
with two pulleys and ropes ; and could see a certain Pair of
Scoundrels mount rapidly thither, what hope is there for anybody ?   A violent crisis does not last, however ; that is one
certainty in it.   Either these agonistic human beings, young
and old, will all die, all go to Bedlam, with their intolerable
woes ; or else something of explosive nature will take place

[1] Guy Dickens's Despatch, 18th July, 1730.

among them.   The maddest boil, unless it kill you with its torments, does at length burst, and become an abscess.

Of course Captain Dickens, the instant Hotham was gone, hastened privily to see the Crown-Prince; saw Katte and him "at the Gate of the Potsdam Palace at midnight," [1] or in some other less romantic way; — read him the Windsor Paper of "*Instructions*" known to us; and preached from that text. No definite countenance from England, the reverse rather, your Highness sees; — how can there be? Give it up, your Highness; at least delay it! — Crown-Prince does not give it up a whit; whether he delays it, we shall see.

A busy week for the Crown-Prince and Katte, this of the Hotham Catastrophe; who have many consultations, the Journey to Anspach being on Saturday next! Crown-Prince has given him in keeping a writing-case with private letters; 1,000 ducats of money, money raised by loan, by picking jewels off some miniatures of honor, and the like sore methods. Katte has his very coat, a gray top-coat or travelling roquelaure, in keeping; — and their schemes are many. Off we must and will be, by some opportunity. Could not Katte get a "Recruiting Furlough," leave to go into the *Reich* on that score; and join one there? Lieutenant Keith is at Wesel; ready, always ready. Into France, into Holland, England? If the English would not, — there is war to be in Italy, say all the Newspapers: why not a campaign as Volunteers in Italy, till we saw how matters went? Anything and all things are preferable to ignominy like this. No dog could endure it!

---

[1] Wilhelmina; Ranke, i. 301.

CHAPTER V.

JOURNEY TO THE REICH.

On Saturday the 15th July, 1730, early in the morning as his wont was, Friedrich Wilhelm, with a small train of official military persons, rolled off from Potsdam, towards Leipzig, on that same journey of his, towards Anspach and the Reich. To Anspach, to see our poor young daughter, lately married there; therefrom we can have a run into the Reich, according to circumstances. In this wide route there lie many Courts and scenes, which it might behoove us to look into; Courts needing to be encouraged to stand for the Kaiser's rights, against those English, French and intrusive Foreigners of the Seville Treaty. We may hope at least to ease our own heavy mind, and have the chaff somewhat blown out of it, by this rushing through the open atmosphere. — Such, so far as I can gather, were Friedrich Wilhelm's objects in this Journey; which turned out to be a more celebrated one than he expected. The authentic records of it are slight, the rumors about it have been many.[1] After painful sifting through mountains of dust and ashes for a poor cinder of a fact here and there, our duty is, to tell the English reader one good time, what certainties, or available cinders, have anywhere turned up.

Crown-Prince Friedrich, it has been decided, after some consultation, shall go with his Majesty. Better he go with us, to be under our own eyes, lest he run away, or do other mischief. Old General Buddenbrock, old Colonel Waldau, and Lieutenant-Colonel Rochow travel in the same carriage with the Prince; are to keep a strict watch over him, one of

[1] Förster (iii. 1–11) contains Seckendorf's Narrative, as sent to Vienna; Preuss (iv. 470), a Prussian *Relatio ex Actis*: these are the only two *original* pieces which I have seen; Excerpts of others (correct doubtless, but not in a very distinct condition) occur in Ranke, i. 294–340.

them at least to be always by him. Old General Buddenbrock, a grim but human old military gentleman, who has
been in all manner of wars : he fought at Steenkirk even,
and in the Siege of Namur, under Dutch William ; stood,
through Malplaquet and much else, under Marlborough ; did
the Siege of Stralsund too, and descent on Rügen there, which
was not his first acquaintance with Karl of Sweden ; and is
a favorite old friend of Friedrich Wilhelm's. A good old
gentleman, though very strict ; now hard on sixty. He is
chief of the Three.

Old Waldau, not younger, though still only Colonel of
Horse, likewise celebrates the Malplaquet anniversary ; a
Pomeranian man, and silent smoker in the Tabagie, well
seen by the master there. To these two elderly authorities,
Lieutenant-Colonel Rochow, still only about forty, and probably sharper of eye, is adjoined as active partner. I conclude,
the Prince and Buddenbrock ride face forward ; Buddenbrock
can tell him about so many things, if he is conversable : about
Dutch William ; about Charles XII., whose Polish fights he
witnessed, as an envoy from Berlin, long ago. A Colonel
Kröcher, I find, is general manager of the Journey ; — and it
does not escape notice that Friedrich, probably out of youthful curiosity, seems always very anxious to know, to the
uttermost settled point, where our future stages are to be.
His Royal Highness laid in a fair stock of District Maps,
especially of the Rhine Countries, at Leipzig, too ;[1] and is
assiduous in studying them, — evidently very desirous to know
the face of Germany, the Rhine Countries in particular ?

Potsdam, Wittenberg, Leipzig, the wheels rush rapidly on,
stage succeeding stage ; and early in the afternoon we are
at Leipzig, — never looking out at Luther's vestiges, or
Karl V.'s, or thinking about Luther, which thou and I, good
English reader, would surely have done, in crossing Wittenberg and the birthplace of Protestantism. At Leipzig we
were thinking to have dined. At the Peter's Gate there, —
where at least fresh horses are, and a topographic Crown-
Prince can send hastily to buy maps, — a General Hopfgarten,

[1] Förster, iii. 2.

Commandant of the Town, is out with the military honors;
he has, as we privately know, an excellent dinner ready in
the Pleissenburg Fortress yonder,[1] — but he compliments to
a dreadful extent! Harangues and compliments in no end
of florid inflated tautologic ornamental balderdash; repeating
and again repeating, What a never-imagined honor it is;
in particular saying three times over, How the Majesty of
Saxony, King August, had he known, would have wished
for wings to fly hither; and bowing to the very ground, "as
if, in the Polish manner, he wished to clasp your feet," said
Friedrich Wilhelm afterwards. I can fancy Friedrich Wilhelm somewhat startled! How, at the first mention of this
idea of big August, with his lame foot, taking wing, and
coming like a gigantic partridge, with lame foot and cocked-
hat, Friedrich Wilhelm grinned. How, at the second mention, and Polish threat of your feet, Friedrich Wilhelm, who
hates all lies, and cares not for salutations in the market-
place, jerks himself impatiently and saves his feet. At the
third mention, clear it is, Friedrich Wilhelm utters the word,
" *Anspannen*, Horses ! " — and in very truth takes to the road
again ; hungry indeed, but still angrier; leaving Hopfgarten
bent into the shape of a parabola, and his grand dinner cooling
futile, in what tragic humor we can imagine.[2] Why has no
Prussian Painter done that scene ? Let another Chodowiecki,
when another comes, try whether he cannot.

Friedrich Wilhelm regretted the dinner, regretted to hurt
the good man's feelings ; but could stand it no longer. He
rushes off for Meuselwitz, where Seckendorf, with at least
silence, and some cold collation instead of dinner, is awaiting
him. Twenty miles off is Meuselwitz; up the flat valley of
the Pleisse River towards Altenburg ; through a region memorable, were we not so hungry. Famed fights have had their
arena here; Lützen, the top of its church-steeple visible on
your right, it is there where the great Gustavus fell two hundred years ago : on that wide champaign, a kind of Bull-ring
of the Nations, how many fights have been, and will be !
Altenburg one does not see to-night : happy were we but at

[1] Fassmann, p. 410.   [2] Ib. p. 411.

Meuselwitz, a few miles nearer, and had seen what dinner the old Feldzeugmeister has.

Dinner enough, we need not doubt. The old Feldzeugmeister has a big fine Schloss at Meuselwitz; his by unexpected inheritance; with uncommonly fine gardens; with a good old Wife, moreover, blithe though childless;—and he is capable of "lighting more than one candle" when a King comes to visit him. Doubtless the man hurls his thrift into abeyance; and blazes out with conspicuous splendor, on this occasion. A beautiful Castle indeed, this Meuselwitz of his; the towers of Altenburg visible in the distance; Altenburg, where Kunz von Kauffungen stole the two little Princes, centuries ago;—where we do not mean to pause at this time. On the morrow morning,—unless they chose to stay over Sunday, which I cannot affirm or deny,—Seckendorf also has made his packages; and joins himself to Friedrich Wilhelm's august travelling party. Doing here a portion of the long space (length of the Terrestrial Equator in all) which he is fated to accomplish in the way of riding with that Monarch.

From Meuselwitz, through Altenburg, Gera, Saalfeld, to Coburg, is our next day's journey. Up one fork of the Leipzig Pleisse, then across the Leipzig Elster, these streams now dwindling to brooks; leading us up to the water-shed or central Hill-countries between the Mayn and Saale Rivers; where the same shower will run partly, on this hand, northward, by the Elster, Pleisse or other labyrinthic course, into the Saale, into the Elbe; and partly, on the other hand,—will flow southward into the Mayn; and so, after endless windings in the Fir Mountains (*Fichtel-Gebirge*), get by Frankfurt into the Rhine at Mainz. Mayn takes the south end of your shower; Saale takes the north,—or farther east yonder, shower will roll down into the same grand Elbe River by the Mulde (over which the Old Dessauer is minded to build a new stone bridge; Wallenstein and others, as well as Time, have ruined many bridges there). That is the line of the primeval mountains, and their ever-flowing rain-courses, in those parts.

At Gera, dim old Town,—does not your Royal Highness well know the "Gera Bond (*Geraische Vertrag*)"? Duhan

did not forget to inform you of that? It is the corner-stone
of the House of Brandenburg's advancement in the world.
Here, by your august ancestors, the Law of Primogeniture
was settled, and much rubbish was annihilated in the House
of Brandenburg : Eldest Son always to inherit the Electorate
unbroken ; after Anspach and Baireuth no more apanages,
upon any cause or pretext whatsoever ; and these themselves
to lapse irrevocable to the main or Electoral House, should
they ever fall vacant again.   Fine fruit of the decisive sense
that was in the Hohenzollerns ; of their fine talent for anni-
hilating rubbish, — which feat, if a man can do it, and keep
doing it, will more than most others accelerate his course in
this world.   It was in this dim old Town of Gera, in the Year
1598, by him that had the twenty-three children, that the
" *Gera Bond* " was brought to parchment.   But indeed it was
intrinsically only a renewal, more solemnly sanctioned, of
Albert Achilles's *Haus Ordnung* (House-Order), done in 1478,
above a century earlier. —

But see, we are under way again.   His Prussian Majesty
rushes forward without pause ; will stop nowhere, except
where business demands ; no Majesty of his day travels at
such a speed.   Orlamünde an hour hence, — your Royal Highness has heard of Orlamünde and its famed Counts of a thousand years back, when Kaiser Redbeard was in the world, and
the Junior Hohenzollern, tired of hawking, came down from
the Hills to him ?   Orlamünde (Orla*mouth*) is not far off, on
our right ; and this itself is the Orla ; this pleasant streamlet
we are now quitting, which has borne us company for some
time : this too will get into the Saale, and be at Magdeburg,
quite beyond the Dessauer's Bridge, early to-morrow.   Ha,
here at last is Saalfeld, Town and Schloss, and the incipient
Saal itself : his Serene Highness Saalfeld-Coburg's little
Residenz ; — probably his Majesty will call on him, in passing ?   I have no doubt he does ; and transacts the civilities
needful.

Christian Ernst, whose Schloss this is, a gentleman of his
Majesty's age (born 1683), married an amiable *Fräulein* not
of quality, whom indeed the Kaiser has ennobled : he lives

here, — I think, courting the shade rather ; and rules con-
jointly with his younger Brother, or Half-Brother, Franz
Josias, who resides at Coburg. Dukes of Saalfeld-Coburg,
such is their style, and in good part their possession ; though,
it is well known to this travelling party and the world, there
has been a Lawsuit about Coburg this half-century and more ;
and though somewhere about 200 *"Conclusa,"* [1] or Decrees of
Aulic Council, have been given in favor of the Saalfelders,
their rivals of Meiningen never end. Nor will end yet, for
five years more to come ; till, in 1735, "206 *Conclusa* being
given," they do end, and leave the Saalfelders in peaceable
possession ; who continue so ever since to this day.[2] How
long his Majesty paused in that Schloss of Saalfeld, or what
he there did, or what he spake, — except perhaps encourage
Christian Ernst to stand by a Kaiser's Majesty against these
French insolences, and the native German, Spanish, English
derelictions of duty, — we are left to the vaguest guess of
fancy. And must get on to Coburg for the night.

At Coburg, in its snug valley, under the *Festung* or Hill
Castle, — where Martin Luther sat solitary during the Diet of
Augsburg (Diet known to us, our old friend Margraf George
of Anspach hypothetically "laying his head on the block"
there, and the great Kaiser, Karl V., practically burning daylight, with pitiable spilling of wax, in the *Corpus-Christi* procession there),[3] — where Martin Luther sat solitary, and wrote
that celebrated Letter about "Crows holding *their* Parliament
all round," and how "the Pillars of the world were never seen
by anybody, and yet the world is held up, in these dumb con-
tinents of space ; " — at Coburg, we will not doubt, his Majesty
found Franz Josias at home, and illuminated to receive him.
Franz Josias, a hearty man of thirty-five, he too will stand by
the Kaiser in these coming storms ? With a weak contingent
truly, perhaps some score or two of fighters : but many a little
makes a mickle ! — remark, however, two points, of a merely

[1] Michaelis, i. 524, 518 ; Büsching, *Erdbeschreibung,* vi. 2464 ; Œrtel, t. 74;
Hübner, t. 166.
[2] Carlyle's *Miscellanies,* vi. § *Prinzenraub.*
[3] Antea, vol. v. p. 197.

genealogical nature. First, that Franz Josias has, or rather is going to have, a Younger Son,[1] who in some sixty years hence will become dreadfully celebrated in the streets of Paris, as "Austrian Coburg." The Austrian Coburg of Robespierre and Company. An immeasurable terror and portent, — not much harm in him, either, when he actually comes, with nothing but the Duke of York and Dunkirk for accompaniment, — to those revolutionary French of 1792–1794. This is point *first*. Point *second* is perhaps still more interesting; this namely: That Franz Josias has an Eldest Son (boy of six when Friedrich Wilhelm makes his visit), — a GRANDSON'S GRANDSON of whom is, at this day, Prince of Wales among the English People, and to me a subject of intense reflection now and then! —

From Coburg, Friedrich Wilhelm, after pause again unknown, rushed on to Bamberg; new scenes and ever new opening on the eyes of our young Hero and his Papa. The course is down the valley of the Itz, one of the many little valleys in the big slope of the Rodach; for the waters are now turned, and all streams and brooks are gurgling incessantly towards the Mayn. Towards Frankfurt, Mainz and the Rhine, — far enough from the Saale, Mulde, or the Old Dessauer's Bridge to-day; towards Rotterdam and the uttermost Dutch swamps to-day. Near upon Bamberg we cross the Mayn itself; Red Mayn and White conjoined, coming from Culmbach and Baireuth, — mark that, your Highness. A country of pleasant hills and vines: and in an hour hence, through thick fir woods, — each side of your road horribly decked with gibbeted thieves swinging aloft,[2] — you arrive at Bamberg, chief of Bishoprics, the venerable town; whose Bishop, famous in old times, is like an Archbishop, and "gets his pallium direct from the Pope," — much good may it do him! "Is bound, however, to give up his Territory, if the Kaiser elected is

---

[1] Friedrich Josias : 1737–1815.

[2] Pöllnitz, *Memoirs and Letters* (English Translation, London, 1745), i. 209. Let me say again, this is a different Book from the "*Memoirs* of Pöllnitz;" and a still different from the *Memoiren*, or "Memoirs of Brandenburg *by* Pöllnitz : " such the excellence of nomenclature in that old fool!

landless," — far enough from likely now.   And so you are at last fairly in the Mayn Valley ; River Mayn itself a little step to north ; — long course and many wide windings between you and Mainz or Frankfurt, not to speak of Rotterdam, and the ultimate Dutch swamps.

At Bamberg why should a Prussian Majesty linger, except for picturesque or for mere baiting purposes ?   At Bamberg are certain fat Catholic Canons, in indolent, opulent circumstances ; and a couple of sublime Palaces, without any Bishop in them at present.   Nor indeed does one much want Papist Bishops, wherever they get their pallium ; of them as well keep to windward ! thinks his Majesty.   And indeed there is no Bishop here.   The present Bishop of Bamberg — one of those Von Schönborns, Counts, sometimes Cardinals, common in that fat Office, — is a Kaiser's Minister of State ; lives at Vienna, enveloped in red tape, as well as red hat and stockings ; and needs no exhortation in the Kaiser's favor.   Let us yoke again, and go. — Fir woods all round, and dead malefactors blackening in the wind : this latter point I know of the then Bamberg ; and have explanation of it.   Namely, that the Prince-Bishop, though a humane Catholic, is obliged to act so. His small Domain borders on some six or seven bigger sovereignties ; and, being Ecclesiastical, is made a cesspool to the neighboring scoundrelism ; which state of things this Prince-Bishop has said shall cease.   Young Friedrich may look, therefore, and old Friedrich Wilhelm and Suite ; and make of it what they can.

"Bamberg, through Erlangen, to Nürnberg ;" so runs the way.   At Erlangen there loiters now, recruiting, a certain Rittmeister von Katte, cousin to our Potsdam Lieutenant and confidant ; to him this transit of the Majesty and Crown-Prince must be an event like few, in that stagnant place. French Refugees are in Erlangen, busy building new straight streets ; no University as yet ; — nay a high Dowager of Baireuth is in it, somewhat exuberant Lady (friend Weissenfels's Sister) on whom Friedrich Wilhelm must call in passing. This high Widow of Baireuth is not Mother of the present Heir-Apparent there, who will wed our Wilhelmina one day ;

— ah no, his Mother was "*divorced* for weighty reasons;"[1] and his Father yet lives, in the single state; a comparatively prosperous gentleman these four years last past; Successor, since four years past, of this Lady's Husband, who was his Cousin-german. Dreadfully poor before that, the present Margraf of Baireuth, as we once explained; but now things are looking up with him again, some jingle of money heard in the coffers of the man; and his eldest Prince, a fine young fellow, only apt to stammer a little when agitated, is at present doing the return part of the Grand Tour, — coming home by Geneva, they say.

Rittmeister von Katte, I doubt not, witnesses this transit of the incognito Majesty, this call upon the exuberant Dowager; but can have little to say to it, he. I hope he is getting tall recruits here in the Reich; that will be the useful point for him. He is our Lieutenant Katte's Cousin, an elder and wiser man than the Lieutenant. A Reichsgraf's and Field-marshal's nephew, he ought to get advanced in his profession; — and can hope to do so when he has deserved it, not sooner at all, in that thrice-fortunate Country. Let the Rittmeister here keep himself well apart from what is *not* his business, and look out for tall men.

Bamberg is halfway-house between Coburg and Nürnberg; whole distance of Coburg and Nürnberg, — say a hundred and odd miles, — is only a fair day's driving for a rapid King. And at Nürnberg, surely, we must lodge for a night and portion of a day, if not for more. On the morrow, it is but a thirty-five miles drive to Anspach; pleasant in the summer evening, after all the sights in this old Nürnberg, "city of the Noricans (*Noricorum Burgum*)." Trading Staple of the German world in old days; Toy-shop of the German world in these new. Albert Dürer's and Hans Sach's City, — mortals infinitely indifferent to Friedrich Wilhelm. But is it not the seed-ground of the Hohenzollerns, this Nürnberg, memorable above cities to a Prussian Majesty? Yes, there in that old white Castle, now very peaceable, they dwelt; considerably liable to bickerings and mutinous heats; and needed all their

---

[1] Hübner, t. 181.

skill and strength to keep matters straight. It is now upon
seven hundred years since the Cadet of Hohenzollern gave his
hawk the slip, patted his dog for the last time, and came down
from the Rough-Alp countries hitherward. And found favor,
not unmerited I fancy, with the great Kaiser Redbeard, and
the fair Heiress of the Vohburgs; and in fact, with the Earth
and with the Heavens in some degree. A loyal, clever, and
gallant kind of young fellow, if your Majesty will think?
Much has grown and waned since that time: but the Hohenzollerns, ever since, are on the waxing hand; — unless this
accursed Treaty of Seville and these English Matches put a
stop to them?

Alas, it is not likely Friedrich Wilhelm, in the hurry and
grating whirl of things, had many poetic thoughts in him, or
pious auroral memories from the Past Ages, instead of grum-
bly dusty provocations from the present, — his feeling, haste
mainly, and need of getting through! The very Crown-Prince,
I should guess, was as good as indifferent to this antique
Cadet of the Hohenzollerns; and looked on Nürnberg and the
old white Castle with little but *ennui:* the Princess of England, and black cares on her beautiful account and his own,
possess him too exclusively. But in truth we do not even
know what day they arrived or departed; much less what they
did or felt in that old City. We know only that the pleasant
little town of Anspach, with its huge unfinished *Schloss,* lay
five-and-thirty miles away; and that thither was the next and
quasi-final bit of driving. Southwestward thirty-five miles;
through fine summer hills and dales; climbing always, gently,
on the southward hand; still drained by the Mayn River, by
the Regnitz and other tributaries of the Mayn: — half-way is
Heilsbronn,[1] with its old Monastery; where the bones of our
Hohenzollern Forefathers rest, and Albert Achilles's "skull,
with no sutures visible." On the gloomy Church-walls their
memorials are still legible: as for the Monastery itself, Mar-

[1] Not Heilbronn, the well-known, much larger Town, in Würtemberg, 80 or
100 miles to westward. Both names (which are applied to still other places)
signify *Health-Well,* or even *Holy-Well,* — these two words, *Healthy* and *Holy*
(what is very remarkable), being the same in old Teutonic speech.

graf George, our memorable Reformation friend, abolished that, — purged the monks away, and put Schoolmasters in their stead; who were long of good renown in those parts, but have since gone to Erlangen, so to speak. The July sunset streaming over those old spires of Heilsbronn might awaken thoughts in a Prussian Majesty, were he not in such haste.

At Anspach, what a thrice-hospitable youthfully joyful welcome from the young married couple there! Margravine Frederika is still not quite sixteen; "beautiful as Day," and rather foolish: fancy her joy at sight of Papa's Majesty and Brother Fritz; and how she dances about, and perhaps bakes "pastries of the finest Anspach flour." Ah, *did* you send me Berlin sausages, then, you untrue Papa? Well, I will bake for you, won't I; — Sarah herself not more loyally (whom we read of in *Genesis*), that time the Angels entered *her* tent in a hungry condition! —

Anspach, as we hint, has an unfinished Palace, of a size that might better beseem Paris or London; Palace begun by former Margraves, left off once and again for want of cash; stands there as a sad monument of several things; — the young family living meanwhile in some solid comfortable wing, or adjacent edifice, of natural dimensions. They are so young, as we say, and not too wise. By and by they had a son, and then a second son; which latter came to manhood, to old age; and made some noise in the foolish parts of the Newspapers, — winding up finally at Hammersmith, as we often explain; — and was the last of the Anspach-Baireuth Margraves. I have heard farther that Frederika did not want for temper, as the Hohenzollerns seldom do; that her Husband likewise had his own stock of it, rather scant of wisdom withal; and that their life was not quite symphonious always, — especially cash being short. The Dowager Margravine, Margraf's Mother, had governed with great prudence during her Son's long minority. I think she is now, since the marriage, gone to reside at her *Wittwensitz* (Dowager-Seat) of Feuchtwang (twenty miles southwest of us); but may have come up to welcome the Majesties into these parts. Very beautiful, I hear; still almost young and charming, though there is a mortal malady upon her, which she knows of.[1] Here are certain Seckendorfs too, this is the Feldzeugmeister's native country; — and there are resources for a Royal Travelling-Party. How long the Royal Party stayed at Anspach I do not know; nor what they did there, — except that Crown-Prince Friedrich is said to have privately asked the young Margraf to lend him a pair of riding-horses, and say nothing of it; who, suspecting something wrong, was obliged to make protestations and refuse.

As to the Crown-Prince, there is no doubt but here at last things are actually coming to a crisis with him. To say truth, it has been the young man's fixed purpose ever since he entered on this Journey, nay was ever since that ignominy in the Camp of Radewitz, to run away; — and indeed all this while he has measures going on with Katte at Berlin of the now-or-never sort. Rash young creatures, elder of them hardly above five-and-twenty yet: not good at contriving measures. But what then? Human nature cannot stand this always; and it is time there were an end of deliberating. Can we ever have such a chance again? — What I find of certain concerning Friedrich while at Anspach is, That there comes by way of Erlangen, guided forward from that place by the Rittmeister von Katte, a certain messenger and message, which proved of deep importance to his Royal Highness. The messenger was Lieutenant Katte's servant: who has come express from Berlin hither. He inquired, on the road, as he was bidden, at Erlangen, of Master's Cousin, the experienced Rittmeister, Where his Royal Highness at present was, that he might deliver a Letter to him? The Master's Cousin, who answered naturally, "At Anspach," knew nothing, and naturally could get to know nothing, of what the message in this Letter was. But he judged, from cross-questionings, added to dim whispering rumors he had heard, that it was questionable, probably in an extreme degree. Wherefore, along with his Cousin the Lieutenant's messenger to Anspach, the Rittmeister forwarded

_____
[1] Pöllnitz, *Memoirs and Letters*, i. 209 (date, 29th September, 1729; — needs *watching* before believing).

a Note of his own to Lieutenant-Colonel Rochow, of this purport, "As a friend, I warn you, have a watchful eye on your
high charge!"—and, for his own share, determined to let
nothing escape him in his corner of the matter. This note to
Rochow, and the Berlin Letter for the Crown-Prince reach
Anspach by the same hand; Lieutenant Katte's express, conscious of nothing, delivering them both. Rochow and the
Rittmeister, though the poor Prince does not know it, are
broad awake to all movements he and the rash Lieutenant
may make.

Lieutenant Katte, in this Letter now arrived, complains:
"That he never yet can get recruiting furlough; whether it
be by accident, or that Rochow has given my Colonel a hint,
no furlough yet to be had: will, at worst, come without furlough and in spite of all men and things, whenever wanted.
Only — Wesel still, if I might advise!" This is the substance of Katte's message by express. Date must be the end
of July, 1730; but neither Date nor Letter is now anywhere
producible, except from Hearsay.

Deeply pondering these things, what shall the poor Prince
do? From Canstatt, close by Stuttgard, a Town on our homeward route, — from Canstatt, where Katte was to "appear in
disguise," had the furlough been got, one might have slipt
away across the Hills. It is but eighty miles to Strasburg,
through the Kniebiss Pass, where the Murg, the Kinzig, and
the intricate winding mountain streams and valleys start
Rhine-ward: a labyrinthic rock-and-forest country, where pursuit or tracking were impossible. Near by Strasburg is Count
Rothenburg's Château; good Rothenburg, long Minister in
Berlin, — who saw those *Profossen*, or Scavenger-Executioners
in French Costume long since, and was always good to me:
— might not that be a method? Lieutenant Keith indeed is
in Wesel, waiting only a signal. Suppose he went to the
Hague, and took soundings there what welcome we should
have? No, not till we have actually run; beware of making
noise!— The poor Prince is in unutterable perplexity; can
only answer Katte by that Messenger of his, to the effect
(date and Letter burnt like the former): "Doubt is on every

hand; doubt,—and yet *certainty*. Will write again before undertaking anything."

And there is no question he did write again; more than once : letters by the post, which his faithful Lieutenant Katte in Berlin received; one of which, however, stuck on the road; and this one, — by some industry of postmasters spirited into vigilance, as is likeliest, though others say by mere misaddressing, by "want of *Berlin* on the address," — fell into the hands of vigilant *Rittmeister* Katte at Erlangen. Who grew pale in reading it, and had to resolve on a painful thing! This was, I suppose, among the last Letters of the series; and must have been dated, as I guess, about the 29th of July, 1730; but they are now all burnt, huddled rapidly into annihilation, and one cannot say!—

Certain it is that the Royal Travelling-Party left Anspach in a few days, to go, southward still, "by the Œttingen Country towards Augsburg."[1] Feuchtwang (*Wet* Wang, not Dürrwang or *Dry* Wang) is the first stage; here lives the Dowager Margravine of Anspach : here the Prince does some inconceivably small fault "lets a knife, which he is handing to or from the Serene Lady, fall,"[2] who, as she is weak, may suffer by the jingle; for which Friedrich Wilhelm bursts out on him like the Irish Rebellion, — to the silent despair of the poor Prince. The poor Prince meditates desperate resolutions, but has to keep them strictly to himself.

Doubtless the Buddenbrock Trio, good old military gentlemen, would endeavor to speak comfort to him, when they were on the road again. Here is Nördlingen, your Highness, where Bernhard of Weimar, for his over-haste, got so beaten in the Thirty-Years War; would not wait till the Swedes were rightly gathered : what general, if he have reinforcement at hand, would not wait for it? The waters now, you observe, run all into the Wörnitz, into the Donau : it is a famed war-country this; known to me well in my young Eugene-Marlborough days! — "Hm, Ha, yes!" For the Prince is preoccupied with black cares; and thinks Blenheim and the Schel-

---

[1] Fassmann, p. 410.

[2] Ranke, i. 304 ("from a Letter the Prince had written to Katte").

lenberg businesses befell long since, and were perhaps simple
to what he has now on hand.   That Feuchtwang scene, it would
appear, has brought him to a resolution.   There is a young
page Keith of the party, Lieutenant Keith of Wesel's Brother;
of this page Keith, who is often busy about horses, he cautiously makes question, What help may be in him ?   A willing
mind traceable in this poor lad, but his terrors great.

To Donauwörth from Anspach, through Feuchtwang and
Nördlingen, is some seventy or eighty miles.   At Donauwörth
one surely ought to lodge, and see the Schellenberg on the
morrow; nay drive to the Field of Hochstädt (Blenheim,
Blindheim), which is but a few miles farther up the River ?
Buddenbrock was there, and Anhalt-Dessau : for their very
sake, were there nothing farther, one surely ought to go ?
Such was the probability, a visit to Blenheim field in passing.
And surely, somewhere in those heart-rending masses of Historical Rubbish, I did at last find express evanescent mention
of the fact, — but cannot now say where ; — the exact record,
or conceivable image of which, would have been a perceptible
pleasure to us.   Alas, in those dim dreary Books, all whirling
dismal round one's soul, like vortices of dim Brandenburg
sand, how should anything human be searched out and mentioned to us ; and a thousand things not-human be searched
out, and eternally suppressed from us, for the sake of that ?
I please myself figuring young Friedrich looking at the vestiges of Marlborough, even in a preoccupied uncertain manner.
Your Majesty too, this is the very "Schellenberg (or *Jingle-
Hill*)," this Hill we are now skirting, on highways, on swift
wheels ; which overhangs Donauwörth, our resting-place this
hot July evening.   Yes, your Majesty, here was a feat of
storming done, — pang, pang ! — such a noise as never jingled
on that Hill before : like Doomsday come ; and a hero-head to
rule the Doomsday, and turn it to heroic marching music.   A
very pretty feat of war, your Majesty !   His Majesty well
knows it; feat of his Marlborough's doing, famed everywhere
for the twenty-six years last past; and will go to see the
Schellenberg and its Lines.   The great Duke is dead four
years; sank sadly, eclipsed under tears of dotage of his own,

and under human stupidity of other men's! But Buddenbrock is still living, Anhalt-Dessau and others of us are still alive a little while!

Hochstädt itself — Blenheim, as the English call it, meaning *Blindheim*, the other village on the Field — is but a short way up the River; well worth such a detour. By what way they drove to the field of honor and back from it, I do not know. But there, northward, towards the heights, is the little wood where Anhalt-Dessau stood at bay like a Molossian dog, of consummate military knowledge; and saved the fight in Eugene's quarter of it. That is visible enough; and worth looking at. Visible enough the rolling Donau, Marlborough's place; the narrow ground, the bordering Hills all green at this season; — and down old Buddenbrock's cheek, and Anhalt's, there would roll an iron tear or two. Augsburg is but some thirty miles off, once we are across the Donau, — by the Bridge of Donauwörth, or the Ferry of Hochstädt, — swift travellers in a long day, the last of July, are soon enough at Augsburg.

As for Friedrich, haunted and whipt onwards by that scene at Feuchtwang, he is inwardly very busy during this latter part of the route. Probably there is some progress towards gaining Page Keith, Lieutenant Keith of Wesel's Brother; some hope that Page Keith, at the right moment, can be gained: the Lieutenant at Wesel is kept duly advised. To Lieutenant Katte at Berlin Friedrich now writes, I should judge from Donauwörth or Augsburg, "That he has had a scene at Feuchtwang; that he can stand it no longer. That Canstatt being given up, as Katte cannot be there to go across the Kniebiss with us, we will endure till we are near enough the Rhine. Once in the Rhineland, in some quiet Town there, handy for Speyer, for French Landau," — say Sinzheim, last stage hitherward of Heidelberg, but this we do not write, — "there might it not be? Be, somewhere, it shall and must! You, Katte, the instant you hear that we are off, speed you towards the Hague; ask for 'M. le Comte d'Alberville;' you will know that gentleman *when* you see him: Keith, our Wesel friend, will have taken the preliminary soundings; — and I tell you, Count d'Alberville, or news of him, will be there. Bring the great-coat with you, and the other things, especially the 1,000 gold ducats. Count d'Alberville at the Hague, if all have gone right: — nay if anything go wrong, cannot he, once across the Rhine, take refuge in the convents in those Catholic regions ? Nobody, under the scapulary, will suspect such a heretic as him. Speed, silence, vigilance! And so adieu ! " A letter of such purport Friedrich did write; which Letter, moreover, the Lieutenant Katte received ; it was not this, it was another, that stuck upon the road, and fell into the Rittmeister's hand. This is the young Prince's ultimate fixed project, brought to birth by that slight accident of dropping the knife at Feuchtwang ; [1] and hanging heavy on his mind during this Augsburg drive. At Augsburg, furthermore, " he bought, in all privacy, red cloth, of quantity to make a top-coat ; " red, the gray being unattainable in Katte's hands : in all privacy ; though the watchful Rochow had full knowledge of it, all the same.

CHAPTER VI.

JOURNEY HOMEWARDS FROM THE REICH ; CATASTROPHE ON JOURNEY HOMEWARDS.

THE travelling Majesty of Prussia went diligently up and down, investigating ancient Augsburg: saw, I doubt not, the *Fuggerei*, or ancient Hospice of the Fuggers, — who were once Weavers in those parts, and are now Princes, and were known to entertain Charles V. with fires of cinnamon, nay with transient flames of Bank-bills on one old occasion. Saw all the Fuggeries, I doubt not ; the ancient Luther-and-Melanchthon relics, Diet-Halls and notabilities of this renowned Free Town ; — perhaps remembered Margraf George, and loud-voiced Kurfürst Joachim with the Bottle-nose (our *direct* Ancestor, though mistaken in opinion on some points !), who were once so audible there.

[1] Ranke, i. 304.

One passing phenomenon we expressly know he saw ; a human, not a historically important one. Driving through the streets from place to place, his Majesty came athwart some questionable quaint procession, ribbony, perhaps musical; Majesty questioned it : " A wedding procession, your Majesty ! " — " Will the Bride step out, then, and let us see how she is dressed ! " " *Vom Herzen gern ;* will have the honor." Bride stept out, with blushes, — handsome we will hope ; Majesty surveyed her, on the streets of Augsburg, having a human heart in him ; and (says Fassmann, as if with insidious insinuation) " is said to have made her a present." She went her way ; fulfilled her destiny in an anonymous manner : Friedrich Wilhelm, loudly named in the world, did the like ; and their two orbits never intersected again. — Some forty-five miles south of Augsburg, up the Wertach River, more properly up the Mindel River, lies Mindelheim, once a name known in England and in Prussia ; once the Duke of Marlborough's " Principality : " given him by a grateful Kaiser Joseph ; taken from him by a necessitous Kaiser Karl, Joseph's Brother, that now is. I know not if his Majesty remembers that transaction, now while in these localities ; but know well, if he does, he must think it a shabby one.

On the same day, 1st August, 1730, we quit Augsburg ; set out fairly homewards again. The route bends westward this time ; towards Frankfurt-on-Mayn ; there yachts are to be ready ; and mere sailing thenceforth, gallantly down the Rhine-stream, — such a yacht-voyage, in the summer weather, with no Tourists yet infesting it, — to end, happily we will hope, at Wesel, in the review of regiments, and other business. First stage, first pause, is to be at Ludwigsburg, and the wicked old Duke of Würtemberg's ; thither first from Augsburg. We cross the Donau at Dillingen, at Günzberg, or I know not where ; and by to-morrow's sunset, being rapid travellers, find ourselves at Ludwigsburg, — clear through Canstatt, Stuttgard, and certainly no Katte waiting there ! Safe across the intermediate uplands, here are we fairly in the Neckar Country, in the Basin of the Rhine again ; and old Duke Eberhard Ludwig of Würtemberg bidding us kindly welcome, poor old bewil-

dered creature, who has become the talk of Germany in those
times. Will English readers consent to a momentary glance
into his affairs and him ? Strange things are going on at
Ludwigsburg; nay the origin of Ludwigsburg, and that the
Duke should be there and not at Stuttgard, is itself strange.
Let us take this Excerpt, headed *Ludwigsburg* in 1730, and
then hasten on : —

Ludwigsburg in 1730.

"Duke Eberhard Ludwig, now an elderly gentleman of fifty-
four, has distinguished himself in his long reign, not by political obliquities and obstinacies, though those also were not
wanting, but by matrimonial and amatory ; which have rendered him conspicuous to his fellow-creatures, and still keep
him mentionable in History, briefly and for a sad reason.
Duke Eberhard Ludwig was duly wedded to an irreproach-
able Princess of Baden-Durlach (Johanna Elizabeth) upwards
of thirty years ago; and he duly produced one Son in consequence, with other good results to himself and her. But in
course of time Duke Eberhard Ludwig took to consorting with
bad creatures; took, in fact, to swashing about at random in
the pool of amatory iniquity, as if there had been no law
known, or of the least validity, in that matter.

"Perceiving which, a certain young fellow, Grävenitz by
name, who had come to him from the Mecklenburg regions, by
way of pushing fortune, and had got some pageship or the
like here in Würtemberg, recollected that he had a young Sister
at home ; pretty and artful, who perhaps might do a stroke of
work here. He sends for the young Sister; very pretty indeed,
and a gentlewoman by birth, though penniless. He borrows
clothes for her (by onerous contract with the haberdashers,
it is said, being poor to a degree) ; he easily gets her introduced to the Ducal Soirées ; bids her — She knows what to do ?
Right well she knows what; catches, with her piquant face,
the dull eye of Eberhard Ludwig, kindles Eberhard Ludwig,
and will not for something quench him. Not she at all: How
can *she ;* your Serene Highness, ask her not ! A virtuous
young lady, she, and come of a stainless Family ! — In brief,

she hooks, she of all the fishes in the pool, this lumber of a
Duke; enchants him, keeps him hooked; and has made such
a pennyworth of him, for the last twenty years and more, as
Germany cannot match.[1] Her brother Grävenitz the page has
become Count Grävenitz the prime minister, or chief of the
Governing Cabal; she Countess Grävenitz and Autocrat of
Würtemberg. Loaded with wealth, with so-called honors, she
and hers, there go they, flaunting sky-high; none else admitted
to more than the liberty of breathing in silence in this Duchy;
— the poor Duke Eberhard Ludwig making no complaint;
obedient as a child to the bidding of his Grävenitz. He is
become a mere enchanted simulacrum of a Duke; bewitched
under worse than Thessalian spells; without faculty of willing,
except as she wills; his People and he the plaything of this
Circe or Hecate, that has got hold of him. So it has lasted
for above twenty years. Grävenitz has become the wonder of
Germany; and requires, on these bad grounds, a slight mention
in Human History for some time to come. Certainly it is by
the Grävenitz alone that Eberhard Ludwig is remembered;
and yet, down since Ulrich with the Thumb,[2] which of those
serene abstruse Beutelsbachers, always an abstruse obstinate
set, has so fixed himself in your memory? —

"Most persons in Würtemberg, for quiet's sake, have complied with the Grävenitz; though not without protest, and
sometimes spoken protest. Thus the Right Reverend Osiander
(let us name Osiander, Head of the Church in Würtemberg)
flatly refused to have her name inserted in the Public Prayers;
'Is not she already prayed for?' said Osiander: 'Do we not
say, *Deliver us from evil?*' said the indignant Protestant
man. And there is one other person that never will comply
with her: the lawful Wife of Eberhard Ludwig. Serene
Lady, she has had a sad existence of it; the voice of her
wrongs audible, to little purpose, this long while, in Heaven
and on Earth. But it is not in the power of reward or
punishment to bend her female will in the essential point:

[1] Michaelis, iii. 440.
[2] Ulricus *Pollex* (right thumb bigger than left); died A.D. 1265 (Michaelis,
iii. 262)..

'Divorce, your Highness? When *I* am found guilty, yes.
Till then, never, your Highness, never, never,' in steady *crescendo* tone: — so that his Highness is glad to escape again,
and drop the subject. On which the Serene Lady again falls
silent. Grävenitz, in fact, hopes always to be wedded with
the right, nay were it only with the left hand: and this
Serene Lady stands like a fateful monument irremovably in
the way. The Serene Lady steadily inhabits her own wing
of the Ducal House, would not exchange it for the Palace
of Aladdin; looks out there upon the grand equipages, high
doings, impure splendors of her Duke and his Grävenitz with
a clear-eyed silence, which seems to say more eloquently than
words, '*Mene, mene,* You are weighed!' In the land of
Würtemberg, or under the Sun, is no reward or punishment
that can abate this silence. Speak of divorce, the answer is
as above: leave divorce lying, there is silence looking forth
clear-eyed from that particular wing of the Palace, on things
which the gods permit for a time.

"Clear-eyed silence, which, as there was no abating of it,
grew at last intolerable to the two sinners. 'Let us remove,' said the Grävenitz, 'since her Serene Highness will
not: build a new charming Palace, — say at our Hunting
Seat, among those pleasant Hills in the Waiblingen region, —
and take the Court out thither.' And they have done so, in
these late bad years; taking out with them by degrees all the
Courtier Gentry, all the *Raths,* Government Boards, public
businesses; and building new houses for them, there.[1] Founding, in fact, a second Capital for Würtemberg, with what
distress, sulky misery and disarrangement to Stuttgard and
the old Capital, readers can fancy. There it stands, that
Ludwigsburg, the second Capital of Würtemberg, some ten
or twenty miles from Stuttgard the first: a lasting memorial
of Circe Grävenitz and her Ludwig. Has not she, by her

---

[1] "From 1727 to 1730" was this latter removal. A hunting-lodge, of
Eberhard Ludwig's building, and named by him *Ludwigsburg,* stood here
since 1705; nucleus of the subsequent palace, with its "Pheasantries," its
"Favoritas," &c. &c. The place had originally been monastic (Büsching,
Erdbeschreibung, vi. 1519).

incantations, made the stone houses dance out hither ? It
remains to this day a pleasant town, and occasional residence
of sovereignty. *Waiblingen,* within an hour's ride, has got
memorability on other grounds ; — what reader has not heard
of *Ghibellines,* meaning Waiblingens ? And in another hour
up the River, you will come to Beutelsbach itself, where
Ulrich with the Thumb had his abode (better luck to him !),
and generated this Lover of the Grävenitz, and much other
nonsense loud now and then for the last four centuries in
the world ! —

"There is something of abstruse in all these Beutelsbachers,
from Ulrich with the Thumb downwards : a mute ennui, an
inexorable obstinacy ; a certain streak of natural gloom which
no illumination can abolish. Veracity of all kinds is great
in them ; sullen passive courage plenty of it ; active courage
rarer ; articulate intellect defective : hence a strange stiff per-
versity of conduct visible among them, often marring what
wisdom they have ; — it is the royal stamp of Fate put upon
these men. What are called fateful or fated men ; such as
are often seen on the top places of the world, making an
indifferent figure there. Something of this, I doubt not, is
concerned in Eberhard Ludwig's fascination ; and we shall
see other instances farther down in this History.

"But so, for twenty years, the absurd Duke, transformed
into a mere Porcus by his Circe in that scandalous miraculous manner, has lived ; and so he still lives. And his Serene Wife, equally obstinate, is living at Stuttgard, happily
out of his sight now. One Son, a weakly man, who had one
heir, but has now none, is her only comfort. His Wife is a
Prussian Margravine (Friedrich Wilhelm's *Half-Aunt*), and
cultivates Calvinism in the Lutheran Country : this Husband
of hers, he too has an abstruse life, not likely to last. We
need not doubt 'the Fates' are busy, and the evil demons,
with those poor fellow-beings ! Nay it is said the Circe is
becoming much of a Hecate now ; if the bewitched Duke
could see it. She is getting haggard beyond the power of
rouge ; her mind, any mind she has, more and more filled
with spleen, malice, and the dregs of pride run sour. A dis-

gusting creature, testifies one Ex-Official gentleman, once a
Hofrath under her, but obliged to run for life, and invoke
free press in his defence:[1] no end to the foul things she
will say, of an unspeakable nature, about the very Duke her
victim, testifies this Ex-Official: malicious as a witch, says he,
and as ugly as one in spite of paint, — '*toujours un lavement
à ses trousses.*'   Good Heavens!"

But here is the august Prussian Travelling-Party: shove
aside your bewitchments and bewilderments; hang a decent
screen over many things! Poor Eberhard Ludwig, who is
infinitely the gentleman, bestirs himself a good deal to welcome old royal friends; nor do we hear that the least thing
went awry during this transit of the royalties. "Field of
Blenheim, says your Majesty? Ah me!" — For Eberhard
Ludwig knows that ground; stood the World-Battle there,
and so much has come and gone since then: Ah me indeed!

Friedrich Wilhelm and he have met before this, and have
much to tell one another; Treaty of Seville by no means
their only topic. Nay the flood of cordiality went at length
so far, that at last Friedrich Wilhelm, the conscientious King,
came upon the most intimate topics: Grävenitz; the Word
of God; scandal to the Protestant Religion: no likely heir
to your Dukedom; clear peril to your own soul. Is not her
Serene Highness an unexceptionable Lady, heroic under sore
woes; and your wedded Wife above all? — '*M-na,* and might
bring Heirs too: only forty come October: — Ah Duke, ah
Friend! *Avisez la fin,* Eberhard Ludwig; consider the end
of it all; we are growing old fellows now! The Duke, I
conceive, who was rather a fat little man, blushed blue, then
red, and various colors; at length settling into steady pale,
as it were, indicating anthracitic white-heat: it is certain
he said at length, with emphasis, "I will!" And he did so

---

[1] *Apologie de Monsieur Forstner de Breitembourg, &c.* (Paris, 1716; or "à
Londres, aux dépens de la Compagnie, 1745"): in Spittler, *Geschichte Wür-
tembergs* (Spittlers *Werke,* Stuttgard und Tübingen, 1828; vol. v.), 497–539.
Michaelis, iii. 428–439, gives (in abstruse Chancery German) a Sequel to
this fine affair of Forstner's.

by and by. Friedrich Wilhelm sent a messenger to Stuttgard to do his reverence to the high injured Lady there,
perhaps to show her afar off some ray of hope if she could
endure. Eberhard Ludwig, raised to a white-heat, perceives
that in fact he is heartily tired of this Circe-Hecate; that
in fact she has long been an intolerable nightmare to him,
could he but have known it.

And his Royal Highness the Crown-Prince all this while?
Well, yes; his Royal Highness has got a Court Tailor at Ludwigsburg; and, in all privacy (seen well by Rochow), has had
the Augsburg red cloth cut into a fine upper wrappage, over-
coat or roquelaure for himself; intending to use the same
before long. Thus they severally, the Father and the Son;
these are their known acts at Ludwigsburg, That the Father
persuaded Eberhard Ludwig of the Grävenitz enormity, and
that the Son got his red top-coat ready. On Thursday, 3d of
August (late in the afternoon, as I perceive), they, well entertained, depart towards Mannheim, Kur-Pfalz (Elector Palatine)
old Karl Philip of the Pfalz's place; hope to be there on the
morrow some time, if all go well. Gloomy much enlightened
Eberhard takes leave of them, with abstruse but grateful feelings; will stand by the Kaiser, and dismiss that Grävenitz
nightmare by the first opportunity.

As accordingly he did. Next Summer, going on a visit
northward, specially to Berlin,[1] he left order that the Grävenitz was to be got out of his sight, safe stowed away, before
his return. Which by the proper officers, military certain of
them, was accomplished, — by fixed bayonets at last, and not
without futile demur on the part of the Grävenitz. Poor
Eberhard Ludwig, "he published in the pulpits, That he was
now minded to lead a better life," — had time now been left
him. Same year, 1731, November being come, gloomy Eberhard Ludwig lost, not unexpectedly, his one Son, — the one
Grandson was gone long since. The serene steadfast Duchess
now had her Duke again, what was left of him: but he was
fallen into the sere and yellow leaf; in two years more, he

[1] There for some three weeks, "till 9th June, 1731, with a suite of above
fifty persons" (Fassmann, pp. 421, 422).

died childless;[1] and his Cousin, Karl Alexander, an Austrian
Feldmarschall of repute, succeeded in Würtemberg. With
whom we may transiently meet, in time coming; with whom,
and perhaps less pleasantly with certain of his children; for
they continue to this day, — with the old abstruse element still
too traceable in them.

Old Karl Philip, Kurfürst of the Pfalz, towards whom
Friedrich Wilhelm is now driving, with intent to be there to-
morrow evening, is not quite a stranger to readers here; and
to Friedrich Wilhelm he is much the reverse, perhaps too
much. This is he who ran away with poor Prince Sobieski's
Bride from Berlin, at starting in life; who fell upon his own
poor Protestant Heidelbergers and their Church of the Holy
Ghost (being himself Papist, ever since that slap on the face
to his ancestor); and who has been in many quarrels with
Friedrich Wilhelm and others. A high expensive sovereign
gentleman, this old Karl Philip; not, I should suppose, the
pleasantest of men to lodge with. One apprehends, he cannot
be peculiarly well disposed to Friedrich Wilhelm, after that
sad Heidelberg passage of fence, twelve or eleven years ago.
Not to mention the inextricable Jülich-and-Berg business,
which is a standing controversy between them.

Poor old Kurfürst, he is now within a year of seventy. He
has had crosses and losses; terrible campaignings against the
Turk, in old times; and always such a stock of quarrels, at
home, as must have been still worse to bear. A life of perpetual arguing, squabbling and battling, — one's neighbors
being such an unreasonable set! Brabbles about Heidelberg
Catechism, and Church of the Holy Ghost, so that foreign
Kings interfered, shaking their whips upon us. Then brabbles
about boundaries; about inheritances, and detached properties
very many, — clearly mine, were the neighbors reasonable!
In fact this sovereign old gentleman has been in the Kaiser's
courts, or even on the edge of fight, oftener than most other
men; and it is as if that first adventure, of the Sobieski wedding turned topsy-turvy, had been symbolical of much that
followed in his life.

[1] 31st October, 1733: Michaelis, iii. 441.

We remember that unpleasant Heidelberg affair : how hopeful it once looked; fact *done*, Church of the Holy Ghost fairly ours ; your *Corpus Evangelicorum* fallen quasi-dead ; and nothing now for it but protocolling by diplomatists, pleading in the Diets by men in bombazine, never like ending at all ; — when Friedrich Wilhelm did suddenly end it ; suddenly locked up his own Catholic establishments and revenues, and quietly inexorable put the key in his pocket ; as it were, drew his own whip, with a "Will you whip *my* Jew ? " — and we had to cower out of the affair, Kaiser himself ordering us, in a most humiliated manner ! Readers can judge whether Kur-Pfalz was likely to have a kindly note of Friedrich Wilhelm in that corner of his memory. The poor man felt so disgusted with Heidelberg, he quitted it soon after. He would not go to Düsseldorf (in the Berg-and-Jülich quarter), as his Forefathers used to do ; but set up his abode at Mannheim, where he still is. Friedrich Wilhelm, who was far from meaning harm or insolence in that Heidelberg affair, hopes there is no grudge remaining. But so stand the facts : it is towards Mannheim, not towards Heidelberg that we are now travelling ! — For the rest, this scheme of reprisals, or whipping your Jew if you whip mine, answered so well, Friedrich Wilhelm has used it, or threatened to use, as the real method, ever since, where needful ; and has saved thereby much bombazine eloquence, and confusion to mankind, on several occasions.

But the worst between these two High Gentlemen is that Jülich-and-Berg controversy ; which is a sore still running, and beyond reach of probable surgery. Old Karl Philip has no male Heir ; and is like to be (what he indeed proved) the last of the *Neuburg* Electors Palatine. What trouble there rose with the first of them, about that sad business ; and how the then Brandenburger, much wrought upon, smote the then Neuburger across the very face, and drove him into Catholicism, we have not forgotten ; how can we ever ? — It is one hundred and sixteen years since that after-dinner scene ; and, O Heavens, what bickering and brabbling and confused negotiation there has been ; lawyers' pens going almost continually ever since, shadowing out the mutual darkness of sovereignties ;

and from time to time the military implements brandishing
themselves, though loath generally to draw blood! For a
hundred and sixteen years: — but the Final Bargain, lying on
parchment in the archives of both parties, and always acknowl-
edged as final, was to this effect: "You serene Neuburg keep
what you have got; we serene Brandenburg the like: Cleve
with detached pertinents ours; Jülich-and-Berg mainly yours.
And let us live in perpetual amity on that footing. And, note
only furthermore, when our Line fails, the whole of these fine
Duchies shall be yours: if your Line fail, ours." That was
the plain bargain, done solemnly in 1624, and again more
solemnly and brought to parchment with signature in 1666, as
Friedrich Wilhelm knows too well. And now the very case
is about to occur; this old man, childless at seventy, is the
last of the Neuburgs. May not one reasonably pretend that
a bargain should be kept?

"Tush," answers old Karl Philip always: "Bargain?"
And will not hear reason against himself on the subject; not
even when the Kaiser asks him, — as the Kaiser really did,
after that Wusterhausen Treaty, but could get only nega-
tives. Karl Philip has no romantic ideas of justice, or of old
parchments tying up a man. Karl Philip had one Daughter
by that dear Radzivil Princess, Sobieski's stolen Bride; and
he never, by the dear Radzivil or her dear successor,[1] had
any son, or other daughter that lived to wed. One Daughter, we say; a first-born, extremely precious to him. Her he
married to the young fortunate Sulzbach Cousin, Karl Joseph
Heir-Apparent of Sulzbach, who, by all laws, was to succeed
in the Pfalz as well, — Karl Philip thinking furthermore, "He
and she, please Heaven, shall hold fast by Düsseldorf too, and
that fine Jülich-and-Berg Territory, which is mine. Bargains?"
Such was, and is, the old man's inflexible notion. Alas, this
one Daughter died lately, and her Husband lately;[2] again
leaving only Daughters; will not this change the notion?
Not a whit, — though Friedrich Wilhelm may have fondly

[1] See Buchholz, i. 61 n.
[2] She in 1728; he in 1729: their eldest Daughter was born 1721 (Hübner,
t. 140; Michaelis, ii. 101, 123).

hoped it by possibility might. Not a whit: Karl Philip cherishes his little Grand-daughter, now a child of nine, as he did her Mother and her Mother's Mother; hopes one day to see her wedded (as he did) to a new Heir-Apparent of the Pfalz and Sulzbach; and, for her behoof, will hold fast by Berg and Jülich, and part with no square inch of it for any parchment.

What is Friedrich Wilhelm to do? Seek justice for himself by his 80,000 men and the iron ramrods? Apparently he will not get it otherwise. He is loath to begin that terrible game. If indeed Europe do take fire, as is likely at Seville or elsewhere — But in the meanwhile how happy if negotiation would but serve! Alas, and if the Kaiser, England, Holland and the others, could be brought to guarantee me, — as indeed they should (to avoid a *casus belli*), and some of them have said they will! Friedrich Wilhelm tried this Jülich-and-Berg Problem by the pacific method, all his life; strenuously, and without effect. Result perhaps was coming nevertheless; at the distance of another hundred years! One thing I know: whatever rectitude and patience, whatever courage, perseverance, or other human virtue he has put into this or another matter, is not lost; not it nor any fraction of it, to Friedrich Wilhelm and his sons' sons; but will well avail him and them, if not soon, then later, if not in Berg and Jülich, then in some other quarter of the Universe, which is a wide Entity and a long-lived! Courage, your Majesty!

So stand matters as Friedrich Wilhelm journeys towards Mannheim: human politeness will have to cloak well, and keep well down, a good many prickly points in the visit ahead. Alas, poor Friedrich Wilhelm has got other matter to think of, by the time we arrive in Mannheim.

Catastrophe on Journey Homewards.

The Royal Party, quitting Ludwigsburg, — on Thursday, 3d August, 1730, some hours after dinner, as I calculate it, — had but a rather short journey before them: journey to a place called Sinzheim, some fifty or sixty miles; a long way

short of Heidelberg; the King's purpose being to lodge in
that dilapidated silent Town of Sinzheim, and leave both
Heidelberg and Mannheim, with their civic noises, for the
next day's work. Sinzheim, such was the program, as the
Prince and others understood it; but by some accident, or
on better calculation, it was otherwise decided in the royal
mind: not at Sinzheim, intricate decayed old Town, shall
we lodge to-night, but five or six miles short of it, in the
naturally silent Village of Steinfurth, where good clean empty
Barns are to be found. Which latter is a favorite method of
his Majesty, fond always of free air and the absence of fuss.
Shake-downs, a temporary cooking apparatus, plenty of tobacco, and a tub to wash in: this is what man requires, and
this without difficulty can be got. His Majesty's tastes are
simple; simple, and yet good and human. Here is a small
Royal Order, which I read once, and ever since remember, —
though the reference is now blown away, and lost in those
unindexed Sibylline Farragos, the terror of human nature; —
let us copy it from memory, till some deliverer arise with
finger on page.[1] "At Magdeburg, on this Review-Journey,
have dinner for me, under a certain Tree you know of, outside
the ramparts." Dinner of one sound portion solid, one ditto
liquid, of the due quality; readied honestly, — and to be
eaten under a shady Tree; on the Review-ground itself, with
the summer sky over one's head. Could Jupiter Tonans,
had he been travelling on business in those parts, have done
better with his dinner? —

"At Sinzheim?" thinks his Royal Highness; and has
spoken privily to the Page Keith. To glide out of their
quarters there, in that waste negligent old Town (where post-
horses can be had), in the gray of the summer's dawn?
Across the Rhine to Speyer is but three hours riding; thence
to Landau, into France, into — ? Enough, Page Keith has

[1] Probably in Rödenbeck's *Beiträge*, — but long sad searching there, and
elsewhere, proves unavailing at present. Historical Farragos without *Index;*
a hundred, or several hundred, blind sacks of Historical clippings, generally
authentic too if useless, and not the least scrap of *label* on them: — are not
these a handy article!

undertaken to get horses, and the flight shall at last be. Husht, husht. To-morrow morning, before the sparrow wake, it is our determination to be upon the road!

Ruins of the Tower of Stauffen, *Hohen* or High *Stauffen,* where Kaiser Barbarossa lived once, young and ruddy, and was not yet a *Myth,* "winking and nodding under the Hill at Salzburg," — yes, it is but a few miles to the right there, were this a deliberate touring party. But this is a rapid driving one; knows nothing about Stauffen, cares nothing. — We cannot fancy Friedrich remembered Barbarossa at all; or much regarded Heilbronn itself, the principal and only famous Town they pass this day. The St. Kilian's Church, your Highness, and big stone giant at the top of the steeple yonder, — adventurous masons and slater people get upon the crown of his head, sometimes, and stand waving flags.[1] The Town-house too (*Rathhaus*), with its amazing old Clock? And Götz von Berlichingen, the Town-Councillors once had him in prison for one night, in the "Götz's Tower" here; your Highness has heard of "Götz with the Iron Hand"? Berlichingens still live at Jaxthausen, farther down the Neckar Valley, in these parts; and show the old *Hand,* considerably rusted now. Heilbronn, the most famous City on the Neckar; and its old miraculous Holy Well — ? What cares his Highness! Weinsberg again, which is but a few miles to the right of us, — there it was that the Besieged Wives did that astonishing feat, 600 years ago; coming out, as the capitulation bore, "with their most valuable property," each brought her Husband on her back (were not the fact a little uncertain!) — whereby the old Castle has, to this day, the name " *Weibertreue,* Faithfulness of Women." Welf's Duchess, Husband on back, was at the head of those women; a Hohenzollern ancestor of yours, I think I have heard, was of the besieging party.[2] Alas, thinks his Royal Highness, is there not a

---

[1] Buddäus, *Lexicon,* ii. § Heilbronn.

[2] Siege is notorious enough; A.D. 1140: Köhler *Reichshistorie,* p. 167, who does not mention the story of the women; Menzel (Wolfgang), *Geschichte der Deutschen,* p. 287, who takes no notice that it is a highly mythical story, — supported only by the testimony of one poor Monk in ·Köln, vaguely chronicling fifty years after date, and at that good distance.

flower of Welfdom now in England; and I, unluckiest of
Hohenzollerns, still far away from her here! It is at Windsor, not in Weinsberg, or among the ruins of *Weibertreue*,
that his Highness wishes to be.

At Heilbronn our road branches off to the left; and we roll
diligently towards Sinzheim, calculating to be there before
nightfall. Whew! Something has gone awry at Sinzheim:
no right lodging in the waste Inns there; or good clean Barns,
of a promising character, are to be had nearer than there: we
absolutely do not go to Sinzheim to-night; we are to stop at
Steinfurth, a small quiet Hamlet with Barns, four or five miles
short of that! This was a great disappointment to the Prince,
—and some say, a highly momentous circumstance in his
History: [1] — however, he rallies in the course of the evening;
speaks again to Page Keith. "Steinfurth [*Stony-ford*, over
the Brook here]; be it at Steinfurth, all the same!" Page
Keith will manage to get horses for us here, no less. And
Speyer and the Ferry of the Rhine are within three hours.
Favor us, Silence and all ye good genii! —

On Friday morning, 4th August, 1730, "usual hour of starting, 3 A.M.," not being yet come, the Royal Party lies asleep
in two clean airy Barns, facing one another, in the Village of
Steinfurth; Barns facing one another, with the Heidelberg
Highway and Village Green asleep in front between them; [2]
for it is little after two in the morning, the dawn hardly
beginning to break. Prince Friedrich, with his Trio of Vigilance, Buddenbrock, Waldau, Rochow, lies in one Barn;
Majesty, with his Seckendorf and party, is in the other: apparently all still locked in sleep? Not all: Prince Friedrich,
for example, is awake; — the Trio is indeed audibly asleep;
unless others watch for them, their six eyes are closed. Friedrich cautiously rises; dresses; takes his money, his new red

---

[1] "Might perhaps have succeeded at Sinzheim" (Seckendorf's *Relation of
the Crown-Prince's meditated Flight*, p. 2; — addressed to Prince Eugene few
days afterwards; given in Förster, iii. 1–13).

[2] Compare Wilhelmina, i. 259 (her Account of the Flight: "Heard it from
my Brother," — and report it loosely after a dozen years!).

roquelaure, unbolts the Barn-door, and walks out. Trio of
Vigilance is sound asleep, and knows nothing: alas, Trio of
Vigilance, while its own six eyes are closed, has appointed
another pair to watch.

Gummersbach the Valet comes to Rochow's bolster: "Hst,
Herr Oberst-Lieutenant, please awaken! Prince Royal is up,
has on his top-coat, and is gone out of doors!" Rochow starts
to his habiliments, or perhaps has them ready on; in a minute
or two, Rochow also is forth into the gray of the morning; —
finds the young Prince actually on the Green there; in his
red roquelaure, leaning pensively on one of the travelling carriages. "*Guten Morgen, Ihro Königliche Hoheit!*" [1] — Fancy
such a salutation to the young man! Page Keith, at this
moment, comes with a pair of horses, too: "Whither with the
nags, Sirrah?" Rochow asked with some sharpness. Keith,
seeing how it was, answered without visible embarrassment,
"Herr, they are mine and Kunz the Page's horses" (which, I
suppose, is true); "ready at the usual hour!" Keith might
add. — "His Majesty does not go till five this morning; —
back to the stables!" beckoned Rochow; and, according to
the best accounts, did not suspect anything, or affected not
to do so.

Page Keith returned, trembling in his saddle. Friedrich
strolled towards the other Barn, — at least to be out of Rochow's company. Seckendorf emerges from the other Barn;
awake at the common hour: "How do you like his Royal
Highness in the red roquelaure?" asks Rochow, as if nothing
had happened. Was there ever such a baffled Royal Highness;
or young bright spirit chained in the Bear's Den in this manner? Our Steinfurth project has gone to water; and it is not
to-day we shall get across the Rhine! — Not to-day; nor any
other day, on that errand, strong as our resolutions are! For
new light, in a few hours afterwards, pours in upon the project; and human finesse, or ulterior schemes, avail nothing
henceforth. "The Crown-Prince's meditated Flight" has tried
itself, and failed. Here and so that long meditation *ends;*
this at Steinfurth was all the over-act it could ever come to.

[1] Ranke, i. 305.

In few hours more it will melt into air; and only the terrible
consequences will remain! —

By last night's arrangement, the Prince with his Trio was
to set out an hour before his Father, which circumstance had
helped Page Keith in his excuses.   Naturally the Prince had
now no wish to linger on the Green of Steinfurth, in such a
posture of affairs: "Towards Heidelberg, then; let us see the
big Tun there: *allons!*"   How the young Prince and his Trio
did this day's journey; where he loitered, what he saw, said
or thought, we have no account: it is certain only that his
Father, who set out from Steinfurth an hour after him, arrived
in Mannheim several hours before him; and, in spite of Kurfürst Karl Philip's welcome, testified the liveliest inquietude
on that unaccountable circumstance.   Beautiful Rhine-stream,
thrice-beautiful trim Mannheim; — yes, all is beautiful indeed,
your Serenity!   But where can the Prince be?   he kept ejacu-
lating.   And Karl Philip had to answer what he could.   Of
course the Prince may be lingering about Heidelberg, looking
at the big Tun and other miracles: — "I had the pleasure to
repair that world-famous Tub or Tun, as your Majesty knows;
which had lain half burnt, ever since Louis XIV. with his
firebrand robberies lay upon us, and burnt the Pfalz in whole,
small honor to him!   I repaired the Tun:[1] it is probably the
successfulest feat I did hitherto; and well worth looking at,
had your Majesty had time!" — "*Ja wohl;* — but he came
away an hour before me!" — The polite Karl Philip, at length,
sent off one of his own Equerries to ride towards Heidelberg,
or even to Steinfurth if needful, and see what was become of
the Prince.   This Official person met the Prince, all in order,
at no great distance; and brought him safe to Papa's presence
again.

Why Papa was in such a fuss about this little circumstance?
Truly there has something come to Papa's knowledge since he

---

[1] Köhler, *Münzbelustigungen* (viii. 418–424; 145–152), who gives a view of
the world's wonder, lying horizontal with stairs running up to it.   Big Tuns
of that kind were not uncommon in Germany; and had uses, if multiplex dues
of wine were to be paid *in naturâ:* the Heidelberg, the biggest of them, is
small to the Whitbread-and-Company, for porter's-ale, in our time.

started, perhaps since he arrived at Mannheim. Page Keith, who rides always behind the King's coach, has ridden this day in an agony of remorse and terror ; and at length (probably in Mannheim, once his Majesty is got to his Apartments, or now that he finds his Majesty so anxious there) has fallen on his knees, and, with tears and obtestations, made a clean breast. Page Keith has confessed that the Crown-Prince and he were to have been in Speyer, or farther, at this time of the day ; flying rapidly into France. "God's Providence alone prevented it ! Pardon, pardon : slay me, your Majesty ; but there is the naked truth, and the whole of it, and I have nothing more to say ! " Hereupon ensues despatch of the Equerry ; and hereupon, as we may conjecture, the Equerry's return with Fritz and the Trio is an unspeakable relief to Friedrich Wilhelm.

Friedrich Wilhelm now summons Buddenbrock and Company straightway ; shows, in a suppressed-volcanic manner, with questions and statements, — obliged to *suppress* oneself in foreign hospitable Serene Houses, — what atrocity of scandal and terror has been on the edge of happening : "And you three, Rochow, Waldau, Buddenbrock, mark it, you three are responsible ; and shall answer, I now tell you, with your heads. Death the penalty, unless you bring *him* to our own Country again, — 'living or dead,' " added the Suppressed-Volcano, in low metallic tone ; and the sparkling eyes of him, the red tint, and rustling gestures, make the words too credible to us.[1]

What Friedrich Wilhelm got to speak about with the old Kur-Pfalz, during their serene psssages of hospitality at Mannheim, is not very clear to me ; his Prussian Majesty is privately in such a desperate humor, and the old Kur-Pfalz privately so discrepant on all manner of points, especially on the Jülich-and-Berg point. They could talk freely about the old Turk Campaigns, Battle of Zentha,[2] and Prince Eugene ;

[1] Ranke, i. 307.

[2] 11th September, 1697 ; Eugene's crowning feat ; — breaking of the Grand Turk's back in this world ; who has staggered about, less and less of a terror and outrage, more and more of a nuisance growing unbearable, ever since that day. See Hormayr (iii. 97–101) for some description of this useful bit of Heroism.

very freely about the Heidelberg Tun. But it is known old
Karl Philip had his agents at the Congress of Soissons, to
secure that Berg-and-Jülich interest for the Sulzbachs and him :
directly in the teeth of Friedrich Wilhelm. How that may
have gone, since the Treaty of Seville broke out to astonish
mankind, — will be unsafe to talk about. For the rest, old
Karl Philip has frankly adopted the Pragmatic Sanction ; but
then he has, likewise, privately made league with France to
secure him in that Jülich-and-Berg matter, should the Kaiser
break promise ; — league which may much obstruct said Sanction. Nay privately he is casting glances on his Bavarian
Cousin, elegant ambitious Karl Albert Kurfürst of Baiern, —
are not we all from the same Wittelsbach stock, Cousins from
of old ? — and will undertake, for the same Jülich-and-Berg
object, to secure Bavaria in *its* claims on the Austrian Heritages in defect of Heirs Male in Austria.[1] Which runs directly
into the throat of said Pragmatic Sanction ; and engages to
make it mere waste sheepskin, so to speak! Truly old Karl
Philip has his abstruse outlooks, this way, that way ; most abstruse politics altogether : — and in fact we had better speak
of the Battle of Zentha and the Heidelberg Tun, while this
Visit lasts.

On the morrow, Saturday, August 5th, certain Frenchmen
from the Garrison of Landau come across to pay their court
and dine. Which race of men Friedrich Wilhelm does not
love ; and now less than ever, gloomily suspicious they may
be come on parricide Fritz's score, — you Rochow and Company keep an eye ! By night and by day an eye upon him !
Friedrich Wilhelm was, no doubt, glad to get away on the
morrow afternoon ; fairly out into the Berg-Strasse, into the
summer breezes and umbrageous woods, with all his pertinents
still safe about him ; rushing towards Darmstadt through the
Sunday stillness, where he will arrive in the evening, time
enough.[2]

The old Prince of Darmstadt, Ernst Ludwig, Landgraf of

---

[1] Michaelis, ii. 99–101.

[2] "Sunday Evening arrive at Darmstadt," says Seckendorf (in Förster,
iii. 3), but by mistake calls it the "7th" instead of "6th."

Hessen-Darmstadt, age now sixty-three, has a hoary venerable appearance, according to Pöllnitz, " but sits a horse well, walks well, and seems to enjoy perfect health," — which we are glad to hear of. What more concerns us, " he lives usually, quite retired, in a small house upon the Square," in this extremely small Metropolis of his, " and leaves his Heir-Apparent to manage all business in the Palace and elsewhere." [1] Poor old Gentleman, he has the biggest Palace almost in the world; only he could not finish it for want of funds; and it lies there, one of the biggest futilities, vexatious to look upon. No doubt the old Gentleman has had vexations, plenty of them, first and last. He is now got disgusted with the affairs of public life, and addicts himself very much to "turning ivory," as the more eligible employment. He lives in that small house of his, among his turning-lathes and ivory shavings; dines in said small house, " at a table for four persons : " only on Sunday, and above all on this Sunday, puts off his apron; goes across to the Palace; dines there in state, with his Heir and the Grandees. He has a kinship by affinity to Friedrich Wilhelm; his Wife (dead long years since), Mother of this Heir-Apparent, was an Anspach Princess, Aunt to the now Queen Caroline of England. Poor old fellow, these insignificancies, and that he descends. direct from Philip the Magnanimous of Hessen (Luther's Philip, who insisted on the supplementary Wife), are all I know of him ; and he is somewhat tragic to me there, turning ivory in this extremely anarchic world. What the passages between him and Friedrich Wilhelm were, on this occasion, shall remain conjectural to all creatures. Friedrich Wilhelm said, this Sunday evening at Darmstadt, to his own Prince: " Still here, then ? I thought you would have been in Paris by this time ! " — To which the Prince, with artificial firmness, answered, He could certainly, if he had wished ; [2] and being familiar with reproaches, perhaps hoped it was nothing.

From Darmstadt to Frankfurt-on-Mayn is not quite forty miles, an easy morning drive ; through the old Country called

[1] Pöllnitz, *Memoirs and Letters*, ii. 66.
[2] Seckendorf (in Förster, iii.), p. 3.

of Katzen-ellenbogen ; *Cats-Elbow*, a name ridiculous to hear.[1]
Berg-Strasse and the Odenwald (*Forest* of the *Otti*) are gone;
but blue on the northeast yonder, if your Royal Highness
will please to look, may be seen summits of the *Spessart*, a
much grander forest, — tall branchy timbers yonder, one day to
be masts of admirals, when floated down as far as Rotterdam,
whitherward one still meets them going.   Spessart ; — and
nearer, well hidden on the right, is an obscure village called
Dettingen, not yet become famous in the Newspapers of an
idle world ; of an England surely very idle to go thither seeking quarrels!   All which is, naturally, in the highest degree
indifferent to a Crown-Prince so preoccupied. — They reach
Frankfurt, Monday, still in good time.

Behold, at Frankfurt, the Trio of Vigilance, Buddenbrock
and Company (horrible to think of!) signify, "That we have
the King's express orders Not to enter the Town at all with
your Royal Highness.   We, for our part, are to go direct into
one of the Royal Yachts, which swing at anchor here, and to
wait in the same till his Majesty have done seeing Frankfurt,
and return to us."   Here is a message for the poor young
Prince : Detected, prisoner, and a volcanic Majesty now likely
to be in full play when he returns ! — Gilt weathercock on the
Mayn Bridge (which one Goethe used to look at, in the next
generation) — this, and the steeple-tops of Frankfurt, especially that steeple-top with the grinning skull of the mutinous malefactor on it, warning to mankind what mutiny leads
to ; this, then, is what we are to see of Frankfurt; and with
such a symphony as our thoughts are playing in the background.   Unhappy Son, unhappy Father, once more !

Nay Friedrich Wilhelm got new lights in Frankfurt : Rittmeister Katte had an estafette waiting for him there.   Estafette with a certain Letter, which the Rittmeister had picked
up in Erlangen, and has shot across by estafette to wait his

---

[1] *Cattimelibocum,* that is, *Cattûm-Melibocum* (*Catti* a famed Nation, *Meli-
bocus* the chief Hill or Fortress of their Country), is said to be the original ; —
which has got changed ; like *Aballaba* into "Appleby," or *God encompass us*
into "The Goat and Compasses," among ourselves.

Majesty here. Majesty has read with open eyes and throat:
Letter from the Crown-Prince to Lieutenant Katte in Berlin:
treasonous Flight-project now indisputable as the sun at noon!
— His Majesty stept on board the Yacht in such humor as
was never seen before : " Detestable rebel and deserter, scandal of scandals — ! " — it is confidently written everywhere
(though Seckendorf diplomatically keeps silence), his Majesty
hustled and tussled the unfortunate Crown-Prince, poked the
handle of his cane into his face and made the nose bleed, —
" Never did a Brandenburg face suffer the like of this!" cried
the poor Prince, driven to the edge of mad ignition and one
knows not what : when the Buddenbrocks, at whatever peril,
interfered; got the Prince brought on board a different Yacht;
and the conflagration moderated for the moment. The Yachts
get under way towards Mainz and down the Rhine-stream.
The Yachts glide swiftly on the favoring current, taking advantage of what wind there may be : were we once ashore
at Wesel in our own country, — wait till then, thinks his
Majesty !

And so it was on these terms that Friedrich made his first
acquaintance with the beauties of the Rhine; — readers can
judge whether he was in a temper very open to the picturesque. I know not that they paused at Mainz, or recollected
Barbarossa's World-Tournament, or the Hochheim vineyards
at all: I see the young man's Yacht dashing in swift gallop,
not without danger, through the Gap of Bingen; dancing
wildly on the boiling whirlpools of St. Goar, well threading
the cliffs ; — the young man gloomily insensible to danger of
life, and charm of the picturesque. Coblenz (*Confluentia*),
the Moselle and Ehrenbreitstein : Majesty, smoking on deck
if he like, can look at these through grimly pacifying tobacco;
but to the Crown-Prince life itself is fallen haggard and bankrupt.

Over against Coblenz, nestled in between the Rhine and the
foot of Ehrenbreitstein,[1] there, perhaps even now, in his Hunting Lodge of Kerlich yonder, is his Serene Highness the fat

[1] Pöllnitz, *Memoirs and Letters*, iii. 180.

little Kurfürst of Trier, one of those Austrian Schönborns
(Brother to him of Bamberg); upon whom why should we
make a call? We are due at Bonn; the fortunate young
Kurfürst of Köln, richest Pluralist in the Church, expects us
at his Residence there. Friedrich Wilhelm views the fine
Fortress of Ehrenbreitstein: — what would your Majesty think
if this were to be yours in a hundred years; this and much
else, by way of compound-interest for the Berg-and-Jülich and
other outstanding debts? Courage, your Majesty! — On the
fat little Kurfürst, at Kerlich here, we do not call: probably
out hunting; "hunts every day," [1] as if it were his trade, poor
little soul.

At Bonn, where we do step ashore to lodge with a lean Kurfürst, Friedrich Wilhelm strictly charges, in my (Seckendorf's)
hearing, the Trio of Vigilance to have an eye; to see that they
bring the Prince on board again, "*living or dead.*" — No fear,
your Majesty. Prince listened with silent, almost defiant
patience, "*mit grosser Geduld.*" [2] At Bonn the Prince contrived to confide to Seckendorf, "That he had in very truth
meant to run away: he could not, at the age he was come to,
stand such indignities, actual strokes as in the Camp of Radewitz; — and he would have gone long since, had it not been
for the Queen and the Princess his Sister's sake. He could
not repent what he had done: and if the King did not cease
beating him in that manner, &c., he would still do it. For
loss of his own life, such a life as his had grown, he cared
little; his chief misery was, that those Officers who had
known of the thing should come to misfortune by his means.
If the King would pardon these poor gentlemen, he would tell
him everything. For the rest, begged Seckendorf to help him
in this labyrinth; — nothing could ever so oblige him as help
now;" and more of the like sort. These things he said, at
Bonn, to Seckendorf, the fountain of all his woes.[3] What
Seckendorf's reflections on this his sad handiwork now were,
we do not know. Probably he made none, being a strong-
minded case-hardened old stager; but resolved to do what he
could for the poor youth. Somewhere on this route, at Bonn

[1] Büsching, *Beiträge*, iv 201.   [2] Seckendorf (in Förster, iii. 4).   [3] Ibid.

more likely than elsewhere, Friedrich wrote in pencil three words to Lieutenant Keith at Wesel, and got it to the Post-Office: " *Sauvez-vous, tout est découvert* (All is found out; — away)! " [1]

Clement August, expensive Kurfürst of Köln (Elector of Cologne, as we call it), who does the hospitalities here at Bonn, in a grand way, with " above a hundred and fifty chamberlains " for one item, — glance at him, reader; perhaps we shall meet the man again. He is younger Brother of the elegant ambitious Karl Albert, Kurfürst of Bavaria, whom we have transiently heard of: sons both of them are of that " Elector of Bavaria " who haunts us in the Marlborough Histories, — who joined Louis XIV. in the Succession War, and got hunted about at such a rate, after Blenheim especially. His Boys, prisoners of the Kaiser, were bred up in a confiscated state, as sons of a mere private gentleman; nothing visibly ahead of them, at one time, but an obscure and extremely limited destiny of that kind; — though now again, on French favor, and the turn of Fortune's inconstant wheel, they are mounting very high. Bavaria came all back to the old Elector of Bavaria; even Marlborough's " Principality of *Mindelheim* " came.[2] And the present Kurfürst, who will not do the Pragmatic Sanction at all, — Kurfürst Karl Albert of Baiern, our old Karl Philip of Mannheim's genealogical " Cousin; " — we heard of abstruse colleaguings there, tendencies to break the Pragmatic Sanction altogether, and reduce it to waste sheepskin! Not impossible Karl Albert will go high enough. And this Clement August the cadet, he is Kurfürst of Köln; by good election-tactics, and favor of the French, he has managed to succeed an Uncle here: has succeeded at Osnabrück in like fashion; — poor old Ernst August of Osnabrück (to whom we

[1] Wilhelmina (i. 265) says it was a Page of the Old Dessauer's, a comrade of Keith's, who, having known in time, gave him warning. Certain it is, this Note of Friedrich's, which the Books generally assign as cause, could not have done it (infrà, p. 275, and the irrefragable date there).

[2] At the Peace of Baden (corollary to *Utrecht*), 1714. Elector had been " banned " (*geächtet*, solemnly drummed out), 1706; nothing but French pay to live upon, till he got back: died 26th February, 1726, when Karl Albert succeeded (Michaelis, ii. 255).

once saw George I. galloping to die, and who himself soon
after died), his successor is this same Clement August, the
turn for a *Catholic* Bishop being come at Osnabrück, and the
French being kind.   Kurfürst of Köln, Bishop of Osnabrück,
ditto of Paderborn and Münster, ditto now of Hildesheim ;
richest Pluralist of the Church.   Goes about here in a languid
expensive manner ; "in green coat trimmed with narrow silver-
lace, small bag-wig done with French garniture (*Schleife*) in
front; and has red heels to his shoes."   A lanky indolent
figure, age now thirty ; "tall and slouching of person, long
lean face, hook-nose, black beard, mouth somewhat open." [1]
Has above one hundred and fifty chamberlains ; — and, I doubt
not, is inexpressibly wearisome to Friedrich Wilhelm in his
Majesty's present mood.   Patience for the moment, and politeness above all things ! — The Trio of Vigilance had no difficulty with Friedrich ; brought him on board safe again next
day, and all proceeded on their voyage ; the Kurfürst in person politely escorting as far as Köln.

Köln, famed old City of the Three Kings, with its famed
Cathedral where those three gentlemen are buried, here the
Kurfürst ceases escorting ; and the flat old City is left, exciting what reflections it can.   The architectural Dilettanti of
the world gather here ; St. Ursula and her Eleven Thousand
Virgins were once massacred here, your Majesty ; an English
Princess she, it is said.   " *Narren-possen* (Pack of nonsense) ! "
grumbles Majesty. — Pleasant Düsseldorf is much more interesting to his Majesty ; the pleasant Capital of Berg, which
ought to be *ours*, if right could be done ; if old Pfalz would
give up his crotchets ; and the bowls, in the big game playing
at Seville and elsewhere, would roll fair !   Düsseldorf and
that fine Palace of the Pfalzers, which ought to be mine ; —
and here next is Kaiserswerth, a place of sieges, cannonadings,
known to those I knew.   '*M-na*, from father to son and grandson it goes on, and there is no end to trouble and war ! —

---

[1] Büsching (*Beiträge*, iv. 201–204 : from a certain Travelling Tutor's *MS.
Diary* of 1731 ; where also is detail of the Kurfürst's mode of Dining, — elaborate but dreary, both mode and detail).   His Schloss is now the Bonn University.

THE REBELLIOUS PRINCE.

Carlyle, Vol. Two, p. 65.

His Majesty's next lodging is at Mörs; old gaunt Castle in the Town of Mörs, which (thanks to Leopold of Anhalt-Dessau and the Iron Ramrods) *is* now his Majesty's in spite of the Dutch. There the lodging is, at an hour's drive westward from the Rhine-shore: — where his Majesty quitted the River, I do not know; nor whether the Crown-Prince went to Mörs with him, or waited in his Yacht; but guess the latter. His Majesty intends for Geldern on the morrow, on matters of business thither, for the Town is his: but what would the Prince, in the present state of things, do there? — At Mörs, Seckendorf found means to address his Majesty privately, and snuffled into him suggestions of mercy to the repentant Prince, and to the poor Officers whom he was so anxious about. "Well, if he *will* confess everything, and leave off his quirks and concealments: but I know he won't!" answered Majesty.

In that dilapidated Castle of Mörs, — look at it, reader, though in the dark; we may see it again, or the shadow of it, perhaps by moonlight. A very gaunt old Castle; next to nothing living in it, since the old Dessauer (by stratagem, and without shot fired) flung out the Dutch, in the Treaty-of-Utrecht time; Mörs Castle and Territory being indisputably ours, though always withheld from us on pretexts.[1]

At Geldern, in the pressure of business next day, his Majesty got word from Wesel, that Lieutenant Keith was not now to be found in Wesel. "Was last seen there (that we can hear of) certain hours before your Majesty's All-gracious Order arrived. Had saddled his own horse; came ambling through the Brünen Gate, 'going out to have a ride,' he said; and did not return." — "Keith gone, scandalous Keith, whom I par-

---

[1] Narrative of the march thither (Night of 7th November, 1712), and dexterous surprisal of the place, in *Leopoldi von Anhalt-Dessau Leben und Thaten* (Anonymous, by *Ranfft*), pp. 85-90; — where the Despatch of the astonished Dutch Commandant himself, to their High Mightinesses, is given. Part of the Orange Heritage, this Mörs, — came by the Great Elector's first Wife; — but had hung *sub lite* (though the Parchments were plain enough) ever since our King William's death, and earlier. Neuchâtel, accepted instead of *Orange*, and not even of the value of Mörs, was another item of the same lot. Besides which, we shall hear of old Palaces at Loo and other dilapidated objects, incidentally in time coming.

doned only few weeks ago; he too is in the Plot! Will the
very Army break its oath, then?" His Majesty bursts into
fire and flame, at these new tidings; orders that Colonel
Dumoulin (our expertest rogue-tracer) go instantly on the
scent of Keith, and follow him till found and caught. Also,
on the other hand, that the Crown-Prince be constituted prisoner; sail down to Wesel, prisoner in his Yacht, and await
upon the Rhine there his Majesty's arrival. Formidable
omens, it is thought.

His Majesty, all business done in Geldern, drives across to
Wesel; can see Fritz's Yacht waiting duly in the River, and
black Care hovering over her. It is on the evening of the 12th
of August, 1730. And so his Majesty ends this memorable
Tour into the Reich; but has not yet ended the gloomy miseries, for himself and others, which plentifully sprung out of
that.

———————•———————

CHAPTER VII.

CATASTROPHE, AND MAJESTY, ARRIVE IN BERLIN.

At Berlin dark rumors of this intended flight, and actual
Arrest of the Crown-Prince, are agitating all the world; especially Lieutenant Katte, and the Queen and Wilhelmina, as
we may suppose. The first news of it came tragically on the
young Princess.[1]

"Mamma had given a ball in honor of Papa's Birthday," —
Tuesday, 15th August, 1730; — and we were all dancing in
the fine saloons of Monbijou, with pretty intervals in the cool
boscages and orangeries of the place: all of us as happy as
could be; Wilhelmina, in particular, dancing at an unusual
rate. "We recommenced the ball after supper. For six years
I had not danced before; it was new fruit, and I took my fill

———

[1] Apparently some rumor *from Frankfurt*, which she confuses in her after-
memory with the specific news *from Wesel;* for her dates here, as usual, are
all awry (Wilhelmina, i. 246; Preuss, i. 42, iv. 473; Seckendorf, in Förster,
iii. 6).

of it, without heeding much what was passing. Madame
Bülow, who with others of them had worn long faces all night,
pleading 'illness' when one noticed it, said to me several
times: 'It is late, I wish you had done.' — '*Eh, mon Dieu!*'
I answered, 'let me have enough of dancing this one new
time; it may be long before it comes again.' — 'That may well
be!' said she. I paid no regard, but continued to divert myself. She returned to the charge half an hour after: 'Will
you end, then!' said she with a vexed air: 'you are so engaged,
you have eyes for nothing.' — 'You are in such a humor,' I
replied, 'that I know not what to make of it.' — 'Look at the
Queen, then, Madam; and you will cease to reproach me!' A
glance which I gave that way filled me with terror. There sat
the Queen, paler than death, in a corner of the room, in low
conference with Sonsfeld and Countess Finkenstein. As my
Brother was most in my anxieties, I asked, If it concerned
him? Bülow shrugged her shoulders, answering, 'I don't
know at all!' A moment after, the Queen gave Good-night;
and got into her carriage with me, — speaking no word all the
way to the Schloss; so that I thought my Brother must be
dead, and I myself took violent palpitations, and Sonsfeld,
contrary to orders, had at last to tell me in the course of the
night." Poor Wilhelmina, and poor Mother of Wilhelmina!

The fact, of Arrest, and unknown mischief to the Prince,
is taken for certain; but what may be the issues of it; who
besides the Prince have been involved in it, especially who will
be found to have been involved, is matter of dire guess to the
three who are most interested here. Lieutenant Katte finds
he ought to dispose of the Prince's effects which were intrusted
to him; of the thousand gold Thalers in particular, and,
beyond and before all, of the locked Writing-desk, in which
lies the Prince's correspondence, the very Queen and Princess
likely to be concerned in it! Katte despatches these two objects, the Money and the little Desk, in all secrecy, to Madam
Finkenstein, as to the surest hand, with a short Note shadowing out what he thinks they are: Countess Finkenstein, old
General von Finkenstein's Wife, and a second mother to the
Prince, she, like her Husband, a sworn partisan of the Prince

and his Mother, shall do with these precious and terrible objects what, to her own wise judgment, seems best.

Madam Finkenstein carries them at once, in deep silence,
to the Queen. Huge dismay on the part of the Queen and
Princess. They know too well what Letters may be there:
and there is a seal on the Desk, and no key to it; neither must
it, in time coming, seem to have been opened, even if we could
now open it. A desperate pinch, and it must be solved.
Female wit and Wilhelmina did solve it, by some pre-eminently
acute device of their despair;[1] and contrived to get the Letters
out: hundreds of Letters, enough to be our death if read, says
Wilhelmina. These Letters they burnt; and set to writing,
fast as the pen would go, other letters in their stead. Fancy
the mood of these two Royal Women, and the black whirlwind
they were in. Wilhelmina's despatch was incredible; pen went
at the gallop night and day: new letters, of old dates and of no
meaning, are got into the Desk again; the Desk closed, without mark of injury, and shoved aside while it is yet time. —
Time presses; his Majesty too, and the events, go at gallop.
Here is a Letter from his Majesty, to a trusty Mistress of
the Robes, or whatever she is; which, let it arrive through
what softening media it likes, will complete the poor Queen's
despair: —

"MY DEAR FRAU VON KAMECKE, — Fritz has attempted to
desert. I have been under the necessity to have him arrested.
I request you to tell my Wife of it in some good way, that the
news may not terrify her. And pity an unhappy Father.
                                   "FRIEDRICH WILHELM."[2]

The same post brought an order to the Colonel of the Gens-
d'Armes to put that Lieutenant Katte of his under close confinement: — we hope the thoughtless young fellow has already
got out of the way? He is getting his saddle altered: fet-
tling about this and that; does not consider what danger he

---

[1] Wilhelmina, i. 253–257.

[2] No date: "arrived" (from Wesel, we conclude), Sunday, "20th August,"
at the Palace of Berlin (Preuss, i. 42).

is in. This same Sunday, his Major met him on the street
of Berlin; said, in a significant tone, "You still *here*,
Katte!" — "I go this night," answered Katte; but he again
put it off, did not go this night; and the order for his arrest
did come in. On the morrow morning, Colonel Pannewitz,
hoping now he was not there, went with the rhadamanthine
order; and finding the unlucky fellow, was obliged to execute it. Katte lies in ward, awaiting what may be prepared
for him.

Friedrich Wilhelm at Wesel has had rough passages with
the Prince and others. On the Saturday evening, 12th August 1730,[1] his Majesty had the Culprit brought on shore,
to the Commandant's House, for an interview. Culprit proving less remorseful than was expected, and evidently not
confessing everything, a loud terrible scene ensued; which
Friedrich Wilhelm, the unhappy Father, winded up by drawing his sword to run the unnatural Son through the body.
Old General Mosel, Commandant of Wesel, sprang between
them, "Sire, cut me to death, but spare your Son!" and the
sword was got back to its scabbard; and the Prince lodged
in a separate room, two sentries with fixed bayonets keeping
watch over him. Friedrich Wilhelm did not see his face
again for twelve months to come, — "twelve months and three
days."

Military gentlemen of due grimness interrogated the Prince
next evening,[2] from a Paper drawn up by his Majesty in the
interim. Prince confesses little: Did design to get across the
Rhine to Landau; thence to Strasburg, Paris, in the strictest
incognito; intended to volunteer there, thought he might take
French service, profoundly incognito, and signalize himself in
the Italian War (just expected to break out), which might have
recovered him some favor from his Majesty: does not tell clearly
where his money came from; shy extremely of elucidating Katte
and Keith; — in fact, as we perceive, struggles against mendacity, but will not tell the whole truth. "Let him lie in ward,
then; and take what doom the Laws have appointed for the like

[1] Preuss, iv. 473; Seckendorf (Förster, iii. 6) says 13th, but *wrong*.
[2] Seckendorf (in Förster, iii. 5).

of him!" Divine Laws, are they not ? Well, yes, your Majesty, divine and human; — or are there perhaps no laws but the human sort, completely explicit in this case ? "He is my Colonel at least," thinks Friedrich Wilhelm, "and tried to desert and make others desert. If a rebellious Crown-Prince, breaking his Father's heart, find the laws still inarticulate; a deserting Colonel of the Potsdam Regiment finds them speak plain enough. Let him take the answer they give him."

Dumoulin, in the mean while, can make nothing of Keith, the runaway Lieutenant. Dumoulin, with his sagacious organ, soon came upon the scent of Keith; and has discovered these things about him: One evening, a week before his Majesty arrived, Sunday evening, 6th August, 1730,[1] Lieutenant Keith, doubtless smelling something, saddled his horse as above mentioned, decided to have a ride in the country this fine evening, and issued out at the Brünen Gate of Wesel. He is on the right bank of the Rhine; pleasant yellow fields on this hand and that. He ambles slowly, for a space; then gradually awakens into speed, into full speed; arrives, within a couple of hours, at Dingden, a Village in the Münster Territory, safe over the Prussian Border, by the shortest line: and from Dingden rides at more leisure, but without losing time, into the Dutch Overyssel region, straight towards the Hague. He must be in the Hague? said Dumoulin to the Official persons, on arriving there, — to Meinertshagen the Prussian Ambassador there,[2] and to Keppel, Dutch Official gentleman who was once Ambassador at Berlin. Prussian Ambassador applies, and again applies, in the highest quarters; but we fear they are slack. Dumoulin discovers that the man was certainly here; Keppel readily admits, He had Keith to dinner a few days ago: but where Keith now is, Keppel cannot form the least guess.

Dumoulin suspects he is with Lord Chesterfield, the English Ambassador here. A light was seen, for a night or two, in one of the garret-rooms of Lord Chesterfield's house, — probably Keith reading? — but Keith is not to be heard of, on inquiry there; and the very light has now gone out. The

---

[1] *Relatio ex Actis:* in Preuss, iv. 473.   [2] Seckendorf (Förster, iii. 7).

distinguished English Lord is gone to England in these days;
but his German Secretary is not gone : the House is inviolable,
impregnable to Prussia. Who knows, in spite of the light
going out, but Keith is still there, merely with a window shut-
ter to screen him ? One morning, it becomes apparent Keith
is not there. One morning, a gentleman at the seaside is admiring Dutch fishing-skiffs, and how they do sail. "Pooh, Sir,
that is nothing!" answers a man in multiplex breeches : "the
other night I went across to England in one, with an Excellency's Messenger who could not wait!" — Truth is, the Chesterfield Secretary, who forbade lights, took the first good night
for conveying Keith to Scheveningen and the seaside ; where
a Fisher-boat was provided for him ; which carried him, frail
craft as it was, safe across to England. Once there, the Authorities took pity on the poor fellow ; — furnished the modicum
of cash and help ; sent him with Admiral Norris to assist the
Portuguese, menaced with Spanish war at this time ; among
whom he gradually rose to be Major of Horse. Friedrich
Wilhelm cited him by tap of drum three times in Wesel, and
also in the Gazettes, native and Dutch ; then, as he did not
come, nailed an Effigy of him (cut in four, if I remember) on
the gallows there ; and confiscated any property he had.
Keith had more pedigree than property ; was of Poberow in
Pommern ; son of poor gentlefolks there. He sent no word
of himself to Prussia, for the next ten years ; so that he had
become a kind of myth to many people ; to his poor Mother
among the rest, who has her tragical surmises about him. He
will appear again ; but not to much purpose. His Brother, the
Page Keith, is packed into the Fusileer Regiment, at Wesel
here ; and there walks sentry, unheard of for the rest of his
life. So much for the Keiths.[1]

Other difficulty there is as to the Prison of the Prince.
Wesel is a strong Town ; but for obvious reasons one nearer
Berlin, farther from the frontier, would be preferable. To-

---

[1] Preuss: *Friedrich mit seinen Verwandten und Freunden*, pp. 380, 392. —
See, on this and the other points, Pöllnitz, *Memoiren*, ii. 352-374 (and correct
his many blunders).

wards Berlin, however, there is no route all on Prussian
ground: from these divided Cleve Countries we have to cross
a bit of Hanover, a bit of Hessen-Cassel: suppose these Serene Highnesses were to interfere ?   Not likely they will
interfere, answer ancient military men, of due grimness; at
any rate, we can go a roundabout road, and they need not
know ! That is the method settled on ; neighborhood of Berlin, clearly somewhere there, must be the place ?   Old Castle
of Mittenwalde, in the Wusterhausen environs, let that be the
first resting-point, then; Rochow, Waldau, and the Wesel
Fusileer-Colonel here, sure men, with a trooper or two for
escort, shall conduct the Prisoner. By Treuenbrietzen, by
circuitous roads : swift, silent, steady, — and with vigilance,
as you shall answer ! — These preliminaries settled, Friedrich
Wilhelm drives off homewards, black Care riding behind him.
He reaches Berlin, Sunday, 27th August ; finds a world gone
all to a kind of doomsday with him there, poor gentleman.

Scene at Berlin on Majesty's Arrival.

On Sunday evening, 27th August, 1730, his Majesty, who
had rested overnight at Potsdam from his rapid journey,
drove into Berlin between four and five in the afternoon.
Deserter Fritz is following, under escort of his three military
gentlemen, at a slower rate and by circuitous routes, so as to
avoid the territories of Hanover and Hessen, — towards Mittenwalde in the Wusterhausen neighborhood. The military
gentlemen are vigilant as Argus, and, though pitying the poor
Prince, must be rigorous as Rhadamanthus. His attempts at
escape, of which tradition mentions more than one, they will
not report to Papa, nor even notice to the Prince himself;
but will take care to render futile, one and all : his Majesty
may be secure on that score.

The scenes that follow are unusual in royal history ; and
having been reported in the world with infinite noise and
censure, made up of laughter and horror, it will behoove us
to be the more exact in relating them as they actually befell.
Very difficult to pull, out of that ravelled cart-load of chaotic

thrums, here a thread and there a thread, capable of being
brought to the straight state, and woven into legible narrative! But perhaps, by that method the mingled laughter and
horror will modify itself a little. What we can well say is,
that pity also ought not to be wanting. The next six months
were undoubtedly by far the wretchedest of Friedrich Wilhelm's life. The poor King, except that he was not conscious
of intending wrong, but much the reverse, walked in the hollow night of Gehenna, all that while, and was often like to be
driven mad by the turn things had taken.

Here is scene first: Wilhelmina reports his Majesty's arrival that Sunday afternoon, to the following effect; she was
present in the adventure, and not a spectatress only: —

"The Queen was alone in his Majesty's Apartment, waiting
for him as he approached. At sight of her, in the distance, he
called out: 'Your losel of a Son (*votre indigne fils*) has ended
at last; you have done with *him*,' or words to that effect.
'What,' cried the Queen, 'you have had the barbarity to kill
him?' 'Yes, I tell you, — but where is the sealed Desk?'
The Queen went to her own Apartment to fetch it; I ran in to
her there for a moment: she was out of herself, wringing her
hands, crying incessantly, and said without ceasing: '*Mon
Dieu, mon fils* (O God, my Son)!' Breath failed me; I fell
fainting into the arms of Madame de Sonsfeld." — The Queen
took away the Writing-case; King tore out the letters, and
went off; upon which the Queen came down again to us.

"We learned from some attendant that, at least, my Brother
was not dead. The King now came back. We all ran to kiss
his hands; but me he no sooner noticed than rage and fury
took possession of him. He became black in the face, his
eyes sparkling fire, his mouth foaming. 'Infamous *canaille*,'
said he; 'darest thou show thyself before me? Go, keep thy
scoundrel of a Brother company!' And so saying, he seized
me with one hand, slapping me on the face with the other,'
— clenched as a fist (*poing*), — 'several blows; one of which
struck me on the temple, so that I fell back, and should have
split my head against a corner of the wainscot, had not
Madame de Sonsfeld caught me by the head-dress and broken

the fall. I lay on the ground without consciousness. The
King, in a frenzy, was for striking me with his feet; had not
the Queen, my Sisters, and the rest, run between, and those
who were present prevented him. They all ranked themselves
round me, which gave Mesdames de Kamecke and Sonsfeld
time to pick me up. They put me in a chair in the embrasure
of a window; threw water on my face to bring me to life:
which care I lamentably reproached them with, death being a
thousand times better, in the pass things had come to. The
Queen kept shrieking, her firmness had quite left her: she
wrung her hands, and ran in despair up and down the room.
The King's face was so disfigured with rage, it was frightful
to look upon. The little ones were on their knees, begging
for me," [1] —

— poor little beings, what a group: Amelia, the youngest
girl, about six; Henri, in his bits of trousers, hardly over
four! — For the rest, I perceive, this room was on the first
or a lower floor, and such noises were very audible. The
Guard had turned out at the noise; and a crowd was col-
lecting to see and hear: "Move on! Move on!"

"The King had now changed his tune: he admitted that
my Brother was still alive; but vowed horribly he would put
him to death, and lay me fast within four walls for the rest
of my life. He accused me of being the Prince's accomplice,
whose crime was high treason; — also of having an intrigue
of love with Katte, to whom, he said, I had borne several
children." The timid Gouvernante flamed up at this unheard-
of insult: " 'That is not true,' said she, fiercely; 'whoever
has told your Majesty such a thing has told a lie!' 'Oh,
spare my Brother, and I will marry the Duke of Weissenfels,'
whimpered I; but in the great noise he did not hear; and
while I strove to repeat it louder, Sonsfeld clapt her handkerchief on my face.

"Hustling aside to get rid of the handkerchief, I saw Katte
crossing the Square. Four soldiers were conducting him to
the King; trunks, my Brother's and his own, sealed, were

[1] Wilhelmina, i. 265–267.

coming on in the rear. Pale and downcast, he took off his
hat to salute me," — poor Katte, to me always so prostrate in
silent respect, and now so unhappy! "A moment after, the
King, hearing he was come, went out exclaiming, 'Now I
shall have proof about the scoundrel Fritz and the offscour-
ing (*canaille*) Wilhelmina; clear proofs to cut the heads off
them.' " — The two Hofdames again interfered ; and one of
them, Kamecke it was, rebuked him ; told him, in the tone
of a prophetess, To take care what he was doing. Whom his
Majesty gazed into with astonishment, but rather with respect than with anger, saying, "Your intentions are good!"

And so his Majesty flung out, seeking Katte ; and vanished : Wilhelmina saw no more of him for about a year
after ; being ordered to her room, and kept prisoner there on
low diet, with sentries guarding her doors, and no outlook but
the worst horror her imagination pleased to paint.

This is the celebrated assault of paternal Majesty on Wilhelmina ; the rumor of which has gone into all lands, exciting
wonder and horror, but could not be so exact as this account
at first hand. Naturally the crowd of street-passengers, once
dispersed by the Guard, carried the matter abroad, and there
was no end of sympathetic exaggerations. Report ran in
Berlin, for example, that the poor Princess was killed, beaten
or trampled to death ; which we clearly see she was not.
Voltaire, in that mass of angry calumnies, very mendacious
indeed, which he calls *Vie Privée du Roi de Prusse*, mentions
the matter with emphasis ; and says farther, The Princess
once did him (Voltaire) the "honor to show him a black mark
she carried on her breast ever after ; " — which is likelier to
be false than true. Captain Guy Dickens, the Legationary
Captain, who seems a clear, ingenuous and ingenious man,
and of course had access to the highest circles of refined
rumor, reports the matter about ten days after, with several
errors, in this manner : —

"*Berlin, 5th September*, 1730. Four or five days ago [by
the Almanac nine, and directly on his Majesty's return,
which Dickens had announced a week ago without that fact·

attached], the King dreadfully ill-treated Wilhelmina in bed
[not in bed at all]; whole Castle (*Schloss* or Palace) was
alarmed; Guard turned out," — to clear away the crowd, as
we perceive. Not properly a crowd, such was not permissible there : but a stagnation of the passers-by would naturally
ensue on that esplanade; till the Guard turned out, and indicated with emphasis, "Move on !" Dickens hears farther
that "the Queen fares no better;" — such is the state of
rumor in Berlin at present.

Poor Katte had a hard audience of it too. He fell at Friedrich Wilhelm's feet; and was spurned and caned; — for the
rest, beyond what was already evident, had little or nothing
to confess : Intention of flight and of accompanying in flight
very undeniable ; although preliminaries and ulterior conditions of said flight not perfectly known to Katte ; known only
that the thought of raising trouble in foreign Courts, or the
least vestige of treason against his Majesty, had not entered
even into their dreams. A name or two of persons who had
known, or guessed, of these operations, is wrung from Katte ;
— name of a Lieutenant Spaen, for one ; who, being on guard,
had admitted Katte into Potsdam once or twice in disguise : —
for him and for the like of him, of whatever rank or which-
ever sex, let arrests be made out, and the scent as with sleuth-
hounds be diligently followed on all sides ; and Katte, stript
of his uniform, be locked up in the grimmest manner. Berlin,
with the rumor of these things, is a much-agitated city.

CHAPTER VIII.

SEQUEL TO CROWN-PRINCE AND FRIENDS.

As for the Crown-Prince, prosecuting his circuitous route,
he arrives safe at Mittenwalde; is lodged in the old Castle
there, I think, for two nights (but the date, in these indexless
Books, is blown away again), in a room bare of all things,
with sentries at the door ; and looks out, expecting Grumkow

and the Officials to make assault on him. One of these Officials, a certain " Gerber, Fiscal General," who, as head of
Prussian Fiscals (kind of Public Prosecutor, or supreme Essence of Bailiffs, Catchpoles and Grand-Juries all in one),
wears a red cloak, — gave the Prince a dreadful start. Red
cloak is the Berlin Hangman's or Headsman's dress ; and poor
Friedrich had the idea his end had summarily come in this
manner. Soon seeing it was otherwise, his spirits recovered,
perhaps rose by the shock.

He fronted Grumkow and the Officials, with a high, almost
contemptuous look ; answered promptly, — if possible, without
lying, and yet without telling anything ; — showed self-posses-
sion, pride ; retorted sometimes, " Have you nothing more to
ask ? "   Grumkow finding there was no way made into anything, not even into the secret of the Writing-case and the
Royal Women's operations there, began at last, as Wilhelmina
says, to hint, That in his Majesty's service there were means
of bringing out the truth in spite of refractory humors ; that
there was a thing called the rack, not yet abolished in his
Prussian Majesty's dominions ! Friedrich owned afterwards,
his blood ran cold. However, he put on a high look : " A
Hangman, such as you, naturally takes pleasure in talking of
his tools and his trade : but on me they will not produce any
effect. I have owned everything ; — and almost regret to have
done so. For it is not my part to stand questionings and
bandy responses with a *coquin comme vous*, scoundrel like you,"
reports Wilhelmina,[1] though we hope the actual term was
slightly less candid ! — Grumkow gathered his notes together ;
and went his ways, with the man in red cloak and the rest ;
thus finishing the scene in Mittenwalde. Mittenwalde, which
we used to know long since, in our Wusterhausen rides with
poor Duhan ; little thinking what awaited us there one
day.

Mittenwalde being finished, Friedrich, on Monday, 5th September, 1730, is sent forward to Cüstrin, a strong little town
in a quiet Country, some sixty or seventy miles eastward of
Berlin. On the evening of the 5th he finds himself lodged in

1 i. 280.

a strong room of the Fortress there, — room consisting of bare
walls lighted from far up; no furniture, not even the needful-
est; everything indicating that the proud spirit and the iron
laws shall here have their duel out at leisure, and see which is
stronger.

His sword was taken from him at Wesel; sword, uniform,
every mark of dignity, all are now gone : he is clad in brown
prison-dress of the plainest cut and cloth; his diet is fixed at
tenpence a day ("to be got from the cook's shop, six groschen
for dinner, four for supper");[1] food to be cut for him, no
knife allowed. Room is to be opened, morning, noon and
evening, "on the average not above four minutes each time;"
lights, or single tallow-light, to be extinguished at seven P.M.
Absolute solitude; no flute allowed, far from it; no books
allowed, except the Bible and a Prayer-Book, — or perhaps Nol-
tenius's *Manual*, if he took a hankering for it. There, shut
out from the babble of fools, and conversing only with the
dumb Veracities, with the huge inarticulate moanings of Destiny, Necessity and Eternity, let the fool of a Fritz bethink
himself, if there is any thought in him! There, among the
Bogs of the Oder, the very sedges getting brown all round
him, and the very curlews flying off for happier climes, let
him wait, till the question of his doom, rather an abstruse
question, ripen in the royal breast.

As for Wilhelmina, she is close prisoner in her apartments
in the Berlin Palace, sentries pacing at every outlet, for many
months to come. Wilhelmina almost rather likes it, such a
dog of an existence has she had hitherto, for want of being
well let alone. She plays, reads; composes music; smuggles
letters to and from Mamma, — one in Pencil, from my Brother
even, O Heavens! Wilhelmina weeps, now and then, with
her good Sonsfeld; hopes nevertheless there will be some
dawn to this *ragnarök*, or general "twilight of the gods."
Friedrich Wilhelm, convinced that England has had a hand
in this treason, signifies officially to his Excellency Captain
Dickens, That the- English negotiations are concluded; that
neither in the way of Single-Marriage nor of Double-Marriage

---

[1] Order, 14th September, 1730 (in Förster, i. 372).

will he have anything more to do with England. "Well,"
answers England, "who can help it? Negotiation was not
quite of our seeking. Let it so end!"[1]—Nay at dinner one
day (Seckendorf reports, while Fritz was on the road to Cüstrin) he proposes the toast, "Downfall of England!"[2] and
would have had the Queen drink it; who naturally wept, but
I conjecture could not be made to drink. Her Majesty is a
weeping, almost broken-hearted woman; his Majesty a raging,
almost broken-hearted man. Seckendorf and Grumkow are,
as it were, too victorious; and now have their apprehensions
on that latter score But they look on with countenances well
veiled, and touch the helm judiciously in Tobacco-Parliament,
intent on the nearest harbor of refuge.

Her Majesty nevertheless steadily persists; merely sinks
deeper out of sight with her English schemes; ducking till
the wave go by. Messages, desperate appeals still go, through
Mamsell Bülow, Wilhelmina's Hofdame, and other channels;
nay Wilhelmina thinks there were still intentions on the part
of England, and that the non-fulfilment of them at the last
moment turned on accident; English "Courier arrived some
hours too late," thinks Wilhelmina.[3] But that is a mistake.
The negotiation, in spite of her Majesty's endeavors, was essentially out; England, after such a message, could not, nor
did, stir farther in the matter.

In that Writing-case his Majesty found what we know;
nothing but mysterious effects of female art, and no light
whatever. It is a great source of wrath and of sorrow to him,
that neither in the Writing-case, nor in Katte's or the Prince's
so-called "Confessions," can the thing be seen into. A deeper
bottom it must have, thinks his Majesty, but knows not what
or where. To overturn the Country, belike; and fling the
Kaiser, and European Balance of Power, bottom uppermost?
Me they presumably meant to poison! he tells Seckendorf one

---

[1] Dickens's Despatch, 25th September, 1730; and Harrington's Answer to it,
of 6th October: Seckendorf (in Förster, iii. 9), 23d September.

[2] Seckendorf (in Förster. iii. 11).

[3] Wilhelmina (i. 369, 384), and Preuss and others after her.

day.[1] Was ever Father more careful for his children, soul and body ? Anxious, to excess, to bring them up in orthodox nurture and admonition: and this is how they reward me, Herr Feldzeugmeister! "Had *he* honestly confessed, and told me the whole truth, at Wesel, I would have made it up with him quietly there. But now it must go its lengths; and the whole world shall be judge between us."[2]

His Majesty is in a flaming height. He arrests, punishes and banishes, where there is trace of co-operation or connection with Deserter Fritz and his schemes. The Bülows, brother and sister, brother in the King's service, sister in Wilhelmina's, respectable goldstick people, originally of Hanover, are hurled out to Lithuania and the world's end : let them live in Memel, and repent as they can. Minister Knyphausen, always of English tendencies, he, with his Wife, — to whom it is specially hard, while General Schwerin, gallant witty Kurt, once of Mecklenburg, stays behind, — is ordered to disappear, and follow his private rural business far off; no minister, ever more. The Lieutenant Spaen of the Giant Regiment, who kept false watch, and did not tell of Katte, gets cashiering and a year in Spandau. He wandered else-whither, and came to something afterwards, poor Spaen.[3] Bookseller Hanau with this bad Fritz's Books : To Memel with him also; let him deal in more orthodox kinds of Literature there.

It is dangerous to have lent the Crown-Prince money, contrary to the Royal Edict; lucky if loss of your money will settle the account. Witness French Montholieu, for one; Count, or whatever he styled himself; nailed to the gallows (in effigy) after he had fled. It is dangerous to have spoken kindly to the Crown-Prince, or almost to have been spoken to by him. Doris Ritter, a comely enough good girl, nothing of a beauty, but given to music, Potsdam *Cantor's* (Precentor's) daughter, has chanced to be standing in the door, perhaps to be singing within doors, once or twice, when the Prince passed that way : Prince inquired about her music, gave her music,

[1] Dickens's Despatch, 16th September, 1730.
[2] Seckendorf (Förster, ubi suprà), 23d September.
[3] Preuss, i. 63, 66.

spoke a civility, as young men will, — nothing more, upon my
honor; though his Majesty believes there was much more;
and condemns poor Doris to be whipt by the Beadle, and beat
hemp for three years. Rhadamanthus is a strict judge, your
Majesty; and might be a trifle better informed! — Poor
Doris got out of this sad Pickle, on her own strength; and
wedded, and did well enough, — Prince and King happily
leaving her alone thenceforth. Voltaire, twenty years after,
had the pleasure of seeing her at Berlin : " Wife of one
Shommers, Clerk of the Hackney-Coach Office," — read, Scho-
mer, *Farmer* of the Berlin Hackney-Coach Enterprise in general; decidedly a poor man. Wife, by this time, was grown
hard enough of feature : " tall, lean ; looked like a Sibyl ; not
the least appearance how she could ever have deserved to be
whipt for a Prince." [1]

The excellent Tutor of the Crown-Prince, good Duhan de
Jandun, for what fault or complicity we know not, is hurled
off to Memel; ordered to live there, — on what resources is
equally unknown. Apparently his fault was the general one,
of having miseducated the Prince, and introduced these
French Literatures, foreign poisonous elements of thought and
practice into the mind of his Pupil, which have ruined the
young man. For his Majesty perceives that there lies the
source of it; that only total perversion of the heart and judgment, first of all, can have brought about these dreadful issues
of conduct. And indeed his Majesty understands, on credible
information, that Deserter Fritz entertains very heterodox
opinions; opinion on Predestination, for one; — which is itself calculated to be the very mother of mischief, in a young
mind inclined to evil. The heresy about Predestination, or
the "*Freie Gnadenwahl* (Election by Free Grace)," as his Majesty terms it, according to which a man is preappointed from
all Eternity either to salvation or the opposite (which is Fritz's
notion, and indeed is Calvin's, and that of many benighted
creatures, this Editor among them), appears to his Majesty an
altogether shocking one; nor would the whole Synod of Dort,

[1] Voltaire, *Œuvres* (calumnious *Vie Privée du Roi de Prusse*), ii. 51, 52.
Preuss, i. 64, 66.

or Calvin, or St. Augustine in person, aided by a Thirty-Editor
power, reconcile his Majesty's practical judgment to such a
tenet.   What!   May not Deserter Fritz say to himself, even
now, or in whatever other deeps of sin he may fall into, " I
was foredoomed to it : how could I, or how can I, help it ? "
The mind of his Majesty shudders, as if looking over the
edge of an abyss.   He is meditating much whether nothing can
be done to save the lost Fritz, at least the soul of him, from
this horrible delusion : — hurls forth your fine Duhan, with his
metaphysics, to remote Memel, as the first step.   And signifies withal, though as yet only historically and in a speculative way, to Finkenstein and Kalkstein themselves, That their
method of training up a young soul, to do God's will, and
accomplish useful work in this world, does by no means appear to the royal mind an admirable one ! [1]   Finkenstein and
Kalkstein were always covertly rather of the Queen's party,
and now stand reprimanded, and in marked disfavor.

That the treasonous mystery of this Crown-Prince (parri-
cidal, it is likely, and tending to upset the Universe) must be
investigated to the very bottom, and be condignly punished,
probably with death, his Majesty perceives too well ; and also
what terrible difficulties, formal and essential, there will be.
But whatever become of his perishable life, ought not, if possible, the soul of him to be saved from the claws of Satan !
" Claws of Satan ; " " brand from the burning ; " " for Christ
our Saviour's sake ; " " in the name of the most merciful God,
Father, Son and Holy Ghost, Amen : " — so Friedrich Wilhelm
phrases it, in those confused old documents and Cabinet Letters of his ; [2] which awaken a strange feeling in the attentive reader ; and show us the ruggedest of human creatures
melted into blubbering tenderness, and growling huskily something which we perceive is real prayer.   Here has a business
fallen out, such as seldom occurred before ! —

[1] His Letter to them (3d December, 1730) in Förster, ii. 382
[2] Förster, i. 374, 379, &c.

CHAPTER IX.

COURT-MARTIAL ON CROWN-PRINCE AND CONSORTS.

THE rumor of these things naturally fills all minds, and
occupies all human tongues, in Berlin and Prussia, though
an Edict threatens, That the tongues shall be *cut out* which
speak of them in any way,[1] and sounds far and wide into
foreign Courts and Countries, where there is no such Edict.
Friedrich Wilhelm's conduct, looked at from without, appears
that of a hideous royal ogre, or blind anthropophagous Poly-
phemus fallen mad. Looked at from within, where the Poly-
phemus has his reasons, and a kind of inner rushlight to
enlighten his path; and is not bent on man-eating, but on
discipline in spite of difficulties, — it is a wild enough piece
of humanity, not so much ludicrous as tragical. Never was
a royal bear so led about before by a pair of conjuring pipers
in the market, or brought to such a pass in his dancing for
them!

"General Ginkel, the Dutch Ambassador here," writes
Dickens, "told me of an interview he had with the King;"
being ordered by their High Mightinesses to solicit his Majesty in this matter. King "harbors 'most monstrous wicked
designs, not fit to be spoken of in words,' reports Ginkel.
'It is certain,' added he, 'if the King of Prussia continue
in the mind he is in at present, we shall see scenes here as
wicked and bloody as any that were ever heard of since the
creation of the world.' 'Will sacrifice his whole family,' not
the Crown-Prince alone; 'everybody except Grumkow being,
as he fancies, in conspiracy against him.' Poor enchanted
King! — 'And all these things he said with such imprecations
and disordered looks, foaming at the mouth all the while, as
it was terrible either to see or hear.'" That is Ginkel's

[1] Dickens, of 7th November, 1730.

report, as Dickens conveys it.[1] Another time, on new order,
a month later, when Ginkel went again to speak a word for
the poor Prisoner, he found his Majesty clothed not in delirious thunder, but in sorrowful thick fog; Ginkel "was the less
able to judge what the King of Prussia meant to do with his
Son, as it was evident the King himself did not know." [2]

Poor Friedrich Wilhelm, through these months, wanders
about, shifting from room to room, in the night-time, like a
man possessed by evil fiends; "orders his carriage for Wusterhausen at two in the morning," but finds he is no better
there, and returns; drinks a great deal, "has not gone to bed
sober for a month past." [3] One night he comes gliding like
a perturbed ghost, about midnight, with his candle in his
hand, into the Queen's apartment; says, wildly staring, "He
thinks there is something haunting him:" — O Feekin, erring disobedient Wife, wilt not thou protect me, after all?
Whither can I fly when haunted, except to thee? Feekin,
like a prudent woman, makes no criticism; orders that his
Majesty's bed be made up in her apartment till these phenomena cease.[4] A much-agitated royal Father.

The question what is to be done with this unhappy Crown-
Prince, a Deserter from the army, a rebel against the paternal
Majesty, and a believer in the doctrine of Election by Free
Grace, or that a man's good or ill conduct is foredoomed
upon him by decree of God, — becomes more intricate the
longer one thinks of it. Seckendorf and Grumkow, alarmed
at being too victorious, are set against violent high methods;
and suggest this and that consideration: "Who is it that can
legally try, condemn, or summon to his bar, a Crown-Prince?
He is Prince of the Empire, as well as your Majesty's Son!"
— "Well, he is Heir of the Sovereign Majesty in Prussia,
too; and Colonel in the Potsdam Guards!" answers Friedrich
Wilhelm.

At length, after six or seven weeks of abstruse meditation,
it is settled in Tobacco-Parliament and the royal breast, That
Katte and the Crown-Prince, as Deserters from the Prussian

---

[1] Despatch, 7th September, 1730.   [2] Ib. 10th October.
[3] Ib. 19th December, 1730.   [4] Ib. 27th February, 1731.

Army, can and shall be tried by Court-Martial; to that no
power, on the earth or out of it, can have any objection worth
attending to. Let a fair Court-Martial of our highest military
characters be selected and got ready. Let that, as a voice of
Rhadamanthus, speak upon the two culprits; and tell us what
is to be done. By the middle of October, things on Friedrich
Wilhelm's side have got so far.

Crown-Prince in Cüstrin.

Poor Friedrich meanwhile has had a grim time of it, these
two months back; left alone, in coarse brown prison-dress,
within his four bare walls at Cüstrin; in uninterrupted,
unfathomable colloquy with the Destinies and the Necessities there. The King's stern orders must be fulfilled to the
letter; the Crown-Prince is immured in that manner. At
Berlin, there are the wildest rumors as to the state he has
fallen into; "covered with rags and vermin, unshaven, no
comb allowed him, lights his own fire," says one testimony,
which Captain Dickens thinks worth reporting. For the truth
is, no unofficial eye can see the Crown-Prince, or know what
state he is in. And we find, in spite of the Edict, "tongues,"
not "cut out," kept wagging at a high rate. "People of all
ranks are unspeakably indignant" at certain heights of the
business: "Margravine Albert said publicly, 'A tyrant as bad
as Nero!'"[1]

How long the Crown-Prince's defiant humor held out, we
are not told. By the middle of October there comes proposal
of "entire confession" from the Prince; and though, when
Papa sends deputies accordingly, there is next to nothing
new confessed, and Papa's anger blazes out again, probably
we may take this as the turning-point on his Son's part.
With him, of course, that mood of mind could not last.
There is no wildest lion but, finding his bars are made of
iron, ceases to bite them. The Crown-Prince there, in his
horror, indignation and despair, had a lucid human judgment
in him, too; loyal to facts, and well knowing their inexorable

[1] Dickens, 7th November, 2d December, 1730.

nature. Just sentiments are in this young man, not capable
of permanent distortion into spasm by any form of injustice
laid on them.   It is not long till he begins to discern, athwart
this terrible, quasi-infernal element, that so the facts are; and
that nothing but destruction, and no honor that were not dis-
honor, will be got by not conforming to the facts.   My Father
may be a tyrant, and driven mad against me : well, well, let
not me at least go mad!

Grumkow is busy on the mild side of the business; of
course Grumkow and all official men.   Grumkow cannot but
ask himself this question among others : How if the King
should suddenly die upon us !   Grumkow is out at Cüstrin,
and again out; explaining to the Prince, what the enormous
situation is; how inflexible, inexorable, and of peril and horror
incalculable to Mother and Sister and self and royal House ;
and that there is one possibility of good issue, and only
one : that of loyally yielding, where one cannot resist.   By
degrees, some lurid troublous but perceptible light-gleam
breaks athwart the black whirlwind of our indignation and
despair; and saner thoughts begin to insinuate themselves.
" Obey, thou art not the strongest, there are stronger than
thou ! All men, the highest among them, are called to learn
obedience."

Moreover, the first sweep of royal fury being past, his Majesty's stern regulations at Cüstrin began to relax in fulfilment ;
to be obeyed only by those immediately responsible, and in
letter rather than in spirit even by those.   President von
Münchow who is head of the Domain-Kammer, chief representative of Government at Cüstrin, and resides in the Fortress there, ventures after a little, the Prince's doors being
closed as we saw, to have an orifice bored through the floor
above, and thereby to communicate with the Prince, and sym-
pathetically ask, What he can do for him ? Many things,
books among others, are, under cunning contrivance, smuggled
in by the judicious Münchow, willing to risk himself in such
a service.   For example, Münchow has a son, a clever boy of
seven years old ; who, to the wonder of neighbors, goes into
child's-petticoats again ; and testifies the liveliest desire to be

admitted to the Prince, and bear him company a little! Surely
the law of No-company does not extend to that of an innocent
child? The innocent child has a row of pockets all round the
inside of his long gown; and goes laden, miscellaneously, like
a ship of the desert, or cockboat not forbidden to cross the
line. Then there are stools, one stool at least indispensable
to human nature; and the inside of this, once you open it, is
a chest-of-drawers, containing paper, ink, new literature and
much else. No end to Münchow's good-will, and his ingenuity
is great.[1]

A Captain Fouquet also, furthered I think by the Old Dessauer, whose man he is, comes to Cüstrin Garrison, on duty or
as volunteer, by and by. He is an old friend of the Prince's;
— ran off, being the Dessauer's little page, to the Siege of
Stralsund, long ago, to be the Dessauer's little soldier there:
— a ready-witted, hot-tempered, highly estimable man; and
his real duty here is to do the Prince what service may be
possible. He is often with the Prince; their light is extinguished precisely at seven o'clock: "Very well, Lieutenant,"
he would say, "you have done your orders to the Crown-
Prince's light. But his Majesty has no concern with Captain
Fouquet's candles!" and thereupon would light a pair. Nay,
I have heard of Lieutenants who punctually blew out the
Prince's light, as a matter of duty and command; and then
kindled it again, as a civility left free to human nature. In
short, his Majesty's orders can only be fulfilled to the letter;
Commandant Lepel and all Officers are willing not to see
where they can help seeing. Even in the letter his Majesty's
orders are severe enough.

Sentence of Court-Martial.

Meanwhile the Court-Martial, selected with intense study,
installs itself at Cöpenick; and on the 25th of October commences work. This Deserter Crown-Prince and his accomplices, especially Katte his chief accomplice, what is to be
done with them? Cöpenick lies on the road to Cüstrin, within

[1] Preuss, i. 46.

a morning's drive of Berlin; there is an ancient Palace here,
and room for a Court-Martial. *"Que faire? ils ont des canons!"* said the old Prussian Raths, wandering about in these
woods, when Gustavus and his Swedes were at the door. *"Que
faire?"* may the new military gentlemen think to themselves,
here again, while the brown leaves rustle down upon them,
after a hundred years!

The Court consists of a President, Lieutenant-General Schulenburg, an elderly Malplaquet gentleman of good experience;
one of the many Schulenburgs conspicuous for soldiering, and
otherwise, in those times. He is nephew of George I.'s lean
mistress; who also was a Schulenburg originally, and conspicuous not for soldiering. Lean mistress we say; not the
Fat one, or cataract of tallow, with eyebrows like a cart-wheel,
and dim coaly disks for eyes, who was George I.'s half-sister,
probably not his mistress at all; and who now, as Countess of
Darlington so called, sits at Isleworth with good fat pensions,
and a tame raven come-of-will, — probably the *soul* of George I.
in some form.[1] Not this one, we say: — but the thread-
paper Duchess of Kendal, actual Ex-mistress; who tore her
hair on the road when apoplexy overtook poor George, and
who now attends chapel diligently, poor old anatomy or lean
human nail-rod. For the sake of the English reader searching
into what is called "History," I, with indignation, endeavor to
discriminate these two beings once again; that each may be
each, till both are happily forgotten to all eternity. It was
the latter, lean may-pole or nail-rod one, that was Aunt of
Schulenburg, the elderly Malplaquet gentleman who now presides at Cöpenick. And let the reader remember him; for he
will turn up repeatedly again.

The Court consisted farther of three Major-Generals, among
whom I name only Grumkow (Major-General by rank though
more of a diplomatist and black-artist than a soldier), and
Schwerin, Kurt von Schwerin of Mecklenburg (whom Madam
Knyphausen regrets, in her now exile to the Country); three
Colonels, Derschau one of them; three Lieutenant-Colonels,
three Majors and three Captains, all of whom shall be name-

[1] See Walpole, *Reminiscences.*

less here. Lastly come three of the "Auditor" or the Judge-Advocate sort: Mylius, the Compiler of sad Prussian Quartos, known to some; Gerber, whose red cloak has frightened us once already; and the Auditor of Katte's regiment. A complete Court-Martial, and of symmetrical structure, by the rule of three; — of whose proceedings we know mainly the result, nor seek much to know more. This Court met on Wednesday, 25th October, 1730, in the little Town of Cöpenick; and in six days had ended, signed, sealed and despatched to his Majesty; and got back to Berlin on the Tuesday next. His Majesty, who is now at Wusterhausen, in hunting time, finds conclusions to the following effect : —

Accomplices of the Crown-Prince are two : *First,* Lieutenant Keith, actual deserter (who cannot be caught) : To be hanged in effigy, cut in four quarters, and nailed to the gallows at Wesel : — *Good,* says his Majesty. *Secondly,* Lieutenant Katte of the Gens-d'Armes, intended deserter, not actually deserting, and much tempted thereto : All things considered, Perpetual Fortress Arrest to Lieutenant Katte : — *Not Good* this ; *Bad* this, thinks Majesty ; this provokes from his Majesty an angry rebuke to the too lax Court-Martial. Rebuke which can still be read, in growling, unlucid phraseology ; but with a rhadamanthine idea clear enough in it, and with a practical purport only too clear : That Katte was a sworn soldier, of the Gens-d'Armes even, or Body-guard of the Prussian Majesty ; and did nevertheless, in the teeth of his oath, "worship the Rising Sun" when minded to desert ; did plot and colleague with foreign Courts in aid of said Rising Sun, and of an intended high crime against the Prussian Majesty itself on Rising Sun's part ; far from at once revealing the same, as duty ordered Lieutenant Katte to do. That Katte's crime amounts to high-treason (*crimen læsæ majestatis*) ; that the rule is, *Fiat justitia, et pereat mundus ;* — and that, in brief, Katte's doom is, and is hereby declared to be, Death. Death by the gallows and hot pincers is the usual doom of Traitors ; but his Majesty will say in this case, Death by the sword and headsman simply ; certain circumstances moving the royal clemency to go so far, no farther. And the Court-Martial has straightway to

apprise Katte of this same : and so doing, "shall say, That his
Majesty is sorry for Katte ; but that it is better he die than
that justice depart out of the world." [1]

This is the iron doom of Katte ; which no prayer or influence
of mortal will avail to alter, — lest justice depart out of the
world. Katte's Father is a General of rank, Commandant
of Königsberg at this moment; Katte's Grandfather by the
Mother's side, old Fieldmarshal Wartensleben, is a man in
good favor with Friedrich Wilhelm, and of high esteem and
mark in his country for half a century past. But all this
can effect nothing. Old Wartensleben thinks of the Daughter
he lost; for happily Katte's Mother is dead long since. Old
Wartensleben writes to Friedrich Wilhelm; his mournful Letter, and Friedrich Wilhelm's mournful but inexorable answer,
can be read in the Histories ; but show only what we already
know.

Katte's Mother, Fieldmarshal Wartensleben's Daughter, died
in 1706 ; leaving Katte only two years old. He is now twenty-
six; very young for such grave issues; and his fate is certainly
very hard. Poor young soul, he did not resist farther, or quarrel with the inevitable and inexorable. He listened to Chaplain
Müller of the Gens-d'Armes ; admitted profoundly, after his
fashion, that the great God was just, and the poor Katte sinful, foolish, only to be saved by miracle of mercy ; and piously
prepared himself to die on these terms. There are three Letters of his to his Grandfather, which can still be read, one of
them in Wilhelmina's Book,[2] the sound of it like that of dirges
borne on the wind. Wilhelmina evidently pities Katte very
tenderly; in her heart she has a fine royal-maiden kind of feeling to the poor youth. He did heartily repent and submit;
left with Chaplain Müller a Paper of pious considerations,
admonishing the Prince to submit. These are Katte's last
employments in his prison at Berlin, after sentence had gone
forth.

<hr>

[1] Preuss, i. 44.   [2] Wilhelmina, i. 302.

Katte's End, 6th November, 1730.

On Sunday evening, 5th November, it is intimated to him, unexpectedly at the moment, that he has to go to Cüstrin, and there die; — carriage now waiting at the gate. Katte masters the sudden flurry; signifies that all is ready, then; and so, under charge of his old Major and two brother Officers, who, and Chaplain Müller, are in the carriage with him, a troop of his own old Cavalry Regiment escorting, he leaves Berlin (rather on sudden summons); drives all night, towards Cüstrin and immediate death. Words of sympathy were not wanting, to which Katte answered cheerily; grim faces wore a cloud of sorrow for the poor youth that night. Chaplain Müller's exhortations were fervent and continual; and, from time to time, there were heard, hoarsely melodious through the damp darkness and the noise of wheels, snatches of "devotional singing," led by Müller.

It was in the gray of the winter morning, 6th November, 1730, that Katte arrived in Cüstrin garrison. He took kind leave of Major and men : Adieu, my brothers; good be with you evermore! — And, about nine o'clock he is on the road towards the Rampart of the Castle, where a scaffold stands. Katte wore, by order, a brown dress exactly like the Prince's; the Prince is already brought down into a lower room to see Katte as he passes (to "see Katte die," had been the royal order; but they smuggled that into abeyance); and Katte knows he shall see him. Faithful Müller was in the death-car along with Katte : and he had adjoined to himself one Besserer, the Chaplain of the Garrison, in this sad function, since arriving. Here is a glimpse from Besserer, which we may take as better than nothing : —

"His (Katte's) eyes were mostly directed to God; and we (Müller and I), on our part, strove to hold his heart up heavenwards, by presenting the examples of those who had died in the Lord, — as of God's Son himself, and Stephen, and the Thief on the Cross, — till, under such discoursing, we approached the Castle. Here, after long wistful looking about, he did get sight of his beloved Jonathan," Royal Highness the

Crown-Prince, "at a window in the Castle; from whom he,
with the politest and most tender expression, spoken in French,
took leave, with no little emotion of sorrow." [1]

President Münchow and the Commandant were with the
Prince; whose emotions one may fancy, but not describe. Seldom did any Prince or man stand in such a predicament. Vain
to say, and again say : "In the name of God, I ask you, stop
the execution till I write to the King !" Impossible that; as
easily stop the course of the stars. And so here Katte comes;
cheerful loyalty still beaming on his face, death now nigh.
"*Pardonnez-moi, mon cher Katte !*" cried Friedrich in a tone :
Pardon me, dear Katte ; oh, that this should be what I have
done for you ! — "Death is sweet for a Prince I love so well,"
said Katte, "*La mort est douce pour un si aimable Prince ;*" [2]
and fared on, — round some angle of the Fortress, it appears ;
not in sight of Friedrich ; who sank into a faint, and had seen
his last glimpse of Katte in this world.

The body lay all day upon the scaffold, by royal order ;
and was buried at night obscurely in the common churchyard ;
friends, in silence, took mark of the place against better times,
— and Katte's dust now lies elsewhere, among that of his own
kindred.

"Never was such a transaction before or since, in Modern
History," cries the angry reader : "cruel, like the grinding of
human hearts under millstones, like — " Or indeed like the
doings of the gods, which are cruel, though not that alone ?
This is what, after much sorting and sifting, I could get to
know about the definite facts of it. Commentary, not likely
to be very final at this epoch, the reader himself shall supply
at discretion.

---

[1] Letter to Katte's Father (Extract, in Preuss, *Friedrich mit Freunden und Verwandten*, p. 7).

[2] Wilhelmina, i. 307 ; Preuss, i. 45.

KATTE, ON THE WAY TO THE SCAFFOLD, SEES HIS BELOVED
PRINCE AT THE CASTLE WINDOW.

Carlyle, Vol. Two, p. 96.

BOOK VIII

CROWN-PRINCE RETRIEVED: LIFE AT CÜSTRIN.

November, 1730–February, 1732.

———◆———

CHAPTER I.

CHAPLAIN MÜLLER WAITS ON THE CROWN-PRINCE.

FRIEDRICH'S feelings at this juncture are not made known to us by himself in the least; or credibly by others in any considerable degree. As indeed in these confused Prussian History-Books, opulent in nugatory pedantisms and learned marine-stores, all that is human remains distressingly obscure to us; so seldom, and then only as through endless clouds of ever-whirling idle dust, can we catch the smallest direct feature of the young man, and of his real demeanor or meaning, on the present or other occasions! But it is evident this last phenomenon fell upon him like an overwhelming cataract; crushed him down under the immensity of sorrow, confusion and despair; his own death not a theory now, but probably a near fact, — a welcome one in wild moments, and then anon so unwelcome. Frustrate, bankrupt, chargeable with a friend's lost life, sure enough he, for one, is: what is to become of him? Whither is he to turn, thoroughly beaten, foiled in all his enterprises? Proud young soul as he was: the ruling Powers, be they just, be they unjust, have proved too hard for him! We hear of tragic vestiges still traceable of Friedrich, belonging to this time: texts of Scripture quoted by him, pencil-sketches of his drawing; expressive of a mind dwelling

in Golgothas, and pathetically, not defiantly, contemplating the
very worst.

Chaplain Müller of the Gens-d'Armes, being found a pious
and intelligent man, has his orders not to return at once from
Cüstrin; but to stay there, and deal with the Prince, on that
horrible Predestination topic and his other unexampled back-
slidings which have ended so. Müller stayed accordingly, for
a couple of weeks, intensely busy on the Predestination topic,
and generally in assuaging, and mutually mollifying, paternal
Majesty and afflicted Son. In all which he had good success;
and especially on the Predestination point was triumphantly
successful. Müller left a little Book in record of his procedures there; which, had it not been bound over to the official
tone, might have told us something. His Correspondence with
the King, during those two weeks, has likewise been mostly
printed;[1] and is of course still more official, — teaching us
next to nothing, except poor Friedrich Wilhelm's profoundly
devotional mood, anxieties about "the claws of Satan" and
the like, which we were glad to hear of above. In Müller
otherwise is small help for us.

But, fifty years afterwards, there was alive a Son of this
Müller's; an innocent Country Parson, not wanting in sense,
and with much simplicity and veracity; who was fished out
by Nicolai, and set to recalling what his Father used to say
of this adventure, much the grandest of his life. In Müller
Junior's Letter of Reminiscences to Nicolai we find some
details, got from his Father, which are worth gleaning: —

"When my Father first attempted, by royal order, to bring
the Crown-Prince to acknowledgment and repentance of the
fault committed, Crown-Prince gave this excuse or explanation: 'As his Father could not endure the sight of him, he
had meant to get out of the way of his displeasure, and go to
a Court with which his Father was in friendship and relation-
ship,'" — clearly indicating England, think the Müllers Junior
and Senior.

"For proof that the intention was towards England this

---

[1] Förster, i. 376–379.

other circumstance serves, that the one confidant — Herr von Keith, if I mistake not [no, you don't mistake], had already bespoken a ship for passage out." — Here is something still more unexpected : —

" My Father used to say, he found an excellent knowledge and conviction of the truths of religion in the Crown-Prince. By the Prince's arrangement, my Father, who at first lodged with the Commandant, had to take up his quarters in the room right above the Prince; who daily, often as early as six in the morning, rapped on the ceiling for him to come down; and then they would dispute and discuss, sometimes half-days long, about the different tenets of the Christian Sects ; — and my Father said, the Prince was perfectly at home in the Polemic Doctrines of the Reformed (Calvinistic) Church, even to the minutest points. As my Father brought him proofs from Scripture, the Prince asked him one time, How he could keep chapter and verse so exactly in his memory ? Father drew from his pocket a little Hand-Concordance, and showed it him as one help. This he had to leave with the Prince for some days. On getting it back, he found inside on the fly-leaf, sketched in pencil," — what is rather notable to History, — " the figure of a man on his knees, with two swords hanging crosswise over his head; and at the bottom these words of Psalm Seventy-third (verses 25, 26), *Whom have I in Heaven but thee ? And there is none upon earth that I desire besides thee. My flesh and my heart fainteth and faileth ; but God is the strength of my heart, and my portion forever."* — Poor Friedrich, this is a very unexpected pencil-sketch on his part ; but an undeniable one ; betokening abtsruse night-thoughts and forebodings in the present juncture ! —

" Whoever considers this fine knowledge of religion, and reflects on the peculiar character and genius of the young Herr, which was ever struggling towards light and clearness (for at that time he had *not* become indifferent to religion, he often prayed with my Father on his knees), — will find that it was morally impossible this young Prince could have thought [as some foolish persons have asserted] of throwing himself into the arms of Papal Superstition [seeking help at Vienna, marry-

ing an Austrian Archduchess, and I know not what] or allow
the intrigues of Catholic Priests to " — Oh no, Herr Müller,
nobody but very foolish persons could imagine such a thing of
this young Herr.

" When my Father, Herr von Katte's execution being ended,
hastened to the Crown-Prince ; he finds him miserably ill (*sehr
alterirt*) ; advises him to take a cooling-powder in water, both
which materials were ready on the table. This he presses on
him : but the Prince always shakes his head." Suspects poison,
you think ? " Hereupon my Father takes from his pocket a
paper, in which he carried cooling-powder for his own use ;
shakes out a portion of it into his hand, and so into his mouth ;
and now the Crown-Prince grips at my Father's powder, and
takes that." Privately to be made away with ; death resolved
upon in some way ! thinks the desperate young man ?[1]

That scene of Katte's execution, and of the Prince's and
other people's position in regard to it, has never yet been
humanly set forth, otherwise the response had been different.
Not humanly set forth, — and so was only barked at, as by the
infinitude of little dogs, in all countries ; and could never yet
be responded to in austere *vox humana*, deep as a *De Profundis*,
terrible as a Chorus of Æschylus, — for in effect that is rather
the character of it, had the barking once pleased to cease.

" King of Prussia cannot sleep," writes Dickens : " the
officers sit up with him every night, and in his slumbers he
raves and talks of spirits and apparitions."[2] We saw him,
ghost-like, in the night-time, gliding about, seeking shelter
with Feekin against ghosts ; Ginkel by daylight saw him, now
clad in thunderous tornado, and anon in sorrowful fog. Here,
farther on, is a new item, — and joined to it and the others, a
remarkable old one : —

" In regard to Wilhelmina's marriage, and whether a Father
cannot give his daughter in wedlock to whom he pleases, there
have been eight Divines consulted, four Lutheran, four Reformed (Calvinist) ; who, all but one [he of the Garrison
Church, a rhadamanthine fellow in serge], have answered,

---

[1] Nicolai, *Anekdoten*, vi. 183–189.
[2] Despatch, 3d October, 1730.

'No, your Majesty!' It is remarkable that his Majesty has not gone to bed sober for this month past."[1]

What Seckendorf and Grumkow thought of all these phenomena? They have done their job too well. They are all for mercy; lean with their whole weight that way, — in black qualms, one of them withal, thinking tremulously to himself, "What if his now Majesty were to die upon us, in the interim!"

CHAPTER II.

CROWN-PRINCE TO REPENT AND NOT PERISH.

In regard to Friedrich, the Court-Martial needs no amendment from the King; the sentence on Friedrich, a Lieutenant-Colonel guilty of desertion, is, from President and all members except two, Death as by law. The two who dissented, invoking royal clemency and pardon, were Major-Generals by rank, — Schwerin, as some write, one of them, or if not Schwerin, then Linger; and for certain, Dönhof, — two worthy gentlemen not 'known to any of my readers, nor to me, except as names. The rest are all coldly of opinion that the military code says Death. Other codes and considerations may say this and that, which it is not in their province to touch upon; this is what the military code says: and they leave it there.

The Junius Brutus of a Royal Majesty had answered in his own heart grimly, Well then! But his Councillors, Old Dessauer, Grumkow, Seckendorf, one and all interpose vehemently. "Prince of the Empire, your Majesty, not a Lieutenant-Colonel only! Must not, cannot;" — nay good old Buddenbrock, in the fire of still unsuccessful pleading, tore open his waistcoat: "If your Majesty requires blood, take mine; that other you shall never get, so long as I can speak!" Foreign Courts interpose; Sweden, the Dutch; the English in a circuitous way, round by Vienna to wit; finally the Kaiser himself sends an

[1] Dickens, 9th and 19th December, 1730.

Autograph; [1] for poor Queen Sophie has applied even to Seckendorf, will be friends with Grumkow himself, and in her
despair is knocking at every door. Junius Brutus is said to
have had paternal affections withal. Friedrich Wilhelm, alone
against the whispers of his own heart and the voices of all men,
yields at last in this cause. To Seckendorf, who has chalked
out a milder didactic plan of treatment, still rigorous enough, [2]
he at last admits that such plan is perhaps good; that the
Kaiser's Letter has turned the scale with him; and the didactic
method, not the beheading one, shall be tried. That Dönhof
and Schwerin, with their talk of mercy, with "their eyes upon
the Rising Sun," as is evident, have done themselves no good,
and shall perhaps find it so one day. But that, at any rate,
Friedrich's life is spared; Katte's execution shall suffice in that
kind. Repentance, prostrate submission and amendment, —
these may do yet more for the prodigal, if he will in heart
return. These points, some time before the 8th of November,
we find to be as good as settled.

The unhappy prodigal is in no condition to resist farther.
Chaplain Müller had introduced himself with Katte's dying
admonition to the Crown-Prince to repent and submit. Chaplain Müller, with his wholesome cooling-powders, with his
ghostly counsels, and considerations of temporal and eternal
nature, — we saw how he prospered almost beyond hope. Even
on Predestination, and the real nature of Election by Free
Grace, all is coming right, or come, reports Müller. The
Chaplain's Reports, Friedrich Wilhelm's grimly mollified Responses on the same: they are written, and in confused form
have been printed; but shall be spared the English reader.

And Grumkow has been out at Cüstrin, preaching to the
same purport from other texts: Grumkow, with the thought
ever present to him, "What if Friedrich Wilhelm should die?"
is naturally an eloquent preacher. Enough, it has been settled
(perhaps before the day of Katte's death, or at the latest three
days after it, as we can see), That if the Prince will, and can

[1] Date, 11th October, 1730 (Förster, i. 380).
[2] His Letter to the King, 1st November, 1730 (in Förster, i. 375, 376).

with free conscience, take an Oath ("no mental reservation," mark you!) of contrite repentance, of perfect prostrate submission, and purpose of future entire obedience and conformity to the paternal mind in all things, " *Gnadenwahl* " included, — the paternal mind may possibly relax his durance a little, and put him gradually on proof again.[1]

Towards which issue, as Chaplain Müller reports, the Crown-Prince is visibly gravitating, with all his weight and will. The very *Gnadenwahl* is settled; the young soul (truly a lover of Truth, your Majesty) taps on his ceiling, my floor being overhead, before the winter sun rises, as a signal that I must come down to him; so eager to have error and darkness purged away. Believes himself, as I believe him, ready to undertake that Oath; desires, however, to see it first, that he may maturely study every clause of it. — Say you verily so? answers Majesty. And *may* my ursine heart flow out again, and blubber gratefully over a sinner saved, a poor Son plucked as brand from the burning? "God, the Most High, give His blessing on it, then!" concludes the paternal Majesty: "And as He often, by wondrous guidances, strange paths and thorny steps, will bring men into the Kingdom of Christ, so may our Divine Redeemer help that this prodigal son be brought into His communion. That his godless heart be beaten till it is softened and changed; and so he be snatched from the claws of Satan. This grant us the Almighty God and Father, for our Lord Jesus Christ and His passion and death's sake! Amen! — I am, for the rest, your well-affectioned King, FRIEL-RICH WILHELM (*Wusterhausen, 8th November*, 1730)."[2]

Crown-Prince begins a new Course.

It was Monday, 6th November, when poor Katte died. Within a fortnight, on the second Sunday after, there has a Select Commission, Grumkow, Borck, Buddenbrock, with three other Soldiers, and the Privy Councillor Thulmeyer, come out to Cüstrin: there and then, Sunday, November

[1] King's Letter to Müller, 8th November (Förster, i. 379)
[2] Förster, i. 379.

19th,[1] these Seven, with due solemnity, administer the Oath
(terms of Oath conceivable by readers) ; Friedrich being found
ready. He signs the Oath, as well as audibly swears it:
whereupon his sword is restored to him, and his prison-door
opened. He steps forth to the Town Church with his Com-
missioners ; takes the sacrament ; listens, with all Cüstrin, to
an illusive Sermon on the subject ; " text happily chosen,
preacher handling it well."   Text was Psalm Seventy-seventh,
verse eleventh (tenth of our English version), *And I said, This
is my infirmity ; but I will remember the years of the right
hand of the Most High ;* or, as Luther's version more intelligi-
bly gives it, *This I have to suffer ; the right hand of the Most
High can change all.* Preacher (not Müller but another) rose
gradually into didactic pathos ; Prince, and all Cüstrin, were
weeping, or near weeping, at the close of the business.[2]

Straight from Church the Prince is conducted, not to the
Fortress, but to a certain Town Mansion, which he is to call
his own henceforth, under conditions : an erring Prince half
liberated, and mercifully put on proof again. His first act
here is to write, of his own composition, or helped by some
official hand, this Letter to his All-serenest Papa ; which must
be introduced, though, except to readers of German who know
the " *Dero* " (Their*o*), " *Allerdurchlauchtigster*," and strange
pipe-clay solemnity of the Court-style, it is like to be in great
part lost in any translation : —

" Cüstrin, 19th November, 1730.

" All-serenest and All-graciousest Father, — To your
Royal Majesty, my All-graciousest Father, have," — *i.e.* " I
have," if one durst write the " I," — " by my disobedience as
Their*o* [Your*o*] subject and soldier, not less than by my
undutifulness as Their*o* Son, given occasion to a just wrath
and aversion against me. With the All-obedientest respect I
submit myself wholly to the grace of my most All-gracious

[1] Nicolai, exactest of men, only that Documents were occasionally less accessible in his time, gives (*Anekdoten*, vi. 187), "Saturday, November 25th,"
as the day of the Oath ; but, no doubt, the later inquirers, Preuss (i. 56) and
others, have found him wrong in this small instance.
[2] Preuss, i. 56.

Father; and beg him, Most All-graciously to pardon me; as it
is not so much the withdrawal of my liberty in a sad arrest
(*malkeureusen Arrest*), as my own thoughts of the fault I have
committed, that have brought me to reason : Who, with all-
obedientest respect and submission, continue till my end,

" My All-graciousest King's and Father's faithfully obedientest Servant and Son,

" FRIEDRICH." [1]

This new House of Friedrich's in the little Town of Cüstrin,
he finds arranged for him on rigorously thrifty principles, yet
as a real Household of his own ; and even in the form of a
Court, with Hofmarschall, Kammerjunkers, and the other
adjuncts ; — Court reduced to its simplest expression, as the
French say, and probably the cheapest that was ever set up.
Hofmarschall (Court-marshal) is one Wolden, a civilian Offi-
cial here. The Kammerjunkers are Rohwedel and Natzmer ;
Natzmer Junior, son of a distinguished Feldmarschall : " a
good-hearted but foolish forward young fellow," says Wilhelmina ; " the failure of a coxcomb (*petit-maître manqué*)." For
example, once, strolling about in a solemn Kaiser's Soirée in
Vienna, he found in some quiet corner the young Duke of
Lorraine, Franz, who it is thought will be the divine Maria
Theresa's husband, and Kaiser himself one day. Foolish
Natzmer found this noble young gentleman in a remote corner
of the Soirée ; went up, nothing loath, to speak graciosities
and insipidities to him : the noble young gentleman yawned,
as was too natural, a wide long yawn ; and in an insipid familiar manner, foolish Natzmer (Wilhelmina and the Berlin circles know it) put his finger into the noble young gentleman's
mouth, and insipidly wagged it there. " Sir, you seem to forget where you are ! " said the noble young gentleman ; and
closing his mouth with emphasis, turned away ; but happily
took no farther notice.[2] This is all we yet know of the history
of Natzmer, whose heedless ways and slap-dash speculations,

[1] Preuss, i. 56, 57 ; and Anonymous, *Friedrichs des Grossen Briefe an seinen
Vater* (Berlin, Posen und Bromberg, 1838), p. 3.
[2] Wilhelmina, i. 310.

tinted with natural ingenuity and good-humor, are not unattractive to the Prince.

Hofmarschall and these two Kammerjunkers are of the lawyer species; men intended for Official business, in which the Prince himself is now to be occupied. The Prince has four lackeys, two pages, one valet. He wears his sword, but has no sword-tash (*porte épée*), much less an officer's uniform: a mere Prince put upon his good behavior again; not yet a soldier of the Prussian Army, only hoping to become so again. He wears a light-gray dress, "*hechtgrauer* (pike-gray) frock with narrow silver cordings;" and must recover his uniform, by proving himself gradually a new man.

For there is, along with the new household, a new employment laid out for him in Cüstrin; and it shall be seen what figure he makes in that, first of all. He is to sit in the *Domänen-Kammer* or Government Board here, as youngest Rath; no other career permitted. Let him learn Economics and the way of managing Domain Lands (a very principal item of the royal revenues in this Country): humble work, but useful; which he had better see well how he will do. Two elder Raths are appointed to instruct him in the Economic Sciences and Practices, if he show faculty and diligence; — which in fact he turns out to do, in a superior degree, having every motive to try.

This kind of life lasted with him for the next fifteen months, all through the year 1731 and farther; and must have been a very singular, and was probably a highly instructive year to him, not in the Domain Sciences alone. He is left wholly to himself. All his fellow-creatures, as it were, are watching him. Hundred-eyed Argus, or the Ear of Dionysius, that is to say, Tobacco-Parliament with its spies and reporters, — no stirring of his finger can escape it here. He has much suspicion to encounter: Papa looking always sadly askance, sadly incredulous, upon him. He is in correspondence with Grumkow; takes much advice from Grumkow (our prompter-general, president in the Dionysius'-Ear, and not an ill-wisher farther); professes much thankfulness to Grumkow,

now and henceforth. Thank you for flinging me out of the
six-story window, and catching me by the coat-skirts ! — Left
altogether to himself, as we said; has in the whole Universe
nothing that will save him but his own good sense, his own
power of discovering what is what, and of doing what will be
behooveful therein.

He is to quit his French literatures and pernicious practices, one and all. His very flute, most innocent " Princess,"
as he used to call his flute in old days, is denied him ever since
he came to Cüstrin ; — but by degrees he privately gets her
back, and consorts much with her ; wails forth, in beautiful
adagios, emotions for which there is no other utterance at
present. He has liberty of Cüstrin and the neighborhood ; out
of Cüstrin he is not to lodge, any night, without leave had of
the Commandant. Let him walk warily ; and in good earnest
study to become a new creature, useful for something in the
Domain Sciences and otherwise.

CHAPTER III.

WILHELMINA IS TO WED THE PRINCE OF BAIREUTH.

CROWN-PRINCE FRIEDRICH being settled so far, his Majesty
takes up the case of Wilhelmina, the other ravelled skein lying
on hand. Wilhelmina has been prisoner in her Apartment at
Berlin all this while : it is proper Wilhelmina be disposed of ;
either in wedlock, filially obedient to the royal mind ; or in
some much sterner way, " within four walls," it is whispered,
if disobedient.

Poor Wilhelmina never thought of disobeying her parents :
only, which of them to obey ? King looks towards the Prince
of Baireuth again, agreed on before those hurly-burlies now
past ; Queen looks far otherwards. Queen Sophie still desperately believes in the English match for Wilhelmina ; and has
subterranean correspondences with that Court ; refusing to see
that the negotiation is extinct there. Grumkow himself, so

over-victorious in his late task, is now heeling towards England; "sincere in his wish to be well with us," thinks Dickens : Grumkow solaces her Majesty with delusive hopes in the English quarter : "Be firm, child; trust in my management; only swear to me, on your eternal salvation, that never, on any compulsion, will you marry another than the Prince of Wales; — give me that oath!"[1] Such was Queen Sophie's last proposal to Wilhelmina, — night of the 27th of January, 1731, as is computable, — her Majesty to leave for Potsdam on the morrow. They wept much together that night, but Wilhelmina dexterously evaded the oath, on a religious ground. Prince of Baireuth, whom Papa may like or may not like, has never yet personally made appearance : who or what will make appearance, or how things can or will turn, except a bad road, is terribly a mystery to Wilhelmina.

What with chagrin and confinement, what with bad diet (for the very diet is bad, quality and quantity alike unspeakable), Wilhelmina sees herself "reduced to a skeleton;" no company but her faithful Sonsfeld, no employment but her Books and Music; — struggles, however, still to keep heart. One day, it is in February, 1731, as I compute, they are sitting, her Sonsfeld and she, at their sad mess of so-called dinner, in their remote upper story of the Berlin Schloss, tramp of sentries the one thing audible; and were "looking mournfully at one another, with nothing to eat but a soup of salt and water, and a ragout of old bones full of hairs and slopperies [nothing else; that was its real quality, whatever fine name they might give it, says the vehement Princess], we heard a sharp tapping at the window; and started up in surprise, to see what it could be. It was a raven, carrying in its beak a bit of bread, which it left on the window-sill, and flew away."[2]

"Tears came into our eyes at this adventure." Are we become as Hebrew Elijahs, then; so that the wild ravens have to bring us food ? Truth is, there was nothing miraculous, as Wilhelmina found by and by. It was a tame raven, — not the soul of old George I., which lives at Isleworth on good pensions; but the pet raven of a certain Margravine, which lost

[1] Wilhelmina, i. 314.   [2] Ib. i. 316.

its way among the intricate roofs here. But the incident was touching. " Well," exclaimed Wilhelmina, " in the Roman Histories I am now reading, it is often said those creatures betoken good luck." All Berlin, such the appetite for gossip, and such the famine of it in Berlin at present, talked of this minute event : and the French Colony — old Protestant Colony, practical considerate people — were so struck by it, they brought baskets of comfortable things to us, and left them daily, as if by accident, on some neutral ground, where the maid could pick them up, sentries refusing to see unless compelled. Which fine procedure has attached Wilhelmina to the French nation ever since, as a dexterous useful people, and has given her a disposition to help them where she could.

The omen of the raven did not at once bring good luck : however, it did chance to be the turning-point, solstice of this long Greenland winter ; after which, amid storms and alarms, daylight came steadily nearer. Storms and alarms : for there came rumors of quarrels out at Potsdam, quarrels on the old score between the Royal Spouses there ; and frightful messages, through one Eversmann, an insolent royal lackey, about wedding Weissenfels, about imprisonment for life and other hard things ; through all which Wilhelmina studied to keep her poor head steady, and answer with dignity yet discreetly. On the other hand, her Sisters are permitted to visit her, and perceptible assuagements come. At length, on the 11th of May, there came solemn Deputation, Borck, Grumkow, Thulmeyer in it, old real friends and pretended new ; which set poor Wilhelmina wringing her hands (having had a Letter from Mamma overnight) ; but did bring about a solution. It was Friday, 11th of May ; a day of crisis in Wilhelmina's history ; Queen commanding one thing, King another, and the hour of decision come.

Entering, announcing themselves, with dreadful solemnity, these gentlemen, Grumkow the spokesman, in soft phrase, but with strict clearness, made it apparent to her, That marry she must, — the Hereditary Prince of Baireuth, — and without the consent of both her parents, which was unattainable at present, but peremptorily under the command of one of them, whose vote was the supreme. Do this (or even say that you will do it, whisper some of the well-affected), his Majesty's paternal favor will return upon you like pent waters; — and the Queen will surely reconcile herself (or perhaps turn it all her own way yet! whisper the well-affected). Refuse to do it, her Majesty, your Royal Brother, you yourself Royal Highness, God only knows what the unheard-of issue will be for you all! Do it, let us advise you: you must, you must!—Wilhelmina wrung her hands; ran distractedly to and fro; the well-affected whispering to her, the others "conversing at a window." At length she did it. Will marry whom her all-gracious Papa appoints; never wished or meant the least disobedience; hopes, beyond all things, his paternal love will now return, and make everybody blessed; — and oh, reconcile Mamma to me, ye well-affected! adds she. — Bravissimo! answer they: her Majesty, for certain, will reconcile herself; Crown-Prince get back from Cüstrin, and all will be well.[1]

Friedrich Wilhelm was overjoyed; Queen Sophie Dorothee was in despair. With his Majesty, who "wept" like a paternal bear, on re-embracing Wilhelmina the obedient some days hence, it became a settled point, and was indicated to Wilhelmina as such, That the Crown-Prince would, on her actual wedding, probably get back from Cüstrin. But her Majesty's reconcilement, — this was very slow to follow. Her Majesty was still in flames of ire at their next interview; and poor Wilhelmina fainted, on approaching to kiss her hand. "Disgraced, vanquished, and my enemies triumphing!" said her Majesty; and vented her wrath on Wilhelmina; and fell ill (so soon as there was leisure), ill, like to die, and said, "Why pretend to weep, when it is you that have killed me!"— and indeed was altogether hard, bitter, upon the poor Princess; a chief sorrow to her in these trying months. Can there be such wrath in celestial minds, venting itself so unreasonably? —

At present there is no leisure for illness; grand visitors in quantity have come and are coming; and the Court is brilliant

[1] Wilhelmina, i. 327-333.

exceedingly ; — his Majesty blazing out into the due magnificence, which was very great on this occasion, domestic matters
looking up with him again.   The Serenities of Brunswick are
here, young and old ; much liked by Friedrich Wilhelm; and
almost reckoned family people, — ever since their Eldest Son
was affianced to the Princess Charlotte here, last visit they
made.   To Princess Charlotte, Wilhelmina's second junior, —
mischievous, coquettish creature she, though very pretty and
insinuating, who seems to think her Intended rather a phlegmatic young gentleman, as Wilhelmina gradually discovers.
Then there is old Duke Eberhard Ludwig, of Würtemberg,
whom we saw at Ludwigsburg last year, in an intricate condition with his female world and otherwise, he too announces
himself, — according to promise then given.   Old Duke Eberhard Ludwig comes, stays three weeks in great splendor of
welcome; — poor old gentleman, his one son is now dead; and
things are getting earnest with him.   On his return home,
this time, he finds, according to order, the foul witch Grävenitz
duly cleared away ; reinstates his injured Duchess, with the
due feelings, better late than never; and dies in a year or two,
still childless. —

These are among the high guests at Berlin ; and there are
plenty of others whom we do not name.   Magnificent dining ;
with "six-and-twenty blackamoors," high-colored creatures,
marching up the grand staircase, round the table, round it,
and then down again, melodious, doing "janizary music," if
you happen to prefer that kind ; — trained creatures these
blackamoors, all got when boys, and set to cymballing and
fifing betimes, adds my authority.[1]   Dining, boar-hunting (if
the boar be huntable), especially reviewing, fail not in those
fine summer days.

One evening, it is Sunday, 27th of May, latish, while the
high guests, with Queen and Wilhelmina, are just passing in
to supper (King's Majesty having "gone to bed at seven," to
be well astir for the review to-morrow), a sound of wheels is
heard in the court.   Modest travelling-equipage rolls up into
the inner court; to the foot of the grand staircase there,

[1] Fassmann, p. 726, &c.

whither only Princes come : — who can it be ? The Queen
sends to inquire. Heavens, it is the Hereditary Prince of
Baireuth ! "Medusa's Head never produced such effect as did
this bit of news : Queen sat petrified ; and I," by reflex, was
petrified too ! Wilhelmina passed the miserablest night, no
wink of sleep ; and felt quite ill in the morning ; — in dread,
too, of Papa's rough jests, — and wretched enough. She had
begged much, last night, to be excused from the review. But
that could not be : "I must go," said the Queen after reflection, "and you with me." Which they did ; — and diversified
the pomp and circumstance of mock-war by a small unexpected scene.

Queen, Princess and the proper Dames had, by his Majesty's
order, to pass before the line : Princess in much trouble, "with
three caps huddled on me, to conceal myself," poor soul. Margraf of Schwedt, at the head of his regiment, "looked swollen
with rage," high hopes gone in this manner ; — and saluted us
with eyes turned away. As for his Mother, the Dessau Margravine in high colors, she was "blue in the face" all day.
Lines passed, and salutations done, her Majesty and Dames
withdrew to the safe distance, to look on : — Such a show, for
pomp and circumstance, Wilhelmina owns, as could not be
equalled in the world. Such wheeling, rhythmic coalescing
and unfolding ; accurate as clock-work, far and wide ; swift big
column here, hitting swift big column there, at the appointed
place and moment ; with their volleyings and trumpetings,
bright uniforms and streamers and field-music, — in equipment and manœuvre perfect all, to the meanest drummer or
black kettle-drummer : — supreme drill-sergeant playing on the
thing, as on his huge piano, several square miles in area !
Comes of the Old Dessauer, all this ; of the "equal step ; " of
the abstruse meditations upon tactics, in that rough head of
his. Very pretty indeed. — But in the mean while an Official
steps up : cap in hand, approaches the Queen's carriage ; says,
He is ordered to introduce his Highness the Prince of Baireuth.
Prince comes up accordingly ; a personable young fellow ; in-
telligent-looking, self-possessed ; makes obeisance to her Majesty, who answers in frosty politeness ; and — and Wilhelmina,

faint, fasting, sleepless all night, fairly falls aswoon. Could
not be helped : and the whole world saw it; and Guy Dickens
and the Diplomatists wrote home about it, and there rose
rumor and gossip enough! [1] But that was the naked truth
of it : hot weather, agitation, want of sleep, want of food; not
aversion to the Hereditary Prince, nothing of that.

Rather the contrary, indeed ; and, on better acquaintance,
much the contrary. For he proved a very rational, honorable
and eligible young Prince : modest, honest, with abundance
of sense and spirit; kind too and good, hot temper well kept,
temper hot not harsh; quietly holds his own in all circles;
good discourse in him, too, and sharp repartee if requisite, —
though he stammered somewhat in speaking. Submissive
Wilhelmina feels that one might easily have had a worse
husband. What glories for you in England! the Queen used
to say to her in old times : "He is a Prince, that Frederick,
who has a good heart, and whose genius is very small. Rather
ugly than handsome; slightly out of shape even (*un peu
contrefait*). But provided you have the complaisance to suffer
his debaucheries, you will quite govern him; and you will be
more King than he, when once his Father is dead. Only see
what a part you will play! It will be you that decide on the
weal or woe of Europe, and give law to the Nation," [2] — in a
manner! Which Wilhelmina did not think a celestial prospect even then. Who knows but, of all the offers she had,
"four" or three "crowned heads" among them, this final
modest honest one may be intrinsically the best? Take your
portion, if inevitable, and be thankful! —

The Betrothal follows in about a week : Sunday, 3d June,
1731; with great magnificence, in presence of the high guests
and all the world: and Wilhelmina is the affianced Bride of
Friedrich of Baireuth : — and that enormous Double-Marriage
Tragi-comedy, of Much Ado about Nothing, is at last ended.
Courage, friends; all things do end ! —

The high guests hereupon go their ways again ; and the

[1] Dickens, of 2d June, 1731 (in pathetic terms) ; Wilhelmina, i. 341 (with
out pathos).

[2] Wilhelmina, i. 143.

Court of Berlin, one cannot but suppose, collapses, as after
a great effort finished. Do not Friedrich Wilhelm and innumerable persons — the readers and the writer of this History
included — feel a stone rolled off their hearts ? — It is now,
and not till now, that Queen Sophie falls sick, and like to
die; and reproaches Wilhelmina with killing her. Friedrich
Wilhelm hopes confidently, not; waits out at Potsdam, for
a few days, till this killing danger pass; then departs, with
double impetuosity, for Preussen, and despatch of Public Business; such a mountain of Domestic Business being victoriously
got under.

Poor King, his life, this long while, has been a series of
earthquakes and titanic convulsions. Narrow miss he has
had, of pulling down his house about his ears, and burying
self, son, wife, family and fortunes, under the ruin-heap, —
a monument to remote posterity. Never was such an enchanted dance, of well-intentioned Royal Bear with poetic
temperament, piped to by two black-artists, for the Kaiser's
and Pragmatic Sanction's sake! Let Tobacco-Parliament also
rejoice; for truly the play was growing dangerous, of late.
King and Parliament, we may suppose, return to Public Business with double vigor.

CHAPTER IV.

CRIMINAL JUSTICE IN PREUSSEN AND ELSEWHERE.

Not that his Majesty, while at the deepest in domestic
intricacies, ever neglects Public Business. This very summer
he is raising Hussar Squadrons; bent to introduce the Hussar kind of soldiery into his Army; — a good deal of horse-
breaking and new sabre-exercise needed for that object.[1]
The affairs of the Reich have at no moment been out of his
eye; glad to see the Kaiser edging round to the Sea-Powers

[1] Fassmann, pp. 417, 418.

again, and things coming into their old posture, in spite of that sad Treaty of Seville.

Nay, for the last two years, while the domestic volcanoes were at their worst, his Majesty has been extensively dealing with a new question which has risen, that of the *Salzburg Protestants;* concerning which we shall hear more anon. Far and wide, in the Diets and elsewhere, he has been diligently, piously and with solid judgment, handling this question of the poor Salzburgers; and has even stored up moneys in intended solace of them (for he foresees what the end will be); — moneys which, it appears about this time, a certain Official over in Preussen has been peculating! In the end of June, his Majesty sets off to Preussen on the usual Inspection Tour; which we should not mention, were it not in regard to that same Official, and to something very rhadamanthine and particular which befell him; significant of what his Majesty can do in the way of prompt justice.

Case of Schlubhut.

The Königsberg Domain-Board (*Kriegs- und Domänen-Kammer*) had fallen awry, in various points, of late; several things known to be out-at-elbows in that Country; the Kammer Raths evidently lax at their post; for which reason they have been sharply questioned, and shaken by the collar, so to speak. Nay there is one Rath, a so-called Nobleman of those parts, by name Schlubhut, who has been found actually defaulting; peculating from that pious hoard intended for the Salzburgers: he is proved, and confesses, to have put into his own scandalous purse no less than 11,000 thalers, some say 30,000 (almost £5,000), which belonged to the Public Treasury and the Salzburg Protestants! These things, especially this latter unheard-of Schlubhut thing, the Supreme Court at Berlin (*Criminal-Collegium*) have been sitting on, for some time; and, in regard to Schlubhut, they have brought out a result, which Friedrich Wilhelm not a little admires at. Schlubhut clearly guilty of the defalcation, say they; but he has moneys, landed properties: let him refund, principal and

interest; and have, say, three or four years' imprisonment,
by way of memento. "Years' imprisonment? Refund? Is
theft in the highest quarters a thing to be let off for refund-
ing?" growls his Majesty; and will not confirm this sentence
of his Criminal-Collegium; but leaves it till he get to the
spot, and see with his own eyes. Schlubhut, in arrest or
mild confinement all this while, ought to be bethinking himself more than he is!

Once on the spot, judge if the Königsberg Domain-Kammer
had not a stiff muster to pass; especially if Schlubhut's drill-
exercise was gentle! Schlubhut, summoned to private interview with his Majesty, carries his head higher than could
be looked for: Is very sorry; knows not how it happened;
meant always to refund; will refund, to the last penny, and
make all good. — "Refund? Does He (*Er*) know what steal-
ing means, then? How the commonest convicted private thief
finds the gallows his portion; much more a public magistrate
convicted of theft? Is He aware that He, in a very especial
manner, deserves hanging, then?" — Schlubhut looks offended
dignity; conscious of rank, if also of quasi-theft: "*Es ist
nicht Manier* (it is not the polite thing) to hang a Prussian
Nobleman on those light terms!" answers Schlubhut, high-
mannered at the wrong time: "I can and will pay the money
back!" — *Noble*-man? Money back? "I will none of His
scoundrelly money." To strait Prison with this *Schurke!* —
And thither he goes accordingly: unhappiest of mortals; to
be conscious of rank, not at the right place, when about to
steal the money, but at the wrong, when answering to Rhadamanthus on it!

And there, sure enough, Schlubhut lies, in his prison on the
Schlossplatz, or Castle Square, of Königsberg, all night; and
hears, close by the *Domänen-Kammer*, which is in the same
Square, *Domänen-Kammer* where his Office used to be, a terrible sound of carpentering go on; — unhappiest of Prussian
Noblemen. And in the morning, see, a high gallows built;
close in upon the Domain-Kammer, looking into the very
windows of it; — and there, sure enough, the unfortunate
Schlubhut dies the thief's death, few hours hence, speaking or

MEETING OF FREDERICK AND WILHELMINA.

Carlyle, Vol. Two, p. 113.

thinking what, no man reports to me. Death was certain for
him; inevitable as fate. And so he vibrates there, admoni-
tory to the other Raths for days, — some say for weeks, —
till by humble petition they got the gallows removed. The
stumps of it, sawed close by the stones, were long after visible
in that Schlossplatz of Königsberg. Here is prompt justice
with a witness ! Did readers ever hear of such a thing ?
There is no doubt about the fact,[1] though in all Prussian
Books it is loosely smeared over, without the least precision
of detail ; and it was not till after long searching that I could
so much as get it dated : July, 1731, while Friedrich Crown-
Prince is still in eclipse at Cüstrin, and some six weeks after
Wilhelmina's betrothal. And here furthermore, direct from
the then Schlubhut precincts, is a stray Note, meteorological
chiefly ; but worth picking up, since it is authentic. "Wehlau," we observe, is on the road homewards again, — on our
return from uttermost Memel, — a day's journey hitherwards
of that place, half a day's thitherwards of Königsberg : —

"*Tuesday, 10th July,* 1731. King dining with General
Dockum at Wehlau," — where he had been again reviewing,
for about forty hours, all manner of regiments brought to
rendezvous there for the purpose, poor "General Katte with
his regiment" among them ; — King at dinner with General
Dockum after all that, "took the resolution to be off to Königsberg ; and arrived here at the stroke of midnight, in a
deluge of rain." This brings us within a day, or two days,
of Schlubhut's death. Terrible "combat of Bisons (*Uri,* or
Auerochsen, with such manes, such heads), of two wild Bisons
against six wild Bears," then ensued ; and the Schlubhut human tragedy ; I know not in what sequence, — rather conjecture the Schlubhut had gone *first.* Pillau, road to Dantzig, on
the narrow strip between the Frische Haf and Baltic, is the
next stage homewards ; at Pillau, General Finkenstein (excellent old Tutor of the Crown-Prince) is Commandant, and expects his rapid Majesty, day and hour given, to me not known.
Majesty goes in three carriages ; Old Dessauer, Grumkow,

[1] Benekendorf (Anonymous), *Karakterzüge aus dem Leben König Friedrich
Wilhelm I.* (Berlin, 1788), vii. 15–20 ; Förster (ii. 268), &c. &c.

Seckendorf, Ginkel are among his suite; weather still very
electric : —

"At Fischhausen, half-way to Pillau, Majesty had a bout of
elk-hunting; killed sixty elks [Melton-Mowbray may consider
it], — creatures of the deer sort, nimble as roes, but strong
as bulls, and four palms higher than the biggest horse, —
to the astonishment of Seckendorf, Ginkel and the strangers
there. Half an hour short of Pillau, furious electricity again;
thunder-bolt shivered an oak-tree fifteen yards from Majesty's
carriage. And at Pillau itself, the Battalion in Garrison there,
drawn out in arms, by Count Finkenstein, to receive his Majesty [rain over by this time, we can hope], had suddenly to
rush forward and take new ground; Frische Haf, on some
pressure from the elements, having suddenly gushed out, two
hundred paces beyond its old watermark in that place." [1]

Pillau, Fischhausen, — this is where the excellent old
Adalbert stamped the earth with his life " in the shape of a
crucifix " eight hundred years ago : and these are the new
phenomena there ! — The General Dockum, Colonel of Dragoons, whom his Majesty dined with at Wehlau, got his death
not many months after. One of Dockum's Dragoon Lieutenants felt insulted at something, and demanded his discharge :
discharge given, he challenged Dockum, duel of pistols, and
shot him dead.[2] Nothing more to be said of Dockum, nor of
that Lieutenant, in military annals.

Case of the Criminal-Collegium itself.

And thus was the error of the Criminal-Collegium rectified
in re Schlubhut. For it is not in name only, but in fact, that
this Sovereign is Supreme Judge, and bears the sword in God's
stead, — interfering now and then, when need is, in this terrible manner. In the same dim authentic Benekendorf (himself
a member of the Criminal-Collegium in later times), and from
him in all the Books, is recorded another interference somewhat in the comic vein; which also we may give. Undisputed

[1] See Mauvillon, ii. 293–297 ; — *correcting* by Fassmann, p. 422.
[2] 7th April, 1732 (*Militair-Lexikon*, i. 365).

fact, again totally without precision or details ; not even datable, except that, on study, we perceive it may have been
before this Schlubhut's execution, and after the Criminal-Collegium had committed their error about him, — must have been
while this of Schlubhut was still vividly in mind.   Here is the
unprecise but indubitable fact, as the Prussian Dryasdust has
left us his smear of it : —

"One morning early" (might be before Schlubhut was
hanged, and while only sentence of imprisonment and restitution lay on him), General Graf von Dönhof, Colonel of a
Musketeer Regiment, favorite old soldier, — who did vote on
the mild side in that Court-Martial on the Crown-Prince lately ;
but I hope has been forgiven by his Majesty, being much
esteemed by him these long years past ; — this Dönhof, early
one morning, calls upon the King, with a grimly lamenting air.
"What is wrong, Herr General ? " — " Your Majesty, my best
musketeer, an excellent soldier, and of good inches, fell into
a mistake lately, — bad company getting round the poor fellow ; they, he among them, slipt into a house and stole something ; trifle and without violence : pay is but three halfpence,
your Majesty, and the Devil tempts men ! Well, the Criminal-Collegium have condemned him to be hanged ; an excellent
soldier and of good inches, for that one fault. Nobleman
Schlubhut was 'to make restitution,' they decreed : that was
their decree on Schlubhut, one of their own set ; and this poor
soldier, six feet three, your Majesty, is to dance on the top of
nothing for a three-halfpenny matter ! " — So would Dönhof
represent the thing, — "fact being," says my Dryasdust, "it
was a case of house-breaking with theft to the value of 6,000
thalers and this musketeer the ringleader ! " — Well ; but
was Schlubhut sentenced to hanging ? Do you keep two
weights and two measures, in that Criminal-Collegium of
yours, then ?

Friedrich Wilhelm feels this sad contrast very much ; the
more, as the soldier is his own chattel withal, and of superlative inches : Friedrich Wilhelm flames up into wrath ; sends off
swift messengers to bring these Judges, one and all instantly
into his presence. The Judges are still in their dressing-

gowns, shaving, breakfasting; they make what haste they can.
So soon as the first three or four are reported to be in the
anteroom, Friedrich Wilhelm, in extreme impatience has
them called in; starts discoursing with them upon the two
weights and two measures. Apologies, subterfuges do but
provoke him farther; it is not long till he starts up, growling
terribly: " *Ihr Schurken* (Ye Scoundrels), how could you? "
and smites down upon the crowns of them with the Royal
Cudgel itself. Fancy the hurry-scurry, the unforensic attitudes
and pleadings! Royal Cudgel rains blows, right and left : blood
is drawn, crowns cracked, crowns nearly broken; and "several
Judges lost a few teeth, and had their noses battered," before
they could get out. The second relay meeting them in this
dilapidated state, on the staircases, dashed home again without the honor of a Royal interview.[1] Let them learn to keep
one balance, and one set of weights, in their Law-Court henceforth. — This is an actual scene, of date Berlin, 1731, or
thereby; unusual in the annals of Themis. Of which no constitutional country can hope to see the fellow, were the need
never so pressing. — I wish his Majesty had been a thought
more equal, when he was so rhadamanthine! Schlubhut he
hanged, Schlubhut being only Schlubhut's chattel; this musketeer, his Majesty's own chattel, he did not hang, but set him
shouldering arms again, after some preliminary dusting! —

His Majesty was always excessively severe on defalcations;
any Chancellor, with his Exchequer-bills gone wrong, would
have fared ill in that country. One Treasury dignitary, named
Wilke (who had "dealt in tall recruits," as a kind of by-
trade, and played foul in some slight measure), the King was
clear for hanging; his poor Wife galloped to Potsdam, shrieking mercy; upon which Friedrich Wilhelm had him whipt by
the hangman, and stuck for life into Spandau. Still more
tragical was poor Hesse's case. Hesse, some domain Rath out
at Königsberg, concerned with moneys, was found with account-books in a state of confusion, and several thousands
short, when the outcome was cleared up. What has become of
these thousands, Sir? Poor old Hesse could not tell: "God is

[1] Benekendorf, vii. 33; Förster, ii. 270.

my witness, no penny of them ever stuck to me," asseverated poor old Hesse; "but where they are — ? My account-books are in such a state; — alas, and my poor old memory is not what it was!" They brought him to Berlin; in the end they actually hanged the poor old soul; — and then afterwards in his dusty lumber-rooms, hidden in pots, stuffed into this nook and that, most or all of the money was found![1] Date and document exist for all these cases, though my Dryasdust gives none; and the cases are indubitable; very rhadamanthine indeed. The soft quality of mercy, — ah, yes, it is beautiful and blessed, when permissible (though thrice-accursed, when not): but it is on the hard quality of justice, first of all, that Empires are built up, and beneficent and lasting things become achievable to mankind, in this world! —

Skipper Jenkins in the Gulf of Florida.

A couple of **weeks** before Schlubhut's death, the English Newspapers are somewhat astir, — in the way of narrative merely, as yet. Ship Rebecca, Captain Robert Jenkins Master, has arrived in the Port of London, with a strange story in her log-book. Of which, after due sifting, this is accurately the substance: —

"*London, 23d–27th June,* 1731. Captain Jenkins left this Port with the Rebecca, several months ago; sailed to Jamaica, for a cargo of sugar. He took in his cargo at Jamaica; put to sea again, 5th April, 1731, and proceeded on the voyage homewards; with indifferent winds for the first fortnight. April 20th, with no wind or none that would suit, he was hanging about in the entrance of the Gulf of Florida, not far from the Havana," — almost too near it, I should think; but these baffling winds! — "not far from the Havana, when a Spanish Guarda-Costa hove in sight; came down on Jenkins, and furiously boarded him: 'Scoundrel, what do *you* want; contrabanding in these seas? Jamaica, say you? Sugar? Likely! Let us see your logwood, hides, Spanish pieces-of-eight!' And broke in upon Jenkins, ship and person, in a most extraor-

---

[1] Förster (ii. 269), &c. &c.

dinary manner. Tore up his hatches; plunged down, seeking logwood, hides, pieces-of-eight; found none, — not the least trace of contraband on board of Jenkins. They brought up his quadrants, sextants, however; likewise his stock of tallow candles: they shook and rummaged him, and all things, for pieces-of-eight; furiously advised him, cutlass in hand, to confess guilt. They slashed the head of Jenkins, his left ear almost off. Order had been given, 'Scalp him!' — but as he had no hair, they omitted that; merely brought away the wig, and slashed: — still no confession, nor any pieces-of-eight. They hung him up to the yard-arm, — actual neck-halter, but it seems to have been tarry, and did not run: — still no confession. They hoisted him higher, tied his cabin-boy to his feet; neck-halter then became awfully stringent upon Jenkins; had not the cabin-boy (without head to speak of) slipt through, noose being tarry; which was a sensible relief to Jenkins. Before very death, they lowered Jenkins, 'Confess, scoundrel, then!' Scoundrel could not confess; spoke of 'British Majesty's flag, peaceable English subject on the high seas.' — 'British Majesty; high seas!' answered they, and again hoisted. Thrice over they tried Jenkins in this manner at the yard-arm, once with cabin-boy at his feet: never had man such a day, outrageous whiskerando cut-throats tossing him about, his poor Rebecca and him, at such rate! Sun getting low, and not the least trace of contraband found, they made a last assault on Jenkins; clutched the bloody slit ear of him; tore it mercilessly off; flung it in his face, 'Carry that to your King, and tell him of it!' Then went their way; taking Jenkins's tallow candles, and the best of his sextants with them; so that he could hardly work his passage home again, for want of latitudes; — and has lost in goods £112, not to speak of his ear. Strictly true all this; ship's company, if required, will testify on their oath." [1]

These surely are singular facts; calculated to awaken a maritime public careful of its honor. Which they did, — after about eight years, as the reader will see! For the present,

[1] *Daily Journal* (and the other London Newspapers), 12th–17th June (o.s.), 1731. Coxe's *Walpole*, i. 579, 560 (indistinct, and needing correction).

there are growlings in the coffee-houses ; and, " *Thursday, 28th June*," say the Newspapers, "This day Captain Jenkins with his Owners," ear in his pocket, I hope, "went out to Hampton Court to lay the matter before his Grace of Newcastle : " "Please your Grace, it is hardly three months since the illustrious Treaty of Vienna was signed ; Dutch and we leading in the Termagant of Spain, and nothing but halcyon weather to be looked for on that side ! " Grace of Newcastle, anxious to avoid trouble with Spain, answers I can only fancy what ; and nothing was done upon Jenkins and his ear ; [1] — may "keep it in cotton," if he like ; shall have " a better ship " for some solacement. This is the first emergence of Jenkins and his ear upon negligent mankind. He and it will marvellously re-emerge, one day ! —

Baby Carlos gets his Apanage.

But in regard to that Treaty of Vienna, seventh and last of the travail-throes for Baby Carlos's Apanage, let the too oblivious reader accept the following Extract, to keep him on a level with Public "Events," as they are pleased to denominate themselves : —

" By that dreadful Treaty of Seville, Cardinal Fleury and the Spaniards should have joined with England, and coerced the Kaiser *vi et armis* to admit Spanish Garrisons [instead of neutral] into Parma and Piacenza, and so secure Baby Carlos his heritage there, which all Nature was in travail till he got. ' War in Italy to a certainty ! ' said all the Newspapers, after Seville : and Crown-Prince Friedrich, we saw, was running off to have a stroke in said War ; — inevitable, as the Kaiser still obstinately refused. And the English, and great George their King, were ready. Nevertheless, no War came. Old Fleury, not wanting war, wanting only to fish out something useful for himself, — Lorraine how welcome, and indeed the smallest contributions are welcome ! — Old Fleury manœuvred, hung back;

---

[1] " The Spaniards own they did a witty thing,
    Who cropt our ears, and sent them to the King."
                                PoPE (date not given me).

till the Spaniards and Termagant Elizabeth lost all patience,
and the very English were weary, and getting suspicious.
Whereupon the Kaiser edged round to the Sea-Powers again,
or they to him; and comfortable *As-you-were* was got accomplished: much to the joy of Friedrich Wilhelm and others.
Here are some of the dates to these sublime phenomena:

"*March* 16*th*, 1731, Treaty of Vienna, England and the
Kaiser coalescing again into comfortable *As-you-were*. Treaty
done by Robinson [Sir Thomas, ultimately Earl of Grantham,
whom we shall often hear of in time coming]; was confirmed
and enlarged by a kind of second edition, 22d July, 1731;
Dutch joining, Spain itself acceding, and all being now right.
Which could hardly have been expected.

"For before the first edition of that Treaty, and while
Robinson at Vienna was still laboring like Hercules in it, —
the poor Duke of Parma died. Died; and no vestige of a
'Spanish Garrison' yet there, to induct Baby Carlos according to old bargain. On the contrary, the Kaiser himself took
possession, — 'till once the Duke's Widow, who declares
herself in the family-way, be brought to bed! If of a Son,
of course he must have the Duchies; if of a Daughter only,
then Carlos *shall* get them, let not Robinson fear.' The due
months ran, but neither son nor daughter came; and the
Treaty of Vienna, first edition and also second, was signed;
and,

"*October* 20*th*, 1731, Spanish Garrisons, no longer an hypothesis, but a bodily fact, 6,000 strong, 'convoyed by the
British Fleet,' came into Leghorn, and proceeded to lodge
themselves in the long-litigated Parma and Piacenza; — and,
in fine, the day after Christmas, blessed be Heaven,

"*December* 26*th*, Baby Carlos in highest person came in:
Baby Carlos (more power to him!) got the Duchies, and we
hope there was an end. No young gentleman ever had such
a pother to make among his fellow-creatures about a little
heritable property. If Baby Carlos's performance in it be anything in proportion, he will be a supereminent sovereign! —

"There is still some haggle about Tuscany, the Duke of
which is old and heirless; Last of the Medici, as he proved.

Baby Carlos would much like to have Tuscany too; but that
is a Fief of the Empire, and might easily be better disposed of,
thinks the Kaiser. A more or less uncertain point, that of
Tuscany; as many points are! Last of the Medici complained,
in a polite manner, that they were parting his clothes before
he had put them off: however, having no strength, he did not
attempt resistance, but politely composed himself, 'Well,
then!'[1] Do readers need to be informed that this same
Baby Carlos came to be King of Naples, and even ultimately
to be Carlos III. of Spain, leaving a younger Son to be King
of Naples, ancestor of the now Majesty there?"

And thus, after such Diplomatic earthquakes and travail of
Nature, there is at last birth; the Seventh Travail-throe has
been successful, in some measure successful. Here actually is
Baby Carlos's Apanage; there probably, by favor of Heaven
and of the Sea-Powers, will the Kaiser's Pragmatic Sanction
be, one day. Treaty of Seville, most imminent of all those
dreadful Imminencies of War, has passed off as they all did;
peaceably adjusts itself into Treaty of Vienna: A Termagant,
as it were, sated; a Kaiser hopeful to be so, Pragmatic Sanction and all: for the Sea-Powers and everybody mere halcyon
weather henceforth, — not extending to the Gulf of Florida
and Captain Jenkins, as would seem! Robinson, who did the
thing, — an expert man, bred to business as old Horace Walpole's Secretary, at Soissons and elsewhere, and now come to
act on his own score, — regards this Treaty of Vienna (which
indeed had its multiform difficulties) as a thing to immortalize
a man.

Crown-Prince has, long since, by Papa's order, written to
the Kaiser, to thank Imperial Majesty for that beneficent
intercession, which has proved the saving of his life, as Papa
inculcates. We must now see a little how the saved Crown-
Prince is getting on, in his eclipsed state, among the Domain
Sciences at Cüstrin.

[1] Schöll, ii. 219-221; Coxe's *Walpole*, i. 346; Coxe's *House of Austria* (London, 1854), iii. 151.

CHAPTER V.

INTERVIEW OF MAJESTY AND CROWN-PRINCE AT CÜSTRIN.

EVER since the end of November last year, Crown-Prince
Friedrich, in the eclipsed state, at Cüstrin, has been prosecuting his probationary course, in the Domain Sciences and
otherwise, with all the patience, diligence and dexterity he
could. It is false, what one reads in some foolish Books,
that Friedrich neglected the functions assigned him as assessor in the *Kriegs- und Domänen-Kammer.* That would not
have been the safe course for him! The truth still evident
is, he set himself with diligence to learn the Friedrich-Wilhelm methods of administering Domains, and the art of
Finance in general, especially of Prussian Finance, the best
extant then or since; — Finance, Police, Administrative Business; — and profited well by the Raths appointed as tutors to
him, in the respective branches. One Hille was his Finance-
tutor; whose "*Kompendium,*" drawn up and made use of on
this occasion, has been printed in our time; and is said to
be, in brief compass, a highly instructive Piece; throwing
clear light on the exemplary Friedrich-Wilhelm methods.[1]
These the Prince did actually learn; and also practise, all his
life, — "essentially following his Father's methods," say the
Authorities, — with great advantage to himself, when the
time came.

Solid Nicolai hunted diligently after traces of him in the
Assessor business here; and found some: Order from Papa,
to "make Report upon the Glass-works of the Neumark:"
Autograph signatures to common Reports, one or two; and
some traditions of his having had a hand in planning certain
Farm-Buildings still standing in those parts: — but as the
Kammer Records of Cüstrin, and Cüstrin itself, were utterly

[1] Preuss, i. 59 n.

burnt by the Russians in 1758, such traces had mostly
vanished thirty years before Nicolai's time.[1] Enough have
turned up since, in the form of Correspondence with the King
and otherwise : and it is certain the Crown-Prince did plan
Farm-Buildings ; — " both Carzig and Himmelstädt (Carzig
now called *Friedrichsfelde* in consequence)," * dim mossy
Steadings, which pious Antiquarianism can pilgrim to if it
likes, were built or rebuilt by him : — and it is remarkable
withal how horoughly instructed Friedrich Wilhelm shows
himself in such matters ; and how paternally delighted to
receive such proposals of improvement introducible at the
said Carzig and Himmelstädt, and to find young Graceless
so diligent, and his ideas even good.[2] Perhaps a momentary
glance into those affairs may be permitted farther on.

The Prince's life, in this his eclipsed state, is one of con-
straint, anxiety, continual liability ; but after the first months
are well over, it begins to be more supportable than we should
think. He is fixed to the little Town ; cannot be absent any
night, without leave from the Commandant; which, however,
and the various similar restrictions, are more formal than real.
An amiable Crown-Prince, no soul in Cüstrin but would run by
night or by day to serve him. He drives and rides about, in
that green peaty country, on Domain business, on visits, on permissible amusement, pretty much at his own modest discretion.
A green flat region, made of peat and sand; human industry
needing to be always busy on it : raised causeways with incessant bridges, black sedgy ditch on this hand and that ; many
meres, muddy pools, stagnant or flowing waters everywhere ;
big muddy Oder, of yellowish-drab color, coming from the
south, big black Warta (Warthe) from the Polish fens in the
east, the black and yellow refusing to mingle for some miles.
Nothing of the picturesque in this country ; but a good deal
of the useful, of the improvable by economic science ; and
more of fine productions in it, too, of the floral, and still more
interesting sorts, than you would suspect at first sight.
Friedrich's worst pinch was his dreadful straitness of income ;

---

[1] Nicolai, *Anekdoten*, vi. 193.   * See Map at p. 349.
[2] Förster, ii. 390, 387, 391.

checking one's noble tendencies on every hand : but the gentry of the district privately subscribed gifts for him (*se coti-
sirent*, says Wilhelmina) ; and one way and other he contrived
to make ends meet.   Münchow, his President in the Kammer,
next to whom sits Friedrich, " King's place standing always
ready but empty there," is heartily his friend ; the Münchows
are diligent in getting up balls, rural gayeties, for him; so the
Hilles, — nay Hille, severe Finance Tutor, has a Mamsell
Hille whom it is pleasant to dance with ;[1] nor indeed is
she the only fascinating specimen, or flower of loveliness, in
those peaty regions, as we shall see.   On the whole, his Royal
Highness, after the first paroxysms of Royal suspicion are
over, and forgiveness beginning to seem possible to the Royal
mind, has a supportable time of it; and possesses his soul in
patience, in activity and hope.

Unpermitted things, once for all, he must avoid to do :
perhaps he will gradually discover that many of them were
foolish things better not done.   He walks warily ; to this all
things continually admonish.   We trace in him some real
desire to be wise, to do and learn what is useful if he can
here.   But the grand problem, which is reality itself to him,
is always, To regain favor with Papa.   And this, Papa being
what he is, gives a twist to all other problems the young man
may have, for they must all shape themselves by this ; and
introduces something of artificial, — not properly of hypocriti-
cal, for that too is fatal if found out, — but of calculated,
reticent, of half-sincere, on the Son's part : an inevitable
feature, plentifully visible in their Correspondence now and
henceforth.   Corresponding with Papa and his Grumkow,
and watched, at every step, by such an Argus as the Tobacco-
Parliament, real frankness of speech is not quite the recommendable thing ; apparent frankness may be the safer !
Besides mastery in the Domain Sciences, I perceive the
Crown-Prince had to study here another art, useful to him
in after life : the art of wearing among his fellow-creatures a
polite cloak-of-darkness.   Gradually he becomes master of it
as few are : a man politely impregnable to the intrusion of

[1] Preuss, i. 59.

human curiosity; able to look cheerily into the very eyes of
men, and talk in a social way face to face, and yet continue
intrinsically invisible to them. An art no less essential to
Royalty than that of the Domain Sciences itself; and, — if at
all consummately done, and with a scorn of mendacity for
help, as in this case, — a difficult art. It is the chief feature
in the Two or Three Thousand *Letters* we yet have of Friedrich's to all manner of correspondents: Letters written with
the gracefulest flowing rapidity; polite, affable, — refusing to
give you the least glimpse into his real inner man, or tell you
any particular you might impertinently wish to know.

As the History of Friedrich, in this Cüstrin epoch, and
indeed in all epochs and parts, is still little other than a
whirlpool of simmering confusions, dust mainly, and sibylline paper-shreds, in the pages of poor Dryasdust, perhaps we
cannot do better than snatch a shred˙or two (of the partly
legible kind, or capable of being made legible) out of that
hideous caldron; pin them down at their proper dates; and
try if the reader can, by such means, catch a glimpse of the
thing with his own eyes. Here is shred first; a Piece in
Grumkow's hand.

This treats of a very grand incident; which forms an era
or turning-point in the Cüstrin life. Majesty has actually,
after hopes long held out of such a thing, looked in upon the
Prodigal at Cüstrin, in testimony of possible pardon in the
distance; — sees him again, for the first time since that scene
at Wesel with the drawn sword, after year and day. Grumkow, for behoof of Seckendorf and the Vienna people, has
drawn a rough "Protocol" of it; and here it is, snatched
from the Dust-whirlwinds, and faithfully presented to the
English reader. His Majesty is travelling towards Sonnenburg, on some grand Knight-of-Malta Ceremony there; and
halts at Cüstrin for a couple of hours as he passes: —

*Grumkow's " Protokoll" of the 15th August, 1731 ; or Summary
of what took place at Cüstrin that day.*

"His Majesty arrived at Cüstrin yesterday [*gestern,* Monday
15th, — hour not mentioned], and proceeded at once to the

Government House, with an attendance of several hundred
persons.   Major-General Lepel," Commandant of Cüstrin,
" Colonel Derschau and myself are immediately sent for to
his Majesty's apartment there.   Privy-Councillor Wolden,"
Prince's Hofmarschall, a solid legal man, " is ordered by his
Majesty to bring the Crown-Prince over from his house; who
accordingly in a few minutes, attended by Rohwedel and Natzmer," the two Kammerjunkers, " entered the room where his
Majesty and we were.

" So soon as his Majesty, turning round, had sight of him,
the Crown-Prince fell at his feet.   Having bidden him rise,
his Majesty said with a severe mien : —

" ' You will now bethink yourself what passed year and day
ago ; and how scandalously you saw fit to behave yourself, and
what a godless enterprise you took in hand.   As I have had
you about me from the beginning, and must know you well, I
did all in the world that was in my power, by kindness and by
harshness, to make an honorable man of you.   As I rather
suspected your evil purpose, I treated you in the harshest and
sharpest way in the Saxon Camp,' at Radewitz, in those gala
days, ' in hopes you would consider yourself, and take another
line of conduct ; would confess your faults to me, and beg forgiveness.   But all in vain ; you grew ever more stiffnecked.
When a young man gets into follies with women, one may try
to overlook it as the fault of his age: but to do with forethought basenesses (*lâchetéen*) and ugly actions ; that is un-
pardonable.   You thought to carry it through with your
headstrong humor : but hark ye, my lad (*höre, mein Kerl*), if
thou wert sixty or seventy instead of eighteen, thou couldst
not cross my resolutions.'   It would take a bigger man to do
that, my lad !   ' And as, up to this date (*bis dato*) I have
managed to sustain myself against any comer, there will be
methods found of bringing thee to reason too ! —

" ' How have not I, on all occasions, meant honorably by
you !   Last time I got wind of your debts, how did I, as a
Father, admonish you to tell me all ; I would pay all, you were
only to tell me the truth.   Whereupon you said, There were
still two thousand thalers beyond the sum named.   I paid

these also at once; and fancied I had made peace with you.
And then it was found, by and by, you owed many thousands
more; and as you now knew you could not pay, it was as good
as if the money had been stolen; — not to reckon how the
French vermin, Montholieu and partner, cheated you with their
new loans.' Pfui! — 'Nothing touched me so much [continues
his Majesty, verging towards the pathetic], as that you had
not any trust in me. All this that I was doing for aggrandize-
ment of the House, the Army and Finances, could only be for
you, if you made yourself worthy of it! I here declare I have
done all things to gain your friendship; — and all has been in
vain!' At which words the Crown-Prince, with a very sorrowful gesture, threw himself at his Majesty's feet," — tears (presumably) in both their eyes by this time.

" 'Was it not your intention to go to England?' asked his
Majesty farther on. The Prince answered '*Ja!*' — 'Then
hear what the consequences would have been. Your Mother
would have got into the greatest misery; I could not but have
suspected she was the author of the business. Your Sister
I would have cast, for life, into a place where she never would
have seen sun and moon again. Then on with my Army into
Hanover, and burn and ravage; yes, if it had cost me life,
land and people. Your thoughtless and godless conduct, see
what it was leading to. I intended to employ you in all
manner of business, civil, military; but how, after such an
action, could I show the face of you to my Officers (soldiers)
and other servants? — The one way of repairing all this
is, That you seek, regardless of your very life in comparison, to make the fault good again!' At which words the
Crown-Prince mournfully threw himself at his Royal Majesty's
feet; begging to be put upon the hardest proofs: He would
endure all things, so as to recover his Majesty's grace and
esteem.

" Whereupon the King asked him: 'Was it thou that
temptedst Katte; or did Katte tempt thee?' The Crown-
Prince without hesitation answered, 'I tempted him.' — 'I am
glad to hear the truth from you, at any rate.' "

The Dialogue now branches out, into complex general form;

out of which, intent upon abridging, we gather the following points. King *loquitur :* —

"How do you like your Cüstrin life ? Still as much aversion to Wusterhausen, and to wearing your shroud [*Sterbekittel*, name for the tight uniform you would now be so glad of, and think quite other than a shroud !] as you called it ? " Prince's answer wanting. — "Likely enough my company does not suit you : I have no French manners, and cannot bring out *bon-mots* in the *petit-maître* way ; and truly regard all that as a thing to be flung to the dogs. I am a German Prince, and mean to live and die in that character. But you can now say what you have got by your caprices and obstinate heart ; hating everything that I liked ; and if I distinguished any one, despising him ! If an Officer was put in arrest, you took to lamenting about him. Your real friends, who intended your good, you hated and calumniated ; those that flattered you, and encouraged your bad purpose, you caressed. You see what that has come to. In Berlin, in all Prussia for some time back, nobody asks after you, Whether you are in the world or not ; and were it not one or the other coming from Cüstrin who reports you as playing tennis and wearing French hair-bags, nobody would know whether you were alive or dead."

Hard sayings ; to which the Prince's answers (if there were any beyond mournful gestures) are not given. We come now upon Predestination, or the *Gnadenwahl ;* and learn (with real interest, not of the laughing sort alone) how his " Majesty, in the most conclusive way, set forth the horrible results of that Absolute-Decree notion ; which makes out God to be the Author of Sin, and that Jesus Christ died only for some ! Upon which the Crown-Prince vowed and declared (*hoch und theuer*), he was now wholly of his Majesty's orthodox opinion."

The King, now thoroughly moved, expresses satisfaction at the orthodoxy ; and adds with enthusiasm, "When godless fellows about you speak against your duties to God, the King and your Country, fall instantly on your knees, and pray with your whole soul to Jesus Christ to deliver you from such wickedness, and lead you on better ways. And if it come in earnest from your heart, Jesus, who would have all men saved, will not leave you unheard." No! And so may God in his mercy aid you, poor son Fritz. And as for me, in hopes the time coming will show fruits, I forgive you what is past. — To which the Crown-Prince answered with monosyllables, with many tears; "kissing his Majesty's feet;" — and as the King's eyes were not dry, he withdrew into another room; revolving many things in his altered soul.

"It being his Majesty's birthday [4th August by *old style*, 15th by *new*, forty-third birthday], the Prince, all bewept and in emotion, followed his Father; and, again falling prostrate, testified such heartfelt joy, gratitude and affection over this blessed anniversary, as quite touched the heart of Papa; who at last clasped him in his arms [poor soul, after all!], and hurried out to avoid blubbering quite aloud. He stept into his carriage," intending for Sonnenburg (chiefly by water) this evening, where a Serene Cousin, one of the Schwedt Margraves, Head Knight of Malta, has his establishment.

"The Crown-Prince followed his Majesty out; and, in the presence of many hundred people, kissed his Majesty's feet" again (linen gaiters, not Day-and-Martin shoes); "and was again embraced by his Majesty, who said, 'Behave well, as I see you mean, and I will take care of you,' which threw the Crown-Prince into such an ecstasy of joy as no pen can express;" and so the carriages rolled away, — towards the Knights-of-Malta business and Palace of the Head Knight of Malta, in the first place.[1]

These are the main points, says Grumkow, reporting next day; and the reader must interpret them as he can. A Crown-Prince with excellent histrionic talents, thinks the reader. Well; a certain exaggeration, immensity of wish becoming itself enthusiasm; somewhat of that: but that is by no means the whole or even the main part of the phenomenon, O reader. This Crown-Prince has a real affection to his Father, as we shall in time convince ourselves. Say, at lowest, a Crown-Prince loyal to fact; able to recognize overwhelming fact, and

[1] Förster, iii. 50-54.

aware that he must surrender thereto. Surrender once made,
the element much clears itself; Papa's side of the question
getting fairly stated for the first time. Sure enough, Papa is
God's Vicegerent in several undeniable respects, most important some of them : better try if we can obey Papa.

Dim old Fassmann yields a spark or two, — as to his Majesty's errand at Sonnenburg. Majesty is going to preside
to-morrow " at the Installation of young Margraf Karl, new
Herrmeister (Grand-Master) of the Knights of St. John "
there ; " the Office having suddenly fallen vacant lately."
Office which is an heirloom ; — usually held by one of the
Margraves, half-uncles of the King, — some junior of them,
not provided for at Schwedt or otherwise. Margraf Albert,
the last occupant, an old gentleman of sixty, died lately, " by
stroke of apoplexy while at dinner ; " [1] — and his eldest Son,
Margraf Karl, with whom his Majesty lodges to-night, is now
Herrmeister. " Majesty came at 6 P.M. to Sonnenburg [must
have left Cüstrin about five] ; forty-two Ritters made at
Sonnenburg next day," — a certain Colonel or Lieutenant-
General von Wreech, whom we shall soon see again, is one of
them ; Seckendorf another. " Fresh *Ritter-Schlag* [" Knight-
stroke," Batch of Knights dubbed] at Sonnenburg, 29th September next," which shall not the least concern us. Note
Margraf Karl, however, the new Herrmeister ; for he proves
a soldier of some mark, and will turn up again in the Silesian Wars ; — as will a poor Brother of his still more
impressively, "shot dead beside the King," on one occasion
there.

We add this of Dickens, for all the Diplomatists, and a discerning public generally, are much struck with the Event at
Cüstrin ; and take to writing of it as news ; — and " Mr. Ginkel," Dutch Ambassador here, an ingenious, honest and observant man, well enough known to us, has been out to sup with
the Prince, next day ; and thus reports of him to Dickens :
" Mr. Ginkel, who supped with the Prince on Thursday last,"
day after the Interview, " tells me that his Royal Highness
is extremely improved since he had seen him ; being grown

[1] 21st June, 1731 : Fassmann, p. 423 ; Pöllnitz, ii. 390.

much taller; and that his conversation is surprising for his age, abounding in good sense and the prettiest turns of expression." [1]

Here are other shreds, snatched from the Witch-Caldron, and pinned down, each at its place; which give us one or two subsequent glimpses : —

Potsdam, 21st August, 1731 (King to Wolden the Hofmarschall). . . . "Crown-Prince shall travel over, and personally inspect, the following Domains : Quartschen, Himmelstädt, Carzig, Massin, Lebus, Gollow and Wollup," dingy moor-farms dear to Antiquarians ; "travel over these and not any other. Permission always to be asked, of his Royal Majesty, in writing, and mention made to which of them the Crown-Prince means to go. Some one to be always in attendance, who can give him fit instruction about the husbandry ; and as the Crown-Prince has yet only learned the theory, he must now be diligent to learn the same practically. For which end it must be minutely explained to him, How the husbandry is managed, — how ploughed, manured, sown, in every particular ; and what the differences of good and bad husbandry are, so that he may be able of himself to know and judge the same. Of Cattle-husbandry too, and the affairs of Brewing (*Viehzucht und Brauwesen*), the due understanding to be given him ; and in the matter of Brewing, show him how things are handled, mixed, the beer drawn off, barrelled, and all how they do with it (*wie überall dabei verfahren*) ; also the malt, how it must be prepared, and what like, when good. Useful discourse to be kept up with him on these journeys ; pointing out how and why this is and that, and whether it could not be better : " — O King of a thousand ! — " Has liberty to shoot stags, moorcocks (*Hühner*) and the like ; and a small-hunt [*kleine Jagd,* not a *Parforce* or big one] can be got up for his amusement now and then; " furthermore "a little duck-shooting from boat," on the sedgy waters there, — if the poor soul should care about it. Wolden, or one of the Kammerjunkers, to accompany always, and be responsible.

[1] Despatch, 18th August, 1731.

" No *Mädchen* or *Frauensmensch*," no shadow of womankind ; —
" keep an eye on him, you three ! "

These things are in the Prussian Archives; of date the
week after that interview. In two weeks farther, follows
the Prince's speculation about Carzig and the Building of a
Farmstead there; with Papa's "real contentment that you
come upon such proposals, and seek to make improvements.
Only " —

Wusterhausen, 11*th September* (King to Crown-Prince). . . .
" Only you must examine whether there is meadow-ground
enough, and how many acres can actually be allotted to that
Farm. [Hear his Majesty !] Take a Land-surveyor with you ;
and have all well considered ; and exactly inform *yourself*
what kind of land it is, whether it can only grow rye, or
whether some of it is barley-land : you must consider it yourself, and do it all out of your own head, though you may
consult with others about it. In grazing-ground (*Hüthung*)
I think it will not fail; if only the meadow-land " —

in fact, it fails in nothing; and is got all done ("wood laid
out to season straightway," and "what digging and stubbing
there is, proceeded with through the winter ") : done in a successful and instructive manner, both Carzig and Himmelstädt,
though we will say nothing farther of them.[1]

Cüstrin, 22*d September* (Crown-Prince to Papa). . . . "Have
been at Lebus; excellent land out there ; fine weather for the
husbandman." "Major Röder," unknown Major, "passed this
way ; and dined with me, last Wednesday. He has got a pretty
fellow (*schönen Kerl*) for my Most All-Gracious Father's regiment [the Potsdam Giants, where I used to be]; whom I
could not look upon without bleeding heart. I depend on my
Most All-Gracious Father's Grace, that he will be good to me :
I ask for nothing and no happiness in the world but what
comes from You ; and hope You will, some day, remember me
in grace, and give me the Blue Coat to put on again ! "[2] — **To**

[1] Förster, i. 387–392.
[2] *Briefwechsel mit Vater* (Œuvres, xxvii. part 3d, p. 27).

which Papa answers nothing, or only "Hm, na, time *may* come!"

Carzig goes on straightway; Papa charmed to grant the moneys; "wood laid out to season," and much "stubbing and digging" set on foot, before the month ends. Carzig; and directly on the heel of it, on like terms, Himmelstädt, — but of all this we must say no more. It is clear the Prince is learning the Domain Sciences; eager to prove himself a perfect son in the eyes of Papa. Papa, in hopeful moments, asks himself: "To whom shall we marry him, then; how settle him?" But what the Prince, in his own heart, thought of it all; how he looked, talked, lived, in unofficial times? Here has a crabbed dim Document turned up, which, if it were not nearly undecipherable to the reader and me, would throw light on the point: —

Schulenburg's Three Letters to Grumkow, on Visits to the Crown-Prince, during the Cüstrin Time.

The reader knows Lieutenant-General Schulenburg; stiff little military gentleman of grave years, nephew of the maypole *Emerita* who is called Duchess of Kendal in England. "Had a horse shot under him at Malplaquet;" battlings and experiences enough, before and since. Has real sense, abundant real pedantry; a Prussian soldier every inch. He presided in the Cöpenick Court-martial; he is deeply concerned in these Crown-Prince difficulties. His Majesty even honors him by expecting he should quietly keep a monitorial eye upon the Crown-Prince; — being his neighbor in those parts; Colonel-Commandant of a regiment of Horse at Landsberg not many miles off. He has just been at Vienna [1] on some "business" (quasi-diplomatic probably, which can remain unknown to us); and has reported upon it, or otherwise finished it off, at Berlin; — whence rapidly home to Landsberg again. On the way homewards, and after getting home, he writes these three Letters; off-hand and in all privacy, and of course with a business sincerity, to Grumkow; — little thinking they would one

[1] September, 1731 (*Militair-Lexikon*, iii. 433).

day get printed, and wander into these latitudes to be scanned
and scrutinized! Undoubtedly an intricate crabbed Document
to us; but then an indubitable one. Crown-Prince, Schulenburg himself, and the actual figure of Time and Place, are
here mirrored for us, with a business sincerity, in the mind of
Schulenburg, — as from an accidental patch of water; ruffled
bog-water, in sad twilight, and with sedges and twigs intervening; but under these conditions we do look with our own
eyes!

Could not one, by any conceivable method, interpret into
legibility this abstruse dull Document; and so pick out here
and there a glimpse, actual face-to-face view, of Crown-Prince
Friedrich in his light-gray frock with the narrow silver tresses,
in his eclipsed condition there in the Cüstrin region? All
is very mysterious about him; his inward opinion about all
manner of matters, from the *Gnadenwahl* to the late Double-
Marriage Question. Even his outward manner of life, in its
flesh-and-blood physiognomy, — we search in vain through
tons of dusty lucubration totally without interest, to catch
here and there the corner of a feature of it. Let us try Schulenburg. We shall know at any rate that to Grumkow, in the
Autumn 1731, these words were luculent and significant: consciously they tell us something of young Friedrich; unconsciously a good deal of Lieutenant-General Schulenburg, who
with his strict theologies, his military stiffnesses, his reticent,
pipe-clayed, rigorous and yet human ways, is worth looking
at, as an antique species extinct in our time. He is just
home from Vienna, getting towards his own domicile from
Berlin, from Cüstrin, and has seen the Prince. He writes
in a wretched wayside tavern, or post-house, between Cüstrin
and Landsberg, — dates his letter "*Wien* (Vienna)," as if he
were still in the imperial City, so off-hand is he.

No. 1. *To his Excellenz* (add a shovelful of other titles) *Lieu-*
tenant-General Herr Baron von Grumkow, President of the
Krieges- und Domänen-Directorium, of the (in fact, Vice-Presi-
dent of the Tobacco-Parliament) *in Berlin.*

"WIEN [properly Berlin-Landsberg Highway,
other side of Cüstrin], 4th October, 1731.

" I regret much to have missed the pleasure of seeing your
Excellency again before I left Berlin. I set off between
seven and eight in the morning yesterday, and got to Cüstrin
[seventy miles or so] before seven at night. But the Prince
had gone, that day, to the Bailliage of Himmelstädt" (up the
Warta Country, eastward some five-and-thirty miles, much
preparatory digging and stubbing there); and he "slept at
Massin [circuitous road back], where he shot a few stags this
morning. As I was told he might probably dine at Kammin
[still nearer Cüstrin, twelve miles from it; half that distance
east of Zorndorf, — mark that, O reader *] with Madam Colonel Schöning, I drove thither. He had arrrived there a moment before me." And who is Madam Schöning, lady of
Kammin here ? — Patience, reader.

"I found him much grown; an air of health and gayety
about him. He caressed me greatly (*me gracieusa fort*); afterwards questioned me about my way of life in Vienna; and
asked, if I had diverted myself well there? I told him what
business had been the occasion of my journey, and that this
rather than amusements had occupied me; for the rest, that
there had been great affluence of company, and no lack of
diversions. He spoke a long time to Madam de Wreech" —

"Wrochem" Schulenburg calls her: young Wife of Lieutenant-General von Wreech, a Marlborough Campaigner, made a
Knight of Malta the other day; [1] — *his* charming young Wife,
and Daughter of Madam Colonel Schöning our hostess here;
lives at Tamsel, in high style, in these parts : mark the young
Lady well, —

---

* Map at p. 349.   [1] *Militair-Lexikon*, iv. 269.

"who did not appear indifferent to him." No! — "and in fact she was in all her beauty; a complexion of lily and rose."

Charming creature; concerning whom there are anecdotes still afloat, and at least verses of this Prince's writing; not too well seen by Wreech, lately made a Knight of Malta, who, though only turning forty, is perhaps twice her age. The beautifulest, cleverest, — fancy it; and whether the peaty Neumark produces nothing in the floral kind!

"We went to dinner; he asked me to sit beside him. The conversation fell, among other topics, on the Elector Palatine's Mistress," crotchety old gentleman, never out of quarrels, with Heidelberg Protestants, heirs of Jülich and Berg, and in general with an unreasonable world, whom we saw at Mannheim last year; has a Mistress, — "Elector Palatine's Mistress, called Taxis. Crown-Prince said: 'I should like to know what that good old gentleman does with a Mistress?' I answered, that the fashion had come so much in vogue, Princes did not think they were Princes unless they had mistresses; and that I was amazed at the facility of women, how they could shut their eyes on the sad reverse of fortune nearly inevitable for them; — and instanced the example of Madam Grävenitz" —

"Grävenitz;" example lately fallen out at Würtemberg, as we predicted. Prayers of the Country, "Deliver us from evil," are now answered there: Grävenitz quite over with it! Alas, yes; lately fallen from her high estate in Würtemberg, and become the topic of dinner-tables; seized by soldiers in the night-time; vain her high refusals, assurances of being too unwell to dress, "Shall go in your shift, then," — is in prison, totally eclipsed.[1] Calming her fury, she will get out; and wearisomely wander about in fashionable capitals, *toujours un lavement à ses trousses !* —

"There were other subjects touched upon; and I always endeavored to deduce something of moral instruction from them," being a military gentleman of the old school.

[1] Michaelis, iii. 440; Pöllnitz, i. 297.

"Among other things, he said, He liked the great world, and was charmed to observe the ridiculous weak side of some people. 'That is excellent,' said I, 'if one profit by it one-self: but if it is only for amusement, such a motive is worth little; we should rather look out for our own ridiculous weak side.' On rising, Hofmarschall Wolden said to me," without much sincerity, "'You have done well to preach a little mo-rality to him.' The Prince went to a window, and beckoned me thither.

"'You have learned nothing of what is to become of me?' said he. I answered: 'It is supposed your Royal Highness will return to Berlin, when the Marriage [Wilhelmina's] takes place; but as to what will come next, I have heard nothing. But as your Highness has friends, they will not fail to do their endeavor; and M. de Grumkow has told me he would try to persuade the King to give you a regiment, in order that your Highness might have something to do.' It seemed as if that would give him pleasure. I then took the liberty of saying: 'Monseigneur, the most, at present, depends on yourself.'— 'How so?' asked he. I answered, 'It is only by showing good conduct, and proofs of real wisdom and worth, that the King's entire favor can be gained. First of all, to fear God'" — And, in fact, I launched now into a moral preachment, or discursive Dialogue, of great length; much needing to have the skirts of it tucked up, in a way of faithful abridgment, for behoof of poor English readers. As follows :—

"*Schulenburg:* If your Highness behave well, the King will accord what you want: but it is absolutely necessary to begin by that. — *Prince:* I do nothing that can displease the King. — *Schulenburg:* It would be a little soon yet! But I speak of the future. Your Highness, the grand thing I recommend is to fear God! Everybody says, you have the sentiments of an honest man; excellent, that, for a beginning; but with-out the fear of God, your Highness, the passions stifle the finest sentiments. Must lead a life clear of reproach; and more particularly on the chapter of women! Need not im-agine you can do the least thing without the King's knowing it: if your Highness take the bad road, he will wish to correct

it; the end will be, he will bring you back to live beside
him; which will not be very agreeable. — *Prince:* Hmph,
No! — *Schulenburg:* Of the ruin to health I do not speak; I
— *Prince:* Pooh, one is young, one is not master of that;" —
and, in fact, on this delicate chapter, which runs to some
length, Prince answers as wildish young fellows will; quizzing my grave self, with glances even at his Majesty, on
alleged old peccadilloes of ours. Which allegations or inferences I rebutted with emphasis. "But, I confess, though I
employed all my rhetoric, his mind did not seem to alter ; and
it will be a miracle if he change on this head." Alas, General! Can't be helped, I fear !

"He said he was not afraid of anything so much as of living
constantly beside the King. — *Schulenburg:* Arm yourself with
patience, Monseigneur, if that happen. God has given you
sense enough; persevere to use it faithfully on all occasions,
you will gain the good graces of the King. — *Prince:* Impossible; beyond my power, indeed, said he ; and made a thousand
objections. — *Schulenburg:* Your Highness is like one that
will not learn a trade because you do not already know it.
Begin; you will certainly never know it otherwise! Before
rising in the morning, form a plan for your day," — in fact,
be moral, oh, be moral !

His Highness now got upon the marriages talked of for
him; an important point for the young man. He spoke, hope-
fully rather, of the marriage with the Princess of Mecklenburg, — Niece of the late Czar Peter the Great ; Daughter of
that unhappy Duke who is in quarrel with his Ritters, and a
trouble to all his neighbors, and to us among the number.
Readers recollect that young Lady's Serene Mother, and a
meeting she once had with her Uncle Peter, — at Magdeburg, a
dozen years ago, in a public drawing-room with alcove near ;
anecdote not lightly to be printed in human types, nor repeated
where not necessary. The Mother is now dead; Father still
up to the eyes in puddle and trouble : but as for the young Lady
herself, she is Niece to the now Czarina Anne; by law of primogeniture Heiress of all the Russias; something of a match truly !

"But there will be difficulties; your Highness to change your religion, for one thing? — *Prince:* Won't, by any means: — *Schulenburg:* And give up the succession to Prussia? — *Prince:* A right fool if I did! — *Schulenburg:* Then this marriage comes to nothing. — Thereupon next he said, If the Kaiser is so strong for us, let him give me his second Daughter;" lucky Franz of Lorraine is to get the first. — "*Schulenburg:* Are you serious? — *Prince:* Why not? with a Duchy or two it would do very well. — *Schulenburg:* No Duchies possible under the Pragmatic Sanction, your Highness: besides, your change of religion? — *Prince:* Oh, as to that, never! — Then this marriage also comes to nothing. Of the English, and their Double-Marriage, and their Hotham brabble, he spoke lightly, as of an extinct matter, — in terms your Excellency will like.

"But, said I, since you speak so much of marriages, I suppose you wish to be married? — *Prince:* No; but if the King absolutely will have it, I will marry to obey him. After that, I will shove my wife into the corner (*planterai là ma femme*), and live after my own fancy. — *Schulenburg:* Horrible to think of! For, in the first place, your Highness, is it not written in the Law of God, Adulterers shall not inherit the Kingdom of Heaven?" And in the second place; and in the third and fourth place! — To all which he answered as wild young fellows do, especially if you force marriage on them. "I can perceive, if he marries, it will only be to have more liberty than now. It is certain, if he had his elbows free, he would strike out (*s'en donnerait à gauche*). He said to me several times: 'I am young; I want to profit by my youth.'" A questionable young fellow, Herr General; especially if you force marriage on him.

"This conversation done," continues the General, "he set to talking with the Madam Wreech," and her complexion of lily and rose; "but he did not stay long; drove off about five [dinner at the stroke of twelve in those countries], inviting me to see him again at Cüstrin, which I promised."

And so the Prince is off in the Autumn sunset, driving down the peaty hollow of the Warta, through unpicturesque

country, which produces Wreechs and incomparable flowers
nevertheless. Yes; and if he look a six miles to the right,
there is the smoke of the evening kettles from Zorndorf,
rising into the sky; and across the River, a twenty miles
to the left, is Kunersdorf: poor sleepy sandy hamlets; where
nettles of the Devil are to be plucked one day! —

"The beautiful Wreech drove off to Tamsel," her fine house;
I to this wretched tavern; where, a couple of hours after that
conversation, I began writing it all down, and have nothing
else to do for the night. Your Excellency's most moral, stiffnecked, pipe-clayed and extremely obedient,

                                   "VON SCHULENBURG." [1]

This young man may be orthodox on Predestination, and
outwardly growing all that a Papa could wish; but here are
strange heterodoxies, here is plenty of mutinous capricious
fire in the interior of him, Herr General! In fact, a young
man unfortunately situated; already become solitary in Creation; has not, except himself, a friend in the world available
just now. Tempestuous Papa storms one way, tempestuous
Mamma Nature another; and between the outside and the
inside there are inconsistencies enough.

Concerning the fair Wreech of Tamsel, with her complexion
of lily and rose, there ensued by and by much whispering,
and rumoring underbreath; which has survived in the apocryphal Anecdote-Books, not in too distinct a form. Here, from
first hand, are three words, which we may take to be the
essence of the whole. Grumkow reporting, in a sordid, occasionally smutty, spy manner, to his Seckendorf, from Berlin,
eight or ten months hence, has this casual expression: "He
[King Friedrich Wilhelm] told me in confidence that Wreech,
the Colonel's Wife, is —— to P. R. (Prince-Royal); and that
Wreech vowed he would not own it for his. And his Majesty
in secret is rather pleased," adds the smutty spy. [2] Elsewhere

---

[1] Förster, iii. 65–71.

[2] Grumkow to Seckendorf, Berlin, 20th August, 1732 (Förster, iii. 112).

I have read that the poor object, which actually came as
anticipated (male or female, I forget), did not live long; —
nor had Friedrich, by any opportunity, another child in this
world. Domestic Tamsel had to allay itself as it best could ;
and the fair Wreech became much a stranger to Friedrich, —
surprisingly so to Friedrich the *King*, as perhaps we may
see. —

Predestination, *Gnadenwahl*, Herr General : what is orthodoxy on Predestination, with these accompaniments ! [1] We
go now to the Second Letter and the Third, — from Landsberg about a fortnight later : —

No. 2. *To his Excellency* (shovelful of titles) *von Grumkow, in
Berlin.*

"LANDSBERG, 19th October, 1731.

"The day before yesterday [that is, Wednesday, 17th Octo-
ber] I received an Order, To have only fifty Horse at that
post, and " — Order which shows us that there has fallen out
some recruiting squabble on the Polish Frontier hereabouts ;
that the Polack gentlemen have seized certain Corporals of
ours, but are about restoring them ; Order and affair which
we shall omit. "Corporals will be got back : but as these
Polack gentlemen will see, by the course taken, that we have
no great stomach for *biting*, I fancy they will grow more insolent ; then, 'ware who tries to recruit there for the future !

"On the same day I was apprised, from Cüstrin, That the
Prince-Royal had resolved on an excursion to Carzig, and
thence to the Bailliage of Himmelstädt [digging and stubbing
now on foot at Himmelstädt too], which is but a couple of
miles [2] from this ; that there would be a little hunt between
the two Bailliages ; and that if I chose to come, I might, and
the Prince would dine with me." — Which I did ; and so, here
again, Thursday, 18th October, 1731, in those remote Warta-
Oder Countries, is a glimpse of his Royal Highness at first

[1] For Wreech, see *Benekendorf*, v. 94 ; for Schulenburg, ib. 26 ; — and *Militair-Lexikon*, iii. 432, 433, and iv. 268, 269. Vacant on the gossiping points ;
cautiously official, both these.

[2] " *Demi-mille* " German.

hand. Schulenburg continues; not even taking a new paragraph, which indeed he never does : —

"They had shut up a couple of *Spiesser* (young roes), and some stags, in the old wreck of a *Saugarten* [Boar-park, between Carzig and Himmelstädt; *fast ruinirten Saugarten*, he calls it, daintily throwing in a touch of German here] : the Prince shot one or two of them, and his companions the like ; but it does not seem as if this amusement were much to his taste. He went on to Himmelstädt; and at noon he arrived here," in my poor Domicile at Landsberg.

"At one o'clock we went to table, and sat till four. He spoke only of very indifferent things ; except saying to me : 'Do you know, the King has promised 400,000 crowns (£60,000) towards disengaging those Bailliages of the Margraf of Baireuth's,'" — old Margraf, Bailliages pawned to raise ready cash ; readers remember what interminable Law-pleading there was, till Friedrich Wilhelm put it into a liquid state, "Pay me back the moneys, then !" [1] — "'400,000 thalers to the old Margraf, in case his Prince (Wilhelmina's now Bridegroom) have a son by my Sister.' I answered, I had heard nothing of it. — 'But,' said he, 'that is a great deal of money ! And some hundred thousands more have gone the like road, to Anspach, who never will be able to repay. For all is much in disorder at Anspach. Give the Margraf his Heron-hunt *(chasse au héron)*, he cares for nothing ; and his people pluck him at no allowance.' I said : That if these Princes would regulate their expenditure, they might, little by little, pay off their debts ; that I had been told at Vienna the Baireuth Bailliages were mortgaged on very low terms, those who now held them making eight or ten per cent of their money ; " — that the Margraf ought to make an effort ; and so on. "I saw very well that these Loans the King makes are not to his mind.

"Directly on rising from table, he went away ; excusing himself to me, That he could not pass the night here ; that the King would not like his sleeping in the Town ; besides that he had still several things to complete in a Report he

[1] Suprà, pp. 161–163.

was sending off to his Majesty. He went to Massin, and slept
there. For my own share, I did not press him to remain;
what I did was rather in the way of form. There were with
him President Münchow," civil gentleman whom we know,
" an Engineer Captain Reger, and the three Gentlemen of his
Court," Wolden, Rohwedel, Natzmer who once twirled his
finger in a certain mouth, the insipid fellow.

"He is no great eater; but I observed he likes the small
dishes (*petits plats*) and the high tastes : he does not care for
fish; though I had very fine trouts, he never touched them.
He does not take brown soup (*soupe au bouillon*). It did not
seem to me he cared for wine : he tastes at all the wines; but
commonly stands by burgundy with water.

" I introduced to him all the Officers of my Regiment who are here ; he received them in the style of a king [*en roi*, plenty of quiet pride in him, Herr General]. It is certain he feels what he is born to ; and if ever he get to it, will stand on the top of it. As to me, I mean to keep myself retired ; and shall see of him as little as I can. I perceive well he does not like advice," especially when administered in the way of preachment, by stiff old military gentlemen of the all-wise stamp ; — "and does not take pleasure except with people inferior to him in mind. His first aim is to find out the ridiculous side of every one, and he loves to banter and quiz. It is a fault in a Prince : he ought to know people's faults, and not to make them known to anybody whatever," — which, we perceive, is not quite the method with private gentlemen of the all-wise type ! —

" I speak to your Excellency as a friend ; and assure you he is a Prince who has talent, but who will be the slave of his passions (*se fera dominer par ses passions*," — not a felicitous prophecy, Herr General) ; "and will like nobody but such as encourage him therein. For me, I think all Princes are cast in the same mould ; there is only a more and a less.

" At parting, he embraced me twice ; and said, 'I am sorry I cannot stay longer ; but another time I will profit better.' Wolden [one of the Three] told me he could not describe how well-intentioned for your Excellency the Prince-Royal is [cunning dog !], who says often to Wolden [doubtless guessing it will be re-said], 'If I cannot show *him* my gratitude, I will his posterity : ' " — profoundly obliged to the Grumkow kindred first and last ! — " I remain your Excellency's " most pipe-clayed   " Von Schulenburg." [1]

And so, after survey of the spademen at Carzig and Himmelstädt (where Colonel Wreech, by the way, is *Amts-Hauptmann*, official Head-Man), after shooting a *Spiesser* or two, and dining and talking in this sort, his Royal Highness goes to sleep at Massin ; and ends one day of his then life. We proceed to Letter No. 3.

[1] Förster, iii. 71–73.

A day or two after No. 2, it would appear, his Majesty, who is commonly at Wusterhausen hunting in this season, has been rapidly out to Crossen, in these Landsberg regions (to south, within a day's drive of Landsberg), rapidly looking after something; Grumkow and another Official attending him : — other Official, "Truchsess," is Truchsess von Waldburg, a worthy soldier and gentleman of those parts, whom we shall again hear of. In No. 3 there is mention likewise of the "Kurfürst of Köln," — Elector of Cologne; languid lanky gentleman of Bavarian breed, whom we saw last year at Bonn, richest Pluralist of the Church; whom doubtless our poor readers have forgotten again. Mention of him; and also considerable sulky humor, of the Majesty's-Opposition kind, on Schulenburg's part; for which reason, and generally as a poor direct reflex of time and place, — reflex by ruffled bog-water, through sedges, and in twilight; dim but indubitable, — we give the Letter, though the Prince is little spoken of in it: —

No. 3. *To the Excellency Grumkow* (as above), *in Berlin.*

"LANDSBERG, 22d October (Monday), 1731.

"MONSIEUR, — I trust your Excellency made your journey to Crossen with all the satisfaction imaginable. Had I been warned sooner, I would have come; not only to see the King, but for your Excellency's sake and Truchsess's: but I received your Excellency's Letter only yesterday morning; so I could not have arrived before yesternight, and that late; for it is fifty miles off, and one has to send relays beforehand; there being no post-horses on that road.

"We are, — not to make comparisons, — like Harlequin! No sooner out of one scrape, than we get into another; and all for the sake of those Big Blockheads (*l'amour de ces grands colosses*). What the Kurfürst of Köln has done, in his character of Bishop of Osnabrück," — a deed not known to this Editor, but clearly in the way of snubbing our recruiting system, — "is too droll: but if we avenge ourselves, there will be high play, and plenty of it, all round our borders! If such things would make any impression on the spirit of our Master: but

they do not; they " — in short, this recruiting system is delirious, thinks the stiff Schulenburg; and scruples not to say so,
though not in his place in Parliament, or even Tobacco-Parliament. For there is a Majesty's Opposition in all lands and
times. "We ruin the Country," says the Honorable Member,
"sending annually millions of money out of it, for a set of
vagabond fellows (*gens à sac et à corde*), who will never do us
the least service. One sees clearly it is the hand of God,"
darkening some people's understanding; "otherwise it might
be possible their eyes would open, one time or another ! " —
A stiff pipe-clayed gentleman of great wisdom, with plenty of
sulphur burning in the heart of him. The rest of his Letter
is all in the Opposition strain (almost as if from his place
in Parliament, only far briefer than is usual "within these
walls"); and winds up with a glance at Victor Amadeus's
strange feat, or rather at the Son's feat done upon Victor, over
in Sardinia; preceded by this interjectionary sentence on a
Prince nearer home : —

"As to the Prince-Royal, depend on it he will do whatever
is required of him [marry anybody you like &c.], if you give
him more elbow-room, for that is whither he aims. — Not a
bad stroke that, of the King of Sardinia " — Grand news of
the day, at that time; now somewhat forgotten, and requiring
a word from us :

Old King Victor Amadeus of Sardinia had solemnly abdicated in favor of his Son ; went, for a twelvemonth or more,
into private felicity with an elderly Lady-love whom he had
long esteemed the first of women ; — tired of such felicity,
after a twelvemonth ; demanded his crown back, and could
not get it ! Lady-love and he are taken prisoners ; lodged in
separate castles : [1] and the wrath of the proud old gentleman is
Olympian in character, — split an oak table, smiting it while
he spoke (say the cicerones) ; — and his silence, and the fiery
daggers he looks, are still more emphatic. But the young

---

[1] 2d September, 1730 abdicated, went to Chambéry ; reclaims, is locked in
Rivoli, 8th October, 1731 (news of it just come to Schulenburg) ; dies there,
31st October, 1732, his 67th year.

fellow holds out; you cannot play handy-dandy with a king's crown, your Majesty! say his new Ministers. Is and will continue King. "Not a bad stroke of him," thinks Schulenburg, —

— "especially if his Father meant to play him the same trick," that is, clap him in prison. Not a bad stroke ; — which perhaps there is another that could imitate, "if *his* Papa gave him the opportunity! But *this* Papa will take good care; and the Queen will not forget the Sardinian business, when he talks again of abdicating," as he does when in ill-humor. —

"But now had not we better have been friends with England, should war rise upon that Sardinian business ? General Schulenburg," — the famed Venetian Field-marshal, bruiser of the Turks in Candia,[1] my honored Uncle, who sometimes used to visit his Sister the Maypole, now *Emerita*, in London, and sip beer and take tobacco on an evening, with George I. of famous memory, — he also "writes me this Victor-Amadeus news, from Paris;" so that it is certain; Ex-King locked in Rivoli near a fortnight ago: "he, General Schulenburg, says farther, To judge by the outside, all appears very quiet; but many think, at the bottom of the bag it will not be the same." —

"I am, with respect," your Excellency's much in buckram,
"LE COMTE DE SCHOULENBOURG."[2]

So far Lieutenant-General Schulenburg; whom we thank for these contemporary glimpses of a young man that has become historical, and of the scene he lived in. And with these three accidental utterances, as if they (which are alone left) had been the sum of all he said in the world, let the Lieutenant-General withdraw now into silence: he will turn up twice again, after half a score of years, once in a nobler than talking attitude, the close-harnessed, stalwart, slightly atrabiliar military gentleman of the old Prussian school.

[1] Same who was beaten by Charles XII. before; a worthy soldier nevertheless, say the Authorities : *Life* of him by Varnhagen von Ense (*Biographische Denkmale*, Berlin, 1845).

[2] Förster, iii. 73–75.

These glimpses of the Crown-Prince, reflected on us in this
manner, are not very luculent to the reader, — light being indifferent, and mirror none of the best : — but some features do
gleam forth, good and not so good ; which, with others coming,
may gradually coalesce into something conceivable. A Prince
clearly of much spirit, and not without petulance ; abundant
fire, much of it shining and burning irregularly at present ;
being sore held down from without, and anomalously situated.
Pride enough, thinks Schulenburg, capricious petulance enough,
— likely to go into "a reign of the passions," if we live. As
will be seen ! —

Wilhelmina was betrothed in June last : Wilhelmina, a Bride
these six months, continues to be much tormented by Mamma.
But the Bridegroom, Prince of Baireuth, is gradually recom-
mending himself to persons of judgment, to Wilhelmina among
others.   One day he narrowly missed an unheard-of accident :
a foolish servant, at some boar-hunt, gave him a loaded piece
on the half-cock ; half-cock slipped in the handling ; bullet
grazed his Majesty's very temple, was felt twitching the hair
there ; — ye Heavens ! Whereupon impertinent remarks from
some of the Dessau people (allies of Schwedt and the Margravine in high colors) ; which were well answered by the
Prince, and noiselessly but severely checked by a well-bred
King.[1] King has given the Prince of Baireuth a regiment ;
and likes him tolerably, though the young man will not always
drink as could be wished. Wedding, in spite of clouds from
her Majesty, is coming steadily on.

His Majesty's Building Operations.

"This year," says Fassmann, "the building operations both
in Berlin and Stettin," — in Stettin where new fortifications
are completed, in Berlin where gradually whole new quarters
are getting built, — " were exceedingly pushed forward (*äus-
serst poussirt*)."   Alas, yes ; this too is a questionable memorable feature of his Majesty's reign. Late Majesty, old King

[1] Wilhelmina, i. 356.

Friedrich I., wishful, as others had been, for the growth of
Berlin, laid out a new Quarter, and called it Friedrichs Stadt;
scraggy boggy ground, planned out into streets, Friedrichs
Strasse the chief street, with here and there a house standing
lonesomely prophetic on it. But it is this present Majesty,
Friedrich Wilhelm, that gets the plan executed, and the
Friedrichs Strasse actually built, not always in a soft or spon-
taneous manner.   Friedrich Wilhelm was the Ædile of his
Country, as well as the Drill-sergeant; Berlin City did not
rise of its own accord, or on the principle of leave-alone, any
more than the Prussian Army itself. Wreck and rubbish
Friedrich Wilhelm will not leave alone, in any kind; but is
intent by all chances to sweep them from the face of the
Earth, that something useful, seemly to the Royal mind, may
stand there instead.   Hence these building operations in
the Friedrich Street and elsewhere, so "exceedingly pushed
forward."

The number of scraggy waste places he swept clear, first
and last, and built tight human dwellings upon, is almost un-
countable. A common gift from him (as from his Son after
him) to a man in favor, was that of a new good House, — an
excellent gift.   Or if the man is himself able to build, Majesty
will help him, incite him: "Timber enough is in the royal
forests; stone, lime are in the royal quarries; scraggy waste
is abundant: why should any man, of the least industry or
private capital, live in a bad house?" By degrees, the pressure of his Majesty upon private men to build with encouragement became considerable, became excessive, irresistible; and
was much complained of, in these years now come. Old
Colonel Derschau is the King's Agent, at Berlin, in this matter; a hard stiff man; squeezes men, all manner of men with
the least capital, till they build.

Nüssler, for example, whom we once saw at Hanover, managing a certain contested Heritage for Friedrich Wilhelm;
adroit Nüssler, though he has yet got no fixed appointment,
nor pay except by the job, is urged to build; — second year
hence, 1733, occurs the case of Nüssler, and is copiously dwelt
upon by Büsching his biographer: "Build yourself a house

in the Friedrichs Strasse !" urges Derschau. "But I have no
pay, no capital !" pleads Nüssler. — "Tush, your Father-in-
law, abstruse Kanzler von Ludwig, in Halle University, monster of law-learning there, is not he a monster of hoarded
moneys withal ? He will lend you, for his own and his
Daughter's sake.[1] Or shall his Majesty compel him ? " urges
Derschau. And slowly, continually turns the screw upon
Nüssler, till he too raises for himself a firm good house in the
Friedrichs Stadt, — Friedrichs Strasse, or *Street*, as they now
call it, which the Tourist of these days knows. Substantial
clear ashlar Street, miles or half-miles long; straight as a
line : — Friedrich Wilhelm found it scrag and quagmire ; and
left it what the Tourist sees, by these hard methods. Thus
Herr Privy-Councillor Klinggräf too, Nüssler's next neighbor :
he did not want to build ; far from it; but was obliged, on
worse terms than Nüssler. You have such work, founding
your house ; — for the Nüssler-Klinggräf spot was a fish-pool,
and "carps were dug up" in founding ; — such piles, bound
platform of solid beams ; "4,000 thalers gone before the first
stone is laid : " and, in fact, the house must be built honestly,
or it will be worse for the house and you. "Cost me 12,000
thalers (£1,800) in all, and is worth perhaps 2,000 !" sorrowfully ejaculates Nüssler, when the job is over. Still worse
with Privy-Councillor Klinggräf : his house, the next to Nüssler's, is worth mere nothing to him when built; a soap-boiler
offers him 800 thalers (£120) for it; and Nüssler, to avoid
suffocation, purchases it himself of Klinggräf for that sum.
Derschau, with his slow screw-machinery, is very formidable ;
— and Büsching knows it for a fact, "that respectable Berlin
persons used to run out of the way of Bürgermeister Koch and
him, when either of them turned up on the streets ! "

These things were heavy to bear. Truly, yes ; where is the
liberty of private capital or liberty of almost any kind, on
those terms ? Liberty to *annihilate* rubbish and chaos, under
known conditions, you may have ; but not the least liberty to
keep them about you, though never so fond of doing it ! What
shall we say ? Nüssler and the Soap-boiler do both live in

[1] Büsching, *Beiträge*, i. 324.

houses more human than they once had. Berlin itself, and
some other things, did not spring from Free-trade. Berlin
City would, to this day, have been a Place of *Scrubs* ("the
Berlin," a mere appellative noun to that effect), had Free-trade
always been the rule there. I am sorry his Majesty trans-
gresses the limits; — and we, my friends, if we can make our
Chaos into Cosmos by firing Parliamentary eloquence into it,
and bombarding it with Blue-Books, we will much triumph
over his Majesty, one day! —

Thus are the building operations exceedingly pushed forward, the Ear of Jenkins torn off, and Victor Amadeus locked
in ward, while our Crown-Prince, in the eclipsed state, is inspected by a Sage in pipe-clay, and Wilhelmina's wedding is
coming on.

———————◆———————

CHAPTER VI.

WILHELMINA'S WEDDING.

TUESDAY, 20th November, 1731, Wilhelmina's wedding-day
arrived, after a brideship of eight months; and that young
Lady's troublesome romance, more happily than might have
been expected, did at last wind itself up. Mamma's unreasonable humors continued, more or less; but these also must
now end. Old wooers and outlooks, "the four or three crowned
heads," — they lie far over the horizon; faded out of one's
very thoughts, all these. Charles XII., Peter II. are dead;
Weissenfels is not, but might as well be. Prince Fred, not
yet wedded elsewhere, is doing French madrigals in Leicester
House; tending towards the "West Wickham" set of Politicians, the Pitt-Lyttelton set; stands ill with Father and
Mother, and will not come to much. August the Dilapidated-
Strong is deep in Polish troubles, in Anti-Kaiser politics, in
drinking-bouts; — his great-toe never mended, never will mend.
Gone to the spectral state all these: here, blooming with life

in its cheeks, is the one practical Fact, our good Hereditary
Prince of Baireuth, — privately our fate all along; — which
we will welcome cheerfully; and be thankful to Heaven that
we have not died in getting it decided for us! —

· Wedding was of great magnificence; Berlin Palace and all
things and creatures at their brightest : the Brunswick-Beverns
here, and other high Guests ; no end of pompous ceremonials,
solemnities and splendors, — the very train of one's gown was
" twelve yards long." Eschewing all which, the reader shall
commodiously conceive it all, by two samples we have picked
out for him : one sample of a Person, high Guest present; one
of an Apartment where the sublimities went on.

The Duchess Dowager of Sachsen-Meiningen, who has come
to honor us on this occasion, a very large Lady, verging towards
sixty ; she is the person. A living elderly Daughter of the
Great Elector himself ; half-sister to the late King, half-aunt
to Friedrich Wilhelm ; widow now of her third husband : a
singular phenomenon to look upon, for a moment, through Wilhelmina's satirical spectacles. One of her three husbands,
" Christian Ernst of Baireuth " (Margraf there, while the
present Line was but expectant), had been a kind of Welsh-
Uncle to the Prince now Bridegroom ; so that she has a double
right to be here. " She had found the secret of totally ruining
Baireuth," says Wilhelmina ; " Baireuth, and Courland as well,
where her first wedlock was ; " — perhaps Meiningen was done
to her hand ? Here is the Portrait of " my Grand-Aunt ; "
dashed off in very high colors, not by a flattering pencil : —

" It is said she was very fond of pleasing, in her youth; one
saw as much still by her affected manners. She would have
made an excellent actress, to play fantastic parts of that kind.
Her flaming red countenance, her shape, of such monstrous
extent that she could hardly walk, gave her the air of a Female
Bacchus. She took care to expose to view her " — a part of her
person, large but no longer beautiful, — " and continually kept
patting it with her hands, to attract attention thither. Though
sixty gone," — fifty-seven in point of fact, — " she was tricked
out like a girl ; hair done in ribbon-locks (*marronnés*), all filled
with gewgaws of rose-pink color, which was the prevailing

tint in her complexion, and so loaded with colored jewels, you would have taken her for the rainbow." [1]

This charming old Lady, daughter of the *Grosse Kurfürst*, and so very fat and rubicund, had a Son once : he too is mentionable in his way, — as a milestone (parish milestone) in the obscure Chronology of those parts. Her first husband was the Duke of Courland ; to him she brought an heir, who became Duke in his turn, — and was the final Duke, *last* of the " Kettler " or native Line of Dukes there. The Kettlers had been Teutsch Ritters, Commandants in Courland ; they picked up that Country, for their own behoof, when the Ritterdom went down ; and this was the last of them. He married Anne of Russia with the big cheek (Czar Peter's Niece, who is since become Czarina) ; and died shortly after, twenty years ago ; with tears doubtless from the poor rose-pink Mother, far away in Baireuth and childless otherwise ; and also in a sense to the sorrow of Courland, which was hereby left vacant, a prey to enterprising neighbors. And on those terms it was that Saxons Moritz (our dissolute friend, who will be *Maréchal de Saxe* one day) made his clutch at Courland, backed by moneys of the French actress ; rumor of which still floats vaguely about. Moritz might have succeeded, could he have done the first part of the feat, fallen in love with swoln-cheeked Anne, Dowager there ; but he could not ; could only pretend it : Courland therefore (now that the Swoln-cheek is become Czarina) falls to one Bieren, a born Courlander, who could.[2] — We hurry to the " Grand Apartment " in Berlin Schloss, and glance rapidly, with Wilhelmina (in an abridged form), how magnificent it is : —

Royal Apartment, third floor of the Palace at Berlin, one

---

[1] Wilhelmina, i. 375.

[2] Last Kettler, Anne's Husband, died (leaving only an old Uncle, fallen into Papistry and other futility, who, till his death some twenty years after, had to reside abroad and be nominal merely), 1711 ; Moritz's attempt with Adrienne Lecouvreur's cash was, 1726 ; Anne became Sovereign of all the Russias (on her poor Cousin Peter II.'s death), 1730 ; Bieren (*Biron* as he tried to write himself, being of poor birth) did not get installed till 1737 ; and had, he and Courland both, several tumbles after that before getting to stable equilibrium.

must say, few things equal it in the world. "From the Outer
Saloon or Antechamber, called *Salle des Suisses* [where the
halberdier and valet people wait] you pass through six grand
rooms, into a saloon magnificently decorated : thence through
two rooms more, and so into what they call the Picture-Gallery, a room ninety feet long. All this is in a line." Grand
all this ; but still only common in comparison. From the
Picture-Gallery you turn (to right or left is not said, nor does
it matter) into a suite of fourteen great rooms, each more
splendid than the other : lustre from the ceiling of the first
room, for example, is of solid silver; weighs, in pounds avoir-
dupois I know not what, but in silver coin " 10,000 crowns : "
ceilings painted as by Correggio ; "wall-mirrors between each
pair of windows are twelve feet high, and their piers (*trumeaux*)
are of massive silver ; in front of each mirror, table can be
laid for twelve ;" twelve Serenities may dine there, flanked by
their mirror, enjoying the Correggiosities above, and the practical sublimities all round. "And this is but the first of the
fourteen ; " and you go on increasing in superbness, till, for
example, in the last, or superlative Saloon, you find " a lustre
weighing 50,000 crowns ; the globe of it big enough to hold a
child of eight years ; and the branches (*guéridons*) of it," I
forget how many feet or fathoms in extent: silver to the heart.
Nay the music-balcony is of silver ; wearied fiddler lays his
elbow on balustrades of that precious metal. Seldom if ever
was seen the like. In this superlative Saloon the Nuptial
Benediction was given.[1]

Old King Friedrich, the expensive Herr, it was he that did
the furnishing and Correggio-painting of these sublime rooms :
but this of the masses of wrought silver, this was done by
Friedrich Wilhelm, — incited thereto by what he saw at Dresden in August the Strong's Establishment ; and reflecting, too,
that silver is silver, whether you keep it in barrels in a coined
form, or work it into chandeliers, mirror-frames and music-
balconies. — These things we should not have mentioned, except to say that the massive silver did prove a hoard available,
in after times, against a rainy day. Massive silver (well mixed

1 Wilhelmina, i. 381 ; Nicolai, ii. 881.

with copper first) was all melted down, stamped into current coins, native and foreign, and sent wandering over the world, before a certain Prince got through his Seven-Years Wars and other pinches that are ahead! —

In fine, Wilhelmina's Wedding was magnificent; though one had rubs too; and Mamma was rather severe. "Hair went all wrong, by dint of over-dressing; and hung on one's face like a boy's. Crown-royal they had put (as indeed was proper) on one's head: hair was in twenty-four locks the size of your arm: such was the Queen's order. Gown was of cloth-of-silver, trimmed with Spanish gold-lace (*avec un point d'Espagne d'or*); train twelve yards long; — one was like to sink to the earth in such equipment." Courage, my Princess! — In fact, the Wedding went beautifully off; with dances and sublimities, slow solemn Torch-dance to conclude with, in those unparalleled upper rooms; Grand-Aunt Meiningen and many other stars and rainbows witnessing; even the Margravine of Schwedt, in her high colors, was compelled to be there. Such variegated splendor, such a dancing of the Constellations; sublunary Berlin, and all the world, on tiptoe round it! Slow Torch-dance, winding it up, melted into the shades of midnight, for this time; and there was silence in Berlin.

But, on the following nights, there were Balls of a less solemn character; far pleasanter for dancing purposes. It is to these, to one of these, that we direct the attention of all readers. Friday, 23d, there was again Ball and Royal Evening Party — "Grand Apartment" so called. Immense Ball, "seven hundred couples, all people of condition:" there were "Four Quadrilles," or dancing places in the big sea of quality-figures; each at its due distance in the grand suite of rooms: Wilhelmina presides in Quadrille *Number One;* place assigned her was in the room called Picture-Gallery; Queen and all the Principalities were with Wilhelmina, she is to lead off their quadrille, and take charge of it. Which she did, with her accustomed fire and elasticity; — and was circling there, on the light fantastic toe, time six in the evening, when Grumkow, whom she had been dunning for his bargain about Friedrich the day before, came up: —

"I liked dancing," says she, "and was taking advantage of my chances. Grumkow came up, and interrupted me in the middle of a minuet: '*Eh, mon Dieu, Madame!*' said Grumkow, 'you seem to have got bit by the tarantula! Don't you see those strangers who have just come in?' I stopt short; and looking all round, I noticed at last a young man dressed in gray, whom I did not know. 'Go, then, embrace the Prince-Royal; there he is before you!' said Grumkow. All the blood in my body went topsy-turvy for joy. 'O Heaven, my Brother?' cried I: 'But I don't see him; where is he? In God's name, let me see him!' Grumkow led me to the young man in gray. Coming near, I recognized him, though with difficulty: he had grown amazingly stouter (*prodigieusement engraissé*), shortened about the neck; his face too had much changed, and was no longer so beautiful as it had been. I sprang upon him with open arms (*sautai au cou*); I was in such a state, I could speak nothing but broken exclamations: I wept, I laughed, like one gone delirious. In my life I have never felt so lively a joy.

"The first sane step was to throw myself at the feet of the King: King said, 'Are you content with me? You see I have kept my word!' I took my Brother by the hand; and entreated the King to restore him his friendship. This scene was so touching, it drew tears from the eyes of everybody. I then approached the Queen. She was obliged to embrace me, the King being close opposite; but I remarked that her joy was only affected." — Why then, O Princess? Guess, if you can, the female humors of her Majesty! —

"I turned to my Brother again; I gave him a thousand caresses, and said the tenderest things to him: to all which he remained cold as ice, and answered only in monosyllables. I presented the Prince (my Husband); to whom he did not say one word. I was astonished at this fashion of procedure! But I laid the blame of it on the King, who was observing us, and who I judged might be intimidating my Brother. But even his countenance surprised me: he wore a proud air, and seemed to look down on everybody."

A much-changed Crown-Prince. What can be the meaning

of it? Neither King nor he appeared at supper: they were
supping elsewhere, with a select circle; and the whisper ran
among us, His Majesty was treating him with great friendliness. At which the Queen, contrary to hope, could not conceal
her secret pique. "In fact," says Wilhelmina, again too hard
on Mamma, "she did not love her children except as they
served her ambitious views." The fact that it was I, and not
she, who had achieved the Prince's deliverance, was painful
to her Majesty: alas, yes, in some degree!

"Ball having recommenced, Grumkow whispered to me,
'That the King was pleased with my frank kind ways to my
Brother; and not pleased with my Brother's cold way of returning it: Does he simulate, and mean still to deceive me?
Or *is* that all the thanks he has for Wilhelmina? thinks his
Majesty. Go on with your sincerity, Madam; and for God's
sake admonish the Crown-Prince to avoid finessing!' Crown-
Prince, when I did, in some interval of the dance, report this
of Grumkow, and say, Why so changed and cold, then, Brother
of my heart? answered, That he was still the same; and that
he had his reasons for what he did." Wilhelmina continues;
and cannot understand her Crown-Prince at all: —

"Next morning, by the King's order, he paid me a visit.
The Prince," my Husband, "was polite enough to withdraw,
and left me and Sonsfeld alone with him. He gave me a re-
cital of his misfortunes; I communicated mine to him," — and
how I had at last bargained to get him free again by my compliance. "He appeared much discountenanced at this last
part of my narrative. He returned thanks for the obligations
I had laid on him, — with some caressings, which evidently did
not proceed from the heart. To break this conversation, he
started some indifferent topic; and, under pretence of seeing
my Apartment, moved into the next room, where the Prince
my Husband was. Him he ran over with his eyes from head
to foot, for some time; then, after some constrained civilities
to him, went his way." What to make of all this? "Madam
Sonsfeld shrugged her shoulders;" no end of Madam Sonsfeld's astonishment at such a Crown-Prince.

Alas, yes, poor Wilhelmina; a Crown-Prince got into terrible cognizance of facts since we last met him! Perhaps already sees, not only what a Height of place is cut out for him in this world, but also in a dim way what a solitude of soul, if he will maintain his height? Top of the frozen Schreckhorn; — have you well considered such a position! And even the way thither is dangerous, is terrible in this case. Be not too hard upon your Crown-Prince. For it is certain he loves you to the last!

Captain Dickens, who alone of all the Excellencies was not at the Wedding, — and never had believed it would be a wedding, but only a rumor to bring England round, — duly chronicles this happy reappearance of the Prince-Royal: "about six, yesterday evening, as the company was dancing, — to the great joy and surprise of the whole Court;" — and adds: "This morning the Prince came to the public Parade; where crowds of people of all ranks flocked to see his Royal Highness, and gave the most open demonstrations of pleasure."[1]

Wilhelmina, these noisy tumults, not all of them delightful, once done, gets out of the perplexed hurly-burly, home towards still Baireuth, shortly after New-year.[2] "Berlin was become as odious to me as it had once been dear. I flattered myself that, renouncing grandeurs, I might lead a soft and tranquil life in my new Home, and begin a happier year than the one that had just ended." Mamma was still perverse; but on the edge of departure Wilhelmina contrived to get a word of her Father, and privately open her heart to him. Poor Father, after all that has come and gone : —

"My discourse produced its effect; he melted into tears, could not answer me for sobs; he explained his thoughts by his embracings of me. Making an effort, at length, he said: 'I am in despair that I did not know thee. They had told me such horrible tales, I hated thee as much as I now love thee. If I had addressed myself direct to thee, I should have escaped much trouble, and thou too. But they hindered me from speaking; said thou wert ill-natured as the Devil, and wouldst drive me to extremities I wanted to avoid. Thy Mother, by

---

[1] Despatch 24th November, 1731.
[2] 11th January, 1732 (Wilhelmina, ii. 2).

her intriguings, is in part the cause of the misfortunes of the
family; I have been deceived and duped on every side. But my
hands are tied; and though my heart is torn in pieces, I must
leave these iniquities unpunished!'" — The Queen's intentions
were always good, urged Wilhelmina. "Let us not enter into
that detail," answered he: "what is past is past; I will try
to forget it;" and assured Wilhelmina that she was the dearest
to him of the family, and that he would do great things for
her still, — only part of which came to effect in the sequel.
"I am too sad of heart to take leave of you," concluded he:
"embrace your Husband on my part; I am so overcome that
I must not see him."[1] And so they rolled away.

Crown-Prince was back to Cüstrin again, many weeks before.
Back to Cüstrin; but under totally changed omens: his history, after that first emergence in Wilhelmina's dance "23d
November about six P.M.," and appearance at Parade on the
morrow (Saturday morning), had been as follows. Monday
November 26th, there was again grand Ball, and the Prince
there, *not* in gray this time. Next day, the old Dessauer
and all the higher Officers in Berlin petitioned, "Let us have
him in the Army again, your Majesty!" Majesty consented:
and so, Friday, 30th, there was grand dinner at Seckendorf's,
Crown-Prince there, in soldier's uniform again; a completely
pardoned youth. His uniform is of the Goltz Regiment, Infantry: Goltz Regiment, which lies at Ruppin, — at and about,
in that moory Country to the Northeast, some thirty or forty
miles from Berlin; — whither his destination now is.

Crown-Prince had to resume his Kammer work at Cüstrin,
and see the Buildings at Carzig, for a three months longer, till
some arrangements in the Regiment Goltz were perfected, and
finishing improvements given to it. But "on the last day of
February" (29th, 1732 being leap-year), his Royal Highness's
Commission to be Colonel Commandant of said Regiment is
made out; and he proceeds, in discharge of the same, to Ruppin, where his men lie. And so puts off the pike-gray coat,
and puts on the military blue one,[2] — never to quit it again,
as turned out.

[1] Wilhelmina, ii. 4; who dates 11th January, 1732.   [2] Preuss, i. 69.

Ruppin is a little Town, in that northwest Fehrbellin region:
Regiment Goltz had lain in detached quarters hitherto; but is
now to lie at Ruppin, the first Battalion of it there, and the
rest within reach. Here, in Ruppin itself, or ultimately at
Reinsberg in the neighborhood, was Friedrich's abode, for the
next eight years. Habitual residence: with transient excursions, chiefly to Berlin in Carnival time, or on other great
occasions, and always strictly on leave; his employment being
that of Colonel of Foot, a thing requiring continual vigilance
and industry in that Country. Least of all to be neglected,
in any point, by one in his circumstances. He did his military
duties to a perfection satisfactory even to Papa; and achieved
on his own score many other duties and improvements, for
which Papa had less value. These eight years, it is always
understood, were among the most important of his life to
him.

BOOK IX.

LAST STAGE OF FRIEDRICH'S APPRENTICESHIP: LIFE IN RUPPIN.

1732–1736.

CHAPTER I.

PRINCESS ELIZABETH CHRISTINA OF BRUNSWICK-BEVERN.

WE described the Crown-Prince as intent to comply, especially in all visible external particulars, with Papa's will and pleasure; — to distinguish himself by real excellence in Commandantship of the Regiment Goltz, first of all. But before ever getting into that, there has another point risen, on which obedience, equally essential, may be still more difficult.

Ever since the grand Catastrophe went off *without* taking Friedrich's head along with it, and there began to be hopes of a pacific settlement, question has been, Whom shall the Crown-Prince marry? And the debates about it in the Royal breast and in Tobacco-Parliament, and rumors about it in the world at large, have been manifold and continual. In the Schulenburg Letters we saw the Crown-Prince himself much interested, and eagerly inquisitive on that head. As was natural: but it is not in the Crown-Prince's mind, it is in the Tobacco-Parliament, and the Royal breast as influenced there, that the thing must be decided. Who in the world will it be, then?

Crown-Prince himself hears now of this party, now of that. England is quite over, and the Princess Amelia sunk below the horizon. Friedrich himself appears a little piqued that Hotham carried his nose so high; that the English would not, in those life-and-death circumstances, abate the least from

their "Both marriages or none," — thinks they should have
saved Wilhelmina, and taken his word of honor for the rest.
England is now out of his head; — all romance is too sorrowfully swept out : and instead of the "sacred air-cities of hope"
in this high section of his history, the young man is looking
into the "mean clay hamlets of reality," with an eye well
recognizing them for real. With an eye and heart already
tempered to the due hardness for them. Not a fortunate
result, though it was an inevitable one. We saw him flirting with the beautiful wedded Wreech; talking to Lieutenant-
General Schulenburg about marriage, in a way which shook
the pipe-clay of that virtuous man. He knows he would not
get his choice, if he had one; strives not to care. Nor does
he, in fact, much care; the romance being all out of it. He
looks mainly to outward advantages; to personal appearance,
temper, good manners; to "religious principle," sometimes
rather in the reverse way (fearing an *overplus* rather); — but
always to likelihood of moneys by the match, as a very direct
item. Ready command of money, he feels, will be extremely
desirable in a Wife; desirable and almost indispensable, in
present straitened circumstances. These are the notions of
this ill-situated Cœlebs.

The parties proposed first and last, and rumored of in Newspapers and the idle brains of men, have been very many, —
no limit to their numbers; it *may* be anybody : an intending
purchaser, though but possessed of sixpence, is in a sense proprietor of the whole Fair! Through Schulenburg we heard
his own account of them, last Autumn; — but the far noblest
of the lot was hardly glanced at, or not at all, on that occasion.
The Kaiser's eldest Daughter, sole heiress of Austria and
these vast Pragmatic-Sanction operations; Archduchess Maria
Theresa herself, — it is affirmed to have been Prince Eugene's
often-expressed wish, That the Crown-Prince of Prussia should
wed the future Empress.[1] Which would indeed have saved
immense confusions to mankind ! Nay she alone of Princesses, beautiful, magnanimous, brave, was the mate for such

---

[1] Hormayr, *Allgemeine Geschichte der neuesten Zeit* (Wien, 1817), i. 13 ; cited
in Preuss, i. 71.

a Prince, — had the Good Fairies been consulted, which seldom happens : — and Romance itself might have become Reality in that case : with high results to the very soul of this young Prince ! Wishes are free : and wise Eugene will have been heard, perhaps often, to express this wish ; but that must have been all. Alas, the preliminaries, political, especially religious, are at once indispensable and impossible : we have to dismiss that day-dream. A Papal-Protestant Controversy still exists among mankind ; and this is one penalty they pay for not having settled it sooner. The Imperial Court cannot afford its Archduchess on the terms possible in that quarter.

What the Imperial Court can do is, to recommend a Niece of theirs, insignificant young Princess, Elizabeth Christina of Brunswick-Bevern, who is Niece to the Empress ; and may be made useful in this way, to herself and us, think the Imperial Majesties ; — will be a new tie upon the Prussians and the Pragmatic Sanction, and keep the Alliance still surer for our Archduchess in times coming, think their Majesties. She, it is insinuated by Seckendorf in Tobacco-Parliament ; ought not she, Daughter of your Majesty's esteemed friend, — modest-minded, innocent young Princess, with a Brother already betrothed in your Majesty's House, — to be the Lady ? It is probable she will.

Did we inform the reader once about Kaiser Karl's young marriage adventures ; and may we, to remind him, mention them a second time ? How Imperial Majesty, some five-and-twenty years ago, then only King of Spain, asked Princess Caroline of Anspach, who was very poor, and an orphan in the world. Who at once refused, declining to think of changing her religion on such a score ; — and now governs England, telegraphing with Walpole, as Queen there instead. How Karl, now Imperial Majesty, then King of Spain, next applied to Brunswick-Wolfenbüttel ; and met with a much better reception there. Applied to old Anton Ulrich, reigning Duke, who writes big Novels, and does other foolish good-natured things ; — who persuaded his Grand-daughter that a change to Catholicism was nothing in such a case, that he himself should not care in the least to change. How the Grand-daughter

changed accordingly, went to Barcelona, and was wedded; —
and had to dun old Grandpapa, "Why don't you change, then?"
Who did change thereupon; thinking to himself, "Plague on
it, I must, then!" the foolish old Herr. He is dead; and his
Novels, in six volumes quarto, are all dead: and the Grand-
daughter is Kaiserinn, on those terms, a serene monotonous
well-favored Lady, diligent in her Catholic exercises; of whom
I never heard any evil, good rather, in her eminent serene
position. Pity perhaps that she had recommended her Niece
for this young Prussian gentleman; whom it by no means did
"attach to the Family" so very careful about him at Vienna!
But if there lay a sin, and a punishment following on it, here
or elsewhere, in her Imperial position, surely it is to be
charged on foolish old Anton Ulrich; not on her, poor Lady,
who had never coveted such height, nor durst for her soul
take the leap thitherward, till the serene old literary gentleman showed her how easy it was.

Well, old Anton Ulrich is long since dead,[1] and his religious
accounts are all settled beyond cavil; and only the sad duty
devolves on me of explaining a little what and who his rather
insipid offspring are, so far as related to readers of this History. Anton Ulrich left two sons; the elder of whom was
Duke, and the younger had an Apanage, Blankenburg by name.
Only this younger had children, — serene Kaiserinn that now
is, one of them. The elder died childless,[2] precisely a few
months before the times we are now got to; reigning Duke of
Brunswick-Wolfenbüttel,[3] all but certain Apanages, and does
not concern us farther. To that supreme dignity the younger
has now come, and his Apanage of Blankenburg and children
with him; — so that there is now only one outstanding Apanage
(Bevern, not known to us yet); which also will perhaps get
reunited, if we cared for it. Ludwig Rudolf is the name of
this new sovereign Duke of Brunswick-Wolfenbüttel, or Duke

---

[1] 1714, age 70. Hübner, t. 190.   [2] 1731, Michaelis, i. 132.

[3] "Welf-*booths*" (Hunted Camp of the Welfs), according to Etymology.
"Brunswick," again, is *Braun's*-Wick; " Braun " (Brown) being an old mili-
tant Welf in those parts, who built some lodge for himself, as a convenience
there, — Year 880, say the uncertain old Books. Hübner, t. 149; Michaelis, &c.

in chief; age now sixty; has a shining, bustling, somewhat irregular Duchess, says Wilhelmina; and a nose — or rather almost no nose, for sad reasons![1] Other qualities or accidents I know not of him, — except that he is Father of the Vienna Kaiserinn; Grandfather of the Princess whom Seckendorf suggests for our Friedrich of Prussia.

In Ludwig Rudolf's insipid offspring our readers are unexpectedly somewhat interested; let readers patiently attend, therefore. He had three Daughters, never any son. Two of his Daughters, eldest and youngest, are alive still; the middle one had a sad fate long ago. She married, in 1711, Alexius the Czarowitz of Peter the Great: foolish Czarowitz, miserable and making others miserable, broke her heart by ill conduct, ill usage, in four years; so that she died; leaving him only a poor small Peter II., who is now dead too, and that matter ended all but the memory of it. Some accounts bear, that *she* did not die; that she only pretended it, and ran and left her intolerable Czarowitz. That she wedded, at Paris, in deep obscurity, an Officer just setting out for Louisiana; lived many years there as a thrifty soldier's wife; returned to Paris with her Officer reduced to half-pay; and told him — or told some select Official person after him, under seven-fold oath, being then a widow and necessitous — her sublime secret. Sublime secret, which came thus to be known to a supremely select circle at Paris; and was published in Books, where one still reads it. No vestige of truth in it, — except that perhaps a necessitous soldier's widow at Paris, considering of ways and means, found that she had some trace of likeness to the Pictures of this Princess, and had heard her tragic story.

Ludwig Rudolf's second Daughter is dead long years ago; nor has this fable as yet risen from her dust. Of Ludwig Rudolf's other two Daughters, we have said that one, the eldest, was the Kaiserinn; Empress Elizabeth Christina, age now precisely forty; with two beautiful Daughters, sublime Maria Theresa the elder of them, and no son that would live. Which last little circumstance has caused the Pragmatic Sanction, and tormented universal Nature for so many years back!

[1] Wilhelmina, ii. 121.

Ludwig Rudolf has a youngest Daughter, also married, and a
Mother in Germany, — to this day conspicuously so ; — of
whom next, or rather of her Husband and Family-circle, we
must say a word.

Her Husband is no other than the esteemed Friend of
Friedrich Wilhelm ; Duke of Brunswick-Bevern, by title ;
who, as a junior branch, lives on the Apanage of Bevern, as
his Father did ; but is sure now to inherit the sovereignty
and be Duke of Brunswick-Wolfenbüttel at large, he or his
Sons, were the present incumbent, Ludwig Rudolf, once out.
Present incumbent, we have just intimated, is his Father-in-
law ; but it is not on that ground that he looks to inherit.
He is Nephew of old Anton Ulrich, Son of a younger Brother
(who was also " Bevern " in Anton's time) ; and is the evident
Heir-male ; old Anton being already fallen into the distaff,
with nothing but three Grand-daughters. Anton's heir will now
be this Nephew ; Nephew has wedded one of the Grand-daughters, youngest of the Three, youngest Daughter of Ludwig
Rudolf, Sovereign Duke that now is ; which Lady, by the
family she brought him, if no otherwise, is memorable or
mentionable here, and may be called a Mother in Germany.[1]

Father Bevern her Husband, Ferdinand Albert the name
of him, is now just fifty, only ten years younger than his

---

[1] Anton Ulrich (1633–1714), Duke in Chief ; that is, Duke of Brunswick-*Wolfenbüttel*.

Ferdinand Albert (1636–1687), his younger Brother apanaged in Bevern ; that is, Duke of Brunswick-*Bevern*.

August Wilhelm, elder Son and Heir (1662, 1714, 1731); had no Children.	Ludwig Rudolf, the younger Son (1671, 1731, 1735), apanaged in Blankenburg ; Duke of Brunswick-*Blankenburg* ; became *Wolfenbüttel*, 1731 ; died, 1st March, 1735. No Son : so that now the Bevern succeeded. Three Daughters :	Ferdinand Albert, eldest Son (an elder had perished, 1704, on the Schellenberg under Marlborough), followed in Bevern (1680, 1687–1704, 1735) ; Kaiser's soldier, Friedrich Wilhelm's friend ; married his Cousin, Antoinette Amelia (" Mother in Germany," as we call her). Duke in Chief, 1st March, 1735, on Ludwig Rudolf's decease ; died himself, 3d September same year.
Elizabeth Christina, **the Kaiserinn** (1691, 1708, 1750).	Charlotte Christina (1694, 1711, 1715), Alexius of Russia's ; had a *fabulous* end.	Antoinette Amelia (1695, 1712, 1762) ; Bevern's Wife,—a " Mother in Germany."	

Born 1713, Karl the Heir (to marry our Friedrich's Sister).	1714, Anton Ulrich (Russia ; tragedy of Czar Iwan).	1715, 8th November, Elizabeth Christina (Crown-Prince's).	1718, Ludwig Ernst (Holland, 1787).	1721, Ferdinand (Chatham's and England's) of the Seven-Years War.	1722, 1724, 1725, 1732, Four others ; Boys the youngest Two, who were both killed in Friedrich's Wars.

serene Father-in-law, Ludwig Rudolf : — whom, I may as well
say here, he does at last succeed, three years hence (1735),
and becomes Duke of Brunswick in General, according to
hope ; but only for a few months, having himself died that
same year. Poor Duke ; rather a good man, by all the accounts I could hear ; though not of qualities that shone. He
is at present "Duke of Brunswick-Bevern," — such his actual
nomenclature in those ever-fluctuating Sibyl's-leaves of German History-Books, Wilhelmina's and the others ; — expectant
Duke of Brunswick in General ; much a friend of Friedrich
Wilhelm. A kind of Austrian soldier he was formerly, and
will again be for brief times ; General-Feldmarschall so styled ;
but is not notable in War, nor otherwise at all, except for the
offspring he had by this serene Spouse of his. Insipid offspring, the impatient reader says ; but permits me to enumer-
ate one or two of them : —

1°. Karl, eldest Son ; who is sure to be Brunswick in General ; who is betrothed to Princess Charlotte of Prussia, —
"a satirical creature, she, fonder of my Prince than of him,"
Wilhelmina thinks. The wedding nevertheless took effect.
Brunswick in General duly fell in, first to the Father ; then,
in a few months more, to Karl with his Charlotte : and from
them proceeded, in due time, another Karl, of whom we shall
hear in this History ; — and of whom all the world heard
much in the French Revolution Wars ; in 1792, and still more
tragically afterwards. Shot, to death or worse, at the Battle
of Jena, October, 1806 ; "battle lost before it was begun," —
such the strategic history they give of it. He peremptorily
ordered the French Revolution to suppress itself ; and that
was the answer the French Revolution made him. From this
Karl, what *new* Queens Caroline of England and portentous
Dukes of Brunswick, sent upon their travels through the
anarchic world, profitable only to Newspapers, we need not
say ! —

2°. Anton Ulrich ; named after his august Great-Grandfather ; does not write novels like him. At present a young
gentleman of eighteen ; goes into Russia before long, hoping
to beget Czars ; which issues dreadfully for himself and the

potential Czars he begot. The reader has heard of a potential "Czar Iwan," violently done to death in his room, one dim moonlight night of 1764, in the Fortress of Schlüsselburg, middle of Lake Ladoga; misty moon looking down on the stone battlements, on the melancholy waters, and saying nothing. — But let us not anticipate.

3°. Elizabeth Christina; to us more important than any of them. Namesake of the Kaiserinn, her august Aunt; age now seventeen; insipid fine-complexioned young lady, who is talked of for the Bride of our Crown-Prince. Of whom the reader will hear more. Crown-Prince fears she is "too religious," — and will have "*cagots*" about her (solemn persons in black, highly unconscious how little wisdom they have), who may be troublesome.

4°. A merry young Boy, now ten, called Ferdinand; with whom England within the next thirty years will ring, for some time, loud enough: the great "Prince Ferdinand" himself, — under whom the Marquis of Granby and others became great; Chatham superintending it. This really was a respectable gentleman, and did considerable things, — a Trismegistus in comparison with the Duke of Cumberland whom he succeeded. A cheerful, singularly polite, modest, well-conditioned man withal. To be slightly better known to us, if we live. He at present is a Boy of ten, chasing the thistle's beard.

5°. Three other sons, all soldiers, two of them younger than Ferdinand; whose names were in the gazettes down to a late period; — whom we shall ignore in this place. The last of them was marched out of Holland, where he had long been Commander-in-chief on rather Tory principles, in the troubles of 1787. Others of them we shall see storming forward on occasion, valiantly meeting death in the field of fight, all conspicuously brave of character; but this shall be enough of them at present.

It is of these that Ludwig Rudolf's youngest daughter, the serene Ferdinand Albert's wife, is Mother in Germany; highly conspicuous in their day. If the question is put, it must be owned they are all rather of the insipid type. Nothing but a kind of albuminous simplicity noticeable in them; no wit, originality, brightness in the way of uttered intellect. If it is asked, How came they to the least distinction in this world ? — the answer is not immediately apparent. But indeed they are Welf of the Welfs, in this respect as in others. One asks, with increased wonder, noticing in the Welfs generally nothing but the same albuminous simplicity, and poverty rather than opulence of uttered intellect, or of qualities that shine, How the Welfs came to play such a part, for the last thousand years, and still to be at it, in conspicuous places ?

Reader, I have observed that uttered intellect is not what permanently makes way, but *un*uttered. Wit, logical brilliancy, spiritual effulgency, true or *false*, — how precious to idle mankind, and to the Newspapers and History-Books, even when it is false : while, again, Nature and Practical Fact care next to nothing for it in comparison, even when it is true ! Two silent qualities you will notice in these Welfs, modern and ancient; which Nature much values: *First*, consummate human Courage ; a noble, perfect, and as it were unconscious superiority to fear. And then *secondly*, much weight of mind, a noble not too conscious Sense of what is Right and Not-Right, I have found in some of them ; — which means mostly *weight*, or good gravitation, good observance of the perpendicular ; and is called justice, veracity, high-honor, and other such names. These are fine qualities indeed, especially with an "albuminous simplicity" as vehicle to them. If the Welfs had not much articulate intellect, let us guess they made a good use, not a bad or indifferent, as is commoner, of what they had.

Who his Majesty's Choice is ; and what the Crown-Prince thinks of it.

Princess Elizabeth Christina, the insipid Brunswick specimen, backed by Seckendorf and Vienna, proves on consideration the desirable to Friedrich Wilhelm in this matter. But his Son's notions, who as yet knows her only by rumor, do not go that way. Insipidity, triviality ; the fear of *" cago-*

tage" and frightful fellows in black supremely unconscious
what blockheads they are, haunts him a good deal. And as
for any money coming, — her sublime Aunt the Kaiserinn
never had much ready money; one's resources on that side
are likely to be exiguous. He would prefer the Princess of
Mecklenburg, Semi-Russian Catharine or Anna, of whom we
have heard; would prefer the Princess of Eisenach (whose
name he does not know rightly); thinks there are many
Princesses preferable. Most of all he would prefer, what is
well known of him in Tobacco-Parliament, but known to be
impossible, this long while back, to go upon a round of travel,
— as for instance the Prince of Lorraine is now doing, — and
look about him a little.

These candid considerations the Crown-Prince earnestly
suggests to Grumkow, and the secret committee of Tobacco-
Parliament; earnestly again and again, in his Correspondence
with that gentleman, which goes on very brisk at present.
"Much of it lost," we hear; — but enough, and to spare,
is saved! Not a beautiful correspondence: the tone of it
shallow, hard of heart; tragically flippant, especially on the
Crown-Prince's part; now and then even a touch of the hypo-
critical from him, slight touch and not with will: alas, what
can the poor young man do? Grumkow — whose ground, I
think, is never quite so secure since that Nosti business —
professes ardent attachment to the real interests of the
Prince; and does solidly advise him of what is feasible, what
not, in head-quarters; very exemplary "attachment;" credible to what length, the Prince well enough knows. And
so the Correspondence is unbeautiful; not very descriptive
even, — for poor Friedrich is considerably under mask, while
he writes to that address; and of Grumkow himself we want
no more " description ; " and is, in fact, on its own score, an
avoidable article rather than otherwise; though perhaps the
reader, for a poor involved Crown-Prince's sake, will wish an
exact Excerpt or two before we quite dismiss it.

Towards turning off the Brunswick speculation, or turning
on the Mecklenburg or Eisenach or any other in its stead, the
Correspondence naturally avails nothing. Seckendorf has his

orders from Vienna: Grumkow has his pension, — his cream-
bowl duly set, — for helping Seckendorf. Though angels
pleaded, not in a tone of tragic flippancy, but with the voice
of breaking hearts, it would be to no purpose. The Imperial
Majesties have ordered, Marry him to Brunswick, "bind him
the better to our House in time coming;" nay the Royal
mind at Potsdam gravitates, of itself, that way, after the first
hint is given. The Imperial will has become the Paternal
one; no answer but obedience. What Grumkow can do will
be, if possible, to lead or drive the Crown-Prince into obeying
smoothly, or without breaking of harness again. Which, accordingly, is pretty much the sum of his part in this unlovely
Correspondence : the geeho-ing of an expert wagoner, who has
got a fiery young Arab thoroughly tied into his dastard sand-
cart, and has to drive him by voice, or at most by slight *crack*
of whip ; and does it. Can we hope, a select specimen or two
of these Documents, not on Grumkow's part, or for Grumkow's unlovely sake, may now be acceptable to the reader ?
A Letter or two picked from that large stock, in a legible
state, will show us Father and Son, and how that tragic
matter went on, better than description could.

Papa's Letters to the Crown-Prince during that final Cüstrin period, when Carzig and Himmelstädt were going on,
and there was such progress in Economics, are all of hopeful
ruggedly affectionate tenor ; and there are a good few of them :
style curiously rugged, intricate, headlong ; and a strong substance of sense and worth tortuously visible everywhere.
Letters so delightful to the poor retrieved Crown-Prince then
and there; and which are still almost pleasant reading to
third-parties, once you introduce grammar and spelling. This
is one exact specimen ; most important to the Prince and us.
Suddenly, one night, by estafette, his Majesty, meaning nothing but kindness, and grateful to Seckendorf and Tobacco-
Parliament for such an idea, proposes, — in these terms
(merely reduced to English and the common spelling) : —

" *To the Crown-Prince at Cüstrin* (from Papa).

"POTSDAM, 4th February, 1732.

"MY DEAR SON FRITZ, — I am very glad you need no more physic. But you must have a care of yourself, some days yet, for the severe weather; which gives me and everybody colds; so pray be on your guard (*nehmet Euch hübsch in Acht*).

"You know, my dear Son, that when my children are obedient, I love them much: so, when you were at Berlin, I from my heart forgave you everything; and from that Berlin time, since I saw you, have thought of nothing but of your well-being and how to establish you, — not in the Army only, but also with a right Step-daughter, and so see you married in my lifetime. You may be well persuaded I have had the Princesses of Germany taken survey of, so far as possible, and examined by trusty people, what their conduct is, their education and so on: and so a Princess has been found, the Eldest one of Bevern, who is well brought up, modest and retiring, as women ought to be.

"You will without delay (*citò*) write me your mind on this. I have purchased the Von Katsch House; the Feldmarschall," old Wartensleben, poor Katte's grandfather, "as Governor" of Berlin, "will get that to live in: and his Government House,[1] I will have made new for you, and furnish it all; and give you enough to keep house yourself there; and will command you into the Army, April coming [which is quite a subordinate story, your Majesty!].

"The Princess is not ugly, nor beautiful. You must mention it to no mortal; — write indeed to Mamma (*der Mama*) that I have written to you. And when you shall have a Son, I will let you go on your Travels, — wedding, however, cannot be before winter next. Meanwhile I will try and contrive opportunity that you see one another, a few times, in all honor,

---

[1] Fine enough old House, or Palace, built by the Great Elector; given by him to Graf Feldmarschall von Schomberg, the "Duke Schomberg" who was killed in the Battle of the Boyne: "same House, opposite the Arsenal, which belongs now (1855) to his Royal Highness Prince Friedrich Wilhelm of Prussia." (Preuss, i. 73; and *Œuvres de Frédéric*, xxvi. 12 n.)

yet so that you get acquainted with her. She is a God-fearing creature (*gottesfürchtiges Mensch*), which is all in all; will suit herself to you [be *comportable* to you] as she does to the Parents-in-law.

"God give his blessing to it; and bless You and your Posterity, and keep Thee as a good Christian. And have God always before your eyes; — and don't believe that damnable *Particular* tenet [Predestination]; and be obedient and faithful: so shall it, here in Time and there in Eternity, go well with thee; — and whoever wishes that from the heart, let him say Amen.

"Your true Father to the death,
"FRIEDRICH WILHELM.

"When the Duke of Lorraine comes, I will have thee come. I think thy Bride will be here then. Adieu; God be with you."[1]

This important Missive reached Cüstrin, by estafette, that same midnight, 4th–5th February; when Wolden, "Hofmarschall of the Prince's Court" (titular Goldstick there, but with abundance of real functions laid on him), had the honor to awaken the Crown-Prince into the joy of reading. Crown-Prince instantly despatched, by another estafette, the requisite responses to Papa and Mamma, — of which Wolden does not know the contents at all, not he, the obsequious Goldstick; — but doubtless they mean "Yes," Crown-Prince appearing so overjoyed at this splendid evidence of Papa's love, as the Goldstick could perceive.[2]

What the Prince's actual amount of joy was, we shall learn better from the following three successive utterances of his, confidentially despatched to Grumkow in the intermediate days, before Berlin or this "Duke of Lorraine" (whom our readers and the Crown-Prince are to wait upon), with actual sight of

[1] *Œuvres de Frédéric*, xxvii. part 3d, p. 55.

[2] Wolden's *Letter* to Friedrich Wilhelm, "5th February, 1732:" in Preuss, :. part 2d (or *Urkundenbuch*), p. 206. Mamma's answer to the message brought her by this return estafette, a mere formal *Very-well*, written from the fingers outward, exists (*Œuvres*, xxvi. 65); the rest have happily vanished.

Papa and the Intended, came in course. Grumkow's Letters
to the Crown-Prince in this important interval are not extant,
nor if they were could we stand them : from the Prince's Answers it will be sufficiently apparent what the tenor of them
was.   Utterance *first* is about a week after that of the estafette
at midnight : —

To General Feldmarschall von Grumkow, at Potsdam (from the
Crown-Prince).

"CÜSTRIN, 11th February, 1732.

"MY DEAR GENERAL AND FRIEND, — I was charmed to learn
by your Letter that my affairs are on so good a footing [Papa
so well satisfied with my professions of obedience]; and you
may depend on it I am docile to follow your advice.   I will
lend myself to whatever is possible for me; and provided
I can secure the King's favor by my obedience, I will do all
that is within my power.

"Nevertheless, in making my bargain with the Duke of
Bevern, manage that the *Corpus delicti* [my Intended] be
brought up under her Grandmother [Duchess of Brunswick-
Wolfenbüttel, Ludwig Rudolf's Spouse, an airy coquettish
Lady, — let her be the tutoress and model of my Intended,
O General].   For I should prefer being made a " — what shall
we say ? by a light wife, — " or to serve under the haughty
fontange[1] of my Spouse [as Ladwig Rudolf does, by all ac-
counts], than to have a blockhead who would drive me mad
by her ineptitudes, and whom I should be ashamed to produce.

"I beg you labor at this affair.   When one hates romance
heroines as heartily as I do, one dreads those ' virtues ' of the
ferocious type [*les vertus farouches,* so terribly aware that they
are virtuous]; and I had rather marry the greatest — [un-
namable] — in Berlin, than a devotee with half a dozen ghastly
hypocrites (*cagots*) at her beck.   If it were still *möglich* [pos-
sible, in German] to make her Calvinist [*Réformée ;* our
Court-Creed, which might have an allaying tendency, and at

---

[1] Species of topknot ; so named from Fontange, an unfortunate female of
Louis Fourteenth's, who invented the ornament.

least would make her go with the stream]? But I doubt that: — I will insist, however, that her Grandmother have the training of her. What you can do to help in this, my dear Friend, I am persuaded you will do.

"It afflicted me a little that the King still has doubts of me, while I am obeying in such a matter, diametrically opposite to my own ideas. In what way shall I offer stronger proofs? I may give myself to the Devil, it will be to no purpose; nothing but the old song over again, doubt on doubt. — Don't imagine I am going to disoblige the Duke, the Duchess or the Daughter, I beseech you! I know too well what is due to them, and too much respect their merits, not to observe the strictest rules of what is proper, — even if I hated their progeny and them like the pestilence.

"I hope to speak to you with open heart at Berlin. — You may think, too, how I shall be embarrassed, having to do the *Amoroso* perhaps without being it, and to take an appetite for mute ugliness, — for I don't much trust Count Seckendorf's taste in this article," — in spite of his testimonies in Tobacco-Parliament and elsewhere. "Monsieur! Once more, get this Princess to learn by heart the *Ecole des Maris* and the *Ecole des Femmes;* that will do her much more good than *True Christianity* by the late Mr. Arndt![1] If, besides, she would learn steadiness of humor (*toujours danser sur un pied*), learn music; and, *nota bene*, become rather too free than too virtuous, — ah then, my dear General, then I should feel some liking for her, and a Colin marrying a Phyllis, the couple would be in accordance: but if she is stupid, naturally I renounce the Devil and her. — It is said she has a Sister, who at least has common sense. Why take the eldest, if so? To the King it must be all one. There is also a Princess Christina Marie of Eisenach [real name being Christina *Wilhelmina*, but no matter], who would be quite my fit, and whom I should like to try for. In fine, I mean to come soon into your Countries;[2] and perhaps will say like Cæsar, *Veni, vidi, vici.*" . . .

---

[1] Johann Arndt ("late" this long while back), *Von wahren Christenthum,* Magdeburg, 1610.

[2] Did come, 26th February, as we shall see.

Paragraph of tragic compliments to Grumkow we omit.
Letter ends in this way : —

" Your Baireuth News is very interesting ; I hope, in September next [time of a grand problem coming there for Wil-
helmina], my Sister will recover her first health. If I go
travelling, I hope to have the consolation of seeing her for a
fortnight or three weeks ; I love her more than my life; and
for all my obediences to the King, surely I shall deserve that
recompense. The diversions for the Duke of Lorraine are
very well schemed; but " — but what mortal can now care
about them ? Close, and seal.[1]

As to this Duke of Lorraine just coming, he is Franz
Stephan, a pleasant young man of twenty-five, son of that
excellent Duke Leopold Joseph, whom young Lyttelton of
Hagley was so taken with, while touring in those parts in the
Congress-of-Soissons time. Excellent Duke Leopold Joseph
is since dead; and this Franz has succeeded to him, — what
succession there was ; for Lorraine as a Dukedom has its neck
under the foot of France this great while, and is evidently not
long for this world. Old Fleury, men say, has his eye upon it.
And in fact it was, as we shall see, eaten up by Fleury within
four years' time ; and this Franz proved the last of all the
Dukes there. Let readers notice him : a man of high destiny
otherwise, of whom we are to hear much. For ten years past
he has lived about Vienna, being a born Cousin of that House
(Grandmother was Kaiser Leopold's own Sister) ; and it is understood, nay it is privately settled he is to marry the transcendent Archduchess, peerless Maria Theresa herself; and
is to reap, he, the whole harvest of that Pragmatic Sanction
sown with such travail of the Universe at large. May be
King of the Romans (which means successor to the Kaisership) any day; and actual Kaiser one day.

We may as well say here, he did at length achieve these
dignities, though not quite in the time or on the terms proposed. King of the Romans old Kaiser Karl never could
quite resolve to make him, — having always hopes of male

[1] Förster, iii. 160–162 ; Œuvres de Frédéric, xvi. 37–39.

progeny yet; which never came. For his peerless Bride he
waited six years still (owing to accidents), "attachment mutual
all the while;" did then wed, 1738, and was the happiest of
men and expectant Kaisers: — but found, at length, the Pragmatic Sanction to have been a strange sowing of dragon's-teeth,
and the first harvest reapable from it a world of armed men!
— For the present he is on a grand Tour, for instruction and
other objects; has been in England last; and is now getting
homewards again, to Vienna, across Germany; conciliating
the Courts as he goes. A pacific friendly eupeptic young
man; Crown-Prince Friedrich, they say, took much to him in
Berlin; did not quite swear eternal friendship; but kept up
some correspondence for a while, and "once sends him a
present of salmon." — But to proceed with the utterances to
Grumkow.

Utterance *second* is probably of prior date; but introducible
here, being an accidental Fragment, with the date lost: —

To the Feldmarschall von Grumkow (from the Crown-Prince;
exact date lost).

"... As to what you tell me of the Princess of Mecklenburg," for whom they want a Brandenburg Prince, — "could
not *I* marry her? Let her come into this Country, and think no
more of Russia: she would have a dowry of two or three millions of roubles, — only fancy how I could live with that! I
think that project might succeed. The Princess is Lutheran;
perhaps she objects to go into the Greek Church? — I find
none of these advantages in this Princess of Bevern; who, as
many people, even of the Duke's Court, say, is not at all beautiful, speaks almost nothing, and is given to pouting (*faisant
la fâchée*). The good Kaiserinn has so little herself, that the
sums she could afford her Niece would be very moderate."[1]

"Given to pouting," too! No, certainly; your Insipidity of
Brunswick, without prospects of ready money; dangerous for
cagotage; "not a word to say for herself in company, and
given to pouting:" I do not reckon her the eligible article! —

[1] Fragment given in *Seckendorfs Leben*, iii. 249 n.

Seckendorf, Schulenburg, Grumkow and all hands are busy in this matter : geeho-ing the Crown-Prince towards the mark set before him. With or without explosion, arrive there he must; other goal for him is none ! — In the mean while, it appears, illustrious Franz of Lorraine, coming on, amid the proper demonstrations, through Magdeburg and the Prussian Towns, has caught some slight illness and been obliged to pause; so that Berlin cannot have the happiness of seeing him quite so soon as it expected. The high guests invited to meet Duke Franz, especially the high Brunswicks, are already there. High Brunswicks, Bevern with Duchess, and still more important, with Son and with Daughter : — insipid *Corpus delicti* herself has appeared on the scene; and Grumkow, we find, has been writing some description of her to the Crown-Prince. Description of an unfavorable nature ; below the truth, not above it, to avert disappointment, nay to create some gleam of inverse joy, when the actual meeting occurs. That is his art in driving the fiery little Arab ignominiously yoked to him; and it is clear he has overdone it, for once. This is Friedrich's *third* utterance to him ; much the most emphatic there is : —

To the General Feldmarschall von Grumkow.

"Cüstrin, 19th February, 1732.

" Judge, my dear General, if I can have been much charmed with the description you give of the abominable object of my desires ! For the love of God, disabuse the King in regard to her [show him that she is a fool, then]; and let him re-member well that fools commonly are the most obstinate of creatures.

"Some months ago he wrote a Letter to Wolden," the ob-sequious Goldstick, "of his giving me the choice of several Princesses : I hope he will not give himself the lie in that. I refer you entirely to the Letter, which Schulenburg will have delivered," — little Schulenburg called here, in passing your way; all hands busy. "For there is no hope of wealth, no reasoning, nor chance of fortune that could change my sen-timent as expressed there [namely, that I will not have her, whatever become of me]; and miserable for miserable, it is all one! Let the King but think that it is not for himself that he is marrying me, but for *my*self; nay he too will have a thousand chagrins, to see two persons hating one another, and the miserablest marriage in the world; — to hear their mutual complaints, which will be to him so many reproaches for having fashioned the instrument of our yoke. As a good Christian, let him consider, If it is well done to wish to force people; to cause divorces, and to be the occasion of all the sins that an ill-assorted marriage leads us to commit! I am determined to front everything in the world sooner : and since things are so, you may in some good way apprise the Duke " of Bevern "that, happen what may, I never will have her.

" I have been unfortunate (*malheureux*) all my life; and I think it is my destiny to continue so. One must be patient, and take the time as it comes. Perhaps a sudden tract of good fortune, on the back of all the chagrins I have made profession of ever since I entered this world, would have made me too proud. In a word, happen what will, I have nothing to reproach myself with. I have suffered sufficiently for an exaggerated crime [that of "attempting to desert ; " — Heavens !] — and I will not engage myself to extend my miseries (*chagrins*) into future times. I have still resources : — a pistol-shot can deliver me from my sorrows and my life : and I think a merciful God would not damn me for that; but, taking pity on me, would, in exchange for a life of wretchedness, grant me salvation. This is whitherward despair can lead a young person, whose blood is not so quiescent as if he were seventy. I have a feeling of myself, Monsieur ; and perceive that, when one hates the methods of force as much as I, our boiling blood will carry us always towards extremities.

. . . "If there are honest people in the world, they must think how to save me from one of the most perilous passages I have ever been in. I waste myself in gloomy ideas ; I fear I shall not be able to hide my grief, on coming to Berlin. This is the sad state I am in ; — but it will never make me change from being," — surely to an excessive degree, the illustrious Grumkow's most &c. &c.   " FRIDERIC."

"I have received a Letter from the King; all agog (*bien coiffé*) about the Princess. I think I may still finish the week here.[1] When his first fire of approbation is spent, you might, praising her all the while, lead him to notice her faults. *Mon Dieu*, has he not already seen what an ill-assorted marriage comes to, — my Sister of Anspach and her Husband, who hate one another like the fire! He has a thousand vexations from it every day. . . . And what aim has the King? If it is to assure himself of me, that is not the way. Madam of Eisenach might do it; but a fool not (*point une bête*); — on the contrary, it is morally impossible to love the cause of our misery. The King is reasonable; and I am persuaded he will understand this himself."[2]

Very passionate pleading; but it might as well address itself to the east-winds. Have east-winds a heart, that they should feel pity? *Jarni-bleu*, Herr Feldzeugmeister, — only take care he don't overset things again!

Grumkow, in these same hours, is writing a Letter to the Prince, which we still have,[3] How charmed his Majesty is at such obedience; "shed tears of joy," writes Grumkow, "and said it was the happiest day of his life." Judge Grumkow's feelings soon after, on this furious recalcitration breaking out! Grumkow's Answer, which also we still have,[4] is truculence itself in a polite form: — horror-struck as a Christian at the suicide notion, at the — in fact at the whole matter; and begs, as a humble individual, not wishful of violent death and destruction upon self and family, to wash his poor hands of it altogether. Dangerous for the like of him; "interfering between Royal Father and Royal Son of such opposite humors, would break the neck of any man," thinks Grumkow; and sums up with this pithy reminiscence: "I remember always what the King said to me at Wusterhausen, when your Royal Highness lay prisoner in the Castle of Cüstrin, and I wished to take your part: '*Nein Grumkow, denket an diese Stelle, Gott gebe dass ich nicht wahr rede, aber mein Sohn stirbt nicht*

---

[1] 26th, did arrive in Berlin: Preuss (in *Œuvres*, xxvii. part 3d, p. 58 n).
[2] *Œuvres de Frédéric*, xvi. 41, 42.   [3] Ib. xvi. 43.   [4] Ib. xvi. pp. 44-46.

eines natürlichen Todes; und Gott gebe dass er nicht unter Henkers Hände komme. No, Grumkow, think of what I now tell you: God grant it do not come true, — but my Son won't die a natural death; God grant he do not come into the Hangman's hands yet!' I shuddered at these words, and the King repeated them twice to me: that is true, or may I never see God's face, or have part in the merits of our Lord." — The Crown-Prince's " pleadings " may fitly terminate here.

Duke of Lorraine arrives in Potsdam and in Berlin.

Saturday, 23d February, 1732, his Serene Highness of Lorraine did at length come to hand. Arrived in Potsdam that day; where the two Majesties, with the Serene Beverns, with the Prince Alexander of Würtemberg, and the other high guests, had been some time in expectation. Suitable persons invited for the occasion: Bevern, a titular Austrian Feldmarschall; Prince Alexander of Würtemberg, an actual one (poor old Eberhard Ludwig's Cousin, and likely to be Heir there soon); high quasi-Austrian Serenities; — not to mention Schulenburg and others officially related to Austria, or acquainted with it. Nothing could be more distinguished than the welcome of Duke Franz; and the things he saw and did, during his three weeks' visit, are wonderful to Fassmann and the extinct Gazetteers. Saw the Potsdam Giants do their *"exercitia,"* transcendent in perfection; had a boar-hunt; "did divine service in the Potsdam Catholic Church;" — went by himself to Spandau, on the Tuesday (26th), where all the guns broke forth, and dinner was ready : King, Queen and Party having made off for Berlin, in the interim, to be ready for his advent there " in the evening about five." Majesties wait at Berlin, with their Party, — among whom, say the old Newspapers, " is his Royal Highness the Crown-Prince : " Crown-Prince just come in from Cüstrin; just blessed with the first sight of his Charmer, whom he finds perceptibly less detestable than he expected.

Serene Highness of Lorraine arrived punctually at five, with outburst of all the artilleries and hospitalities; balls, soirées, *exercitia* of the Kleist Regiment, of the Gens-d'Armes; dinners with Grumkow, dinners with Seckendorf, evening party with the Margravine Philip (Margravine in high colors); — one scenic miracle succeeding another, for above a fortnight to come.

The very first spectacle his Highness saw, a private one, and of no intense interest to him, we shall mention here for our own behoof. "An hour after his arrival the Duke was carried away to his Excellency Herr Creutz the Finance-Minister's; to attend a wedding there, along with his Majesty. Wedding of Excellency Creutz's only Daughter to the Herr *Hofjägermeister* von Hacke." — *Hofjägermeister* (Master of the Hunt), and more specifically Captain Hacke, of the Potsdam Guard or Giant regiment, much and deservedly a favorite with his Majesty. Majesty has known, a long while, the merits military and other of this Hacke; a valiant expert exact man, of good stature, good service among the Giants and otherwise, though not himself gigantic; age now turned of thirty; — and unluckily little but his pay to depend on. Majesty, by way of increment to Hacke, small increment on the pecuniary side, has lately made him "Master of the Hunt;" will, before long, make him Adjutant-General, and his right-hand man in Army matters, were he only rich; — has, in the mean while, made this excellent match for him; which supplies that defect. Majesty was the making of Creutz himself; who is grown very rich, and has but one Daughter: "Let Hacke have her!" his Majesty advised; — and snatches off the Duke of Lorraine to see it done.[1]

Did the reader ever hear of Finance-Minister Creutz, once a poor Regiment's Auditor, when his Majesty, as yet Crown-Prince, found talent in him? Can readers fish up from their memory, twenty years back, anything of a terrific Spectre walking in the Berlin Palace, for certain nights, during that "Stralsund Expedition" or famed Swedish-War time, to the terror of mankind? Terrific Spectre, thought to be in Swedish pay, — properly a spy Scullion, in a small concern of Grumkow *versus* Creutz?[2] This is the same Creutz; of whom we have

[1] Fassmann, p. 430.   [2] Antea, vol. v. pp. 356–358; Wilhelmina.

never spoken more, nor shall again, now that his rich Daughter is well married to Hacke, a favorite of his Majesty's and ours. It was the Duke's first sight in Berlin; February 26th; prologue to the flood of scenic wonders there.

But perhaps the wonderfulest thing, had he quite understood it, was that of the 10th March, which he was invited to. Last obligation laid upon the Crown-Prince, "to bind him to the House of Austria," that evening. Of which take this account, external and internal, from authentic Documents in our hand.

Betrothal of the Crown-Prince to the Brunswick Charmer, Niece of Imperial Majesty, Monday Evening, 10th March, 1732.

Document *first* is of an internal nature, from the Prince's own hand, written to his Sister four days before :—

To the Princess Wilhelmina at Baireuth.

"BERLIN, 6th March, 1732.

"MY DEAREST SISTER,— Next Monday comes my Betrothal, which will be done just as yours was. The Person in question is neither beautiful nor ugly, not wanting for sense, but very ill brought up, timid, and totally behind in manners and social behavior (*manières du savoir-vivre*): that is the candid portrait of this Princess. You may judge by that, dearest Sister, if I find her to my taste or not. The greatest merit she has is that she has procured me the liberty of writing to you; which is the one solacement I have in your absence.

"You never can believe, my adorable Sister, how concerned I am about your happiness; all my wishes centre there, and every moment of my life I form such wishes. You may see by this that I preserve still that sincere friendship which has united our hearts from our tenderest years :— recognize at least, my dear Sister, that you did me a sensible wrong when you suspected me of fickleness towards you, and believed false reports of my listening to tale-bearers; me, who love only you, and whom neither absence nor lying rumors could change

9.9

in respect of you. At least don't again believe such things on
my score, and never mistrust me till you have had clear proof,
— or till God has forsaken me, and I have lost my wits. And
being persuaded that such miseries are not in store to overwhelm me, I here repeat how much I love you, and with what
respect and sincere veneration, — I am and shall be till death,
my dearest Sister, — Your most humble and faithful Brother
and Valet,   FRIDERICH." [1]

That was on the Thursday; Betrothal is on the Monday
following. Document *second* is from poor old Fassmann, and
quite of external nature; which we much abridge : —

"Monday evening, all creatures are in gala, and the Royal
Apartments upstairs are brilliantly alight; Duke of Lorraine
with the other high strangers are requested to take their place
up there, and wait for a short while. Prussian Majesty, Queen
and Crown-Prince with him, proceeds then, in a solemn official
manner, to the Durchlaucht of Bevern's Apartment, in a lower
floor of the Palace; where the Bevern Party, Duke, Duchess,
Son and intended Charmer are. Prussian Majesty asks the
Durchlaucht and Spouse, 'Whether the Marriage, some time
treated of, between that their Princess here present, and this
his Crown-Prince likewise here, is really a thing to their
mind?' Serene Spouses answer, to the effect, 'Yea, surely,
very much!' Upon which they all solemnly ascend to the
Royal Apartments [upstairs where we have seen Wilhelmina
dancing before now], where Lorraine, Würtemberg and the
other sublimities are in waiting. Lorraine and the sublimities form a semicircle; with the two Majesties, and pair of
young creatures, in the centre. You young creatures, you
are of one intention with your parents in this matter? Alas,
there is no doubt of it. Pledge yourselves, then, by exchange
of rings! said his Majesty with due business brevity. The
rings are exchanged : Majesty embraces the two young creatures with great tenderness;" as do Queen and Serenities;
and then all the world takes to embracing and congratulat-
ing; and so the betrothal is a finished thing. Bassoons and

[1] *Œuvres de Frédéric*, xxvii. part 1st, p. 5.

violins, striking up, whirl it off in universal dancing, — in
"supper of above two hundred and sixty persons," princely
or otherwise sublime in rank, with "spouses and noble ladies
there" in the due proportion.[1]

Here is fraction of another Note from the Crown-Prince to
his Sister at Baireuth, a fortnight after that event : —

Berlin, 24th March, 1732 (to Princess Wilhelmina). — . . .
"God be praised that you are better, dearest Sister! For nobody can love you more tenderly than I do. — As to the Princess of Bevern [my Betrothed], the Queen [Mamma, whom
you have been consulting on these etiquettes] bids me answer,
That you need not style her 'Highness,' and that you may
write to her quite as to an indifferent Princess. As to 'kissing of the hands,' I assure you I have not kissed them, nor
will kiss them; they are not pretty enough to tempt one
that way. God long preserve you in perfect health! And you,
preserve for me always the honor of your good graces; and
believe, my charming Sister, that never brother in the world
loved with such tenderness a sister so charming as mine; in
short, believe, dear Sister, that without compliments, and in
literal truth, I am yours wholly (*tout à vous*),

"FRIDERICH."

This is the Betrothal of the Crown-Prince to an Insipidity
of Brunswick. Insipidity's private feelings, perhaps of a
languidly glad sort, are not known to us; Crown-Prince's we
have in part seen. He has decided to accept his fate without a murmur farther. Against his poor Bride or her qualities
not a word more. In the Schloss of Berlin, amid such tem-
pests of female gossip (Mamma still secretly corresponding
with England), he has to be very reserved, on this head especially. It is understood he did not, in his heart, nearly so
much dislike the insipid Princess as he wished Papa to think
he did.

Duke Franz of Lorraine went off above a week ago, on the
Saturday following the Betrothal; an amiable serene young

[1] Fassmann, pp. 432, 433.   [2] Ib. xxvii. part 1st, p. 5.

gentleman, well liked by the Crown-Prince and everybody.
" He avoided the Saxon Court, though passing near it," on
his way to old Kur-Mainz; "which is a sign," thinks Fassmann, "that mutual matters are on a weak footing in that
quarter;"—Pragmatic Sanction never accepted there, and
plenty of intricacies existing. Crown-Prince Friedrich may
now go to Ruppin and the Regiment Goltz; his business and
destinies being now all reduced to a steady condition;—
steady sky, rather leaden, instead of the tempestuous thunder-
and-lightning weather which there heretofore was. Leaden
sky, he, if left well to himself, will perhaps brighten a little.
Study will be possible to him; improvement of his own faculties, at any rate. It is much his determination. Outwardly,
besides drilling the Regiment Goltz, he will have a steady
correspondence to keep up with his Brunswick Charmer;—
let him see that he be not slack in that.

CHAPTER II.

SMALL INCIDENTS AT RUPPIN.

FRIEDRICH, after some farther pause in Berlin, till things
were got ready for him, went to Ruppin. This is in the
Spring of 1732;[1] and he continued to have his residence
there till August, 1736. Four important years of young life;
of which we must endeavor to give, in some intelligible condition, what traces go hovering about in such records as there
are.

Ruppin, where lies the main part of the Regiment Goltz,
and where the Crown-Prince Colonel of it dwells, is a quiet
dull little Town, in that northwestern region; inhabitants,
grown at this day to be 10,000, are perhaps guessable then

---

[1] Still in Berlin, 6th March; dates from *Nauen* (in the Ruppin neighborhood) for the first time, 25th April, 1732, among his *Letters* yet extant : Preuss,
Œuvres de Frédéric, xxvii. part 1st, p. 4; xvi. 49.

at 2,000. Regiment Goltz daily rolls its drums in Ruppin : Town otherwise lifeless enough, except on market-days : and the grandest event ever known in it, this removal of the Crown-Prince thither, — which is doubtless much a theme, and proud temporary miracle, to Ruppin at present. Of society there or in the neighborhood, for such a resident, we hear nothing.

Quiet Ruppin stands in grassy flat country, much of which is natural moor, and less of it reclaimed at that time than now. The environs, except that they are a bit of the Earth, and have a bit of the sky over them, do not set up for loveliness. Natural woods abound in that region, also peat-bogs not yet drained ; and fishy lakes and meres, of a dark complexion : plenteous cattle there are, pigs among them ; — thick-soled husbandmen inarticulately toiling and moiling. Some glass-furnaces, a royal establishment, are the only manufactures we hear of. Not a picturesque country ; but a quiet and innocent, where work is cut out, and one hopes to be well left alone after doing it. This Crown-Prince has been in far less desirable localities.

He had a reasonable house, two houses made into one for him, in the place. He laid out for himself a garden in the outskirts, with what they call a "temple" in it, — some more or less ornamental garden-house, — from which I have read of his "letting off rockets" in a summer twilight. Rockets to amuse a small dinner-party, I should guess, — dinner of Officers, such as he had weekly or twice a week. On stiller evenings we can fancy him there in solitude ; reading meditative, or musically fluting ; — looking out upon the silent death of Day : how the summer gloaming steals over the moorlands, and over all lands ; shutting up the toil of mortals ; their very flocks and herds collapsing into silence, and the big Skies and endless Times overarching him and them. With thoughts perhaps sombre enough now and then, but profitable if he face them piously.

His Father's affection is returning ; would so fain return if it durst. But the heart of Papa has been sadly torn up : it is too good news to be quite believed, that he has a son grown

wise, and doing son-like! Rumor also is very busy, rumor and
the Tobacco-Parliament for or against; a little rumor is capable
of stirring up great storms in the suspicious paternal mind.
All along during Friedrich's abode at Ruppin, this is a constantly recurring weather-symptom; very grievous now and
then; not to be guarded against by any precaution; — though
steady persistence in the proper precaution will abate it, and
as good as remove it, in course of time. Already Friedrich
Wilhelm begins to understand that "there is much in this
Fritz," — who knows how much, though of a different type
from Papa's? — and that it will be better if he and Papa, so
discrepant in type, and ticklishly related otherwise, live not
too constantly together as heretofore. Which is emphatically
the Crown-Prince's notion too.

I perceive he read a great deal at Ruppin: what Books I
know not specially: but judge them to be of more serious solid
quality than formerly; and that his reading is now generally
a kind of studying as well. Not the express Sciences or Tech-
nologies; not these, in any sort, — except the military, and
that an express exception. These he never cared for, or regarded as the noble knowledges for a king or man. History
and Moral Speculation; what mankind have done and been in
this world (so far as "History" will give one any glimpse of
that), and what the wisest men, poetical or other, have thought
about mankind and their world: this is what he evidently had
the appetite for; appetite insatiable, which lasted with him to
the very end of his days. Fontenelle, Rollin, Voltaire, all the
then French lights, and gradually others that lay deeper in
the firmament: — what suppers of the gods one may privately
have at Ruppin, without expense of wine! Such an opportunity for reading he had never had before.

In his soldier business he is punctual, assiduous; having an
interest to shine that way. And is, in fact, approvable as a
practical officer and soldier, by the strictest judge then living.
Reads on soldiering withal; studious to know the rationale of
it, the ancient and modern methods of it, the essential from
the unessential in it; to understand it thoroughly, — which
he got to do. One already hears of conferences, correspond-

ences, with the Old Dessauer on this head : " Account of the
Siege of Stralsund," with plans, with didactic commentaries,
drawn up by that gunpowder Sage for behoof of the Crown-
Prince, did actually exist, though I know not what has become
of it. Now and afterwards this Crown-Prince must have been
a great military reader. From Cæsar's *Commentaries*, and
earlier, to the Chevalier Folard, and the Marquis Feuquière ;[1]
from Epaminondas at Leuctra to Charles XII. at Pultawa, all
manner of Military Histories, we perceive, are at his finger-
ends ; and he has penetrated into the essential heart of each,
and learnt what it had to teach him. Something of this,
how much we know not, began at Ruppin ; and it did not end
again.

On the whole, Friedrich is prepared to distinguish himself
henceforth by strictly conforming, in all outward particulars
possible, to the paternal will, and becoming the most obedient
of sons. Partly from policy and necessity, partly also from
loyalty ; for he loves his rugged Father, and begins to perceive
that there is more sense in his peremptory notions than at first
appeared. The young man is himself rather wild, as we have
seen, with plenty of youthful petulance and longings after forbidden fruit. And then he lives in an element of gossip ; his
whole life enveloped in a vast Dionysius'-Ear, every word and
action liable to be debated in Tobacco-Parliament. He is very
scarce of money, too, Papa's allowance being extremely moderate, " not above 6,000 thalers (£900)," says Seckendorf once.[2]
There will be contradictions enough to settle : caution, silence,
every kind of prudence will be much recommendable.

In all outward particulars the Crown-Prince will conform ;
in the inward, he will exercise a judgment, and if he cannot
conform, will at least be careful to hide. To do his Commandant duties at Ruppin, and avoid offences, is much his
determination. We observe he takes great charge of his men's

[1] *Mémoires sur la Guerre* (specially on the Wars of Louis XIV., in which
Feuquière had himself shone) : a new Book at this time (Amsterdam, 1731 ;
first *complete* edition is, Paris, 1770, 4 vols. 4to) ; at Ruppin, and afterwards, a
chief favorite with Friedrich.

[2] Förster, iii. 114 (Seckendorf to Prince Eugene).

health; has the Regiment Goltz in a shiningly exact condition
at the grand reviews; — is very industrious now and afterwards to get tall recruits, as a dainty to Papa.   Knows that
nothing in Nature is so sure of conciliating that strange old
gentleman; corresponds, accordingly, in distant quarters; lays
out, now and afterwards, sums far too heavy for his means
upon tall recruits for Papa.   But it is good to conciliate in
that quarter, by every method, and at every expense; — Argus
of Tobacco-Parliament still watching one there; and Rumor
needing to be industriously dealt with, difficult to keep down.

Such, so far as we can gather, is the general figure of Friedrich's life at Ruppin.   Specific facts of it, anecdotes about it,
are few in those dim Books; are uncertain as to truth, and
without importance whether true or not.   For all his gravity
and Colonelship, it would appear the old spirit of frolic has
not quitted him.   Here are two small incidents, pointing that
way; which stand on record; credible enough, though vague
and without importance otherwise.   Incident *first* is to the
following feeble effect; indisputable though extremely unmo-
mentous: Regiment Goltz, it appears, used to have gold trim-
mings; the Colonel Crown-Prince petitioned that they might
be of silver, which he liked better.   Papa answers, Yes.   Regiment Goltz gets its new regimentals done in silver; the Colonel proposes they shall solemnly *burn* their old regimentals.
And they do it, the Officers of them, *sub dio*, perhaps in the
Prince's garden, stripping successively in the " Temple " there,
with such degree of genial humor, loud laughter, or at least
boisterous mock-solemnity, as may be in them.   This is a true
incident of the Prince's history, though a small one.

Incident *second* is of slightly more significance; and intimates, not being quite alone in its kind, a questionable habit
or method the Crown-Prince must have had of dealing with
Clerical Persons hereabouts when they proved troublesome.
Here are no fewer than three such Persons, or Parsons, of the
Ruppin Country, who got mischief by him.   How the first
gave offence shall be seen, and how he was punished: offences
of the second and the third we can only guess to have been
perhaps pulpit-rebukes of said punishments: perhaps general

preaching against military levities, want of piety, nay open sinfulness, in thoughtless young men with cockades. Whereby the thoughtless young men were again driven to think of nocturnal charivari? We will give the story in Dr. Büsching's own words, who looks before and after to great distances, in a way worth attending to. The Herr Doctor, an endless Collector and Compiler on all manner of subjects, is very authentic always, and does not want for natural sense: but he is also very crude, — and here and there not far from stupid, such his continual haste, and slobbery manner of working up those Hundred and odd Volumes of his: — [1]

"The sanguine-choleric temperament of Friedrich," says this Doctor, "drove him, in his youth, to sensual enjoyments and wild amusements of different kinds; in his middle age, to fiery enterprises; and in his old years to decisions and actions of a rigorous and vehement nature; yet so that the primary form of utterance, as seen in his youth, never altogether ceased with him. There are people still among us (1788) who have had, in their own experience, knowledge of his youthful pranks; and yet more are living, who know that he himself, at table, would gayly recount what merry strokes were done by him, or by his order, in those young years. To give an instance or two.

"While he was at Neu-Ruppin as Colonel of the Infantry Regiment there, the Chaplain of it sometimes waited upon him about the time of dinner, — having been used to dine occasionally with the former Colonel. The Crown-Prince, however, put him always off, did not ask him to dinner; spoke contemptuously of him in presence of the Officers. The Chaplain was so inconsiderate, he took to girding at the Crown-Prince in his sermons. 'Once on a time,' preached he, one day, 'there was Herod who had Herodias to dance before him; and he, — he gave her John the Baptist's head for her pains!'" This *Herod*, Büsching says, was understood to mean, and meant, the Crown-Prince; *Herodias*, the merry corps of Officers who made sport for him; *John the Baptist's head* was no other

[1] See his Autobiography, which forms *Beiträge*, B. vi. (the biggest and last volume).

than the Chaplain not invited to dinner! "To punish him
for such a sally, the Crown-Prince with the young Officers of
his Regiment went, one night, to the Chaplain's house," somewhere hard by, with cow's-grass adjoining to it, as we see:
and "first, they knocked in the windows of his sleeping-room
upon him [*hinge*-windows, glass not entirely broken, we may
hope]; next there were crackers [*Schwärmer*, "enthusiasts,"
so to speak!] thrown in upon him; and thereby the Chaplain,
and his poor Wife," more or less in an interesting condition,
poor woman, "were driven out into the court-yard, and at last
into the dung-heap there;" — and so left, with their Head on
a Charger to that terrible extent!

That is Büsching's version of the story; no doubt substantially correct; of which there are traces in other quarters, —
for it went farther than Ruppin; and the Crown-Prince had
like to have got into trouble from it. "Here is piety!" said
Rumor, carrying it to Tobacco-Parliament. The Crown-Prince
plaintively assures Grumkow that it was the Officers, and that
they got punished for it. A likely story, the Prince's!

"When King Friedrich, in his old days, recounted this after
dinner, in his merry tone, he was well pleased that the guests,
and even the pages and valets behind his back, laughed aloud
at it." Not a pious old King, Doctor, still less an orthodox
one! The Doctor continues: "In a like style, at Nauen, where
part of his regiment lay, he had — by means of Herr von der
Gröben, his First-Lieutenant," much a comrade of his, as we
otherwise perceive — "the Diaconus of Nauen and his Wife
hunted out of bed, and thrown into terror of their lives, one
night:" — offence of the Diaconus not specified. "Nay he
himself once pitched his gold-headed stick through Salpius
the Church Inspector's window," — offence again not specified,
or perhaps merely for a little artillery practice? — "and the
throw was so dexterous that it merely made a round hole in the
glass; stick was lying on the floor; and the Prince," on some
excuse or other, "sent for it next morning." "Margraf Heinrich of Schwedt," continues the Doctor, very trustworthy on
points of fact, "was a diligent helper in such operations.
Kaiserling," whom we shall hear of, "First-Lieutenant von

der Gröben," these were prime hands; "Lieutenant Buddenbrock [old Feldmarschall's son] used, in his old days, when
himself grown high in rank and dining with the King, to be
appealed to as witness for the truth of these stories." [1]

These are the two Incidents at Ruppin, in such light as
they have. And these are all. Opulent History yields from
a ton of broken nails these two brass farthings, and shuts her
pocket on us again. A Crown-Prince given to frolic, among
other things ; though aware that gravity would beseem him
better. Much gay bantering humor in him, cracklings, radia-
tions, — which he is bound to keep well under cover, in present circumstances.

CHAPTER III.

THE SALZBURGERS.

For three years past there has been much rumor over
Germany, of a strange affair going on in the remote Austrian
quarter, down in Salzburg and its fabulous Tyrolese valleys.
Salzburg, city and territory, has an Archbishop, not theoretically Austrian, but sovereign Prince so styled; it is from him
and his orthodoxies, and pranks with his sovereign crosier, that
the noise originates. Strange rumor of a body of the population discovered to be Protestant among the remote Mountains,
and getting miserably ill-used, by the Right Reverend Father
in those parts. Which rumor, of a singular, romantic, religious
interest for the general Protestant world, proves to be but too

---

[1] Büsching, *Beiträge zu der Lebensgeschichte denkwürdiger Personen*, v. 19–21.
Vol. v. — wholly occupied with *Friedrich II. King of Prussia* (Halle, 1788), —
is accessible in French and other languages ; many details, and (as Büsching's
wont is) few or none not authentic, are to be found in it; a very great secret
spleen against Friedrich is also traceable, — for which the Doctor may have
had his reasons, not obligatory upon readers of the Doctor. The truth is,
Friedrich never took the least special notice of him : merely employed and
promoted him, when expedient for both parties ; and he really was a man of
considerable worth, in an extremely crude form.

well founded. It has come forth in the form of practical complaint to the *Corpus Evangelicorum* at the Diet, without result
from the *Corpus ;* complaint to various persons ; — in fine, to
his Majesty Friedrich Wilhelm, *with* result.

   With result at last; actual "Emigration of the Salzburgers:"
and Germany — in these very days while the Crown-Prince is
at Berlin betrothing himself, and Franz of Lorraine witnessing
the *exercitia* and wonders there — sees a singular phenomenon
of a touching idyllic nature going on; and has not yet quite
forgotten it in our days. Salzburg Emigration was all in
motion, flowing steadily onwards, by various routes, towards
Berlin, at the time the Betrothal took place ; and seven weeks
after that event, when the Crown-Prince had gone to Ruppin,
and again could only hear of it, the First Instalment of Emigrants arrived bodily at the Gates of Berlin, "30th April, at
four in the afternoon;" Majesty himself, and all the world
going out to witness it, with something of a poetic, almost of
a psalmist feeling, as well as with a practical on the part of
his Majesty. First Instalment this ; copiously followed by
others, all that year ; and flowing on, in smaller rills and
drippings, for several years more, till it got completed. A
notable phenomenon, full of lively picturesque and other
interest to Brandenburg and Germany ; — which was not forgotten by the Crown-Prince in coming years, as we shall
transiently find ; nay which all Germany still remembers,
and even occasionally sings. Of which this is in brief the
history.

   The Salzburg Country, northeastern slope of the Tyrol
(Donau draining that side of it, Etsch or Adige the Italian
side), is celebrated by the Tourist for its airy beauty, rocky
mountains, smooth green valleys, and swift-rushing streams ;
perhaps some readers have wandered to Bad-Gastein, or
Ischl, in these nomadic summers ; have looked into Salzburg,
Berchtesgaden, and the Bavarian-Austrian boundary-lands ;
seen the wooden-clock makings, salt-works, toy-manufactures,
of those simple people in their slouch-hats ; and can bear
some testimony to the phenomena of Nature there. Salzburg
is the Archbishop's City, metropolis of his bit of sovereignty

that then was.[1] A romantic City, far off among its beautiful Mountains, shadowing itself in the Salza River, which rushes down into the Inn, into the Donau, now becoming great with the tribute of so many valleys. Salzburg we have not known hitherto except as the fabulous resting-place of Kaiser Barbarossa: but we are now slightly to see it in a practical light; and mark how the memory of Friedrich Wilhelm makes an incidental lodgment for itself there.

It is well known there was extensive Protestantism once in those countries. Prior to the Thirty-Years War, the fair chance was, Austria too would all become Protestant; an extensive minority among all ranks of men in Austria too, definable as the serious intelligence of mankind in those countries, having clearly adopted it, whom the others were sure to follow. In all ranks of men; only not in the highest rank, which was pleased rather to continue Official and Papal. Highest rank had its Thirty-Years War, "its sleek Fathers Lämmerlein and Hyacinth in Jesuit serge, its terrible Fathers Wallenstein in chain-armor;" and, by working late and early then and afterwards, did manage at length to trample out Protestantism, — they know with what advantage by this time. Trample out Protestantism; or drive it into remote nooks, where under sad conditions it might protract an unnoticed existence. In the Imperial Free-Towns, Ulm, Augsburg, and the like, Protestantism continued, and under hard conditions contrives to continue: but in the country parts, except in unnoticed nooks, it is extinct. Salzburg Country is one of those nooks; an extensive Crypto-Protestantism lodging, under the simple slouch-hats, in the remote valleys there. Protestantism peaceably kept concealed, hurting nobody; wholesomely forwarding the wooden-clock manufacture, and arable or grazier husbandries,

---

[1] Tolerable description of it in the Baron Riesbeck's *Travels through Germany* (London, 1787, Translation by Maty, 3 vols. 8vo), i. 124–222; — whose details otherwise, on this Emigration business, are of no authenticity or value. A kind of Play-actor and miscellaneous Newspaper-man in that time (not so opulent to his class as ours is); who takes the title of "Baron" on this occasion of coming out with a Book of Imaginary "*Travels.*" Had personally lived, practising the miscellaneous arts, about Lintz and Salzburg, — and may be heard on the look of the Country, if on little else.

of those poor people. More harmless sons of Adam, probably,
did not breathe the vital air, than those dissentient Salzburgers; generation after generation of them giving offence to no
creature.

Successive Archbishops had known of this Crypto-Protestantism, and in remote periods had made occasional slight
attempts upon it; but none at all for a long time past. All
attempts that way, as ineffectual for any purpose but stirring
up strife, had been discontinued for many generations;[1] and
the Crypto-Protestantism was again become a mythical romantic object, ignored by Official persons. However, in 1727, there
came a new Archbishop, one "Firmian," Count Firmian by
secular quality, of a strict lean character, zealous rather than
wise; who had brought his orthodoxies with him in a rigid
and very lean form.

Right Reverend Firmian had not been long in Salzburg till
he smelt out the Crypto-Protestantism, and determined to haul
it forth from the mythical condition into the practical: and
in fact, to see his law-beagles there worry it to death as they
ought. Hence the rumors that had risen over Germany, in
1729: Law-terriers penetrating into human cottages in those
remote Salzburg valleys, smelling out some German Bible or
devout Book, making lists of Bible-reading cottagers; haling
them to the Right Reverend Father-in-God; thence to prison,
since they would not undertake to cease reading. With fine,
with confiscation, tribulation: for the peaceable Salzburgers,
respectful creatures, doffing their slouch-hats almost to mankind in general, were entirely obstinate in that matter of the
Bible. "Cannot, your Reverence; must not, dare not!" and
went to prison or whithersoever rather; a wide cry rising,
Let us sell our possessions and leave Salzburg then, according to Treaty of Westphalia, Article so-and-so. "Treaty of
Westphalia? Leave Salzburg?" shrieked the Right Reverend
Father: "Are we getting into open mutiny, then? Open extensive mutiny!" shrieked he. Borrowed a couple of Austrian
regiments, — Kaiser and we always on the pleasantest terms,
— and marched the most refractory of his Salzburgers over

[1] Buchholz, i. 148-151.

the frontiers (retaining their properties and families); whereupon noise rose louder and louder.

Refractory Salzburgers sent Deputies to the Diet; appealed,
complained to the *Corpus Evangelicorum*, Treaty of Westphalia in hand, — without result. *Corpus*, having verified matters,
complained to the Kaiser, to the Right Reverend Father. The
Kaiser, intent on getting his Pragmatic Sanction through the
Diet, and anxious to offend nobody at present, gave good words;
but did nothing : the Right Reverend Father answered a Letter or two from the *Corpus ;* then said at last, He wished to
close the Correspondence, had the honor to be, — and answered
no farther, when written to. *Corpus* was without result. So
it lasted through 1730 ; rumor, which rose in 1729, waxing
ever louder into practicable or impracticable shape, through
that next year; tribulation increasing in Salzburg; and noise
among mankind. In the end of 1730, the Salzburgers sent
Two Deputies to Friedrich Wilhelm at Berlin ; solid-hearted,
thick-soled men, able to answer for themselves, and give real
account of Salzburg and the phenomena : this brought matters
into a practicable state.

" Are you actual Protestants, the Treaty of Westphalia ap-
plicable to you ? Not mere fanatic mystics, as Right Reverend
Firmian asserts; protectible by no Treaty ? " That was Friedrich Wilhelm's first question ; and he set his two chief Berlin
Clergymen, learned Roloff one of them, a divine of much fame,
to catechise the two Salzburg Deputies, and report upon the
point. Their Report, dated Berlin, 30th November, 1730, with
specimens of the main questions, I have read; [1] and can fully
certify, along with Roloff and friend, That here are orthodox
Protestants, apparently of very pious peaceable nature, suffering hard wrong ; — orthodox beyond doubt, and covered by
the Treaty of Westphalia. Whereupon his Majesty dismisses
them with assurance, " Return, and say there shall be help ! "
— and straightway lays hand on the business, strong swift
steady hand as usual, with a view that way.

Salzburg being now a clear case, Friedrich Wilhelm writes
to the Kaiser ; to the King of England, King of Denmark ; —

[1] Fassmann, pp. 446–448.

orders preparations to be made in Preussen, vacant messuages
to be surveyed, moneys to be laid up; — bids his man at the
Regensburg Diet signify, That unless this thing is rectified,
his Prussian Majesty will see himself necessitated to take
effectual steps : " reprisals " the first step, according to the
old method of his Prussian Majesty.   Rumor of the Salzburg
Protestants rises higher and higher.   Kaiser intent on conciliating every *Corpus,* Evangelical and other, for his Pragmatic
Sanction's sake, admonishes Right Reverend Firmian; intimates at last to him, That he will actually have to let those
poor people emigrate if they demand it ; Treaty of Westphalia
being express.   In the end of 1731 it has come thus far.

"Emigrate, says your Imperial Majesty ?   Well, they shall
emigrate," answers Firmian; "the sooner the better ! "   And
straightway, in the dead of winter, marches, in convenient
divisions, some nine hundred of them over the frontiers : "Go
about your business, then ; emigrate — to the Old One, if you
like ! " — "And our properties, our goods and chattels ? " ask
they. — "Be thankful you have kept your skins.   Emigrate, I
say ! "   And the poor nine hundred had to go out, in the rigor
of winter, "hoary old men among them, and women coming
near their time;" and seek quarters in the wide world mostly
unknown to them.   Truly Firmian is an orthodox Herr; acquainted with the laws of fair usage and the time of day.   The
sleeping Barbarossa does not awaken upon him within the Hill
here : — but in the Roncalic Fields, long ago, I should not
have liked to stand in his shoes !

Friedrich Wilhelm, on this procedure at Salzburg, intimates
to his Halberstadt and Minden Catholic gentlemen, That their
Establishments must be locked up, and incomings suspended ;
that they can apply to the Right Reverend Firmian upon
it ; — and bids his man at Regensburg signify to the Diet that
such is the course adopted here.   Right Reverend Firmian
has to hold his hand ; finds both that there shall be Emigration, and that it must go forward on human terms, not inhuman ; and that in fact the Treaty of Westphalia will have
to guide it, not he henceforth.   Those poor ousted Salzburgers
eower into the Bavarian cities, till the weather mend, and his

Prussian Majesty's arrangements be complete for their brethren and them.

His Prussian Majesty has been maturing his plans, all this while; — gathering moneys, getting lands ready. We saw him hanging Schlubhut in the autumn of 1731, who had peculated from said moneys; and surveying Preussen, under storms of thunder and rain on one occasion. Preussen is to be the place for these people; Tilsit and Memel region, same where the big Fight of Tannenberg and ruin of the Teutsch Ritters took place: in that fine fertile Country there are homes got ready for this Emigration out of Salzburg.

Long ago, at the beginning of this History, did not the reader hear of a pestilence in Prussian Lithuania? Pestilence in old King Friedrich's time; for which the then Crown-Prince, now Majesty Friedrich Wilhelm, vainly solicited help from the Treasury, and only brought about partial change of Ministry and no help. "Fifty-two Towns" were more or less entirely depopulated; hundreds of thousands of fertile acres fell to waste again, the hands that had ploughed them being swept away. The new Majesty, so soon as ever the Swedish War was got rid of, took this matter diligently in hand; built up the fifty-two ruined Towns; issued Proclamations once and again (Years 1719, 1721) to the Wetterau, to Switzerland, Saxony, Schwaben;[1] inviting Colonists to come, and, on favorable terms, till and reap there. His terms are favorable, well-considered; and are honestly kept. He has a fixed set of terms for Colonists: their road-expenses thither, so much a day allowed each travelling soul; homesteads, ploughing implements, cattle, land, await them at their journey's end; their rent and services, accurately specified, are light not heavy; and "immunities" from this and that are granted them, for certain years, till they get well nestled. Excellent arrangements: and his Majesty has, in fact, got about 20,000 families in that way. And still there is room for thousands more. So that if the tyrannous Firmian took to tribulating Salzburg in that manner, Heaven had provided remedies and a Prussian Majesty. Heaven is very opulent; has alchemy to change the

[1] Buchholz, i. 148.

ugliest substances into beautifulest. Privately to his Majesty,
for months back, this Salzburg Emigration is a most manageable matter.   Manage well, it will be a god-send to his Majesty, and fit, as by pre-established harmony, into the ancient
Prussian sorrow ; and " two afflictions well put together shall
become a consolation," as the proverb promises ! Go along
then, Right Reverend Firmian, with your Emigration there :
only no foul-play in it, — or Halberstadt and Minden get
locked : — for the rest of the matter we will undertake.

And so, February 2d, 1732, Friedrich Wilhelm's Proclamation [1] flew abroad over the world ; brief and business-like,
cheering to all but Firmian ; — to this purport : " Come, ye
poor Salzburgers, there are homes provided for you. Apply
at Regensburg, at Halle : Commissaries are appointed ; will
take charge of your long march and you. Be kind, all Christian German Princes : do not hinder them and me." And in
a few days farther, still early in February (for the matter is
all ready before proclaiming), an actual Prussian Commissary
hangs out his announcements and officialities at Donauwörth,
old City known to us, within reach of the Salzburg Boundaries ; collects, in a week or two, his first lot of Emigrants, near
a thousand strong ; and fairly takes the road with them.

A long road and a strange : I think, above five hundred
miles before we get to Halle, within Prussian land ; and then
seven hundred more to our place there, in the utmost East.
Men, women, infants and hoary grandfathers are here ; —
most of their property sold, — still on ruinous conditions,
think of it, your Majesty. Their poor bits of preciosities and
heirlooms they have with them ; made up in succinct bundles,
stowed on ticketed baggage-wains ; " some have their own poor
cart and horse, to carry the too old and the too young, those
that cannot walk." A pilgrimage like that of the Children of
Israel : such a pilgrim caravan as was seldom heard of in our
Western Countries. Those poor succinct bundles, the making
of them up and stowing of them ; the pangs of simple hearts,
in those remote native valleys ; the tears that were not seen,
the cries that were addressed to God only : and then at last

[1] Copy of it in Mauvillon, February, 1732, ii. 311.

the actual turning out of the poor caravan, in silently practical condition, staff in hand, no audible complaint heard from
it; ready to march; practically marching here : — which of
us can think of it without emotion, sad, and yet in a sort
blessed !

Every Emigrant man has four *groschen* a day (fourpence odd)
allowed him for road expenses, every woman three groschen,
every child two : and regularity itself, in the shape of Prussian Commissaries, presides over it. Such marching of the
Salzburgers : host after host of them, by various routes, from
February onwards ; above seven thousand of them this year,
and ten thousand more that gradually followed, — was heard
of at all German firesides, and in all European lands. A phenomenon much filling the general ear and imagination ; especially at the first emergence of it. We will give from poor
old authentic Fassmann, as if caught up by some sudden pho-
tograph apparatus, a rude but undeniable glimpse or two into
the actuality of this business : the reader will in that way
sufficiently conceive it for himself.

Glimpse *first* is of an Emigrant Party arriving, in the cold
February days of 1732, at Nördlingen, Protestant Free-Town
in Bavaria : three hundred of them ; first section, I think, of
those nine hundred who were packed away unceremoniously
by Firmian last winter, and have been wandering about Bavaria, lodging " in Kaufbeuern " and various preliminary Towns,
till the Prussian arrangements became definite. Prussian
Commissaries are, by this time, got to Donauwörth ; but these
poor Salzburgers are ahead of them, wandering under the vol-
untary principle as yet. Nördlingen, in Bavaria, is an old
Imperial Free-Town ; Protestantism not suppressed there, as
it has been all round ; scene of some memorable fighting in
the Thirty-Years War, especially of a bad defeat to the Swedes
and Bernhard of Weimar, the worst they had in the course
of that bad business. The Salzburgers are in number three
hundred and thirty-one ; time, " first days of February, 1732,
weather very cold and raw." The charitable Protestant Town
has been expecting such an advent : —

" Two chief Clergymen, and the Schoolmaster and Scholars,

with some hundreds of citizens and many young people, went out to meet them ; there, in the open field, stood the Salzburgers, with their wives and their little ones, with their bullock-carts and baggage-wains," pilgriming towards unknown parts of the Earth. " 'Come in, ye blessed of the Lord ! Why stand ye without ?' said the Parson solemnly, by way of welcome ; and addressed a Discourse to them," devout and yet human, true every word of it, enough to draw tears from any Fassmann that were there ; — Fassmann and we not far from weeping without words. " Thereupon they ranked themselves two and two, and marched into the Town," straight to the Church, I conjecture, Town all out to participate ; "and there the two reverend gentlemen successively addressed them again, from appropriate texts : Text of the first reverend gentleman was, *And every one that hath forsaken houses, or brethren, or sisters, or father, or mother, or wife, or children, or lands, for my name's sake, shall receive an hundred-fold, and shall inherit everlasting life.*[1] Text of the second was, *Now the Lord had said unto Abraham, Get thee out of thy country, and from thy kindred, and from thy father's house, unto a land that I will show thee.*" [2] Excellent texts ; well handled, let us hope, — especially with brevity. After which the strangers were distributed, some into public-houses, others taken home by the citizens to lodge.

" Out of the Spital there was distributed to each person, for the first three days, a half-pound of flesh-meat, bread, and a measure of beer. The remaining days they got in money six *creutzers* (twopence) each, and bread. On Sunday, at the Church-doors there was a collection ; no less than eight hundred *gulden* [£80 ; population, say, three thousand] for this object. At Sermon they were put into the central part of the Church," all Nördlingen lovingly encompassing them ; "and were taught in two sermons," texts not given, *What the true Church is built of*, and then *Of true Faith, and what love a Christian ought to have ;* Nördlingen copiously shedding tears the while (*viele Thränen vergossen*), as it well might. " Going to Church, and coming from it, each Landlord walked ahead

[1] Matthew xix. 29.   [2] Genesis xii. 1.

of his party; party followed two and two. On other days, there was much catechising of them at different parts of the Town;" — orthodox enough, you see, nothing of superstition or fanaticism in the poor people; — " they made a good testimony of their Evangelical truth.

"The Baggage-wagons which they had with them, ten in number, upon which some of their old people sat, were brought into the Town. The Baggage was unloaded, and the packages, two hundred and eighty-one of them in all [for Fassmann is Photography itself], were locked in the Zoll-Haus. Over and above what they got from the Spital, the Church-collection and the Town-chest, Citizens were liberal; daily sent them food, or daily had them by fours and fives to their own houses to meat." And so let them wait for the Prussian Commissary, who is just at hand: "they would not part from one another, these three hundred and thirty-one," says Fassmann, "though their reunion was but of that accidental nature." [1]

Glimpse *second:* not dated; perhaps some ten days later; and a Prussian Commissary with this party : —

" On their getting to the Anspach Territory, there was so incredible a joy at the arrival of these exiled Brothers in the Faith (*Glaubens-Brüder*) that in all places, almost in the smallest hamlets, the bells were set a-tolling; and nothing was heard but a peal of welcome from far and near." Prussian Commissary, when about quitting Anspach, asked leave to pass through Bamberg; Bishop of Bamberg, too orthodox a gentleman, declined; so the Commissary had to go by Nürnberg and Baireuth. Ask not if his welcome was good, in those Protestant places. " At Erlangen, fifteen miles from Nürnberg, where are French Protestants and a Dowager Margravine of Baireuth," — Widow of Wilhelmina's Father-in-law's predecessor (if the reader can count that); *daughter* of Weissenfels who was for marrying Wilhelmina not long since ! — " at Erlangen, the Serene Dowager snatched up fifty of them into her own House for Christian refection; and Burghers of means had twelve, fifteen and even eighteen of them, following such example set. Nay certain French

[1] Fassmann, pp. 439, 440.

Citizens, prosperous and childless, besieged the Prussian Commissary to allow them a few Salzburg children for adoption; especially one Frenchman was extremely urgent and specific: but the Commissary, not having any order, was obliged to refuse." [1] These must have been interesting days for the two young Margravines; forwarding Papa's poor pilgrims in that manner.

"At Baireuth," other side of Nürnberg, "it was towards Good Friday when the Pilgrims under their Commissarius arrived. They were lodged in the villages about, but came copiously into the Town; came all in a body to Church on Good Friday; and at coming out, were one and all carried off to dinner, a very scramble arising among the Townsfolk to get hold of Pilgrims and dine them. Vast numbers were carried to the Schloss:" one figures Wilhelmina among them, figures the Hereditary Prince and old Margraf: their treatment there was "beyond belief," says Fassmann; "not only dinner of the amplest quality and quantity, but much money added and other gifts." From Baireuth the route is towards Gera and Thüringen, circling the Bamberg Territory: readers remember Gera, where the Gera Bond was made? — "At Gera, a commercial gentleman dined the whole party in his own premises, and his wife gave four groschen to each individual of them; other two persons, brothers in the place, doing the like. One of the poor pilgrim women had been brought to bed on the journey, a day or two before: the Commissarius lodged her in his own inn, for greater safety; Commissarius returning to his inn, finds she is off, nobody at first can tell him whither: a lady of quality (*vornehme Dame*) has quietly sent her carriage for the poor pilgrim sister, and has her in the right softest keeping. No end to people's kindness: many wept aloud, sobbing out, ' Is this all the help we can give ? ' Commissarius said, 'There will others come shortly; them also you can help.' "

In this manner march these Pilgrims. "From Donauwörth, by Anspach, Nürnberg, Baireuth, through Gera, Zeitz, Weissenfels, to Halle," where they are on Prussian ground, and

[1] Fassmann, p. 441.

within few days of Berlin. Other Towns, not upon the first
straight route to Berlin, demand to have a share in these grand
things; share is willingly conceded: thus the Pilgrims, what
has its obvious advantages, march by a good variety of routes.
Through Augsburg, Ulm (instead of Donauwörth), thence to
Frankfurt; from Frankfurt some direct to Leipzig : some
through Cassel, Hanover, Brunswick, by Halberstadt and
Magdeburg instead of Halle. Starting all at Salzburg, landing all at Berlin; their routes spread over the Map of Germany
in the intermediate space.

"Weissenfels Town and Duke distinguished themselves by
liberality: especially the Duke did; " — poor old drinking
Duke ; very Protestant all these Saxon Princes, except the
Apostate or Pseudo-Apostate the Physically Strong, for sad
political reasons. "In Weissenfels Town, while the Pilgrim
procession walked, a certain rude foreign fellow, flax-pedler
by trade,[1] by creed Papist or worse, said floutingly, 'The
Archbishop ought to have flung you all into the river,
you — !' Upon which a menial servant of the Duke's suddenly broke in upon him in the way of actuality, the whole
crowd blazing into flame ; and the pedler would certainly have
got irreparable damage, had not the Town-guard instantly
hooked him away."

April 21st, 1732, the first actual body, a good nine hundred
strong,[2] got to Halle ; where they were received with devout
jubilee, psalm-singing, spiritual and corporeal refection, as at
Nördlingen and the other stages ; "Archidiaconus Franke"
being prominent in it, — I have no doubt, a connection of that
"chien de Franke," whom Wilhelmina used to know. They
were lodged in the Waisenhaus (old Franke's Orphan-house);
Official List of them was drawn up here, with the fit specifi-
cality ; and, after three days, they took the road again for
Berlin. Useful Buchholz, then a very little boy, remembers
the arrival of a Body of these Salzburgers, not this but a later
one in August, which passed through his native Village, Pritz-

[1] "Hecheltrüger," Hawker of flax-combs or heckles ; — is oftenest a Slavonic
Austrian (I am told).
[2] Buchholz, i. 156.

walk in the Priegnitz: How village and village authorities
were all awake, with opened stores and hearts; how his Father,
the Village Parson, preached at five in the afternoon. The
same Buchholz, coming afterwards to College at Halle, had
the pleasure of discovering two of the Commissaries, two of
the three, who had mainly superintended in this Salzburg Pilgrimage. Let the reader also take a glance at them, as specimens worth notice:—

Commissarius First: "Herr von Reck was a nobleman from
the Hanover Country; of very great piety; who, after his
Commission was done, settled at Halle; and lived there, without servant, in privacy, from the small means he had;— seeking his sole satisfaction in attendance on the Theological and
Ascetic College-Lectures, where I used to see him constantly
in my student time."

Commissarius Second: "Herr Göbel was a medical man by
profession; and had the regular degree of Doctor; but was in
no necessity to apply his talents to the gaining of bread. His
zeal for religion had moved him to undertake this Commission.
Both these gentlemen I have often seen in my youth," but do
not tell you what they were like farther; "and both their
Christian names have escaped me."

A third Commissarius was of Preussen, and had religious-
literary tendencies. I suppose these three served gratis;—
volunteers; but no doubt under oath, and tied by strict enough
Prussian law. Physician, Chaplain, Road-guide, here they are,
probably of supreme quality, ready to our hand.[1]

Buchholz, after "his student time," became a poor Country-
Schoolmaster, and then a poor Country-Parson, in his native
Altmark. His poor Book is of innocent, clear, faithful nature,
with some vein of "unconscious geniality" in it here and
there;— a Book by no means so destitute of human worth as
some that have superseded it. This was posthumous, this
"*Newest History*," and has a *Life* of the Author prefixed. He
has four previous Volumes on the "*Ancient History of Brandenburg*," which are not known to me. — About the Year 1745,

[1] Buchholz, *Neueste Preussisch-Brandenburgische Geschichte* (Berlin, 1775,
2 vols. 4to), i. 155 n.

there were four poor Schoolmasters in that region (two at
Havelberg, one at Seehausen, one at Werben), of extremely
studious turn; who, in spite of the Elbe which ran between,
used to meet on stated nights, for colloquy, for interchange of
Books and the like. One of them, the Werben one, was this
Buchholz; another, Seehausen, was the Winckelmann so celebrated in after years. A third, one of the Havelberg pair,
"went into Mecklenburg in a year or two, as Tutor to Karl
Ludwig the Prince of Strelitz's children," — whom also mark.
For the youngest of these Strelitz children was no other than
the actual "Old Queen Charlotte" (ours and George III.'s),
just ready for him with her Hornbooks about that time: Let
the poor man have what honor he can from that circumstance!
"Prince Karl Ludwig," rather a foolish-looking creature, we
may fall in with personally by and by.

It was the 30th April, 1732, seven weeks and a day since
Crown-Prince Friedrich's Betrothal, that this first body of
Salzburg Emigrants, nine hundred strong, arrived at Berlin;
"four in the afternoon, at the Brandenburg Gate;" Official
persons, nay Majesty himself, or perhaps both Majesties, waiting there to receive them. Yes, ye poor footsore mortals,
there is the dread King himself; stoutish short figure in blue
uniform and white wig, straw-colored waistcoat, and white
gaiters; stands uncommonly firm on his feet; reddish, blue-
reddish face, with eyes that pierce through a man: look upon
him, and yet live if you are true men. His Majesty's reception of these poor people could not but be good; nothing now
wanting in the formal kind. But better far, in all the essen-
tialities of it, there had not been hitherto, nor was henceforth,
the least flaw. This Salzburg Pilgrimage has found for itself,
and will find, regulation, guidance, ever a stepping-stone at
the needful place; a paved road, so far as human regularity
and punctuality could pave one. That is his Majesty's shining
merit. "Next Sunday, after sermon, they [this first lot of
Salzburgers] were publicly catechised in church; and all the
world could hear their pertinent answers, given often in the
very Scripture texts, or express words of Luther."

His Majesty more than once took survey of these Pilgrim-

age Divisions, when they got to Berlin. A pleasant sight, if
there were leisure otherwise. On various occasions, too, her
Majesty had large parties of them over to Monbijou, to supper
there in the fine gardens; and "gave them Bibles," among
other gifts, if in want of Bibles through Firmian's industry.
Her Majesty was Charity itself, Charity and Grace combined,
among these Pilgrims. On one occasion she picked out a
handsome young lass among them, and had Painter Pesne
over to take her portrait. Handsome lass, by Pesne, in her
Tyrolese Hat, shone thenceforth on the walls of Monbijou;
and fashion thereupon took up the Tyrolese Hat, "which has
been much worn since by the beautiful part of the Creation,"
says Buchholz; "but how many changes they have introduced
in it no pen can trace."

At Berlin the Commissarius ceased; and there was usually
given the Pilgrims a Candidatus Theologiæ, who was to conduct them the rest of the way, and be their Clergyman when
once settled. Five hundred long miles still. Some were
shipped at Stettin; mostly they marched, stage after stage, —
four groschen a day. At the farther end they found all ready;
tight cottages, tillable fields, all implements furnished, and
stock, — even to "*Federvieh*," or Chanticleer with a modicum
of Hens. Old neighbors, and such as liked each other, were
put together: fields grew green again, desolate scrubs and
scrags yielding to grass and corn. Wooden clocks even came
to view, — for Berchtesgaden neighbors also emigrated; and
Swiss came, and Bavarians and French: — and old trades were
revived in those new localities.

Something beautifully real-idyllic in all this, surely: — Yet
do not fancy that it all went on like clock-work; that there
were not jarrings at every step, as is the way in things real.
Of the Prussian Minister chiefly concerned in settling this new
Colony I have heard one saying, forced out of him in some
pressure: "There must be somebody for a scolding-stock and
scape-goat; I will be it, then!" And then the Salzburg Officials, what a humor they were in! No Letters allowed from
those poor Emigrants; the wickedest rumors circulated about
them: "All cut to pieces by inroad of the Poles;" "Pressed

for soldiers by the Prussian drill-sergeant;" "All flung into
the Lakes and stagnant waters there; drowned to the last
individual;" and so on. Truth nevertheless did slowly pierce
through. And the "*Grosse Wirth*," our idyllic-real Friedrich
Wilhelm, was wanting in nothing. Lists of their unjust losses
in Salzburg were, on his Majesty's order, made out and au-
thenticated, by the many who had suffered in that way there,
— forced to sell at a day's notice, and the like : — with these
his Majesty was diligent in the Imperial Court; and did get
what human industry could of compensation, a part but not
the whole. Contradictory noises had to abate. In the end,
sound purpose, built on fact and the Laws of Nature, carried
it ; lies, vituperations, rumors and delusion sank to zero; and
the true result remained. In 1738, the Salzburg Emigrant
Community in Preussen held, in all their Churches, a Day of
Thanksgiving; and admitted piously that Heaven's blessing,
of a truth, had been upon this King and them. There we
leave them, a useful solid population ever since in those
parts ; increased by this time we know not how many fold.

It cost Friedrich Wilhelm enormous sums, say the Old
Histories ; probably "ten *tons of gold*," — that is to say, ten
hundred thousand thalers ; almost £150,000, no less! But
he lived to see it amply repaid, even in his own time ; how
much more amply since ; — being a man skilful in investments to a high degree indeed. Fancy £150,000 invested
there, in the Bank of Nature herself ; and a hundred millions
invested, say at Balaclava, in the Bank of Newspaper rumor :
and the respective rates of interest they will yield, a million
years hence ! This was the most idyllic of Friedrich Wilhelm's feats, and a very real one the while.

We have only to add or repeat, that Salzburgers to the
number of about 7,000 souls arrived at their place this first
year ; and in the year or two following, less noted by the public, but faring steadily forward upon their four groschen a day,
10,000 more. Friedrich Wilhelm would have gladly taken
the whole ; "but George II. took a certain number," say the
Prussian Books (George II., or pious Trustees instead of him),
"and settled them at Ebenezer in Virginia," — read, Ebenezer

in Georgia, where General Oglethorpe was busy founding a
Colony.[1] There at Ebenezer I calculate they might go ahead,
too, after the questionable fashion of that country, and increase
and swell; — but have never heard of them since.

Salzburg Emigration was a very real transaction on Friedrich Wilhelm's part; but it proved idyllic too, and made a
great impression on the German mind. Readers know of a
Book called *Hermann and Dorothea?* It is written by the
great Goethe, and still worth reading. The great Goethe had
heard, when still very little, much talk among the elders about
this Salzburg Pilgrimage; and how strange a thing it was,
twenty years ago and more.[2] In middle life he threw it into
Hexameters, into the region of the air; and did that unreal
Shadow of it; a pleasant work in its way, since he was not
inclined for more.

CHAPTER IV.

PRUSSIAN MAJESTY VISITS THE KAISER.

MAJESTY seeing all these matters well in train, — Salzburgers under way, Crown-Prince betrothed according to his
Majesty's and the Kaiser's (not to *her* Majesty's, and high-
flying little George of England my Brother the Comedian's)
mind and will, — begins to think seriously of another enterprise, half business, half pleasure, which has been hovering in
his mind for some time. " Visit to my Daughter at Baireuth,"
he calls it publicly; but it means intrinsically Excursion into
Böhmen, to have a word with the Kaiser, and see his Imperial
Majesty in the body for once. Too remarkable a thing to be
omitted by us here.

Crown-Prince does not accompany on this occasion; Crown-
Prince is with his Regiment all this while; busy minding his

----

[1] Petition to Parliament, 10th (21st) May, 1733, by Oglethorpe and his
Trustees, for £10,000 to carry over these Salzburgers; which was granted:
Tindal's *Rapin* (London, 1769), xx. 184.

[2] 1749 was Goethe's birth-year.

own affairs in the Ruppin quarter ; — only hears, with more
or less interest, of these Salzburg-Pilgrim movements, of this
Excursion into Böhmen.   Here are certain scraps of Letters ;
which, if once made legible, will assist readers to conceive his
situation and employments there.   Letters otherwise of no
importance ; but worth reading on that score.   The *first* (or
rather first three, which we huddle into one) is from " Nauen,"
few miles off Ruppin ; where one of our Battalions lies ; requiring frequent visits there : —

1.   *To Grumkow, at Berlin* (from the Crown-Prince).

"NAUEN, 25th April, 1732.

" MONSIEUR MY DEAREST FRIEND, — I send you a big mass
of papers, which a certain gentleman named Plötz has trans-
mitted me.   In faith, I know not in the least what it is : I
pray you present it [to his Majesty, or in the proper quarter],
and make me rid of it.

" To-morrow I go to Potsdam [a drive of forty miles south-
ward], to see the exercise, and if we do it here according to
pattern.   *Neue Besen kehren gut* [New brooms sweep clean,
in German]; I shall have to illustrate my new character" of
Colonel; "and show that I am *ein tüchtiger Officier* (a right
Officer).   Be what I may, I shall to you always be," &c. &c.

Nauen, 7th May, 1732.   " . . . Thousand thanks for informing me how everything goes on in the world.   Things far
from agreeable, those leagues [imaginary, in Tobacco-Parlia-
ment] suspected to be forming against our House!   But if
the Kaiser don't abandon us ; . . . if God second the valor of
80,000 men resolved to spend their life, . . . let us hope there
will nothing bad happen.

" Meanwhile, till events arrive, I make a pretty stir here
(*me trémousse ici d'importance*), to bring my Regiment to its
requisite perfection, and I hope I shall succeed.   The other
day I drank your dear health, Monsieur ; and I wait only the
news from my Cattle-stall that the Calf I am fattening there
is ready for sending to you.   I unite Mars and Housekeeping,
you see.   Send me your Secretary's name, that I may address

your Letters that way," — our Correspondence needing to
be secret in certain quarters. . . . "With a" truly infinite
esteem,   " FRÉDÉRIC."

Nauen, 10th May, 1732.   "You will see by this that I am
exact to follow your instruction ; and that the *Schulz* of Trem-
men [Village in the Brandenburg quarter, with a *Schulz* or
Mayor to be depended on], becomes for the present the mainspring of our correspondence.   I return you all the things
(*pièces*) you had the goodness to communicate to me, — except
Charles Douze,[1] which attaches me infinitely.   The particulars
hitherto unknown which he reports ; the greatness of that
Prince's actions, and the perverse singularity (*bizarrerie*) of
his fortune : all this, joined to the lively, brilliant and
charming way the Author has of telling it, renders this Book
interesting to the supreme degree. . . . I send you a fragment of my correspondence with the most illustrious Sieur
Crochet," some French Envoy or Emissary, I conclude : "you
perceive we go on very sweetly together, and are in a high
strain.   I am sorry I burnt one of his Letters, wherein he
assured me he would in the Versailles Antechamber itself
speak of me to the King, and that my name had actually
been mentioned at the King's Levee.   It certainly is not my
ambition to choose this illustrious mortal to publish my
renown ; on the contrary, I should think it soiled by such a
mouth, and prostituted if he were the publisher.   But enough
of the Crochet : the kindest thing we can do for so contemptible an object is to say nothing of him at all."[2] — . . .

Letter *second* is to Jägermeister Hacke, Captain of the Potsdam Guard ; who stands in great nearness to the King's
Majesty ; and, in fact, is fast becoming his factotum in Army-
details.   We, with the Duke of Lorraine and Majesty in person, saw his marriage to the Excellency Creutz's Fräulein
Daughter not long since ; who we trust has made him happy ;
— rich he is at any rate, and will be Adjutant-General before

---

[1] Voltaire's new Book ; lately come out, "Bâle, 1731."
[2] *Œuvres de Frédéric,* xvi. 49, 51.

long; powerful in such intricacies as this that the Prince has fallen into.

The Letter has its obscurities; turns earnestly on Recruits tall and short; nor have idle Editors helped us, by the least hint towards "reading" it with more than the *eyes*. Old Dessauer at this time is Commandant at Magdeburg; Buddenbrock, perhaps now passing by Ruppin, we know for a high old General, fit to carry messages from Majesty, — or, likelier, it may be Lieutenant Buddenbrock, his Son, merely *returning* to Ruppin? We can guess, that the flattering Dessauer has sent his Majesty five gigantic men from the Magdeburg regiments, and that Friedrich is ordered to hustle out thirty of insignificant stature from his own, by way of counter-gift to the Dessauer; — which Friedrich does instantly, but cannot, for his life, see how (being totally cashless) he is to replace them with better, or replace them at all!

2. *To Captain Hacke, of the Potsdam Guard.*

"RUPPIN, 15th July, 1732.

" *Mein Gott,* what a piece of news Buddenbrock has brought me! I am to get nothing out of Brandenburg, my dear Hacke? Thirty men I had to shift out of my company in consequence [of Buddenbrock's order]; and where am I now to get other thirty? I would gladly give the King tall men, as the Dessauer at Magdeburg does; but I have no money; and I don't get, or set up for getting, six men for one [thirty short for five tall], as he does. So true is that Scripture: To him that hath shall be given; and from him that hath not shall be taken away even that he hath.

" Small art, that the Prince of Dessau's and the Magdeburg Regiments are fine, when they have money at command, and thirty men *gratis* over and above! I, poor devil, have nothing; nor shall have, all my days. Prithee, dear Hacke (*bitte Ihn, lieber Hacke*), think of all that: and if I have no money allowed, I must bring Asmus [1] alone as Recruit next year;

---

[1] Recruit unknown to me.

and my Regiment will to a certainty be rubbish (*Kroop*).
Once I had learned a German Proverb —

> ' *Versprechen und halten* (To promise and to keep)
> *Ziemt wohl Jungen und Alten* (Is pretty for young and for old) ! '

"I depend alone on you (*Ihn*), dear Hacke ; unless you help,
there is a bad outlook.   To-day I have knocked again [written
to Papa for money]; and if that does not help, it is over.
If I could get any money to borrow, it would do ; but I need
not think of that.   Help me, then, dear Hacke !   I assure you
I will ever remember it ; who, at all times, am my dear Herr
Captain's devoted (*ganz ergebener*) servant and friend,

"FRIDERICH."[1]

To which add only this Note, two days later, to Seckendorf ;
indicating that the process of "borrowing" has already, in
some form, begun, — process which will have to continue, and
to develop itself ; — and that his Majesty, as Seckendorf well
knows, is resolved upon his Bohemian journey : —

3. *To the General Feldzeugmeister Graf von Seckendorf.*

"RUPPIN, 17th July, 1732.

"MY VERY DEAR GENERAL, — I have written to the King,
that I owed you 2,125 *thalers* for the Recruits; of which he
says there are 600 paid : there remain, therefore, 1,525, which
he will pay you directly.

"The King is going to Prague : I shall not be of the party
[as you will].   To say truth, I am not very sorry; for it
would infallibly give rise to foolish rumors in the world.   At
the same time, I should have much wished to see the Emperor, Empress, and Prince of Lorraine, for whom I have a
quite particular esteem.   I beg you, Monsieur, to assure him
of it ; — and to assure yourself that I shall always be, —
with a great deal of consideration, *Monsieur, mon très-cher
Général,* &c.   FRÉDÉRIC."

[1] In German : *Œuvres,* xxvii. part 3d, p. 177.

And now for the Bohemian Journey, "Visit at Kladrup" as they call it; — Ruppin being left in this assiduous and wholesome, if rather hampered condition.

Kaiser Karl and his Empress, in this summer of 1732, were at Karlsbad, taking the waters for a few weeks. Friedrich Wilhelm, who had long, for various reasons, wished to see his Kaiser face to face, thought this would be a good opportunity. The Kaiser himself, knowing how it stood with the Jülich-and-Berg and other questions, was not anxious for such an interview: still less were his official people; among whom the very ceremonial for such a thing was matter of abstruse difficulty. Seckendorf accordingly had been instructed to hunt wide, and throw in discouragements, so far as possible; — which he did, but without effect. Friedrich Wilhelm had set his heart upon the thing; wished to behold for once a Head of the Holy Roman Empire, and Supreme of Christendom; — also to see a little, with his own eyes, into certain matters Imperial.

And so, since an express visit to Karlsbad might give rise to newspaper rumors, and will not suit, it is settled, there shall be an accidental intersection of routes, as the Kaiser travels homeward, — say in some quiet Bohemian Schloss or Hunting-seat of the Kaiser's own, whither the King may come incognito; and thus, with a minimum of noise, may the needful passage of hospitality be done. Easy all of this: only the Vienna Ministers are dreadfully in doubt about the ceremonial, Whether the Imperial hand can be given (I forget if for kissing or for shaking)? — nay at last they manfully declare that it cannot be given; and wish his Prussian Majesty to understand that it must be refused.[1] " *Res summæ consequentiæ*," say they; and shake solemnly their big wigs. — Nonsense (*Narrenpossen*)! answers the Prussian Majesty: You, Seckendorf, settle about quarters, reasonable food, reasonable lodgings; and I will do the ceremonial.

Seckendorf — worth glancing into, for biographical purposes, in this place — has written to his Court: That as to the victual department, his Majesty goes upon good common meat; flesh, to which may be added all manner of river-fish

[1] Förster, i. 328.

and crabs: sound old Rhenish is his drink, with supplements
of brown and of white beer. Dinner-table to be spread always
in some airy place, garden-house, tent, big clean barn, — Majesty likes air, of all things ; — will sleep, too, in a clean barn
or garden-house : better anything than being stifled, thinks
his Majesty. Who, for the rest, does not like mounting stairs.[1]
These are the regulations ; and we need not doubt they were
complied with.

Sunday, 27th July, 1732, accordingly, his Majesty, with five
or six carriages, quits Berlin, before the sun is up, as is his
wont : eastward, by the road for Frankfurt-on-Oder ; "intends
to look at Schulenburg's regiment," which lies in those parts,
— Schulenburg's regiment for one thing : the rest is secret
from the profane vulgar. Schulenburg's regiment (drawn up
for Church, I should suppose) is soon looked at ; Schulenburg
himself, by preappointment, joins the travelling party, which
now consists of the King and Eight : — known figures, seven,
Buddenbrock, Schulenburg, Waldau, Derschau, Seckendorf,
Grumkow, Captain Hacke of the Potsdam Guard ; and for
eighth the Dutch Ambassador, Ginkel, an accomplished knowing kind of man, whom also my readers have occasionally seen.
Their conversation, road-colloquy, could it interest any modern reader ? It has gone all to dusk ; we can know only that
it was human, solid, for most part, and had much tobacco
intermingled. They were all of the Calvinistic persuasion,
of the military profession ; knew that life is very serious, that
speech without cause is much to be avoided. They travelled
swiftly, dined in airy places : they are a *fact*, they and their
summer dust-cloud there, whirling through the vacancy of
that dim Time ; and have an interest for us, though an unimportant one.

The first night they got to Grünberg ; a pleasant Town, of
vineyards and of looms, across the Silesian frontier. They are
now turning more southeastward ; they sleep here, in the
Kaiser's territory, welcomed by some Official persons ; who

[1] Seckendorf's Report (in Förster, i. 330).

signify that the overjoyed Imperial Majesty has, as was extremely natural, paid the bill everywhere.   On the morrow,
before the shuttles awaken, Friedrich Wilhelm is gone again;
towards the Glogau region, intending for Liegnitz that night.
Coursing rapidly through the green Silesian Lowlands, blue
Giant Mountains (*Riesengebirge*) beginning to rise on the
southwestward far away.   Dines, at noon, under a splendid
tent, in a country place called Polkwitz,[1] with country Nobility (sorrow on them, and yet thanks to them) come to do reverence.   At night he gets to Liegnitz.

Here is Liegnitz, then.   Here are the Katzbach and the
Blackwater (*Schwarzwasser*), famed in war, your Majesty;
here they coalesce; gray ashlar houses (not without inhabitants unknown to us) looking on.   Here are the venerable
walls and streets of Liegnitz; and the Castle which defied
Baty Khan and his Tartars, five hundred years ago.[2] — Oh,
your Majesty, this Liegnitz, with its princely Castle, and wide
rich Territory, the bulk of the Silesian Lowland, whose is it
if right were done?   Hm, his Majesty knows full well; in
Seckendorf's presence, and going on such an errand, we must
not speak of certain things.   But the undisputed truth is,
Duke Friedrich II., come of the Sovereign Piasts, made that
Erbverbrüderung, and his Grandson's Grandson died childless:
so the heirship fell to *us*, as the biggest wig in the most benighted Chancery would have to grant; — only the Kaiser
will not, never would; the Kaiser plants his armed self on
Schlesien, and will hear no pleading.   Jägerndorf too, which
we purchased with our own money — No more of that; it is
too miserable!   Very impossible too, while we have Berg and
Jülich in the wind! —

At Liegnitz, Friedrich Wilhelm " reviews the garrison, cavalry and infantry," before starting; then off for Glatz, some
sixty miles before we can dine.   The goal is towards Bohemia,
all this while; and his Majesty, had he liked the mountain-
passes, and unlevel ways of the Giant Mountains, might have

---

[1] "Balkowitz," say Pöllnitz (ii. 407) and Förster; which is not the correct
name.

[2] 1241, the Invasion, and Battle here, of this unexpected Barbarian.

found a shorter road and a much more picturesque one. Road abounding in gloomy valleys, intricate rock-labyrinths, haunts of Sprite *Rübezahl,* sources of the Elbe and I know not what. Majesty likes level roads, and interesting rock-labyrinths built by man rather than by Nature. Majesty makes a wide sweep round to the east of all that; leaves the Giant Mountains, and their intricacies, as a blue Sierra far on his right, — had rather see Glatz Fortress than the caverns of the Elbe; and will cross into Bohemia, where the Hills are fallen lowest. At Glatz during dinner, numerous Nobilities are again in waiting. Glatz is in Jägerndorf region; Jägerndorf, which we purchased with our own money, is and remains ours, in spite of the mishaps of the Thirty-Years War; — *ours,* the darkest Chancery would be obliged to say, from under the immensest wig! Patience, your Majesty; Time brings roses! —

From Glatz, after viewing the works, drilling the guard a little, not to speak of dining, and despatching the Nobilities, his Majesty takes the road again; turns now abruptly westward, across the Hills at their lowest point; into Bohemia, which is close at hand. Lewin, Nachod, these are the Bohemian villages, with their remnant of Czechs; not a prosperous population to look upon: but it is the Kaiser's own Kingdom: "King of Bohemia" one of his Titles ever since Sigismund *Super-Grammaticam's* time. And here now, at the meeting of the waters (*Elbe* one of them, a brawling mountain-stream) is Jaromierz, respectable little Town, with an Imperial Officiality in it, — where the Official Gentlemen meet us all in gala, "Thrice welcome to this Kingdom, your Majesty!" — and signify that they are to wait upon us henceforth, while we do the Kaiser's Kingdom of Bohemia that honor.

It is Tuesday night, 29th July, this first night in Bohemia. The Official Gentlemen lead his Majesty to superb rooms, new-hung with crimson velvet, and the due gold fringes and tresses, — very grand indeed; but probably not so airy as we wish. "This is the way the Kaiser lodges in his journeys; and your Majesty is to be served like him." The goal of our journey is now within few miles. Wednesday, 30th July, 1732, his Majesty awakens again, within these crimson-velvet hangings with the gold tresses and fringes, not so airy as he could wish; despatches Grumkow to the Kaiser, who is not many miles off, to signify what honor we would do ourselves.

It was on Saturday last that the Kaiser and Kaiserinn, returning from Karlsbad, illuminated Prag with their serene presence; "attended high-mass, vespers," and a good deal of other worship, as the meagre old Newspapers report for us, on that and the Sunday following. And then, "on Monday, at six in the morning," both the Majesties left Prag, for a place called Chlumetz, southwestward thirty miles off, in the Elbe region, where they have a pretty Hunting Castle; Kaiser intending "sylvan sport for a few days," says the old rag of a Newspaper, "and then to return to Prag." It is here that Grumkow, after a pleasant morning's drive of thirty miles with the sun on his back, finds Kaiser Karl VI.; and makes his announcements, and diplomatic inquiries what next.

Had Friedrich Wilhelm been in Potsdam or Wusterhausen, and heard that Kaiser Karl was within thirty miles of him, Friedrich Wilhelm would have cried, with open arms, Come, come! But the Imperial Majesty is otherwise hampered; has his rhadamanthine Aulic Councillors, in vast amplitude of wig, sternly engaged in study of the etiquettes: they have settled that the meeting cannot be in Chlumetz; lest it might lead to night's lodgings, and to intricacies. "Let it be at Kladrup," say the Ample-wigged; Kladrup, an Imperial Stud, or Horse-Farm, half a dozen miles from this; where there is room for nothing more than dinner. There let the meeting be, to-morrow at a set hour; and, in the mean time, we will take precautions for the etiquettes. So it is settled, and Grumkow returns with the decision in a complimentary form.

Through Königsgrätz, down the right bank of the Upper Elbe, on the morrow morning, Thursday, 31st July, 1732, Friedrich Wilhelm rushes on towards Kladrup; finds that little village, with the Horse-edifices, looking snug enough in the valley of Elbe;—alights, welcomed by Prince Eugenio von Savoye, with word that the Kaiser is not come, but steadily expected soon. Prince Eugenio von Savoye: *Ach Gott,* it is another thing, your Highness, than when we met in the Flanders Wars, long since ; — at Malplaquet that morning, when your Highness had been to Brussels, visiting your Lady Mother in case of the worst! Slightly grayer your Highness is grown; I too am nothing like so nimble ; the great Duke, poor man, is dead! — Prince Eugenio von Savoye, we need not doubt, took snuff, and answered in a sprightly appropriate manner.

Kladrup is a Country House as well as a Horse-Farm : a square court is the interior, as I gather ; the Horse-buildings at a reverent distance forming the fourth side. In the centre of this court, — see what a contrivance the Aulic Councillors have hit upon, — there is a wooden stand built, with three staircases leading up to it, one for each person, and three galleries leading off from it into suites of rooms : no question of precedence here, where each of you has his own staircase and own gallery to his apartment! Friedrich Wilhelm looks down like a rhinoceros on all those cobwebberies. No sooner are the Kaiser's carriage-wheels heard within the court, than Friedrich Wilhelm rushes down, by what staircase is readiest ; forward to the very carriage-door ; and flings his arms about the Kaiser, embracing and embraced, like mere human friends glad to see one another. On these terms, they mount the wooden stand, Majesty of Prussia, Kaiser, Kaiserinn, each by his own staircase ; see, for a space of two hours, the Kaiser's foals and horses led about, — which at least fills up any gap in conversation that may threaten to occur. The Kaiser, a little man of high and humane air, is not bright in talk ; the Empress, a Brunswick Princess of fine carriage, Grand-daughter of old Anton Ulrich who wrote the Novels, is likewise of mute humor in public life ; but old Nord-Teutschland, cradle of one's existence ; Brunswick reminiscences ; news of your Imperial Majesty's serene Father, serene Sister, Brother-in-law the Feldmarschall, and Insipid Niece whom we have had the satisfaction to betroth lately, — furnish small-talk where needful.

Dinner being near, you go by your own gallery to dress. From the drawing-room, Friedrich Wilhelm leads out the

Kaiserinn; the Kaiser, as Head of the world, walks first,
though without any lady. How they drank the healths, gave
and received the ewers and towels, is written duly in the old
Books, but was as indifferent to Friedrich Wilhelm as it is to
us; what their conversation was, let no man presume to ask.
Dullish, we should apprehend, — and perhaps *better* lost to us?
But where there are tongues, there are topics: the Loom of
Time wags always, and with it the tongues of men. Kaiser
and Kaiserinn have both been in Karlsbad lately; Kaiser and
Kaiserinn both have sailed to Spain, in old days, and been in
sieges and things memorable: Friedrich Wilhelm, solid Squire
Western of the North, does not want for topics, and talks as
a solid rustic gentleman will. Native politeness he knows on
occasion; to etiquette, so far as concerns his own pretensions,
he feels callous altogether, — dimly sensible that the Eighteenth Century is setting in, and that solid musketeers and
not goldsticks are now the important thing. "I felt mad to
see him so humiliate himself," said Grumkow afterwards to
Wilhelmina, "*j'enrageais dans ma peau:* " why not ?

Dinner lasted two hours; the Empress rising, Friedrich
Wilhelm leads her to her room; then retires to his own, and
"in a quarter of an hour" is visited there by the Kaiser;
"who conducts him," in so many minutes exact by the watch,
"back to the Empress," — for a sip of coffee, as one hopes;
which may wind up the Interview well. The sun is still a
good space from setting, when Friedrich Wilhelm, after cordial
adieus, neglectful of etiquette, is rolling rapidly towards Nimburg, thirty miles off on the Prag Highway; and Kaiser Karl
with his Spouse move deliberately towards Chlumetz to hunt
again. In Nimburg Friedrich Wilhelm sleeps, that night; —
Imperial Majesties, in a much-tumbled world, of wild horses,
ceremonial ewers, and Eugenios of Savoy and Malplaquet,
probably peopling his dreams. If it please Heaven, there
may be another private meeting, a day or two hence.

Nimburg, ah your Majesty, Son Fritz will have a night in
Nimburg too; — riding slowly thither amid the wrecks of Kolin
Battle, not to sleep well; — but that happily is hidden from
your Majesty. Kolin, Czaslau (Chotusitz), Elbe Teinitz, —

here in this Kladrup region, your Majesty is driving amid
poor Villages which will be very famous by and by. And
Prag itself will be doubly famed in war, if your Majesty knew
it, and the Ziscaberg be of bloodier memory than the Weissenberg itself! — His Majesty, the morrow's sun having risen
upon Nimburg, rolls into Prag successfully about eleven A.M.,
Hill of Zisca not disturbing him; goes to the Klein-Seite
Quarter, where an Aulic Councillor with fine Palace is ready;
all the cannon thundering from the walls at his Majesty's
advent; and Prince Eugenio, the ever-present, being there to
receive his Majesty, — and in fact to invite him to dinner this
day at half-past twelve. It is Friday, 1st of August, 1732.

By a singular chance, there is preserved for us in Fassmann's
Book, what we may call an Excerpt from the old *Morning Post*
of Prag, bringing that extinct Day into clear light again; recalling the vanished Dinner-Party from the realms of Hades, as
a thing that once actually *was*. The List of the Dinner-guests
is given complete; vanished ghosts, whom, in studying the
old History-Books, you can, with a kind of interest, fish up
into visibility at will. There is Prince Eugenio von Savoye
at the bottom of the table, in the Count-Thun Palace where
he lodges; there bodily, the little man, in gold-laced coat of
unknown cut; the eyes and the temper bright and rapid,
as usual, or more; nose not unprovided with snuff, and lips
in consequence rather open. Be seated, your Majesty, high
gentlemen all.

A big chair-of-state stands for his Majesty at the upper end
of the table : his Majesty will none of it; sits down close by
Prince Eugene at the very bottom, and opposite Prince Alexander of Würtemberg, whom we had at Berlin lately, a General
of note in the Turkish and other wars : here probably there
will be better talk; and the big chair may preside over us in
vacancy. Which it does. Prince Alexander, Imperial General
against the Turks, and Heir-Apparent of Würtemberg withal,
can speak of many things, — hardly much of his serene Cousin
the reigning Duke; whose health is in a too interesting state,
the good though unlucky man. Of the Grävenitz sitting now
in limbo, or travelling about disowned, *toujours un lavement à*

ses trousses, let there be deep silence. But the Prince Alexander can answer abundantly on other heads. He comes to his inheritance a few months hence; actual reigning Duke, the poor serene Cousin having died: and perhaps we shall meet him transiently again.

He is Ancestor of the Czars of Russia, this Prince Alexander, who is now dining here in the body, along with Friedrich Wilhelm and Prince Eugene: Paul of Russia, unbeautiful Paul, married the second time, from Mümpelgard (what the French call Montbeillard, in Alsace), a serene Grand-daughter of his, from whom come the Czars, — thanks to her or not. Prince Alexander is Ancestor withal of our present "Kings of Würtemberg," if that mean anything: Father (what will mean something) to the serene Duke, still in swaddling-clothes,[1] who will be son-in-law to Princess Wilhelmina of Baireuth (could your Majesty foresee it); and will do strange pranks in the world, upon poet Schiller and others. Him too, and Brothers of his, were they born and become of size, we shall meet. A noticeable man, and not without sense, this Prince Alexander; who is now of a surety eating with us, — as we find by the extinct *Morning Post* in Fassmann's old Book.

Of the others eating figures, Stahrembergs, Sternbergs, Kinsky Ambassador to England, Kinsky Ambassador to France, high Austrian dignitaries, we shall say nothing; — who would listen to us? Hardly can the Hof-Kanzler Count von Sinzendorf, supreme of Aulic men, who holds the rudder of Austrian State-Policy, and probably feels himself loaded with importance beyond most mortals now eating here or elsewhere, — gain the smallest recognition from oblivious English readers of our time. It is certain he eats here on this occasion; and to his Majesty he does not want for importance. His Majesty, intent on Jülich and Berg and other high matters, spends many hours next day, in earnest private dialogue with him. We mention farther, with satisfaction, that Grumkow and Ordnance-Master Seckendorf are both on the list, and all our Prussian party, down to Hacke of the Potsdam grenadiers, friend

---

[1] Born 21st January, 1732; Karl Eugen the name of him (Michaelis, iii. 450).

Schulenburg visibly eating among the others. Also that the
dinner was glorious (*herrlich*), and ended about five.[1] After
which his Majesty went to two evening parties, of a high order,
in the Hradschin Quarter or elsewhere; cards in the one (unless you liked to dance, or grin idle talk from you), and supper
in the other.

His Majesty amused himself for four other days in Prag,
interspersing long earnest dialogues with Sinzendorf, with
whom he spent the greater part of Saturday,[2] — results as to
Jülich and Berg of a rather cloudy nature. On Saturday came
the Kaiser, too, and Kaiserinn, to their high House, the Schloss
in Prag; and there occurred, in the incognito form, "as if by
accident," three visits or counter-visits, two of them of some
length. The King went dashing about; saw, deliberately or
in glimpses, all manner of things, — from "the Military Hospital" to "the Tongue of St. Nepomuk" again. Nepomuk,
an imaginary Saint of those parts; pitched into the Moldau,
as is fancied and fabled, by wicked King Wenzel (King and
Deposed-Kaiser, whom we have heard of), for speaking and
refusing to speak; Nepomuk is now become the Patron of
Bridges, in consequence; stands there in bronze on the Bridge
of Prag; and still shows a dried Tongue in the world:[3] this
latter, we expressly find, his Majesty saw.

On Sunday, his Majesty, nothing of a strait-laced man,
attended divine or quasi-divine worship in the Cathedral
Church, — where high Prince Bishops delivered *palliums*, did
histrionisms; "manifested the *Absurdität* of Papistry" more
or less. Coming out of the Church, he was induced to step in
and see the rooms of the Schloss, or Imperial Palace. In one
of the rooms, as if by accident, the Kaiser was found lounging: — "Extremely delighted to see your Majesty!" — and
they had the first of their long or considerable dialogues together; purport has not transpired. The second considerable
dialogue was on the morrow, when Imperial Majesty, as if by

[1] Fassmann, p. 474.   [2] Pöllnitz, ii. 411.
[3] *Die Legende vom heiligen Johann von Nepomuk*, von D. Otto Abel (Berlin
1855); an acute bit of Historical Criticism.

accident, found himself in the Count-Nostitz Palace, where
Friedrich Wilhelm lodges. Delighted to be so fortunate again!
Hope your Majesty likes Prag? Eternal friendship, *Oh ja:* —
and as to Jülich and Berg? Particulars have not transpired.

Prag is a place full of sights: his Majesty, dashing about in
all quarters, has a busy time; affairs of state (Jülich and Berg
principally) alternating with what we now call the *lions.*
Zisca's drum, for instance, in the Arsenal here? Would your
Majesty wish to see Zisca's own skin, which he bequeathed to
be a drum when *he* had done with it? "*Narrenpossen!*" — for
indeed the thing is fabulous, though in character with Zisca.
Or the Council-Chamber window, out of which "the Three
Prag Projectiles fell into the Night of things," as a modern
Historian expresses it? Three Official Gentlemen, flung out
one morning,[1] 70 feet, but fell on "sewerage," and did not die,
but set the whole world on fire? That is too certain, as his
Majesty knows: that brought the crowning of the Winter-
King, Battle of the Weissenberg, Thirty-Years War; and lost
us Jägerndorf and much else.

Or Wallenstein's Palace, — did your Majesty look at that?
A thing worth glancing at, on the score of History and even
of Natural-History. That rugged son of steel and gunpowder
could not endure the least noise in his sleeping-room or even
sitting-room, — a difficulty in the soldiering way of life; — and
had, if I remember, one hundred and thirty houses torn away
in Prag, and sentries posted all round in the distance, to secure
silence for his much-meditating indignant soul. And yonder
is the Weissenberg, conspicuous in the western suburban region: and here in the eastern, close by, is the Ziscaberg; —
O Heaven, your Majesty, on this Zisca-Hill will be a new "Battle of Prag," which will throw the Weissenberg into eclipse;
and there is awful fighting coming on in these parts again!

The *third* of the considerable dialogues in Prag was on this
same Monday night; when his Majesty went to wait upon the
Kaiserinn, and the Kaiser soon accidentally joined them.
Precious gracious words passed; — on Berg and Jülich nothing particular, that we hear; — and the High Personages, with

[1] 13th (23d) May, 1618 (Köhler, p. 507).

assurances of everlasting friendship, said adieu; and met no more in this world. On his toilet-table Friedrich Wilhelm found a gold Tobacco-box, sent by the highest Lady extant; gold Tobacco-box, item gold Tobacco-stopper or Pipe-picker: such the parting gifts of her Imperial Majesty. Very precious indeed, and grateful to the honest heart; — yet testifying too (as was afterwards suggested to the royal mind) what these high people think of a rustic Orson King; and how they fling their nose into the air over his Tabagies and him.

On the morrow morning early, Friedrich Wilhelm rolls away again homewards, by Karlsbad, by Baireuth; all the cannon of Prag saying thrice, Good speed to him. "He has had a glorious time," said the Berlin Court-lady to Queen Sophie one evening, "no end of kindness from the Imperial Majesties: but has he brought Berg and Jülich in his pocket?" — Alas, not a fragment of them; nor of any solid thing whatever, except it be the gold Tobacco-box; and the confirmation of our claims on East-Friesland (cheap liberty to let us vindicate them if we can), if you reckon that a solid thing. These two Imperial gifts, such as they are, he has consciously brought back with him; — and perhaps, though as yet unconsciously, a third gift of much more value, once it is developed into clearness: some dim trace of insight into the no-meaning of these high people; and how they consider *us* as mere Orsons and wild Bisons, whom they will do the honor to consume as provision, if we behave well!

The great King Friedrich, now Crown-Prince at Ruppin, writing of this Journey long afterwards, — hastily, incorrectly, as his wont is, in regard to all manner of minute outward particulars; and somewhat maltreating, or at least misplacing, even the inward meaning, which was well known to him *without* investigation, but which he is at no trouble to *date* for himself, and has dated at random, — says, in his thin rapid way, with much polished bitterness: —

"His [King Friedrich Wilhelm's] experience on this occasion served to prove that good-faith and the virtues, so contrary to the corruption of the age, do not succeed in it. Politicians have banished sincerity (*la candeur*) into private life: they

look upon themselves as raised quite above the laws which
they enjoin on other people; and give way without reserve
to the dictates of their own depraved mind.

" The guaranty of Jülich and Berg, which Seckendorf had
formally promised in the name of the Emperor, went off in
smoke; and the Imperial Ministers were in a disposition so
opposed to Prussia, the King saw clearly [not for some years
yet] that if there was a Court in Europe intending to cross
his interests, it was certainly that of Vienna.   This Visit of his
to the Emperor was like that of Solon to Crœsus [Solon not
recognizable, in the grenadier costume, amid the tobacco-smoke,
and dim accompaniments ?] — and he returned to Berlin, rich
still in his own virtue.   The most punctilious censors could
find no fault in his conduct, except a probity carried to excess.
The Interview ended as those of Kings often do : it cooled
[not for some time yet], or, to say better, it extinguished the
friendship there had been between the two Courts.   Friedrich
Wilhelm left Prag full of contempt [dimly, altogether unconsciously, *tending* to have some contempt, and in the end to be
full of it] for the deceitfulness and pride of the Imperial
Court : and the Emperor's Ministers disdained a Sovereign who
looked without interest on frivolous ceremonials and prece-
dences.   Him they considered too ambitious in aiming at the
Berg-and-Jülich succession : them he regarded [came to re-
gard] as a pack of knaves, who had broken their word, and
were not punished for it."

Very bitter, your Majesty; and, in all but the dates, true
enough.   But what a drop of concentrated absinthe follows
next, by way of finish, — which might itself have corrected the
dating !

"In spite of so many subjects of discontent, the King
wedded his Eldest Son [my not too fortunate self], out of
complaisance to the Vienna Court, with a Princess of Brunswick-Bevern, Niece to the Empress :" — bitter fact; necessitat-
ing change of date in the paragraphs just written.[1]

Friedrich Wilhelm, good soul, cherishes the Imperial gifts,
Tobacco-box included; — claps the Arms of East-Friesland on

[1] *Œuvres de Frédéric* (*Mémoires de Brandebourg*), i. 162, 163.

his escutcheon; will take possession of Friesland, if the present Duke die heirless, let George of England say what he will. And so he rolls homeward, by way of Baireuth. He stayed but a short while in Karlsbad; has warned his Wilhelmina that he will be at Baireuth on the 9th of the month.[1]

Wilhelmina is very poorly; "near her time," as wives say; rusticating in "the Hermitage," a Country-House in the vicinity of Baireuth; Husband and Father-in-law gone away, towards the Bohemian frontier, to hunt boars. Oh, the bustle and the bother that high Lady had; getting her little Country-House stretched out to the due pitch to accommodate everybody, — especially her foolish Sister of Anspach and foolish Brother-in-law and suite, — with whom, by negligence of servants and otherwise, there had like to have risen incurable quarrel on the matter. But the dexterous young Wife, gladdest, busiest and weakliest of hopeful creatures, contrived to manage everything, like a Female Fieldmarshal, as she was. Papa was delighted; bullied the foolish Anspach people, — or would have done so, had not I intervened, that the matter might die. Papa was gracious, happy; very anxious about me in my interesting state. "Thou hast lodged me to perfection, good Wilhelmina. Here I find my wooden stools, tubs to wash in; all things as if I were at Potsdam : — a good girl; and thou must take care of thyself, my child (mein Kind)."

At dinner, his Majesty, dreading no ill, but intent only on the practical, got into a quiet, but to me most dreadful, lecture to the old Margraf (my Father-in-law) upon debt and money and arrears : How he, the Margraf, was cheated at every turn, and led about by the nose, and kept weltering in debt : how he should let the young Margraf go into the Offices, to supervise, and withal to learn tax-matters and economics betimes. How he (Friedrich Wilhelm) would send him a fellow from Berlin who understood such things, and would drill his scoundrels for him ! To which the old Margraf, somewhat flushed in the face, made some embarrassed assent, knowing it in fact to be true; and accepted the Berlin man : — but he made me

---

[1] Wilhelmina, ii. 55.

(his poor Daughter-in-law) smart for it afterwards : "Not quite dead *yet*, Madam ; you will have to wait a little ! " — and other foolish speech ; which required to be tempered down again by a judicious female mind.

Grumkow himself was pleasant on this occasion ; told us of Kladrup, the Prag etiquettes ; and how he was like to go mad seeing his Majesty so humiliate himself. Fräulein Grumkow, a niece of his, belonging to the Austrian court, who is over here with the rest, a satirical intriguing baggage, she, I privately perceive, has made a conquest of my foolish Brother-in-law, the Anspach Margraf here ; — and there will be jealousies, and a cat-and-dog life over yonder, worse than ever ! Tush, why should we talk ? — These are the phenomena at Baireuth ; Husband and Father-in-law having quitted their boar-hunt and hurried home.

After three days, Friedrich Wilhelm rolled away again ; lodged, once more, at Meuselwitz, with abstruse Seckendorf, and his good old Wife, who do the hospitalities well when they must, in spite of the single candle once visible. On the morrow after which, 14th August, 1732, his Majesty is off again, "at four in the morning," towards Leipzig, intending to be home that night, though it is a long drive. At Leipzig, not to waste time, he declines entering the Town ; positively will not, though the cannon-salvos are booming all round ; — "breakfasts in the suburbs, with a certain Horse-dealer (*Ross-Händler*) now deceased : " a respectable Centaur, capable, no doubt, of bargaining a little about cavalry mountings, while one eats, with appetite and at one's ease. Which done, Majesty darts off again, the cannon-salvos booming out a second time ; — and by assiduous driving gets home to Potsdam about eight at night. And so has happily *ended* this Journey to Kladrup.[1]

[1] Fassmann, pp. 474–479 ; Wilhelmina, ii. 46–55 ; Pöllnitz, ii. 407–412 ; Förster, i. 328–334.

CHAPTER V.

GHOST OF THE DOUBLE-MARRIAGE RISES; TO NO PURPOSE.

WE little expected to see the "Double-Marriage" start up
into vitality again, at this advanced stage; or, of all men,
Seckendorf, after riding 25,000 miles to kill the Double-Marriage, engaged in resuscitating it! But so it is: by endless
intriguing, matchless in History or Romance, the Austrian
Court had, at such expense to the parties and to itself, achieved
the first problem of stifling the harmless Double-Marriage;
and now, the wind having changed, it is actually trying its
hand the opposite way.

Wind is changed: consummate Robinson has managed to do
his thrice-salutary "Treaty of Vienna;" [1] to clout up all differences between the Sea-Powers and the Kaiser, and restore the
old Law of Nature, — Kaiser to fight the French, Sea-Powers
to feed and pay him while engaged in that necessary job. And
now it would be gratifying to the Kaiser, if there remained,
on this side of the matter, no rent anywhere, if between his
chief Sea ally and his chief Land one, the Britannic Majesty
and the Prussian, there prevailed a complete understanding,
with no grudge left.

The honor of this fine resuscitation project is ascribed to
Robinson by the Vienna people: "Robinson's suggestion,"
they always say: how far it was, or whether at all it was or
not, nobody at present knows. Guess rather, if necessary, it
had been the Kaiser's own! Robinson, as the thing proceeds,
is instructed from St. James's to "look on and not interfere;" [2]
Prince Eugene, too, we can observe, is privately against it,
though officially urgent, and doing his best. Who knows, —
or need know?

---

[1] 16th March, 1731, the *tail* of it (accession of the Dutch, of Spain, &c.)
not quite coiled up till 20th February, 1732: Schöll, i. 218–222.

[2] Despatches, in State-Paper Office.

Enough that High Heads are set upon it ; that the diplomatic wigs are all wagging with it, from about the beginning of October, 1732 ; and rumors are rife and eager, occasionally spurting out into the Newspapers : Double-Marriage after all, hint the old Rumors : Double-Marriage somehow or other ; Crown-Prince to have his English Princess, Prince Fred of England to console the Brunswick one for loss of her Crown-Prince ; or else Prince Karl of Brunswick to — And half a dozen other ways ; which Rumor cannot settle to its satisfaction. The whispers upon it, from Hanover, from Vienna, at Berlin, and from the Diplomatic world in general, occasionally whistling through the Newspapers, are manifold and incessant, — not worthy of the least attention from us here.[1] What is certain is, Seckendorf, in the end of October, is corresponding on it with Prince Eugene ; has got instructions to propose the matter in Tobacco-Parliament ; and does not like it at all. Grumkow, who perhaps has seen dangerous clouds threatening to mount upon him, and never been quite himself again in the Royal Mind since that questionable *Nosti* business, dissuades earnestly, constantly. "Nothing but mischief will come of such a proposal," says Grumkow steadily ; and for his own share absolutely declines concern in it.

But Prince Eugene's orders are express ; remonstrances, cunctations only strengthen the determination of the High Heads or Head : Forward with this beautiful scheme ! Seckendorf, puckered into dangerous anxieties, but summoning all his cunning, has at length, after six weeks' hesitation, to open it, as if casually, in some favorable hour, to his Prussian Majesty. December 5th, 1732, as we compute ; — a kind of epoch in his Majesty's life. Prussian Majesty stares wide-eyed ; the breath as if struck out of him ; repeats, " Jülich and Berg absolutely secured, say you ? But — hm, na ! " — and has not yet taken in the unspeakable dimensions of the occurrence. " What ? Imperial Majesty will make me break my word before all the world ? Imperial Majesty has been whirling me about, face now to the east, face straightway round to the west : Imperial Majesty does not feel that I am a man and

[1] Förster, iii. 111, 120, 108, 113, 122.

king at all; takes me for a mere machine, to be seesawed and whirled hither and thither, like a rotatory Clothes-horse, to dry his Imperial Majesty's linen upon. *Tausend Himmel — !*"

The full dimensions of all this did not rise clear upon the intellect of Prussian Majesty, — a slow intellect, but a true and deep, with terrible earthquakes and poetic fires lying under it, — not at once, or for months, perhaps years to come. But they had begun to dawn upon him painfully here; they rose gradually into perfect clearness : all things seen at last as what they were; — with huge submarine earthquake for consequence, and total change of mind towards Imperial Majesty and the drying of his Pragmatic linen, in Friedrich Wilhelm. Amiable Orson, true to the heart; amiable, though terrible when too much put upon!

This dawning process went on for above two years to come, painfully, reluctantly, with explosions, even with tears. But here, directly on the back of Seckendorf's proposal, and recorded from a sure hand, is what we may call the peep-of-day in that matter : First Session of Tobacco-Parliament, close after that event. Event is on the 5th December, 1732; Tobacco Session is of the 6th; — glimpse of it is given by Speaker Grumkow himself; authentic to the bone.

Session of Tobacco-Parliament, 6th December, 1732.

Grumkow, shattered into "headache" by this Session, writes Report of it to Seckendorf before going to bed. Look, reader, into one of the strangest Political Establishments; and how a strange Majesty comports himself there, directly after such proposal from Vienna to marry with England still ! — "Schwerin" is incidentally in from Frankfurt-on-Oder, where his Regiment and business usually lie : the other Honorable Members we sufficiently know. Majesty has been a little out of health lately; perceptibly worse the last two days. "Syberg" is a Gold-cook (Alchemical gentleman, of very high professions), came to Berlin some time ago; whom his Majesty, after due investigation, took the liberty to hang.[1] Readers can now

[1] Förster, iii. 126.

understand what speaker Grumkow writes, and despatches by
his lackey, in such haste: —

"I never saw such a scene as this evening.   Derschau,
Schwerin, Buddenbrock, Rochow, Flanz were present.   We had
been about an hour in the Red Room [languidly doing our tobacco off and on], when he [the King] had us shifted into the
Little Room : drove out the servants ; and cried, looking fixedly
at me : 'No, I cannot endure it any longer!   *Es stosset mir das
Herz ab,*' cried he, breaking into German : ' It crushes the heart
out of me ; to make me do a bit of scoundrelism, me, me !   No,
I say ; no, never !   Those damned intrigues ; may the Devil
take them !' —

"*Ego* (Grumkow).   'Of course, I know of nothing.   But I
do not comprehend your Majesty's inquietude, coming thus on
the sudden, after our common indifferent mood.'

"*King*. 'What, make me a villain !   I will tell it right out.
Certain damned scoundrels have been about betraying me.
People that should have known me better have been trying to
lead me into a dishonorable scrape ' — (" Here I called in the
hounds, *Je rompis les chiens*," reports Grumkow, " for he was
going to blab everything; I interrupted, saying) : —

"*Ego*. 'But, your Majesty, what is it ruffles you so ?   I
know not what you talk of.   Your Majesty has honorable
people about you ;· and the man who lets himself be employed
in things against your Majesty must be a traitor.'

"*King*. 'Yes, *ja, ja.*   I will do things that will surprise
them.   I —'

" And, in short, a torrent of exclamations : which I strove to
soften by all manner of incidents and contrivances ; succeeding
at last," — by dexterity and time (but, at this point, the light is
now blown out, and we *see* no more) : — " so that he grew quite
calm again, and the rest of the evening passed gently enough.

" Well, you see what the effect of your fine Proposal is,
which you said he would like !   I can tell you, it is the most
detestable incident that could have turned up.   I know, you
had your orders : but you may believe and depend on it, he
has got his heart driven rabid by the business, and says, ' Who

knows now whether that villain Syberg' Gold-cook, that was hanged the other day, 'was not set on by some people to poison me?' In a word, he was like a madman.

"What struck me most was when he repeated, 'Only think! Think! Who would have expected it of people that should have known me; and whom I know, and have known, better than they fancy!'"—Pleasant passage for Seckendorf to chew the cud upon, through the night-watches!

"In fine, as I was somewhat confused; and anxious, above all, to keep him from exploding with the secret, I cannot remember everything. But Derschau, who was more at his ease, will be able to give you a full account. He [the King] said more than once: '*This* was his sickness; the thing that ailed him, this: it gnawed his heart, and would be the death of him!' He certainly did not affect; he was in a very convulsive condition. [*Jarni-bleu*, here is a piece of work, Herr Seckendorf!]—Adieu, I have a headache." Whereupon to bed.

"GRUMKOW." [1]

This Hansard Report went off direct to Prince Eugene; and ought to have been a warning to the high Vienna heads and him. But they persisted not the less to please Robinson or themselves; considering his Prussian Majesty to be, in fact, a mere rotatory Clothes-horse for drying the Imperial linen on; and to have no intellect at all, because he was without guile, and had no vulpinism at all. In which they were very much mistaken indeed. History is proud to report that the guileless Prussian Majesty, steadily attending to his own affairs in a wise manner, though hoodwinked and led about by Black-Artists as he had been, turned out when Fact and Nature subsequently pronounced upon it, to have had more intellect than the whole of them together,—to have been, in a manner, the only one of them that had any real "intellect," or insight into Fact and Nature, at all. Consummate Black-art Diplomacies overnetting the Universe, went entirely to water, running down the gutters to the last drop; and a prosperous Drilled Prussia, compact, organic in every

[1] Förster, iii. 135, 136.

part, from diligent plough-sock to shining bayonet and iron
ramrod, remained standing. "A full Treasury and 200,000
well-drilled men would be the one guarantee to your Pragmatic
Sanction," Prince Eugene had said. But that bit of insight
was not accepted at Vienna; Black-art, and Diplomatic spider-
webs from pole to pole, being thought the preferable method.

Enough, Seckendorf was ordered to manipulate and soothe
down the Prussian Majesty, as surely would be easy; to continue his galvanic operations on the Double-Match, or produce
a rotation in the purposes of the royal breast. Which he
diligently strove to do, when once admitted to speech again;
— Grumkow steadily declining to meddle, and only Queen
Sophie, as we can fancy, auguring joyfully of it. Seckendorf,
admitted to speech the third day after that explosive Session,
snuffles his softest, his cunningest; — continues to ride diligently, the concluding portion (such it proved) of his 25,000
miles with the Prussian Majesty up and down through winter
and spring; but makes not the least progress, the reverse
rather.

Their dialogues and arguings on the matter, here and
elsewhere, are lost in air; or gone wholly to a single point
unexpectedly preserved for us. One day, riding through some
village, Priort some say his Majesty calls it, some give another
name, — advocate Seckendorf, in the fervor of pleading and
arguing, said some word, which went like a sudden flash of
lightning through the dark places of his Majesty's mind, and
never would go out of it again while he lived after. In
passionate moments, his Majesty spoke of it sometimes, a
clangorous pathos in his tones, as of a thing hideous, horrible,
never to be forgotten, which had killed him, — death from
a friend's hand. "It was the 17th of April, 1733,[1] riding
through Priort, a man said something to me: it was as if
you had turned a dagger about in my heart. That man was
he that killed me; there and then I got my death!"

---

[1] All the Books (Förster, ii. 142, for one) mention this utterance of his
Majesty, on what occasion we shall see farther on; and give the date "1732,"
not 1733: but except as amended above, it refuses to have any sense visible
at this distance. The Village of Priort is in the Potsdam region.

A strange passion in that utterance: the deep dumb soul
of his Majesty, of dumb-poetic nature, suddenly brought to
a fatal clearness about certain things. "O Kaiser, Kaiser
of the Holy Roman Empire; and this is your return for my
loyal faith in you? I had nearly killed my Fritz, my Wilhelmina, broken my Feekin's heart and my own, and reduced
the world to ruins for your sake. And because I was of
faith more than human, you took me for a dog? O Kaiser,
Kaiser!"—Poor Friedrich Wilhelm, he spoke of this often,
in excited moments, in his later years; the tears running
down his cheeks, and the whole man melted into tragic
emotion: but if Fritz were there, the precious Fritz whom he
had almost killed for their sake, he would say, flashing out
into proud rage, "There is one that will avenge me, though;
that one! *Da steht Einer, der mich rächen wird!*"[1] Yes, your
Majesty; perhaps that one. And it will be seen whether *you*
were a rotatory Clothes-horse to dry their Pragmatic linen
upon, or something different a good deal.

CHAPTER VI.

KING AUGUST MEDITATING GREAT THINGS FOR POLAND.

IN the New-year's days of 1733, the topic among diplomatic
gentlemen, which set many big wigs wagging, and even tremulously came out in the gray leaves of gazetteers and garreteers
of the period, was a royal drama, dimly supposed to be getting itself up in Poland at this time. Nothing known about
it for certain; much guessed. "Something in the rumor!"
nods this wig; "Nothing!" wags that, slightly oscillating;
and gazetteers, who would earn their wages, and have a peck
of coals apiece to glad them in the cold weather, had to
watch with all eagerness the movements of King August, our
poor old friend, the Dilapidated-Strong, who is in Saxony at

[1] Förster, ii. 153.

present; but bound for Warsaw shortly, — just about lifting the curtain on important events, it is thought and not thought. Here are the certainties of it, now clear enough, so far as they deserve a glance from us.

January 10th, 1733, August the Dilapidated-Strong of Poland has been in Saxony, looking after his poor Electorate a little; and is on the road from Dresden homewards again; — will cross a corner of the Prussian Dominions, as his wont is on such occasions. Prussian Majesty, if not appearing in person, will as usual, by some Official of rank, send a polite Well-speed-you as the brother Majesty passes. This time, however, it was more than politeness; the Polish Majesty having, as was thought, such intricate affairs in the wind. Let Grumkow, the fittest man in all ways, go, and do the greeting to his old Patroon: greeting, or whatever else may be needed.

Patroon left Dresden, — "having just opened the Carnival" or fashionable Season there, opened and nothing more, — January 10th, 1733; [1] being in haste home for a Polish Diet close at hand. On which same day Grumkow, we suppose, drives forth from Berlin, to intersect him, in the Neumark, about Crossen; and have a friendly word again, in those localities, over jolly wine. Intersection took place duly; — there was exuberant joy on the part of the Patroon; and such a dinner and night of drinking, as has seldom been. Abstruse things lie close ahead of August the Dilapidated-Strong, important to Prussia, and for which Prussia is important; let Grumkow try if he can fish the matter into clearness out of these wine-cups. And then August, on his side, wishes to know what the Kaiser said at Kladrup lately; there is much to be fished into clearness.

Many are the times August the Strong has made this journey; many are the carousals, on such and other occasions, Grumkow and he have had. But there comes an end to all things. This was their last meeting, over flowing liquor or otherwise, in the world. Satirical History says, they drank all night, endeavoring to pump one another, and with such enthusiasm that they never recovered it; drank themselves to

---

[1] Fassmann, *Leben Friedrich Augusti des Grossen*, p. 994.

death at Crossen on that occasion.[1] It is certain August died
within three weeks; and people said of Grumkow, who lived
six years longer, he was never well after this bout. Is it
worth any human creature's while to look into the plans of
this precious pair of individuals? Without the least expense
of drinking, the secrets they were pumping out of each other
are now accessible enough, — if it were of importance now.
One glance I may perhaps commend to the reader, out of these
multifarious Note-books in my possession : —

"August, by change of his religion, and other sad operations, got to be what they called the King of Poland, thirty-
five years ago ; but, though looking glorious to the idle public,
it has been a crown of stinging-nettles to the poor man, — a
sedan-chair running on rapidly, with the bottom broken out!
To say nothing of the scourgings he got, and poor Saxony
along with him, from Charles XII., on account of this Sovereignty so called, what has the thing itself been to him? In
Poland, for these thirty-five years, the individual who had
least of his real will done in public matters has been, with infinite management, and display of such good-humor as at least
deserves credit, the nominal Sovereign Majesty of Poland.
Anarchic Grandees have been kings over him; ambitious, contentious, unmanageable ; — very fanatical too, and never persuaded that August's Apostasy was more than a sham one,
not even when he made his Prince apostatize too. Their
Sovereignty has been a mere peck of troubles, disgraces and
vexations: for those thirty-five years, an ever-boiling pot of
mutiny, contradiction, insolence, hardly tolerable even to such
nerves as August's.

" August, for a long time back, has been thinking of schemes
to clap some lid upon all that. To make the Sovereignty
hereditary in his House: that, with the good Saxon troops
we have, would be a remedy ; — and in fact it is the only
remedy. John Casimir (who abdicated long ago, in the Great
Elector's time, and went to Paris, — much charmed with Ninon
de l'Enclos there) told the Polish Diets, With their *liberum
veto*, and 'right of confederation' and rebellion, they would

[1] *Œuvres de Frédéric (Mémoires de Brandebourg)*, i. 163.

bring the country down under the feet of mankind, and reduce
their Republic to zero one day, if they persisted. They have
not failed to persist. With some hereditary King over it,
and a regulated Saxony to lean upon : truly might it not
be a change to the better ? To the worse, it could hardly be,
thinks August the Strong ; and goes intent upon that method,
this long while back ; — and at length hopes now, in few days
longer, at the Diet just assembling, to see fruits appear, and
the thing actually begin.

"The difficulties truly are many ; internal and external : —
but there are calculated methods, too. For the internal : Get
up, by bribery, persuasion, some visible minority to countenance you ; with these manœuvre in the Diets ; on the back
of these, the 30,000 Saxon troops. But then what will the
neighboring Kings say ? The neighboring Kings, with their
big-mouthed manifestoes, pities for an oppressed Republic,
overwhelming forces, and invitations to 'confederate' and
revolt : without their tolerance first had, nothing can be done.
That is the external difficulty. For which too there is a remedy. Cut off sufficient outlying slices of Poland ; fling these
to the neighboring Kings to produce consent : Partition of
Poland, in fact ; large sections of its Territory sliced away :
that will be the method, thinks King August.

"Neighboring Kings, Kaiser, Prussia, Russia, to them it is
not grievous that Poland should remain in perennial anarchy,
in perennial impotence ; the reverse rather : a dead horse, or
a dying, in the next stall, — he at least will not kick upon us,
think the neighboring Kings. And yet, — under another simil-
itude, — you do not like your next-door neighbor to be always
on the point of catching fire ; smoke issuing, thicker or thin-
ner, through the slates of his roof, as a perennial phenomenon ? August will conciliate the neighboring Kings. Russia,
big-cheeked Anne Czarina there, shall have not only Courland
peaceably henceforth, but the Ukraine, Lithuania, and other
large outlying slices ; that surely will conciliate Russia. To
Austria, on its Hungarian border, let us give the Country of
Zips ; — nay there are other sops we have for Austria. Pragmatic Sanction, hitherto refused as contrary to plain rights of

ours, — that, if conceded to a spectre-hunting Kaiser ?   To
Friedrich Wilhelm we could give West-Preussen ; West-Preussen torn away three hundred years ago, and leaving a hiatus
in the very continuity of Friedrich Wilhelm : would not that
conciliate him ?   Of all enemies or friends, Friedrich Wilhelm,
close at hand with 80,000 men capable of fighting at a week's
notice, is by far the most important.

" These are August's plans : West-Preussen for the nearest
Neighbor ; Zips for Austria ; Ukraine, Lithuania, and appendages for the Russian Czarina : handsome Sections to be sliced
off, and flung to good neighbors ; as it were, all the outlying
limbs and wings of the Polish Territory sliced off ; compact
body to remain, and become, by means of August and Saxon
troops, a Kingdom with government, not an imaginary Republic without government any longer.   In fact, it was the 'Partition of Poland,' such as took effect forty years after, and has
kept the Newspapers weeping ever since.   Partition of Poland, — *minus* the compact interior held under government,
by a King with Saxon troops or otherwise.   Compact interior,
in that effective partition, forty years after, was left as anarchic as ever ; and had to be again partitioned, and cut away
altogether, — with new torrents of loud tears from the Newspapers, refusing to be comforted to this day.

" It is not said that Friedrich Wilhelm had the least intention of countenancing August in these dangerous operations,
still less of going shares with August ; but he wished much,
through Grumkow, to have some glimpse into the dim program of them ; and August wished much to know Friedrich
Wilhelm's and Grumkow's humor towards them.   Grumkow
and August drank copiously, or copiously pressed drink on
one another, all night (11th–12th January, 1733, as I compute ;
some say at Crossen, some say at Frauendorf a royal domain
near by), with the view of mutually fishing out those secrets ;
— and killed one another in the business, as is rumored."

What were Grumkow's news at home-coming, I did not
hear ; but he continues very low and shaky ; — refuses, almost
with horror, to have the least hand in Seckendorf's mad project of resuscitating the English Double-Marriage, and break-

ing off the Brunswick one, at the eleventh hour and after word pledged. Seckendorf himself continues to dislike and dissuade : but the High Heads at Vienna are bent on it; and command new strenuous attempts ; — literally at the last moment ; which is now come.

CHAPTER VII.

CROWN-PRINCE'S MARRIAGE.

SINCE November last, Wilhelmina is on visit at Berlin, — first visit since her marriage ; — she stays there for almost ten months ; not under the happiest auspices, poor child. Mamma's reception of her, just off the long winter journey, and extenuated with fatigues and sickly chagrins, was of the most cutting cruelty : " What do you want here ? What is a mendicant like you come hither for ? " And next night, when Papa himself came home, it was little better. " Ha, ha," said he, " here you are ; I am glad to see you." Then holding up a light, to take view of me : " How changed you are ! " said he : " What is little Frederika [my little Baby at Baireuth] doing ? " And on my answering, continued : " I am sorry for you, on my word. You have not bread to eat ; and but for me you might go begging. I am a poor man myself, not able to give you much ; but I will do what I can. I will give you now and then a twenty or a thirty shillings (*par dix ou douze florins*), as my affairs permit : it will always be something to assuage your want. And you, Madam," said he, turning to the Queen, " you will sometimes give her an old dress ; for the poor child has n't a shift to her back." [1] This rugged paternal banter was taken too literally by Wilhelmina, in her weak state ; and she was like " to burst in her skin," poor Princess.

So that, — except her own good Hereditary Prince, who was here, " over from Pasewalk " and his regimental duties,

[1] Wilhelmina, ii. 85.

waiting to welcome her; in whose true heart, full of honest
human sunshine towards her, she could always find shelter
and defence, — native Country and Court offer little to the
brave Wilhelmina. Chagrins enough are here: chagrins also
were there. At Baireuth our old Father Margraf has his
crotchets, his infirmities and outbreaks; takes more and more
to liquor; and does always keep us frightfully bare in money.
No help from Papa here, either, on the finance side; no real
hope anywhere (thinks Seckendorf, when we consult him),
except only in the Margraf's death: "old Margraf will soon
drink himself dead," thinks Seckendorf; "and in the mean
while there is Vienna, and a noble Kaiserinn who knows *her*
friends in case of extremity!" thinks he.[1] Poor Princess, in
her weak shattered state, she has a heavy time of it; but
there is a tough spirit in her; bright, sharp, like a swift
sabre, not to be quenched in any coil; but always cutting its
way, and emerging unsubdued.

One of the blessings reserved for her here, which most of
all concerns us, was the occasional sight of her Brother.
Brother in a day or two[2] ran over from Ruppin, on short
leave, and had his first interview. Very kind and affectionate;
quite the old Brother again; and "blushed" when, at supper,
Mamma and the Princesses, especially that wicked Charlotte
(Papa not present), tore up his poor Bride at such a rate.
"Has not a word to answer you, but *Yes* or *No*," said they;
"stupid as a block." "But were you ever at her toilette?" said
the wicked Charlotte: "Out of shape, completely: considerable waddings, I promise you: and then " — still worse features,
from that wicked Charlotte, in presence of the domestics here.
Wicked Charlotte; who is to be her Sister-in-law soon; — and
who is always flirting with my Husband, as if she liked that
better! — Crown-Prince retired, directly after supper: as did
I, to my apartment, where in a minute or two he joined me.

"To the question, How with the King and you? he answered, 'That his situation was changing every moment; that

[1] Wilhelmina, ii. 81–111.

[2] "18th November," she says; which date is wrong, if it were of moment
(see *Œuvres de Frédéric*, xxvii. part 1st, where their *Correspondence* is).

sometimes he was in favor, sometimes in disgrace; — that his chief happiness consisted in absence. That he led a soft and tranquil life with his Regiment at Ruppin; study and music his principal occupations; he had built himself a House there, and laid out a Garden, where he could read, and walk about.' Then as to his Bride, I begged him to tell me candidly if the portrait the Queen and my Sister had been making of her was the true one. 'We are alone,' replied he, 'and I will conceal nothing from you. The Queen, by her miserable intrigues, has been the source of our misfortunes. Scarcely were you gone when she began again with England; wished to substitute our Sister Charlotte for you; would have had me undertake to contradict the King's will again, and flatly refuse the Brunswick Match; — which I declined. That is the source of her venom against this poor Princess. As to the young Lady herself, I do not hate her so much as I pretend; I affect complete dislike, that the King may value my obedience more. She is pretty, a complexion lily-and-rose; her features delicate; face altogether of a beautiful person. True, she has no breeding, and dresses very ill: but I flatter myself, when she comes hither, you will have the goodness to take her in hand. I recommend her to you, my dear Sister; and beg your protection for her.' It is easy to judge, my answer would be such as he desired." [1]

For which small glimpse of the fact itself, at first-hand, across a whirlwind of distracted rumors new and old about the fact, let us be thankful to Wilhelmina. Seckendorf's hopeless attempts to resuscitate extinct English things, and make the Prussian Majesty break his word, continue to the very last; but are worth no notice from us. Grumkow's Drinking-bout with the Dilapidated-Strong at Crossen, which follows now in January, has been already noticed by us. And the Dilapidated-Strong's farewell next morning, — "Adieu, dear Grumkow; I think I shall not see you again!" as he rolled off towards Warsaw and the Diet, — will require farther notice; but must stand over till this Marriage be got done. Of which latter Event, — Wilhelmina once more kindling the

[1] Wilhelmina, ii. 89.

old dark Books into some light for us, — the essential particulars are briefly as follows.

Monday, 8th June, 1733, the Crown-Prince is again over from Ruppin: King, Queen and Crown-Prince are rendezvoused at Potsdam; and they set off with due retinues towards Wolfenbüttel, towards Salzdahlum the Ducal Schloss there; Sister Wilhelmina sending blessings, if she had them, on a poor Brother in such interesting circumstances. Mamma was "plunged in black melancholy;" King not the least; in the Crown-Prince nothing particular to be remarked. They reached Salzdahlum, Duke Ludwig Rudolf the Grandfather's Palace, one of the finest Palaces, with Gardens, with antiques, with Picture-Galleries no end; a mile or two from Wolfenbüttel; built by old Anton Ulrich, and still the ornament of those parts; — reached Salzdahlum, Wednesday the 10th; where Bride, with Father, Mother, much more Grandfather, Grandmother, and all the sublimities interested, are waiting in the highest gala; Wedding to be on Friday next.

Friday morning, this incident fell out, notable and somewhat contemptible: Seckendorf, who is of the retinue, following his bad trade, visits his Majesty who is still in bed: — "Pardon, your Majesty: what shall I say for excuse? Here is a Letter just come from Vienna; in Prince Eugene's hand; — Prince Eugene, or a Higher, will say something, while it is still time!" Majesty, not in impatience, reads the little Prince's and the Kaiser's Letter. "Give up this, we entreat you for the last time; marry with England after all!" Majesty reads, quiet as a lamb; lays the Letter under his pillow; will himself answer it; and does straightway, with much simple dignity, to the effect, "For certain, Never, my always respected Prince!"[1] Seckendorf, having thus shot his last bolt, does not stay many hours longer at Salzdahlum; — may as well quit Friedrich Wilhelm altogether, for any good he will henceforth do upon him. This is the one incident between the Arrival at Salzdahlum and the Wedding there.

[1] Account of the Interview by Seckendorf, in Förster, iii. 143–155; Copy of the answer itself is in the State-Paper Office here.

Same Friday, 12th June, 1733, at a more advanced hour, the Wedding itself took effect; Wedding which, in spite of the mad rumors and whispers, in the Newspapers, Diplomatic Despatches and elsewhere, went off, in all respects, precisely as other weddings do; a quite human Wedding now and afterwards. Officiating Clergyman was the Reverend Herr Mosheim: readers know with approval the *Ecclesiastical History* of Mosheim: he, in the beautiful Chapel of the Schloss, with Majesties and Brunswick Sublimities looking on, performed the ceremony: and Crown-Prince Friedrich of Prussia has fairly wedded the Serene Princess Elizabeth Christina of Brunswick-Bevern, age eighteen coming, manners rather awkward, complexion lily-and-rose; — and History is right glad to have done with the wearisome affair, and know it settled on any tolerable terms whatever. Here is a Note of Friedrich's to his dear Sister, which has been preserved:—

To Princess Wilhelmina of Baireuth, at Berlin.

"SALZDAHLUM, Noon, 12th June, 1733.

"MY DEAR SISTER, — A minute since, the whole Ceremony was got finished; and God be praised it is over! I hope you will take it as a mark of my friendship that I give you the first news of it.

"I hope I shall have the honor to see you again soon; and to assure you, my dear Sister, that I am wholly yours (*tout à vous*). I write in great haste; and add nothing that is merely formal. Adieu.[1]   FRÉDÉRIC."

One Keyserling, the Prince's favorite gentleman, came over express, with this Letter and the more private news; Wilhelmina being full of anxieties. Keyserling said, The Prince was inwardly "well content with his lot; though he had kept up the old farce to the last; and pretended to be in frightful humor, on the very morning; bursting out upon his valets in the King's presence, who reproved him, and looked rather pensive," — recognizing, one hopes, what a sacrifice it was. The

[1] *Œuvres*, xxvii. part 1st, p. 9.

Queen's Majesty, Keyserling reported, "was charmed with the
style and ways of the Brunswick Court; but could not endure
the Princess-Royal [new Wife], and treated the two Duchesses
like dogs (*comme des chiens*)." [1] Reverend Abbot Mosheim
(such his title ; Head Churchman, theological chief of Helm-
städt University in those parts, with a couple of extinct little
Abbacies near by, to help his stipend) preached next Sunday,
" On the Marriage of the Righteous," — felicitous appropriate
Sermon, said a grateful public ; [2] — and in short, at Salzdahlum
all goes, if not as merry as some marriage-bells, yet without
jarring to the ear.

On Tuesday, both the Majesties set out towards Potsdam
again ; "where his Majesty," having business waiting, "arrived some time before the Queen." Thither also, before the
week ends, Crown-Prince Friedrich with his Bride, and all the
Serenities of Brunswick escorting, are upon the road, — duly
detained by complimentary harangues, tedious scenic evolutions at Magdeburg and the intervening Towns ; — grand entrance of the Princess-Royal into Berlin is not till the 27th,
last day of the week following. That was such a day as Wilhelmina never saw ; no sleep the night before ; no breakfast
can one taste : between Charlottenburg and Berlin, there is a
review of unexampled splendor ; "above eighty carriages of
us," and only a tent or two against the flaming June sun :
think of it ! Review begins at four A.M. ; — poor Wilhelmina
thought she would verily have died, of heat and thirst and
hunger, in the crowded tent, under the flaming June sun ;
before the Review could end itself, and march into Berlin,
trumpeting and salvoing, with the Princess-Royal at the head
of it. [3]

Of which grand flaming day, and of the unexampled balls
and effulgent festivities that followed, "all Berlin ruining
itself in dresses and equipages," we will say nothing farther ;
but give only, what may still have some significance for readers, Wilhelmina's Portrait of the Princess-Royal on their first

1 Wilhelmina, ii. 114.
2 Text, Psalm, xcii. 12; "Sermon printed in Mosheim's *Works.*"
3 Wilhelmina, ii. 127-129.

meeting, which had taken place at Potsdam two days before. The Princess-Royal had arrived at Potsdam too, on that occasion, across a grand Review; Majesty himself riding out, Majesty and Crown-Prince, who had preceded her a little, to usher in the poor young creature; — Thursday, June 25th, 1733: —

"The King led her into the Queen's Apartment; then seeing, after she had saluted us all, that she was much heated and dispowdered (*dépoudrée*), he bade my Brother take her to her own room. I followed them thither. My Brother said to her, introducing me: 'This is a Sister I adore, and am obliged to beyond measure. She has had the goodness to promise me that she will take care of you, and help you with her good counsel; I wish you to respect her beyond even the King and Queen, and not to take the least step without her advice: do you understand?' I embraced the Princess-Royal, and gave her every assurance of my attachment; but she remained like a statue, not answering a word. Her people not being come, I repowdered her myself, and readjusted her dress a little, without the least sign of thanks from her, or any answer to all my caressings. My Brother got impatient at last; and said aloud: 'Devil's in the blockhead (*Peste soit de la bête*): thank my Sister, then!' She made me a courtesy, on the model of that of Agnès in the *Ecole des Femmes*. I took her back to the Queen's Apartment; little edified by such a display of talent.

"The Princess-Royal is tall; her figure is not fine: stooping slightly, or hanging forward, as she walks or stands, which gives her an awkward air. Her complexion is of dazzling whiteness, heightened by the liveliest colors: her eyes are pale blue, and not of much promise for spiritual gifts. Mouth small; features generally small, — dainty (*mignons*) rather than beautiful: — and the countenance altogether is so innocent and infantine, you would think this head belonged to a child of twelve. Her hair is blond, plentiful, curling in natural locks. Teeth are unhappily very bad, black and ill set; which are a disfigurement in this fine face. She has no manners, nor the least vestige of tact; has much difficulty in speaking and making herself understood : for most part you are obliged to guess what she means; which is very embarrassing." [1]

The Berlin gayeties — for Karl, Heir-Apparent of Brunswick, brother to this Princess-Royal, wedded his Charlotte, too, about a week hence [2] — did not end, and the serene Guests disappear, till far on in July. After which an Inspection with Papa; and then Friedrich got back to Ruppin and his old way of life there. Intrinsically the old studious, quietly diligent way of life; varied by more frequent excursions to Berlin; — where as yet the Princess-Royal usually resides, till some fit residence be got ready in the Ruppin Country for a wedded Crown-Prince and her.

The young Wife had an honest guileless heart ; if little articulate intellect, considerable inarticulate sense; did not fail to learn tact, perpendicular attitude, speech enough; — and I hope kept well clear of pouting (*faire la fâchée*), a much more dangerous rock for her. With the gay temper of eighteen, and her native loyalty of mind, she seems to have shaped herself successfully to the Prince's taste ; and growing yearly gracefuler and better-looking was an ornament and pleasant addition to his Ruppin existence. These first seven years, spent at Berlin or in the Ruppin quarter, she always regarded as the flower of her life. [3]

Papa, according to promise, has faithfully provided a Crown-Prince Palace at Berlin ; all trimmed and furnished, for occasional residences there ; the late "Government House" (originally *Schomberg* House), new-built, — which is, to this day, one of the distinguished Palaces of Berlin. Princess-Royal had Schönhausen given her ; a pleasant Royal Mansion some miles out of Berlin, on the Ruppin side. Furthermore, the Prince-Royal, being now a wedded man, has, as is customary in such case, a special *Amt* (Government District) set apart for his support; the "Amt of Ruppin," where his business lies. What the exact revenues of Ruppin are, is not communicated; but we can justly fear they were far too frugal, — and excused

[1] Wilhelmina, ii. 119–12i.   [2] 2d July, 1733.
[3] Büsching (Autobiography, *Beiträge*, vi.) heard her say so, in advanced years.

the underhand borrowing, which is evident enough as a painful shadow in the Prince's life henceforth. He does not seem to have been wasteful; but he borrows all round, under sevenfold secrecy, from benevolent Courts, from Austria, Russia, England: and the only pleasant certainty we notice in such painful business is, that, on his Accession, he pays with exactitude, — sends his Uncle George of England, for example, the complete amount in rouleaus of new coin, by the first courier that goes.[1]

A thought too frugal, his Prussian Majesty; but he means to be kind, bountiful; and occasionally launches out into handsome munificence. This very Autumn, hearing that the Crown-Prince and his Princess fancied Reinsberg, an old Castle in their Amt Ruppin, some miles north of them, — his Majesty, without word spoken, straightway purchased Reinsberg, Schloss and Territory, from the owner; gave it to his Crown-Prince, and gave him money to new-build it according to his mind.[2] Which the Crown-Prince did with much interest, under very wise architectural advice, for the next three years; then went into it, to reside; — yet did not cease newbuilding, improving, artistically adorning, till it became in all points the image of his taste.

A really handsome princely kind of residence, that of Reinsberg: — got up with a thrift that most of all astonishes us. In which improved locality we shall by and by look in upon him again. For the present we must to Warsaw, where tragedies and troubles are in the wind, which turn out to be not quite without importance to the Crown-Prince and us.

[1] Despatch (of adjacent date) in the State-Paper Office here.
[2] 23d Oct. 1733–16th March, 1734 (Preuss, i. 75).

CHAPTER VIII.

KING AUGUST DIES ; AND POLAND TAKES FIRE.

MEANWHILE, over at Warsaw, there has an Event fallen out. Friedrich, writing rapidly from vague reminiscence, as he often does, records it as " during the marriage festivities ; "[1] but it was four good months earlier. Event we must now look at for a moment.

In the end of January last, we left Grumkow in a low and hypochondriacal state, much shaken by that drinking-bout at Crossen, when the Polish Majesty and he were so anxious to pump one another, by copious priming with Hungary wine. About a fortnight after, in the first days of February following (day is not given), Grumkow reported something curious. " In my presence," says Wilhelmina, "and that of forty persons," for the thing was much talked about, " Grumkow said to the King one morning : 'Ah Sire, I am in despair ; the poor Patroon is dead ! I was lying broad awake, last night : all on a sudden, the curtains of my bed flew asunder : I saw him ; he was in a shroud : he gazed fixedly at me : I tried to start up, being dreadfully taken ; but the phantom disappeared !' " Here was an illustrious ghost-story for Berlin, in a day or two when the Courier came. " Died at the very time of the phantom ; Death and phantom were the same night," say Wilhelmina and the miraculous Berlin public, — but do not say *what* night for either of them it was.[2] By help of which latter circumstance the phantom becomes reasonably unmiraculous again, in a nervous system tremulous from drink. " They had been sad at parting," Wilhelmina says, " having drunk immensities of Hungary wine ; the Patroon almost weeping over his

---

[1] Œuvres (Mémoires de Brandebourg), i. 163.

[2] Wilhelmina, ii. 98. Event happened, 1st February ; news of it came to Berlin, 4th February : Fassmann (p. 485) ; Buchholz ; &c.

Grumkow: 'Adieu, my dear Grumkow,' said he; 'I shall never see you more!'"

Miraculous or not, the catastrophe is true: August, the once Physically Strong, lies dead; — and there will be no Partition of Poland for the present. He had the Diet ready to assemble; waiting for him, at Warsaw; and good trains laid in the Diet, capable of fortunate explosion under a good engineer. Engineer, alas! The Grumkow drinking-bout had awakened that old sore in his foot: he came to Warsaw, eager enough for business; but with his stock of strength all out, and Death now close upon him. The Diet met, 26th–27th January; engineer all alert about the good trains laid, and the fortunate exploding of them; when, almost on the morrow — "Inflammation has come on!" said the Doctors, and were futile to help farther. The strong body, and its life, was done; and nothing remained but to call in the Archbishop, with his extreme unctions and soul-apparatus.

August made no moaning or recalcitrating; took, on the prescribed terms, the inevitable that had come. Has been a very great sinner, he confesses to the Archbishop: "I have not at present strength to name my many and great sins to your Reverence," said he; "I hope for mercy on the" — on the usual rash terms. Terms perhaps known to August to be rash; to have been frightfully rash; but what can he now do? Archbishop thereupon gives absolution of his sins; Archbishop does, — a baddish, unlikely kind of man, as August well knows. August "laid his hand on his eyes," during such sad absolution-mummery; and in that posture had breathed his last, before it was well over.[1] Unhappy soul; who shall judge him? — transcendent King of edacious Flunkies; not without fine qualities, which he turned to such a use amid the temptations of this world!

Poland has to find a new King.

His death brought vast miseries on Poland; kindled foolish Europe generally into fighting, and gave our Crown-Prince his

---

[1] "Sunday, 1st February, 1733, quarter past 4 A.M." (Fassmann, *Leben Frederici Augusti Königs in Pohlen*, pp. 994–997).

first actual sight and experience of the facts of War. For
which reason, hardly for another, the thing having otherwise little memorability at present, let us give some brief
synopsis of it, the briefer the better. Here, excerpted from
multifarious old Note-books, are some main heads of the
affair : —

"On the disappearance of August the Strong, his plans of
Partitioning Poland disappeared too, and his fine trains in the
Diet abolished themselves. The Diet had now nothing to do,
but proclaim the coming Election, giving a date to it; and go
home to consider a little whom they would elect.[1] A question
weighty to Poland. And not likely to be settled by Poland
alone or chiefly ; the sublime Republic, with *liberum veto*, and
Diets capable only of anarchic noise, having now reached such
a stage that its Neighbors everywhere stood upon its skirts ;
asking, 'Whitherward, then, with your anarchy ? Not this
way ; — we say, that way !' — and were apt to get to battle
about it, before such a thing could be settled. A house, in
your street, with perpetual smoke coming through the slates
of it, is not a pleasant house to be neighbor to ! One honest
interest the neighbors have, in an Election Crisis there, That
the house do not get on fire, and kindle them. Dishonest
interests, in the way of theft and otherwise, they may have
without limit.

"The poor house, during last Election Crisis, — when August
the Strong was flung out, and Stanislaus brought in ; Crisis
presided over by Charles XII., with Czar Peter and others
hanging on the outskirts, as Opposition party, — fairly got
into flame ;[2] but was quenched down again by that stout
Swede ; and his Stanislaus, a native Pole, was left peaceably
as King for the years then running. Years ran ; and Stanislaus was thrown out, Charles himself being thrown out ; and
had to make way for August the Strong again : — an ejected

---

[1] "Interregnum proclaimed," 11th February ; Preliminary Diet to meet
21st April ; — meets ; settles, before May is done, that the Election shall
begin 25th August : it must *end* in six weeks thereafter, by law of the
land.
[2] Description of it in Köhler, *Münzbelustigungen*, vi. 228-230.

Stanislaus : King only in title ; known to most readers of this
time.[1]

"Poor man, he has been living in Zweibrück, in Weissenburg and such places, in that Debatable French-German region, — which the French are more and more getting stolen to
themselves, in late centuries : — generally on the outskirts of
France he lives ; having now connections of the highest quality with France. He has had fine Country-houses in that Zwei-
bruck (*Two-Bridge*, Deux-Ponts) region ; had always the ghost
of a Court there ; plenty of money, — a sinecure Country-
gentleman life ; — and no complaints have been heard from
him. Charles XII., as proprietor of Deux-Ponts, had first of
all sent him into those parts for refuge ; and in general, easy
days have been the lot of Stanislaus there.

" Nor has History spoken of him since, except on one small
occasion : when the French Politician Gentlemen, at a certain
crisis of their game, chose a Daughter of his to be Wife for
young Louis XV., and bring royal progeny, of which they were
scarce. This was in 1724–1725 ; Duc de Bourbon, and other
Politicians male and female, finding that the best move. A
thing wonderful to the then Gazetteers, for nine days ; but
not now worth much talk. The good young Lady, it is well
known, a very pious creature, and sore tried in her new station, did bring royal progeny enough, — and might as well
have held her hand, had she foreseen what would become of
them, poor souls ! This was a great event for Stanislaus, the
sinecure Country-gentleman, in his French-German rustication.
One other thing I have read of him, infinitely smaller, out of
those ten years : in Zweibrück Country, or somewhere in that
French-German region, he 'built a pleasure-cottage,' conceivable to the mind, 'and called it *Schuhflick* (Shoe-Patch),'[2] — a

---

[1] Stanislaus Lesczinsky, "Woywode of Posen," born 1677 : King of Poland, Charles XII. superintending, 1704 (age then 27) ; driven out 1709, went
to Charles XII. at Bender ; to Zweibrück, 1714 ; thence, on Charles's death,
to Weissenburg (Alsace, or Strasburg Country) : Daughter married to
Louis XV., 1725. Age now 56. — Hübner, t. 97 ; *Histoire de Stanislas I., Roi
de Pologne* (English Translation, London, 1741), pp. 96–126 ; &c.

[2] Büsching, *Erdbeschreibung*, v. 1194.

name that touches one's fancy on behalf of the innocent soul.
Other fact I will not remember of him. He is now to quit
Shoe-Patch and his pleasant Weissenburg Castle; to come on
the public stage again, poor man; and suffer a second season of
mischances and disgraces still worse than the first. As we shall
see presently; — a new Polish Election Crisis having come !

"What individual the Polish Grandees would have chosen
for King if entirely left alone to do it ? is a question not important; and indeed was never asked, in this or in late Elections. Not the individual who could have *been* a King among
them were they, for a long time back, in the habit of seeking
after; not him, but another and indeed reverse kind of individual, — the one in whom there lay most *nourishment*, nourishment of any kind, even of the cash kind, for a practical
Polish Grandee. So that the question was no longer of the
least importance, to Poland or the Universe; and in point of
fact, the frugal Destinies had ceased to have it put, in that
quarter. Not Grandees of Poland; but Intrusive Neighbors,
carrying Grandees of Poland ' in their breeches-pocket ' (as
our phrase is), were the voting parties. To that pass it was
come. Under such stern penalty had Poland and its Grandees
fallen, by dint of false voting: the frugal Destinies had ceased
to ask about their vote; and they were become machines for
voting with, or pistols for fighting with, by bad Neighbors
who cared to vote ! Nor did the frugal Destinies consider
that the proper method, either ; but had, as we shall see, determined to abolish that too, in about forty years more."

*Of the Candidates ; of the Conditions. How the Election
went.*

It was under such omens that the Polish Election of 1733
had to transact itself. Austria, Russia, Prussia, as next
Neighbors, were the chief voting parties, if they cared to
intrude ; — which Austria and Russia were clear for doing;
Prussia not clear, or not beyond the indispensable or evidently profitable. Seckendorf, and one Löwenwolde the Rus-

sian Ambassador at Berlin, had, some time ago, in foresight of this event, done their utmost to bring Friedrich Wilhelm into co-operation, — offering fine baits, " Berg and Jülich" again, among others ; — but nothing definite came of it : peaceable, reasonably safe Election in Poland, other interest Friedrich Wilhelm has not in the matter ; and compliance, not co-operation, is what can be expected of him by the Kaiser and Czarina.   Co-operating or even complying, these three could have settled it ; and would, — had no other Neighbor interfered.   But other neighbors *can* interfere ; any neighbor that has money to spend, or likes to bully in such a matter ! And that proved to be the case, in this unlucky instance.

Austria and Russia, with Prussia complying, had, — a year ago, before the late August's decease, his life seeming then an extremely uncertain one, and foresight being always good, — privately come to an understanding,[1] in case of a Polish Election : —

"1°. That France was to have no hand in it whatever, — no tool of France to be King ; or, as they more politely expressed it, having their eye upon Stanislaus, No Piast or native Pole could be eligible.

"2°. That neither could August's Son, the new August, who would then be Kurfürst of Saxony, be admitted King of Poland. — And, on the whole,

"3°. That an Emanuel Prince of Portugal would be the eligible man."   Emanuel of Portugal, King of Portugal's Brother ; a gentleman without employment, as his very Title tells us : gentleman never heard of before or since, in those parts or elsewhere ; but doubtless of the due harmless quality, as Portugal itself was : he is to be the Polish King, — vote these Intrusive Neighbors.   What the vote of Poland itself may be, the Destinies do not, of late, ask ; finding it a superfluous question.

So had the Three Neighbors settled this matter : — or rather, I should say, so had Two of them ; for Friedrich Wilhelm wanted, now or afterwards, nothing in this Election, but that

---

[1] 31st December, 1731, " Treaty of Löwenwolde" (which never got completed or became valid) : Schöll, ii. 223.

it should not take fire and kindle him. Two of the Neighbors: and of these two, perhaps we might guess the Kaiser was the principal contriver and suggester; France and Saxony being both hateful to him, — obstinate refusers of the Pragmatic Sanction, to say nothing more. What the Czarina, Anne with the big cheek, specially wanted, I do not learn, — unless it were peaceable hold of Courland; or perhaps merely to produce herself in these parts, as a kind of regulating Pallas, along with the Jupiter Kaiser of Western Europe; — which might have effects by and by.

Emanuel of Portugal was not elected, nor so much as spoken of in the Diet. Nor did one of these Three Regulations take effect; but much the contrary, — other Neighbors having the power to interfere. France saw good to interfere, a rather distant neighbor; Austria, Russia, could not endure the French vote at all; and so the whole world got on fire by the business.

France is not a near Neighbor; but it has a Stanislaus much concerned, who is eminently under the protection of France: — who may be called the "*Father* of France," in a sense, or even the "Grandfather;" his Daughter being Mother of a young creature they call Dauphin, or "Child of France." Fleury and the French Court decide that Stanislaus, Grandfather of France, was once King of Poland: that it will behoove, for various reasons, he be King again. Some say old Fleury did not care for Stanislaus; merely wanted a quarrel with the Kaiser, — having got himself in readiness, "with Lorraine in his eye;" and seeing the Kaiser not ready. It is likelier the hot young spirits, Belléisle and others, controlled old Fleury into it. At all events, Stanislaus is summoned from his rustication; the French Ambassador at Warsaw gets his instructions. French Ambassador opens himself largely, at Warsaw, by eloquent speech, by copious money, on the subject of Stanislaus; finds large audience, enthusiastic receptivity; — and readers will now understand the following chronological phenomena of the Polish Election: —

"*August 25th,* 1733. This day the Polish Election begins. So has the Preliminary Diet (kind of Polish *Caucus*) ordered

it; — Preliminary Diet itself a very stormy matter; minority
like to be 'thrown out of window,' to be 'shot through the
head,' on some occasions.[1] Actual Election begins; continues
sub dio, 'in the Field of Wola,' in a very tempestuous fashion; bound to conclude within six weeks. Kaiser has his
troops assembled over the border, in Silesia, 'to protect the
freedom of election;' Czarina has 30,000 under Marshal Lacy,
lying on the edge of Lithuania, bent on a like object; will
increase them to 50,000, as the plot thickens.

"So that Emanuel of Portugal is not heard of; and French
interference is, with a vengeance, — and Stanislaus, a born
Piast, is overwhelmingly the favorite. Intolerable to Austria,
to Russia; the reverse to Friedrich Wilhelm, who privately
thinks him the right man. And Kurfürst August of Saxony
is the other Candidate, — with troops of his own in the distance, but without support in Poland; and depending wholly
on the Kaiser and Czarina for his chance. And our 'three
settled points' are gone to water in this manner!

"August seeing there was not the least hope in Poland's
own vote, judiciously went to the Kaiser first of all: 'Imperial Majesty, I will accept your Pragmatic Sanction root
and branch, swallow it whole; make me King of Poland!' —
'Done!' answers Imperial Majesty;[2] brings the Czarina over,
by good offers of August's and his; — and now there is an
effective Opposition Candidate in the field, with strength of
his own, and good backing close at hand. Austrian, Russian
Ambassadors at Warsaw lift up their voice, like the French
one; open their purse, and bestir themselves; but with no
success in the Field of Wola, except to the stirring up of noise
and tumult there. They must look to other fields for success.
The voice of Wola and of Poland, if it had now a voice, is
enthusiastic for Stanislaus.

"*September 7th.* A couple of quiet-looking Merchants
arrive in Warsaw, — one of whom is Stanislaus in person.
Newspapers say he is in the French Fleet of War, which is
sailing minatory towards these Coasts: and there is in truth a

---

[1] *History of Stanislaus* (cited above), p. 136.
[2] 16th July, 1733; Treaty in Schöll, ii. 224–231.

Gentleman in Stanislaus's clothes on board there; — to make
the Newspapers *believe*. Stanislaus himself drove through Berlin, a day or two ago; gave the sentry a ducat at the Gate,
to be speedy with the Passports, — whom Friedrich Wilhelm
affected to put under arrest for such negligent speed. And so,
on the 10th of the month, Stanislaus being now rested and
trimmed, makes his appearance on the Field of Wola itself;
and captivates all hearts by the kind look of him. So that,
on the second day after, 12th September, 1733, he is, as it
were, unanimously elected; with acclamation, with enthusiasm; and sees himself actual King of Poland, — if France
send proper backing to continue him there. As, surely, she
will not fail? — But there are alarming news that the Russians
are advancing: Marshal Lacy with 30,000; and reinforcements
in the rear of him.

"*September* 22d. Russians advancing more and more, no
French help arrived yet, and the enthusiastic Polish Chivalry
being good for nothing against regular musketry, — King Stanislaus finds that he will have to quit Warsaw, and seek covert
somewhere. Quits Warsaw this day; gets covert in Dantzig.
And, in fact, from this 22d of September, day of the autumnal
equinox, 1733, is a fugitive, blockaded, besieged Stanislaus:
an Imaginary King thenceforth. His real Kingship had lasted
precisely ten days.

"*October* 3d. Lacy and his Russians arrive in the suburbs of
Warsaw, intent upon 'protecting freedom of election.' Bridges
being broken, they do not yet cross the River, but invite the
free electors to come across and vote: 'A real King is very
necessary, — Stanislaus being an imaginary one, brought in by
compulsion, by threats of flinging people out of window, and
the like.' The free electors do not cross. Whereupon a small
handful, now free enough, and *not* to be thrown out of window,
whom Lacy had about him, proceed to elect August of Saxony;
he, on the 5th of October, still one day within the legal six
weeks, is chosen and declared the real King: — 'twelve sena-
tors and about six hundred gentlemen' voting for him there,
free they in Lacy's quarters, the rest of Poland having lain
under compulsion when voting for Stanislaus. That is the

Polish Election, so far as Poland can settle it. We said the
Destinies had ceased, some time since, to ask Poland for its
vote; it is other people who have now got the real power
of voting. But that is the correct state of the poll at Warsaw, if important to anybody."

August is crowned in Cracow before long; "August III.,"
whom we shall meet again in important circumstances. Lacy
and his Russians have voted for August; able, they, to dis-
perse all manner of enthusiastic Polish Chivalry; which indeed, we observe, usually stands but one volley from the
Russian musketry; and flies elsewhither, to burn and plunder
its own domestic enemies. Far and wide, robbery and arson
are prevalent in Poland; Stanislaus lying under covert in
Dantzig, — an imaginary King ever since the equinox, but well
trusting that the French will give him a plumper vote. French
War-fleet is surely under way hither.

Poland on Fire ; Dantzig stands Siege.

These are the news our Crown-Prince hears at Ruppin, in
the first months of his wedded life there. With what interest we may fancy. Brandenburg is next neighbor; and these
Polish troubles reach far enough; — the ever-smoking house
having taken fire; and all the street threatening to get on
blaze. Friedrich Wilhelm, nearest neighbor, stands anxious
to quench, carefully sweeping the hot coals across again from
his own borders; and will not interfere on one or the other
side, for any persuasion.

Dantzig, strong in confidence of French help, refuses to
give up Stanislaus when summoned; will stand siege rather.
Stands siege, furious lengthy siege, — with enthusiastic defence; "a Lady of Rank firing off the first gun," against the
Russian batteries. Of the Siege of Dantzig, which made the
next Spring and Summer loud for mankind (February–June,
1734), we shall say nothing, — our own poor field, which also
grows loud enough, lying far away from Dantzig, — except:

First, That no French help came, or as good as none; the
minatory War-fleet having landed a poor 1,500 men, headed

by the Comte de Plelo, who had volunteered along with them;
that they attempted one onslaught on the Russian lines, and
that Plelo was shot, and the rest were blown to miscellaneous
ruin, and had to disappear, not once getting into Dantzig.
Secondly, That the Saxons, under Weissenfels, our poor old
friend, with proper siege-artillery, though not with enough,
did, by effort (end of May), get upon the scene ; in which this
is to be remarked, that Weissenfels's siege-artillery " came
by post ; " two big mortars expressly passing through Berlin,
marked as part of the Duke of Weissenfels's Luggage.   And
thirdly, That Münnich, who had succeeded Lacy as Besieging
General, and was in hot haste, and had not artillery enough,
made unheard-of assaults (2,000 men, some say 4,000, lost in
one night-attack upon a post they call the Hagelberg ; rash attack, much blamed by military men) ; [1] — but nevertheless, having now (by Russian Fleet, middle of June) got siege-artillery
enough, advances irrepressibly day by day.

So that at length, things being now desperate, Stanislaus,
disguised as a cattle-dealer, privately quitted Dantzig, night
of 27th June, 1734 ; got across the intricate mud-and-water
difficulties of the Weichsel and its mouths, flying perilously
towards Preussen and Friedrich Wilhelm's protection.[2] Whereby the Siege of Dantzig ended in chamade, and levying of
penalties ; penalties severe to a degree, though Friedrich
Wilhelm interceded what he could.   And with the Siege of
Dantzig, the blazing Polish Election went out in like manner ; [3]
— having already kindled, in quarters far away from it, conflagrations quite otherwise interesting to us.   Whitherward
we now hasten.

---

[1] *Œuvres de Frédéric,* xxvii. part 2d, p. 31.

[2] Narrative by himself, in *History,* pp. 235–248.

[3] Clear account, especially of Siege, in Mannstein (pp. 71–83), who was
there as Münnich's Aide-de-Camp.

CHAPTER IX.

KAISER'S SHADOW-HUNT HAS CAUGHT FIRE.

FRANZ of Lorraine, the young favorite of Fortune, whom we once saw at Berlin on an interesting occasion, was about this time to have married his Imperial Archduchess ; Kaiser's consent to be formally demanded and given ; nothing but joy and splendor looked for in the Court of Vienna at present. Nothing to prevent it, — had there been no Polish Election; had not the Kaiser, in his Shadow-Hunt (coursing the Pragmatic Sanction chiefly, as he has done these twenty years past), gone rashly into that combustible foreign element. But so it is : this was the fatal limit. The poor Kaiser's Shadow-Hunt, going scot-free this long while, and merely tormenting other people, has, at this point, by contact with inflammable Poland, unexpectedly itself caught fire ; goes now plunging, all in mad flame, over precipices one knows not how deep : and there will be a lamentable singeing and smashing before the Kaiser get out of this, if he ever get ! Kaiser Karl, from this point, plunges down and down, all his days ; and except in that Shadow of a Pragmatic Sanction, if he can still save that, has no comfort left. Marriages are not the thing to be thought of at present ! —

Scarcely had the news of August's Election, and Stanislaus's flight to Dantzig, reached France, when France, all in a state of readiness, informed the Kaiser, ready for nothing, his force lying in Silesia, doing the Election functions on the Polish borders there, "That he the Kaiser had, by such treatment of the Grandfather of France and the Polish Kingdom fairly fallen to him, insulted the most Christian Majesty ; that in consequence the most Christian Majesty did hereby declare

War against the said Kaiser," — and in fact had, that very
day (14th of October, 1733), begun it.   Had marched over into
Lorraine, namely, secured Lorraine against accidents; and,
more specially, gone across from Strasburg to the German side
of the Rhine, and laid siege to Kehl.   Kehl Fortress; a dilapidated outpost of the Reich there, which cannot resist many
hours.   Here is news for the Kaiser, with his few troops all on
the Polish borders; minding his neighbors' business, or chasing
Pragmatic Sanction, in those inflammable localities.

Pacific Fleury, it must be owned, if he wanted a quarrel with
the Kaiser, could not have managed it on more advantageous
terms.   Generals, a Duc de Berwick, a Noailles, Belleisle;
generals, troops, artillery, munitions, nothing is wanting to
Fleury; to the Kaiser all things.   It is surmised, the French
had their eye on Lorraine, not on Stanislaus, from the first.
For many centuries, especially for these last two, — ever since
that Siege of Metz, which we once saw, under Kaiser Karl V.
and Albert Alcibiades, — France has been wrenching and
screwing at this Lorraine, wriggling it off bit by bit; till now,
as we perceived on Lyttelton junior of Hagley's visit, Lorraine
seems all lying unscrewed; and France, by any good opportunity, could stick it in her pocket.   Such opportunity sly
Fleury contrived, they say; — or more likely it might be Belleisle and the other adventurous spirits that urged it on pacific
Fleury; — but, at all events, he has got it.   Dilapidated Kehl
yields straightway:[1] Sardinia, Spain, declare alliance with
Fleury; and not Lorraine only, and the Swabian Provinces,
but Italy itself lies at his discretion, — owing to your treatment of the Grandfather of France, and these Polish Elective
methods.

The astonished Kaiser rushes forward to fling himself into
the arms of the Sea-Powers, his one resource left: "Help!
moneys, subsidies, ye Sea-Powers!"   But the Sea-Powers stand
obtuse, arms not open at all, hands buttoning their pockets:
"Sorry we cannot, your Imperial Majesty.   Fleury engages
not to touch the Netherlands, the Barrier Treaty; Polish

[1] 29th October, 1733.   *Mémoires du Maréchal de Berwick* (in Petitot's Collection, Paris, 1828), ii. 303.

Elections are not our concern!" and callously decline. The
Kaiser's astonishment is extreme; his big heart swelling even
with a martyr-feeling; and he passionately appeals : "Ungrateful, blind Sea-Powers! No money to fight France, say
you? Are the Laws of Nature fallen void?" Imperial astonishment, sublime martyr-feeling, passionate appeals to the
Laws of Nature, avail nothing with the blind Sea-Powers :
"No money in us," answer they : "we will help you to nego-
tiate." — "Negotiate!" answers he; and will have to pay his
own Election broken-glass, with a sublime martyr-feeling, without money from the Sea-Powers.

Fleury has got the Sardinian Majesty; "Sardinian doorkeeper of the Alps," who opens them now this way, now that,
for a consideration : "A slice of the Milanese, your Majesty;"
bargains Fleury. Fleury has got the Spanish Majesty (our
violent old friend the Termagant of Spain) persuaded to join :
"Your infant Carlos made Duke of Parma and Piacenza, with
such difficulty : what is that? Naples itself, crown of the
Two Sicilies, lies in the wind for Carlos; — and your junior
infant, great Madam, has he no need of apanages?" The
Termagant of Spain, "offended by Pragmatic Sanction" (she
says), is ready on those terms; the Sardinian Majesty is ready :
and Fleury, this same October, with an overwhelming force,
Spaniards and Sardinians to join, invades Italy; great Marshal Villars himself taking the command. Marshal Villars,
an extremely eminent old military gentleman, — somewhat of
a friend, or husband of a lady-friend, to M. de Voltaire, for one
thing; — and capable of slicing Italy to pieces at a fine rate,
in the condition it was in.

Never had Kaiser such a bill of broken-glass to pay for
meddling in neighbors' elections before. The year was not
yet ended, when Villars and the Sardinian Majesty had done
their stroke on Lombardy; taken Milan Citadel, taken Piz-
zighetone, the Milanese in whole, and appropriated it; swept
the poor unprepared Kaiser clear out of those parts. Baby
Carlos and the Spaniards are to do the Two Sicilies, Naples or
the land one to begin with, were the Winter gone. For the
present, Louis XV. "sings *Te Deum* at Paris, 23d December,

1733 "[1] — a merry Christmas there. Villars, now above four-score, soon died of those fatigues; various Marshals, Broglio, Coigny, Noailles, succeeding him, some of whom are slightly notable to us; and there was one Maillebois, still a subordinate under them, whose name also may reappear in this History.

Subsequent Course of the War, in the Italian Part of it.

The French-Austrian War, which had now broken out, lasted a couple of years; the Kaiser steadily losing, though he did his utmost; not so much a War, on his part, as a Being Beaten and Being Stript. The Scene was Italy and the Upper-Rhine Country of Germany; Italy the deciding scene; where, except as it bears on Germany, our interest is nothing, as indeed in Germany too it is not much. The principal events, on both stages, are chronologically somewhat as follows; — beginning with Italy : —

" *March 29th*, 1734. Baby Carlos with a Duke of Montemar for General, a difficult impetuous gentleman, very haughty to the French allies and others, lands in Naples Territory; intending to seize the Two Sicilies, according to bargain. They find the Kaiser quite unprepared, and their enterprise extremely feasible.

" *May 10th*. Baby Carlos — whom we ought to call Don Carlos, who is now eighteen gone, and able to ride the great horse — makes triumphant entry into Naples, having easily swept the road clear ; styles himself ' King of the Two Sicilies ' (Papa having surrendered him his ' right ' there) ; whom Naples, in all ranks of it, willingly homages as such. Wrecks of Kaiser's forces intrench themselves, rather strongly, at a place called Bitonto, in Apulia, not far off.

" *May 25th*. Montemar, in an impetuous manner, storms them there : — which feat procures for him the title, Duke of Bitonto; and finishes off the First of the Sicilies. And indeed, we may say, finishes Both the Sicilies : our poor Kaiser having no considerable force in either, nor means of sending any ; the

---

[1] *Fastes du Règne de Louis XV.* (Paris, 1766), i. 248.

Sea-Powers having buttoned their pockets, and the Combined
Fleet of France and Spain being on the waters there.

"We need only add, on this head, that, for ten months more.
Baby Carlos and Montemar went about besieging, Gaeta, Mes-
sina, Syracuse; and making triumphal entries; — and that, on
the 30th of June, 1735, Baby Carlos had himself fairly crowned
at Palermo.[1] 'King of the Two Sicilies' *de facto;* in which
eminent post he and his continue, not with much success, to
this day.

"That will suffice for the Two Sicilies. As to Lombardy
again, now that Villars is out of it, and the Coignys and
Broglios have succeeded: —

"*June 29th*, 1734. Kaiser, rallying desperately for recovery
of the Milanese, has sent an Army thither, Graf von Mercy
leader of it : Battle of Parma between the French and it (29th
June) ; — totally lost by the Kaiser's people, after furious
fighting; Graf von Mercy himself killed in the action. Graf
von Mercy, and what comes nearer us, a Prince of Culmbach,
amiable Uncle of our Wilhelmina's Husband, a brave man
and Austrian Soldier, who was much regretted by Wilhelmina
and the rest; his death and obsequies making a melancholy
Court of Baireuth in this agitated year. The Kaiser, doing his
utmost, is beaten at every point.

"*September 15th*. Surprisal of the Secchia. Kaiser's people
rally, — under a General Graf von Königseck worth noting by
us, — and after some manœuvring, in the Guastalla-Modena
region, on the Secchia and Po rivers there, dexterously steal
across the Secchia that night (15th September), cutting off the
small guard-party at the ford of the Secchia, then wading
silently ; and burst in upon the French Camp in a truly alarming manner.[2] So that Broglio, in command there, had to gallop
with only one boot òn, some say 'in his shirt,' till he got
some force rallied, and managed to retreat more Parthian-like
upon his brother Maréchal's Division. Artillery, war-chest,
secret correspondence, 'King of Sardinia's tent,' and much
cheering plunder beside Broglio's odd boot, were the conse-

---

[1] *Fastes de Louis XV.*, i. 278.
[2] Hormayr, xx. 84 ; *Fastes,* as it is liable to do, misdates.

quences; the Kaiser's one success in this War; abolished, unluckily, in four days! — The Broglio who here gallops is the
second French Maréchal of the name, son of the first; a military gentleman whom we shall but too often meet in subsequent
stages. A son of this one's, a third Maréchal Broglio, present
at the Secchia that bad night, is the famous War-god of the
Bastille time, fifty-five years hence, — unfortunate old War-
god, the Titans being all up about him. As to Broglio with
the one boot, it is but a triumph over him till —

" *September* 19*th*. Battle of Guastalla, that day. Battle lost
by the Kaiser's people, after eight hours' hot fighting; who
are then obliged to hurry across the Secchia again; — and
in fact do not succeed in fighting any more in that quarter,
this year or afterwards. For, next year (1735), Montemar is
so advanced with the Two Sicilies, he can assist in these
Northern operations; and Noailles, a better Maréchal, replaces
the Broglio and Coigny there; who, with learned strategic
movements, sieges, threatenings of siege, sweeps the wrecks
of Austria, to a satisfactory degree, into the Tyrol, without
fighting, or event mentionable thenceforth.

" This is the Kaiser's War of two Campaigns, in the Italian,
which was the decisive part of it: a continual Being Beaten,
as the reader sees; a Being Stript, till one was nearly bare in
that quarter."

Course of the War, in the German Part of it.

In Germany the mentionable events are still fewer; and indeed, but for one small circumstance binding on us, we might
skip them altogether. For there is nothing comfortable in it
to the human memory otherwise.

Maréchal Duc de Berwick, a cautious considerable General
(Marlborough's Nephew, on what terms is known to readers),
having taken Kehl and plundered the Swabian outskirts last
Winter, had extensive plans of operating in the heart of Germany, and ruining the Kaiser there. But first he needs, and
the Kaiser is aware of it, a " basis on the Rhine; " free bridge
over the Rhine, not by Strasburg and Kehl alone: and for

this reason, he will have to besiege and capture Philipsburg
first of all. Strong Town of Philipsburg, well down towards
Speyer-and-Heidelberg quarter on the German side of the
Rhine : * here will be our bridge. Lorraine is already occupied, since the first day of the War ; Trarbach, strong-place
of the Moselle and Electorate of Trier, cannot be difficult to
get. Thus were the Rhine Country, on the French side, secure
to France ; and so Berwick calculates he will have a basis on
the Rhine, from which to shoot forth into the very heart of
the Kaiser.

Berwick besieged Philipsburg accordingly (Summer and
Autumn) ; Kaiser doing his feeble best to hinder : at the
Siege, Berwick lost his life, but Philipsburg surrendered to
his successor, all the same ; — Kaiser striving to hinder ; but
in a most paralyzed manner, and to no purpose whatever.
And — and this properly *was* the German War ; the sum of all
done in it during those two years.

Seizure of Nanci (that is, of Lorraine), seizure of Kehl we
already heard of ; then, prior to Philipsburg, there was siege
or seizure of Trarbach by the French ; and, posterior to it,
seizure of Worms by them ; and by the Germans there was
"burning of a magazine in Speyer by bombs." And, in brief,
on both sides, there was marching and manœuvring under
various generals (our old rusty Seckendorf one of them), till
the end of 1735, when the Italian decision arrived, and Truce
and Peace along with it ; but there was no other action worth
naming, even in the Newspapers as a wonder of nine days.
The Siege of Philipsburg, and what hung flickering round that
operation, before and after, was the sum-total of the German
War.

Philipsburg, key of the Rhine in those parts, has had many
sieges ; nor would this one merit the least history from us,
were it not for one circumstance : That our Crown-Prince was
of the Opposing Army, and made his first experience of arms
there. A Siege of Philipsburg slightly memorable to us, on
that one account. What Friedrich did there, which in the
military way was as good as nothing ; what he saw and ex-

* Map at p. 499.

perienced there, which, with some "eighty Princes of the
Reich," a Prince Eugene for General, and three months under
canvas on the field, may have been something: this, in outline,
by such obscure indications as remain, we would fain make
conceivable to the reader.   Indications, in the History-Books,
we have as good as none ; but must gather what there is from
Wilhelmina and the Crown-Prince's *Letters*, — much studying
to be brief, were it possible !

———————•———————

CHAPTER X.

CROWN-PRINCE GOES TO THE RHINE CAMPAIGN.

THE Kaiser — with Kehl snatched from him, the Rhine
open, and Louis XV. singing *Te Deum* in the Christmas time
for what Villars in Italy had done — applied, in passionate
haste, to the Reich.   The Reich, though Fleury tried to cajole
it, and apologize for taking Kehl from it, declares for the
Kaiser's quarrel; War against France on his behalf; [1] — it
was in this way that Friedrich Wilhelm and our Crown-Prince
came to be concerned in the Rhine Campaign.   The Kaiser
will have a Reich's-Army (were it good for much, as is not
likely) to join to his own Austrian one.   And if Prince
Eugene, who is Reich's-Feldmarschall, one of the *two* Feldmarschalls, get the Generalship as men hope, it is not doubted
but there will be great work on the Rhine, this Summer
of 1734.

Unhappily the Reich's-Army, raised from multifarious contingents, and guided and provided for by many heads, is
usually good for little.   Not to say that old Kur-Pfalz, with
an eye to French help in the Berg-and-Jülich matter; old
Kur-Pfalz, and the Bavarian set (*Kur-Baiern* and *Kur-Köln*,
Bavaria and Cologne, who are Brothers, and of old cousinship
to Kur-Pfalz), — quite refuse their contingents; protest in

[1] 13th March, 1734 (Buchholz, i. 131).

the Diet, and openly have French leanings. These are bad
omens for the Reich's-Army. And in regard to the Reich's-
Feldmarschall Office, there also is a difficulty. The Reich, as
we hinted, keeps two supreme Feldmarschalls; one Catholic,
one Protestant, for equilibrium's sake; illustrious Prince
Eugenio von Savoye is the Catholic; — but as to the Protestant, it is a difficulty worth observing for a moment.

Old Duke Eberhard Ludwig of Würtemberg, the unfortunate old gentleman bewitched by the Grävenitz "Deliver us
from evil," used to be the Reich's-Feldmarschall of Protestant persuasion; — Commander-in-Chief for the Reich, when it
tried fighting. Old Eberhard had been at Blenheim, and had
marched up and down: I never heard he was much of a General; perhaps good enough for the Reich, whose troops were
always bad. But now that poor Duke, as we intimated once
or more, is dead; there must be, of Protestant type, a new
Reich's-Feldmarschall had. One Catholic, unequalled among
Captains, we already have; but where is the Protestant, Duke
Eberhard being dead?

Duke Eberhard's successor in Würtemberg, Karl Alexander
by name, whom we once dined with at Prag on the Kladrup
journey, he, a General of some worth, would be a natural person. Unluckily Duke Karl Alexander had, while an Austrian
Officer and without outlooks upon Protestant Würtemberg,
gone over to Papacy, and is now Catholic. "Two Catholic
Feldmarschalls!" cries the *Corpus Evangelicorum;* "that will
never do!"

Well, on the other or Protestant side there appear two Candidates; one of them not much expected by the reader: no
other than Ferdinand Duke of Brunswick-Bevern, our Crown-
Prince's Father-in-law; whom we knew to be a worthy man,
but did not know to be much of a soldier, or capable of these
ambitious views. He is Candidate First. Then there is a
Second, much more entitled: our gunpowder friend the Old
Dessauer; who, to say nothing of his soldier qualities, has
promises from the Kaiser, — he surely were the man, if it
did not hurt other people's feelings. But it surely does and
will. There is Ferdinand of Bevern applying upon the score

of old promises too. How can people's feelings be saved ?
Protestants these two last : but they cannot both have it ; and
what will Würtemberg say to either of them ? The Reich
was in very great affliction about this preliminary matter.
But Friedrich Wilhelm steps in with a healing recipe : " Let
there be four Reich's-Feldmarschalls," said Friedrich Wilhelm ; " two Protestant and two Catholic : won't that do ? "
— Excellent ! answers the Reich : and there are four Feldmarschalls for the time being ; no lack of commanders to the
Reich's-Army. Brunswick-Bevern tried it first ; but only till
Prince Eugene were ready, and indeed he had of himself come
to nothing before that date. Prince Eugene next ; then Karl
Alexander next ; and in fact they all might have had a stroke
at commanding, and at coming to nothing or little, — only the
Old Dessauer sulked at the office in this its fourfold state, and
never would fairly have it, till, by decease of occupants, it
came to be twofold again. This glimpse into the distracted
effete interior of the poor old Reich and its Politics, with
friends of ours concerned there, let it be welcome to the
reader.[1]

Friedrich Wilhelm was without concern in this War, or in
what had led to it. Practical share in the Polish Election
(after that preliminary theoretic program of the Kaiser's and
Czarina's went to smoke) Friedrich Wilhelm steadily refused
to take : though considerable offers were made him on both
sides, — offer of West Preussen (Polish part of Prussia, which
once was known to us) on the French side.[2] But his primary
fixed resolution was to stand out of the quarrel ; and he abides
by that ; suppresses any wishes of his own in regard to the
Polish Election ; — keeps ward on his own frontiers, with good
military besom in hand, to sweep it out again if it intruded
there. " What King you like, in God's name ; only don't
come over my threshold with his brabbles and him ! "

But seeing the Kaiser got into actual French War, with the
Reich consenting, he is bound, by Treaty of old date (date
older than *Wusterhausen*, though it was confirmed on that

[1] *Leopoldi von Anhalt-Dessau Leben* (by Ranfft), p. 127 ; Buchholz, i. 131.
[2] By De la Chétardie, French Ambassador at Berlin (Buchholz, i. 130).

famous occasion), "To assist the Kaiser with ten thousand men;" and this engagement he intends amply to fulfil. No sooner, therefore, had the Reich given sure signs of assenting ("Reich's assent" is the condition of the ten thousand), than Friedrich Wilhelm's orders were out, "Be in readiness!" Friedrich Wilhelm, by the time of the Reich's actual assent, or Declaration of War on the Kaiser's behalf, has but to lift his finger: squadrons and battalions, out of Pommern, out of Magdeburg, out of Preussen, to the due amount, will get on march whitherward you bid, and be with you there at the day you indicate, almost at the hour. Captains, not of an imaginary nature, these are always busy; and the King himself is busy over them. From big guns and wagon-horses down to gun-flints and gaiter-straps, all is marked in registers; nothing is wanting, nothing out of its place at any time, in Friedrich Wilhelm's Army.

From an early period, the French intentions upon Philipsburg might be foreseen or guessed: and in the end of March, Maréchal Berwick, "in three divisions," fairly appears in that quarter; his purpose evident. So that the Reich's-Army, were it in the least ready, ought to rendezvous, and reinforce the handful of Austrians there. Friedrich Wilhelm's part of the Reich's-Army does accordingly straightway get on march; leaves Berlin, after the due reviewing, "8th April:" [1] eight regiments of it, three of Horse and five of Foot, Goltz Foot-regiment one of them; — a General Röder, unexceptionable General, to command in chief; — and will arrive, though the farthest off, "first of all the Reich's-Contingents;" 7th of June, namely. The march, straight south, must be some four hundred miles.

Besides the Official Generals, certain high military dignitaries, Schulenburg, Bredow, Majesty himself at their head, propose to go as volunteers; — especially the Crown-Prince, whose eagerness is very great, has got liberty to go. "As volunteer" he too: as Colonel of Goltz, it might have had its unsuitabilities, in etiquette and otherwise. Few volunteers are more interested than the Crown-Prince. Watching the

[1] Fassmann, p. 495.

great War-theatre uncurtain itself in this manner, from Dantzig down to Naples; and what his own share in it shall be:
this, much more than his Marriage, I suppose, has occupied
his thoughts since that event. Here out of Ruppin, dating six
or seven weeks before the march of the Ten Thousand, is a
small sign, one among many, of his outlooks in this matter.
Small Note to his Cousin, Margraf Heinrich, the ill-behaved
Margraf, much his comrade, who is always falling into scrapes;
and whom he has just, not without difficulty, got delivered out
of something of the kind.[1] He writes in German and in the
intimate style of *Thou :* —

"*Ruppin,* 23d *February,* 1734. My dear Brother, — I can
with pleasure answer that the King hath spoken of thee altogether favorably to me [scrape now abolished, for the time]:
— and I think it would not have an ill effect, wert thou to
apply for leave to go with the ten thousand whom he is sending to the Rhine, and do the Campaign with them as volunteer.
I am myself going with that corps; so I doubt not the King
would allow thee.

"I take the freedom to send herewith a few bottles of Champagne; and wish" all manner of good things.

"Friedrich." [2]

This Margraf Heinrich goes; also his elder Brother, Margraf
Friedrich Wilhelm, — who long persecuted Wilhelmina with
his hopes; and who is now about getting Sophie Dorothee,
a junior Princess, much better than he merits : Betrothal is
the week after these ten thousand march; [3] he thirty, she fifteen. He too will go; as will the other pair of Cousin Margraves, — Karl, who was once our neighbor in Cüstrin; and
the *Younger* Friedrich Wilhelm, whose fate lies at Prag if he
knew it. Majesty himself will go as volunteer. Are not great
things to be done, with Eugene for General ? — To understand
the insignificant Siege of Philipsburg, sum-total of the Rhine
Campaign, which filled the Crown-Prince's and so many other

---

[1] *Œuvres de Frédéric,* xxvii. part 2d, pp. 8, 9.
[2] Ib. xxvii. part 2d, p. 10.
[3] 16th April, 1734 (Ib. part 1st, p. 14 n).

minds brimful, that Summer, and is now wholly out of every
mind, the following Excerpt may be admissible : —

"The unlucky little Town of Philipsburg, key of the Rhine
in that quarter, fortified under difficulties by old Bishops of
Speyer who sometimes resided there,[1] has been dismantled and
refortified, has had its Rhine-bridge torn down and set up
again ; been garrisoned now by this party, now by that, who
had 'right of garrison there;' nay France has sometimes had
'the right of garrison;'— and the poor little Town has
suffered much, and been tumbled sadly about in the Succes-
sion-Wars and perpetual controversies between France and
Germany in that quarter. In the time we are speaking of,
it has a 'flying-bridge' (of I know not what structure), with
fortified 'bridge-head (tête-de-pont),' on the western or France-
ward side of the River. Town's bulwarks, and complex engi-
neering defences, are of good strength, all put in repair for this
occasion : Reich and Kaiser have an effective garrison there,
and a commandant determined on defence to the uttermost :
what the unfortunate Inhabitants, perhaps a thousand or so
in number, thought or did under such a visitation of ruin
and bombshells, History gives not the least hint anywhere.
'Quite used to it!' thinks History, and attends to other
points.

"The Rhine Valley here is not of great breadth : eastward
the heights rise to be mountainous in not many miles. By
way of defence to this Valley, in the Eugene-Marlborough
Wars, there was, about forty miles southward, or higher up
the River than Philipsburg, a military line or chain of posts ;
going from Stollhofen, a boggy hamlet on the Rhine, with cunning indentations, and learned concatenation of bog and bluff,
up into the inaccessibilities, — Lines of Stollhofen, the name of
it, — which well-devised barrier did good service for certain
years. It was not till, I think, the fourth year of their existence, year 1707, that Villars, the same Villars who is now
in Italy, 'stormed the Lines of Stollhofen;' which made him
famous that year.

"The Lines of Stollhofen have now, in 1734, fallen flat

[1] Köhler, Münzbelustigungen, vi. 169.

again; but Eugene remembers them, and, I could guess, it was
he who suggests a similar expedient.   At all events, there is
a similar expedient fallen upon : *Lines of Ettlingen* this time;
one-half nearer Philipsburg; running from Mühlburg on the
Rhine-brink up to Ettlingen in the Hills.*   Nearer, by twenty
miles; and, I guess, much more slightly done.   We shall see
these Lines of Ettlingen, one point of them, for a moment : —
and they would not be worth mentioning at all, except that
in careless Books they too are called 'Lines of *Stollhofen*,'[1]
and the ingenuous reader is sent wandering on his map to no
purpose."

   "Lines of *Ettlingen*" they are; related, as now said, to the
Stollhofen set.   Duke Ferdinand of Brunswick-Bevern, one of
the four Feldmarschalls, has some ineffectual handful of Imperial troops dotted about, within these Lines and on the skirts
of Philipsburg; — eagerly waiting till the Reich's-Army gather
to him; otherwise he must come to nothing.   Will at any rate,
I should think, be happy to resign in favor of Prince Eugene,
were that little hero once on the ground.

   On Mayday, Maréchal Berwick, who has been awake in this
quarter, " in three divisions," for a month past, — very impatient till Belleisle with the first division should have taken
Trarbach, and made the Western interior parts secure, — did
actually cross the Rhine, with his second division, "at Fort
Louis," well up the River, well south of Philipsburg; intending to attack the Lines of Ettlingen, and so get in upon the
Town.   There is a third division, about to lay pontoons for
itself a good way farther down, which will attack the Lines
simultaneously from within, — that is to say, shall come upon
the *back* of poor Bevern and his defensive handful of troops,
and astonish him there.   All prospers to Berwick in this
matter : Noailles his lieutenant (not yet gone to Italy till next
year), with whom is Maurice Comte de Saxe (afterwards Maréchal de Saxe), an excellent observant Officer, marches up to

   * Map at p. 499.
   [1] Wilhelmina (ii. 206), for instance; who, or whose Printer, calls them
"Lines of *Stokoff*" even.

Ettlingen, May 3d; bivouacs "at the base of the mountain" (no great things of a mountain); ascends the same in two columns, horse and foot, by the first sunlight next morning; forms on a little plain on the top; issues through a thin wood, — and actually beholds those same *Lines of Ettlingen,* the outmost eastern end of them : a somewhat inconsiderable matter, after all!   Here is Noailles's own account : —

"These retrenchments, made in Turk fashion, consisted of big trees set zigzag (*en échiquier*), twisted together by the branches; the whole about five fathoms thick.   Inside of it were a small forlorn of Austrians : these steadily await our grenadiers, and do not give their volley till we are close.   Our grenadiers receive their volley; clear the intertwisted trees, after receiving a second volley (total loss seventy-five killed and wounded); and — the enemy quits his post; and the Lines of Ettlingen *are* stormed!"[1]   This is not like storming the Lines of Stollhofen; a thing to make Noailles famous in the Newspapers for a year.   But it was a useful small feat, and well enough performed on his part.   The truth is, Berwick was about attacking the Lines simultaneously on the other or Mühlburg end of them (had not Noailles, now victorious, galloped to forbid); and what was far more considerable, those other French, to the northward, "upon pontoons," are fairly across; like to be upon the *back* of Duke Ferdinand and his handful of defenders.   Duke Ferdinand perceives that he is come to nothing; hastily collects his people from their various posts; retreats with them that same night, unpursued, to Heilbronn; and gives up the command to Prince Eugene, who is just arrived there, — who took quietly two pinches of snuff on hearing this news of Ettlingen, and said, "No matter, after all!"

Berwick now forms the Siege, at his discretion; invests Philipsburg, 13th May;[2] begins firing, night of the 3d–4th June; — Eugene waiting at Heilbronn till the Reich's-Army come up.   The Prussian ten thousand do come, all in order, on the 7th: the rest by degrees, all later, and all *not* quite in

---

[1] Noailles, *Mémoires* (in Petitot's Collection), iii. 207.
[2] Berwick, ii. 312; 23d, says Noailles's Editor (iii. 210).

order. Eugene, the Prussians having joined him, moves down
towards Philipsburg and its cannonading; encamps close to
rearward of the besieging French. "Camp of Wiesenthal"
they call it; Village of Wiesenthal with bogs, on the left,
being his head-quarters; Village of Waghäusel, down near the
River, a five miles distance, being his limit on the right. Berwick, in front, industriously battering Philipsburg into the
River, has thrown up strong lines behind him, strongly manned,
to defend himself from Eugene; across the River, Berwick has
one Bridge, and at the farther end one battery with which he
plays upon the rear of Philipsburg. He is much criticised
by unoccupied people, "Eugene's attack will ruin us on those
terms!" — and much incommoded by overflowings of the
Rhine; Rhine swoln by melting of the mountain-snows, as is
usual there. Which inundations Berwick had well foreseen,
though the War-minister at Paris would not: "Haste!"
answered the War-minister always: "We shall be in right
time. I tell you there have fallen no snows this winter:
how can inundation be?" — "Depends on the heat," said
Berwick; "there are snows enough always in stock up
there!"

And so it proves, though the War-minister would not believe;
and Berwick has to take the inundations, and to take the circumstances; — and to try if, by his own continual best exertions, he can but get Philipsburg into the bargain. On the
12th of June, visiting his posts, as he daily does, the first
thing, Berwick stept out of the trenches, anxious for clear
view of something; stept upon "the crest of the sap," a place
exposed to both French and Austrian batteries, and which had
been forbidden to the soldiers, — and there, as he anxiously
scanned matters through his glass, a cannon-ball, unknown
whether French or Austrian, shivered away the head of Berwick; left others to deal with the criticisms, and the inundations, and the operations big or little, at Philipsburg and
elsewhere! Siege went on, better or worse, under the next in
command; "Paris in great anxiety," say the Books.

It is a hot siege, a stiff defence; Prince Eugene looks on,
but does not attack in the way apprehended. Southward in

Italy, we hear there is marching, strategying in the Parma Country; Graf von Mercy likely to come to an action before long. Northward, Dantzig by this time is all wrapt in fire-whirlwinds; its sallyings and outer defences all driven in; mere torrents of Russian bombs raining on it day and night; French auxiliaries, snapt up at landing, are on board Russian ships; and poor Stanislaus and "the Lady of Quality who shot the first gun" have a bad outlook there. Towards the end of the month, the Berlin volunteer Generals, our Crown-Prince and his Margraves among them, are getting on the road for Philipsburg; — and that is properly the one point we are concerned with. Which took effect in manner following.

Tuesday evening, 29th June, there is Ball at Monbijou; the Crown-Prince and others busy dancing there, as if nothing special lay ahead. Nevertheless, at three in the morning he has changed his ball-dress for a better, he and certain more; and is rushing southward, with his volunteer Generals and Margraves, full speed, saluted by the rising sun, towards Philipsburg and the Seat of War. And the same night, King Stanislaus, if any of us cared for him, is on flight from Dantzig, "disguised as a cattle-dealer;" got out on the night of Sunday last, Town under such a rain of bombshells being palpably too hot for him: got out, but cannot get across the muddy intricacies of the Weichsel; lies painfully squatted up and down, in obscure alehouses, in that Stygian Mud-Delta, — a matter of life and death to get across, and not a boat to be had, such the vigilance of the Russian. Dantzig is capitulating, dreadful penalties exacted, all the heavier as no Stanislaus is to be found in it; and search all the keener rises in the Delta after him. Through perils and adventures of the sort usual on such occasions,[1] Stanislaus does get across; and in time does reach Preussen; where, by Friedrich Wilhelm's order, safe opulent asylum is afforded him, till the Fates (when this War ends) determine what is to become of the poor Imaginary Majesty. We leave him, squatted in the intricacies

[1] Credible modest detail of them, in a *Letter* from Stanislaus himself (*History of Stanislaus*, already cited, pp. 235–248).

of the Mud-Delta, to follow our Crown-Prince, who in the same
hour is rushing far elsewhither.

Margraves, Generals and he, in their small string of carriages, go on, by extra-post, day and night; no rest till they
get to Hof, in the Culmbach neighborhood, a good two hundred miles off, — near Wilhelmina, and more than half-way to
Philipsburg. Majesty Friedrich Wilhelm is himself to follow
in about a week : he has given strict order against waste of
time : " Not to part company; go together, and *not* by Anspach
or Baireuth," — though they lie almost straight for you.

This latter was a sore clause to Friedrich, who had counted
all along on seeing his dear faithful Wilhelmina, as he passed :
therefore, as the Papa's Orders, dangerous penalty lying in
them, cannot be literally disobeyed, the question rises, How
see Wilhelmina and not Baireuth ? Wilhelmina, weak as she
is and unfit for travelling, will have to meet him in some
neutral place, suitablest for both. After various shiftings, it
has been settled between them that Berneck, a little town
twelve miles from Baireuth on the Hof road, will do; and that
Friday, probably early, will be the day. Wilhelmina, accordingly, is on the road that morning, early enough; Husband
with her, and ceremonial attendants, in honor of such a Brother;
morning is of sultry windless sort; day hotter and hotter;
— at Berneck is no Crown-Prince, in the House appointed
for him; hour after hour, Wilhelmina waits there in vain. The
truth is, one of the smallest accidents has happened : the Generals " lost a wheel at Gera yesterday; " were left behind there
with their smiths, have not yet appeared; and the insoluble
question among Friedrich and the Margraves is, " We dare not
go on without them, then ? We dare; — dare we ? " Question
like to drive Friedrich mad, while the hours, at any rate, are
slipping on ! Here are three Letters of Friedrich, legible at
last; which, with Wilhelmina's account from the other side,
represent a small entirely human scene in this French-Austrian
War, — nearly all of human we have found in the beggarly
affair : —

1. *To Princess Wilhelmina, at Baireuth, or on the road to*
Berneck.

"HOF, 2d July [not long after 4 A.M.], 1734.

"MY DEAR SISTER, — Here am I within six leagues [say eight
or more, twenty-five miles English] of a Sister whom I love;
and I have to decide that it will be impossible to see her, after
all!" — Does decide so, accordingly, for reasons known to us.

"I have never so lamented the misfortune of not depending
on myself as at this moment! The King being but very sour-
sweet on my score, I dare not risk the least thing; Monday
come a week, when he arrives himself, I should have a pretty
scene (*serais joliment traité*) in the Camp, if I were found to
have disobeyed orders.

". . . The Queen commands me to give you a thousand
regards from her. She appeared much affected at your illness;
but for the rest, I could not warrant you how sincere it was;
for she is totally changed, and I have quite lost reckoning of
her (*n'y connais rien*). That goes so far that she has done me
hurt with the King, all she could : however, that is over now.
As to Sophie [young Sister just betrothed to the eldest Margraf whom you know], she also is no longer the same; for she
approves all that the Queen says or does; and she is charmed
with her big clown (*gros nigaud*) of a Bridegroom.

"The King is more difficult than ever; he is content with
nothing, so as to have lost whatsoever could be called gratitude
for all pleasures one can do him," — marrying against one's
will, and the like. "As to his health, it is one day better,
another worse; but the legs, they are always swelled. Judge
what my joy must be to get out of that turpitude, — for the
King will only stay a fortnight, at most, in the Camp.

"Adieu, my adorable Sister : I am so tired, I cannot stir;
having left on Tuesday night, or rather Wednesday morning
at three o'clock, from a Ball at Monbijou, and arrived here this
Friday morning at four. I recommend myself to your gracious
remembrance; and am, for my own part, till death, dearest
Sister," — Your —   "FRIEDRICH."

¹ *Œuvres de Frédéric,* xxvii. part 1st, p. 13.

This is Letter First; written Friday morning, on the edge
of getting into bed, after such fatigue; and it has, as natural
in that mood, given up the matter in despair. It did not meet
Wilhelmina on the road; and she had left Baireuth; — where
it met her, I do not know; probably at home, on her return,
when all was over. Let Wilhelmina now speak her own lively
experiences of that same Friday: —

"I got to Berneck at ten. The heat was excessive; I found
myself quite worn out with the little journey I had done. I
alighted at the House which had been got ready for my
Brother. We waited for him, and in vain waited, till three in
the afternoon. At three we lost patience; had dinner served
without him. Whilst we were at table, there came on a frightful thunder-storm. I have witnessed nothing so terrible: the
thunder roared and reverberated among the rocky cliffs which
begirdle Berneck; and it seemed as if the world was going
to perish: a deluge of rain succeeded the thunder.

"It was four o'clock; and I could not understand what had
become of my Brother. I had sent out several persons on
horseback to get tidings of him, and none of them came back.
At length, in spite of all my prayers, the Hereditary Prince
[my excellent Husband] himself would go in search. I remained waiting till nine at night, and nobody returned. I
was in cruel agitations: these cataracts of rain are very dangerous in the mountain countries; the roads get suddenly
overflowed, and there often happen misfortunes. I thought
for certain, there had one happened to my Brother or to the
Hereditary Prince." Such a 2d of July, to poor Wilhelmina!

"At last, about nine, somebody brought word that my
Brother had changed his route, and was gone to Culmbach
[a House of ours, lying westward, known to readers]; there
to stay overnight. I was for setting out thither, — Culmbach
is twenty miles from Berneck; but the roads are frightful,"
White Mayn, still a young River, dashing through the rock-
labyrinths there, "and full of precipices: — everybody rose in
opposition, and, whether I would or not, they put me into the
carriage for Himmelkron [partly on the road thither], which
is only about ten miles off. We had like to have got drowned

on the road; the waters were so swoln [White Mayn and its angry brooks], the horses could not cross but by swimming.

"I arrived at last, about one in the morning. I instantly threw myself on a bed. I was like to die with weariness; and in mortal terrors that something had happened to my Brother or the Hereditary Prince. This latter relieved me on his own score; he arrived at last, about four o'clock, — had still no news farther of my Brother. I was beginning to doze a little, when they came to warn me that 'M. von Knobelsdorf wished to speak with me from the Prince-Royal.' I darted out of bed, and ran to him. He," handing me a Letter, "brought word that "—

But let us now give Letter Second, which has turned up lately, and which curiously completes the picture here. Friedrich, on rising refreshed with sleep at Hof, had taken a cheerfuler view; and the Generals still lagging rearward, he thinks it possible to see Wilhelmina after all. Possible; and yet so very dangerous, — perhaps not possible? Here is a second Letter written from München, some fifteen miles farther on, at an after period of the same Friday: purport still of a perplexed nature, " I will, and I dare not; " — practical outcome, of itself uncertain, is scattered now by torrents and thunderstorms. This is the Letter, which Knobelsdorf now hands to Wilhelmina at that untimely hour of Saturday : —

2. To Princess Wilhelmina (by Knobelsdorf).

"MÜNCHBERG, 2d July, 1734.

" MY DEAREST SISTER, — I am in despair that I cannot satisfy my impatience and my duty, — to throw myself at your feet this day. But alas, dear Sister, it does not depend on me : we poor Princes," the Margraves and I, "are obliged to wait here till our Generals [Bredow, Schulenburg and Company] come up; we dare not go along without them. They broke a wheel in Gera [fifty miles behind us]; hearing nothing of them since, we are absolutely forced to wait here. Judge in what a mood I am, and what sorrow must be mine! Express order not to go by Baireuth or Anspach : — forbear, dear Sister, to torment me on things not depending on myself at all.

"I waver between hope and fear of paying my court to you. I hope it might still be at Berneck," this evening, — "if you could contrive a road into the Nürnberg Highway again; avoiding Baireuth: otherwise I dare not go. The Bearer, who is Captain Knobelsdorf [excellent judicious man, old acquaintance from the Cüstrin time, who attends upon us, actual Captain once, but now titular merely, given to architecture and the fine arts [1]], will apprise you of every particular : let Knobelsdorf settle something that may be possible. This is how I stand at present; and instead of having to expect some favor from the King [after what I have done by his order], I get nothing but chagrin. But what is crueler upon me than all, is that you are ill. God, in his grace, be pleased to help you, and restore the precious health which I so much wish you!. . .   FRIEDRICH." [2]

Judicious Knobelsdorf settles that the meeting is to be this very morning at eight; Wilhelmina (whose memory a little fails her in the insignificant points) does not tell us where : but, by faint indications, I perceive it was in the Lake-House, pleasant Pavilion in the ancient artificial Lake, or big ornamental Fish-pond, called *Brandenburger Weiher*, a couple of miles to the north of Baireuth : there Friedrich is to stop, — keeping the Paternal Order from the teeth outwards in this manner. Eight o'clock : so that Wilhelmina is obliged at once to get upon the road again, — poor Princess, after such a day and night. Her description of the Interview is very good : —

"My Brother overwhelmed me with caresses; but found me in so pitiable a state, he could not restrain his tears. I was not able to stand on my limbs; and felt like to faint every

---

[1] Seyfarth (Anonymous), *Lebens- und Regierungs-Geschichte Friedrichs des Andern* (Leipzig, 1786), ii. 200. *Œuvres de Frédéric*, vii. 33. Preuss, *Friedrich mit seinen Verwandten* (Berlin, 1838), pp. 8, 17.

[2] *Œuvres de Frédéric*, xxvii. part 1st, p. 15.

moment, so weak was I. He told me the King was much angered at the Margraf [my Father-in-Law] for not letting his Son make the Campaign," — concerning which point, said Son, my Husband, being Heir-Apparent, there had been much arguing in Court and Country, here at Baireuth, and endless anxiety on my poor part, lest he should get killed in the Wars. "I told him all the Margraf's reasons; and added, that surely they were good, in respect of my dear Husband. 'Well,' said he, 'let him quit soldiering, then, and give back his regiment to the King. But for the rest, quiet yourself as to the fears you may have about him if he do go; for I know, by certain information, that there will be no blood spilt.' — 'They are at the Siege of Philipsburg, however.' — 'Yes,' said my Brother; 'but there will not be a battle risked to hinder it.'

"The Hereditary Prince," my Husband, "came in while we were talking so; and earnestly entreated my Brother to get him away from Baireuth. They went to a window, and talked a long time together. In the end, my Brother told me he would write a very obliging Letter to the Margraf, and give him such reasons in favor of the Campaign, that he doubted not it would turn the scale. 'We will stay together,' said he, addressing the Hereditary Prince; 'and I shall be charmed to have my dear Brother always beside me.' He wrote the Letter; gave it to Baron Stein [Chamberlain or Goldstick of ours], to deliver to the Margraf. He promised to obtain the King's express leave to stop at Baireuth on his return; — after which he went away. It was the last time I saw him on the old footing with me: he has much changed since then! — We returned to Baireuth; where I was so ill that, for three days, they did not think I should get over it." [1]

Crown-Prince dashes off, southwestward, through cross country, into the Nürnberg Road again; gets to Nürnberg that same Saturday night; and there, among other Letters, writes the following; which will wind up this little Incident for us, still in a human manner: —

[1] Wilhelmina, ii. 200–202.

3. *To Princess Wilhelmina at Baireuth.*

"Nürnberg, 3d July, 1734.

" My dearest (*très-chère*) Sister, — It would be impossible
to quit this place without signifying, dearest Sister, my lively
gratitude for all the marks of favor you showed me in the
Weiherhaus [House on the Lake, to-day]. The highest of all
that it was possible to do, was that of procuring me the satisfaction of paying my court to you. I beg millions of pardons for so putting you about, dearest Sister; but I could not
help it; for you know my sad circumstances well enough. In
my great joy, I forgot to give you the Enclosed. I entreat
you, write me often news of your health ! Question the Doctors; and " — and in certain contingencies, the Crown-Prince
"would recommend goat's-milk" for his poor Sister. Had
already, what was noted of him in after life, a tendency to
give medical advice, in cases interesting to him ? —

" Adieu, my incomparable and dear Sister. I am always the
same to you, and will remain so till my death.

"Friedrich." [1]

Generals with their wheel mended, Margraves, Prince and
now the Camp Equipage too, are all at Nürnberg; and start
on the morrow; hardly a hundred miles now to be done, —
but on slower terms, owing to the Equipage. Heilbronn,
place of arms or central stronghold of the Reich's-Army, they
reach on Monday : about Eppingen, next night, if the wind
is westerly, one may hear the cannon, — not without interest.
It was Wednesday forenoon, 7th July, 1734, on some hill-top
coming down from Eppingen side, that the Prince first saw
Philipsburg Siege, blotting the Rhine Valley yonder with its
fire and counter-fire; and the Tents of Eugene stretching on
this side : first view he ever had of the actualities of war.
His account to Papa is so distinct and good, we look through
it almost as at first-hand for a moment : —

"Camp at Wiesenthal, Wednesday, 7th July, 1734.

" Most All-gracious Father, — . . . We left Nürnberg
[nothing said of our Baireuth affair], 4th early, and did not

---

[1] *Œuvres de Frédéric*, xxvii. part 1st, p. 57.

stop till Heilbronn; where, along with the Equipage, I arrived on the 5th. Yesterday I came with the Equipage to Eppingen [twenty miles, a slow march, giving the fourgons time]; and this morning we came to the Camp at Wiesenthal. I have dined with General Röder [our Prussian Commander]; and, after dinner, rode with Prince Eugene while giving the parole. I handed him my All-gracious Father's Letter, which much rejoiced him. After the parole, I went to see the relieving of our outposts [change of sentries there], and view the French retrenchment.

"We," your Majesty's Contingent, "are throwing up three redoubts: at one of them to-day, three musketeers have been miserably shot [*geschossen*, wounded, not quite killed]; two are of Röder's, and one is of Finkenstein's regiment.

"To-morrow I will ride to a village which is on our right wing; Waghäusel is the name of it [1] [some five miles off, north of us, near by the Rhine]; there is a steeple there, from which one can see the French Camp; from this point I will ride down, between the two Lines," French and ours, "to see what they are like.

"There are quantities of hurdles and fascines being made; which, as I hear, are to be employed in one of two different plans. The first plan is, To attack the French retrenchment generally; the ditch which is before it, and the morass which lies on our left wing, to be made passable with these fascines. The other plan is, To amuse the Enemy by a false attack, and throw succor into the Town. — One thing is certain, in a few days we shall have a stroke of work here. Happen what may, my All-gracious Father may be assured that" &c., "and that I will do nothing unworthy of him.

"FRIEDRICH." [2]

Neither of those fine plans took effect; nor did anything take effect, as we shall see. But in regard to that "survey from the steeple of Waghäusel, and ride home again between the Lines," — in regard to that, here is an authentic fraction of anecdote, curiously fitting in, which should not be omitted.

[1] Büsching, v. 1152.   [2] Œuvres, xxvii. part 3d, p. 79.

A certain Herr von Suhm, Saxon Minister at Berlin, occasionally mentioned here, stood in much Correspondence with the
Crown-Prince in the years now following : Correspondence
which was all published at the due distance of time; Suhm
having, at his decease, left the Prince's Letters carefully
assorted with that view, and furnished with a Prefatory
"Character of the Prince-Royal (*Portrait du Prince-Royal, par
M. de Suhm*)." Of which Preface this is a small paragraph,
relating to the Siege of Philipsburg ; offering us a momentary
glance into one fibre of the futile War now going on there.
Of Suhm, and how exact he was, we shall know a little by
and by. Of "Prince von Lichtenstein," an Austrian man and
soldier of much distinction afterwards, we have only to say
that he came to Berlin next year on Diplomatic business, and
that probably enough he had been eye-witness to the little
fact, — fact credible perhaps without much proving. One
rather regretted there was no date to it, no detail to give it
whereabout and fixity in our conception ; that the poor little
Anecdote, though indubitable, had to hang vaguely in the air.
Now, however, the above dated *Letter* does, by accident, date
Suhm's Anecdote too ; date "July 8" as good as certain for it;
the Siege itself having ended (July 18) in ten days more.
Herr von Suhm writes (not for publication till after Friedrich's death and his own) : —

"It was remarked in the Rhine Campaign of 1734, that this
Prince has a great deal of intrepidity (*beaucoup de valeur*).
On one occasion, among others [to all appearance, this very
day, "July 8," riding home from Waghäusel between the
lines], when he had gone to reconnoitre the Lines of Philipsburg, with a good many people about him, — passing, on his
return, along a strip of very thin wood, the cannon-shot from
the Lines accompanied him incessantly, and crashed down
several trees at his side; during all which he walked his horse
along at the old pace, precisely as if nothing were happening,
nor in his hand upon the bridle was there the least trace of
motion perceptible. Those who gave attention to the matter
remarked, on the contrary, that he did not discontinue speaking very tranquilly to some Generals who accompanied him;

and who admired his bearing, in a kind of danger with which he had not yet had occasion to familiarize himself. It is from the Prince von Lichtenstein that I have this anecdote." [1]

On the 15th arrived his Majesty in person, with the Old Dessauer, Buddenbrock, Derschau and a select suite; in hopes of witnessing remarkable feats of war, now that the crisis of Philipsburg was coming on. Many Princes were assembled there, in the like hope: Prince of Orange (honeymoon well ended [2]), a vivacious light gentleman, slightly crooked in the back; Princes of Baden, Darmstadt, Waldeck: all manner of Princes and distinguished personages, fourscore Princes of them by tale, the eyes of Europe being turned on this matter, and on old Eugene's guidance of it. Prince Fred of England, even he had a notion of coming to learn war.

It was about this time, not many weeks ago, that Fred, now falling into much discrepancy with his Father, and at a loss for a career to himself, appeared on a sudden in the Antechamber at St. James's one day; and solemnly demanded an interview with his Majesty. Which his indignant Majesty, after some conference with Walpole, decided to grant. Prince Fred, when admitted, made three demands: 1°. To be allowed to go upon the Rhine Campaign, by way of a temporary career for himself; 2°. That he might have something definite to live upon, a fixed revenue being suitable in his circumstances; 3°. That, after those sad Prussian disappointments, some suitable Consort might be chosen for him, — heart and household lying in such waste condition. Poor Fred, who of us knows what of sense might be in these demands? Few creatures more absurdly situated are to be found in this world. To go where his equals were, and learn soldiering a little, might really have been useful. Paternal Majesty received Fred and his Three Demands with fulminating look; answered, to the first two, nothing; to the third, about a Consort,

---

[1] *Correspondance de Frédéric II. avec M. de Suhm* (Berlin, 1787); Avant-propos, p. xviii. (written 28th April, 1740). The *Correspondance* is all in *Œuvres de Frédéric* (xvi. 247–408); but the Suhm Preface not.

[2] Had wedded Princess Anne, George II.'s eldest, 25th (14th) March, 1734; to the joy of self and mankind, in England here.

" Yes, you shall; but be respectful to the Queen; — and now
off with you; away!"[1]

Poor Fred, he has a circle of hungry Parliamenteers about
him; young Pitt, a Cornet of Horse, young Lyttelton of
Hagley, our old Soissons friend, not to mention others of
worse type; to whom this royal Young Gentleman, with his
vanities, ambitions, inexperiences, plentiful inflammabilities,
is important for exploding Walpole. He may have, and with
great justice I should think, the dim consciousness of talents
for doing something better than "write madrigals" in this
world; infinitude of wishes and appetites he clearly has; —
he is full of inflammable materials, poor youth. And he is
the Fireship those older hands make use of for blowing Walpole and Company out of their anchorage. What a school of
virtue for a young gentleman; — and for the elder ones concerned with him! He did not get to the Rhine Campaign;
nor indeed ever to anything, except to writing madrigals, and
being very futile, dissolute and miserable with what of talent
Nature had given him. Let us pity the poor constitutional
Prince. Our Fritz was only in danger of losing his life;
but what is that, to losing your sanity, personal identity
almost, and becoming Parliamentary Fireship to his Majesty's
Opposition?

Friedrich Wilhelm stayed a month campaigning here;
graciously declined Prince Eugene's invitation to lodge in
Head-quarters, under a roof and within built walls; preferred a tent among his own people, and took the common
hardships, — with great hurt to his weak health, as was afterwards found.

In these weeks, the big Czarina, who has set a price
(100,000 rubles, say £15,000) upon the head of poor Stanislaus, hears that his Prussian Majesty protects him; and
thereupon signifies, in high terms, That she, by her Feldmarschall Münnich, will come across the frontiers and seize
the said Stanislaus. To which his Prussian Majesty answers
positively, though in proper Diplomatic tone, "Madam, I will

[1] Coxe's *Walpole*, i. 322.

in no wise permit it!" Perhaps his Majesty's remarkablest transaction, here on the Rhine, was this concerning Stanislaus. For Seckendorf the Feldzeugmeister was here also, on military function, not forgetful of the Diplomacies; who busily assailed his Majesty, on the Kaiser's part, in the same direction: "Give up Stanislaus, your Majesty! How ridiculous (*lächerlich*) to be perhaps ruined for Stanislaus!" But without the least effect, now or afterwards.

Poor Stanislaus, in the beginning of July, got across into Preussen, as we intimated; and there he continued, safe against any amount of rubles and Feldmarschalls, entreaties and menaces. At Angerburg, on the Prussian frontier, he found a steadfast veteran, Lieutenant-General von Katte, Commandant in those parts (Father of a certain poor Lieutenant, whom we tragically knew of long ago!) — which veteran gentleman received the Fugitive Majesty,[1] with welcome in the King's name, and assurances of an honorable asylum till the times and roads should clear again for his Fugitive Majesty. Fugitive Majesty, for whom the roads and times were very dark at present, went to Marienwerder; talked of going "to Pillau, for a sea-passage," of going to various places; went finally to Königsberg, and there — with a considerable Polish Suite of Fugitives, very moneyless, and very expensive, most of them, who had accumulated about him — set up his abode. There for almost two years, in fact till this War ended, the Fugitive Polish Majesty continued; Friedrich Wilhelm punctually protecting him, and even paying him a small Pension (£50 a month), — France, the least it could do for the Grandfather of France, allowing a much larger one; larger, though still inadequate. France has left its Grandfather strangely in the lurch here; with "100,000 rubles on his head." But Friedrich Wilhelm knows the sacred rites, and will do them; continues deaf as a door-post alike to the menaces and the entreaties of Kaiser and Czarina; strictly intimating to Münnich, what the Laws of Neutrality are, and that they must be observed. Which, by his Majesty's good arrangements, Münnich, willing enough to the

[1] *Militair-Lexikon,* ii. 254.

contrary had it been feasible, found himself obliged to comply
with.   Prussian Majesty, like a King and a gentleman, would
listen to no terms about dismissing or delivering up, or otherwise failing in the sacred rites to Stanislaus ; but honorably
kept him there till the times and routes cleared themselves
again.[1] A plain piece of duty; punctually done : the beginning of it falls here in the Camp at Philipsburg, July–August
1734; in May, 1736, we shall see some glimpse of the end !—

His Prussian Majesty in Camp at Philipsburg — so distinguished a volunteer, doing us the honor to encamp here—
"was asked to all the Councils-of-war that were held," say the
Books.   And he did attend, the Crown-Prince and he, on important occasions : but, alas, there was, so to speak, nothing to
be consulted of.   Fascines and hurdles lay useless ; no attempt
was made to relieve Philipsburg.   On the third day after his
Majesty's arrival, July 18th, Philipsburg, after a stiff defence
of six weeks, growing hopeless of relief, had to surrender ;—
French then proceeded to repair Philipsburg, no attempt on
Eugene's part to molest them there.   If they try ulterior
operations on this side the River, he counter-tries ; and that
is all.

Our Crown-Prince, somewhat of a judge in after years, is
maturely of opinion, That the French Lines were by no means
inexpugnable ; that the French Army might have been ruined
under an attack of the proper kind.[2] Their position was
bad ; no room to unfold themselves for fight, except with the
Town's cannon playing on them all the while ; only one Bridge
to get across by, in case of coming to the worse : defeat of
them probable, and ruin to them inevitable in case of defeat.
But Prince Eugene, with an Army little to his mind (Reich's-
Contingents not to be depended on, thought Eugene), durst
not venture : "Seventeen victorious Battles, and if we should
be defeated in the eighteenth and last ? "

It is probable the Old Dessauer, had he been Generalissimo,
with this same Army, — in which, even in the Reich's part of
it, we know ten thousand of an effective character, — would

[1] Förster, ii. 132, 134–136.   [2] Œuvres de Frédéric, i. 167.

have done some stroke upon the French; but Prince Eugene
would not try.   Much dimmed from his former self this old
hero; age now 73; — a good deal wearied with the long march
through Time.   And this very Summer, his Brother's Son, the
last male of his House, had suddenly died of inflammatory
fever; left the old man very mournful: " Alone, alone, at
the end of one's long march; laurels have no fruit, then ? "
He stood cautious, on the defensive; and in this capacity is
admitted to have shown skilful management.

But Philipsburg being taken, there is no longer the least
event to be spoken of; the Campaign passed into a series
of advancings, retreatings, facings, and then right-about
facings, — painful manœuvrings, on both sides of the Rhine
and of the Neckar, — without result farther to the French,
without memorability to either side.   About the middle of
August, Friedrich Wilhelm went away ; — health much hurt
by his month under canvas, amid Rhine inundations, and
mere distressing phenomena.   Crown-Prince Friedrich and
a select party escorted his Majesty to Mainz, where was a
Dinner of unusual sublimity by the Kurfürst there ; [1] — Dinner done, his Majesty stept on board " the Electoral Yacht ; "
and in this fine hospitable vehicle went sweeping through
the Binger Loch, rapidly down towards Wesel ; and the
Crown-Prince and party returned to their Camp, which is
upon the Neckar at this time.

Camp shifts about, and Crown-Prince in it : to Heidelberg,
to Waiblingen, Weinheim ; close to Mainz at one time : but it
is not worth following : nor in Friedrich's own Letters, or in
other documents, is there, on the best examination, anything
considerable to be gleaned respecting his procedures there.
He hears of the ill-success in Italy, Battle of Parma at the
due date, with the natural feelings ; speaks with a sorrowful
gayety, of the muddy fatigues, futilities here on the Rhine ;
— has the sense, however, not to blame his superiors unreasonably.   Here, from one of his Letters to Colonel Camas,
is a passage worth quoting for the credit of the writer.   With
Camas, a distinguished Prussian Frenchman, whom we men-

[1] 15th August (Fassmann, p. 511).

tioned elsewhere, still more with Madame Camas in time coming, he corresponded much, often in a fine filial manner : —

"The present Campaign is a school, where profit may be reaped from observing the confusion and disorder which reigns in this Army : it has been a field very barren in laurels ; and those who have been used, all their life, to gather such, and on Seventeen distinguished occasions have done so, can get none this time." Next year, we all hope to be on the Moselle, and to find that a fruitfuler field. . . . "I am afraid, dear Camas, you think I am going to put on the cothurnus ; to set up for a small Eugene, and, pronouncing with a doctoral tone what each should have done and not have done, condemn and blame to right and left. No, my dear Camas ; far from carrying my arrogance to that point, I admire the conduct of our Chief, and do not disapprove that of his worthy Adversary ; and far from forgetting the esteem and consideration due to persons who, scarred with wounds, have by years and long service gained a consummate experience, I shall hear them more willingly than ever as my teachers, and try to learn from them how to arrive at honor, and what is the shortest road into the secret of this Profession." [1]

This other, to Lieutenant Gröben, three weeks earlier in date, shows us a different aspect ; which is at least equally authentic ; and may be worth taking with us. Gröben is Lieutenant, — I suppose still of the Regiment Goltz, though he is left there behind ; — at any rate, he is much a familiar with the Prince at Ruppin ; was ringleader, it is thought, in those midnight pranks upon parsons, and the other escapades there ; [2] a merry man, eight years older than the Prince, — with whom it is clear enough he stands on a very free footing. Philipsburg was lost a month ago ; French are busy repairing it ; and manœuvring, with no effect, to get into the interior of Germany a little. Weinheim is a little Town on the north side of the Neckar, a dozen miles or so from Mannheim ; — out of which, and into which, the Prussian Corps

---

[1] "Camp at Heidelberg, 11th September, 1734" (Œuvres, xvi. 131).
[2] Büsching, v. 20.

goes shifting from time to time, as Prince Eugene and the
French manœuvre to no purpose in that Rhine-Neckar Country. "*Herdek Teremtetem*," it appears, is a bit of Hungarian
swearing; should be *Ordek teremtete;* and means "The Devil
made you!"

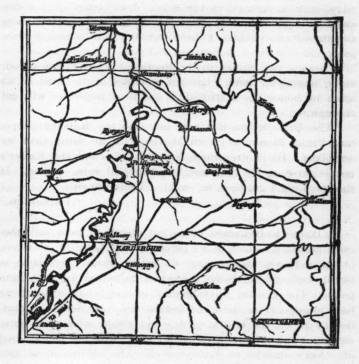

"WEINHEIM, 17th August, 1734.

"*Herdek Teremtetem!* 'Went with them, got hanged with
them,'[1] said the Bielefeld Innkeeper! So will it be with me,
poor devil; for I go dawdling about with this Army here;
and the French will have the better of us. We want to be
over the Neckar again [to the South or Philipsburg side], and
the rogues won't let us. What most provokes me in the matter is, that while we are here in such a wilderness of trouble,

[1] "*Mitgegangen mitgehangen:*" Letter is in German.

doing our utmost, by military labors and endurances, to make ourselves heroic, thou sittest, thou devil, at home!

" Duc de Bouillon has lost his equipage ; our Hussars took it at Landau [other side the Rhine, a while ago]. Here we stand in mud to the ears ; fifteen of the Regiment Alt-Baden have sunk altogether in the mud. Mud comes of a water-spout, or sudden cataract of rain, there was in these Heidelberg Countries ; two villages, Fuhrenheim and Sandhausen, it swam away, every stick of them (*ganz und gar*).

"Captain von Stojentin, of Regiment Flans," one of our eight Regiments here, " has got wounded in the head, in an affair of honor ; he is still alive, and it is hoped he will get through it.

" The Drill-Demon has now got into the Kaiser's people too : Prince Eugene is grown heavier with his drills than we ourselves. He is often three hours at it ; — and the Kaiser's people curse us for the same, at a frightful rate. Adieu. If the Devil don't get thee, he ought. Therefore *vale*.[1]

"FRIEDRICH."

No laurels to be gained here ; but plenty of mud, and laborious hardship, — met, as we perceive, with youthful stoicism, of the derisive, and perhaps of better forms. Friedrich is twenty-two and some months, when he makes his first Campaign. The general physiognomy of his behavior in it we have to guess from these few indications. No doubt he profited by it, on the military side ; and would study with quite new light and vivacity after such contact with the fact studied of. Very didactic to witness even " the confusions of this Army," and what comes of them to Armies ! For the rest, the society of Eugene, Lichtenstein, and so many Princes of the Reich, and Chiefs of existing mankind, could not but be entertaining to the young man ; and silently, if he wished to read the actual Time, as sure enough he, with human and with royal eagerness, did wish, — they were here as the *alphabet* of it to him : important for years coming. Nay it is not doubted, the insight he here got into the condition of the

[1] *Œuvres de Frédéric*, xxvii. part 3d, p. 181.

Austrian Army and its management — " Army left seven days without bread," for one instance — gave him afterwards the highly important notion, that such Army could be beaten if necessary ! —

Wilhelmina says, his chief comrade was Margraf Heinrich; — the *Ill* Margraf; who was *cut* by Friedrich, in after years, for some unknown bad behavior. Margraf Heinrich "led him into all manner of excesses," says Wilhelmina, — probably in the language of exaggeration. He himself tells her, in one of his *Letters*, a day or two before Papa's departure : "The Camp is soon to be close on Mainz, nothing but the Rhine between Mainz and our right wing, where my place is; and so soon as Serenissimus goes [*Le Sérénissime*, so he irreverently names Papa], I mean to be across for some sport," [1] — no doubt the Ill Margraf with me ! With the Elder Margraf, little Sophie's Betrothed, whom he called " big clown " in a Letter we read, he is at this date in open quarrel, — " *brouillé à toute outrance* with the mad Son-in-law, who is the wildest wild-beast of all this Camp." [2]

Wilhelmina's Husband had come, in the beginning of August; but was not so happy as he expected. Considerably cut out by the Ill Heinrich. Here is a small adventure they had; mentioned by Friedrich, and copiously recorded by Wilhelmina : adventure on some River, — which we could guess, if it were worth guessing, to have been the Neckar, not the Rhine. French had a fortified post on the farther side of this River; Crown-Prince, Ill Margraf, and Wilhelmina's Husband were quietly looking about them, riding up the other side : Wilhelmina's Husband decided to take a pencil-drawing of the French post, and paused for that object. Drawing was proceeding unmolested, when his foolish Baireuth Hussar, having an excellent rifle (*arquebuse rayée*) with him, took it into his head to have a shot at the French sentries at long range. His shot hit nothing; but it awakened the French animosity, as was natural; the French began diligently firing; and might easily have done mischief. My Husband, volleying out some rebuke upon the blockhead of a Hussar, finished his drawing,

---

[1] *Œuvres de Frédéric*, xxvii. part 1st, p. 17 (10th August).   [2] Ibid.

in spite of the French bullets; then rode up to the Crown-
Prince and Ill Margraf, who had got their share of what was
going, and were in no good-humor with him. Ill Margraf
rounded things into the Crown-Prince's ear, in an unmannerly
way, with glances at my Husband; — who understood it well
enough; and promptly coerced such ill-bred procedures, intimating, in a polite impressive way, that they would be dangerous if persisted in. Which reduced the Ill Margraf to a
spiteful but silent condition. No other harm was done at that
time; the French bullets all went awry, or "even fell short,
being sucked in by the river," thinks Wilhelmina.[1]

A more important feature of the Crown-Prince's life in
these latter weeks is the news he gets of his father. Friedrich Wilhelm, after quitting the Electoral Yacht, did his reviewing at Wesel, at Bielefeld, all his reviewing in those
Rhine and Weser Countries; then turned aside to pay a promised visit to Ginkel the Berlin Dutch Ambassador, who has a
fine House in those parts; and there his Majesty has fallen
seriously ill. Obliged to pause at Ginkel's, and then at his
own Schloss of Moyland, for some time; does not reach Potsdam till the 14th September, and then in a weak, worsening,
and altogether dangerous condition, which lasts for months
to come.[2] Wrecks of gout, they say, and of all manner of
nosological mischief; falling to dropsy. Case desperate, think
all the Newspapers, in a cautious form; which is Friedrich
Wilhelm's own opinion pretty much, and that of those better
informed. Here are thoughts for a Crown-Prince; well affected
to his Father, yet suffering much from him which is grievous.
To by-standers, one now makes a different figure: "A Crown-
Prince, who may be King one of these days, — whom a little
adulation were well spent upon!" From within and from
without come agitating influences; thoughts which must be
rigorously repressed, and which are not wholly repressible.
The soldiering Crown-Prince, from about the end of September, for the last week or two of this Campaign, is secretly no
longer quite the same to himself or to others.

[1] Wilhelmina, ii. 208, 209; Œuvres de Frédéric, xxvii. part 1st, p. 19.
[2] Fassmann, pp. 512–533: September, 1734–January, 1735.

Glimpse of Lieutenant Chasot, and of other Acquisitions.

We have still two little points to specify, or to bring up from the rearward whither they are fallen, in regard to this Campaign. After which the wearisome Campaign shall terminate; Crown-Prince leading his Ten Thousand to Frankfurt, towards their winter-quarters in Westphalia; and then himself running across from Frankfurt (October 5th), to see Wilhelmina for a day or two on the way homewards: — with much pleasure to all parties, my readers and me included!

First point is, That, some time in this Campaign, probably towards the end of it, the Crown-Prince, Old Dessauer and some others with them, "procured passports," went across, and "saw the French Camp," and what new phenomena were in it for them. Where, when, how, or with what impression left on either side, we do not learn. It was not much of a Camp for military admiration, this of the French.[1] There were old soldiers of distinction in it here and there; a few young soldiers diligently studious of their art; and a great many young fops of high birth and high ways, strutting about "in red-heeled shoes," with "Commissions got from Court" for this War, and nothing of the soldier but the epaulettes and plumages, — apt to be "insolent" among their poorer comrades. From all parties, young and old, even from that insolent red-heel party, nothing but the highest finish of politeness could be visible on this particular occasion. Doubtless all passed in the usual satisfactory manner; and the Crown-Prince got his pleasant excursion, and materials, more or less, for after thought and comparison. But as there is nothing whatever of it on record for us but the bare fact, we leave it to the reader's imagination, — fact being indubitable, and details not inconceivable to lively readers. Among the French dignitaries doing the honors of their Camp on this occasion, he was struck by the General's Adjutant, a "Count de Rottembourg" (properly *von Rothenburg,* of German birth, kinsman to the Rothenburg whom we have seen as French

---

[1] *Mémoires de Noailles* (passim).

Ambassador at Berlin long since); a promising young soldier;
whom he did not lose sight of again, but acquired in due time
to his own service, and found to be of eminent worth there.
A Count von Schmettau, two Brothers von Schmettau, here
in the Austrian service; superior men, Prussian by birth, and
very fit to be acquired by and by; these the Crown-Prince
had already noticed in this Rhine Campaign, — having always
his eyes open to phenomena of that kind.

The *second* little point is of date perhaps two months anterior to that of the French Camp; and is marked sufficiently
in this Excerpt from our confused manuscripts.

Before quitting Philipsburg, there befell one slight adventure,
which, though it seemed to be nothing, is worth recording here.
One day, date not given, a young French Officer, of ingenuous prepossessing look, though much flurried at the moment,
came across as involuntary deserter; flying from a great peril
in his own camp. The name of him is Chasot, Lieutenant of
such and such a Regiment: "Take me to Prince Eugene!" he
entreats, which is done. Peril was this: A high young gentleman, one of those fops in red heels, ignorant, and capable of
insolence to a poorer comrade of studious turn, had fixed a
duel upon Chasot. Chasot ran him through, in fair duel; dead,
and is thought to have deserved it. "But Duc de Boufflers is
his kinsman: run, or you are lost!" cried everybody. The
Officers of his Regiment hastily redacted some certificate for
Chasot, hastily signed it; and Chasot ran, scarcely waiting to
pack his baggage.

"Will not your Serene Highness protect me?"—"Certainly!" said Eugene; — gave Chasot a lodging among his own
people; and appointed one of them, Herr Brender by name,
to show him about, and teach him the nature of his new quarters. Chasot, a brisk, ingenuous young fellow, soon became a
favorite; eager to be useful where possible; and very pleasant
in discourse, said everybody.

By and by, — still at Philipsburg, as would seem, though it
is not said, —the Crown-Prince heard of Chasot; asked Brender to bring him over. Here is Chasot's own account: through

which, as through a small eyelet-hole, we peep once more, and for the last time, direct into the Crown-Prince's Campaign-life on this occasion : —

"Next morning, at ten o'clock the appointed hour, Brender having ordered out one of his horses for me, I accompanied him to the Prince ; who received us in his Tent, — behind which he had, hollowed out to the depth of three or four feet, a large Dining-room, with windows, and a roof," I hope of good height, "thatched with straw. His Royal Highness, after two hours' conversation, in which he had put a hundred questions to me [a Prince desirous of knowing the facts], dismissed us ; and at parting, bade me return often to him in the evenings.

"It was in this Dining-room, at the end of a great dinner, the day after next, that the Prussian guard introduced a Trumpet from Monsieur d'Asfeld [French Commander-in-Chief since Berwick's death], with my three horses, sent over from the French Army. Prince Eugene, who was present, and in good humor, said, 'We must sell those horses, they don't speak German ; Brender will take care to mount you some way or other.' Prince Lichtenstein immediately put a price on my horses ; and they were sold on the spot at three times their worth. The Prince of Orange, who was of this Dinner [slightly crook-backed witty gentleman, English honeymoon well over], said to me in a half-whisper, ' Monsieur, there is nothing like selling horses to people who have dined well.'

"After this sale, I found myself richer than I had ever been in my life. The Prince-Royal sent me, almost daily, a groom and led horse, that I might come to him, and sometimes follow him in his excursions. At last, he had it proposed to me, by M. de Brender, and even by Prince Eugene, to accompany him to Berlin." Which, of course, I did ; taking Ruppin first. "I arrived at Berlin from Ruppin, in 1734, two days after the marriage of Friedrich Wilhelm Margraf of Schwedt [Ill Margraf's elder Brother, wildest wild-beast of this camp] with the Princess Sophie," — that is to say, 12th of November ; Marriage having been on the 10th, as the Books teach us. Chasot remembers that, on the 14th, "the Crown-Prince gave, in his

Berlin mansion, a dinner to all the Royal Family," in honor
of that auspicious wedding.[1]

Thus is Chasot established with the Crown-Prince. He will
turn up fighting well in subsequent parts of this History ; and
again duelling fatally, though nothing of a quarrelsome man,
as he asserts.

Crown-Prince's Visit to Baireuth on the Way home.

October 4th, the Crown-Prince has parted with Prince Eugene, — not to meet again in this world; "an old hero gone
to the shadow of himself," says the Crown-Prince; [2] — and is
giving his Prussian War-Captains a farewell dinner at Frankfurt-on-Mayn ; having himself led the Ten Thousand so far,
towards Winter-quarters, and handing them over now to their
usual commanders. They are to winter in Westphalia, these
Ten Thousand, in the Paderborn-Münster Country ; where they
are nothing like welcome to the Ruling Powers; nor are intended to be so, — Kur-Köln (proprietor there) and his Brother
of Bavaria having openly French leanings. The Prussian Ten
Thousand will have to help themselves to the essential, therefore, without welcome; — and things are not pleasant. And
the Ruling Powers, by protocolling, still more the Commonalty
if it try at mobbing,[3] can only make them worse. Indeed it is
said the Ten Thousand, though their bearing was so perfect
otherwise, generally behaved rather ill in their marches over
Germany, during this War, — and always worst, it was remarked by observant persons, in the countries (Bamberg and
Würzburg, for instance) where their officers had in past years
been in recruiting troubles. Whereby observant persons explained the phenomenon to themselves. But we omit all
that; our concern lying elsewhere. " Directly after dinner
at Frankfurt," the Crown-Prince drives off, rapidly as his
wont is, towards Baireuth. He arrives there on the morrow;

---

[1] Kurd von Schlözer, *Chasot* (Berlin, 1856), pp. 20–22. A pleasant little
Book ; tolerably accurate, and of very readable quality.

[2] *Œuvres (Mémoires de Brandebourg)*, i. 167.

[3] " 28th March, 1735 " (Fassmann, p. 547) ; Buchholz, i. 136.

"October 5th," says Wilhelmina, — who again illuminates him
to us, though with oblique lights, for an instant.

Wilhelmina was in low spirits : — weak health ; add funeral
of the Prince of Culmbach (killed in the Battle of Parma),
illness of Papa, and other sombre events : — and was by
no means content with the Crown-Prince, on this occasion.
Strangely altered since we met him in July last ! It may be,
the Crown-Prince, looking, with an airy buoyancy of mind,
towards a certain Event probably near, has got his young head
inflated a little, and carries himself with a height new to this
beloved Sister ; — but probably the sad humor of the Princess
herself has a good deal to do with it. Alas, the contrast
between a heart knowing secretly its own bitterness, and a
friend's heart conscious of joy and triumph, is harsh and
shocking to the former of the two ! Here is the Princess's
account; with the subtrahend, twenty-five or seventy-five per
cent, *not* deducted from it : —

"My Brother arrived, the 5th of October. He seemed to
me put out (*décontenancé*) ; and to break off conversation with
me, he said he had to write to the King and Queen. I ordered
him pen and paper. He wrote in my room ; and spent more
than a good hour in writing a couple of Letters, of a line or
two each. He then had all the Court, one after the other, introduced to him ; said nothing to any of them, looked merely
with a mocking air at them ; after which we went to dinner.

"Here his whole conversation consisted in quizzing (*turlu-
piner*) whatever he saw ; and repeating to me, above a hundred times over, the words 'little Prince,' 'little Court.' I was
shocked ; and could not understand how he had changed so
suddenly towards me. The etiquette of all Courts in the Empire is, that nobody who has not at the least the rank of Captain can sit at a Prince's table : my Brother put a Lieutenant
there, who was in his suite ; saying to me, 'A King's Lieutenants are as good as a Margraf's Ministers.' I swallowed
this incivility, and showed no sign.

"After dinner, being alone with me, he said," — turning up
the flippant side of his thoughts, truly, in a questionable way :
— "'Our Sire is going to end (*tire à sa fin*); he will not live

out this month. I know I have made you great promises ; but
I am not in a condition to keep them. I will give you up the
Half of the sum which the late King [our Grandfather] lent
you ;[1] I think you will have every reason to be satisfied with
that.' I answered, That my regard for him had never been of
an interested nature ; that I would never ask anything of him,
but the continuance of his friendship ; and did not wish one
sou, if it would in the least inconvenience him. 'No, no,' said
he, 'you shall have those 100,000 thalers ; I have destined them
for you. — People will be much surprised,' continued he, 'to
see me act quite differently from what they had expected.
They imagine I am going to lavish all my treasures, and that
money will become as common as pebbles at Berlin: but they
will find I know better. I mean to increase my Army, and to
leave all other things on the old footing. I will have every
consideration for the Queen my Mother, and will sate her
(*rassasierai*) with honors ; but I do not mean that she shall
meddle in my affairs ; and if she try it, she will find so.' "
What a speech ; what an outbreak of candor in the young
man, preoccupied with his own great thoughts and difficulties,
— to the exclusion of any other person's !

"I fell from the clouds, on hearing all that ; and knew not
if I was sleeping or waking. He then questioned me on the
affairs of this Country. I gave him the detail of them. He
said to me : 'When your goose (*benêt*) of a Father-in-law dies,
I advise you to break up the whole Court, and reduce yourselves to the footing of a private gentleman's establishment,
in order to pay your debts. In real truth, you have no need
of so many people ; and you must try also to reduce the wages
of those whom you cannot help keeping. You have been accustomed to live at Berlin with a table of four dishes ; that is
all you want here : and I will invite you now and then to Berlin ; which will spare table and housekeeping.'

"For a long while my heart had been getting big ; I could
not restrain my tears, at hearing all these indignities. 'Why
do you cry ?' said he : 'Ah, ah, you are in low spirits, I see.
We must dissipate that dark humor. The music waits us ;

[1] Suprà, pp. 161, 162.

I will drive that fit out of you by an air or two on the flute.'
He gave me his hand, and led me into the other room. I sat
down to the harpsichord; which I inundated (*inondai*) with
my tears. Marwitz [my artful Demoiselle d'Atours, perhaps
too artful in time coming] placed herself opposite me, so as to
hide from the others what disorder I was in." [1]

For the last two days of the visit, Wilhelmina admits her
Brother was a little kinder. But on the fourth day there
came, by estafette, a Letter from the Queen, conjuring him to
return without delay, the King growing worse and worse.
Wilhelmina, who loved her Father, and whose outlooks in
case of his decease appeared to be so little flattering, was overwhelmed with sorrow. Of her Brother, however, she strove
to forget that strange outbreak of candor; and parted with
him as if all were mended between them again. Nay, the day
after his departure, there goes a beautifully affectionate Letter to him; which we could give, if there were room: [2] " the
happiest time I ever in my life had;" "my heart so full
of gratitude and so sensibly touched;" "every one repeating
the words 'dear Brother' and 'charming Prince-Royal:'" —
a Letter in very lively contrast to what we have just been reading. A Prince-Royal not without charm, in spite of the hard
practicalities he is meditating, obliged to meditate! —

As to the outbreak of candor, offensive to Wilhelmina and
us, we suppose her report of it to be in substance true, though
of exaggerated, perhaps perverted tone; and it is worth the
reader's notice, with these deductions. The truth is, our
charming Princess is always liable to a certain subtrahend.
In 1744, when she wrote those *Mémoires*, "in a Summer-house
at Baireuth," her Brother and she, owing mainly to go-betweens
acting on the susceptible female heart, were again in temporary
quarrel (the longest and worst they ever had), and hardly on
speaking terms; which of itself made her heart very heavy;
— not to say that Marwitz, the too artful Demoiselle, seemed
to have stolen her Husband's affections from the poor Princess, and made the world look all a little grim to her. These

[1] Wilhelmina, ii. 216–218.
[2] *Œuvres*, xxvii. part 1st, p. 23.

14.14

circumstances have given their color to parts of her Narrative, and are not to be forgotten by readers.

The Crown-Prince — who goes by Dessau, lodging for a night with the Old Dessauer, and writes affectionately to his Sister from that place, their Letters crossing on the road — gets home on the 12th to Potsdam. October 12th, 1734, he has ended his Rhine Campaign, in that manner; — and sees his poor Father, with a great many other feelings besides those expressed in the dialogue at Baireuth.

1732–1736.

————

CHAPTER XI.

IN PAPA'S SICK-ROOM; PRUSSIAN INSPECTIONS: END OF WAR.

IT appears, Friedrich met a cordial reception in the sick-room at Potsdam; and, in spite of his levities to Wilhelmina, was struck to the heart by what he saw there. For months to come, he seems to be continually running between Potsdam and Ruppin, eager to minister to his sick Father, when military leave is procurable. Other fact, about him, other aspect of him, in those months, is not on record for us.

Of his young Madam, or Princess-Royal, peaceably resident at Berlin or at Schönhausen, and doing the vacant officialities, formal visitings and the like, we hear nothing; of Queen Sophie and the others, nothing: anxious, all of them, no doubt, about the event at Potsdam, and otherwise silent to us. His Majesty's illness comes and goes; now hope, and again almost none. Margraf of Schwedt and his young Bride, we already know, were married in November; and Lieutenant Chasot (two days old in Berlin) told us, there was Dinner by the Crown-Prince to all the Royal Family on that occasion; —

poor Majesty out at Potsdam languishing in the background, meanwhile.

His Carnival the Crown-Prince passes naturally at Berlin. We find he takes a good deal to the French Ambassador, one Marquis de la Chétardie ; a showy restless character, of fame in the Gazettes of that time ; who did much intriguing at Petersburg some years hence, first in a signally triumphant way, and then in a signally untriumphant ; and is not now worth any knowledge but a transient accidental one. Chétardie came hither about Stanislaus and his affairs ; tried hard, but in vain, to tempt Friedrich Wilhelm into interference ; — is naturally anxious to captivate the Crown-Prince, in present circumstances.

Friedrich Wilhelm lay at Potsdam, between death and life, for almost four months to come ; the Newspapers speculating much on his situation ; political people extremely anxious what would become of him, — or in fact, when he would die ; for that was considered the likely issue. Fassmann gives dolorous clippings from the *Leyden Gazette*, all in a blubber of tears, according to the then fashion, but full of impertinent curiosity withal. And from the Seckendorf private Papers there are Extracts of a still more inquisitive and notable character : Seckendorf and the Kaiser having an intense interest in this painful occurrence.

Seckendorf is not now himself at Berlin ; but running much about, on other errands ; can only see Friedrich Wilhelm, if at all, in a passing way. And even this will soon cease ; — and in fact, to us it is by far the most excellent result of this French-Austrian War, that it carries Seckendorf clear away ; who now quits Berlin and the Diplomatic line, and obligingly goes out of our sight henceforth. The old Ordnance-Master, as an Imperial General of rank, is needed now for War-Service, if he has any skill that way. In those late months, he was duly in attendance at Philipsburg and the Rhine-Campaign, in a subaltern torpid capacity, like Brunswick-Bevern and the others ; ready for work, had there been any : but next season, he expects to have a Division of his own, and to do something considerable. — In regard to Berlin and the Diplomacies, he

has appointed a Nephew of his, a Seckendorf Junior, to take
his place there; to keep the old machinery in gear, if nothing
more; and furnish copious reports during the present crisis.
These Reports of Seckendorf Junior — full of eavesdroppings,
got from a *Kammermohr* (Nigger Lackey), who waits in the
sick-room at Potsdam, and is sensible to bribes — have been
printed; and we mean to glance slightly into them. But
as to Seckendorf Senior, readers can entertain the fixed hope
that they have at length done with him; that, in these
our premises, we shall never see him again; — nay shall
see him, on extraneous dim fields, far enough away, smarting
and suffering, till even we are almost sorry for the old
knave ! —

Friedrich Wilhelm's own prevailing opinion is, that he
cannot recover. His bodily sufferings are great: dropsically
swollen, sometimes like to be choked: no bed that he can bear
to lie on; — oftenest rolls about in a Bath-chair; very heavy-
laden indeed; and I think of tenderer humor than in former sicknesses. To the Old Dessauer he writes, few days
after getting home to Potsdam: "I am ready to quit the
world, as Your Dilection knows, and has various times heard
me say. One ship sails faster, another slower; but they
come all to one haven. Let it be with me, then, as the Most
High has determined for me." [1] He has settled his affairs,
Fassmann says, so far as possible; settled the order of his
funeral, How he is to be buried, in the Garrison Church of
Potsdam, without pomp or fuss, like a Prussian Soldier; and
what regiment or regiments it is that are to do the triple
volley over him, by way of finis and long farewell. His soul's
interests too, — we need not doubt he is in deep conference,
in deep consideration about these; though nothing is said on
that point. A serious man always, much feeling what immense facts he was surrounded with; and here is now the
summing up of all facts. Occasionally, again, he has hopes;
orders up "two hundred of his Potsdam Giants to march
through the sick-room," since he cannot get out to them; or

---

[1] Orlich, *Geschichte der Schlesischen Kriege* (Berlin, 1841), i. 14. "From the
Dessau Archives; date, 21st September, 1734."

old Generals, Buddenbrock, Waldau, come and take their pipe
there, in reminiscence of a Tabagie. Here, direct from the
fountain-head, or Nigger Lackey bribed by Seckendorf Junior,
is a notice or two : —

"*Potsdam, September* 30*th,* 1734. Yesterday, for half an
hour, the King could get no breath : he keeps them continually rolling him about" in his Bath-chair, "over the room, and
cries '*Luft, Luft* (Air, air) !'

"*October* 2*d.* The King is not going to die just yet; but
will scarcely see Christmas. He gets on his clothes; argues
with the Doctors, is impatient; won't have people speak of
his illness ; — is quite black in the face ; drinks nothing but
Moll [which we suppose to be small bitter beer], takes physic,
writes in bed.

"*October* 5*th.* The Nigger tells me things are better. The
King begins to bring up phlegm ; drinks a great deal of oat-
meal water [*Hafergrützwasser,* comfortable to the sick]; says
to the Nigger : 'Pray diligently, all of you ; perhaps I shall
not die !'"

October 5th : this is the day the Crown-Prince arrives
at Baireuth ; to be called away by express four days after.
How valuable, at Vienna or elsewhere, our dark friend the
Lackey's medical opinion is, may be gathered from this other
Entry, three weeks farther on, — enough to suffice us on that
head : —

"The Nigger tells me he has a bad opinion of the King's
health. If you roll the King a little fast in his Bath-chair,
you hear the water jumble in his body," — with astonishment! "King gets into passions; has beaten the pages
[may we hope, our dark friend among the rest ?], so that
it was feared apoplexy would take him."

This will suffice for the physiological part; let us now hear
our poor friend on the Crown-Prince and his arrival : —

"*October* 12*th.* Return of the Prince-Royal to Potsdam ;
tender reception. — *October* 21*st.* Things look ill in Potsdam.

The other leg is now also begun running; and above a quart
(*maas*) of water has come from it. Without a miracle, the
King cannot live," — thinks our dark friend. "The Prince-
Royal is truly affected (*véritablement attendri*) at the King's
situation; has his eyes full of water, has wept the eyes out
of his head : has schemed in all ways to contrive a commo-
dious bed for the King; would n't go away from Potsdam.
King forced him away ; he is to return Saturday afternoon.
The Prince-Royal has been heard to say, 'If the King will
let me live in my own way, I would give an arm to lengthen
his life for twenty years.' King always calls him Fritzchen.
But Fritzchen," thinks Seckendorf Junior, "knows nothing
about business. The King is aware of it; and said in the
face of him one day : ' If thou begin at the wrong end with
things, and all go topsy-turvy after I am gone, I will laugh at
thee out of my grave ! ' " [1]

So Friedrich Wilhelm; laboring amid the mortal quicksands ; looking into the Inevitable, in various moods. But
the memorablest speech he made to Fritzchen or to anybody
at present, was that covert one about the Kaiser and Seckendorf, and the sudden flash of insight he got, from some word
of Seckendorf's, into what they had been meaning with him
all along. Riding through the village of Priort, in debate
about Vienna politics of a strange nature, Seckendorf said
something, which illuminated his Majesty, dark for so many
years, and showed him where he was. A ghastly horror of a
country, yawning indisputable there; revealed to one as if
by momentary lightning, in that manner ! This is a speech
which all the ambassadors report, and which was already
mentioned by us, — in reference to that opprobrious Proposal
about the Crown-Prince's Marriage, " Marry with England,
after all ; never mind breaking your word ! " Here is the
manner of it, with time and place : —

"Sunday last," Sunday, 17th October, 1734, reports Seckendorf, Junior, through the Nigger or some better witness, "the

[1] Seckendorf (*Baron*), *Journal Secret;* cited in Förster, ii. 142.

King said to the Prince-Royal : 'My dear Son, I tell thee I
got my death at Priort. I entreat thee, above all things in
the world, don't trust those people (*denen Leuten*), however
many promises they make. That day, it was April 17th,
1733, there was a man said something to me : it was as if you
had turned a dagger round in my heart.' "[1] —

Figure that, spoken from amid the dark sick whirlpools, the
mortal quicksands, in Friedrich Wilhelm's voice, clangorously
plaintive; what a wild sincerity, almost pathos, is in it; and
whether Fritzchen, with his eyes all bewept even for what
Papa had suffered in that matter, felt lively gratitudes to the
House of Austria at this moment ! —

It was four months after, "21st January, 1735,"[2] when the
King first got back to Berlin, to enlighten the eyes of the
Carnival a little, as his wont had been. The crisis of his
Majesty's illness is over, present danger gone; and the Car-
nival people, not without some real gladness, though proba-
bly with less than they pretend, can report him well again.
Which is far from being the fact, if they knew it. Friedrich
Wilhelm is on his feet again; but he never more was well.
Nor has he forgotten that word at Priort, "like the turning
of a dagger in one's heart;" — and indeed gets himself con-
tinually reminded of it by practical commentaries from the
Vienna Quarter.

In April, Prince Lichtenstein arrives on Embassy with
three requests or demands from Vienna : "1°. That, besides
the Ten Thousand due by Treaty, his Majesty would send
his Reich's-Contingent," *not* comprehended in those Ten Thousand, thinks the Kaiser. "2°. That he would have the goodness
to dismiss Marquis de la Chétardie the French Ambassador, as
a plainly superfluous person at a well-affected German Court
in present circumstances ; " — person excessively dangerous,
should the present Majesty die, Crown-Prince being so fond
of that Chétardie. "3°. That his Prussian Majesty do give
up the false Polish Majesty Stanislaus, and no longer harbor

[1] Seckendorf (*Baron*), *Journal Secret;* cited in Förster, ii. 142.
[2] Fassmann, p. 533.

him in East Preussen or elsewhere." The whole of which demands his Prussian Majesty refuses; the latter two especially, as something notably high on the Kaiser's part, or on any mortal's, to a free Sovereign and Gentleman. Prince Lichtenstein is eloquent, conciliatory; but it avails not. He has to go home empty-handed; — manages to leave with Herr von Suhm, who took care of it for us, that Anecdote of the Crown-Prince's behavior under cannon-shot from Philipsburg last year; and does nothing else recordable, in Berlin.

The Crown-Prince's hopes were set, with all eagerness, on getting to the Rhine-Campaign next ensuing; nor did the King refuse, for a long while, but still less did he consent; and in the end there came nothing of it. From an early period of the year, Friedrich Wilhelm sees too well what kind of campaigning the Kaiser will now make; at a certain Wedding-dinner where his Majesty was, — precisely a fortnight after his Majesty's arrival in Berlin, — Seckendorf Junior has got, by eavesdropping, this utterance of his Majesty's: "The Kaiser has not a groschen of money. His Army in Lombardy is gone to twenty-four thousand men, will have to retire into the Mountains. Next campaign [just coming], he will lose Mantua and the Tyrol. God's righteous judgment it is: a War like this! Comes of flinging old principles overboard, — of meddling in business that was none of yours;" and more, of a plangent alarming nature.[1]

Friedrich Wilhelm sends back his Ten Thousand, according to contract; sends, over and above, a beautiful stock of "copper pontoons" to help the Imperial Majesty in that River Country, says Fassmann; — sends also a supernumerary Troop of Hussars, who are worth mentioning, "Six-score horse of Hussar type," under one Captain Ziethen, a taciturn, much-enduring, much-observing man, whom we shall see again: these are to be diligently helpful, as is natural; but they are also, for their own behoof, to be diligently observant, and learn the Austrian Hussar methods, which his Majesty last year saw to be much superior. Nobody that knows Ziethen doubts but he learnt; Hussar-Colonel Baronay, his Austrian

[1] Förster, ii. 144 (and *date* it from *Militair-Lexikon*, ii. 54).

teacher here, became too well convinced of it when they met
on a future occasion.[1] All this his Majesty did for the ensuing campaign: but as to the Crown-Prince's going thither,
after repeated requests on his part, it is at last signified to
him, deep in the season, that it cannot be: "Won't answer
for a Crown-Prince to be sharer in such a Campaign; — be
patient, my good Fritzchen, I will find other work for thee."[2]
Fritzchen is sent into Preussen, to do the Reviewings and
Inspections there; Papa not being able for them this season;
and strict manifold Inspection, in those parts, being more than
usually necessary, owing to the Russian-Polish troubles. On
this errand, which is clearly a promotion, though in present
circumstances not a welcome one for the Crown-Prince, he
sets out without delay; and passes there the equinoctial and
autumnal season, in a much more useful way than he could
have done in the Rhine-Campaign.

In the Rhine-Moselle Country and elsewhere the poor Kaiser does exert himself to make a Campaign of it; but without
the least success. Having not a groschen of money, how
could he succeed? Noailles, as foreseen, manœuvres him,
hitch after hitch, out of Italy; French are greatly superior,
more especially . when Montemar, having once got Carlos
crowned in Naples and put secure, comes to assist the French;
Kaiser has to lean for shelter on the Tyrol Alps, as predicted.
Italy, all but some sieging of strong-places, may be considered
as lost for the present.

Nor on the Rhine did things go better. Old Eugene, "the
shadow of himself," had no more effect this year than last:
nor, though Lacy and Ten Thousand Russians came as allies,
Poland being all settled now, could the least good be done.
Reich's-Feldmarschall Karl Alexander of Würtemberg did
"burn a Magazine" (probably of hay among better provender)
by his bomb-shells, on one occasion. Also the Prussian Ten

---

[1] *Life of Ziethen* (veridical but inexact, by the Frau von Blumenthal, a
kinswoman of his; English Translation, very ill printed, Berlin, 1803), p. 54.

[2] Friedrich's Letter, 5th September, 1735; Friedrich Wilhelm's Answer
next day (*Œuvres de Frédéric*, xxvii. part 3d, 93-95).

Thousand — Old Dessauer leading them, General Röder having fallen ill — burnt something: an Islet in the Rhine, if
I recollect, "Islet of Lorch near Bingen," where the French
had a post; which and whom the Old Dessauer burnt away.
And then Seckendorf, at the head of thirty thousand, he,
after long delays, marched to Trarbach in the interior Moselle Country; and got into some explosive sputter of battle
with Belleisle, one afternoon, — some say, rather beating
Belleisle; but a good judge says, it was a mutual flurry and
terror they threw one another into.[1] Seckendorf meant to
try again on the morrow: but there came an estafette that
night: "Preliminaries signed (Vienna, 3d October, 1735); —
try no farther!"[2] And this was the second Rhine-Campaign,
and the end of the Kaiser's French War. The Sea-Powers,
steadily refusing money, diligently run about, offering terms
of arbitration; and the Kaiser, beaten at every point, and
reduced to his last groschen, is obliged to comply. He will
have a pretty bill to pay for his Polish-Election frolic, were
the settlement done! Fleury is pacific, full of bland candor
to the Sea-Powers; the Kaiser, after long higgling upon articles, will have to accept the bill.

The Crown-Prince, meanwhile, has a successful journey into
Preussen; sees new interesting scenes, Salzburg Emigrants,
exiled Polish Majesties; inspects the soldiering, the schooling,
the tax-gathering, the domain-farming, with a perspicacity, a
dexterity and completeness that much pleases Papa. Fractions of the Reports sent home exist for us: let the reader
take a glance of one only; the first of the series; dated *Marienwerder* (just across the Weichsel, fairly out of Polish Preussen and into our own), 27th September, 1735, and addressed
to the "Most All-gracious King and Father;" — abridged for
the reader's behoof: —

. . . "In Polish Preussen, lately the Seat of War, things
look hideously waste; one sees nothing but women and a few

[1] *Œuvres de Frédéric*, i. 168.
[2] "Cessation is to be, 5th November for Germany, 15th for Italy; Preliminaries" were, Vienna, "3d October," 1735 (Schöll, ii. 245).

children; it is said the people are mostly running away," —
owing to the Russian-Polish procedures there, in consequence
of the blessed Election they have had. King August, whom
your Majesty is not in love with, has prevailed at this rate of
expense. King Stanislaus, protected by your Majesty in spite
of Kaisers and Czarinas, waits in Königsberg, till the Peace,
now supposed to be coming, say what is to become of him :
once in Königsberg, I shall have the pleasure to see him. " A
detachment of five-and-twenty Saxon Dragoons of the Regiment Arnstedt, marching towards Dantzig, met me : their
horses were in tolerable case; but some are piebald, some
sorrel, and some brown among them," which will be shocking
to your Majesty, " and the people did not look well." . . .

" Got hither to Marienwerder, last night : have inspected
the two Companies which are here, that is to say, Lieutenant-
Col. Meier's and Rittmeister Hans's. In very good trim, both
of them; and though neither the men nor their horses are
of extraordinary size, they are handsome well-drilled fellows,
and a fine set of stiff-built horses (gedrungenen Pferden). The
fellows sit them like pictures (reiten wie die Puppen); I saw
them do their wheelings. Meier has some fine recruits; in
particular two ; " — nor has the Rittmeister been wanting in
that respect. " Young horses " too are coming well on, sleek
of skin. In short, all is right on the military side.[1]

Civil business, too, of all kinds, the Crown-Prince looked
into, with a sharp intelligent eye ; — gave praise, gave censure
in the right place; put various things on a straight footing,
which were awry when he found them. In fact, it is Papa's
second self ; looks into the bottom of all things quite as Papa
would have done, and is fatal to mendacities, practical or
vocal, wherever he meets them. What a joy to Papa : "Here,
after all, is one that can replace me, in case of accident. This
Apprentice of mine, after all, he has fairly learned the Art;
and will continue it when I am gone ! " —
Yes, your Majesty, it is a Prince-Royal wise to recognize
your Majesty's rough wisdom, on all manner of points; will

---

[1] Œuvres de Frédéric, xxvii. part 3d, p. 97.

not be a Devil's-*friend*, I think, any more than your Majesty
was. Here truly are rare talents; like your Majesty and unlike ; — and has a steady swiftness in him, as of an eagle, over
and above! Such powers of practical judgment, of skilful
action, are rare in one's twenty-third year. And still rarer,
have readers noted what a power of holding his peace this
young man has? Fruit of his sufferings, of the hard life he
has had. Most important power; under which all other useful ones will more and more ripen for him. This Prince
already knows his own mind, on a good many points; privately, amid the world's vague clamor jargoning round him to
no purpose, he is capable of having *his* mind made up into
definite Yes and No, — so as will surprise us one day.

Friedrich Wilhelm, we perceive,[1] was in a high degree content with this performance of the Prussian Mission: a very
great comfort to his sick mind, in those months and afterwards. Here are talents, here are qualities, — visibly the
Friedrich-Wilhelm stuff throughout, but cast in an infinitely
improved type : — what a blessing we did not cut off that young
Head, at the Kaiser's dictation, in former years ! —

At Königsberg, as we learn in a dim indirect manner, the
Crown-Prince sees King Stanislaus twice or thrice, — not
formally, lest there be political offence taken, but incidentally
at the houses of third-parties; — and is much pleased with the
old gentleman; who is of cultivated good-natured ways, and
has surely many curious things, from Charles XII. downwards,
to tell a young man.[2] Stanislaus has abundance of useless
refugee Polish Magnates about him, with their useless crowds
of servants, and no money in pocket; Königsberg all on flutter, with their draperies and them, " like a little Warsaw : "
so that Stanislaus's big French pension, moderate Prussian
monthly allowance, and all resources, are inadequate ; and, in
fact, in the end, these Magnates had to vanish, many of them,
without settling their accounts in Königsberg.[3] For the
present they wait here, Stanislaus and they, till Fleury and

---

[1] His Letter, 24th October, 1735.   (Ib. p. 99).
[2] Came 8th October, went 21st (*Œuvres de Frédéric*, xxvii. part 3d, p. 98).
[3] *History of Stanislaus*.

the Kaiser, shaking the urn of doom in abstruse treaty after
battle, decide what is to become of them.

Friedrich returned to Dantzig : saw that famous City, and
late scene of War; tracing with lively interest the footsteps
of Münnich and his Siege operations, — some of which are
much blamed by judges, and by this young Soldier among the
rest. There is a pretty Letter of his from Dantzig, turning
mainly on those points. Letter written to his young Brother-
in-law, Karl of Brunswick, who is now become Duke there;
Grandfather and Father both dead; [1] and has just been blessed
with an Heir, to boot. Congratulation on the birth of this
Heir is the formal purport of the Letter, though it runs ever
and anon into a military strain. Here are some sentences in a
condensed form : —

" *Dantzig, 26th October,* 1735. . . . Thank my dear Sister for
her services. I am charmed that she has made you papa with
so good a grace. I fear you won't stop there; but will go on
peopling the world " — one knows not to what extent — " with
your amiable race. Would have written sooner; but I am
just returning from the depths of the barbarous Countries;
and having been charged with innumerable commissions which
I did not understand too well, had no good possibility to think
or to write.

"I have viewed all the Russian labors in these parts; have
had the assault on the Hagelsberg narrated to me ; been on the
grounds ; — and own I had a better opinion of Marshal Münnich than to think him capable of so distracted an enterprise.[2]
. . . Adieu, my dear Brother. My compliments to the amiable young Mother. Tell her, I beg you, that her proof-essays
are masterpieces (*coups d'essai sont des coups de maître*)." . . .

" Your most," &c.,

" FRÉDÉRIC."

---

[1] Grandfather, 1st March, 1735 ; Father (who lost the *Lines of Ettlingen*
lately in our sight), 3d September, 1735. Suprà, vol. vi. p. 372.

[2] *Œuvres de Frédéric*, xxvii. part 2d, p. 31. Pressed for time, and in want
of battering-cannon, he attempted to seize this Hagelsberg, one of the outlying
defences of Dantzig, by nocturnal storm ; lost two thousand men ; and retired, *without* doing "what was flatly impossible," thinks the Crown-Prince.
See Mannstein, pp. 77–79, for an account of it.

The Brunswick Masterpiece, achieved on this occasion, grew
to be a man and Duke, famous enough in the Newspapers in
time coming: Champagne, 1792; Jena, 1806; George IV.'s
Queen Caroline; these and other distracted phenomena (pretty
much blotting out the earlier better sort) still keep him hanging painfully in men's memory. From his birth, now in this
Prussian Journey of our Crown-Prince, to his death-stroke on
the Field of Jena, what a seventy-one years! —

Fleury and the Kaiser, though it is long before the signature and last finish can take place, are come to terms of settlement, at the Crown-Prince's return; and it is known, in
political circles, what the Kaiser's Polish-Election damages
will probably amount to. Here are, in substance, the only conditions that could be got for him: —

" 1°. Baby Carlos, crowned in Naples, cannot be pulled out
again: Naples, the Two Sicilies, are gone without return.
That is the first loss; please Heaven it be the worst! On
the other hand, Baby Carlos will, as some faint compensation,
surrender to your Imperial Majesty his Parma and Piacenza
apanages; and you shall get back your Lombardy, — all but
a scantling which we fling to the Sardinian Majesty; who is
a good deal huffed, having had possession of the Milanese
these two years past, in terms of his bargain with Fleury.
Pacific Fleury says to him: ' Bargain cannot be kept, your
Majesty; please to quit the Milanese again, and put up with
this scantling.'

" 2°. The Crown of Poland, August III. has got it, by Russian bombardings and other measures: Crown shall stay with
August, — all the rather as there would be no dispossessing
him, at this stage. He was your Imperial Majesty's Candidate; let him be the winner there, for your Imperial Majesty's
comfort.

" 3°. And then as to poor Stanislaus? Well, let Stanislaus
be Titular Majesty of Poland for life; — which indeed will do
little for him: — but in addition, we propose, That, the Dukedom of Lorraine being now in our hands, Majesty Stanislaus
have the life-rent of Lorraine to subsist upon; and — and that

Lorraine fall to us of France on his decease! — 'Lorraine?'
exclaim the Kaiser, and the Reich, and the Kaiser's intended
Son-in-law Franz Duke of Lorraine. There is indeed a loss
and a disgrace; a heavy item in the Election damages!

"4°. As to Duke Franz, there is a remedy. The old Duke
of Florence, last of the Medici, is about to die childless: let
the now Duke of Lorraine, your Imperial Majesty's intended
Son-in-law, have Florence instead. — And so it had to be
settled. 'Lorraine? To Stanislaus, to France?' exclaimed
the poor Kaiser, still more the poor Reich, and poor Duke
Franz. This was the bitterest cut of all; but there was no
getting past it. This too had to be allowed, this item for the
Election breakages in Poland. And so France, after nibbling
for several centuries, swallows Lorraine whole. Duke Franz
attempted to stand out; remonstrated much, with Kaiser and
Hofrath, at Vienna, on this unheard-of proposal: but they told
him it was irremediable; told him at last (one Bartenstein, a
famed Aulic Official, told him), 'No Lorraine, no Archduchess,
your Serenity!' — and Franz had to comply. Lorraine is gone;
cunning Fleury has swallowed it whole. 'That was what he
meant in picking this quarrel!' said Teutschland mournfully.
Fleury was very pacific, candid in aspect to the Sea-Powers
and others; and did not crow afflictively, did not say what he
had meant.

"5°. One immense consolation for the Kaiser, if for no
other, is : France guarantees the Pragmatic Sanction, —
though with very great difficulty; spending a couple of years,
chiefly on this latter point as was thought.[1] How it kept
said guarantee, will be seen in the sequel."

And these were the damages the poor Kaiser had to pay for
meddling in Polish Elections; for galloping thither in chase
of his Shadows. No such account of broken windows was
ever presented to a man before. This may be considered as
the consummation of the Kaiser's Shadow-Hunt; or at least its
igniting and exploding point. His Duel with the Termagant
has at last ended; in total defeat to him on every point.
Shadow-Hunt does not end; though it is now mostly vanished;

---

[1] **Treaty** on *it* not signed till 18th November, 1738 (Schöll, ii. 246).

exploded in fire.　Shadow-Hunt is now gone all to Pragmatic Sanction, as it were: that now is the one thing left in Nature for a Kaiser; and that he will love, and chase, as the summary of all things.　From this point he steadily goes down, and at a rapid rate; — getting into disastrous Turk Wars, with as little preparation for War or Fact as a life-long Hunt of *Shadows* presupposes; Eugene gone from him, and nothing but Seckendorfs to manage for him; — and sinks to a low pitch indeed. We will leave him here; shall hope to see but little more of him.

In the Summer of 1736, in consequence of these arrangements, — which were completed so far, though difficulties on Pragmatic Sanction and other points retarded the final signature for many months longer, — the Titular Majesty Stanislaus girt himself together for departure towards his new Dominion or Life-rent; quitted Königsberg; traversed Prussian Poland, safe this time, "under escort of Lieutenant-General von Katte [our poor Katte of Cüstrin's Father] and fifty cuirassiers;" reached Berlin in the middle of May, under flowerier aspects than usual.　He travelled under the title of "Count" Something, and alighted at the French Ambassador's in Berlin: but Friedrich Wilhelm treated him like a real Majesty, almost like a real Brother; had him over to the Palace; rushed out to meet him there, I forget how many steps beyond the proper limits; and was hospitality itself and munificence itself; — and, in fact, that night and all the other nights, "they smoked above thirty pipes together," for one item.　May 21st, 1736,[1] Ex-Majesty Stanislaus went on his way again; towards France, — towards Meudon, a quiet Royal House in France, — till Lunéville, Nanci, and their Lorraine Palaces are quite ready.　There, in these latter, he at length does find resting-place, poor innocent insipid mortal, after such tossings to and fro: and M. de Voltaire, and others of

---

[1] Förster (i. 227), following loose Pöllnitz (ii. 478), dates it 1735: a more considerable error, if looked into, than is usual in Herr Förster; who is not an ill-informed nor inexact man; — though, alas, in respect of method (that is to say, *want* of visible method, indication, or human arrangement), probably the most confused of all the Germans!

mark, having sometimes enlivened the insipid Court there,
Titular King Stanislaus has still a kind of remembrance among
mankind.

Of his Prussian Majesty we said that, though the Berlin
populations reported him well again, it was not so. The truth
is, his Majesty was never well again. From this point, age
only forty-seven, he continues broken in bodily constitution;
clogged more and more with physical impediments; and his
History, personal and political withal, is as that of an old man,
finishing his day. To the last he pulls steadily, neglecting no
business, suffering nothing to go wrong. Building operations
go on at Berlin; pushed more than ever, in these years, by the
rigorous Derschau, who has got that in charge. No man of
money or rank in Berlin but Derschau is upon him, with
heavier and heavier compulsion to build: which is felt to be
tyrannous; and occasions an ever-deepening grumble among
the moneyed classes. At Potsdam his Majesty himself is the
Builder; and gives the Houses away to persons of merit.[1]

Nor is the Army less an object, perhaps almost more. Nay,
at one time, old Kur-Pfalz being reckoned in a dying condition,
Friedrich Wilhelm is about ranking his men, prepared to fight
for his rights in Jülich and Berg; Kaiser having openly gone
over, and joined with France against his Majesty in that matter. However, the old Kur-Pfalz did not die, and there came
nothing of fight in Friedrich Wilhelm's time. But his History,
on the political side, is henceforth mainly a commentary to
him on that "word" he heard in Priort, "which was as if
you had turned a dagger in my heart!" With the Kaiser he
has fallen out: there arise unfriendly passages between them,
sometimes sarcastic on Friedrich Wilhelm's part, in reference
to this very War now ended. Thus, when complaint rose
about the Prussian misbehaviors on their late marches (misbehaviors notable in Countries where their recruiting operations
had been troubled), the Kaiser took a·high severe tone, not
assuaging, rather aggravating the matter; and, for his own
share, winded up by a strict prohibition of Prussian recruiting

[1] Pöllnitz, ii. 469.

in any and every part of the Imperial Dominions. Which
Friedrich Wilhelm took extremely ill. This is from a letter
of his to the Crown-Prince, and after the first gust of wrath
had spent itself: "It is a clear disadvantage, this prohibition
of recruiting in the Kaiser's Countries. That is our thanks for
the Ten Thousand men sent him, and for all the deference I
have shown the Kaiser at all times; and by this you may see
that it would be of no use if one even sacrificed oneself to him.
So long as they need us, they continue to flatter; but no sooner
is the strait thought to be over, and help not wanted, than
they pull off the mask, and have not the least acknowledgment. The considerations that will occur to you on this
matter may put it in your power to be prepared against similar
occasions in time coming." [1]

Thus, again, in regard to the winter-quarters of the Ziethen
Hussars. Prussian Majesty, we recollect, had sent a Supernumerary Squadron to the last Campaign on the Rhine. They
were learning their business, Friedrich Wilhelm knew; but
also were fighting for the Kaiser, — that was what the Kaiser
knew about them. Somewhat to his surprise, in the course of
next year, Friedrich Wilhelm received, from the Vienna War-
Office, a little Bill of 10,284 florins (£1,028 8s.) charged to *him*
for the winter-quarters of these Hussars. He at once paid the
little Bill, with only this observation: "Heartily glad that I
can help the Imperial *Ærarium* with that £1,028 8s. With
the sincerest wishes for hundred-thousandfold increase to it
in said *Ærarium;* otherwise it won't go very far!" [2]

At a later period, in the course of his disastrous Turk
War, the Kaiser, famishing for money, set about borrowing
a million gulden (£100,000) from the Banking House Splittgerber and Daun at Berlin. Splittgerber and Daun had not
the money, could not raise it: "Advance us that sum, in their
name, your Majesty," proposes the Vienna Court: "There
shall be three-per-cent bonus, interest six per cent, and secu-
rity beyond all question!" To which fine offer his Majesty
answers, addressing Seckendorf Junior: "Touching the pro-

---

[1] 6th February, 1736: *Œuvres de Frédéric*, xxvii. part 3d, p. 102.
[2] Letter to Seckendorf (*Senior*): Förster, ii. 150.

posal of my giving the Bankers Splittgerber and Daun a lift, with a million gulden, to assist in that loan of theirs, — said proposal, as I am not a merchant accustomed to deal in profits and percentages, cannot in that form take effect. Out of old friendship, however, I am, on Theiro Imperial Majesty's request, extremely ready to pay down, once and away (*à fond perdu*), a couple of million gulden, provided the Imperial Majesty will grant me *the conditions* known to your Uncle [*fulfilment* of that now oldish Jülich-and-Berg promise, namely!] which are *fair*. In such case the thing shall be rapidly completed!"[1]

In a word, Friedrich Wilhelm falls out with the Kaiser more and more; experiences more and more what a Kaiser this has been towards him. Queen Sophie has fallen silent in the History Books; both the Majesties may look remorsefully, but perhaps best in silence, over the breakages and wrecks this Kaiser has brought upon them. Friedrich Wilhelm does not meanly hate the Kaiser: good man, he sometimes pities him; sometimes, we perceive, has a touch of authentic contempt for him. But his thoughts, in that quarter, premature old age aggravating them, are generally of a tragic nature, not to be spoken without tears; and the tears have a flash at the bottom of them, when he looks round on Fritz and says, "There is one, though, that will avenge me!" Friedrich Wilhelm, to the last a broad strong phenomenon, keeps wending downward, homeward, from this point; the Kaiser too, we perceive, is rapidly consummating his enormous Spectre-Hunts and Duels with Termagants, and before long will be at rest. We have well-nigh done with both these Majesties.

The Crown-Prince, by his judicious obedient procedures in these Four Years at Ruppin, at a distance from Papa, has, as it were, completed his *Apprenticeship;* and, especially by this last Inspection-Journey into Preussen, may be said to have delivered his *Proof-Essay* with a distinguished success. He is now out of his Apprenticeship; entitled to take up his Indentures, whenever need shall be. The rugged old Master cannot but declare him competent, qualified to try his own

[1] Förster, ii. 151 (without *date* there).

hand without supervision : — after all those unheard-of confusions, like to set the shop on fire at one time, it is a blessedly
successful Apprenticeship !   Let him now, theoretically at
least, in the realms of Art, Literature, Spiritual Improvement,
do his *Wanderjahre,* over at Reinsberg, still in the old region,
—still well apart from Papa, who agrees best *not* in immediate contact ; — and be happy in the new Domesticities, and
larger opportunities, provided for him there ; till a certain
time come, which none of us are in haste for.

BOOK X.

AT REINSBERG.

1736–1740.

CHAPTER I.

MANSION OF REINSBERG.

On the Crown-Prince's Marriage, three years ago, when the *Amt* or Government-District *Ruppin*, with its incomings, was assigned to him for revenue, we heard withal of a residence getting ready. Hint had fallen from the Prince, that Reinsberg, an old Country-seat, standing with its Domain round it in that little Territory of Ruppin, and probably purchasable as was understood, might be pleasant, were it once his and well put in repair. Which hint the kind paternal Majesty instantly proceeded to act upon. He straightway gave orders for the purchase of Reinsberg; concluded said purchase, on fair terms, after some months' bargaining; [1] — and set his best Architect, one Kemeter, to work, in concert with the Crown-Prince, to new-build and enlarge the decayed Schloss of Reinsberg into such a Mansion as the young Royal Highness and his Wife would like.

Kemeter has been busy, all this while; a solid, elegant, yet frugal builder: and now the main body of the Mansion is complete, or nearly so, the wings and adjuncts going steadily forward; Mansion so far ready that the Royal Highnesses can take up their abode in it. Which they do, this Autumn, 1736;

---

[1] 23d October, 1733, order given, — 16th March, 1734, purchase completed (Preuss, i. 75).

and fairly commence Joint Housekeeping, in a permanent manner. Hitherto it has been intermittent only: hitherto the Crown-Princess has resided in their Berlin Mansion, or in her own Country-house at Schönhausen; Husband not habitually with her, except when on leave of absence from Ruppin, in Carnival time or for shorter periods. At Ruppin his life has been rather that of a bachelor, or husband abroad on business, up to this time. But now at Reinsberg they do kindle the sacred hearth together; "6th August, 1736," the date of that important event. They have got their Court about them, dames and cavaliers more than we expected; they have arranged the furnitures of their existence here on fit scale, and set up their Lares and Penates on a thrifty footing. Majesty and Queen come out on a visit to them next month; [1] — raising the sacred hearth into its first considerable blaze, and crowning the operation in a human manner.

And so there has a new epoch arisen for the Crown-Prince and his Consort. A new, and much-improved one. It lasted into the fourth year; rather improving all the way: and only Kingship, which, if a higher sphere, was a far less pleasant one, put an end to it. Friedrich's happiest time was this at Reinsberg; the little Four Years of Hope, Composure, realizable Idealism: an actual snatch of something like the Idyllic, appointed him in a life-pilgrimage consisting otherwise of realisms oftenest contradictory enough, and sometimes of very grim complexion. He is master of his work, he is adjusted to the practical conditions set him; conditions once complied with, daily work done, he lives to the Muses, to the spiritual improvements, to the social enjoyments; and has, though not without flaws of ill-weather, — from the Tobacco-Parliament perhaps rather less than formerly, and from the Finance-quarter perhaps rather more, — a sunny time. His innocent insipidity of a Wife, too, appears to have been happy. She had the charm of youth, of good looks; a wholesome perfect loyalty of character withal; and did not "take to pouting," as was once apprehended of her, but pleasantly gave and received of what was going. This poor Crown-Princess, afterwards Queen, has been

[1] 4th September, 1736 (Ib.).

heard, in her old age, reverting, in a touching transient way,
to the glad days she had at Reinsberg. Complaint openly was
never heard from her, in any kind of days; but these doubtless
were the best of her life.

Reinsberg, we said, is in the *Amt* Ruppin; naturally under
the Crown-Prince's government at present: the little Town or
Village of Reinsberg stands about ten miles north of the Town
Ruppin; — not quite a third-part as big as Ruppin is in our
time, and much more pleasantly situated. The country about
is of comfortable, not unpicturesque character; to be distinguished almost as beautiful, in that region of sand and moor.
Lakes abound in it; tilled fields; heights called "hills;" and
wood of fair growth, — one reads of "beech-avenues," of "high
linden-avenues:" — a country rather of the ornamented sort,
before the Prince with his improvements settled there. Many
lakes and lakelets in it, as usual hereabouts; the loitering
waters straggle, all over that region, into meshes of lakes.
Reinsberg itself, Village and Schloss, stands on the edge of a
pleasant Lake, last of a mesh of such: the *summary*, or outfall, of which, already here a good strong brook or stream, is
called the *Rhein*, Rhyn or Rein; and gives name to the little
place. We heard of the Rein at Ruppin: it is there counted
as a kind of river; still more, twenty miles farther down,
where it falls into the Havel, on its way to the Elbe. The
waters, I think, are drab-colored, not peat-brown: and here,
at the source, or outfall from that mesh of lakes, where Reinsberg is, the country seems to be about the best; — sufficient, in
picturesqueness and otherwise, to satisfy a reasonable man.

The little Town is very old; but, till the Crown-Prince settled there, had no peculiar vitality in it. I think there are
now some potteries, glass-manufactories: Friedrich Wilhelm,
just while the Crown-Prince was removing thither, settled a
first Glass-work there; which took good root, and rose to eminence in the crystal, Bohemian-crystal, white-glass, cut-glass,
and other commoner lines, in the Crown-Prince's time.[1]

Reinsberg stands on the east or southeast side of its pretty

[1] *Beschreibung des Lustschlosses &c. zu Reinsberg* (Berlin, 1788); Author, a
"Lieutenant Hennert," thoroughly acquainted with his subject.

Lake : Lake is called "the *Grinerick See*" (as all those remote Lakes have their names) ; Mansion is between the Town
and Lake. A Mansion fronting, we may say, four ways ; for
it is of quadrangular form, with a wet moat from the Lake
begirdling it, and has a spacious court for interior : but the
principal entrance is from the Town side ; for the rest, the
Building is ashlar on all sides, front and rear. Stands there,
handsomely abutting on the Lake with two Towers, a Tower
at each angle, which it has on that lakeward side ; and looks,
over Reinsberg, and its steeple rising amid friendly umbrage
which hides the house-tops, towards the rising sun. Townward there is room for a spacious esplanade ; and then for the
stables, outbuildings, well masked ; which still farther shut off
the Town. To this day, Reinsberg stands with the air of a
solid respectable Edifice ; still massive, rain-tight, though long
since deserted by the Princeships, — by Friedrich nearly sixscore years ago, and nearly threescore by Prince Henri, a
Brother of Friedrich's, who afterwards had it. Last accounts
I got were, of talk there had risen of planting an extensive
Normal-School there ; which promising plan had been laid
aside again for the time.

The old Schloss, residence of the Bredows and other feudal
people for a long while, had good solid masonry in it, and
around it orchards, potherb gardens ; which Friedrich Wilhelm's Architects took good care to extend and improve, not to
throw away : the result of their art is what we see, a beautiful
Country-House, what might be called a Country-Palace with
all its adjuncts ; — and at a rate of expense which would
fill English readers, of this time, with amazement. Much
is admirable to us as we study Reinsberg, what it had
been, what it became, and how it was made ; but nothing
more so than the small modicum of money it cost. To our
wondering thought, it seems as if the shilling, in those parts,
were equal to the guinea in these ; and the reason, if we ask
it, is by no means flattering altogether. "Change in the value
of money ? " Alas, reader, no ; that is not above the fourth
part of the phenomenon. Three-fourths of the phenomenon
are change in the methods of administering money, — differ-

ence between managing it with wisdom and veracity on both
sides, and managing it with unwisdom and mendacity on both
sides. Which is very great indeed; and infinitely sadder
than any one, in these times, will believe! — But we cannot
dwell on this consideration. Let the reader take it with him,
as a constant accompaniment in whatever work of Friedrich
Wilhelm's or of Friedrich his Son's, he now or at any other
time may be contemplating. Impious waste, which means
disorder and dishonesty, and loss of much other than money
to all parties, — disgusting aspect of human creatures, master
and servant, working together as if they were not human, —
will be spared him in those foreign departments; and in an
English heart thoughts will arise, perhaps, of a wholesome
tendency, though very sad, as times are.

It would but weary the reader to describe this Crown-
Prince Mansion; which, by desperate study of our abstruse
materials, it is possible to do with auctioneer minuteness.
There are engraved *Views* of Reinsberg and its Environs; which
used to lie conspicuous in the portfolios of collectors, — which
I have not seen.[1] Of the House itself, engraved Frontages
(*Façades*), Ground-plans, are more accessible; and along with
them, descriptions which are little descriptive, — wearisomely
detailed, and as it were dark by excess of light (auctioneer
light) thrown on them. The reader sees, in general, a fine
symmetrical Block of Buildings, standing in rectangular shape,
in the above locality : — about two hundred English feet, each,
the two longer sides measure, the Townward and the Lakeward,
on their outer front : about a hundred and thirty, each, the
two shorter; or a hundred and fifty, taking in their Towers
just spoken of. The fourth or Lakeward side, however,
which is one of the longer pair, consists mainly of "Colonnade;" spacious Colonnade "with vases and statues;" catching up the outskirts of said Towers, and handsomely uniting
everything.

Beyond doubt, a dignified, substantial pile of stone-work;
all of good proportions. Architecture everywhere of cheerfully serious, solidly graceful character; all of sterling ashlar;

[1] See Hennert, just cited, for the titles of them.

the due *risalites* (projecting spaces) with their attics and statues atop, the due architraves, cornices and corbels, — in short the due opulence of ornament being introduced, and only the due. Genuine sculptors, genuine painters, artists have been busy; and in fact all the suitable fine arts, and all the necessary solid ones, have worked together, with a noticeable fidelity, comfortable to the very beholder to this day. General height is about forty feet; two stories of ample proportions: the Towers overlooking them are sixty feet in height. Extent of outer frontage, if you go all round, and omit the Colonnade, will be five hundred feet and more: this, with the rearward face, is a thousand feet of room frontage: — fancy the extent of lodging space. For "all the kitchens and appurtenances are underground;" the "left front" (which is a new part of the Edifice) rising comfortably over these. Windows I did not count; but they must go high up into the Hundreds. No end to lodging space. Nay in a detached side-edifice subsequently built, called Cavalier House, I read of there being, for one item, "fifty lodging rooms," and for another "a theatre." And if an English Duke of Trumps were to look at the bills for all that, — his astonishment would be extreme, and perhaps in a degree painful and salutary to him.

In one of these Towers the Crown-Prince has his Library: a beautiful apartment; nothing wanting to it that the arts could furnish, "ceiling done by Pesne" with allegorical geniuses and what not; looks out on mere sky, mere earth and water in an ornamental state: silent as in Elysium. It is there we are to fancy the Correspondence written, the Poetries and literary industries going on. There, or stepping down for a turn in the open air, or sauntering meditatively under the Colonnade with its statues and vases (where weather is no object), one commands the Lake, with its little tufted Islands, "Remus Island" much famed among them, and "high beech-woods" on the farther side. The Lake is very pretty, all say; lying between you and the sunset; — with perhaps some other lakelet, or solitary pool in the wilderness, many miles away, "revealing itself as a cup of molten gold,"

at that interesting moment. What the Book-Collection was,
in the interior, I know not except by mere guess.

The Crown-Princess's Apartment, too, which remained un-
altered at the last accounts had of it,[1] is very fine; — take
the anteroom for specimen: "This fine room," some twenty
feet height of ceiling, "has six windows; three of them, in
the main front, looking towards the Town, the other three
towards the Interior Court. The light from these windows
is heightened by mirrors covering all the piers (*Schäfte*,
interspaces of the walls), to an uncommonly splendid pitch;
and shows the painting of the ceiling, which again is by
the famous Pesne, to much perfection. The Artist himself,
too, has managed to lay on his colors there so softly, and with
such delicate skill, that the light-beams seem to prolong
themselves in the painted clouds and air, as if it were the
real sky you had overhead." There in that cloud-region
"Mars is being disarmed by the Love-goddesses, and they are
sporting with his weapons. He stretches out his arm towards
the Goddess, who looks upon him with fond glances. Cupids
are spreading out a draping." That is Pesne's luxurious
performance in the ceiling. — "Weapon-festoons, in basso-
relievo, gilt, adorn the walls of this room; and two Pictures,
also by Pesne, which represent, in life size, the late King and
Queen [our good friends Friedrich Wilhelm and his Sophie],
are worthy of attention. Over each of the doors, you find in
low-relief the Profiles of Hannibal, Pompey, Scipio, Cæsar,
introduced as Medallions."

All this is very fine; but all this is little to another ceiling,
in some big Saloon elsewhere, Music-saloon, I think: Black
Night, making off, with all her sickly dews, at one end of the
ceiling; and at the other end, the Steeds of Phœbus bursting
forth, and the glittering shafts of Day, — with Cupids, Love-
goddesses, War-gods, not omitting Bacchus and his vines, all
getting beautifully awake in consequence. A very fine room
indeed; — used as a Music-saloon, or I know not what, — and
the ceiling of it almost an ideal, say the connoisseurs.

Endless gardens, pavilions, grottos, hermitages, orangeries,

[1] From Hennert, namely, in 1778.

artificial ruins, parks and pleasances surround this favored
spot and its Schloss; nothing wanting in it that a Prince's
establishment needs, — except indeed it be hounds, for which
this Prince never had the least demand.

Except the old Ruppin duties, which imply continual journeyings thither, distance only a morning's ride ; except these,
and occasional commissions from Papa, Friedrich is left master
of his time and pursuits in this new Mansion. There are visits
to Potsdam, periodical appearances at Berlin; some Correspondence to keep the Tobacco-Parliament in tune. But Friedrich's taste is for the Literatures, Philosophies : a young
Prince bent seriously to cultivate his mind ; to attain some
clear knowledge of this world, so all-important to him. And
he does seriously read, study and reflect a good deal; his main
recreations, seemingly, are Music, and the converse of well-
informed, friendly men. In Music we find him particularly
rich. Daily, at a fixed hour of the afternoon, there is concert
held; the reader has seen in what kind of room : and if the
Artists entertained here for that function were enumerated
(high names, not yet forgotten in the Musical world), it would
still more astonish readers. I count them to the number
of twenty or nineteen; and mention only that "the two
Brothers Graun " and "the two Brothers Benda" were of the
lot; suppressing four other Fiddlers of eminence, and "a
Pianist who is known to everybody." [1] The Prince has a fine
sensibility to Music: does himself, with thrilling adagios on
the flute, join in these harmonious acts; and, no doubt, if
rightly vigilant against the Nonsenses, gets profit, now and
henceforth, from this part of his resources.

He has visits, calls to make, on distinguished persons within
reach; he has much Correspondence, of a Literary or Social
nature. For instance, there is Suhm the Saxon Envoy translating *Wolf's Philosophy* into French for him; sending it in
fascicles ; with endless Letters to and from, upon it, — which
were then highly interesting, but are now dead to every reader.
The Crown-Prince has got a Post-Office established at Reins-

[1] Hennert, p. 21.

berg; leathern functionary of some sort comes lumbering
round, southward, "from the Mecklenburg quarter twice a
week, and goes by Fehrbellin," for the benefit of his Correspondences. Of his calls in the neighborhood, we mean to
show the reader one sample, before long; and only one.

There are Lists given us of the Prince's "Court" at Reinsberg; and one reads, and again reads, the dreariest unmemorable accounts of them; but cannot, with all one's industry,
attain any definite understanding of what they were employed
in, day after day, at Reinsberg: — still more are their salaries
and maintenance a mystery to us, in that frugal establishment.
There is Wolden for Hofmarschall, our old Cüstrin friend;
there is Colonel Senning, old Marlborough Colonel with the
wooden leg, who taught Friedrich his drillings and artillery-
practices in boyhood, a fine sagacious old gentleman this latter.
There is a M. Jordan, Ex-Preacher, an ingenious Prussian-
Frenchman, still young, who acts as "Reader and Librarian;"
of whom we shall hear a good deal more. "Intendant" is
Captain (Ex-Captain) Knobelsdorf; a very sensible accomplished man, whom we saw once at Baireuth; who has been
to Italy since, and is now returned with beautiful talents for
Architecture: it is he that now undertakes the completing of
Reinsberg,[1] which he will skilfully accomplish in the course
of the next three years. Twenty Musicians on wind or string;
Painters, Antoine Pesne but one of them; Sculptors, Glume
and others of eminence; and Hof-Cavaliers, to we know not
what extent: — how was such a Court kept up, in harmonious
free dignity, and no halt in its finances, or mean pinch of any
kind visible? The Prince did get in debt; but not deep, and
it was mainly for the tall recruits he had to purchase. His
money-accounts are by no means fully known to me: but I
should question if his expenditure (such is my guess) ever
reached £3,000 a year; and am obliged to reflect more and
more, as the ancient Cato did, what an admirable revenue
frugality is!

Many of the Cavaliers, I find, for one thing, were of the
Regiment Goltz; that was one evident economy. "Rittmeister

[1] Hennert, p. 29.

von Chasot," as the Books call him : readers saw that Chasot
flying to Prince Eugene, and know him since the Siege of
Philipsburg.   He is not yet Rittmeister, or Captain of Horse,
as he became ; but is of the Ruppin Garrison ; Hof-Cavalier ;
"attended Friedrich on his late Prussian journey ; " and is
much a favorite, when he can be spared from Ruppin.   Captain Wylich, afterwards a General of mark ; the Lieutenant
Buddenbrock who did the parson-charivari at Ruppin, but is
now reformed from those practices : all these are of Goltz.
Colonel Keyserling, not of Goltz, nor in active military duty
here, is a friend of very old standing ; was officially named as
" Companion " to the Prince, a long while back ; and got into
trouble on his account in the disastrous Ante-Cüstrin or Flight
Epoch : one of the Prince's first acts, when he got pardoned
after Cüstrin, was to beg for the pardon of this Keyserling ;
and now he has him here, and is very fond of him.   A Courlander, of good family, this Keyserling ; of good gifts too, —
which, it was once thought, would be practically sublime ; for
he carried off all manner of college prizes, and was the Admi-
rable-Crichton of Königsberg University and the Graduates
there.   But in the end they proved to be gifts of the vocal
sort rather : and have led only to what we see.   A man, I
should guess, rather of buoyant vivacity than of depth or
strength in intellect or otherwise.   Excessively buoyant, ingenious ; full of wit, kindly exuberance ; a loyal-hearted, gay-
tempered man, and much a favorite in society as well as with
the Prince.   If we were to dwell on Reinsberg, Keyserling
would come prominently forward.

Major von Stille, ultimately Major-General von Stille, I
should also mention : near twenty years older than the Prince ;
a wise thoughtful soldier (went, by permission, to the Siege
of Dantzig lately, to improve himself) ; a man capable of rugged
service, when the time comes.   His military writings were once
in considerable esteem with professional men ; and still im-
press a lay reader with favorable notions towards Stille, as a
man of real worth and sense.[1]

---

[1] *Campagnes du Roi de Prusse ;* — a posthumous Book ; *anterior* to the Seven-
Years War.

Of Monsieur Jordan and the Literary Set.

There is, of course, a Chaplain in the Establishment: **a**
Reverend "M. Deschamps;" who preaches to them all,— in
French no doubt. Friedrich never hears Deschamps: Friedrich is always over at Ruppin on Sundays; and there "himself reads a sermon to the Garrison," as part of the day's
duties. Reads finely, in a melodious feeling manner, says
Formey, who can judge: "even in his old days, he would incidentally," when some Emeritus Parson, like Formey, chanced
to be with him, "roll out choice passages from Bossuet, from
Massillon," in a voice and with a look, which would have been
perfection in the pulpit, thinks Formey.[1]

M. Jordan, though he was called "*Lecteur* (Reader)," did
not read to him, I can perceive ; but took charge of the
Books; busied himself honestly to be useful in all manner
of literary or quasi-literary ways. He was, as his name
indicates, from the French-refugee department: a recent ac-
quisition, much valued at Reinsberg. As he makes a figure
afterwards, we had better mark him a little.

Jordan's parents were wealthy religious persons, in trade at
Berlin; this Jordan (Charles Etienne, age now thirty-six) was
their eldest son. It seems they had destined him from birth,
consulting their own pious feelings merely, to be a Preacher
of the Gospel; the other sons, all of them reckoned clever too,
were brought up to secular employments. And preach he, this
poor Charles Etienne, accordingly did; what best Gospel he
had; in an honest manner, all say,— though never with other
than a kind of reluctance on the part of Nature, forced out of
her course. He had wedded, been clergyman in two successive
country places; when his wife died, leaving him one little
daughter, and a heart much overset by that event. Friends,
wealthy Brothers probably, had pushed him out into the free
air, in these circumstances: "Take a Tour; Holland, England; feel the winds blowing, see the sun shining, as in times
past: it will do you good!"

Jordan, in the course of his Tour, came to composure on

[1] *Souvenirs d'un Citoyen* (2de édition, Paris, 1797), i. 37.

several points. He found that, by frugality, by wise management of some peculium already his, his little Daughter and he might have quietness at Berlin, and the necessary food and raiment ; — and, on the whole, that he would altogether cease preaching, and settle down there, among his Books, in a frugal manner. Which he did ; — and was living so, when the Prince, searching for that kind of person, got tidings of him. And here he is at Reinsberg ; bustling about, in a brisk, modestly frank and cheerful manner : well liked by everybody ; by his Master very well and ever better, who grew into real regard, esteem and even friendship for him, and has much Correspondence, of a freer kind than is common to him, with little Jordan, so long as they lived together. Jordan's death, ten years hence, was probably the one considerable pain he had ever given his neighbors, in this the ultimate section of his life.

I find him described, at Reinsberg, as a small nimble figure, of Southern-French aspect ; black, uncommonly bright eyes ; and a general aspect of adroitness, modesty, sense, sincerity ; good prognostics, which on acquaintance with the man were pleasantly fulfilled.

For the sake of these considerations, I fished out, from the Old-Book Catalogues and sea of forgetfulness, some of the poor Books he wrote ; especially a *Voyage Littéraire*,[1] Journal of that first Sanitary Excursion or Tour he took, to get the clouds blown from his mind. A *Literary Voyage* which awakens a kind of tragic feeling ; being itself dead, and treating of matters which are all gone dead. So many immortal writers, Dutch chiefly, whom Jordan is enabled to report as having effloresced, or being soon to effloresce, in such and such forms, of Books important to be learned : leafy, blossomy Forest of Literature, waving glorious in the then sunlight to Jordan ; — and it lies all now, to Jordan and us, not withered only, but abolished ; compressed into a film of indiscriminate *peat*. Consider what that *peat* is made of, O celebrated or uncelebrated reader, and take a moral from Jordan's Book !

[1] *Histoire d'un Voyage Littéraire fait*, en MDCCXXXIII., *en France, en Angleterre et en Hollande* (2de édition, à La Haye, 1736).

Other merit, except indeed clearness and commendable brevity, the *Voyage Littéraire* or other little Books of Jordan's have not now. A few of his Letters to Friedrich, which exist, are the only writings with the least life left in them, and this an accidental life, not momentous to him or us. Dryasdust informs me, "Abbé Jordan, alone of the Crown-Prince's cavaliers, sleeps in the Town of Reinsberg, not in the Schloss:" and if I ask, Why? — there is no answer. Probably his poor little Daughterkin was beside him there? —

We have to say of Friedrich's Associates, that generally they were of intelligent type, each of them master of something or other, and capable of rational discourse upon that at least. Integrity, loyalty of character, was indispensable; good humor, wit if it could be had, were much in request. There was no man of shining distinction there; but they were the best that could be had, and that is saying all. Friedrich cannot be said, either as Prince or as King, to have been superlatively successful in his choice of associates. With one single exception, to be noticed shortly, there is not one of them whom we should now remember except for Friedrich's sake; — uniformly they are men whom it is now a weariness to hear of, except in a cursory manner. One man of shining parts he had, and one only; no man ever of really high and great mind. The latter sort are not so easy to get; rarely producible on the soil of this Earth! Nor is it certain how Friedrich might have managed with one of this sort, or he with Friedrich; — though Friedrich unquestionably would have tried, had the chance offered. For he loved intellect as few men on the throne, or off it, ever did; and the little he could gather of it round him often seems to me a fact tragical rather than otherwise.

With the outer Berlin social world, acting and reacting, Friedrich has his connections, which obscurely emerge on us now and then. Literary Eminences, who are generally of Theological vesture; any follower of Philosophy, especially if he be of refined manners withal, or known in fashionable life, is sure to attract him; and gains ample recognition at

Reinsberg or on Town-visits.   But the Berlin Theological or
Literary world at that time, still more the Berlin Social, like
a sunk extinct object, continues very dim in those old records;
and to say truth, what features we have of it do not invite to
miraculous efforts for farther acquaintance.   Venerable Beausobre, with his *History of the Manicheans*,[1] and other learned
things, — we heard of him long since, in Toland and the Republican Queen's time, as a light of the world.   He is now
fourscore, grown white as snow; very serene, polite, with a
smack of French noblesse in him, perhaps a smack of affecta-
tion traceable too.   The Crown-Prince, on one of his Berlin
visits, wished to see this Beausobre; got a meeting appointed,
in somebody's rooms "in the French College," and waited
for the venerable man.   Venerable man entered, loftily serene
as a martyr Preacher of the Word, something of an ancient
Seigneur de Beausobre in him, too; for the rest, soft as sunset, and really with fine radiances, in a somewhat twisted state,
in that good old mind of his.   " What have you been reading
lately, M. de Beausobre ? " said the Prince, to begin conversation.   " Ah, Monseigneur, I have just risen from reading
the sublimest piece of writing that exists." — " And what ? "
" The exordium of St. John's Gospel : *In the Beginning was
the Word ; and the Word was with God, and the Word was —*"
Which somewhat took the Prince by surprise, as Formey reports ; though he rallied straightway, and got good conversation out of the old gentleman.   To whom, we perceive, he
writes once or twice,[2] — a copy of his own verses to correct,
on one occasion, — and is very respectful and considerate.

Formey tells us of another French sage, personally known
to the Prince since Boyhood; for he used to be about the
Palace, doing something.   This is one La Croze ; Professor of,
I think, "Philosophy" in the French College : sublime Mon-

---

[1] *Histoire critique de Manichée et du Manichéisme :* wrote also *Remarques
&c. sur le Nouveau Testament,* which were once famous ; *Histoire de la Réfor-
mation ;* &c. &c.   He is Beausobre *Senior ;* there were two Sons (one of them
born in second wedlock, after Papa was 70), who were likewise given to
writing. — See Formey, *Souvenirs d'un Citoyen,* i. 33–39.

[2] *Œuvres de Frédéric,* xvi. 121–126.   Dates are all of 1737 ; the last of
Beausobre's years.

ster of Erudition, at that time; forgotten now, I fear, by
everybody. Swag-bellied, short of wind; liable to rages, to
utterances of a coarse nature; a decidedly ugly, monstrous
and rather stupid kind of man. Knew twenty languages, in
a coarse inexact way. Attempted deep kinds of discourse, in
the lecture-room and elsewhere; but usually broke off into
endless welters of anecdote, not always of cleanly nature; and
after every two or three words, a desperate sigh, not for
sorrow, but on account of flabbiness and fat. Formey gives
a portraiture of him; not worth copying farther. The same
Formey, standing one day somewhere on the streets of Berlin,
was himself, he cannot doubt, *seen* by the Crown-Prince in
passing; "who asked M. Jordan, who that was," and got answer : — is not that a comfortable fact ? Nothing farther
came of it; — respectable Ex-Parson Formey, though ever
ready with his pen, being indeed of very vapid nature, not
wanted at Reinsberg, as we can guess.

There is M. Achard, too, another Preacher, supreme of his
sort, in the then Berlin circles; to whom or from whom a
Letter or two exist. Letters worthless, if it were not for one
dim indication : That, on inquiry, the Crown-Prince had been
consulting this supreme Achard on the difficulties of Orthodoxy;[1] and had given him texts, or a text, to preach from.
Supreme Achard did not abolish the difficulties for his inquiring Prince, — who complains respectfully that "his faith is
weak," and leaves us dark as to particulars. This Achard
passage is almost the only hint we have of what might have
been an important chapter : Friedrich's Religious History at
Reinsberg. The expression "weak faith" I take to be meant
not in mockery, but in ingenuous regret and solicitude ; much
painful fermentation, probably, on the religious question in
those Reinsberg years ! But the old " *Gnadenwahl* " business,
the Free-Grace controversy, had taught him to be cautious as
to what he uttered on those points. The fermentation, therefore, had to go on under cover ; what the result of it was, is
notorious enough ; though the steps of the process are not in
any point known.

---

[1] *Œuvres de Frédéric*, xvi. pp. 112–117 : date, March–June, 1736.

Enough now of such details. Outwardly or inwardly, there is no History, or almost none, to be had of this Reinsberg Period; the extensive records of it consisting, as usual, mainly of chaotic nugatory matter, opaque to the mind of readers. There is copious correspondence of the Crown-Prince, with at least dates to it for most part: but this, which should be the main resource, proves likewise a poor one; the Crown-Prince's Letters, now or afterwards, being almost never of a deep or intimate quality; and seldom turning on events or facts at all, and then not always on facts interesting, on facts clearly apprehensible to us in that extinct element.

The Thing, we know always, *is* there; but vision of the Thing is only to be had faintly, intermittently. Dim inane twilight, with here and there a transient *spark* falling somewhither in it; — you do at last, by desperate persistence, get to discern outlines, features: — "The Thing cannot *always* have been No-thing," you reflect! Outlines, features: — and perhaps, after all, those are mostly what the reader wants on this occasion.

CHAPTER II.

OF VOLTAIRE AND THE LITERARY CORRESPONDENCES.

ONE of Friedrich's grand purposes at Reinsberg, to himself privately the grandest there, which he follows with constant loyalty and ardor, is that of scaling the heights of the Muses' Hill withal; of attaining mastership, discipleship, in Art and Philosophy; — or in candor let us call it, what it truly was, that of enlightening and fortifying himself with clear knowledge, clear belief, on all sides; and acquiring some spiritual panoply in which to front the coming practicalities of life. This, he feels well, will be a noble use of his seclusion in those still places; and it must be owned, he struggles and endeavors towards this, with great perseverance, by all the methods in his power, here, or wherever afterwards he might be.

Here at Reinsberg, one of his readiest methods, his pleasantest if not his usefulest, is that of getting into correspondence with the chief . spirits of his time. Which accordingly he forthwith sets about, after getting into Reinsberg, and continues, as we shall see, with much assiduity. Rollin, Fontenelle, and other French lights of the then firmament, — his Letters to them exist; and could be given in some quantity: but it is better not. They are intrinsically the common Letters on such occasions: "O sublime demi-god of literature, how small are princely distinctions to such a glory as thine; thou who enterest within the veil of the temple, and issuest with thy face shining!" — To which the response is: "Hm, think you so, most happy, gracious, illustrious Prince, with every convenience round you, and such prospects ahead? Well, thank you, at any rate, — and, as the Irish say, more power to your Honor's Glory!" This really is nearly all that said Sets of Letters contain; and except perhaps the Voltaire Set, none of them give symptoms of much capacity to contain more.

Certainly there was no want of Literary Men discernible from Reinsberg at that time; and the young Prince corresponds with a good many of them; temporal potentate saluting spiritual, from the distance, — in a way highly interesting to the then parties, but now without interest, except of the reflex kind, to any creature. A very cold and empty portion, this, of the Friedrich Correspondence; standing there to testify what his admiration was for literary talent, or the great reputation of such; but in itself uninstructive utterly, and of freezing influence on the now living mind. Most of those French lights of the then firmament are gone out. Forgotten altogether; or recognized, like Rollin and others, for polished dullards, university big-wigs, and long-winded commonplace persons, deserving nothing but oblivion. To Montesquieu, — not yet called "Baron de Montesquieu" with *Esprit des Lois*, but "M. de Secondat" with (Anonymous) *Lettres Persanes*, and already known to the world for a person of sharp audacious eyesight, — it does not appear that Friedrich addressed any Letter, now or afterwards. No notice of Montesquieu nor of some others, the absence of whom is a little unexpected. Probably it was want of knowledge mainly; for his appetite was not fastidious at this time. And certainly he did hit the centre of the mark, and get into the very kernel of French literature, when, in 1736, hardly yet established in his new quarters, he addressed himself to the shining figure known to us as "Arouet Junior" long since, and now called *M. de Voltaire;* which latter is still a name notable in Friedrich's History and that of Mankind. Friedrich's first Letter, challenging Voltaire to correspondence, dates itself 8th August, 1736; and Voltaire's Answer — the Reinsberg Household still only in its second month — was probably the brightest event which had yet befallen there.

On various accounts it will behoove us to look a good deal more strictly into this Voltaire; and, as his relations to Friedrich and to the world are so multiplex, endeavor to disengage the real likeness of the man from the circumambient noise and confusion which in his instance continue very great. "Voltaire was the spiritual complement of Friedrich," says Sauerteig once: "what little of lasting their poor Century produced lies mainly in these Two. A very somnambulating Century! But what little it *did*, we must call Friedrich; what little it *thought*, Voltaire. Other fruit we have not from it to speak of, at this day. Voltaire, and what *can* be faithfully done on the Voltaire Creed; 'Realized Voltairism;' — admit it, reader, not in a too triumphant humor, — is not that pretty much the net historical product of the Eighteenth Century? The rest of its history either pure somnambulism; or a mere Controversy, to the effect, 'Realized Voltairism? How soon shall it be realized, then? Not at once, surely!' So that Friedrich and Voltaire are related, not by accident only. They are, they for want of better, the two Original Men of their Century; the chief and in a sense the sole products of their Century. They alone remain to us as still living results from it, — such as they are. And the rest, truly, *ought* to depart and vanish (as they are now doing); being mere ephemera; contemporary eaters, scramblers for

provender, talkers of acceptable hearsay; and related merely
to the butteries and wiggeries of their time, and not related to
the Perennialities at all, as these Two were." — With more
of the like sort from Sauerteig.

M. de Voltaire, who used to be M. François-Marie Arouet,
was at this time about forty,[1] and had gone through various
fortunes; a man, now and henceforth, in a high degree conspicuous, and questionable to his fellow-creatures. Clear
knowledge of him ought, at this stage, to be common; but
unexpectedly it is not. What endless writing and biography-
ing there has been about this man; in which one still reads,
with a kind of lazy satisfaction, due to the subject, and to
the French genius in that department! But the man himself,
and his environment and practical aspects, what the actual
physiognomy of his life and of him can have been, is dark
from beginning to ending; and much is left in an ambiguous
undecipherable condition to us. A proper History of Voltaire,
in which should be discoverable, luminous to human creatures,
what he was, what element he lived in, what work he did:
this is still a problem for the genius of France! —

His Father's name is known to us; the name of his Father's
profession, too, but not clearly the nature of it; still less
his Father's character, economic circumstances, physiognomy
spiritual or social: not the least possibility granted you of
forming an image, however faint, of that notable man and
household, which distinguished itself to all the earth by pro-
ducing little François into the light of this sun. Of Madame
Arouet, who, or what, or how she was, nothing whatever is
known. A human reader, pestered continually with the
Madame-Denises, Abbé-Mignots and enigmatic nieces and
nephews, would have wished to know, at least, what children,
besides François, Madame Arouet had: once for all, How
many children? Name them, with year of birth, year of
death, according to the church-registers: they all, at any rate,

[1] Born 20th February, 1694; the younger of two sons: Father, "François
Arouet, a Notary of the Châtelet, ultimately Treasurer of the Chamber of
Accounts;" Mother, "Marguerite d'Aumart, of a noble family of Poitou."

had that degree of history! No; even that has not been done. Beneficent correspondents of my own make answer, after some research, No register of the Arouets anywhere to be had. The very name VOLTAIRE, if you ask whence came it? there is no answer, or worse than none. — The fit "History" of this man, which might be one of the shining Epics of his Century, and the lucid summary and soul of any *History* France then had, but which would require almost a French demi-god to do it, is still a great way off, if on the road at all! For present purposes, we select what follows from a well-known hand: —

" *Youth of Voltaire* (1694–1725). — French Biographers have left the Arouet Household very dark for us; meanwhile we can perceive, or guess, that it was moderately well in economic respects; that François was the second of the Two Sons; and that old Arouet, a steady, practical and perhaps rather sharp-tempered old gentleman, of official legal habits and position, 'Notary of the Châtelet' and something else, had destined him for the Law Profession; as was natural enough to a son of M. Arouet, who had himself succeeded well in Law, and could there, best of all, open roads for a clever second son. François accordingly sat 'in chambers,' as we call it; and his fellow-clerks much loved him, — the most amusing fellow in the world. Sat in chambers, even became an advocate; but did not in the least take to advocateship; — took to poetry, and other airy dangerous courses, speculative, practical; causing family explosions and rebukes, which were without effect on him. A young fool, bent on sportful pursuits instead of serious; more and more shuddering at Law. To the surprise and indignation of M. Arouet Senior. Law, with its wigs and sheepskins, pointing towards high honors and deep flesh-pots, had no charms for the young fool; he could not be made to like Law.

"Whereupon arose explosions, as we hint; family explosions on the part of M. Arouet Senior; such that friends had to interfere, and it was uncertain what would come of it. One judicious friend, 'M. Caumartin,' took the young fellow home

to his house in the country for a time ; — and there, incidentally, brought him acquainted with old gentlemen deep in the
traditions of Henri Quatre and the cognate topics; which
much inflamed the young fellow, and produced big schemes in
the head of him.

" M. Arouet Senior stood strong for Law; but it was becoming daily more impossible. Madrigals, dramas (not without
actresses), satirical wit, airy verse, and all manner of adventurous speculation, were what this young man went upon;
and was getting more and more loved for; introduced, even,
to the superior circles, and recognized there as one of the
brightest young fellows ever seen. Which tended, of course,
to confirm him in his folly, and open other outlooks and harbors of refuge than the paternal one.

" Such things, strange to M. Arouet Senior, were in vogue
then ; wicked Regent d'Orléans having succeeded sublime
Louis XIV., and set strange fashions to the Quality. Not
likely to profit this fool François, thought M. Arouet Senior;
and was much confirmed in his notion, when a rhymed Lam-
poon against the Government having come out (*Les j'ai vu*, as
they call it[1]), and become the rage, as a clever thing of the
kind will, it was imputed to the brightest young fellow in
France, M. Arouet's Son. Who, in fact, was not the Author;
but was not believed on his denial; and saw himself, in spite
of his high connections, ruthlessly lodged in the Bastille in
consequence. ' Let him sit,' thought M. Arouet Senior, ' and
come to his senses there ! ' He sat for eighteen months
(age still little above twenty); but privately employed his
time, not in repentance, or in serious legal studies, but in
writing a Poem on his Henri Quatre. ' Epic Poem,' no less ;
La Ligue, as he then called it; which it was his hope the
whole world would one day fall in love with ; — as it did. Nay,
in two years more, he had done a Play, *Œdipe* the renowned
name of it; which 'ran for forty-eight nights' (18th November, 1718, the first of them); and was enough to turn any

[1] " I have seen (*j'ai vu*) " this ignominy occur, " I have seen " that other, —
to the amount of a dozen or two ; — " and am not yet twenty." Copy of it,
and guess as to authorship, in *Œuvres de Voltaire*, i. 321.

head of such age. Law may be considered hopeless, even by
M. Arouet Senior.

"Try him in the Diplomatic line; break these bad habits
and connections, thought M. Arouet, at one time; and sent
him to the French Ambassador in Holland, — on good behavior, as it were, and by way of temporary banishment. But
neither did this answer. On the contrary, the young fellow
got into scrapes again; got into amatory intrigues, — young
lady visiting you in men's clothes, young lady's mother invei-
gling, and I know not what; — so that the Ambassador was
glad to send him home again unmarried; marked, as it were,
'Glass, with care!' And the young lady's mother printed
his Letters, not the least worth reading: — and the old
M. Arouet seems now to have flung up his head; to have settled some small allowance on him, with peremptory no-hope
of more, and said, 'Go your own way, then, foolish junior : the
elder shall be my son.' M. Arouet disappears at this point,
or nearly so, from the history of his son François; and I think
must have died in not many years. Poor old M. Arouet closed
his old eyes without the least conception what a prodigious
ever-memorable thing he had done unknowingly, in sending
this François into the world, to kindle such universal 'dry
dung-heap of a rotten world,' and set it blazing! François, his
Father's synonym, came to be representative of the family,
after all; the elder Brother also having died before long. Except certain confused niece-and-nephew personages, progeny
of the sisters, François has no more trouble or solacement
from the paternal household. François meanwhile is his
Father's synonym, and signs Arouet Junior, 'François Arouet
l. j. (le jeune).'

"'All of us Princes, then, or Poets!' said he, one night at
supper, looking to right and left: the brightest fellow in the
world, well fit to be Phœbus Apollo of such circles; and great
things now ahead of him. Dissolute Regent d'Orléans, politest, most debauched of men, and very witty, holds the helm;
near him Dubois the Devil's Cardinal, and so many bright
spirits. All the Luciferous Spiritualism there is in France
is lifting anchor, under these auspices, joyfully towards new

latitudes and Isles of the Blest. What may not François hope
to become? 'Hmph!' answers M. Arouet Senior, steadily,
so long as he lives. Here are one or two subsequent phases,
epochs or turning-points, of the young gentleman's career.

"*Phasis First* (1725–1728). — The accomplished Duc de
Sulli (Year 1725, day not recorded), is giving in his hôtel a
dinner, such as usual; and a bright witty company is assembled; — the brightest young fellow in France sure to be there;
and with his electric coruscations illuminating everything, and
keeping the table in a roar. To the delight of most; not to
that of a certain splenetic ill-given Duc de Rohan; grandee
of high rank, great haughtiness, and very ill-behavior in the
world; who feels impatient at the notice taken of a mere civic
individual, Arouet Junior. ' *Quel est donc ce jeune homme qui
parle si haut,* Who is this young man that talks so loud, then ?'
exclaims the proud splenetic Duke. 'Monseigneur,' flashes
the young man back upon him in an electric manner, 'it is
one who does not drag a big name about with him; but who
secures respect for the name he has!' Figure that, in the
penetrating grandly clangorous voice (*voix sombre et majes-
tueuse*), and the momentary flash of eyes that attended it. Duc
de Rohan rose, in a sulphurous frame of mind; and went his
ways. What date? You ask the idle French Biographer in
vain; — see only, after more and more inspection, that the
incident is true; and with labor date it, summer of the Year
1725. Treaty of Utrecht itself, though all the Newspapers
and Own Correspondents were so interested in it, was perhaps
but a foolish matter to date in comparison!

"About a week after, M. Arouet Junior was again dining
with the Duc de Sulli, and a fine company as before. A servant whispers him, That somebody has called, and wants him
below. 'Cannot come,' answers Arouet; 'how can I, so engaged?' Servant returns after a minute or two: 'Pardon,
Monsieur; I am to say, it is to do an act of beneficence that
you are wanted below!' Arouet lays down his knife and
fork; descends instantly to see what act it is. A carriage is
in the court, and hackney-coach near it: 'Would Monsieur

have the extreme goodness to come to the door of the carriage,
in a case of necessity ?' At the door of the carriage, hands
seize the collar of him, hold him as in a vice ; diabolic visage
of Duc de Rohan is visible inside, who utters, looking to the
hackney-coach, some ' *Voilà*, Now then !' Whereupon the
hackney-coach opens, gives out three porters, or hired bullies,
with the due implements : scandalous actuality of horsewhipping descends on the back of poor Arouet, who shrieks and
execrates to no purpose, nobody being near. 'That will do,'
says Rohan at last, and the gallant ducal party drive off ;
young Arouet, with torn frills and deranged hair, rushing upstairs again, in such a mood as is easy to fancy. Everybody
is sorry, inconsolable, everybody shocked ; nobody volunteers
to help in avenging. 'Monseigneur de Sulli, is not such
atrocity done to one of your guests, an insult to yourself ?'
asks Arouet. 'Well, yes perhaps, but' —Monseigneur de
Sulli shrugs his shoulders, and proposes nothing. Arouet
withdrew, of course in a most blazing condition, to consider
what he could, on his own strength, do in this conjuncture.

"His Biographer Duvernet says, he decided on doing two
things : learning English and the small-sword exercise.[1] He
retired to the country for six months, and perfected himself
in these two branches. Being perfect, he challenged Duc de
Rohan in the proper manner ; applying ingenious compulsives
withal, to secure acceptance of the challenge. Rohan accepted,
not without some difficulty, and compulsion at the Theatre or
otherwise : — accepted, but withal confessed to his wife. The
result was. no measuring of swords took place ; and Rohan
only blighted by public opinion, or incapable of farther blight
that way, went at large ; a convenient *Lettre de Cachet* having put Arouet again in the Bastille. Where for six months

---

[1] *La Vie de Voltaire*, par M—— (à Genève, 1786), pp. 55-57 ; or pp. 60-63,
in his *second* form of the Book. The "M——" is an Abbé Duvernet ;
of no great mark otherwise. He got into Revolution trouble afterwards, but
escaped with his head ; and republished his Book, swollen out somewhat by
new "Anecdotes" and republican bluster, in this second instance ; signing
himself T. J. D. V—— (Paris, 1797). A vague but not dark or mendacious little Book ; with traces of real *eyesight* in it, — by one who had personally known Voltaire, or at least seen and heard him.

Arouet lodged a second time, the innocent not the guilty;
making, we can well suppose, innumerable reflections on the
phenomena of human life. Imprisonment once over, he hastily quitted for England; shaking the dust of ungrateful
France off his feet, — resolved to change his unhappy name,
for one thing.

"Smelfungus, denouncing the torpid fatuity of Voltaire's
Biographers, says he never met with one Frenchman, even
of the Literary classes, who could tell him whence this name
VOLTAIRE originated. 'A *petite terre*, small family estate,'
they said; and sent him hunting through Topographies, far
and wide, to no purpose. Others answered, 'Volterra in Italy,
some connection with Volterra,' — and seemed even to know
that this was but fatuity. 'In ever-talking, ever-printing Paris,
is it as in Timbuctoo, then, which neither prints nor has
anything to print?' exclaims poor Smelfungus! He tells us
at last, the name *Voltaire* is a mere Anagram of *Arouet l. j.* —
you try it; A.R.O.U.E.T.L.J. = V.O.L.T.A.I.R.E; and perceive at
once, with obligations to Smelfungus, that he has settled this
small matter for you, and that you can be silent upon it
forever thenceforth.

"The anagram VOLTAIRE, gloomily settled in the Bastille in
this manner, can be reckoned a very famous wide-sounding
outer result of the Rohan impertinence and blackguardism;
but it is not worth naming beside the inner intrinsic result,
of banishing Voltaire to England at this point of his course.
England was full of Constitutionality and Freethinking; To-
lands, Collinses, Wollastons, Bolingbrokes, still living; very
free indeed. England, one is astonished to see, has its royal-
republican ways of doing; something Roman in it, from Peerage down to Plebs; strange and curious to the eye of M. de
Voltaire. Sciences flourishing; Newton still alive, white with
fourscore years, the venerable hoary man; Locke's Gospel of
Common Sense in full vogue, or even done into verse, by incomparable Mr. Pope, for the cultivated upper classes. In
science, in religion, in politics, what a surprising 'liberty'
allowed or taken! Never was a freer turn of thinking. And
(what to M. de Voltaire is a pleasant feature) it is Freethinking

with ruffles to its shirt and rings on its fingers ; — never yet,
the least, dreaming of the shirtless or *sansculottic* state that
lies ahead for it ! That is the palmy condition of English
Liberty, when M. de Voltaire arrives there.

"In a man just out of the Bastille on those terms, there is
a mind driven by hard suffering into seriousness, and provoked
by indignant comparisons and remembrances. As if you had
elaborately ploughed and pulverized the mind of this Voltaire
to receive with its utmost avidity, and strength of fertility,
whatever seed England may have for it. That was a notable
conjuncture of a man with circumstances. The question, Is
this man to grow up a Court Poet ; to do legitimate dramas,
lampoons, witty verses, and wild spiritual and practical mag-
nificences, the like never seen ; Princes and Princesses recognizing him as plainly divine, and keeping him tied by
enchantments to that poor trade as his task in life ? is an
swered in the negative. No : and it is not quite to decorate
and comfort your 'dry dung-heap' of a world, or the fortunate
cocks that scratch on it, that the man Voltaire is here ; but
to shoot lightnings into it, and set it ablaze one day ! That
was an important alternative ; truly of world-importance to
the poor generations that now are ; and it was settled, in good
part, by this voyage to England, as one may surmise. Such
is sometimes the use of a dissolute Rohan in this world ; for
the gods make implements of all manner of things.

"M. de Voltaire (for we now drop the Arouet altogether, and
never hear of it more) came to England — when ? Quitted
England — when ? Sorrow on all fatuous Biographers, who
spend their time not in laying permanent foundation-stones,
but in fencing with the wind ! — I at last find indisputably, it
was in 1726 that he came to England :[1] and he himself tells
us that he quitted it 'in 1728.' Spent, therefore, some two
years there in all, — last year of George I.'s reign, and first
of George II.'s. But mere inanity and darkness visible reign,
in all his Biographies, over this period of his life, which was
above all others worth investigating : seek not to know it ; no

[1] Got out of the Bastille, with orders to leave France, "29th April" of that
year (*Œuvres de Voltaire,* i. 40 n.).

man has inquired into it, probably no competent man now ever
will. By hints in certain Letters of the period, we learn that
he lodged, or at one time lodged, in 'Maiden Lane, Covent
Garden;' one of those old Houses that yet stand in Maiden
Lane: for which small fact let us be thankful. His own Letters of the period are dated now and then from 'Wandsworth.'
Allusions there are to Bolingbroke; but the Wandsworth is
not Bolingbroke's mansion, which stood in Battersea; the
Wandsworth was one Edward Fawkener's; a man somewhat
admirable to young Voltaire, but extinct now, or nearly so, in
human memory. He had been a Turkey Merchant, it would
seem, and nevertheless was admitted to speak his word in in-
tellectual, even in political circles; which was wonderful to
young Voltaire. This Fawkener, I think, became Sir Edward
Fawkener, and some kind of 'Secretary to the Duke of Cumberland:' — I judge it to be the same Fawkener; a man highly
unmemorable now, were it not for the young Frenchman he
was hospitable to. Fawkener's and Bolingbroke's are perhaps
the only names that turn up in Voltaire's *Letters* of this English Period: over which generally there reigns, in the French
Biographies, inane darkness, with an intimation, half involuntary, that it *should* have been made luminous, and would it
perfectly easy.

"We know, from other sources, that he had acquaintance
with many men in England, with all manner of important
men: Notes to Pope in Voltaire-English, visit of Voltaire to
Congreve, Notes even to such as Lady Sundon in the interior
of the Palace, are known of. The brightest young fellow in
the world did not want for introductions to the highest quarters, in that time of political alliance, and extensive private
acquaintance, between his Country and ours. And all this he
was the man to improve, both in the trivial and the deep
sense. His bow to the divine Princess Caroline and suite,
could it fail in graceful reverence or what else was needed?
Dexterous right words in the right places, winged with *esprit*
so called: that was the man's supreme talent, in which he had
no match, to the last. A most brilliant, swift, far-glancing
young man, disposed to make himself generally agreeable.

For the rest, his wonder, we can see, was kept awake; wonder readily inclining, in his circumstances, towards admiration. The stereotype figure of the Englishman, always the same, which turns up in Voltaire's *Works,* is worth noting in this respect. A rugged surly kind of fellow, much-enduring, not intrinsically bad; splenetic without complaint, standing oddly inexpugnable in that natural stoicism of his; taciturn, yet with strange flashes of speech in him now and then, something which goes beyond laughter and articulate logic, and is the taciturn elixir of these two, what they call 'humor' in their dialect: this is pretty much the *reverse* of Voltaire's own self, and therefore all the welcomer to him; delineated always with a kind of mockery, but with evident love. What excellences are in England, thought Voltaire; no Bastille in it, for one thing! Newton's Philosophy annihilated the vortexes of Descartes for him; Locke's Toleration is very grand (especially if all is uncertain, and *you* are in the minority); then Collins, Wollaston and Company,—no vile Jesuits here, strong in their mendacious mal-odorous stupidity, despicablest yet most dangerous of creatures, to check freedom of thought! Illustrious Mr. Pope, of the *Essay on Man,* surely he is admirable; as are Pericles Bolingbroke, and many others. Even Bolingbroke's high-lacquered brass is gold to this young French friend of his. — Through all which admirations and exaggerations the progress of the young man, toward certain very serious attainments and achievements, is conceivable enough.

"One other man, who ought to be mentioned in the Biographies, I find Voltaire to have made acquaintance with, in England: a German M. Fabrice, one of several Brothers called Fabrice or Fabricius, — concerning whom, how he had been at Bender, and how Voltaire picked *Charles Douze* from the memory of him, there was already mention. The same Fabrice who held poor George I. in his arms while they drove, galloping, to Osnabrück, that night, *in extremis:* — not needing mention again. The following is more to the point.

"Voltaire, among his multifarious studies while in England, did not forget that of economics: his Poem *La Ligue,* — sur-

reptitiously printed, three years since, under that title (one
Desfontaines, a hungry Ex-Jesuit, the perpetrator),[1] — he now
took in hand for his own benefit; washed it clean of its blots;
christened it *Henriade*, under which name it is still known
over all the world; — and printed it; published it here, by
subscription, in 1726; one of the first things he undertook.
Very splendid subscription; headed by Princess Caroline, and
much favored by the opulent of quality. Which yielded an
unknown but very considerable sum of thousands sterling, and
grounded not only the world-renown but the domestic finance
of M. de Voltaire. For the fame of the 'new epic,' as this
Henriade was called, soon spread into all lands. And such
fame, and other agencies on his behalf, having opened the
way home for Voltaire, he took this sum of Thousands Sterling
along with him; laid it out judiciously in some city lottery, or
profitable scrip then going at Paris, which at once doubled
the amount: after which he invested it in Corn-trade, Army
Clothing, Barbary-trade, Commissariat Bacon-trade, all manner
of well-chosen trades, — being one of the shrewdest financiers
on record; — and never from that day wanted abundance of
money, for one thing. Which he judged to be extremely expedient for a literary man, especially in times of Jesuit and
other tribulation. 'You have only to watch,' he would say,
'what scrips, public loans, investments in the field of agio,
are offered; if you exert any judgment, it is easy to gain
there: do not the stupidest of mortals gain there, by intensely
attending to it?'

"Voltaire got almost nothing by his Books, which he generally had to disavow, and denounce as surreptitious supposi-
tious scandals, when some sharp-set Book-seller, in whose way
he had laid the savory article as bait, chose to risk his ears
for the profit of snatching and publishing it. Next to nothing
by his Books; but by his fine finance-talent otherwise, he had
become possessed of ample moneys. Which were so cunningly
disposed, too, that he had resources in every Country; and
no conceivable combination of confiscating Jesuits and dark
fanatic Official Persons could throw him out of a livelihood,

---

[1] 1723, *Vie*, par T. J. D. V. (that is, "M—— " in the *second* form), p. 59.

whithersoever he might be forced to run. A man that looks
facts in the face; which is creditable of him. The vulgar
call it avarice and the like, as their way is : but M. de Voltaire
is convinced that effects will follow causes; and that it well
beseems a lonely Ishmaelite, hunting his way through the
howling wildernesses and confused ravenous populations of
this world, to have money in his pocket. He died with a
revenue of some £7,000 a year, probably as good as £20,000
at present; the richest literary man ever heard of hitherto,
as well as the remarkablest in some other respects. But we
have to mark the second phasis of his life [in which Friedrich
now sees him], and how it grew out of this first one.

"*Phasis Second* (1728–1733). — Returning home as if quietly
triumphant, with such a talent in him, and such a sanction put
upon it and him by a neighboring Nation, and by all the world,
Voltaire was warmly received, in his old aristocratic circles,
by cultivated France generally; and now in 1728, in his thirty-
second year, might begin to have definite outlooks of a sufficiently royal kind, in Literature and otherwise. Nor is he
slow, far from it, to advance, to conquer and enjoy. He writes
successful literature, falls in love with women of quality;
encourages the indigent and humble ; eclipses, and in case of
need tramples down, the too proud. He elegizes poor Adrienne
Lecouvreur, the Actress, — our poor friend the Comte de
Saxe's female friend ; who loyally emptied out her whole purse
for him, £30,000 in one sum, that he might try for Courland,
and whether he could fall in love with her of the Swollen
Cheek there ; which proved impossible. Elegizes Adrienne, we
say, and even buries her under cloud of night : ready to protect
unfortunate females of merit. Especially theatrical females ;
having much to do in the theatre, which we perceive to be the
pulpit or real preaching-place of cultivated France in those
years. All manner of verse, all manner of prose, he dashes
off with surprising speed and grace : showers of light spray
for the moment ; and always some current of graver enterprise,
Siècle de Louis Quatorze or the like, going on beneath it. For
he is a most diligent, swift, unresting man ; and studies and

learns amazingly in such a rackety existence. Victorious
enough in some senses; defeat, in Literature, never visited
him. His Plays, coming thick on the heels of one another,
rapid brilliant pieces, are brilliantly received by the unofficial
world; and ought to dethrone dull Crébillon, and the sleepy
potentates of Poetry that now are. Which in fact is their
result with the public; but not yet in the highest courtly
places; — a defect much to be condemned and lamented.

"Numerous enemies arise, as is natural, of an envious ven-
omous description; this is another ever-widening shadow in the
sunshine. In fact we perceive he has, besides the inner obsta-
cles and griefs, two classes of outward ones: There are Lions
on his path and also Dogs. Lions are the Ex-Bishop of Mirepoix, and certain other dark Holy Fathers, or potent orthodox
Official Persons. These, though Voltaire does not yet declare
his heterodoxy (which, indeed, is but the *ortho*doxy of the cultivated private circles), perceive well enough, even by the
Henriade, and its talk of 'tolerance,' horror of 'fanaticism'
and the like, what this one's *'doxy* is; and how dangerous he,
not a mere mute man of quality, but a talking spirit with
winged words, may be; — and they much annoy and terrify
him, by their roaring in the distance. Which roaring cannot,
of course, convince; and since it is not permitted to kill, can
only provoke a talking spirit into still deeper strains of heterodoxy for his own private behoof. These are the Lions on his
path: beasts conscious to themselves of good intentions; but
manifesting from Voltaire's point of view, it must be owned,
a physiognomy unlovely to a degree. 'Light is superior to
darkness, I should think,' meditates Voltaire; 'power of
thought to the want of power! The *Ane de Mirepoix* (Ass of
Mirepoix),[1] pretending to use me in this manner, is it other,
in the court of Rhadamanthus, than transcendent Stupidity,

---

[1] Poor joke of Voltaire's, continually applied to this Bishop, or Ex-Bishop,
— who was thought, generally, a rather tenebrific man for appointment to the
Feuille des Bénéfices (charge of nominating Bishops, keeping King's conscience, &c.); and who, in that capacity, signed himself *Anc* (by no means
"*Ane*," but "*Ancien,* Whilom") *de Mirepoix,* — to the enragement of Voltaire often enough.

with transcendent Insolence superadded?' Voltaire grows
more and more heterodox; and is ripening towards dangerous
utterances, though he strives to hold in.

"The Dogs upon his path, again, are all the disloyal envious
persons of the Writing Class, whom his success has offended;
and, more generally, all the dishonest hungry persons who can
gain a morsel by biting him: and their name is legion. It
must be owned, about as ugly a Doggery ('*infâme Canaille*'
he might well reckon them) as has, before or since, infested
the path of a man. They are not hired and set on, as angry
suspicion might suggest; but they are covertly somewhat
patronized by the Mirepoix, or orthodox Official class. Scandalous Ex-Jesuit Desfontaines, Thersites Fréron, — these are but
types of an endless Doggery; whose names and works should
be blotted out; whose one claim to memory is, that the riding
man so often angrily sprang down, and tried horsewhipping
them into silence. A vain attempt. The individual hound
flies howling, abjectly petitioning and promising; but the rest
bark all with new comfort, and even *he* starts again straightway. It is bad travelling in those woods, with such Lions
and such Dogs. And then the sparsely scattered *Human*
Creatures (so we may call them in contrast, persons of Quality
for most part) are not always what they should be. The
grand mansions you arrive at, in this waste-howling solitude,
prove sometimes essentially Robber-towers; — and there may
be Armida Palaces, and divine-looking Armidas, where your
ultimate fate is still worse.

   ' *Que le monde est rempli d'enchanteurs, je ne dis rien d'enchanteresses!* '

To think of it, the solitary Ishmaelite journeying, never so
well mounted, through such a wilderness: with lions, dogs,
human robbers and Armidas all about him; himself lonely,
friendless under the stars: — one could pity him withal, though
that is not the feeling he solicits; nor gets hitherto, even at
this impartial distance.

"One of the beautiful creatures of Quality, — we hope, not
an Armida, — who came athwart Voltaire, in these times, was
a Madame du Châtelet; distinguished from all the others by a

love of mathematics and the pure sciences, were it nothing
else. She was still young, under thirty; the literary man
still under forty. With her Husband, to whom she had
brought a child, or couple of children, there was no formal
quarrel; but they were living apart, neither much heeding the
other, as was by no means a case without example at that
time; Monsieur soldiering, and philandering about, in garrison
or elsewhere; Madame, in a like humor, doing the best for
herself in the high circles of society, to which he and she
belonged. Most wearisome barren circles to a person of
thought, as both she and M. de Voltaire emphatically admitted
to one another, on first making acquaintance. But is there no
help?

"Madame had tried the pure sciences and philosophies, in
Books: but how much more charming, when they come to you
as a Human Philosopher; handsome, magnanimous, and the
wittiest man in the world! Young Madame was not regularly
beautiful; but she was very piquant, radiant, adventurous;
understood other things than the pure sciences, and could be
abundantly coquettish and engaging. I have known her scut-
tle off, on an evening, with a couple of adventurous young
wives of Quality, to the remote lodging of the witty M. de
Voltaire, and make his dim evening radiant to him.[1] Then
again, in public crowds, I have seen them; obliged to dis-
mount to the peril of Madame's diamonds, there being a jam
of carriages, and no getting forward for half the day. In
short, they are becoming more and more intimate, to the ex-
tremest degree; and, scorning the world, thank Heaven that
they are mutually indispensable. Cannot we get away from
this scurvy wasp's-nest of a Paris, thought they, and live to
ourselves and our books?

"Madame was of high quality, one of the Breteuils; but
was poor in comparison, and her Husband the like. An old
Château of theirs, named Cirey, stands in a pleasant enough
little valley in Champagne; but so dilapidated, gaunt and
vacant, nobody can live in it. Voltaire, who is by this time a
man of ample moneys, furnishes the requisite cash; Madame

[1] One of Voltaire's Letters.

and he, in sweet symphony, concert the plans : Cirey is repaired, at least parts of it are, into a boudoir of the gods,
regardless of expense; nothing ever seen so tasteful, so magnificent; and the two withdraw thither to study, in peace,
what sciences, pure and other, they have a mind to. They
are recognized as lovers, by the Parisian public, with little
audible censure from anybody there, — with none at all from
the easy Husband; who occasionally even visits Cirey, if he be
passing that way; and is content to take matters as he finds
them, without looking below the surface.[1] For the Ten Commandments are at a singular pass in cultivated France at this
epoch. Such illicit-idyllic form of life has been the form of
Voltaire's since 1733," — for some three years now, when
Friedrich and we first make acquaintance with him. " It
lasted above a dozen years more : an illicit marriage after its
sort, and subject only to the liabilities of such. Perhaps we
may look in upon the Cirey Household, ourselves, at some
future time; and " — This Editor hopes not !

" Madame admits that for the first ten years it was, on the
whole, sublime; a perfect Eden on Earth, though stormy now
and then.[2] After ten years, it began to grow decidedly
dimmer; and in the course of few years more, it became un-
deniably evident that M. de Voltaire ' did not love me as formerly : ' — in fact, if Madame could have seen it, M. de Voltaire
was growing old, losing his teeth, and the like; and did not care
for anything as formerly ! Which was a dreadful discovery,
and gave rise to results by and by.

" In this retreat at Cirey, varied with flying visits to Paris,
and kept awake by multifarious Correspondences, the quantity

[1] See (whosoever is curious) Madame de Grafigny, *Vie Privée de Voltaire
et de Madame du Châtelet* (Paris, 1820). A six months of actual Letters written by poor Grafigny, while sheltering at Cirey, Winter and Spring, 1738-
1739 ; straitened there in various respects, — extremely ill off for fuel, among
other things. Rugged practical Letters, shadowing out to us, unconsciously
oftenest, and like a very mirror, the splendid and the sordid, the seamy side
and the smooth, of Life at Cirey, in her experience of it. Published, fourscore years after, under the above title.

[2] *Lettres Inédites de Madame la Marquise du Chastelet ; auxquelles on a joint
une Dissertation* (&c. of hers) : Paris, 1806.

of Literature done by the two was great and miscellaneous.
By Madame, chiefly in the region of the pure sciences, in
Newtonian Dissertations, competitions for Prizes, and the like:
really sound and ingenious Pieces, entirely forgotten long
since. By Voltaire, in serious Tragedies, Histories, in light
Sketches and deep Dissertations: — mockery getting ever
wilder with him; the satirical vein, in prose and verse, amazingly copious, and growing more and more heterodox, as we
can perceive. His troubles from the ecclesiastical or Lion
kind in the Literary forest, still more from the rabid Doggery
in it, are manifold, incessant. And it is pleasantly notable, —
during these first ten years, — with what desperate intensity,
vigilance and fierceness, Madame watches over all his interests
and liabilities and casualties great and small; leaping with
her whole force into M. de Voltaire's scale of the balance,
careless of antecedences and consequences alike; flying, with
the spirit of an angry brood-hen, at the face of mastiffs, in
defence of any feather that is M. de Voltaire's. To which
Voltaire replies, as he well may, with eloquent gratitude;
with Verses to the divine Emilie, with Gifts to her, verses
and gifts the prettiest in the world; — and industriously
celebrates the divine Emilie to herself and all third parties.

"An ardent, aerial, gracefully predominant, and in the end
somewhat termagant female figure, this divine Emilie. Her
temper, radiant rather than bland, was none of the patientest
on occasion; nor was M. de Voltaire the least of a Job, if you
came athwart him the wrong way. I have heard, their domestic symphony was liable to furious flaws, — let us hope
at great distances apart: — that 'plates,' in presence of the
lackeys, actual crockery or metal, have been known to fly
from end to end of the dinner-table; nay they mention
'knives' (though only in the way of oratorical action); and
Voltaire has been heard to exclaim, the sombre and majestic
voice of him risen to a very high pitch: ' *Ne me regardez tant
de ces yeux hagards et louches,* Don't fix those haggard side-
long eyes on me in that way!' — mere shrillness of pale rage
presiding over the scene. But we hope it was only once in

the quarter, or seldomer: after which the element would be clearer for some time. A lonesome literary man, who has got a Brood Phœnix to preside over him, and fly at the face of gods and men for him in that manner, ought to be grateful.

"Perhaps we shall one day glance, personally, as it were, into Cirey with our readers;"—Not with this Editor or his! "It will turn out beyond the reader's expectation. Tolerable illicit resting-place, so far as the illicit can be tolerable, for a lonesome Man of Letters, who goes into the illicit. Helpfulness, affection, or the flattering image of such, are by no means wanting: squalls of infirm temper are not more frequent than in the most licit establishments of a similar sort. Madame, about this time, has a swift Palfrey, ' *Rossignol* (Nightingale) ' the name of him; and gallops fairy-like through the winding valleys; being an ardent rider, and well-looking on horseback. Voltaire's study is inlaid with — the Grafigny knows all what: — mere china tiles, gilt sculptures, marble slabs, and the supreme of taste and expense: study fit for the Phœbus Apollo of France, so far as Madame could contrive it. Takes coffee with Madame, in the Gallery, about noon. And his bedroom, I expressly discern,[1] looks out upon a running brook, the murmur of which is pleasant to one."

Enough, enough. We can perceive what kind of Voltaire it was to whom the Crown-Prince now addressed himself; and how luminous an object, shining afar out of the solitudes of Champagne, upon the ardent young man, still so capable of admiration. Model Epic, *Henriade;* model History, *Charles Douze;* sublime Tragedies, *César, Alzire* and others, which readers still know though with less enthusiasm, are blooming fresh in Friedrich's memory and heart; such Literature as man never saw before; and in the background Friedrich has inarticulately a feeling as if, in this man, there were something grander than all Literatures: a Reform of human Thought itself; a new "Gospel," good-tidings or God's-Message, by this man;—which Friedrich does not suspect, as the

[1] *Letters of Voltaire.*

world with horror does, to be a new *Ba'spel*, or Devil's-Message of bad-tidings! A sublime enough Voltaire; radiant
enough, over at Cirey yonder. To all lands, a visible Phœbus
Apollo, climbing the eastern steeps; with arrows of celestial
"new light" in his quiver; capable of stretching many a big
foul Python, belly uppermost, in its native mud, and ridding
the poor world of her Nightmares and Mud-Serpents in some
measure, we may hope! —

And so there begins, from this point, a lively Correspondence between Friedrich and Voltaire; which, with some interruptions of a notable sort, continued during their mutual Life;
and is a conspicuous feature in the Biographies of both. The
world talked much of it, and still talks; and has now at last
got it all collected, and elucidated into a dimly legible form
for studious readers.[1] It is by no means the diabolically
wicked Correspondence it was thought to be; the reverse,
indeed, on both sides; — but it has unfortunately become
a very dull one, to the actual generation of mankind. Not
without intrinsic merit; on the contrary (if you read intensely,
and bring the extinct alive again), it sparkles notably with
epistolary grace and vivacity; and, on any terms, it has still
passages of biographical and other interest: but the substance
of it, then so new and shining, has fallen absolutely commonplace, the property of all the world, since then; and is now
very wearisome to the reader. No doctrine or opinion in it
that you have not heard, with clear belief or clear disbelief,
a hundred times, and could wish rather not to hear again.
The common fate of philosophical originalities in this world.
As a Biographical Document, it is worth a very strict perusal,
if you are interested that way in either Friedrich or Voltaire:
finely significant hints and traits, though often almost evanescent, so slight are they, abound in this Correspondence;
frankness, veracity under graceful forms, being the rule of it,
strange to say! As an illustration of Two memorable Characters, and of their Century; showing on what terms the sage
Plato of the Eighteenth Century and his Tyrant Dionysius

---

[1] Preuss, *Œuvres de Frédéric*, (xxi. xxii. xxiii., Berlin, 1853); who super-
sedes the lazy French Editors in this matter.

correspond, and what their manners are to one another, it may long have a kind of interest to mankind : otherwise it has not much left.

In Friedrich's History it was, no doubt, an important fact, that there lived a Voltaire along with him, twenty years his senior. With another Theory of the Universe than the Voltaire one, how much *other* had Friedrich too been! But the Theory called by Voltaire's name was not properly of Voltaire's creating, but only of his uttering and publishing; it lay ready for everybody's finding, and could not well have been altogether missed by such a one as Friedrich. So that perhaps we exaggerate the effects of Voltaire on him, though undoubtedly they were considerable. Considerable; but not derived from this express correspondence, which seldom turns on didactic points at all; derived rather from Voltaire's Printed *Works,* where they lay derivable to all the world. Certain enough it is, Voltaire was at this time, and continued all his days, Friedrich's chief Thinker in the world; unofficially, the chief Preacher, Prophet and Priest of this Working King; — no better off for a spiritual Trismegistus was poor Friedrich in the world! On the practical side, Friedrich soon outgrew him, — perhaps had already outgrown, having far more veracity of character, and an intellect far better built in the silent parts of it, and trained too by hard experiences to know shadow from substance; — outgrew him, and gradually learned to look down upon him, occasionally with much contempt, in regard to the practical. But in all changes of humor towards Voltaire, Friedrich, we observe, considers him as plainly supreme in speculative intellect; and has no doubt but, for thinking and speaking, Nature never made such another. Which may be taken as a notable feature of Friedrich's History; and gives rise to passages between Voltaire and him, which will make much noise in time coming.

Here, meanwhile, faithfully presented though in condensed form, is the starting of the Correspondence; First Letter of it, and first Response. Two Pieces which were once bright as the summer sunrise on both sides, but are now fallen very dim; and have much needed condensation, and abridgment by omission of the unessential, — so lengthy are they, so extinct and almost dreary to us! Sublime "Wolf" and his "Philosophy," how he was hunted out of Halle with it, long since; and now shines from Marburg, his "Philosophy" and he supreme among mankind: this, and other extinct points, the reader's fancy will endeavor to rekindle in some slight measure: —

To M. de Voltaire, at Cirey (from the Crown-Prince).

"BERLIN, 8th August, 1736.

"MONSIEUR, — Although I have not the satisfaction of knowing you personally, you are not the less known to me through your Works. They are treasures of the mind, if I may so express myself; and they reveal to the reader new beauties at every fresh perusal. I think I have recognized in them the character of their ingenious Author, who does honor to our age and to human nature. If ever the dispute on the comparative merits of the Moderns and the Ancients should be revived, the modern great men will owe it to you, and to you only, that the scale is turned in their favor. With the excellent quality of Poet you join innumerable others more or less related to it. Never did Poet before put Metaphysics into rhythmic cadence: to you the honor was reserved of doing it first.

"This taste for Philosophy manifested in your writings, induces me to send you a translated Copy of the *Accusation and defence of M. Wolf,* the most celebrated Philosopher of our days; who, for having carried light into the darkest places of Metaphysics, is cruelly accused of irreligion and atheism. Such is the destiny of great men; their superior genius exposes them to the poisoned arrows of calumny and envy. I am about getting a Translation made of the *Treatise on God, the Soul, and the World,*" — Translation done by an Excellency Suhm, as has been hinted, — "from the pen of the same Author. I will send it you when it is finished; and I am sure that the force of evidence in all his propositions, and their close geometrical sequence, will strike you.

"The kindness and assistance you afford to all who devote

themselves to the Arts and Sciences, makes me hope that you
will not exclude me from the number of those whom you find
worthy of your instructions: — it is so I would call your intercourse by Correspondence of Letters; which cannot be other
than profitable to every thinking being. . . .

. . . "beauties without number in your works. Your *Henriade* delights me. The tragedy of *César* shows us sustained
characters; the sentiments in it are magnificent and grand, and
one feels that Brutus is either a Roman, or else an Englishman
(*ou un Romain ou un Anglais*). Your *Alzire*, to the graces of
novelty adds . . .

"Monsieur, there is nothing I wish so much as to possess
all your Writings," even those not printed hitherto. "Pray,
Monsieur, do communicate them to me without reserve. If
there be amongst your Manuscripts any that you wish to conceal from the eyes of the public, I engage to keep them in the
profoundest secrecy. I am unluckily aware, that the faith of
Princes is an object of little respect in our days; nevertheless
I hope you will make an exception from the general rule in
my favor. I should think myself richer in the possession of
your Works than in that of all the transient goods of Fortune.
These the same chance grants and takes away: your Works
one can make one's own by means of memory, so that they
last us whilst it lasts. Knowing how weak my own memory
is, I am in the highest degree select in what I trust to it.

"If Poetry were what it was before your appearance, a
strumming of wearisome idyls, insipid eclogues, tuneful noth-
ings, I should renounce it forever:" but in your hands it becomes ennobled; a melodious "course of morals; worthy of
the admiration and the study of cultivated minds (*des honnêtes gens*). You" — in fine, "you inspire the ambition to
follow in your footsteps. But I, how often have I said to
myself: '*Malheureux*, throw down a burden which is above
thy strength! One cannot imitate Voltaire, without being
Voltaire!'

"It is in such moments that I have felt how small are those
advantages of birth, those vapors of grandeur, with which
vanity would solace us! They amount to little, properly to

nothing (*pour mieux dire, à rien*). Nature, when she pleases, forms a great soul, endowed with faculties that can advance the Arts and Sciences ; and it is the part of Princes to recompense his noble toils. Ah, would Glory but make use of me to crown your successes ! My only fear would be, lest this Country, little fertile in laurels, proved unable to furnish enough of them.

"If my destiny refuse me the happiness of being able to possess you, may I, at least, hope one day to see the man whom I have admired so long now from afar ; and to assure you, by word of mouth, that I am, — With all the esteem and consideration due to those who, following the torch of truth for guide, consecrate their labors to the Public, — Monsieur, your affectionate friend,

"FRÉDÉRIC, P. R. of Prussia." [1]

By what route or conveyance this Letter went, I cannot say. In general, it is to be observed, these Friedrich-Voltaire Letters — liable perhaps to be considered contraband at *both* ends of their course — do not go by the Post ; but by French-Prussian Ministers, by Hamburg Merchants, and other safe subterranean channels. Voltaire, with enthusiasm, and no doubt promptly, answers within three weeks : —

To the Crown-Prince, at Reinsberg (from Voltaire).

"CIREY, 26th August, 1736.

"MONSEIGNEUR, — A man must be void of all feeling who were not infinitely moved by the Letter which your Royal Highness has deigned to honor me with. My self-love is only too much flattered by it : but my love of Mankind, which I have always nourished in my heart, and which, I venture to say, forms the basis of my character, has given me a very much purer pleasure, — to see that there is, now in the world, a Prince who thinks as a man ; a *Philosopher* Prince, who will make men happy.

"Permit me to say, there is not a man on the earth but

<hr>

[1] *Œuvres de Frédéric*, xxi. 6.

owes thanks for the care you take to cultivate by sound philosophy a soul that is born for command. Good kings there
never were except those that had begun by seeking to instruct
themselves; by knowing good men from bad; by loving what
was true, by detesting persecution and superstition. No
Prince, persisting in such thoughts, but might bring back the
golden age into his Countries! And why do so few Princes
seek this glory? You feel it, Monseigneur, it is because they
all think more of their Royalty than of Mankind. Precisely
the reverse is your case : — and, unless, one day, the tumult of
business and the wickedness of men alter so divine a character, you will be worshipped by your People, and loved by the
whole world. Philosophers, worthy of the name, will flock to
your States; thinkers will crowd round that throne, as the
skilfulest artisans do to the city where their art is in request.
The illustrious Queen Christina quitted her kingdom to go in
search of the Arts; reign you, Monseigneur, and the Arts will
come to seek you.

"May you only never be disgusted with the Sciences by the
quarrels of their Cultivators! A race of men no better than
Courtiers; often enough as greedy, intriguing, false and cruel
as these," and still more ridiculous in the mischief they do.
"And how sad for mankind that the very Interpreters of
Heaven's commandments, the Theologians, I mean, are sometimes the most dangerous of all! Professed messengers of the
Divinity, yet men sometimes of obscure ideas and pernicious
behavior; their soul blown out with mere darkness; full of
gall and pride, in proportion as it is empty of truths. Every
thinking being who is not of their opinion is an Atheist; and
every King who does not favor them will be damned. Dangerous to the very throne; and yet intrinsically insignificant : "
best way is, leave their big talk and them alone; speedy col-
lapse will follow. . . .

"I cannot sufficiently thank your Royal Highness for the
gift of that little Book about Monsieur Wolf. I respect Meta-
physical ideas; rays of lightning they are in the midst of deep
night. More, I think, is not to be hoped from Metaphysics.
It does not seem likely that the First-principles of things will

ever be known. The mice that nestle in some little holes of
an immense Building, know not whether it is eternal, or who
the Architect, or why he built it. Such mice are we ; and the
Divine Architect who built the Universe has never, that I
know of, told his secret to one of us. If anybody could pretend to guess correctly, it is M. Wolf." Beautiful in your
Royal Highness to protect such a man. And how beautiful it
will be, to send me his chief Book, as you have the kindness
to promise ! "The Heir of a Monarchy, from his palace, attending to the wants of a recluse far off ! Condescend to afford
me the pleasure of that Book, Monseigneur. . . .

"What your Royal Highness thinks of poetry is just :
verses that do not teach men new and touching truths, do not
deserve to be read." As to my own poor verses — But, after
all, "that *Henriade* is the writing of an Honest Man : fit, in
that sense, that it find grace with a Philosopher Prince.

"I will obey your commands as to sending those unpublished
Pieces. You shall be my public, Monseigneur ; your criticisms
will be my reward : it is a price few Sovereigns can pay. I am
sure of your secrecy : your virtue and your intellect must be
in proportion. I should indeed consider it a precious happiness to come and pay my court to your Royal Highness ! One
travels to Rome to see paintings and ruins : a Prince such
as you is a much more singular object ; worthier of a long
journey ! But the friendship [divine Emilie's] which keeps
me in this retirement does not permit my leaving it. No
doubt you think with Julian, that great and much calumniated man, who said, 'Friends should always be preferred to
Kings.'

"In whatever corner of the world I may end my life, be assured, Monseigneur, my wishes will continually be for you, —
that is to say, for a whole People's happiness. My heart will
rank itself among your subjects ; your glory will ever be dear
to me. I shall wish, May you always be like yourself, and
may other Kings be like you ! — I am, with profound respect,
your Royal Highness's most humble

                                        "VOLTAIRE." [1]

---

[1] *Œuvres de Frédéric,* xxi. 10.

The Correspondence, once kindled, went on apace; and soon burst forth, finding nourishment all round, into a shining little household fire, pleasant to the hands and hearts of both parties. Consent of opinions on important matters is not wanting; nor is emphasis in declaring the same. The mutual admiration, which is high, — high and intrinsic on Friedrich's side; and on Voltaire's, high if in part *extrinsic*, — by no means wants for emphasis of statement: superlatives, tempered by the best art, pass and repass. Friedrich, reading Voltaire's immortal Manuscripts, confesses with a blush, before long, that he himself is a poor Apprentice that way. Voltaire, at sight of the Princely Productions, is full of admiration, of encouragement; does a little in correcting, solecisms of grammar chiefly; a little, by no means much. But it is a growing branch of employment; now and henceforth almost the one reality of function Voltaire can find for himself in this beautiful Correspondence. For, "Oh what a Crown-Prince, ripening forward to be the delight of human nature, and realize the dream of sages, Philosophy upon the Throne!" And on the other side, "Oh what a Phœbus Apollo, mounting the eastern sky, chasing the Nightmares, — sowing the Earth with Orient pearl, to begin with!" — In which fine duet, it must be said, the Prince is perceptibly the truer singer; singing within compass, and from the heart; while the Phœbus shows himself acquainted with art, and warbles in seductive quavers, now and then beyond the pitch of his voice. We must own also, Friedrich proves little seducible; shows himself laudably indifferent to such siren-singing; — perhaps more used to flattery, and knowing by experience how little meal is to be made of chaff. Voltaire, in an ungrateful France, naturally plumes himself a good deal on such recognition by a Foreign Rising Sun; and, of the two, though so many years the elder, is much more like losing head a little.

Elegant gifts are despatched to Cirey; gold-amber trinkets for Madame, perhaps an amber inkholder for Monsieur: priceless at Cirey as the gifts of the very gods. By and by, a messenger goes express: the witty Colonel Keyserling, witty but experienced, whom we once named at Reinsberg; he is to go

and see with his eyes, since his Master cannot.   What a messenger there; ambassador from star to star!   Keyserling's
report at Reinsberg is not given; but we have Grafigny's,
which is probably the more impartial.   Keyserling's embassy
was in the end of next year;[1] and there is plenty of airy
writing about it and him, in these Letters.

Friedrich has translated the name *Keyserling* (diminutive
of *Kaiser*) into "Cæsarion;" — and I should have said, he
plays much upon names and also upon things, at Reinsberg,
in that style; and has a good deal of airy symbolism, and
cloud-work ingeniously painted round the solidities of his life
there.   Especially a "Bayard Order," as he calls it: Twelve
of his selectest Friends made into a Chivalry Brotherhood,
the names of whom are all changed, "Cæsarion '& one of
them; with dainty devices, and mimetic procedures of the
due sort.   Which are not wholly mummery; but have a spice
of reality, to flavor them to a serious young heart.   For the
selection was rigorous, superior merit and behavior a strict
condition; and indeed several of these Bayard Chevaliers
proved notable practical Champions in time coming; — for
example Captain Fouquet, of whom we have heard before, in
the dark Cüstrin days.   This is a mentionable feature of the
Reinsberg life, and of the young Prince's character there:
pleasant to know of, from this distance; but not now worth
knowing more in detail.

The Friedrich-Voltaire Correspondence contains much in-
cense; due whiffs of it, from Reinsberg side, to the "divine
Emilie," Voltaire's quasi better-half or worse-half; who re-
sponds always in her divinest manner to Reinsberg, eager for
more acquaintance there.   The Du Châtelets had a Lawsuit
in Brabant; very inveterate, perhaps a hundred years old or
more; with the "House of Honsbrouck:"[2] this, not to speak
of other causes, flights from French peril and the like, often
brought Voltaire and his Dame into those parts; and gave
rise to occasional hopes of meeting with Friedrich; which
could not take effect.   In more practical style, Voltaire solicits

---

[1] 3d November, 1737 (as we gather from the Correspondence).
[2] *Lettres Inédites de Voltaire* (Paris, 1826), p. 9.

of him : " Could not your Royal Highness perhaps graciously speak to some of those Judicial Big wigs in Brabant, and flap them up a little ! " Which Friedrich, I think, did, by some good means. Happily, by one means or other, Voltaire got the Lawsuit ended, — 1740, we might guess, but the time is not specified ; — and Friedrich had a new claim, had there been need of new, to be regarded with worship by Madame.[1] But the proposed meeting with Madame could never take effect ; not even when Friedrich's hands were free. Nay I notice at last, Friedrich had privately determined it never should ; Madame evidently an inconvenient element to him. A young man not wanting in private power of eyesight ; and able to distinguish chaff from meal ! Voltaire and he will meet ; meet, and also part ; and there will be passages between them : — and the reader will again hear of this Correspondence of theirs, where it has a biographical interest. We are to conceive it, at present, as a principal light of life to the young heart at Reinsberg ; a cheerful new fire, almost an altar-fire, irradiating the common dusk for him there.

Of another Correspondence, beautifully irradiative for the young heart, we must say almost nothing : the Correspondence with Suhm. Suhm the Saxon Minister, whom we have occasionally heard of, is an old Friend of the Crown-Prince's, dear and helpful to him : it is he who is now doing those *Translations* of *Wolf*, of which Voltaire lately saw specimens ; translating *Wolf* at large, for the young man's behoof. The young man, restless to know the best Philosophy going, had tried reading of Wolf's chief Book ; found it too abstruse, in Wolf's German : wherefore Suhm translates ; sends it to him in limpid French ; fascicle by fascicle, with commentaries ; young man doing his best to understand and admire, — gratefully, not too successfully, we can perceive. That is the staple of the famous *Suhm Correspondence ;* staple which nobody could now bear to be concerned with.

Suhm is also helpful in finance difficulties, which are pretty

---

[1] Record of all this, left, like innumerable other things there, in an intrinsically dark condition, lies in Voltaire's *Letters*, — not much worth hunting up into clear daylight, the process being so difficult to a stranger.

frequent; works out subventions, loans under a handsome
form, from the Czarina's and other Courts. Which is an operation of the utmost delicacy; perilous, should it be heard of
at Potsdam. Wherefore Suhm and the Prince have a covert
language for it: and affect still to be speaking of "Publish-
ers" and "new Volumes," when they mean Lenders and
Bank-Draughts. All these loans, I will hope, were accurately
paid one day, as that from George II. was, in "rouleaus of
new gold." We need not doubt the wholesome charm and
blessing of so intimate a Correspondence to the Crown-Prince:
and indeed his real love of the amiable Suhm, as Suhm's of
him, comes beautifully to light in these Letters: but otherwise
they are not now to be read without weariness, even dreari-
ness, and have become a biographical reminiscence merely.

Concerning Graf von Manteufel, a third Literary Correspondent, and the only other considerable one, here, from a
German Commentator on this matter, is a Clipping that will
suffice: —

"Manteufel was Saxon by birth, long a Minister of August
the Strong, but quarrelled with August, owing to some frail
female it is said, and had withdrawn to Berlin a few years
ago. He shines there among the fashionable philosophical
classes; underhand, perhaps does a little in the volunteer
political line withal; being a very busy pushing gentleman.
Tall of stature, 'perfectly handsome at the age of sixty;'[1]
great partisan of Wolf and the Philosophies, awake to the
Orthodoxies too. Writes flowing elegant French, in a softly
trenchant, somewhat too all-knowing style. High manners
traceable in him; but nothing of the noble loyalty, natural
politeness and pious lucency of Suhm. One of his Letters to
Friedrich has this slightly impertinent passage; — Friedrich,
just getting settled in Reinsberg, having transiently mentioned 'the quantity of fair sex' that had come about him
there: —

"'*Berlin, 26th August,* 1736 (to the Crown-Prince). . . .
I am well persuaded your Royal Highness will regulate all

[1] Formey, *Souvenirs d'un Citoyen,* i. 39–45.

that to perfection, and so manage that your fair sex will be charmed to find themselves with you at Reinsberg, and you charmed to have them there. But permit me, your Royal Highness, to repeat in this place, what I one day took the liberty of saying here at Berlin: Nothing in the world would better suit the present interests of your Royal Highness and of us all, than some Heir of your Royal Highness's making! Perhaps the tranquil convenience with which your Royal Highness at Reinsberg can now attend to that object, will be of better effect than all those hasty and transitory visits at Berlin were. At least I wish it with the best of my heart. I beg pardon, Monseigneur, for intruding thus into everything which concerns your Royal Highness;'—In truth, I am a rather impudent busybodyish fellow, with superabundant dashing manner, speculation, utterance; and shall get myself ordered out of the Country, by my present correspondent, by and by.— 'Being ever,' with the due enthusiasm, 'MANTEUFEL.' [1]

"To which Friedrich's Answer is of a kind to put a gag in the foul mouth of certain extraordinary Pamphleteerings, that were once very copious in the world; and, in particular, to set at rest the Herr Dr. Zimmermann, and his poor puddle of calumnies and credulities, got together in that weak pursuit of physiology under obscene circumstances;—

"Which is the one good result I have gathered from the Manteufel Correspondence," continues our German friend; whom I vote with!—Or if the English reader never saw those Zimmermann or other dog-like Pamphleteerings and surmisings, let this Excerpt be mysterious and superfluous to the thankful English reader.

On the whole, we conceive to ourselves the abundant nature of Friedrich's Correspondence, literary and other; and what kind of event the transit of that Post functionary "from Fehrbellin northwards," with his leathern bags, "twice a week," may have been at Reinsberg, in those years.

[1] *Œuvres de Frédéric*, xxv. 487;—Friedrich's Answer is, Reinsberg, 23d September (Ib. 489).

CHAPTER III.

CROWN-PRINCE MAKES A MORNING CALL.

THURSDAY, 25th October, 1736, the Crown-Prince, with Lieutenant Buddenbrock and an attendant or two, drove over into
Mecklenburg, to a Village and serene Schloss called Mirow,
intending a small act of neighborly civility there; on which
perhaps an English reader of our time will consent to accompany him. It is but some ten or twelve miles off, in a north-
erly direction; Reinsberg being close on the frontier there.
A pleasant enough morning's-drive, with the October sun shining on the silent heaths, on the many-colored woods and you.

Mirow is an Apanage for one of the Mecklenburg-Strelitz
junior branches: Mecklenburg-Strelitz being itself a junior
compared to the Mecklenburg-Schwerin of which, and its infatuated Duke, we have heard so much in times past. Mirow
and even Strelitz are not in a very shining state, — but indeed,
we shall see them, as it were, with eyes. And the English
reader is to note especially those Mirow people, as perhaps of
some small interest to him, if he knew it. The Crown-Prince
reports to Papa, in a satirical vein, not ungenially, and with
much more freedom than is usual in those Reinsberg letters
of his: —

" *To his Prussian Majesty* (from the Crown-Prince).

" REINSBERG, 26th October, 1736.

. . . "Yesterday I went across to Mirow. To give my Most
All-gracious Father an idea of the place, I cannot liken it to
anything higher than Gross-Kreutz [term of comparison lost
upon us; say *Garrat*, at a venture, or the *Clachan of Aber-
foyle*]: the one house in it, that can be called a house, is not
so good as the Parson's there. I made straight for the Schloss;
which is pretty much like the Garden-house in Bornim: only

there is a rampart round it; and an old Tower, considerably in ruins, serves as a Gateway to the House.

" Coming on the Drawbridge, I perceived an old stocking-knitter disguised as Grenadier, with his cap, cartridge-box and musket laid to a side, that they might not hinder him in his knitting-work. As I advanced, he asked, 'Whence I came, and whitherward I was going?' I answered, that 'I came from the Post-house, and was going over this Bridge:' whereupon the Grenadier, quite in a passion, ran to the Tower; where he opened a door, and called out the Corporal. The Corporal seemed to have hardly been out of bed; and in his great haste, had not taken time to put on his shoes, nor quite button his breeches; with much flurry he asked us, 'Where we were for, and how we came to treat the Sentry in that manner?' Without answering him at all, we went our way towards the Schloss.

" Never in my life should I have taken this for a Schloss, had it not been that there were two glass lamps fixed at the door-posts, and the figures of two Cranes standing in front of them, by way of Guards. We made up to the House; and after knocking almost half an hour to no purpose, there peered out at last an exceedingly old woman, who looked as if she might have nursed the Prince of Mirow's father. The poor woman, at sight of strangers, was so terrified, she slammed the door to in our faces. We knocked again; and seeing there could nothing be made of it, we went round to the stables; where a fellow told us, 'The young Prince with his Consort was gone to Neu-Strelitz, a couple of miles off [ten miles English]; and the Duchess his Mother, who lives here, had given him, to make the better figure, all her people along with him; keeping nobody but the old woman to herself.'

" It was still early; so I thought I could not do better than profit by the opportunity, and have a look at Neu-Strelitz. We took post-horses; and got thither about noon. Neu-Strelitz is properly a Village; with only one street in it, where Chamberlains, Office-Clerks, Domestics all lodge, and where there is an Inn. I cannot better describe it to my Most All-gracious

Father than by that street in Gumbinnen where you go up to
the Town-hall, — except that no house here is whitewashed.
The Schloss is fine, and lies on a lake, with a big garden;
pretty much like Reinsberg in situation.

"The first question I asked here was for the Prince of
Mirow: but they told me he had just driven off again to a
place called Kanow; which is only a couple of miles English
from Mirow, where we had been. Buddenbrock, who is acquainted with Neu-Strelitz, got me, from a chamberlain, something to eat; and in the mean while, that Böhme came in, who
was Adjutant in my Most All-gracious Father's Regiment [not
of Goltz, but King's presumably]: Böhme did not know me
till I hinted to him who I was. He told me, ' The Duke of
Strelitz was an excellent seamster;'" fit to be Tailor to your
Majesty in a manner, had not Fate been cruel, "'and that he
made beautiful dressing-gowns (*cassaquins*) with his needle.'
This made me curious to see him: so we had ourselves presented as Foreigners; and it went off so well that nobody
recognized me. I cannot better describe the Duke than by
saying he is like old Stahl [famed old medical man at Berlin,
dead last year, physiognomy not known to actual readers],
in a blond Abbé's-periwig. He is extremely silly (*blöde*); his
Hofrath Altrock tells him, as it were, everything he has to
say." About fifty, this poor Duke; shrunk into needlework,
for a quiet life, amid such tumults from Schwerin and elsewhere.

"Having taken leave, we drove right off to Kanow; and
got thither about six. It is a mere Village; and the Prince's
Pleasure-House (*Lusthaus*) here is nothing better than an or-
dinary Hunting-Lodge, such as any Forest-keeper has. I
alighted at the Miller's; and had myself announced" at the
Lusthaus, "by his maid: upon which the Major-Domo (*Haus-
Hofmeister*) came over to the Mill, and complimented me; with
whom I proceeded to the Residenz," that is, back again to
Mirow, "where the whole Mirow Family were assembled. The
Mother is a Princess of Schwartzburg, and still the cleverest
of them all," still under sixty; good old Mother, intent that
her poor Son should appear to advantage, when visiting the

more opulent Serenities. " His Aunt also," mother's sister,
" was there. The Lady Spouse is small; a Niece to the Prince
of Hildburghausen, who is in the Kaiser's service : she was in
the family-way ; but (*aber*) seemed otherwise to be a very
good Princess.

" The first thing they entertained me with was, the sad misfortune come upon their best Cook; who, with the cart that
was bringing the provisions, had overset, and broken his arm ;
so that the provisions had all gone to nothing. Privately I
have had inquiries made ; there was not a word of truth in
the story. At last we went to table ; and, sure enough, it
looked as if the Cook and his provisions had come to some
mishap ; for certainly in the Three Crowns at Potsdam [worst
inn, one may guess, in the satirical vein], there is better eating
than here.

" At table, there was talk of nothing but of all the German
Princes who are not right in their wits (*nicht recht klug*)," as
Mirow himself, your Majesty knows, is reputed to be ! " There
was Weimar,[1] Gotha, Waldeck, Hoym, and the whole lot of
them, brought upon the carpet : — and after our good Host had
got considerably drunk, we rose, — and he lovingly promised
me that ' he and his whole Family would come and visit Reinsberg.' Come he certainly will ; but how I shall get rid of him,
God knows.

" I most submissively beg pardon of my Most All-gracious
Father for this long Letter ; and " — we will terminate here.[2]

Dilapidated Mirow and its inmates, portrayed in this satirical way, except as a view of Serene Highnesses fallen into
Sleepy Hollow, excites little notice in the indolent mind ; and
that little, rather pleasantly contemptuous than really profitable. But one fact ought to kindle momentary interest in Eng-

---

[1] Wilhelmina's acquaintance ; wedded, not without difficulty, to a superfluous Baireuth Sister-in-law by Wilhelmina (*Mémoires de Wilhelmina*, ii. 185–
194): Grandfather of Goethe's Friend ; — is nothing like fairly out of his
wits ; only has a flea (as we may say) dancing occasionally in the ear of him.
Perhaps it is so with the rest of these Serenities, here fallen upon evil tongues ?

[2] *Œuvres de Frédéric*, xxvii. part 3d, pp. 104–106.

lish readers : the young foolish Herr, in this dilapidated place, is no other than our "Old Queen Charlotte's" Father that is to be, — a kind of Ancestor of ours, though we little guessed it! English readers will scan him with new curiosity, when he pays that return visit at Reinsberg. Which he does within the fortnight : —

"*To his Prussian Majesty* (from the Crown-Prince).

"REINSBERG, 8th November, 1736.

. . . "that my Most All-gracious Father has had the graciousness to send us some Swans. My Wife also has been exceedingly delighted at the fine Present sent her. . . . General Prætorius," Danish Envoy, with whose Court there is some tiff of quarrel, " came hither yesterday to take leave of us; he seems very unwilling to quit Prussia.

"This morning about three o'clock, my people woke me, with word that there was a Stafette come with Letters," — from your Majesty or Heaven knows whom! "I spring up in all haste ; and opening the Letter, — find it is from the Prince of Mirow; who informs me that 'he will be here to-day at noon.' I have got all things in readiness to receive him, as if he were the Kaiser in person ; and I hope there will be material for some amusement to my Most All-gracious Father, by next post." — Next post is half a week hence : —

"*To his Prussian Majesty* (from the Crown-Prince).

"REINSBERG, 11th November.

. . . "The Prince of Mirow's visit was so curious, I must give my Most All-gracious Father a particular report of it. In my last, I mentioned how General Prætorius had come to us : he was in the room, when I entered with the Prince of Mirow; at sight of him Prætorius exclaimed, loud enough to be heard by everybody, ' *Voilà le Prince Cajuca !* ' [1] Not one of us could help laughing; and I had my own trouble to turn it so that he did not get angry.

"Scarcely was the Prince got in, when they came to tell me,

[1] Nickname out of some Romance, fallen extinct long since.

for his worse luck, that Prince Heinrich," the Ill Margraf, "was come; — who accordingly trotted him out, in such a way that we thought we should all have died with laughing. Incessant praises were given him, especially for his fine clothes, his fine air, and his uncommon agility in dancing. And indeed I thought the dancing would never end.

"In the afternoon, to spoil his fine coat," — a contrivance of the Ill Margraf's, I should think, — "we stept out to shoot at target in the rain: he would not speak of it, but one could observe he was in much anxiety about the coat. In the evening, he got a glass or two in his head, and grew extremely merry; said at last, 'He was sorry that, for divers state-reasons and businesses of moment, he must of necessity return home;' — which, however, he put off till about two in the morning. I think, next day he would not remember very much of it.

"Prince Heinrich is gone to his Regiment again;" Prætorius too is off; — and we end with the proper *Kow-tow*.[1]

These Strelitzers, we said, are juniors to infatuated Schwerin; and poor Mirow is again junior to Strelitz: plainly one of the least opulent of Residences. At present, it is Dowager Apanage (*Wittwen-Sitz*) to the Widow of the late Strelitz of blessed memory: here, with her one Child, a boy now grown to what manhood we see, has the Serene Dowager lived, these twenty-eight years past; a Schwartzburg by birth, "the cleverest head among them all." Twenty-eight years in dilapidated Mirow: so long has that Tailoring Duke, her eldest *stepson* (child of a prior wife) been Supreme Head of Mecklenburg-Strelitz; employed with his needle, or we know not how, — collapsed plainly into tailoring at this date. There was but one other Son; this clever Lady's, twenty years junior, — "Prince of Mirow" whom we now see. Karl Ludwig Friedrich is the name of this one; age now twenty-eight gone. He, ever since the third month of him, when the poor Serene Father died ("May, 1703"), has been at Mirow with Mamma; getting what education there was, — not too successfully, as

[1] *Œuvres de Frédéric*, xvii. part 3d, p. 109.

would appear.   Eight years ago, " in 1726," Mamma sent him
off upon his travels; to Geneva, Italy, France : he looked in
upon Vienna, too ; got a Lieutenant-Colonelcy in the Kaiser's
Service, but did not like it ; soon gave it up ; and returned home
to vegetate, perhaps to seek a wife, — having prospects of
succession in Strelitz.   For the Serene Half-Brother proves
to have no children : were *his* tailoring once finished in the
world, our Prince of Mirow is Duke in Chief.   On this basis
he wedded last year; the little Wife has already brought him
one child, a Daughter ; and has (as Friedrich notices) another
under way, if it prosper.   No lack of Daughters, nor of Sons
by and by : eight years hence came the little Charlotte, — subsequently Mother of England : much to her and our astonishment.[1]

The poor man did not live to be Duke of Strelitz; he
died, 1752, in little Charlotte's eighth year ; Tailor Duke
surviving him a few months.   Little Charlotte's Brother did
then succeed, and lasted till 1794; after whom a second
Brother, father of the now Serene Strelitzes; — who also is
genealogically notable.   For from him there came another still
more famous Queen : Louisa of Prussia; beautiful to look
upon, as "Aunt Charlotte" was not, in a high degree ; and
who showed herself a Heroine in Napoleon's time, as Aunt
Charlotte never was called to do.   Both Aunt and Niece
were women of sense, of probity, propriety ; fairly beyond
the average of Queens.   And as to their early poverty, ridiculous to this gold-nugget generation, I rather guess it may have
done them benefits which the gold-nugget generation, in its
Queens and otherwise, stands far more in want of than it
thinks.

But enough of this Prince of Mirow, whom Friedrich has accidentally unearthed for us.   Indeed there is no farther history
of him, for or against.   He evidently was not thought to have
invented gunpowder, by the public.   And yet who knows but,

---

[1] Born (at Mirow) 19th May, 1744 ; married (London), 8th September, 1761 ;
died, 18th November, 1818 (Michaelis, ii. 445, 446 ; Hübner, t. 195 ; Œrtel,
pp. 43, 22).

in his very simplicity, there lay something far beyond the Ill
Margraf to whom he was so quizzable? Poor down-pressed
brother mortal; somnambulating so pacifically in Sleepy Hollow yonder, and making no complaint!

He continued, though soon with less enthusiasm, and in the
end very rarely, a visitor of Friedrich's during this Reinsberg
time. Patriotic English readers may as well take the few
remaining vestiges, too, before quite dismissing him to Sleepy
Hollow. Here they are, swept accurately together, from that
Correspondence of Friedrich with Papa:—

"*Reinsberg, 18th November,* 1736. . . . report most submissively that the Prince of Mirow has again been here, with his
Mother, Wife, Aunt, Hofdames, Cavaliers and entire Household; so that I thought it was the Flight out of Egypt [Exo-
dus of the Jews]. I begin to have a fear of those good
people, as they assured me they would have such pleasure in
coming often!"

"*Reinsberg, 1st February,* 1737." Let us give it in the Original too, as a specimen of German spelling:—

"*Der Printz von Mihrau ist vohr einigen thagen hier gewes-
sen und haben wier einige Wasser schwermer in der See ihm zu
Ehren gesmissen, seine frau ist mit einer thoten Printzesin nie-
der geKomen. — Der General schulenburg ist heute hier gekom-
men und wirdt morgen*" — That is to say:—

"The Prince of Mirow was here a few days ago; and we
let off, in honor of him, a few water-rockets over the Lake:
his Wife has been brought to bed of a dead Princess. General Schulenburg [with a small *s*] came hither to-day; and
to-morrow will" . . .

"*Reinsberg, 28th March,* 1737. . . . Prince von Mirow was
here yesterday; and tried shooting at the popinjay with us;
he cannot see rightly, and shoots always with help of an opera-
glass."

"*Ruppin, 20th October,* 1737. The Prince of Mirow was
with us last Friday; and babbled much in his high way;
among other things, white-lied to us, that the Kaiserinn gave
him a certain porcelain snuff-box he was handling; but on

being questioned more tightly, he confessed to me he had
bought it in Vienna." [1]

And so let him somnambulate yonder, till the two Queens,
like winged Psyches, one after the other, manage to emerge
from him.

Friedrich's Letters to his Father are described by some
Prussian Editors as "very attractive, *sehr anziehende Briefe ;*"
which, to a Foreign reader, seems a strange account of them.
Letters very hard to understand completely ; and rather insignificant when understood. They turn on Gifts sent to and
sent from, "swans," "hams," with the unspeakable thanks
for them ; on recruits of so many inches ; on the visitors
that have been ; they assure us that "there is no sickness in
the regiment," or tell expressly how much : — wholly small
facts ; nothing of speculation, and of ceremonial pipe-clay a
great deal. We know already under what nightmare conditions Friedrich wrote to his Father! The attitude of the
Crown-Prince, sincerely reverent and filial, though obliged
to appear ineffably so, and on the whole struggling under
such mountains of encumbrance, yet loyally maintaining his
equilibrium, does at last acquire, in these Letters, silently a
kind of beauty to the best class of readers. But that is nearly
their sole merit. By far the most human of them, that on
the first visit to Mirow, the reader has now seen ; and may
thank us much that we show him no more of them. [2]

[1] *Briefe an Vater*, p. 71 (*caret* in *Œuvres*) ; pp. 85–114. — See Ib. 6th November, 1737, for faint trace of a visit ; and 25th September, 1739, for another
still fainter, the last there is.

[2] *Friedrich des Grossen Briefe an seinen Vater* (Berlin, 1838). Reduced in
size, by suitable omissions ; and properly spelt ; but with little other elucida-
tion for a stranger : in *Œuvres*, xxvii. part 3d, pp. 1–123 (Berlin, 1856).

CHAPTER IV.

NEWS OF THE DAY.

WHILE these Mirow visits are about their best, and much
else at Reinsberg is in comfortable progress, Friedrich's first
year there just ending, there come accounts from England
of quarrels broken out between the Britannic Majesty and
his Prince of Wales. Discrepancies risen now to a height;
and getting into the very Newspapers; — the Rising Sun
too little under the control of the Setting, in that unquiet
Country!

Prince Fred of England did not get to the Rhine Campaign, as we saw: he got some increase of Revenue, a Household of his own; and finally a Wife, as he had requested:
a Sachsen-Gotha Princess; who, peerless Wilhelmina being
unattainable, was welcome to Prince Fred. She is in the
family-way, this summer 1737, a very young lady still; result
thought to be due — When? Result being potential Heir to
the British Nation, there ought to have been good calculation
of the time when! But apparently nobody had well turned
his attention that way. Or if Fred and Spouse had, as
is presumable, Fred had given no notice to the Paternal
Majesty, — "Let Paternal Majesty, always so cross to me,
look out for himself in that matter." Certain it is, Fred
and Spouse, in the beginning of August, 1737, are out at
Hampton Court; potential Heir due before long, and no preparation made for it. August 11th in the evening, out at
solitary Hampton Court; the poor young Mother's pains came
on; no Chancellor there, no Archbishop to see the birth,
— in fact, hardly the least medical help, and of political
altogether none. Fred, in his flurry, or by forethought, —
instead of dashing off expresses, at a gallop as of Epsom, to
summon the necessary persons and appliances, yoked wheeled

vehicles and rolled off to the old unprovided Palace of St.
James's, London, with his poor Wife in person! Unwarned,
unprovided; where nevertheless she was safely delivered
that same night, — safely, as if by miracle. The crisis might
have taken her on the very highway: never was such an
imprudence. Owing, I will believe, to Fred's sudden flurry
in the unprovided moment, — unprovided, by reason of prior
desuetudes and discouragements to speech, on Papa's side.
A shade of malice there might also be. Papa doubts not, it
was malice aforethought all of it. "Had the potential Heir
of the British Nation gone to wreck, or been born on the
highway, from my quarrels with this bad Fred, what a scrape
had I been in!" thinks Papa, and is in a towering permanence
of wrath ever since; the very Newspapers and coffee-houses
and populaces now all getting vocal with it.

Papa, as it turned out, never more saw the face of Fred.
Judicious Mamma, Queen Caroline, could not help a visit,
one visit to the poor young Mother, so soon as proper: coming out from the visit, Prince Fred obsequiously escorting
her to her carriage, found a crowd of people and populace,
in front of St. James's; and there knelt down on the street,
in his fine silk breeches, careless of the mud, to "beg a
Mother's blessing," and show what a son he was, he for his
part, in this sad discrepancy that had risen! Mamma threw
a silent glance on him, containing volumes of mixed tenor;
drove off; and saw no more of Fred, she either. I fear, this
kneeling in the mud tells against Prince Fred; but in truth
I do not know, nor even much care.[1] What a noise in England about nothing at all!— What a noisy Country, your
Prussian Majesty! Foolish "rising sun" not restrainable
there by the setting or shining one; opposition parties
bowling him about among the constellations, like a very
mad object!—

But in a month or two, there comes worse news out of England; falling heavy on the heart of Prussian Majesty: news
that Queen Caroline herself is dead.[2] Died as she had lived,

---

[1] Lord Hervey, *Memoirs of George the Second*, ii. 362–370, 409.

[2] "Sunday evening, 1st December (20th Nov.), 1737." Ib. pp. 510–539.

with much constancy of mind, with a graceful modest courage
and endurance; sinking quietly under the load of private miseries long quietly kept hidden, but now become too heavy, and
for which the appointed rest was now here. Little George
blubbered a good deal; fidgeted and flustered a good deal:
much put about, poor foolish little soul. The dying Caroline
recommended *him* to Walpole; advised his Majesty to marry
again. "*Non, j'aurai des maîtresses* (No, I'll have mistresses)!"
sobbed his Majesty passionately. "*Ah, mon Dieu, cela n'em-
pêche pas* (that does not hinder)!" answered she, from long
experience of the case. There is something stoically tragic in
the history of Caroline with her flighty vaporing little King:
seldom had foolish husband so wise a wife. "Dead!" thought
Friedrich Wilhelm, looking back through the whirlwinds of
life, into sunny young scenes far enough away: "Dead!" —
Walpole continued to manage the little King; but not for
long; England itself rising in objection. Jenkins's Ear, I understand, is lying in cotton; and there are mad inflammable
strata in that Nation, capable of exploding at a great rate.

From the Eastern regions our Newspapers are very full of
events: War with the Turk going on there; Russia and Austria
both doing their best against the Turk. The Russians had
hardly finished their Polish-Election fighting, when they decided to have a stroke at the Turk, — Turk always an especial
eye-sorrow to them, since that "Treaty of the Pruth," and Czar
Peter's sad rebuff there: — Münnich marched direct out of
Poland through the Ukraine, with his eye on the Crimea and
furious business in that quarter. This is his second Campaign
there, this of 1737; and furious business has not failed. Last
year he stormed the Lines of Perecop, tore open the Crimea;
took Azoph, he or Lacy under him; took many things: this
year he had laid his plans for Oczakow; — takes Oczakow, —
fiery event, blazing in all the Newspapers, at Reinsberg and
elsewhere. Concerning which will the reader accept this condensed testimony by an eye-witness?

"*Oczakow*, 13*th July*, 1737. Day before yesterday, Feldmarschall Münnich got to Oczakow, as he had planned," —
strong Turkish Town in the nook between the Black Sea and

the estuary of the Dnieper; — " with intention to besiege it.
Siege-train, stores of every sort, which he had set afloat upon
the Dnieper in time enough, were to have been ready for him
at Oczakow. But the flotilla had been detained by shallows,
by waterfalls; not a boat was come, nor could anybody say
when they were coming. Meanwhile nothing is to be had
here; the very face of the earth the Turks have burnt: not
a blade of grass for cavalry within eight miles, nor a stick of
wood for engineers; not a hole for covert, and the ground so
hard you cannot raise redoubts on it: Münnich perceives he
must attempt, nevertheless.

" On his right, by the sea-shore, Münnich finds some remains
of gardens, palisades; scrapes together some vestige of shelter
there (five thousand, or even ten thousand pioneers working
desperately all that first night, 11th July, with only half success); and on the morrow commences firing with what artillery
he has. Much outfired by the Turks inside; — his enterprise
as good as desperate, unless the Dnieper flotilla come soon.
July 12th, all day the firing continues, and all night; Turks
extremely furious : about an hour before daybreak, we notice
burning in the interior, 'Some wooden house kindled by us,
town got on fire yonder,' — and, praise to Heaven, they do not
seem to succeed in quenching it again. Münnich turns out, in
various divisions; intent on trying something, had he the least
engineer furniture; — hopes desperately there may be promise
for him in that internal burning still visible.

" In the centre of Münnich's line is one General Keith, a
deliberate stalwart Scotch gentleman, whom we shall know
better; Münnich himself is to the right: Could not one try it
by scalade; keep the internal burning free to spread, at any
rate ? 'Advance within musket-shot, General Keith!' orders
Münnich's Aide-de-Camp cantering up. 'I have been this good
while within it,' answers Keith, pointing to his dead men.
Aide-de-Camp canters up a second time : 'Advance within
half musket-shot, General Keith, and quit any covert you
have !' Keith does so; sends, with his respects to Feldmarschall Münnich, his remonstrance against such a waste of
human life. Aide-de-Camp canters up a third time : 'Feld-

marschall Münnich is for trying a scalade; hopes General Keith will do his best to co-operate!' 'Forward, then!' answers Keith; advances close to the glacis; finds a wet ditch twelve feet broad, and has not a stick of engineer furniture. Keith waits there two hours; his men, under fire all the while, trying this and that to get across; Münnich's scalade going off ineffectual in like manner: — till at length Keith's men, and all men, tire of such a business, and roll back in great confusion out of shot-range. Münnich gives himself up for lost. And indeed, says Mannstein, had the Turks sallied out in pursuit at that moment, they might have chased us back to Russia. But the Turks did not sally. And the internal conflagration is not quenched, far from it; — and about nine A.M. their Powder-Magazine, conflagration reaching it, roared aloft into the air, and killed seven thousand of them," [1] —

So that Oczakow was taken, sure enough; terms, life only: and every remaining Turk packs off from it, some "twenty thousand inhabitants young and old" for one sad item. — A very blazing semi-absurd event, to be read of in Prussian military circles, — where General Keith will be better known one day.

Russian War with the Turk: that means withal, by old Treaties, aid of thirty thousand men from the Kaiser to Russia. Kaiser, so ruined lately, how can he send thirty thousand, and keep them recruited, in such distant expedition? Kaiser, much meditating, is advised it will be better to go frankly into the Turk on his own score, and try for slices of profit from him in this game. Kaiser declares war against the Turk; and what is still more interesting to Friedrich Wilhelm and the Berlin Circles, Seckendorf is named General of it. Feldzeugmeister now Feldmarschall Seckendorf, envy may say what it will, he has marched this season into the Lower-Donau Countries, — going to besiege Widdin, they say, — at the head of a big Army (on paper, almost a hundred and fifty thousand, light troops and heavy) — virtually Commander-in-Chief; though nominally our fine young friend Franz of Lorraine bears the title of Commander, whom Seckendorf is to dry-nurse in the

[1] Mannstein, pp. 151–156.

way sometimes practised. Going to besiege Widdin, they say.
So has the poor Kaiser been advised. His wise old Eugene is
now gone;[1] I fear his advisers,—a youngish Feldzeugmeister,
Prince of Hildburghausen, the chief favorite among them,—
are none of the wisest. All Protestants, we observe, these
favorite Hildburghausens, Schmettaus, Seckendorfs of his;
and Vienna is an orthodox papal Court;—and there is a Hofkriegsrath (Supreme Council of War), which has ruined many
a General, poking too meddlesomely into his affairs! On the
whole, Seckendorf will have his difficulties. Here is a scene,
on the Lower Donau, different enough from that at Oczakow,
not far from contemporaneous with it. The Austrian Army
is at Kolitz, a march or two beyond Belgrade:—

"*Kolitz, 2d July,* 1737. This day, the Army not being on
march, but allowed to rest itself, Grand Duke Franz went into
the woods to hunt. Hunting up and down, he lost himself;
did not return at evening; and, as the night closed in and no
Generalissimo visible, the Generalissimo *ad Latus* (such the
title they had contrived for Seckendorf) was in much alarm.
Generalissimo *ad Latus* ordered out his whole force of drum-
mers, trumpeters : To fling themselves, postwise, deeper and
deeper into the woods all round; to drum there, and blow, in
ever-widening circle, in prescribed notes, and with all energy,
till the Grand Duke were found. Grand Duke being found,
Seckendorf remonstrated, rebuked ; a thought too earnestly,
some say, his temper being flurried,"—voice snuffling somewhat in alt, with lisp to help:—"so that the Grand Duke
took offence; flung off in a huff : and always looked askance
on the Feldmarschall from that time;"[2]—quitting him altogether before long; and marching with Khevenhüller, Wallis,
Hildburghausen, or any of the subordinate Generals rather.
Probably Widdin will not go the road of Oczakow, nor the
Austrians prosper like the Russians, this summer.

Pöllnitz, in Tobacco-Parliament, and in certain Berlin circles foolishly agape about this new Feldmarschall, maintains

---

[1] Died 30th April, 1736.

[2] See *Lebensgeschichte des Grafen von Schmettau* (by his Son : Berlin, 1806),
i. 27.

always, Seckendorf will come to nothing; which his Majesty
zealously contradicts, — his Majesty, and some short-sighted
private individuals still favorable to Seckendorf.[1] Exactly
one week after that singular drum-and-trumpet operation on
Duke Franz, the Last of the Medici dies at Florence;[2] and
Serene Franz, if he knew it, is Grand Duke of *Tuscany,* according to bargain: a matter important to himself chiefly,
and to France, who, for Stanislaus and Lorraine's sake, has
had to pay him some £200,000 a year during the brief intermediate state.

Of Berg and Jülich again; and of Luiscius with the One Razor.

These remote occurrences are of small interest to his Prussian Majesty, in comparison with the Pfalz affair, the Cleve-
Jülich succession, which lies so near home. His Majesty is
uncommonly anxious to have this matter settled, in peace, if
possible. Kaiser and Reich, with the other Mediating Powers,
go on mediating; but when will they decide? This year the
old Bishop of Augsburg, one Brother of the older Kur-Pfalz
Karl Philip, dies; nothing now between us and the event
itself, but Karl Philip alone, who is verging towards eighty:
the decision, to be peaceable, ought to be speedy! Friedrich
Wilhelm, in January last, sent the expert Degenfeld, once of
London, to old Karl Philip; and has him still there, with the
most conciliatory offers: "Will leave your Sulzbachs a part,
then; will be content with part, instead of the whole, which
is mine if there be force in sealed parchment; will do anything
for peace!" To which the old Kur-Pfalz, foolish old creature,
is steadily deaf; answers vaguely, negatively always, in a
polite manner; pushing his Majesty upon extremities painful
to think of. "We hate war; but cannot quite do without
justice, your Serenity," thinks Friedrich Wilhelm: "must it
be the eighty thousand iron ramrods, then?" Obstinate Serenity continues deaf; and Friedrich Wilhelm's negotiations, there

[1] Pöllnitz, *Memoiren,* ii. 497–502.
[2] 9th July (*Fastes de Louis XV.,* p. 304).

at Mannheim, over in Holland, and through Holland with England, not to speak of Kaiser and Reich close at hand, become very intense; vehemently earnest, about this matter, for the next two years. The details of which, inexpressibly uninteresting, shall be spared the reader.

Summary is, these Mediating Powers will be of no help to his Majesty; not even the Dutch will, with whom he is specially in friendship: nay, in the third year it becomes fatally manifest, the chief Mediating Powers, Kaiser and France, listening rather to political convenience, than to the claims of justice, go direct in Kur-Pfalz's favor; — by formal treaty of their own,[1] France and the Kaiser settle, "That the Sulzbachers shall, as a preliminary, get provisional possession, on the now Serenity's decease; and shall continue undisturbed for two years, till Law decide between his Prussian Majesty and them." Two years; Law decide; — and we know what are the *nine-points* in a Law-case! This, at last, proved too much for his Majesty. Majesty's abstruse dubitations, meditations on such treatment by a Kaiser and others, did then, it appears, gloomily settle into fixed private purpose of trying it by the iron ramrods, when old Kur-Pfalz should die, — of marching with eighty thousand men into the Cleve Countries, and *so* welcoming any Sulzbach or other guests that might arrive. Happily old Kur-Pfalz did not die in his Majesty's time; survived his Majesty several years: so that the matter fell into other hands, — and was settled very well, near a century after.

Of certain wranglings with the little Town of Herstal, — Prussian Town (part of the Orange Heritage, once *King Pepin's* Town, if that were any matter now) in the Bishop of Liége's neighborhood, Town highly insignificant otherwise, — we shall say nothing here, as they will fall to be treated, and be settled, at an after stage. Friedrich Wilhelm was much grieved by the contumacies of that paltry little Herstal; and by the Bishop of Liége's high-flown procedures in countenancing them; — especially in a recruiting case that had fallen out there, and

---

[1] "Versailles, 13th January, 1739" (Olrich, *Geschichte der Schlesischen Kriege*, i. 13); Mauvillon, ii. 405–446; &c.

brought matters to a head.[1] The Kaiser too was afflictively
high in countenancing the Bishop; — for which both Kaiser
and Bishop got due payment in time. But his Prussian Majesty would not kindle the world for such a paltriness; and so
left it hanging in a vexatious condition. Such things, it is
remarked, weigh heavier on his now infirm Majesty than they
were wont. He is more subject to fits of hypochondria, to
talk of abdicating. "All gone wrong!" he would say, if any
little flaw rose, about recruiting or the like. "One might go
and live at Venice, were one rid of it!"[2] And his deep-stung
clangorous growl against the Kaiser's treatment of him bursts
out, from time to time; though he oftenest pities the Kaiser,
too; seeing him at such a pass with his Turk War and otherwise.

It was in this Pfalz business that Herr Luiscius, the Prussian Minister in Holland, got into trouble; of whom there is
a light dash of outline-portraiture by Voltaire, which has made
him memorable to readers. This "fat King of Prussia," says
Voltaire, was a dreadfully avaricious fellow, unbeautiful to a
high degree in his proceedings with mankind: —
"He had a Minister at the Hague called Luiscius; who
certainly of all Ministers of Crowned Heads was the worst
paid. This poor man, to warm himself, had made some trees
be felled in the Garden of Honslardik, which belonged at that
time to the House of Prussia; he thereupon received despatches from the King, intimating that a year of his salary
was forfeited. Luiscius, in despair, cut his throat with probably the one razor he had (*seul rasoir qu'il eût*); an old valet
came to his assistance, and unhappily saved his life. In
after years, I found his Excellency at the Hague; and have
occasionally given him an alms at the door of the *Vieille Cour*
(Old Court), a Palace belonging to the King of Prussia, where
this poor Ambassador had lived a dozen years. It must be

---

[1] "December, 1738," is crisis of the recruiting case (*Helden-Geschichte*, ii.
63); "17th February, 1739," Bishop's high-flown appearance in it (ib. 67);
Kaiser's in consequence, "10th April, 1739."

[2] Förster (place *lost*).

owned, Turkey is a republic in comparison to the despotism
exercised by Friedrich Wilhelm." [1]

Here truly is a witty sketch; consummately dashed off, as
nobody but Voltaire could; "round as Giotto's O," done at
one stroke. Of which the prose facts are only as follows.
Luiscius, Prussian Resident, not distinguished by salary or
otherwise, had, at one stage of these negotiations, been told,
from head-quarters, He might, in casual extra-official ways, if
it seemed further;ome, give their High Mightinesses the hope,
or notion, that his Majesty did not intend actual war about
that Cleve-Jülich Succession, — being a pacific Majesty, and
unwilling to involve his neighbors and mankind. Luiscius,
instead of casual hint delicately dropped in some good way,
had proceeded by direct declaration; frank assurance to the
High Mightinesses, That there would be no war. Which had
never been quite his Majesty's meaning, and perhaps was now
becoming rather the reverse of it. Disavowal of Luiscius
had to ensue thereupon; who produced defensively his instruction from head-quarters; but got only rebukes for such heavy-
footed clumsy procedure, so unlike Diplomacy with its shoes
of felt; — and, in brief, was turned out of the Diplomatic
function, as unfit for it; and appointed to manage certain
Orange Properties, fragments of the Orange Heritage which
his Majesty still has in those Countries. This misadventure
sank heavily on the spirits of Luiscius, otherwise none of the
strongest-minded of men. Nor did he prosper in managing
the Orange Properties : on the contrary, he again fell into
mistakes; got soundly rebuked for injudicious conduct there, —
"cutting trees," planting trees, or whatever it was; — and this
produced such an effect on Luiscius, that he made an attempt
on his own throat, distracted mortal; and was only stopped
by somebody rushing in. "It was not the first time he had
tried that feat," says Pöllnitz, "and been prevented; nor was
it long till he made a new attempt, which was again frus-
trated : and always afterwards his relations kept him close
in view :" Majesty writing comfortable forgiveness to the
perturbed creature, and also "settling a pension on him;"

---

[1] *Œuvres de Voltaire* (*Vie Privée*, or what they now call *Mémoires*), ii. 15.

adequate, we can hope, and not excessive; "which Luiscius continued to receive, at the Hague, so long as he lived." These are the prose facts; not definitely dated to us, but perfectly clear otherwise.[1]

Voltaire, in his Dutch excursions, did sometimes, in after years, lodge in that old vacant Palace, called *Vieille Cour*, at the Hague; where he gracefully celebrates the decayed forsaken state of matters; dusky vast rooms with dim gilding; forgotten libraries "veiled under the biggest spider-webs in Europe;" for the rest, an uncommonly quiet place, convenient for a writing man, besides costing nothing. A son of this Luiscius, a good young lad, it also appears, was occasionally Voltaire's amanuensis there; him he did recommend zealously to the new King of Prussia, who was not deaf on the occasion. This, in the fire of satirical wit, is what we can transiently call "giving alms to a Prussian Excellency;" — not now excellent, but pensioned and cracked; and the reader perceives, Luiscius had probably more than one razor, had not one been enough, when he did the rash act' Friedrich employed Luiscius Junior, with no result that we hear of farther; and seems to have thought Luiscius Senior an absurd fellow, not worth mentioning again: "ran away from the Cleve Country [probably some mad-house there] above a year ago, I hear; and what is the matter where such a crackbrain end?"[2]

CHAPTER V.

VISIT AT LOO.

THE Pfalz question being in such a predicament, and Luiscius diplomatizing upon it in such heavy-footed manner, his Majesty thinks a journey to Holland, to visit one's Kinsfolk

---

[1] Pöllnitz, ii. 495, 496; — the "*new* attempt" seems to have been "June, 1739" (*Gentleman's Magazine*, in mense, p. 331).

[2] Voltaire, *Œuvres* (Letter to Friedrich, 7th October, 1740), lxxii. 261; and Friedrich's answer (wrong dated), ib. 265; Preuss, xxii. 33.

there, and incidentally speak a word with the High Mightinesses upon Pfalz, would not be amiss. Such journey is
decided on; Crown-Prince to accompany. Summer of 1738:
a short visit, quite without fuss; to last only three days; —
mere sequel to the Reviews held in those adjacent Cleve
Countries; so that the Gazetteers may take no notice. All
which was done accordingly: Crown-Prince's first sight of
Holland; and one of the few reportable points of his
Reinsberg life, and not quite without memorability to him
and us.

On the 8th of July, 1738, the Review Party got upon the
road for Wesel: all through July, they did their reviewing
in those Cleve Countries; and then struck across for the
Palace of Loo in Geldern, where a Prince of Orange countable kinsman to his Prussian Majesty, and a Princess still
more nearly connected, — English George's Daughter, own
niece to his Prussian Majesty, — are in waiting for this distinguished honor. The Prince of Orange we have already
seen, for a moment once; at the siege of Philipsburg four
years ago, when the sale of Chasot's horses went off so well.
"Nothing like selling horses when your company have dined
well," whispered he to Chasot, at that time; since which date
we have heard nothing of his Highness.

He is not a beautiful man; he has a crooked back, and
features conformable; but is of prompt vivacious nature, and
does not want for sense and good-humor. Paternal George,
the gossips say, warned his Princess, when this marriage was
talked of, "You will find him very ill-looking, though!" "And
if I found him a baboon — !" answered she; being so heartily
tired of St. James's. And in fact, for anything I have heard,
they do well enough together. She is George II.'s eldest
Princess; — next elder to our poor Amelia, who was once so
interesting to us! What the Crown-Prince now thought of all
that, I do not know; but the Books say, poor Amelia wore the
willow, and specially wore the Prince's miniature on her breast
all her days after, which were many. Grew corpulent, somewhat a huddle in appearance and equipment, "eyelids like
upper-*lips*," for one item: but when life itself fled, the minia-

ture was found in its old place, resting on the old heart
after some sixty years. O Time, O Sons and Daughters of
Time! —

His Majesty's reception at Loo was of the kind he liked, —
cordial, honorable, unceremonious; and these were three
pleasant days he had. Pleasant for the Crown-Prince too;
as the whole Journey had rather been; Papa, with covert
satisfaction, finding him a wise creature, after all, and "more
serious" than formerly. "Hm, you don't know what things
are in that Fritz!" his Majesty murmured sometimes, in these
later years, with a fine light in his eyes.

Loo itself is a beautiful Palace: "Loo, close by the Village
Appeldoorn, is a stately brick edifice, built with architectural
regularity; has finely decorated rooms, beautiful gardens, and
round are superb alleys of oak and linden." [1] There saunters
pleasantly our Crown-Prince, for these three days; — and one
glad incident I do perceive to have befallen him there: the
arrival of a Letter from Voltaire. Letter much expected,
which had followed him from Wesel; and which he answers
here, in this brick Palace, among the superb avenues and
gardens. [2]

No doubt a glad incident, irradiating, as with a sudden sun-
burst in gray weather, the commonplace of things. Here is
news worth listening to; news as from the empyrean! Free
interchange of poetries and proses, of heroic sentiments and
opinions, between the Unique of Sages and the Paragon of
Crown-Princes; how charming to both! Literary business,
we perceive, is brisk on both hands; at Cirey the *Discours sur
l'Homme* ("Sixth *Discours*" arrives in this packet at Loo,
surely a deathless piece of singing); nor is Reinsberg idle:
Reinsberg is copiously doing verse, such verse! and in prose,
very earnestly, an "*Anti-Machiavel;*" which soon afterwards
filled all the then world, though it has now fallen so silent
again. And at Paris, as Voltaire announces with a flourish,
"M. de Maupertuis's excellent Book, *Figure de la Terre*, is

[1] Büsching, *Erdbeschreibung*, viii. 69.
[2] *Œuvres*, xxi. 203, the Letter, "Cirey, June, 1738;" Ib. 222, the Answer
to it, "Loo, 6th August, 1738."

out;"[1] M. de Maupertuis, home from the Polar regions and from measuring the Earth there; the sublimest miracle in Paris society at present. Might build, new-build, an *Academy of Sciences* at Berlin for your Royal Highness, one day? suggests Voltaire, on this occasion: and Friedrich, as we shall see, takes the hint. One passage of the Crown-Prince's Answer is in these terms; — fixing this Loo visit to its date for us, at any rate: —

"*Loo in Holland, 6th August,* 1739. . . . I write from a place where there lived once a great man [William III. of England, our Dutch William]; which is now the Prince of Orange's House. The demon of Ambition sheds its unhappy poisons over his days. He might be the most fortunate of men; and he is devoured by chagrins in his beautiful Palace here, in the middle of his gardens and of a brilliant Court. It is pity in truth; for he is a Prince with no end of wit (*infiniment d'esprit*), and has respectable qualites." Not Stadtholder, unluckily; that is where the shoe pinches; the Dutch are on the Republican tack, and will not have a Stadtholder at present. No help for it in one's beautiful gardens and avenues of oak and linden.

"I have talked a great deal about Newton with the Princess," — about Newton; never hinted at Amelia; not permissible! — "from Newton we passed to Leibnitz; and from Leibnitz to the Late Queen of England," Caroline lately gone, "who, the Prince told me, was of Clarke's sentiment" on that important theological controversy now dead to mankind. — And of Jenkins and his Ear did the Princess say nothing? That is now becoming a high phenomenon in England! But readers must wait a little.

Pity that we cannot give these two Letters in full; that no reader, almost, could be made to understand them, or to care

---

[1] Paris, 1738: Maupertuis's "measurement of a degree," in the utmost North, 1736–1737 (to prove the Earth flattened there). Vivid Narrative; somewhat gesticulative, but duly brief. The only Book of that great Maupertuis which is now readable to human nature.

for them when understood. Such the cruelty of Time upon
this Voltaire-Friedrich Correspondence, and some others ;
which were once so rosy, sunny, and are now fallen drearily
extinct, — studiable by Editors only ! In itself the Friedrich-
Voltaire Correspondence, we can see, was charming; very
blossomy at present : businesses increasing ; mutual admiration
now risen to a great height, — admiration sincere on both
sides, most so on the Prince's, and extravagantly expressed on
both sides, most so on Voltaire's.

Crown-Prince becomes a Freemason ; and is harangued by Monsieur de Bielfeld.

His Majesty, we said, had three pleasant days at Loo ; discoursing, as with friends, on public matters, or even on more
private matters, in a frank unconstrained way. He is not to
be called "Majesty " on this occasion; but the fact, at Loo,
and by the leading Mightinesses of the Republic, who come
copiously to compliment him there, is well remembered. Talk
there was, with such leading Mightinesses, about the Jülich-
and-Berg question, aim of this Journey : earnest enough private talk with some of them : but it availed nothing ; and
would not be worth reporting now to any creature, if we even
knew it. In fact, the Journey itself remains mentionable
chiefly by one very trifling circumstance ; and then by another,
not important either, which followed out of that. The trifling
circumstance is, — That Friedrich, in the course of this Journey, became a Freemason : and the unimportant sequel was,
That he made acquaintance with one Bielfeld, on the occasion ;
who afterwards wrote a Book about him, which was once much
read, though never much worth reading, and is still citable,
with precaution, now and then.[1] Trifling circumstance, of
Freemasonry, as we read in Bielfeld and in many Books after
him, befell in manner following.

Among the dinner-guests at Loo, one of those three days,
was a Prince of Lippe-Bückeburg, — Prince of small territory,

---

[1] Monsieur le Baron de Bielfeld, *Lettres Familières et Autres*, 1763 ; —
second edition, 2 vols. à Leide, 1767, is the one we use here.

but of great speculation; whose territory lies on the Weser,
leading to Dutch connections; and whose speculations stretch
over all the Universe, in a high fantastic style: — he was a
dinner-guest; and one of the topics that came up was Freemasonry; a phantasmal kind of object, which had kindled
itself, or rekindled, in those years, in England first of all;
and was now hovering about, a good deal, in Germany and
other countries; pretending to be a new light of Heaven, and
not a bog-meteor of phosphorated hydrogen, conspicuous in
the murk of things.   Bog-meteor, foolish putrescent will-o'-
wisp, his Majesty promptly defined it to be: Tom-foolery and
Kinderspiel, what else?   Whereupon ingenious Bückeburg,
who was himself a Mason, man of forty by this time, and had
high things in him of the Quixotic type, ventured on defence;
and was so respectful, eloquent, dexterous, ingenious, he quite
captivated, if not his Majesty, at least the Crown-Prince, who
was more enthusiastic for high things.   Crown-Prince, after
table, took his Durchlaucht of Bückeburg aside; talked farther
on the subject, expressed his admiration, his conviction, — his
wish to be admitted into such a Hero Fraternity.   Nothing
could be welcomer to Durchlaucht.   And so, in all privacy, it
was made up betweeen them, That Durchlaucht, summoning
as many mystic Brothers out of Hamburg as were needful,
should be in waiting with them, on the Crown-Prince's road
homeward, — say at Brunswick, night before the Fair, where
we are to be, — and there make the Crown-Prince a Mason.[1]

This is Bielfeld's account, repeated ever since; substantially
correct, except that the scene was not Loo at all: dinner and
dialogue, it now appears, took place in Durchlaucht's own
neighborhood, during the Cleve Review time; "probably at
Minden, 17th July;" and all was settled into fixed program
before Loo came in sight.[2]   Bielfeld's report of the subsequent

---

[1] Bielfeld, i. 14–16 ; Preuss, i. 111 ; Preuss, *Buch für Jedermann*, i. 41.

[2] *Œuvres de Frédéric*, xvs. 201 : Friedrich's Letter to this Durchlaucht,
"Comte de Schaumbourg-Lippe" he calls him ; date, " Moyland, 26th July,
1738 : " Moyland, a certain *Schloss*, or habitable Mansion, of his Majesty's,
few miles to north of Mörs in the Cleve Country; where his Majesty used
often to pause; — and where (what will be much more remarkable to readers)
the Crown-Prince and Voltaire had their first meeting, two years hence.

procedure at Brunswick, as he saw it and was himself part of it, is liable to no mistakes, at least of the involuntary kind; and may, for anything we know, be correct in every particular.

He says (veiling it under discreet asterisks, which are now decipherable enough), The Durchlaucht of Lippe-Bückeburg had summoned six Brethren of the Hamburg Lodge ; of whom we mention only a Graf von Kielmannsegge, a Baron von Oberg, both from Hanover, and Bielfeld himself, a Merchant's Son, of Hamburg ; these, with "Kielmannsegge's Valet to act as Tiler," Valet being also a Mason, and the rule equality of mankind, — were to have the honor of initiating the Crown-Prince. They arrived at the Western Gate of Brunswick on the 11th of August, as prearranged ; Prussian Majesty not yet come, but coming punctually on the morrow. It is Fair-time ; all manner of traders, pedlers, showmen rendezvousing ; many neighboring Nobility too, as was still the habit. "Such a bulk of light luggage ? " said the Custom-house people at the Gate ; — but were pacified by slipping them a ducat. Upon which we drove to "Korn's Hôtel " (if anybody now knew it); and there patiently waited. No great things of a Hôtel, says Bielfeld; but can be put up with ; — worst feature is, we discover a Hanover acquaintance lodging close by, nothing but a wooden partition between us : How if he should over-hear ! —

Prussian Majesty and suite, under universal cannon-salvos, arrived, Sunday the 12th ; to stay till Wednesday (three days) with his august Son-in-law and Daughter here. Durchlaucht Lippe presents himself at Court, the rest of us not ; privately settles with the Prince : "Tuesday night, eve of his Majesty's departure ; that shall be the night : at Korn's Hôtel, late enough ! " And there, accordingly, on the appointed night, 14th–15th August, 1738, the light-luggage trunks have yielded their stage-properties ; Jachin and Boaz are set up, and all things are ready ; Tiler (Kielmannsegge's Valet) watching with drawn sword against the profane. As to our Hanover neighbor, on the other side the partition, says Bielfeld, we waited on him. this day after dinner, successively paying our respects; successively pledged him in so many bumpers, he is lying dead drunk hours ago, could not overhear a cannon-battery, he. And soon after midnight, the Crown-Prince glides in, a Captain Wartensleben accompanying, who is also a candidate; and the mysterious rites are accomplished on both of them, on the Crown-Prince first, without accident, and in the usual way.

Bielfeld could not enough admire the demeanor of this Prince, his clearness, sense, quiet brilliancy; and how he was so "intrepid," and "possessed himself so gracefully in the most critical instants." Extremely genial air, and so young, looks younger even than his years: handsome to a degree, though of short stature. Physiognomy, features, quite charming; fine auburn hair (*beau brun*), a negligent plenty of it; "his large blue eyes have something at once severe, sweet and gracious." Eligible Mason indeed. Had better make despatch at present, lest Papa be getting on the road before him!—Bielfeld delivered a small address, composed beforehand; with which the Prince seemed to be content. And so, with masonic grip, they made their adieus for the present; and the Crown-Prince and Wartensleben were back at their posts, ready for the road along with his Majesty.

His Majesty came on Sunday; goes on Wednesday, home now at a stretch; and, we hope, has had a good time of it here, these three days. Daughter Charlotte and her Serene Husband, well with their subjects, well with one another, are doing well; have already two little Children; a Boy the elder, of whom we have heard: Boy's name is Karl, age now three; sprightly, reckoned very clever, by the fond parents;—who has many things to do in the world, by and by; to attack the French Revolution, and be blown to pieces by it on the Field of Jena, for final thing! That is the fate of little Karl, who frolics about here, so sunshiny and ingenuous at present.

Karl's Grandmother, the Serene Dowager Duchess, Friedrich's own Mother-in-law, his Majesty and Friedrich would also of course see here. Fine Younger Sons of hers are coming forward; the reigning Duke beautifully careful about the

furtherance of these Cadets of the House. Here is Prince
Ferdinand, for instance; just getting ready for the Grand
Tour; goes in a month hence :[1] a fine eupeptic loyal young
fellow; who, in a twenty years more, will be Chatham's Generalissimo, and fight the French to some purpose. A Brother
of his, the next elder, is now fighting the Turks for his
Kaiser; does not like it at all, under such Seckendorfs and
War-Ministries as there are. Then, elder still, eldest of all
the Cadets, there is Anton Ulrich, over at Petersburg for some
years past, with outlooks high enough : To wed the Mecklenburg Princess there (Daughter of the unutterable Duke), and
be as good as Czar of all the Russias one day. Little to his
profit, poor soul ! — These, historically ascertainable, are the
aspects of the Brunswick Court during those three days of
Royal Visit, in Fair-time ; and may serve to date the Masonic
Transaction for us, which the Crown-Prince has just accomplished over at Korn's.

As for the Transaction itself, there is intrinsically no harm
in this initiation, we will hope : but it behooves to be kept
well hidden from Papa. Papa's good opinion of the Prince
has sensibly risen, in the course of this Journey, " so rational,
serious, not dangling about among the women as formerly ; "
— and what a shock would this of Korn's Hôtel be, should
Papa hear of it ! Poor Papa, from officious tale-bearers he
hears many things : is in distress about Voltaire, about Heterodoxies ; — and summoned the Crown-Prince, by express,
from Reinsberg, on one occasion lately, over to Potsdam, " to
take the Communion " there, by way of case-hardening against
Voltaire and Heterodoxies ! Think of it, human readers ! —
We will add the following stray particulars, more or less
illustrative of the Masonic Transaction; and so end that
trifling affair.

The Captain Wartensleben, fellow-recipient of the mysteries
at Brunswick, is youngest son, by a second marriage, of old
Feldmarschall Wartensleben, now deceased; and is consequently Uncle, Half-Uncle, of poor Lieutenant Katte, though

---

[1] Mauvillon (Fils, son of him whom we cite otherwise), Geschichte Ferdi-
nands Herzogs von Braunschweig-Lüneburg (Leipzig, 1794), i. 17–25.

some years younger than Katte would now have been. Tender
memories hang by Wartensleben, in a silent way! He is
Captain in the Potsdam Giants; somewhat an intimate, and
not undeservedly so, of the Crown-Prince;— succeeds Wolden
as Hofmarschall at Reinsberg, not many months after this;
Wolden having died of an apoplectic stroke. Of Bielfeld
comes a Book, slightly citable; from no other of the Brethren,
or their Feat at Korn's, comes (we may say) anything whatever. The Crown-Prince prosecuted his Masonry, at Reinsberg
or elsewhere, occasionally, for a year or two; but was never
ardent in it; and very soon after his Accession, left off altogether: "Child's-play and *ignis fatuus* mainly!" A Royal
Lodge was established at Berlin, of which the new King consented to be patron; but he never once entered the place; and
only his Portrait (a welcomely good one, still to be found
there) presided over the mysteries in that Establishment.
Harmless "fire," but too "fatuous;" mere flame-circles cut in
the air, for infants, we know how!—

With Lippe-Bückeburg there ensued some Correspondence,
high enough on his Serenity's side; but it soon languished on
the Prince's side; and in private Poetry, within a two years
of this Brunswick scene, we find Lippe used proverbially for
a type-specimen of Fools.[1] A windy fantastic individual;—
overwhelmed in finance-difficulties too! Lippe continued writing; but "only Secretaries now answered him" from Berlin.
A son of his, son and successor, something of a Quixote too,
but notable in Artillery-practice and otherwise, will turn up at
a future stage.

Nor is Bielfeld with his Book a thing of much moment to
Friedrich or to us. Bielfeld too has a light airy vein of talk;
loves Voltaire and the Philosophies in a light way;—knows
the arts of Society, especially the art of flattering; and would
fain make himself agreeable to the Crown-Prince, being anxious
to rise in the world. His Father is a Hamburg Merchant,
Hamburg "Sealing-wax Manufacturer," not ill off for money:

---

[1] "Taciturne, Caton, avec mes bons parents,
Aussi fou que la Lippe avec les jeunes gens."
Œuvres, xi. 80 (*Discours sur la Fausseté*, written 1740).

Son has been at schools, high schools, under tutors, posture-
masters; swashes about on those terms, with French *esprit* in
his mouth, and lace ruffles at his wrists; still under thirty;
showy enough, sharp enough; considerably a coxcomb, as is
still evident. He did transiently get about Friedrich, as we
shall see; and hoped to have sold his heart to good purpose
there; — was, by and by, employed in slight functions; not
found fit for grave ones. In the course of some years, he got
a title of Baron; and sold his heart more advantageously, to
some rich Widow or Fräulein; with whom he retired to Saxony, and there lived on an Estate he had purchased, a stranger
to Prussia thenceforth.

His Book (*Lettres Familières et Autres,* all turning on Friedrich), which came out in 1763, at the height of Friedrich's
fame, and was much read, is still freely cited by Historians as
an Authority. But the reading of a few pages sufficiently intimates that these " Letters " never can have gone through a
terrestrial Post-office; that thay are an afterthought, composed
from vague memory and imagination, in that fine Saxon retreat; — a sorrowful ghost-like " *Travels of Anacharsis,*" instead
of living words by an eye-witness! Not to be cited " freely "
at all, but sparingly and under conditions. They abound in
small errors, in misdates, mistakes; small fictions even, and
impossible pretensions : — foolish mortal, to write down his
bit of knowledge in that form! For the man, in spite of his
lace ruffles and gesticulations, has brisk eyesight of a superficial kind : he *could* have done us this little service (apparently his one mission in the world, for which Nature gave him
bed and board here); and he, the lace ruffles having gone into
his soul, has been tempted into misdoing it! — Bielfeld and
Bielfeld's Book, such as they are, appear to be the one conquest Friedrich got of Freemasonry; no other result now
traceable to us of that adventure in Korn's Hôtel, crowning
event of the Journey to Loo.

Seckendorf gets lodged in Grätz.

Feldmarschall Seckendorf, after unheard-of wrestlings with
the Turk War, and the Vienna War-Office (*Hofkriegsrath*), is
sitting, for the last three weeks, — where thinks the reader ?
— in the Fortress of Grätz among the Hills of Styria; a State-
Prisoner, not likely to get out soon ! Seckendorf led forth,
in 1737, "such an Army, for number, spirit and equipment,"
say the Vienna people, "as never marched against the Turk
before ; " and it must be owned, his ill success has been unparalleled. The blame was not altogether his; not chiefly
his, except for his rash undertaking of the thing, on such terms
as there were. But the truth is, that first scene we saw of him,
— an Army all gone out trumpeting and drumming into the
woods to *find* its Commander-in-Chief, — was an emblem of the
Campaign in general. Excellent Army ; but commanded by nobody in particular; commanded by a *Hofkriegsrath* at Vienna,
by a Franz Duke of Tuscany, by Feldmarschall Seckendorf,
and by subordinates who were disobedient to him : which accordingly, almost without help of the Turk and his disorderly
ferocity, rubbed itself to pieces before long. Roamed about,
now hither now thither, with plans laid and then with plans
suddenly altered, Captain being Chaos mainly ; in swampy
countries, by overflowing rivers, in hunger, hot weather, forced
marches ; till it was marched gradually off its feet ; and the
clouds of chaotic Turks, who did finally show face, had a cheap
pennyworth of it. Never was such a campaign seen as this of
Seckendorf in 1737, said mankind. Except indeed that the
present one, Campaign of 1738, in those parts, under a different hand, is still worse ; and the Campaign of 1739, under
still a different, will be worst of all ! — Kaiser Karl and his
Austrians do not prosper in this Turk War, as the Russians do,
— who indeed have got a General equal to his task : Münnich, a
famed master in the art of handling Turks and War-Ministries :
real father of Russian Soldiering, say the Russians still.[1]

---

[1] See *Mannstein* for Münnich's plans with the Turk (methods and devices
of steady Discipline in small numbers *versus* impetuous Ferocity in great) ;
and Berenhorst (*Betrachtungen über die Kriegskunst*, Leipzig, 1796), a first-rate
Authority, for examples and eulogies of them.

Campaign 1737, with clouds of chaotic Turks now sabring on the skirts of it, had not yet ended, when Seckendorf was called out of it; on polite pretexts, home to Vienna; and the command given to another. At the gates of Vienna, in the last days of October, 1737, an Official Person, waiting for the Feldmarschall, was sorry to inform him, That he, Feldmarschall Seckendorf, was under arrest; arrest in his own house, in the *Kohlmarkt* (Cabbage-market so called), a captain and twelve musketeers to watch over him with fixed bayonets there; strictly private, till the *Hofkriegsrath* had satisfied themselves in a point or two. "Hmph!" snuffled he; with brow blushing slate-color, I should think, and gray eyes much alight. And ever since, for ten months or so, Seckendorf, sealed up in the Cabbage-market, has been fencing for life with the *Hofkriegsrath;* who want satisfaction upon "eighty-six" different "points;" and make no end of chicaning to one's clear answers. And the Jesuits preach, too: "A Heretic, born enemy of Christ and his Kaiser; what is the use of questioning!" And the Heathen rage, and all men gnash their teeth, in this uncomfortable manner.

Answering done, there comes no verdict, much less any acquittal; the captain and twelve musketeers, three of them with fixed bayonets in one's very bedroom, continue. One evening, 21st July, 1738, glorious news from the seat of War — not *till* evening, as the Imperial Majesty was out hunting — enters Vienna; blowing trumpets; shaking flags: "Grand Victory over the Turks!" so we call some poor skirmish there has been; and Vienna bursting all into three-times-three, the populace get very high. Populace rush to the Kohlmarkt: break the Seckendorf windows; intent to massacre the Seckendorf, had not fresh military come, who were obliged to fire and kill one or two. "The house captain and his twelve musketeers, of themselves, did wonders; Seckendorf and all his domestics were in arms:" "*Jarnibleu*" for the last time! — This is while the Crown-Prince is at Wesel; sound asleep, most likely; Loo, and the Masonic adventure, perhaps twinkling prophetically in his dreams.

At two next morning, an Official Gentleman informs Seckendorf, That he, for his part, must awaken, and go to Grätz. And in one hour more (3 A.M.), the Official Gentleman rolls off with him; drives all day; and delivers his Prisoner at Grätz : — "Not so much as a room ready there; Prisoner had to wait an hour in the carriage," till some summary preparation were made. Wall-neighbors of the poor Feldmarschall, in his Fortress here, were "a *Gold-Cook* (swindling Alchemist), who had gone crazy; and an Irish Lieutenant, confined thirty-two years for some love-adventure, likewise pretty crazy; their noises in the night-time much disturbed the Feldmarschall." [1] One human thing there still is in his lot, the Feldmarschall's old Gräfinn. True old Dame, she, both in the Kohlmarkt and at Grätz, stands by him, "imprisoned along with him" if it must be so; ministering, comforting, as only a true Wife can; — and hope has not quite taken wing.

Rough old Feldmarschall; now turned of sixty : never made such a Campaign before, as this of 1737 followed by 1738! There sits he; and will not trouble us any more during the present Kaiser's lifetime. Friedrich Wilhelm is amazed at these sudden cantings of Fortune's wheel, and grieves honestly as for an old friend : even the Crown-Prince finds Seckendorf punished unjustly; and is almost sorry for him, after all that has come and gone.

The Ear of Jenkins re-emerges.

We must add the following, distilled from the English Newspapers, though it is now almost four months after date : —

"*London*, 1st *April*, 1738. In the English House of Commons, much more in the English Public, there has been furious debating for a fortnight past : Committee of the whole House, examining witnesses, hearing counsel; subject, the Termagant of Spain, and her West-Indian procedures; — she, by her procedures somewhere, is always cutting out work for mankind! How English and other strangers, fallen-in with in those seas, are treated by the Spaniards, readers have heard,

---

[1] *Seckendorfs Leben*, ii. 170-277. See *Schmettau*, pp. 27-59.

nay have chanced to see; and it is a fact painfully known to all nations. Fact which England, for one nation, can no longer put up with. Walpole and the Official Persons would fain smooth the matter; but the West-India Interest, the City, all Mercantile and Navigation Interests are in dead earnest: Committee of the whole House, 'Presided by Alderman Perry,' has not ears enough to hear the immensities of evidence offered; slow Public is gradually kindling to some sense of it. This had gone on for two weeks, when — what shall we say ? — the *Ear of Jenkins* re-emerged for the second time; and produced important effects !

" Where Jenkins had been all this while, — steadfastly navigating to and fro, steadfastly eating tough junk with a wetting of rum; not thinking too much of past labors, yet privately ' always keeping his lost Ear in cotton ' (with a kind of ursine piety, or other dumb feeling), — no mortal now knows. But to all mortals it is evident he was home in London at this time; no doubt a noted member of Wapping society, the much-enduring Jenkins. And witnesses, probably not one but many, had mentioned him to this Committee, as a case eminently in point. Committee, as can still be read in its Rhadamanthine Journals, orders : ' *Die Jovis,* 16° *Martii* 1737–1738, That Captain Robert Jenkins do attend this House immediately ; ' and then more specially, ' 17° *Martii,*' captious objections having risen in Official quarters, as we guess, — 'That Captain Robert Jenkins do attend upon Tuesday morning next.' [1] Tuesday next is 21st March, — 1st of April, 1738, by our modern Calendar ; — and on that day, not a doubt, Jenkins does attend; narrates that tremendous passage we already heard of, seven years ago, in the entrance of the Gulf of Florida; and produces his Ear wrapt in cotton : — setting all on flame (except the Official persons) at sight of it."

Official persons, as their wont is in the pressure of debate, endeavored to deny, to insinuate in their vile Newspapers, That Jenkins lost his Ear nearer home and not for nothing;

[1] *Commons Journals,* xxiii. (in diebus).

as one still reads in the History Books.[1] Sheer calumnies,
we now find. Jenkins's account was doubtless abundantly
emphatic; but there is no ground to question the substantial
truth of him and it. And so, after seven years of unnotice-
able burning upon the thick skin of the English Public, the
case of Jenkins accidentally burns through, and sets England
bellowing; such a smart is there of it, — not to be soothed
by Official wet-cloths; but getting worse and worse, for the
nineteen months ensuing. And in short — But we will not
anticipate!

CHAPTER VI.

LAST YEAR OF REINSBERG; JOURNEY TO PREUSSEN.

THE Idyllium of Reinsberg — of which, except in the way
of sketchy suggestion, there can no history be given — lasted
less than four years; and is now coming to an end, unexpectedly soon. A pleasant Arcadian Summer in one's life; —
though it has not wanted its occasional discords, flaws of ill
weather in the general sunshine. Papa, always in uncertain
health of late, is getting heavier of foot and of heart under
his heavy burdens; and sometimes falls abstruse enough, liable to bewilderments from bad people and events: not much
worth noticing here.[2] But the Crown-Prince has learned to
deal with all this; all this is of transient nature; and a bright
long future seems to lie ahead at Reinsberg; — brightened especially by the Literary Element; which, in this year of 1739,
is brisker than it had ever been. Distinguished Visitors, of a
literary turn, look in at Reinsberg; the Voltaire Correspondence is very lively; on Friedrich's part there is copious pro-
duction, various enterprise, in the form of prose and verse;
thoughts even of going to press with some of it: in short, the
Literary Interest rises very prominent at Reinsberg in 1739.

---

[1] Tindal (xx. 372), Coxe, &c.

[2] See Pöllnitz, ii. 509-515; Friedrich's Letter to Wilhelmina (" Berlin, 20th
January, 1739 :" in *Œuvres*, xxvii. part 1st, pp. 60, 61) ; &c. &c.

Biography is apt to forget the Literature there (having her reasons) ; but must at last take some notice of it, among the phenomena of the year.

To the young Prince himself, "courting tranquillity," as his door-lintel intimated,[1] and forbidden to be active except within 'limits, this of Literature was all along the great light of existence at Reinsberg ; the supplement to all other employments or wants of employment there. To Friedrich himself, in those old days, a great and supreme interest ; while again, to the modern Biographer of him, it has become dark and vacant ; a thing to be shunned, not sought. So that the fact as it stood with Friedrich differs far from any description that can be given of the fact. Alas, we have said already, and the constant truth is, Friedrich's literatures, his distinguished literary visitors and enterprises, which were once brand-new and brilliant, have grown old as a garment, and are a sorrow rather than otherwise to existing mankind ! Conscientious readers, who would represent to themselves the vanished scene at Reinsberg, in this point more especially, must make an effort.

As biographical documents, these Poetries and Proses of the young man give a very pretty testimony of him ; but are not of value otherwise. In fact, they promise, if we look well into them, That here is probably a practical faculty and intellect of the highest kind ; which again, on the speculative, especially on the poetical side, will never be considerable, nor has even tried to be so. This young soul does not deal in meditation at all, and his tendencies are the reverse of sentimental. Here is no introspection, morbid or other, no pathos or complaint, no melodious informing of the public what dreadful emotions you labor under : here, in rapid prompt form, indicating that it is truth and not fable, are generous aspirations for the world and yourself, generous pride, disdain of the ignoble, of the dark, mendacious ; — here, in short, is a swift-handed, valiant, *steel*-bright kind of soul ; very likely for a King's, if other things answer, and not likely for a Poet's. No doubt he could have made something of Literature too ; could have written Books,

---

[1] "*Frederico tranquillitatem colenti*" (Infrà, p. 123).

and left some stamp of a veracious, more or less victorious intellect, in that strange province too. But then he must have
applied himself to it, as he did to reigning : done in the cursory style, we see what it has come to.

It is certain, Friedrich's reputation suffers, at this day, from
his writing. From his *not* having written nothing, he stands
lower with the world. Which seems hard measure ; — though
perhaps it is the law of the case, after all. " Nobody in these
days," says my poor Friend, "has the least notion of the sinful
waste there is in talk, whether by pen or tongue. Better probably that King Friedrich had written no Verses ; nay I know
not that David's Psalms did David's Kingship any good ! "
Which may be truer than it seems. Fine aspirations, generous convictions, purposes, — they are thought very fine : but
it is good, on various accounts, to keep them rather silent ;
strictly unvocal, except on call of real business ; so dangerous
are they for becoming conscious of themselves ! Most things
do not ripen at all except underground. And it is a sad but
sure truth, that every time you *speak* of a fine purpose, especially if with eloquence and to the admiration of by-standers,
there is the *less* chance of your ever making a fact of it in
your poor life. — If Reinsberg, and its vacancy of great employment, was the cause of Friedrich's verse-writing, we will
not praise Reinsberg on that head ! But the truth is, Friedrich's verses came from him with uncommon fluency ; and
were not a deep matter, but a shallow one, in any sense. Not
much more to him than speaking with a will ; than fantasying
on the flute in an animated strain. Ever and anon through
his life, on small hint from without or on great, there was
found a certain leakage of verses, which he was prompt to
utter ; — and the case at Reinsberg, or afterwards, is not so
serious as we might imagine.

Pine's Horace ; and the Anti-Machiavel.

In late months Friedrich had conceived one notable project ;
which demands a word in this place. Did modern readers
ever hear of "John Pine, the celebrated English Engraver " ?

John Pine, a man of good scholarship, good skill with his burin, did "Tapestries of the House of Lords," and other things of a celebrated nature, famous at home and abroad : but his peculiar feat, which had commended him at Reinsberg, was an Edition of *Horace :* exquisite old *Flaccus* brought to perfection, as it were ; all done with vignettes, classical borderings, symbolic marginal ornaments, in fine taste and accuracy, the Text itself engraved ; all by the exquisite burin of Pine.[1] This Edition had come out last year, famous over the world ; and was by and by, as rumor bore, to be followed by a *Virgil* done in the like exquisite manner.

The Pine *Horace,* part of the Pine *Virgil* too, still exist in the libraries of the curious ; and are doubtless known to the proper parties, though much forgotten by others of us. To Friedrich, scanning the Pine phenomenon with interest then brand-new, it seemed an admirable tribute to classical genius ; and the idea occurred to him, "Is not there, by Heaven's blessing, a living genius, classical like those antique Romans, and worthy of a like tribute ? " Friedrich's idea was, That Voltaire being clearly the supreme of Poets, the *Henriade,* his supreme of Poems, ought to be engraved like *Flaccus ;* text and all, with vignettes, tail-pieces, classical borderings beautifully symbolic and exact ; by the exquisite burin of Pine. Which idea the young hero-worshipper, in spite of his finance-difficulties, had resolved to realize ; and was even now busy with it, since his return from Loo. "Such beautiful enthusiasm," say some readers ; "and in behalf of that particular demi-god ! " Alas, yes ; to Friedrich he was the best demigod then going ; and Friedrich never had any doubt about him.

For the rest, this heroic idea could not realize itself ; and we are happy to have nothing more to do with Pine or the *Henriade.* Correspondences were entered into with Pine, and some pains taken : Pine's high prices were as nothing ; but Pine was busy with his *Virgil ;* probably, in fact, had little stomach for the *Henriade ;* "could not for seven years to come enter upon it : " so that the matter had to die away ;

[1] "London, 1737 " (*Biographie Universelle,* xxxiv. 465).

and nothing came of it but a small *Dissertation*, or Introductory Essay, which the Prince had got ready, — which is still to be found printed in Voltaire's Works [1] and in Friedrich's, if anybody now cared much to read it. Preuss says it was finished, "the 10th August, 1739;" and that minute fact in Chronology, with the above tale of Hero-worship hanging to it, will suffice my readers and me.

But there is another literary project on hand, which did take effect; — much worthy of mention, this year; the whole world having risen into such a Chorus of *Te Deum* at sight of it next year. In this year falls, what at any rate was a great event to Friedrich, as literary man, the printing of his first Book, — assiduous writing of it with an eye to print. The Book is that "celebrated *Anti-Machiavel*," ever-praiseworthy Refutation of Machiavel's *Prince;* concerning which there are such immensities of Voltaire Correspondence, now become, like the Book itself, inane to all readers. This was the chosen soul's employment of Friedrich, the flower of life to him, at Reinsberg, through the year 1739. It did not actually get to press till Spring 1740; nor actually come out till Autumn, — by which time a great change had occurred in Friedrich's title and circumstances: but we may as well say here what little is to be said of it for modern readers.

"The Crown-Prince, reading this bad Book of Machiavel's, years ago, had been struck, as all honest souls, especially governors or apprentices to governing, must be, if they thought of reading such a thing, with its badness, its falsity, detestability; and came by degrees, obliquely fishing out Voltaire's opinion as he went along, on the notion of refuting Machiavel; and did refute him, the best he could. Set down, namely, his own earnest contradiction to such ungrounded noxious doctrines; elaborating the same more and more into clear logical utterance, till it swelled into a little Volume; which, so excellent was it, so important to mankind, Voltaire and friends were clear for publishing. Published accordingly it was; goes through the press next Summer (1740), under

[1] *Œuvres*, xiii. 393–402.

Voltaire's anxious superintendence : [1] for the Prince has at
length consented ; and Voltaire hands the Manuscript, with
mystery yet with hints, to a Dutch Bookseller, one Van Duren
at the Hague, who is eager enough to print such an article.
Voltaire himself — such his magnanimous friendship, especially if one have Dutch Lawsuits, or business of one's own,
in those parts — takes charge of correcting ; lodges himself
in the 'Old Court' (Prussian Mansion, called *Vieille Cour*, at
the Hague, where 'Luiscius,' figuratively speaking, may 'get
an alms' from us) ; and therefrom corrects, alters ; corresponds with the Prince and Van Duren, at a great rate. Keeps
correcting, altering, till Van Duren thinks he is spoiling it for
sale ; — and privately determines to preserve the original Manuscript, and have an edition of that, with only such corrections
as seem good to Van Duren. A treasonous step on this mule
of a Bookseller's part, thinks Voltaire ; but mulishly persisted
in by the man. Endless correspondence, to right and left,
ensues ; intolerably wearisome to every reader. And, in fine,
there came out, in Autumn next," — the Crown-Prince no
longer a Crown-Prince by that time, but shining conspicuous
under Higher Title, — "not one *Anti-Machiavel* only, but a
couple or a trio of *Anti-Machiavels ;* as printed ' at the
Hague ;' as reprinted ' at London ' or elsewhere ; the confused Bibliography of which has now fallen very insignificant.
First there was the Voltaire text, Authorized Edition, 'end of
September, 1740 ;' then came, in few weeks, the Van Duren
one ; then, probably, a third, combining the two, the variations
given as foot-notes : — in short, I know not how many editions,
translations, printings and reprintings ; all the world being

---

[1] Here, gathered from Friedrich's Letters to Voltaire, is the Chronology of
the little Enterprise : —

1738, *March* 2!, *June* 17, "Machiavel a baneful man," thinks Friedrich.
"Ought to be refuted by somebody ? " thinks he (date not known).

1739, *March* 22, Friedrich thinks of doing it himself. Has done it, *December* 4 ; — "a Book which ought to be printed," say Voltaire and the literary
visitors.

1740, *April* 26, Book given up to Voltaire for printing. Printing finished ;
Book appears, "end of *September*," when a great change had occurred in
Friedrich's title and position.

much taken up with such a message from the upper regions,
and eager to read it in any form.

"As to Friedrich himself, who of course says nothing of the
Anti-Machiavel in public, he privately, to Voltaire, disowns
all these editions; and intends to give a new one of his own,
which shall be the right article; but never did it, having far
other work cut out for him in the months that came. But
how zealous the world's humor was in that matter, no modern
reader can conceive to himself. In the frightful Compilation
called *Helden-Geschichte,* which we sometimes cite, there are,
excerpted from the then 'Bibliothèques' (*Nouvelle Bibliothèque*
and another; shining Periodicals of the time, now gone quite
dead), two 'reviews' of the *Anti-Machiavel,* which fill modern
readers with amazement : such a *Domine dimittas* chanted
over such an article ! — These details, in any other than the
Biographical point of view, are now infinitely unimportant."

Truly, yes! The Crown-Prince's *Anti-Machiavel,* final correct edition (in two forms, Voltaire's as corrected, and the
Prince's own as written), stands now in clear type;[1] and, after
all that jumble of printing and counter-printing, we can any of
us read it in a few hours; but, alas, almost none of us with the
least interest, or, as it were, with any profit whatever. So different is present tense from past, in all things, especially in
things like these ! It is sixscore years since the *Anti-Machiavel*
appeared. The spectacle of one who was himself a King (for the
mysterious fact was well known to Van Duren and everybody)
stepping forth to say with conviction, That Kingship was not
a thing of attorney mendacity, to be done under the patronage
of Beelzebub, but of human veracity, to be set about under quite
Other patronage ; and that, in fact, a King was the "born servant of his People" (*domestique* Friedrich once calls it), rather
than otherwise : this, naturally enough, rose upon the then populations, unused to such language, like the dawn of a new day ;
and was welcomed with such applauses as are now incredible,
after all that has come and gone ! Alas, in these sixscore
years, it has been found so easy to profess and speak, even
with sincerity ! The actual Hero-Kings were long used to be

[1] Preuss, *Œuvres de Frédéric,* viii. **61–163.**

silent; and the Sham-Hero kind grow only the more desperate for us, the more they speak and profess! — This *Anti-Machiavel* of Friedrich's is a clear distinct Treatise; confutes, or at least heartily contradicts, paragraph by paragraph, the incredible sophistries of Machiavel. Nay it leaves us, if we sufficiently force our attention, with the comfortable sense that his Royal Highness is speaking with conviction, and honestly from the heart, in the affair: but that is all the conquest we get of it, in these days. Treatise fallen more extinct to existing mankind it would not be easy to name.

Perhaps indeed mankind is getting weary of the question altogether. Machiavel himself one now reads only by compulsion. "What is the use of arguing with anybody that can believe in Machiavel?" asks mankind, or might well ask; and, except for Editorial purposes, eschews any *Anti-Machiavel;* impatient to be rid of bane and antidote both. Truly the world has had a pother with this little Nicolò Machiavelli and his perverse little Book: — pity almost that a Friedrich Wilhelm, taking his rounds at that point of time, had not had the "refuting" of him; Friedrich Wilhelm's method would have been briefer than Friedrich's! But let us hope the thing is now, practically, about completed. And as to the other question, "Was the Signor Nicolò serious in this perverse little Book; or did he only do it ironically, with a serious inverse purpose?" we will leave that to be decided, any time convenient, by people who are much at leisure in the world! —

The printing of the *Anti-Machiavel* was not intrinsically momentous in Friedrich's history; yet it might as well have been dispensed with. He had here drawn a fine program, and needlessly placarded it for the street populations: and afterwards there rose, as could not fail on their part, comparison between program and performance; scornful cry, chiefly from men of weak judgment, "Is this King an *Anti*-Machiavel, then? Pfui!" Of which, — though Voltaire's voice, too, was heard in it, in angry moments, — we shall say nothing: the reader, looking for himself, will judge by and by. And herewith enough of the *Anti-Machiavel*. Composition of *Anti-*

Machiavel and speculation of the Fine *Henriade* lasted, both
of them, all through this Year 1739, and farther : from these
two items, not to mention any other, readers can figure sufficiently how literary a year it was.

*Friedrich in Preussen again ; at the Stud of Trakehnen.
A tragically great Event coming on.*

In July this year the Crown-Prince went with Papa on
the Prussian Review-journey.[1] Such attendance on Review-
journeys, a mark of his being well with Papa, is now becoming
usual ; they are agreeable excursions, and cannot but be instructive as well. On this occasion, things went beautifully with
him. Out in those grassy Countries, in the bright Summer,
once more he had an unusually fine time ; — and two very
special pleasures befell him. First was, a sight of the Emigrants, our Salzburgers and other, in their flourishing condition, over in Lithuania yonder. Delightful to see how the
waste is blossoming up again ; busy men, with their industries,
their steady pious husbandries, making all things green and
fruitful: horse-droves, cattle-herds, waving cornfields ; — a very
" *Schmalzgrube* (Butter-pit) " of those Northern parts, as it is
since called.[2] The Crown-Prince's own words on this matter
we will give ; they are in a Letter of his to Voltaire, perhaps
already known to some readers ; — and we can observe he
writes rather copiously from those localities at present, and in
a cheerful humor with everybody.

" *Insterburg, 27th July,* 1739 (Crown-Prince to Voltaire). . . .
Prussian Lithuania is a Country a hundred and twenty miles
long, by from sixty to forty broad ;[3] it was ravaged by Pestilence at the beginning of this Century ; and they say
three hundred thousand people died of disease and famine."
Ravaged by Pestilence and the neglect of King Friedrich I. ;
till my Father, once his hands were free, made personal survey
of it, and took it up, in earnest.

[1] " Set out, 7th July " (*Œuvres*, xxvii. part 1st, 67 n.).

[2] Büsching, *Erdbeschreibung*, ii. 1049.

[3] " Miles *English*," we always mean, *unless* &c.

" Since that time," say twenty years ago, " there is no expense that the King has been afraid of, in order to succeed in
his salutary views. He made, in the first place, regulations
full of wisdom ; he rebuilt wherever the Pestilence had deso-
lated : thousands of families, from the ends of Europe," seventeen thousand Salzburgers for the last item, " were conducted
hither ; the Country repeopled itself ; trade began to flourish
again ; — and now, in these fertile regions, abundance reigns
more than it ever did.

" There are above half a million of inhabitants in Lithuania ;
there are more towns than there ever were, more flocks than
formerly, more wealth and more productiveness than in any
other part of Germany. And all this that I tell you of is due
to the King alone : who not only gave the orders, but superintended the execution of them ; it was he that devised the plans,
and himself got them carried to fulfilment ; and spared neither
care nor pains, nor immense expenditures, nor promises nor
recompenses, to secure happiness and life to this half-million
of thinking beings, who owe to him alone that they have possessions and felicity in the world.

" I hope this detail does not weary you. I depend on your
humanity extending itself to your Lithuanian brethren, as well
as to your French, English, German, or other, — all the more
as, to my great astonishment, I passed through villages where
you hear nothing spoken but French. — I have found something so heroic, in the generous and laborious way in which the
King addressed himself to making this desert flourish with
inhabitants and happy industries and fruits, that it seemed to
me you would feel the same sentiments in learning the circumstances of such a re-establishment.

" I daily expect news of you from Enghien [in those Dutch-
Lawsuit Countries]. . . . The divine Emilie ; . . . the Duke
[D'Aremberg, Austrian Soldier, of convivial turn, — remote
Welsh-Uncle to a certain little Prince de Ligne, now spinning
tops in those parts ; [1] not otherwise interesting], whom Apollo

---

[1] Born 23d May, 1735, this latter little Prince ; lasted till 13th December,
1814 (" danse, mais il ne marche pas ").

contends for against Bacchus. . . . Adieu. *Ne m'oubliez pas,
mon cher ami.*" [1]

This is one pleasant scene, to the Crown-Prince and us, in
those grassy localities. And now we have to mention that,
about a fortnight later, at Königsberg one day, in reference
to a certain Royal Stud or Horse-breeding Establishment in
those same Lithuanian regions, there had a still livelier satisfaction happened him; satisfaction of a personal and filial
nature. The name of this Royal Stud, inestimable on such
ground, is Trakehnen, — lies south of Tilsit, in an upper valley
of the Pregel river; — very extensive Horse-Establishment,
"with seven farms under it," say the Books, and all "in the
most perfect order," they need hardly add, Friedrich Wilhelm
being master of it. Well, the Royal Party was at Königsberg,
so far on the road homewards again from those outlying parts,
when Friedrich Wilhelm said one day to his Son, quite in a
cursory manner, "I give thee that Stud of Trakehnen; thou
must go back and look to it;" which struck Fritz quite dumb
at the moment.

For it is worth near upon £2,000 a year (12,000 thalers);
a welcome new item in our impoverished budget; and it is an
undeniable sign of Papa's good-humor with us, which is more
precious still. Fritz made his acknowledgments, eloquent with
looks, eloquent with voice, on coming to himself; and is, in
fact, very proud of his gift, and celebrates it to his Wilhelmina,
to Camas and others who have a right to know such a thing.
Grand useful gift; and handed over by Papa grandly, in three
business words, as if it had been a brace of game: "I give
it thee, Fritz!" A thing not to be forgotten. "At bottom,
Friedrich Wilhelm was not avaricious" (not a miser, only a
man grandly abhorring waste, as the poor vulgar cannot do),
"not avaricious," says Pöllnitz once; "he made munificent
gifts, and never thought of them more." This of Trakehnen,
— perhaps there might be a whiff of coming Fate concerned
in it withal: "I shall soon be dead, not able to give thee anything, poor Fritz!" To the Prince and us it is very beautiful;

1 *Œuvres,* xxi. 304, 305.

a fine effulgence of the inner man of Friedrich Wilhelm. The
Prince returned to Trakehnen, on this glad errand; settled
the business details there; and, after a few days, went home
by a route of his own; — well satisfied with this Prussian-
Review journey, as we may imagine.

One sad thing there was, though Friedrich did not yet know
how sad, in this Review-journey : the new fit of illness that
overtook his Majesty. From Pöllnitz, who was of the party,
we have details on that head. In his Majesty's last bad illness, five years ago, when all seemed hopeless, it appears the
surgeons had relieved him, — in fact recovered him, bringing
off the bad humors in quantity, — by an incision in the foot
or leg. In the course of the present fatigues, this old wound
broke out again; which of course stood much in the way of
his Majesty; and could not be neglected, as probably the
causes of it were. A regimental surgeon, Pöllnitz says, was
called in; who, in two days, healed the wound, — and declared
all to be right again; though in fact, as we may judge, it
was dangerously worse than before. " All well here," writes
Friedrich; " the King has been out of order, but is now entirely
recovered *(tout à fait remis)*." [1]

Much reviewing and heavy business followed at Königsberg;
— gift of Trakehnen, and departure of the Crown-Prince for
Trakehnen, winding it up. Directly on the heel of which, his
Majesty turned homewards, the Crown-Prince not to meet him
till once at Berlin again. Majesty's first stage was at Pillau,
where we have been. At Pillau, or next day at Dantzig, Pöllnitz observed a change in his Majesty's humor, which had been
quite sunshiny all this journey hitherto. At Dantzig Pöllnitz
first noticed it; but at every new stage it grew worse, evil
accidents occurring to worsen it; and at Berlin it was worst
of all; — and, alas, his poor Majesty never recovered his sunshine in this world again ! Here is Pöllnitz's account of the
journey homewards: —

" Till now," till Pillau and Dantzig, " his Majesty had been
in especially good humor; but in Dantzig his cheerfulness for

---

[1] " Königsberg, 30th July, 1739," to his Wife (*Œuvres*, xxvi. 6).

sook him; — and it never came back. He arrived about ten at night in that City [Wednesday, 12th August, or thereby]; slept there; and was off again next morning at five. He drove only thirty miles this day; stopped in Lupow [coast road through Pommern], with Herr von Grumkow [the late Grumkow's Brother], Kammer President in this Pommern Province. From Lupow he went to a poor Village near Belgard, eighty miles farther;" — last village on the great road, Belgard lying to left a little, on a side road; — "and stayed there overnight.

"At Belgard, next morning, he reviewed the Dragoon Regiment von Platen; and was very ill content with it. And nobody, with the least understanding of that business, but must own that never did Prussian Regiment manœuvre worse. Conscious themselves how bad it was, they lost head, and got into open confusion. The King did all that was possible to help them into order again. He withdrew thrice over, to give the Officers time to recover themselves; but it was all in vain. The King, contrary to wont, restrained himself amazingly, and would not show his displeasure in public. He got into his carriage, and drove away with the Fürst of Anhalt," Old Dessauer, "and Von Winterfeld," Captain in the Giant Regiment, "who is now Major-General von Winterfeld;[1] not staying to dine with General von Platen, as was always his custom with Commandants whom he had reviewed. He bade Prince Wilhelm and the rest of us stay and dine; he himself drove away," — towards the great road again, and some uncertain lodging there.

"We stayed accordingly; and did full justice to the good cheer," — though poor Platen would certainly look flustered, one may fancy. "But as the Prince was anxious to come up with his Majesty again, and knew not where he would meet him, we had to be very swift with the business.

"We found the King with Anhalt and Winterfeld, by and by; sitting in a village, in front of a barn, and eating a cold pie there, which the Fürst of Anhalt had chanced to have with him; his Majesty, owing to what he had seen on the parade-

---

[1] Major-General since 1743, of high fame; fell in fight, 7th September, 1757.

ground, was in the utmost ill-humor (*höchst übler Laune*). Next day, Saturday, he went a hundred and fifty or two hundred miles ; and arrived in Berlin at ten at night. Not expected there till the morrow ; so that his rooms were locked, — her Majesty being over in Monbijou, giving her children a Ball; "[1] — and we can fancy what a frame of mind there was !

Nobody, not at first even the Doctors, much heeded this new fit of illness ; which went and came : " changed temper," deeper or less deep gloom of " bad humor," being the main phenomenon to by-standers. But the sad truth was, his Majesty never did recover his sunshine ; from Pillau onwards he was slowly entering into the shadows of the total Last Eclipse ; and his journeyings and reviewings in this world were all done. Ten months hence, Pöllnitz and others knew better what it had been ! —

CHAPTER VII.

LAST YEAR OF REINSBERG : TRANSIT OF BALTIMORE AND OTHER PERSONS AND THINGS.

FRIEDRICH had not been long home again from Trakehnen and Preussen, when the routine of things at Reinsberg was illuminated by Visitors, of brilliant and learned quality ; some of whom, a certain Signor Algarotti for one, require passing mention here. Algarotti, who became a permanent friend or satellite, very luminous to the Prince, and was much about him in coming years, first shone out upon the scene at this time, — coming unexpectedly, and from the Eastward as it chanced.

On his own score, Algarotti has become a wearisome literary man to modern readers : one of those half-remembered men ; whose books seem to claim a reading, and do not repay it you when given. Treatises, of a serious nature, *On the Opera ;* setting forth, in earnest, the potential " moral uses " of

[1] Pöllnitz, ii. 534–537.

the Opera, and dedicated to Chatham; *Neutonianismo per le Donne* (Astronomy for Ladies): the mere Titles of such things are fatally sufficient to us; and we cannot, without effort, nor with it, recall the brilliancy of Algarotti and them to his contemporary world.

Algarotti was a rich Venetian Merchant's Son, precisely about the Crown-Prince's age; shone greatly in his studies at Bologna and elsewhere; had written Poesies (*Rime*); written especially that *Newtonianism for the Dames* (equal to Fontenelle, said Fame, and orthodox Newtonian withal, not heterodox or Cartesian); and had shone, respected, at Paris, on the strength of it, for three or four years past: friend of Voltaire in consequence, of Voltaire and his divine Emilie, and a welcome guest at Cirey; friend of the cultivated world generally, which was then laboring, divine Emilie in the van of it, to understand Newton and be orthodox in this department of things. Algarotti did fine Poesies, too, once and again; did Classical Scholarships, and much else: everywhere a clearheaded, methodically distinct, concise kind of man. A high style of breeding about him, too; had powers of pleasing, and used them: a man beautifully lucent in society, gentle yet impregnable there; keeping himself unspotted from the world and its discrepancies, — really with considerable prudence, first and last.

He is somewhat of the Bielfeld type; a Merchant's Son, we observe, like Bielfeld; but a Venetian Merchant's, not a Hamburg's; and also of better natural stuff than Bielfeld. Concentrated himself upon his task with more seriousness, and made a higher thing of it than Bielfeld; though, after all, it was the same task the two had. Alas, our "Swan of Padua" (so they sometimes called him) only sailed, paddling grandly, no-whither, — as the Swan-Goose of the Elbe did, in a less stately manner! One cannot well bear to read his Books. There is no light upon Friedrich to tempt us; better light than Bielfeld's there could have been, and much of it: but he prudently, as well as proudly, forbore such topics. He approaches very near fertility and geniality in his writings, but never reaches it. Dilettantism become serious and strenuous, in those departments — Well, it was beautiful to young Friedrich and the world at that time, though it is not to us ! — Young Algarotti, twenty-seven this year, has been touring about as a celebrity these four years past, on the strength of his fine manners and *Newtonianism for the Dames.*

It was under escort of Baltimore, " an English Milord," recommended from Potsdam itself, that Algarotti came to Reinsberg; the Signor had much to do with English people now and after. Where Baltimore first picked him up, I know not : but they have been to Russia together; Baltimore by twelve years the elder of the two : and now, getting home towards England again, they call at Reinsberg in the fine Autumn weather; — and considerably captivate the Crown-Prince, Baltimore playing chief, in that as in other points. The visit lasted five days :[1] there was copious speech on many things; — discussion about Printing of the *Anti-Machiavel ;* Algarotti to get it printed in England, Algarotti to get Pine and his Engraved *Henriade* put under way; neither of which projects took effect; — readers can conceive what a charming five days these were. Here, in the Crown-Prince's own words, are some brief glimmerings which will suffice us : —

Reinsberg, 25th Sept. 1739 (Crown-Prince to Papa). . . . that "nothing new has occurred in the Regiment, and we have few sick. Here has the English Milord, who was at Potsdam, passing through [stayed five days, though we call it passing, and suppress the Algarotti, Baltimore being indeed chief]. He is gone towards Hamburg, to take ship for England there. As I heard that my Most All-gracious Father wished I should show him courtesy, I have done for him what I could. The Prince of Mirow has also been here," — our old Strelitz friend. Of Baltimore nothing more to Papa. But to another Correspondent, to the good Suhm (who is now at Petersburg, and much in our intimacy, ready to transact loans for us, translate Wolf, or do what is wanted), there is this passage next day : —

Reinsberg, 26th September, 1739 (to Suhm). " We have had Milord Baltimore here, and the young Algarotti ; both of them

[1] 20th-25th September, 1739 (*Œuvres de Frédéric,* xiv. p. xiv).

men who, by their accomplishments, cannot but conciliate the esteem and consideration of all who see them. We talked much of you [Suhm], of Philosophy, of Science, Art; in short, of all that can be included in the taste of cultivated people (*honnêtes gens*)." [1] And again to another, about two weeks hence : —

Reinsberg, 10th October, 1739 (to Voltaire). "We have had Milord Baltimore and Algarotti here, who are going back to England. This Milord is a very sensible man (*homme très-sensé*); who possesses a great deal of knowledge, and thinks, like us, that sciences can be no disparagement to nobility, nor degrade an illustrious rank. I admired the genius of this *Anglais,* as one does a fine face through a crape veil. He speaks French very ill, yet one likes to hear him speak it; and as for his English, he pronounces it so quick, there is no possibility of following him. He calls a Russian ' a mechanical animal.' He says ' Petersburg is the eye of Russia, with which it keeps civilized countries in sight; if you took this eye from it, Russia would fall again into barbarism, out of which it is just struggling.' [2] . . . Young Algarotti, whom you know, pleased me beyond measure. He promised that he " — But Baltimore, promise or not, is the chief figure at present.

Evidently an original kind of figure to us, *cet Anglais.* And indeed there is already finished a rhymed *Epistle* to Baltimore ; *Epître sur la Liberté* (copy goes in that same *Letter,* for Voltaire's behoof), which dates itself likewise October 10th ; beginning, —

> " *L'esprit libre, Milord, qui règne en Angleterre,*"

which, though it is full of fine sincere sentiments, about human dignity, papal superstition, Newton, Locke, and aspirations for progress of culture in Prussia, no reader could stand at this epoch.

What Baltimore said in answer to the *Epître,* we do not know ; probably not much : it does not appear he ever saw or spoke to Friedrich a second time. Three weeks after, Friedrich writing to Algarotti, has these words : " I pray you make

[1] *Œuvres de Frédéric,* xvi. 378.   [2] Ib. xxi. 326, 327.

my friendships to Milord Baltimore, whose character and
manner of thinking I truly esteem. I hope he has, by this
time, got my *Epître* on the English Liberty of Thought." [1]
And so Baltimore passes on, silent in History henceforth, —
though Friedrich seems to have remembered him to late times,
as a kind of type-figure when England came into his head.
For the sake of this small transit over the sun's disk, I have
made some inquiry about Baltimore; but found very little; —
perhaps enough: —

"He was Charles, Sixth Lord Baltimore, it appears; Sixth,
and last but one. First of the Baltimores, we know, was
Secretary Calvert (1618–1624), who colonized Maryland; last
of them (1774) was the Son of this Charles; something of a
fool, to judge by the face of him in Portraits, and by some of
his doings in the world. He, that Seventh Baltimore, printed
one or two little Volumes ('now of extreme rarity,' — cannot
be too rare); and winded up by standing an ugly Trial at
Kingston Assizes (plaintiff an unfortunate female). After
which he retired to Naples, and there ended, 1774, the last of
these Milords. [2]

"He of the Kingston Assizes, we say, was not this Charles;
but his Son, whom let the reader forget. Charles, age forty
at this time, had travelled about the Continent a good deal:
once, long ago, we imagined we had got a glimpse of him (but
it was a guess merely) lounging about Lunéville and Lorraine,
along with Lyttelton, in the Congress-of-Soissons time? Not
long after that, it is certain enough, he got appointed a Gentleman of the Bedchamber to Prince Fred; who was a friend of
speculative talkers and cultivated people. In which situation
Charles Sixth Baron Baltimore continued all his days after;
and might have risen by means of Fred, as he was anxious
enough to do, had both of them lived; but they both died;
Baltimore first, in 1751, a year before Fred. Bubb Dodding-
ton, diligent laborer in the same Fred vineyard, was much infested by this Baltimore, — who, drunk or sober (for he occa-

---

[1] 29th October 1739, To Algarotti in London (*Œuvres*, xviii. 5).

[2] Walpole (by Park), *Catalogue of Royal and Noble Authors* (London, 1806),
v. 278.

sionally gets into liquor), is always putting out Bubb, and
stands too well with our Royal Master, one secretly fears!
Baltimore's finances, I can guess, were not in too good order;
mostly an Absentee; Irish Estates not managed in the first
style, while one is busy in the Fred vineyard! 'The best and
honestest man in the world, with a good deal of jumbled
knowledge,' Walpole calls him once: 'but not capable of conducting a party.'"[1]   Oh no; — and died, at any rate, Spring
1751:[2] and we will not mention him farther.

Bielfeld, what he saw at Reinsberg and around.

Directly on the rear of these fine visitors, came, by invitation, a pair of the Korn's-Hôtel people; Masonic friends; one
of whom was Bielfeld, whose dainty Installation Speech and
ways of procedure had been of promise to the Prince on that
occasion. "Baron von Oberg" was the other: — Hanoverian
Baron: the same who went into the Wars, and was a "General von Oberg" twenty years hence? The same or another,
it does not much concern us. Nor does the visit much, or at
all; except that Bielfeld, being of writing nature, professes
to give ocular account of it. Honest transcript of what a
human creature actually saw at Reinsberg, and in the Berlin
environment at that date, would have had a value to mankind:
but Bielfeld has adopted the fictitious form; and pretty much
ruined for us any transcript there is. Exaggeration, gesticu-
lation, fantastic uncertainty afflict the reader; and prevent
comfortable belief, except where there is other evidence than
Bielfeld's.

At Berlin the beautiful straight streets, Linden Avenues
(perhaps a better sample than those of our day), were notable
to Bielfeld; bridges, statues very fine; grand esplanades, and
such military drilling and parading as was never seen. He
had dinner-invitations, too, in quantity; likes this one and
that (all in prudent asterisks), — likes Truchsess von Waldburg

---

[1] Walpole's *Letters to Mann* (London, 1843), ii. 175: 27th January, 1747.
See ib. i. 82.

[2] *Peerage of Ireland* (London, 1768), ii. 172-174.

very much, and his strange mode of bachelor housekeeping,
and the way he dines and talks among his fellow-creatures,
or sits studious among his Military Books and Paper-litters.
But all is loose far-off sketching, in the style of *Anacharsis the
Younger ;* and makes no solid impression.

Getting to Reinsberg, to the Town, to the Schloss, he crosses
the esplanade, the moat ; sees what we know, beautiful square
Mansion among its woods and waters ; — and almost nothing
that we do not know, except the way the moat-bridge is
lighted : "Bridge furnished," he says, "with seven Statues
representing the seven Planets, each holding in her hand a
glass lamp in the form of a globe ; " — which is a pretty object
in the night-time. The House is now finished ; Knobelsdorf
rejoicing in his success ; Pesne and others giving the last
touch to some ceilings of a sublime nature. On the lintel of
the gate is inscribed *Frederico Tranquillitatem Colenti* (To
Friedrich courting Tranquillity). The gardens, walks, hermitages, grottos, are very spacious, fine : not yet completed, —
perhaps will never be. A Temple of Bacchus is just now on
hand, somewhere in those labyrinthic woods : "twelve gigantic
Satyrs as caryatides, crowned by an inverted Punch-bowl for
dome ; " that is the ingenious Knobelsdorf's idea, pleasant
to the mind. Knobelsdorf is of austere aspect ; austere, yet
benevolent and full of honest sagacity ; the very picture of
sound sense, thinks Bielfeld. M. Jordan is handsome, though
of small stature ; agreeable expression of face ; eye extremely
vivid ; brown complexion, bushy eyebrows as well as beard are
black.[1]

Or did the reader ever hear of "M. Fredersdorf," Head
Valet at this time ? Fredersdorf will become, as it were,
Privy-Purse, House-Friend, and domestic Factotum, and play
a great part in coming years. "A tall handsome man ; " much
"silent sense, civility, dexterity ; " something "magnificently
clever in him," thinks Bielfeld (now, or else twenty years
afterwards) ; whom we can believe.[2] He was a gift from General Schwerin, this Fredersdorf ; once a Private in Schwerin's
regiment, at Frankfurt-on-Oder, — excellent on the flute, for

---

[1] Bielfeld (abridged), i. 45.   [2] Ib. p. 49.

one quality. Schwerin, who had an eye for men, sent him
to Friedrich, in the Cüstrin time; hoping he might suit in
fluting and otherwise. Which he conspicuously did. Bielfeld's account, we must candidly say, appears to be an afterthought; but readers can make their profit of it, all the
same.

As to the Crown-Prince and Princess, words fail to express
their gracious perfections, their affabilities, polite ingenui-
ties: — Bielfeld's words do give us some pleasant shadowy
conceivability of the Crown-Princess: —

"Tall, and perfect in shape; bust such as a sculptor might
copy; complexion of the finest; features ditto; nose, I confess, smallish and pointed, but excellent of that kind; hair of
the supremest flaxen, 'shining' like a flood of sunbeams, when
the powder is off it. A humane ingenuous Princess; little
negligences in toilet or the like, if such occur, even these set
her off, so ingenuous are they. Speaks little; but always to
the purpose, in a simple, cheerful and wise way. Dances
beautifully; heart (her soubrette assures me) is heavenly; —
and 'perhaps no Princess living has a finer set of diamonds.'"

Of the Crown-Princess there is some pleasant shadow traced
as on cobweb, to this effect. But of the Crown-Prince there
is no forming the least conception from what he says: — this
is mere cobweb with Nothing elaborately painted on it. Nor
do the portraits of the others attract by their verisimilitude.
Here is Colonel Keyserling, for instance; the witty Courlander, famous enough in the Friedrich circle; who went on
embassy to Cirey, and much else: he "whirls in with uproar
(*fracas*) like Boreas in the Ballet;" fowling-piece on shoulder,
and in his "dressing-gown" withal, which is still stranger;
snatches off Bielfeld, unknown till that moment, to sit by him
while dressing; and there, with much capering, pirouetting,
and indeed almost ground-and-lofty tumbling, for accompaniment, "talks of Horses, Mathematics, Painting, Architecture,
Literature, and the Art of War," while he dresses. This gentleman was once Colonel in Friedrich Wilhelm's Army; is
now fairly turned of forty, and has been in troubles: we hope

he is not *like* in the Bielfeld Portrait; — otherwise, how happy
that we never had the honor of knowing him! Indeed, the
Crown-Prince's Household generally, as Bielfeld paints it in
flourishes of panegyric, is but unattractive; barren to the
modern on-looker; partly the Painter's blame, we doubt not.
He gives details about their mode of dining, taking coffee,
doing concert; — and describes once an incidental drinking-
bout got up aforethought by the Prince; which is probably in
good part fiction, though not ill done. These fantastic sketch-
ings, rigorously winnowed into the credible and actual, leave
no great residue in that kind; but what little they do leave
is of favorable and pleasant nature.

Bielfeld made a visit privately to Potsdam, too: saw the
Giants drill; made acquaintance with important Captains of
theirs (all in *asterisks*) at Potsdam; with whom he dined, not
in a too credible manner, and even danced. Among the asterisks, we easily pick out Captain Wartensleben (of the Korn's-
Hôtel operation), and Winterfeld, a still more important Captain, whom we saw dining on cold pie with his Majesty, at
a barn-door in Pommern, not long since. Of the Giants, or
their life at Potsdam, Bielfeld's word is not worth hearing, —
worth suppressing rather; his knowledge being so small, and
hung forth in so fantastic a way. This transient sight he had
of his Majesty in person; this, which is worth something to
us, — fact being evidently lodged in it. "After church-
parade," Autumn Sunday afternoon (day uncertain, Bielfeld's
date being fictitious, and even impossible), Majesty drove out
to Wusterhausen, "where the quantities of game surpass all
belief;" and Bielfeld had one glimpse of him : —

"I saw his Majesty only, as it were, in passing. If I may
judge by his Portraits, he must have been of a perfect beauty
in his young time; but it must be confessed there is nothing
left of it now. His eyes truly are fine; but the glance of
them is terrible: his complexion is composed of the strongest
tints of red, blue, yellow, green," — not a lovely complexion
at all; "big head; the thick neck sunk between the shoulders; figure short and heavy (*courte et ramassée*)."[1]

---

[1] Bielfeld, p. 35.

"Going out to Wusterhausen," then, that afternoon, "October, 1739." How his Majesty is crushed down; quite bulged out of shape in that sad way, by the weight of time and its pressures: his thoughts, too, most likely, of a heavy-laden and abstruse nature! The old Pfalz Controversy has misgone with him: Pfalz, and so much else in the world; — the world in whole, probably enough, near ending to him; the final shadows, sombre, grand and mournful, closing in upon him!

Turk War ends; Spanish War begins. A Wedding in Petersburg.

Last news come to Potsdam in these days is, The Kaiser has ended his disastrous Turk War; been obliged to end it; sudden downbreak, and as it were panic terror, having at last come upon his unfortunate Generals in those parts. Duke Franz was passionate to be out of such a thing; Franz, General Neipperg and others; and now, "2d September, 1739," like lodgers leaping from a burning house, they are out of it. The Turk gets Belgrade itself, not to mention wide territories farther east, — Belgrade without shot fired; — nay the Turk was hardly to be kept from hanging the Imperial Messenger (a General Neipperg, Duke Franz's old Tutor, and chief Confidant, whom we shall hear more of elsewhere), whose passport was not quite right on this occasion! — Never was a more disgraceful Peace. But also never had been worse fighting; planless, changeful, powerless, melting into futility at every step: — not to be mended by imprisonments in Grätz, and still harsher treatment of individuals. "Has all success forsaken me, then, since Eugene died?" said the Kaiser; and snatched at this Turk Peace; glad to have it, by mediation of France, and on any terms.

Has not this Kaiser lost his outlying properties at a fearful rate? Naples is gone; Spanish Bourbon sits in our Naples; comparatively little left for us in Italy. And now the very Turk has beaten us small; insolently fillips the Imperial nose of us, — threatening to hang our Neipperg, and the like. Were it not for Anne of Russia, whose big horse-

whip falls heavy on this Turk, he might almost get to Vienna
again, for anything we could do! A Kaiser worthy to be
pitied; — whom Friedrich Wilhelm, we perceive, does honestly
pity. A Kaiser much beggared, much disgraced, in late years;
who has played a huge life-game so long, diplomatizing, war-
ring; and, except the Shadow of Pragmatic Sanction, has
nothing to retire upon.

The Russians protested, with astonishment, against such
Turk Peace on the Kaiser's part. But there was no help for
it. One ally is gone, the Kaiser has let go this Western skirt
of the Turk; and "Thamas Kouli Khan" (called also Nadir
Shah, famed Oriental slasher and slayer of that time) no
longer stands upon the Eastern skirt, but "has entered India,"
it appears: the Russians — their cash, too, running low —
do themselves make peace, "about a month after;" restoring
Azoph and nearly all their conquests; putting off the ruin of
the Turk till a better time.

War is over in the East, then; but another in the West,
England against Spain (Spain and France to help), is about
beginning. Readers remember how Jenkins's Ear re-emerged,
Spring gone a year, in a blazing condition? Here, through
Sylvanus Urban himself, are two direct glimpses, a twelvemonth nearer hand, which show us how the matter has been
proceeding since: —

"*London, 19th February,* 1739. The City Authorities," —
laying or going to lay "the foundation of the Mansion-House"
(Edifice now very black in our time), and doing other things
of little moment to us, "had a Masquerade at the Guildhall
this night. There was a very splendid appearance at the
Masquerade; but among the many humorous and whimsical
characters, what seemed most to engage attention was a Span-
iard, who called himself 'Knight of the Ear;' as Badge of
which Order he wore on his breast the form of a Star, with its
points tinged in blood; and on the body of it an Ear painted,
and in capital letters the word JENKINS encircling it. Across
his shoulder there hung, instead of ribbon, a large Halter;
which he held up to several persons dressed as English Sailors,

who seemed in great terror of him, and falling on their knees
suffered him to rummage their pockets; which done, he would
insolently dismiss them with strokes of his halter. Several of
the Sailors had a bloody Ear hanging down from their heads;
and on their hats were these words, *Ear for Ear;* on others,
No Search or no Trade; with the like sentences." [1] The conflagration evidently going on; not likely to be damped down
again, by ministerial art! —

"*London, 19th March,* 1739." Grand Debate in Parliament,
on the late "Spanish Convention," pretended Bargain of re-
dress lately got from Spain: Approve the Convention, or Not
approve? "A hundred Members were in the House of Commons before seven, this morning; and four hundred had taken
their seat by ten; which is an unheard-of thing. Prince of
Wales," Fred in person, "was in the gallery till twelve at
night, and had his dinner sent to him. Sir Robert Walpole
rose: 'Sir, the great pains that have been taken to influence
all ranks and degrees of men in this Nation — . . . But give
me leave to'" — apply a wet cloth to Honorable Gentlemen.
Which he does, really with skill and sense. France and the
others are so strong, he urges; England so unprepared;
Kaiser at such a pass; 'War like to be, about the Palati-
nate Dispute [our friend Friedrich Wilhelm's]: Where is
England to get allies?' — and hours long of the like sort. A
judicious wet cloth; which proved unavailing.

For "William Pitts" (so they spell the great Chatham that
is to be) was eloquent on the other side: "Despairing Merchants," "Voice of England," and so on. And the world was
all in an inflamed state. And Mr. Pulteney exclaimed: Palat-
inate? Allies? "We need no allies; the case of Mr. Jenkins will raise us volunteers everywhere!" And in short, —
after eight months more of haggling, and applying wet cloths,
— Walpole, in the name of England, has to declare War
against Spain; [2] the public humor proving unquenchable on

---

[1] *Gentleman's Magazine* for 1739, p. 103; — our *dates,* as always, are N. S.
[2] "3d November (23d October), 1739."

that matter. War; and no Peace to be, "till our undoubted right," to roadway on the oceans of this Planet, become permanently manifest to the Spanish Majesty.

Such the effect of a small Ear, kept about one in cotton, from ursine piety or other feelings. Has not Jenkins's Ear re-emerged, with a vengeance? It has kindled a War: dangerous for kindling other Wars, and setting the whole world on fire, — as will be too evident in the sequel! The *Ear of Jenkins* is a singular thing. Might have mounted to be a constellation, like *Berenice's Hair,* and other small facts become mythical, had the English People been of poetic turn! Enough of *it,* for the time being. —

This Summer, Anton Ulrich, at Petersburg, did wed his Serene Mecklenburg Princess, Heiress of all the Russias: "July 14th, 1739," — three months before that Drive to Wusterhausen, which we saw lately. Little Anton Ulrich, Cadet of Brunswick; our Friedrich's Brother-in-Law; — a noticeably small man in comparison to such bulk of destiny, thinks Friedrich, though the case is not without example![1]

" Anton Ulrich is now five-and-twenty," says one of my Notebooks; " a young gentleman of small stature, shining courage in battle, but somewhat shy and bashful; who has had his troubles in Petersburg society, till the trial came, — and will have. Here are the stages of Anton Ulrich's felicity: —

" *Winter,* 1732–1733. He was sent for to Petersburg (his Serene Aunt the German Kaiserinn, and Kaiser Karl's diplomatists, suggesting it there), with the view of his paying court to the young Mecklenburg Princess, Heiress of all the Russias, of whom we have often heard. February, 1733, he arrived on this errand; — not approved of at all by the Mecklenburg Princess, by Czarina Anne or anybody there: what can be done with such an uncomfortable little creature? They gave him the Colonelcy of Cuirassiers: ' Drill there, and endure.'

[1] A Letter of his to Suhm; touching on Franz of Lorraine and this Anton Ulrich.

" *Spring*, 1737. Much-enduring, diligently drilling, for four years past, he went this year to the Turk War under Mün-nich; — much pleased Münnich, at Oczakow and elsewhere; who reports in the War-Office high things of him. And on the whole, — the serene Vienna people now again bestirring themselves, with whom we are in copartnery in this Turk business, — little Anton Ulrich is encouraged to proceed. Proceeds; formally demands his Mecklenburg Princess; and,

" *July 14th*, 1739, weds her; the happiest little man in all the Russias, and with the biggest destiny, if it prosper. Next year, too, there came a son and heir; whom they called Iwan, in honor of his Russian Great-grandfather. Shall we add the subsequent felicities of Anton Ulrich here; or wait till another opportunity? "

Better wait. This is all, and more than all, his Prussian Majesty, rolling out of Wusterhausen that afternoon, ever knew of them, or needed to know! —

CHAPTER VIII.

DEATH OF FRIEDRICH WILHELM.

At Wusterhausen, this Autumn, there is game as usual, but little or no hunting for the King. He has to sit drearily within doors, for most part; listening to the rustle of falling leaves, to dim Winter coming with its rains and winds. Field-sports are a rumor from without: for him now no joyous sow-baiting, deer-chasing; — that, like other things, is past.

In the beginning of November, he came to Berlin; was worse there, and again was better; — strove to do the Carnival, as had been customary; but, in a languid, lamed manner. One night he looked in upon an evening-party which General Schulenburg was giving: he returned home, chilled, shiver-ing; could not, all night, be brought to heat again. It was the

last evening-party Friedrich Wilhelm ever went to.[1] Lieutenant-General Schulenburg: the same who doomed young
Friedrich to death, as President of the Court-Martial; and
then wrote the Three Letters about him which we once looked
into : illuminates himself in this manner in Berlin society, —
Carnival season, 1740, weather fiercely cold. Maypole Schulenburg the lean Aunt, Ex-Mistress of George I., over in London, — I think she must now be dead ? Or if not dead, why
not! Memory, for the tenth time, fails me, of the humanly
unmemorable, whom perhaps even flunkies should forget;
and I will try it no more. The stalwart Lieutenant-General
will reappear on us once, twice at the utmost, and never
again. He gave the last evening-party Friedrich Wilhelm
ever went to.

Poor Friedrich Wilhelm is in truth very ill; tosses about
all day, in and out of bed, — bed and wheeled-chair drearily
alternating; suffers much ; — and again, in Diplomatic circles,
the rumors are rife and sinister. Ever from this chill at
Schulenburg's the medicines did him no good, says Pöllnitz:
if he rallied, it was the effect of Nature, and only temporary.
He does daily, with punctuality, his Official business ; perhaps
the best two hours he has of the four-and-twenty, for the time
hangs heavy on him. His old Generals sit round his bed, talking, smoking, as it was five years ago; his Feekin and his
Children much about him, out and in : the heavy-laden, weary
hours roll round as they can. In general there is a kind of
constant Tabaks-Collegium, old Flans, Camas, Hacke, Pöllnitz,
Derschau, and the rest by turns always there ; the royal
Patient cannot be left alone, without faces he likes: other
Generals, estimable in their way, have a physiognomy displeas-
ing to the sick man ; and will smart for it if they enter, —
"At sight of *him* every pain grows painfuler!" — the poor
King being of poetic temperament, as we often say. Friends
are encouraged to smoke, especially to keep up a stream of
talk; if at any time he fall into a doze and they cease talk-
ing, the silence will awaken him.

He is worst off in the night; sleep very bad: and among

[1] Pöllnitz (ii. 538) ; who gives no date.

his sore bodily pains, ennui falls very heavy to a mind so restless. He can paint, he can whittle, chisel: at last they even
mount him a table, in his bed, with joiner's tools, mallets,
glue-pots, where he makes small carpentry, — the talk to go on
the while; — often at night is the sound of his mallet audible
in the Palace Esplanade; and Berlin townsfolk pause to listen,
with many thoughts of a sympathetic or at least inarticulate
character: "*Hm, Weh, Ihro Majestät: ach Gott,* pale Death
knocks with impartial foot at the huts of poor men and the
Palaces of Kings!"[1] Reverend Herr Roloff, whom they call
Provost (*Probst,* Chief Clergyman) Roloff, a pious honest man
and preacher, he, I could guess, has already been giving spiritual counsel now and then; later interviews with Roloff are
expressly on record: for it is the King's private thought,
ever and anon borne in upon him, that death itself is in this
business.

Queen and Children, mostly hoping hitherto, though fearing too, live in much anxiety and agitation. The Crown-
Prince is often over from Reinsberg; must not come too
often, nor even inquire too much: his affectionate solicitude
might be mistaken for solicitude of another kind! It is
certain he is in no haste to be King; to quit the haunts of
the Muses, and embark on Kingship. Certain, too, he loves
his Father; shudders at the thought of losing *him.* And yet
again there will gleams intrude of a contrary thought; which
the filial heart disowns, with a kind of horror, "Down, thou
impious thought!" — We perceive he manages in general to
push the crisis away from him; to believe that real danger
is still distant. His demeanor, so far as we can gather from
his Letters or other evidence, is amiable, prudent, natural;
altogether that of a human Son in those difficult circumstances.
Poor Papa is heavy-laden: let us help to bear his burdens; —
let us hope the crisis is still far off! —

Once, on a favorable evening, probably about the beginning
of April, when he felt as if improving, Friedrich Wilhelm
resolved to dress, and hold Tobacco-Parliament again in a
formal manner. Let us look in there, through the eyes

[1] Pöllnitz, ii. 539.

of Pöllnitz, who was of it, upon the last Tobacco-Parliament : —

"A numerous party; Schwerin, Hacke, Derschau, all the chiefs and commandants of the Berlin Garrison are there; the old circle full; social human speech once more, and pipes alight; pleasant to the King. He does not himself smoke on this occasion; but he is unusually lively in talk; much enjoys the returning glimpse of old days; and the Tobacco circle was proceeding through its phases, successful beyond common. All at once the Crown-Prince steps in; direct from Reinsberg : [1] an unexpected pleasure. At sight of whom the Tobacco circle, taken on the sudden, simultaneously started up, and made him a bow. Rule is, in Tobacco-Parliament you do not rise for anybody; and they have risen. Which struck the sick heart in a strange painful way. 'Hm, the Rising Sun ?' thinks he; 'Rules broken through, for the Rising Sun. But I am not dead yet, as you shall know!' ringing for his servants in great wrath; and had himself rolled out, regardless of protestations and excuses. 'Hither, you Hacke!' said he.

"Hacke followed; but it was only to return on the instant, with the King's order, 'That you instantly quit the Palace, all of you, and don't come back!' Solemn respectful message to his Majesty was of no effect, or of less; they had to go, on those terms; and Pöllnitz, making for his Majesty's apartment next morning as usual, was twitched by a Gens-d'arme, 'No admittance!' And it was days before the matter would come round again, under earnest protestations from the one side, and truculent rebukes from the other." [2] Figure the Crown-Prince, figure the poor sick Majesty; and what a time in those localities !

With the bright spring weather he seemed to revive; towards the end of April he resolved for Potsdam, everybody thinking him much better, and the outer Public reckoning the crisis of the illness over. He himself knew other. It was on the 27th of the month that he went; he said, "Fare thee

---

[1] 12th April, 1740 ? (*Œuvres*, xxvii. part 1st, p. 29); Pöllnitz is dateless.
[2] Pöllnitz (abridged), ii. 540.

well, then, Berlin; I am to die in Potsdam, then (*ich werde in Potsdam sterben*) ! " The May-flowers came late; the weather was changeful, ungenial for the sick man: this winter of 1740 had been the coldest on record; it extended itself into the very summer; and brought great distress of every kind; — of which some oral rumor still survives in all countries. Friedrich Wilhelm heard complaints of scarcity among the people; admonitions to open his Corn-granaries (such as he always has in store against that kind of accident); but he still hesitated and refused; unable to look into it himself, and fearing deceptions.

For the rest, he is struggling between death and life; in general persuaded that the end is fast hastening on. He sends for Chief Preacher Roloff out to Potsdam; has some notable dialogues with Roloff, and with two other Potsdam Clergymen, of which there is record still left us. In these, as in all his demeanor at this supreme time, we see the big rugged block of manhood come out very vividly; strong in his simplicity, in his veracity. Friedrich Wilhelm's wish is to know from Roloff what the chances are for him in the other world, — which is not less certain than Potsdam and the giant grenadiers to Friedrich Wilhelm; and where, he perceives, never half so clearly before, he shall actually peel off his Kinghood, and stand before God Almighty, no better than a naked beggar. Roloff's prognostics are not so encouraging as the King had hoped. Surely this King "never took or coveted what was not his; kept true to his marriage-vow, in spite of horrible examples everywhere; believed the Bible, honored the Preachers, went diligently to Church, and tried to do what he understood God's commandments were ? " To all which Roloff, a courageous pious man, answers with discreet words and shak ngs of the head. "Did I behave ill, then; did I ever do injustice ? " Roloff mentions Baron Schlubhut the defalcating Amtmann, hanged at Königsberg without even a trial. "He had no trial; but was there any doubt *he* had justice ? A public thief, confessing he had stolen the taxes he was set to gather; insolently offering, as if that were all, to repay the money, and saying, It was not

Manier (good manners) to hang a nobleman!" Roloff shakes his head, Too violent, your Majesty, and savoring of the tyrannous. The poor King must repent.

"Well, — is there anything more? Out with it, then; better now than too late!" — Much oppression, forcing men to build in Berlin. — "Oppression? was it not their benefit, as well as Berlin's and the Country's? I had no interest in it other. Derschau, you who managed it?" and his Majesty turned to Derschau. For all the smoking generals and company are still here; nor will his Majesty consent to dismiss them from the presence and be alone with Roloff: "What is there to conceal? They are people of honor, and my friends." Derschau, whose feats in the building way are not unknown even to us, answers with a hard face, It was all right and orderly; nothing out of square in his building operations. To which Roloff shakes his head: "A thing of public notoriety, Herr General." — "I will prove everything before a Court," answers the Herr General with still harder face; Roloff still austerely shaking his head. Hm! — And then there is forgiveness of enemies; your Majesty is bound to forgive all men, or how can you ask to be forgiven? "Well, I will, I do; you Feekin, write to your Brother (unforgivablest of beings), after I am dead, that I forgave him, died in peace with him." — Better her Majesty should write at once, suggests Roloff. — "No, after I am dead," persists the Son of Nature, — that will be safer!" [1] An unwedgeable and gnarled big block of manhood and simplicity and sincerity; such as we rarely get sight of among the modern sons of Adam, among the crowned sons nearly never. At parting he said to Roloff, "You (*Er*, He) do not spare me; it is right. You do your duty like an honest Christian man." [2]

---

[1] Wrote accordingly, "not able to finish without many tears;" honest sensible Letter (though indifferently spelt), "Berlin, 1st June, 1740;" — lies now in State-Paper Office: "*Royal Letters*, vol. xciv., Prussia, 1689–1777."

[2] *Notata ex ore Roloffi* ("found among the Seckendorf Papers," no date but "May, 1740"), in Förster, ii. 154, 155; in a fragmentary state: completed in Pöllnitz, ii. 545–549.

Roloff, I perceive, had several Dialogues with the King; and stayed in Potsdam some days for that object. The above bit of jotting is from the Seckendorf Papers (probably picked up by Seckendorf Junior), and is dated only "May." Of the two Potsdam Preachers, one of whom is "Oesfeld, Chaplain of the Giant Grenadiers," and the other is "Cochius, Calvinist Hofprediger," each published on his own score some Notes of dialogue and circumstance;[1] which are to the same effect, so far as they concern us; and exhibit the same rugged Son of Nature, looking with all his eyesight into the near Eternity, and sinking in a human and not inhuman manner amid the floods of Time. "Wa, Wa, what great God is this, that pulls down the strength of the strongest Kings!" —

The poor King's state is very restless, fluctuates from day to day; he is impatient of bed; sleeps very ill; is up whenever possible; rolls about in his wheeled-chair, and even gets into the air: at one time looking strong, as if there were still months in him, and anon sunk in fainting weakness, as if he had few minutes to live. Friedrich at Reinsberg corresponds very secretly with Dr. Eller; has other friends at Potsdam whose secret news he very anxiously reads. To the last he cannot bring himself to think it serious.[2]

On Thursday, 26th of May, an express from Eller, or the Potsdam friends, arrives at Reinsberg: He is to come quickly, if he would see his Father again alive! The step may have danger, too; but Friedrich, a world of feelings urging him, is on the road next morning before the sun. His journey may be fancied; the like of it falls to all men. Arriving at last, turning hastily a corner of the Potsdam Schloss, Friedrich

---

[1] Cochius the *Hofprediger's* (Calvinist Court-Chaplain's) *Account* of his Interviews (first of them "Friday, 27th May, 1740, about 9 P.M."); followed by ditto from Oesfeld (Chaplain of the Giants), who usually accompanied Cochius, — are in Seyfarth, *Geschichte Friedrich des Grossen* (Leipzig, 1783–1788), i. (Beylage) 24–40. Seyfarth was "Regiments-Auditor" in Halle: his Work, solid though stupid, consists nearly altogether of multifarious *Beylagen* (Appendices) and *Notes;* which are creditably accurate, and often curious; and, as usual, have no Index for an unfortunate reader.

[2] Letter to Eller, 25th May, 1740 (*Œuvres*), xvi. 184.

sees some gathering in the distance: it is his Father in his *rollwagen* (wheeled-chair), — not dying; but out of doors, giving orders about founding a House, or seeing it done. House for one Philips, a crabbed Englishman he has; whose tongue is none of the best, not even to Majesty itself, but whose merits as a Groom, of English and other Horses, are without parallel in those parts. Without parallel, and deserve a House before we die. Let us see it set agoing, this blessed May-day! Of Philips, who survived deep into Friedrich's time, and uttered rough sayings (in mixed intelligible dialect) when put upon in his grooming, or otherwise disturbed, I could obtain no farther account: the man did not care to be put in History (a very small service to a man); cared to have a house with trim fittings, and to do his grooming well, the fortunate Philips.

At sight of his Son, Friedrich Wilhelm threw out his arms; the Son kneeling sank upon his breast, and they embraced with tears. My Father, my Father; My Son, my Son! It was a scene to make all by-standers and even Philips weep. — Probably the emotion hurt the old King; he had to be taken in again straightway, his show of strength suddenly gone, and bed the only place for him. This same Friday he dictated to one of his Ministers (Boden, who was in close attendance) the Instruction for his Funeral; a rude characteristic Piece, which perhaps the English reader knows. Too long and rude for reprinting here.[1]

He is to be buried in his uniform, the Potsdam Grenadiers his escort; with military decorum, three volleys fired (and take care they be well fired, "*nicht plackeren*"), so many cannon-salvos; — and no fuss or flaunting ceremony: simplicity and decency is what the tenant of that oak coffin wants, as he always did when owner of wider dominions. The coffin, which he has ready and beside him in the Palace this good while, is a stout piece of carpentry, with leather straps and other improvements; he views it from time to time; solaces his truculent imagination with the look of it:

---

[1] Copy of it, in Seyfarth (ubi suprà), i. 19–24. Translated in Mauvillon (ii. 432–437); in &c. &c.

"I shall sleep right well *there*," he would say. The image he has of his Burial, we perceive, is of perfect visuality, equal to what a Defoe could do in imagining. All is seen, settled to the last minuteness : the coffin is to be borne out by so and so, at such and such a door ; this detachment is to fall-in here, that there, in the attitude of "cover arms" (musket inverted under left arm) ; and the band is to play, with all its blacka-moors, *O Haupt voll Blut und Wunden* (O Head, all bleeding wounded) ; a Dirge his Majesty had liked, who knew music, and had a love for it, after his sort. Good Son of Nature : a dumb Poet, as I say always ; most dumb, but real ; the value of him great, and unknown in these babbling times. It was on this same Friday night that Cochius was first sent for ; Cochius, and Oesfeld with him, "about nine o'clock."

For the next three days (Saturday to Monday) when his cough and many sufferings would permit him, Friedrich Wilhelm had long private dialogues with his Son ; instruct-ing him, as was evident, in the mysteries of State ; in what knowledge, as to persons and to things, he reckoned might be usefulest to him. What the lessons were, we know not ; the way of taking them had given pleasure to the old man : he was heard to say, perhaps more than once, when the Generals were called in, and the dialogue interrupted for a while : "Am not I happy to have such a Son to leave behind me !" And the grimly sympathetic Generals testified assent ; endeavored to talk a little, could at least smoke, and look friendly ; till the King gathered strength for continuing his instructions to his Successor. All else was as if settled with him ; this had still remained to do. This once done (finished, Monday night), why not abdicate altogether ; and die dis-engaged, be it in a day or in a month, since that is now the one work left ? Friedrich Wilhelm does so purpose.

His state, now as all along, was fluctuating, uncertain, restless. He was heard murmuring prayers ; he would say sometimes, "Pray for me ; *Betet, betet.*" And more than once, in deep tone : "Lord, enter not into judgment with Thy servant, for in Thy sight shall no man living be jus-tified !" The wild Son of Nature, looking into Life and

Death, into Judgment and Eternity, finds that these things
are very great. This too is a characteristic trait : In a certain German Hymn (*Why fret or murmur, then ?* the title of
it), which they often sang to him, or along with him, as he
much loved it, are these words, "Naked I came into the
world, and naked shall I go," — "No," said he, "always
with vivacity," at this passage; "not quite naked, I shall
have my uniform on : " Let us be exact, since we are at it!
After which the singing proceeded again. "The late Graf
Alexander von Wartenberg" — Captain Wartenberg, whom
we know, and whose opportunities — "was wont to relate
this." [1]

Tuesday, 31st May, "about one in the morning," Cochius
was again sent for. He found the King in very pious mood,
but in great distress, and afraid he might yet have much pain
to suffer. Cochius prayed with him; talked piously. "I can
remember nothing," said the King; "I cannot pray, I have
forgotten all my prayers." — "Prayer is not in words, but
in the thought of the heart," said Cochius; and soothed the
heavy-laden man as he could. "Fare you well," said Friedrich Wilhelm, at length; "most likely we shall not meet again
in this world." Whereat Cochius burst into tears, and withdrew. About four, the King was again out of bed; wished to
see his youngest Boy, who had been ill of measles, but was
doing well : "Poor little Ferdinand, adieu, then, my little
child!" This is the Father of that fine Louis Ferdinand, who
was killed at Jena; concerning whom Berlin, in certain eman-
cipated circles of it, still speaks with regret. He, the Louis
Ferdinand, had fine qualities; but went far a-roving, into radi-
calism, into romantic love, into champagne; and was cut down
on the threshold of Jena, desperately fighting, — perhaps
happily for him.

From little Ferdinand's room Friedrich Wilhelm has himself
rolled into Queen Sophie's. "Feekin, O my Feekin, thou must
rise this day, and help me what thou canst. This day I am
going to die; thou wilt be with me this day!" The good Wife
rises : I know not that it was the first time she had been so

[1] Büsching (in 1786), *Beiträge,* iv. 100.

called; but it did prove the last. Friedrich Wilhelm has decided, as the first thing he will do, to abdicate; and all the Official persons and companions of the sick-room, Pöllnitz among them, not long after sunrise, are called to see it done. Pöllnitz, huddling on his clothes, arrived about five: in a corridor he sees the wheeled-chair and poor sick King; steps aside to let him pass: " 'It is over (*Das ist vollbracht*),' said the King, looking up to me as he passed: he had on his nightcap, and a blue mantle thrown round him." He was wheeled into his anteroom; there let the company assemble: many of them are already there.

The royal stables are visible from this room: Friedrich Wilhelm orders the horses to be ridden out: you old Fürst of Anhalt-Dessau my oldest friend, you Colonel Hacke faithfulest of Adjutant-Generals, take each of you a horse, the best you can pick out: it is my last gift to you. Dessau, in silence, with dumb-show of thanks, points to a horse, any horse: "You have chosen the very worst," said Friedrich Wilhelm: "Take that other, I will warrant him a good one!" The grim old Dessauer thanks in silence; speechless grief is on that stern gunpowder face, and he seems even to be struggling with tears. "Nay, nay, my friend," Friedrich Wilhelm said, "this is a debt we have all to pay."

The Official people, Queen, Friedrich, Minister Boden, Minister Podewils, and even Pöllnitz, being now all present, Friedrich Wilhelm makes his Declaration, at considerable length; old General Bredow repeating it aloud,[1] sentence by sentence, the King's own voice being too weak; so that all may hear: "That he abdicates, gives up wholly, in favor of his good Son Friedrich; that foreign Ambassadors are to be informed; that you are all to be true and loyal to my Son as you were to me"— and what else is needful. To which the judicious Podewils makes answer, "That there must first be a written Deed of his high Transaction executed, which shall be straightway set about; the Deed once executed, signed and sealed, — the high Royal will, in all points, takes effect." Alas, before Podewils has done speaking, the King is like falling into a

[1] Pöllnitz, ii. 561.

faint; does faint, and is carried to bed: too unlikely any Deed
of Abdication will be needed.

Ups and downs there still were; sore fluctuating labor, as
the poor King struggles to his final rest, this morning. He
was at the window again, when the *Wacht-parade* (Grenadiers
on Guard) turned out; he saw them make their evolutions for
the last time.[1] After which, new relapse, new fluctuation. It
was about eleven o'clock, when Cochius was again sent for.
The King lay speechless, seemingly still conscious, in bed;
Cochius prays with fervor, in a loud tone, that the dying King
may hear and join. "Not so loud!" says the King, rallying
a little. He had remembered that it was the season when
his servants got their new liveries; they had been ordered to
appear this day in full new costume: "O vanity! O vanity!"
said Friedrich Wilhelm, at sight of the ornamented plush.
"Pray for me, pray for me; my trust is in the Saviour!" he
often said. His pains, his weakness are great; the cordage of
a most tough heart rending itself piece by piece. At one time,
he called for a mirror: that is certain: — rugged wild man,
son of Nature to the last. The mirror was brought; what he
said at sight of his face is variously reported: "Not so worn
out as I thought," is Pöllnitz's account, and the likeliest; —
though perhaps he said several things, "ugly face," "as good
as dead already;" and continued the inspection for some
moments.[2] A grim, strange thing.

"Feel my pulse, Pitsch," said he, noticing the Surgeon of
his Giants: "tell me how long this will last." — "Alas, not
long," answered Pitsch. — "Say not, alas; but how do you (He)
know?" — "The pulse is gone!" — "Impossible," said he, lifting his arm: "how could I move my fingers so, if the pulse
were gone?" Pitsch looked mournfully steadfast. "Herr
Jesu, to thee I live; Herr Jesu, to thee I die; in life and in
death thou art my gain (*Du bist mein Gewinn*)." These were
the last words Friedrich Wilhelm spoke in this world. He
again fell into a faint. Eller gave a signal to the Crown-Prince
to take the Queen away. Scarcely were they out of the room,
when the faint had deepened into death; and Friedrich Wil-

---

[1] Pauli, viii. 280.   [2] Pöllnitz, ii. 564; Wilhelmina, ii. 321.

helm, at rest from all his labors, slept with the primeval sons of Thor.

No Baresark of them, nor Odin's self, I think, was a bit of truer human stuff; — I confess his value to me, in these sad times, is rare and great. Considering the usual Histrionic, Papin's-Digester, Truculent-Charlatan and other species of "Kings," alone attainable for the sunk flunky populations of an Era given up to Mammon and the worship of its own belly, what would not such a population give for a Friedrich Wilhelm, to guide it on the road *back* from Orcus a little? "Would give," I have written; but alas, it ought to have been "*should* give." What *they* "would" give is too mournfully plain to me, in spite of ballot-boxes: a steady and tremendous truth from the days of Barabbas downwards and upwards! — Tuesday, 31st May, 1740, between one and two o'clock in the afternoon, Friedrich Wilhelm died; age fifty-two, coming 15th August next. Same day, Friedrich his Son was proclaimed at Berlin; quilted heralds, with sound of trumpet and the like, doing what is customary on such occasions.

On Saturday, 4th June, the King's body is laid out in state; all Potsdam at liberty to come and see. He lies there, in his regimentals, in his oaken coffin, on a raised place in the middle of the room; decent mortuary draperies, lamps, garlands, banderols furnishing the room and him: at his feet, on a black-velvet *tabouret* (stool), are the chivalry emblems, helmet, gauntlets, spurs; and on similar stools, at the right hand and the left, lie his military insignia, hat and sash, sword, guidon, and what else is fit. Around, in silence, sit nine veteran military dignitaries; Buddenbrock, Waldau, Derschau, Einsiedel, and five others whom we omit to name. Silent they sit. A grim earnest sight in the shine of the lamplight, as you pass out of the June sun. Many went, all day; looked once again on the face that was to vanish. Precisely at ten at night, the coffin-lid is screwed down: twelve Potsdam Captains take the coffin on their shoulders; four-and-twenty Corporals with wax torches, four-and-twenty Sergeants with inverted halberts lowered; certain Generals on order, and very many following as volunteers; these perform the actual burial, — carry the body to the Garrison Church, where are clergy waiting, which is but a small step off; see it lodged, oak coffin and all, in a marble coffin in the side vault there, which is known to Tourists.[1] It is the end of the week, and the actual burial is done, — hastened forward for reasons we can guess.

Filial piety by no means intends to defraud a loved Father of the Spartan ceremonial contemplated as obsequies by him: very far from it. Filial piety will conform to that with rigor; only adding what musical and other splendors are possible, to testify his love still more. And so, almost three weeks hence, on the 23d of the month, with the aid of Dresden Artists, of Latin Cantatas and other pomps (not inexcusable, though somewhat out of keeping), the due Funeral is done, no Corpse but a Wax Effigy present in it; — and in all points, that of the Potsdam Grenadiers not forgotten, there was rigorous conformity to the Instruction left. In all points, even to the extensive funeral dinner, and drinking of the appointed cask of wine, "the best cask in my cellar." Adieu, O King.

The Potsdam Grenadiers fired their three volleys (not "*plackering*," as I have reason to believe, but well); got their allowance, dinner-liquor, and appointed coin of money: it was the last service required of them in this world. That same night they were dissolved, the whole Four Thousand of them, at a stroke; and ceased to exist as Potsdam Grenadiers. Colonels, Captains, all the Officers known to be of merit, were advanced, at least transferred. Of the common men, a minority, of not inhuman height and of worth otherwise, were formed into a new Regiment on the common terms: the stupid splay-footed eight-feet mass were allowed to stalk off whither they pleased, or vegetate on frugal pensions; Irish Kirkman, and a few others neither knock-kneed nor without head, were appointed *heyducs*, that is, porters to the King's or other Palaces; and did that duty in what was considered an ornamental manner.

[1] Pauli, viii. 281.

Here are still two things capable of being fished up from
the sea of nugatory matter; and meditated on by readers, till
the following Books open.

The last breath of Friedrich Wilhelm having fled, Friedrich
hurried to a private room; sat there all in tears; looking back
through the gulfs of the Past, upon such a Father now rapt
away forever. Sad all, and soft in the moonlight of memory,
— the lost Loved One all in the right as we now see, we all
in the wrong!— This, it appears, was the Son's fixed opinion.
Seven years hence, here is how Friedrich concludes the *History* of his Father, written with a loyal admiration throughout: "We have left under silence the domestic chagrins of
this great Prince: readers must have some indulgence for the
faults of the Children, in consideration of the virtues of such
a Father."[1] All in tears he sits at present, meditating these
sad things.

In a little while the Old Dessauer, about to leave for Dessau,
ventures in to the Crown-Prince, Crown-Prince no longer;
"embraces his knees;" offers, weeping, his condolence, his
congratulation;—hopes withal that his sons and he will be
continued in their old posts, and that he, the Old Dessauer,
"will have the same authority as in the late reign." Friedrich's eyes, at this last clause, flash out tearless, strangely
Olympian. "In your posts I have no thought of making
change: in your posts, yes; — and as to authority, I know of
none there can be but what resides in the King that is sovereign!" Which, as it were, struck the breath out of the Old
Dessauer; and sent him home with a painful miscellany of
feelings, astonishment not wanting among them.

At an after hour, the same night, Friedrich went to Berlin;
met by acclamation enough. He slept there, not without
tumult of dreams, one may fancy; and on awakening next
morning, the first sound he heard was that of the Regiment
Glasenap under his windows, swearing fealty to the new
King. He sprang out of bed in a tempest of emotion; bustled
distractedly to and fro, wildly weeping. Pöllnitz, who came
into the anteroom, found him in this state, "half-dressed,

[1] *Œuvres*, i. 174 (*Mémoires de Brandebourg*: finished about 1747).

with dishevelled hair, in tears, and as if beside himself."
"These huzzaings only tell me what I have lost!" said the
new King. — "*He* was in great suffering," suggested Pöllnitz ;
"he is now at rest." "True, he suffered ; but he was here
with us : and now — !" [1]

[1] Ranke (ii. 46, 47), from certain Fragments, still in manuscript, of Pöllnitz's *Memoiren*.

BOOK XI.

FRIEDRICH TAKES THE REINS IN HAND.

June–December, 1740.

·——·

CHAPTER I.

PHENOMENA OF FRIEDRICH'S ACCESSION.

In Berlin, from Tuesday, 31st May, 1740, day of the late King's death, till the Thursday following, the post was stopped and the gates closed; no estafette can be despatched, though Dickens and all the Ambassadors are busy writing. On the Thursday, Regiments, Officers, principal Officials having sworn, and the new King being fairly in the saddle, estafettes and post-boys shoot forth at the top of their speed; and Rumor, towards every point of the compass, apprises mankind what immense news there is.[1]

A King's Accession is always a hopeful phenomenon to the public; more especially a young King's, who has been talked of for his talents and aspirings, — for his sufferings, were it nothing more, — and whose *Anti-Machiavel* is understood to be in the press. Vaguely everywhere there has a notion gone abroad that this young King will prove considerable. Here at last has a Lover of Philosophy got upon the throne, and great philanthropies and magnanimities are to be expected, think rash editors and idle mankind. Rash editors in England and elsewhere, we observe, are ready to believe that Friedrich has not only disbanded the Potsdam Giants; but means to "reduce

[1] Dickens (in State-Paper Office), 4th June, 1740.

DEATH OF THE OLD KING.

Carlyle, Vol. Two, p. 459.

the Prussian Army one half" or so, for ease (temporary ease,
which we hope will be lasting) of parties concerned; and to
go much upon emancipation, political rose-water, and friendship to humanity, as we now call it.

At his first meeting of Council, they say, he put this question, "Could not the Prussian Army be reduced to 45,000?"
The excellent young man.   To which the Council had answered, "Hardly, your Majesty! The Jülich-and-Berg affair
is so ominous hitherto!" These may be secrets, and dubious
to people out of doors, thinks a wise editor; but one thing
patent to the day was this, surely symbolical enough: On one
of his Majesty's first drives to Potsdam or from it, a thousand
children, — in round numbers a thousand of them, all with the
red string round their necks, and liable to be taken for soldiers,
if needed in the regiment of their Canton, — "a thousand
children met this young King at a turn of his road; and with
shrill unison of wail, sang out: "Oh, deliver us from slavery,"
— from the red threads, your Majesty.   Why should poor we
be liable to suffer hardship for our Country or otherwise, your
Majesty!   Can no one else be got to do it? sang out the thousand children.   And his Majesty assented on the spot, thinks
the rash editor.[1]   "Goose, Madam?" exclaimed a philanthro-
pist projector once, whose scheme of sweeping chimneys by
pulling a live goose down through them was objected to:
"Goose, Madam?   You can take two ducks, then, if you are
so sorry for the goose!" — Rash editors think there is to be
a reign of Astræa Redux in Prussia, by means of this young
King; and forget to ask themselves, as the young King must
by no means do, How far Astræa may be possible, for Prussia
and him?

At home, too, there is prophesying enough, vague hope
enough, which for most part goes wide of the mark.   This
young King, we know, did prove considerable; but not in the
way shaped out for him by the public; — it was in far other
ways!   For no public in the least knows, in such cases: nor
does the man himself know, except gradually and if he strive
to learn.   As to the public, — "Doubtless," says a friend of

[1] *Gentleman's Magazine* (London, 1740), x 318; Newspapers, &c.

mine, "doubtless it was the Atlantic Ocean that carried Columbus to America; lucky for the Atlantic, and for Columbus and us: but the Atlantic did not quite vote that way from the first; nay *its* votes, I believe, were very various at different stages of the matter!" This is a truth which kings and men, not intending to be drift-logs or waste brine obedient to the Moon, are much called to have in mind withal, from perhaps an early stage of their voyage.

Friedrich's actual demeanor in these his first weeks, which is still decipherable if one study well, has in truth a good deal of the brilliant, of the popular-magnanimous; but manifests strong solid quality withal, and a head steadier than might have been expected. For the Berlin world is all in a rather Auroral condition; and Friedrich too is, — the chains suddenly cut loose, and such hopes opened for the young man. He has great things ahead; feels in himself great things, and doubtless exults in the thought of realizing them. Magnanimous enough, popular, hopeful enough, with Voltaire and the highest of the world looking on: — but yet he is wise, too; creditably aware that there are limits, that this is a bargain, and the terms of it inexorable. We discern with pleasure the old veracity of character shining through this giddy new element; that all these fine procedures are at least unaffected, to a singular degree true, and the product of nature, on his part; and that, in short, the complete respect for Fact, which used to be a quality of his, and which is among the highest and also rarest in man, has on no side deserted him at present.

A trace of airy exuberance, of natural exultancy, not quite repressible, on the sudden change to freedom and supreme power from what had gone before: perhaps that also might be legible, if in those opaque bead-rolls which are called Histories of Friedrich anything human could with certainty be read! He flies much about from place to place; now at Potsdam, now at Berlin, at Charlottenburg, Reinsberg; nothing loath to run whither business calls him, and appear in public: the gazetteer world, as we noticed, which has been hitherto a most mute world, breaks out here and there into a kind of husky jubilation over the great things he is daily doing, and rejoices in the pros-

pect of having a Philosopher King; which function the young
man, only twenty-eight gone, cannot but wish to fulfil for the
gazetteers and the world. He is a busy man; and walks boldly
into his grand enterprise of "making men happy," to the admiration of Voltaire and an enlightened public far and near.

Bielfeld speaks of immense concourses of people crowding
about Charlottenburg, to congratulate, to solicit, to &c.; tells
us how he himself had to lodge almost in outhouses, in that
royal village of hope. His emotions at Reinsberg, and everybody's, while Friedrich Wilhelm lay dying, and all stood like
greyhounds on the slip; and with what arrow-swiftness they
shot away when the great news came : all this he has already
described at wearisome length, in his fantastic semi-fabulous
way.[1] Friedrich himself seemed moderately glad to see Bielfeld; received his high-flown congratulations with a benevolent
yet somewhat composed air; and gave him afterwards, in the
course of weeks, an unexpectedly small appointment: To go
to Hanover, under Truchsess von Waldburg, and announce our
Accession. Which is but a simple, mostly formal service; yet
perhaps what Bielfeld is best equal to.

The Britannic Majesty, or at least his Hanover people have
been beforehand with this civility; Baron Münchhausen, no
doubt by orders given for such contingency, had appeared at
Berlin with the due compliment and condolence almost on the
first day of the New Reign; first messenger of all on that
errand; Britannic Majesty evidently in a conciliatory humor,
— having his dangerous Spanish War on hand. Britannic
Majesty in person, shortly after, gets across to Hanover; and
Friedrich despatches Truchsess, with Bielfeld adjoined, to
return the courtesy.

Friedrich does not neglect these points of good manners;
along with which something of substantial may be privately
conjoined. For example, if he had in secret his eye on Jülich
and Berg, could anything be fitter than to ascertain what the
French will think of such an enterprise ? What the French;
and next to them what the English, that is to say, Hanoverians,
who meddle much in affairs of the Reich. For these reasons

[1] Bielfeld, i. 68–77; ib. 81.

and others he likewise, probably with more study than in the Bielfeld case, despatches Colonel Camas to make his compliment at the French Court, and in an expert way take soundings there. Camas, a fat sedate military gentleman, of advanced years, full of observation, experience and sound sense, — "with one arm, which he makes do the work of two, and nobody can notice that the other arm resting in his coat-breast is of cork, so expert is he," — will do in this matter what is feasible; probably not much for the present. He is to call on Voltaire, as he passes, who is in Holland again, at the Hague for some months back; and deliver him " a little cask of Hungary Wine," which probably his Majesty had thought exquisite. Of which, and the other insignificant passages between them, we hear more than enough in the writings and correspondences of Voltaire about this time.

In such way Friedrich disposes of his Bielfelds; who are rather numerous about him now and henceforth. Adventurers from all quarters, especially of the literary type, in hopes of being employed, much hovered round Friedrich through his whole reign. But they met a rather strict judge on arriving; it cannot be said they found it such a Goshen as they expected.

Favor, friendly intimacy, it is visible from the first, avails nothing with this young King; beyond and before all things he will have his work done, and looks out exclusively for the man ablest to do it. Hence Bielfeld goes to Hanover, to grin out euphuisms, and make graceful court-bows to our sublime little Uncle there. On the other hand, Friedrich institutes a new Knighthood, *Order of Merit* so called; which indeed is but a small feat, testifying mere hope and exuberance as yet; and may even be made worse than nothing, according to the Knights he shall manage to have. Happily it proved a successful new Order in this last all-essential particular; and, to the end of Friedrich's life, continued to be a great and coveted distinction among the Prussians.

Beyond doubt this is a radiant enough young Majesty; entitled to hope, and to be the cause of hope. Handsome, to

begin with; decidedly well-looking, all say, and of graceful
presence, though hardly five feet seven, and perhaps stouter
of limb than the strict Belvedere standard.[1] Has a fine free
expressive face; nothing of austerity in it; not a proud face,
or not too proud, yet rapidly flashing on you all manner of
high meanings.[2] Such a man, in the bloom of his years; with
such a possibility ahead, and Voltaire and mankind waiting
applausive! — Let us try to select, and extricate into coherence
and visibility out of those Historical dust-heaps, a few of the
symptomatic phenomena, or physiognomic procedures of Friedrich in his first weeks of Kingship, by way of contribution to
some Portraiture of his then inner-man.

Friedrich will make Men happy : Corn-Magazines.

On the day after his Accession, Officers and chief Ministers
taking the Oath, Friedrich, to his Officers, "on whom he counts
for the same zeal now which he had witnessed as their comrade," recommends mildness of demeanor from the higher to
the lower, and that the common soldier be not treated with
harshness when not deserved: and to his Ministers he is still
more emphatic, in the like or a higher strain. Officially announcing to them, by Letter, that a new Reign has commenced,
he uses these words, legible soon after to a glad Berlin public:
"Our grand care will be, To further the Country's well-being,
and to make every one of our subjects (*einen jeden unserer
Unterthanen*) contented and happy. Our will is, not that you
strive to enrich Us by vexation of Our subjects; but rather
that you aim steadily as well towards the advantage of the
Country as Our particular interest, forasmuch as We make no
difference between these two objects," but consider them one

---

[1] Height, it appears, was five feet five inches (Rhenish), which in English measure is five feet seven or a hair's-breadth less. Preuss, twice over, by
a mistake unusual with him, gives "five feet two inches three lines" as the
correct cipher (which it is of *Napoleon's* measure in *French* feet); then settles
on the above dimensions from unexceptionable authority (Preuss, *Buch für
Jedermann*, i. 18; Preuss, *Friedrich der Grosse*, i. 39 and 419).

[2] Wille's Engraving after Pesne (excellent, both Picture and Engraving)
is reckoned the best Likeness in that form.

and the same. This is written, and gets into print within the month; and his Majesty, that same day (Wednesday, 2d June), when it came to personal reception, and actual taking of the Oath, was pleased to add in words, which also were printed shortly, this comfortable corollary: " My will henceforth is, If it ever chance that my particular interest and the general good of my Countries should seem to go against each other, — in that case, my will is, That the latter always be preferred." [1]

This is a fine dialect for incipient Royalty; and it is brand-new at that time. It excites an admiration in the then populations, which to us, so long used to it and to what commonly comes of it, is not conceivable at once. There can be no doubt the young King does faithfully intend to develop himself in the way of making men happy; but here, as elsewhere, are limits which he will recognize ahead, some of them perhaps nearer than was expected.

Meanwhile his first acts, in this direction, correspond to these fine words. The year 1740, still grim with cold into the heart of summer, bids fair to have a late poor harvest, and famine threatens to add itself to other hardships there have been. Recognizing the actualities of the case, what his poor Father could not, he opens the Public Granaries, — a wise resource they have in Prussian countries against the year of scarcity; — orders grain to be sold out, at reasonable rates, to the suffering poor; and takes the due pains, considerable in some cases, that this be rendered feasible everywhere in his dominions. "Berlin, 2d June," is the first date of this important order; fine program to his Ministers, which, we read, is no sooner uttered, than some performance follows. An evident piece of wisdom and humanity; for which doubtless blessings of a very sincere kind rise to him from several millions of his fellow-mortals.

Nay furthermore, as can be dimly gathered, this scarcity continuing, some continuous mode of management was set on

---

[1] Dickens, Despatch, 4th June, 1740 : Preuss, *Friedrichs Jugend und Thron-besteigung* (Berlin, 1840), p. 325; — quoting from the Berlin Newspapers of 28th June and 2d July, 1740.

foot for the Poor; and there is nominated, with salary, with
outline of plan and other requisites, as "Inspector of the
Poor," to his own and our surprise, M. Jordan, late Reader
to the Crown-Prince, and still much the intimate of his royal
Friend. Inspector who seems to do his work very well.
And in the November coming this is what we see: "One
thousand poor old women, the destitute of Berlin, set to
spin," at his Majesty's charges; vacant houses, hired for
them in certain streets and suburbs, have been new-planked,
partitioned, warmed; and spinning is there for any diligent
female soul. There a thousand of them sit, under proper
officers, proper wages, treatment; — and the hum of their
poor spindles, and of their poor inarticulate old hearts, is
a comfort, if one chance to think of it. — Of "distressed
needlewomen" who cannot sew, nor be taught to do it; who,
in private truth, are mutinous maid-servants come at last to
the net upshot of their anarchies; of these, or of the like
incurable phenomena, I hear nothing in Berlin; and can
believe that, under this King, Indigence itself may still have
something of a human aspect, not a brutal or diabolic as is
commoner in some places. — This is one of Friedrich's first
acts, this opening of the Corn-magazines, and arrangements
for the Destitute; [1] and of this there can be no criticism.
The sound of hungry pots set boiling, on judicious principles;
the hum of those old women's spindles in the warm rooms :
gods and men are well pleased to hear such sounds; and
accept the same as part, real though infinitesimally small, of
the sphere-harmonies of this Universe !

Abolition of Legal Torture.

Friedrich makes haste, next, to strike into Law-improve-
ments. It is but the morrow after this of the Corn-magazines,

---

[1] *Helden-Geschichte,* i. 367.   Rödenbeck, *Tagebuch aus Friedrichs des Grossen
Regentenleben* (Berlin, 1840), i. 2, 26 (2d June, October, 1740) : a meritorious,
laborious, though essentially chaotic Book, unexpectedly futile of result to the
reader; settles for each Day of Friedrich's Reign, so far as possible, where
Friedrich was and what doing; fatally wants all index &c., as usual.

by *Kabinets-Ordre* (Act of Parliament such as they can have
in that Country, where the Three Estates sit all under one
Three-cornered Hat, and the debates are kept silent, and only
the upshot of them, more or less faithfully, is made public),
— by Cabinet Order, 3d June, 1740, he abolishes the use of
Torture in Criminal Trials.[1] Legal Torture, "Question" as
they mildly call it, is at an end from this date. Not in any
Prussian Court shall a "question" try for answer again by
that savage method. The use of Torture had, I believe, fallen
rather obsolete in Prussia; but now the very threat of it
shall vanish, — the threat of it, as we may remember, had
reached Friedrich himself, at one time. Three or four years
ago, it is farther said, a dark murder happened in Berlin:
Man killed one night in the open streets; murderer discoverable by no method, — unless he were a certain *Candidatus*
of Divinity to whom some trace of evidence pointed, but
who sorrowfully persisted in absolute and total denial. This
poor Candidatus had been threatened with the rack; and
would most likely have at length got it, had not the real
murderer been discovered, — much to the discredit of the
rack in Berlin. This Candidatus was only threatened; nor
do I know when the last actual instance in Prussia was;
but in enlightened France, and most other countries, there
was as yet no scruple upon it. Barbier, the Diarist at Paris,
some time after this, tells us of a gang of thieves there, who
were regularly put to the torture; and "they blabbed too,
ils ont jasé," says Barbier with official jocosity.[2]

Friedrich's Cabinet Order, we need not say, was greeted
everywhere, at home and abroad, by three rounds of applause;
— in which surely all of us still join; though the *per contra*
also is becoming visible to some of us, and our enthusiasm
grows less complete than formerly. This was Friedrich's
first step in Law-Reform, done on his fourth day of Kingship.
A long career in that kind lies ahead of him; in reform of

---

[1] Preuss, *Friedrichs Jugend und Thronbesteigung* (Berlin, 1840, — a minor
Book of Preuss's), p. 340. Rödenbeck, i. 14 ("3d June").

[2] Barbier, *Journal Historique du Règne de Louis XV.* (Paris, 1849), ii. 338
(date "Dec. 1742").

Law, civil as well as criminal, his efforts ended with life
only. For his love of Justice was really great; and the
mendacities and wiggeries, attached to such a necessary of
life as Law, found no favor from him at any time.

Will have Philosophers about him, and a real Academy of Sciences.

To neglect the Philosophies, Fine Arts, interests of Human
Culture, he is least of all likely. The idea of building up the
Academy of Sciences to its pristine height, or far higher,
is evidently one of those that have long lain in the Crown-
Prince's mind, eager to realize themselves. Immortal Wolf,
exiled but safe at Marburg, and refusing to return in Friedrich Wilhelm's time, had lately dedicated a Book to the
Crown-Prince; indicating that perhaps, under a new Reign,
he might be more persuadable. Friedrich makes haste to
persuade; instructs the proper person, Reverend Herr Rein-
beck, Head of the Consistorium at Berlin, to write and negotiate. "All reasonable conditions shall be granted" the
immortal Wolf, — and Friedrich adds with his own hand as
Postscript: "I request you (*Ihn*) to use all diligence about
Wolf. A man that seeks truth, and loves it, must be reckoned
precious in any human society; and I think you will make
a conquest in the realm of truth if you persuade Wolf hither
again."[1] This is of date June 6th; not yet a week since
Friedrich came to be King. The Reinbeck-Wolf negotiation
which ensued can be read in Büsching by the curious.[2] It
represents to us a croaky, thrifty, long-headed old Herr Professor, in no haste to quit Marburg except for something
better: "obliged to wear woollen shoes and leggings;" "bad
at mounting stairs;" and otherwise needing soft treatment.
Willing, though with caution, to work at an Academy of
Sciences; — but dubious if the French are so admirable as they
seem to themselves in such operations. Veteran Wolf, one
dimly begins to learn, could himself build a German Academy

[1] In *Œuvres de Frédéric* (xxvii. ii. 185), the Letter given.
[2] Büsching's *Beiträge* (§ Freiherr von Wolf), i. 63–137.

of Sciences, to some purpose, if encouraged! This latter was probably the stone of stumbling in that direction. Veteran Wolf did not get to be President in the New Academy of Sciences; but was brought back, "streets all in triumph," to his old place at Halle; and there, with little other work that was heard of, but we hope in warm shoes and without much mounting of stairs, lived peaceably victorious the rest of his days.

Friedrich's thoughts are not of a German home-built Academy, but of a French one: and for this he already knows a builder; has silently had him in his eye, these two years past, —Voltaire giving hint, in the *Letter* we once heard of at Loo. Builder shall be that sublime Maupertuis; scientific lion of Paris, ever since his feat in the Polar regions, and the charming Narrative he gave of it. "What a feat, what a book!" exclaimed the Parisian cultivated circles, male and female, on that occasion; and Maupertuis, with plenty of bluster in him carefully suppressed, assents in a grandly modest way. His Portraits are in the Printshops ever since; one very singular Portrait, just coming out (at which there is some laughing): a coarse-featured, blusterous, rather triumphant-looking man, blusterous, though finely complacent for the nonce; in copious dressing-gown and fur cap; comfortably *squeezing* the Earth and her meridians flat (as if *he* had done it), with his left hand; and with the other, and its outstretched finger, asking mankind, "Are not you aware, then?"—"Are not we!" answers Voltaire by and by, with endless waggeries upon him, though at present so reverent. Friedrich, in these same days, writes this Autograph; which who of men or lions could resist?

To Monsieur de Maupertuis, at Paris.

(No date; —datable, June, 1740.)

"My heart and my inclination excited in me, from the moment I mounted the throne, the desire of having you here, that you might put our Berlin Academy into the shape you alone are capable of giving it. Come, then, come and insert into this wild crab-tree the graft of the Sciences, that it may

VIEW OF THE ROYAL PALACE.

Carlyle, Vol. Two, p. 453.

bear fruit. You have shown the Figure of the Earth to mankind; show also to a King how sweet it is to possess such a
man as you.

> "Monsieur de Maupertuis, — *Votre très-affectionné*
> "FÉDÉRIC" (*sic*).[1]

This Letter — how could Maupertuis prevent some accident
in such a case? — got into the Newspapers; glorious for Friedrich, glorious for Maupertuis; and raised matters to a still
higher pitch. Maupertuis is on the road, and we shall see
him before long.

And Every One shall get to Heaven in his own Way.

Here is another little fact which had immense renown at
home and abroad, in those summer months and long afterwards.

June 22d, 1740, the *Geistliche Departement* (Board of Religion, we may term it) reports that the Roman-Catholic Schools,
which have been in use these eight years past, for children of
soldiers belonging to that persuasion, "are, especially in Berlin, perverted, directly in the teeth of Royal Ordinance, 1732,
to seducing Protestants into Catholicism;" annexed, or ready
for annexing, "is the specific Report of Fiscal-General to this
effect:" — upon which, what would it please his Majesty to
direct us to do?

His Majesty writes on the margin these words, rough and
ready, which we give with all their grammatical blotches on
them; indicating a mind made up on one subject, which was
much more dubious then, to most other minds, than it now
is : —

"Die Religionen Müsen (*müssen*) alle Tollerirt (*tolerirt*) werden, und Mus (*muss*) der Fiscal nuhr (*nur*) das Auge darauf
haben, das (*dass*) keine der andern abrug Tuhe (*Abbruch thue*),
den (*denn*) hier mus (*muss*) ein jeder nach seiner Fasson Selich
(*Façon selig*) werden."[2]

---

[1] *Œuvres*, xvii. i. 334. The fantastic "Fédéric," instead of Frédéric," is,
by this time, the common signature to French Letters.

[2] **Preuss**, *Thronbesteigung*, p. 333; Rödenbeck, *in die*.

Which in English might run as follows : —

"All Religions must be tolerated (*Tollerated*), and the Fiscal must have an eye that none of them make unjust encroachment on the other; for in this Country every man must get to Heaven in his own way."

Wonderful words; precious to the then leading spirits, and which (the spelling and grammar being mended) flew abroad over all the world : the enlightened Public everywhere answering his Majesty, once more, with its loudest "Bravissimo !" on this occasion. With what enthusiasm of admiring wonder, it is now difficult to fancy, after the lapse of sixscore years ! And indeed, in regard to all these worthy acts of Human Improvement which we are now concerned with, account should be held (were it possible) on Friedrich's behalf how extremely original, and bright with the splendor of new gold, they then were : and how extremely they are fallen dim, by general circulation, since that. Account should be held ; and yet it is not possible, no human imagination is adequate to it, in the times we are now got into.

Free Press, and Newspapers the best Instructors.

Toleration, in Friedrich's spiritual circumstances, was perhaps no great feat to Friedrich : but what the reader hardly expected of him was Freedom of the Press, or an attempt that way ! From England, from Holland, Friedrich had heard of Free Press, of Newspapers the best Instructors : it is a fact that he hastens to plant a seed of that kind at Berlin ; sets about it "on the second day of his reign," so eager is he. Berlin had already some meagre *Intelligenz-Blatt* (Weekly or Thrice-Weekly Advertiser), perhaps two ; but it is a real Newspaper, frondent with genial leafy speculation, and food for the mind, that Friedrich is intent upon : a "Literary-Political Newspaper," or were it even two Newspapers, one French, one German ; and he rapidly makes the arrangements for it ; despatches Jordan, on the second day, to seek some fit Frenchman. Arrangements are soon made : a Bookselling

Printer, Haude, Bookseller once to the Prince-Royal, — whom
we saw once in a domestic flash-of-lightning long ago,[1]—is
encouraged to proceed with the improved German article, *Mercury* or whatever they called it; vapid Formey, a facile pen,
but not a forcible, is the Editor sought out by Jordan for the
French one. And, in short, No. 1 of Formey shows itself in
print within a month;[2] and Haude and he, Haude picking up
some grand Editor in Hamburg, do their best for the instruction of mankind.

In not many months, Formey, a facile and learned but
rather vapid gentleman, demitted or was dismissed; and the
Journals coalesced into one, or split into two again; and went
I know not what road, or roads, in time coming, — none that
led to results worth naming. Freedom of the Press, in the
case of these Journals, was never violated, nor was any need
for violating it. General Freedom of the Press Friedrich did
not grant, in any quite Official or steady way; but in practice,
under him, it always had a kind of real existence, though a
fluctuating, ambiguous one. And we have to note, through
Friedrich's whole reign, a marked disinclination to concern
himself with Censorship, or the shackling of men's poor
tongues and pens; nothing but some officious report that
there was offence to Foreign Courts, or the chance of offence,
in a poor man's pamphlet, could induce Friedrich to interfere
with him or it, — and indeed his interference was generally
against his Ministers for having wrong informed him, and in
favor of the poor Pamphleteer appealing at the fountain-head.[3]
To the end of his life, disgusting Satires against him, *Vie
Privée* by Voltaire, *Matinées du Roi de Prusse*, and still worse
Lies and Nonsenses, were freely sold at Berlin, and even bore
to be printed there, Friedrich saying nothing, caring nothing.

[1] Anteà, Book vi. c. 7.

[2] " 2d July, 1740: " Preuss, *Thronbesteigung*, p. 330; and Formey, *Souvenirs*,
i. 107, rectified by the exact Herr Preuss.

[3] Anonymous (Laveaux), *Vie de Frédéric II., Roi de Prusse* (Strasbourg,
1787), iv. 82. A worthless, now nearly forgotten Book; but competent on
this point, if on any; Laveaux (a handy fellow, fugitive Ex-Monk, with
fugitive Ex-Nun attached) having lived much at Berlin, always in the pamphleteering line.

He has been known to burn Pamphlets publicly, — one Pamphlet we shall ourselves see on fire yet ; — but it was without the least hatred to them, and for official reasons merely. To the last, he would answer his reporting Ministers, "*La presse est libre* (Free press, you must consider)!"—grandly reluctant to meddle with the press, or go down upon the dogs barking at his door. Those ill effects of Free Press (first stage of the ill effects) he endured in this manner; but the good effects seem to have fallen below his expectation. Friedrich's enthusiam for freedom of the press, prompt enough, as we see, never rose to the extreme pitch, and it rather sank than increased as he continued his experiences of men and things. This of Formey and the two Newspapers was the only express attempt he made in that direction; and it proved a rather disappointing one. The two Newspapers went their way thenceforth, Friedrich sometimes making use of them for small purposes, once or twice writing an article himself, of wildly quizzical nature, perhaps to be noticed by us when the time comes; but are otherwise, except for chronological purposes, of the last degree of insignificance to gods or men.

"Freedom of the Press," says my melancholic Friend, "is a noble thing ; and in certain Nations, at certain epochs, produces glorious effects, — chiefly in the revolutionary line, where that has grown indispensable. Freedom of the Press is possible, where everybody disapproves the least abuse of it; where the 'Censorship' is, as it were, exercised by all the world. When the world (as, even in the freest countries, it almost irresistibly tends to become) is no longer in a case to exercise that salutary function, and cannot keep down loud unwise speaking, loud unwise persuasion, and rebuke it into silence whenever printed, Freedom of the Press will not answer very long, among sane human creatures : and indeed, in Nations not in an exceptional case, it becomes impossible amazingly soon !"—

All these are phenomena of Friedrich's first week. Let these suffice as sample, in that first kind. Splendid indications surely ; and shot forth in swift enough succession, flash

following flash, upon an attentive world. Betokening, shall
we say, what internal sea of splendor, struggling to disclose
itself, probably lies in this young King; and how high his
hopes go for mankind and himself ? Yes, surely ; — and introducing, we remark withal, the "New Era," of Philanthropy,
Enlightenment and so much else; with French Revolution,
and a "world well suicided" hanging in the rear! Clearly
enough, to this young ardent Friedrich, foremost man of his
Time, and capable of *doing* its inarticulate or dumb aspirings,
belongs that questionable honor; and a very singular one it
would have seemed to Friedrich, had he lived to see what it
meant !

Friedrich's rapidity and activity, in the first months of his
reign, were wonderful to mankind; as indeed through life he
continued to be a most rapid and active King. He flies about;
mustering Troops, Ministerial Boards, passing Edicts, inspecting, accepting Homages of Provinces ; — decides and does,
every day that passes, an amazing number of things. Writes
many Letters, too ; finds moments even for some verses ; and
occasionally draws a snatch of melody from his flute.

His Letters are copiously preserved; but, as usual, they are
in swift official tone, and tell us almost nothing. To his Sisters he writes assurances ; to his friends, his Suhms, Duhans,
Voltaires, eager invitations, general or particular, to come to
him. "My state has changed," is his phrase to Voltaire and
other dear intimates; a tone of pensiveness, at first even of
sorrow and pathos traceable in it ; "Come to me," — and the
tone, in an old dialect, different from Friedrich's, might have
meant, "Pray for me." An immense new scene is opened, full
of possibilities of good and bad. His hopes being great, his
anxieties, the shadow of them, are proportionate. Duhan (his
good old Tutor) does arrive, Algarotti arrives, warmly welcomed, both : with Voltaire there are difficulties; but surely
he too will, before long, manage to arrive. The good Suhm,
who had been Saxon Minister at Petersburg to his sorrow
this long while back, got in motion soon enough; but, alas,
his lungs were ruined by the Russian climate, and he did not
arrive. Something pathetic still in those final *Letters* of Suhm.

Passionately speeding on, like a spent steed struggling home-ward; he has to pause at Warsaw, and in a few days dies there, — in a way mournful to Friedrich and us! To Duhan, and Duhan's children afterwards, he was punctually, not too lavishly, attentive; in like manner to Suhm's Nephews, whom the dying man had recommended to him. — We will now glance shortly at a second and contemporaneous phasis of Friedrich's affairs.

Intends to be Practical withal, and every inch a King.

Friedrich is far indeed from thinking to reduce his Army, as the Foreign Editor imagines. On the contrary, he is, with all industry, increasing it. He changed the Potsdam Giants into four regiments of the usual stature; he is busy bargaining with his Brother-in-law of Brunswick, and with other neigh-bors, for still new regiments; — makes up, within the next few months, Eight Regiments, an increase of, say, 16,000 men. It would appear he means to keep an eye on the practicalities withal; means to have a Fighting-Apparatus of the utmost potentiality, for one thing! Here are other indications.

We saw the Old Dessauer, in a sad hour lately, speaking beside the mark; and with what Olympian glance, suddenly tearless, the new King flashed out upon him, knowing nothing of "authority" that could reside in any Dessauer. Nor was that a solitary experience; the like befell wherever needed. Heinrich of Schwedt, the Ill Margraf, advancing with jocose countenance in the way of old comradeship, in those first days, met unexpected rebuff, and was reduced to gravity on the sudden: "*Jetzt bin ich König*, — My Cousin, I am now King!" a fact which the Ill Margraf could never get forgotten again. Lieutenant-General Schulenburg, too, the didactic Schulenburg, presuming on old familiarity, and willing to wipe out the misfortune of having once condemned us to death, which nobody is now upbraiding him with, rushes up from Landsberg, unbidden, to pay his congratulations and condo-lences, driven by irresistible exuberance of loyalty: to his astonishment, he is reminded (thing certain, manner of the

thing not known), That an Officer cannot quit his post without order; that he, at this moment, ought to be in Landsberg![1]   Schulenburg has a hard old military face; but here
is a young face too, which has grown unexpectedly rigorous.
Fancy the blank look of little Schulenburg; the light of him
snuffed out in this manner on a sudden.   It is said he had
thoughts of resigning, so indignant was he: no doubt he went
home to Landsberg gloomily reflective, with the pipe-clay of
his mind in such a ruinous condition.   But there was no
serious anger, on Friedrich's part; and he consoled his little
Schulenburg soon after, by expediting some promotion he had
intended him.   "Terribly proud young Majesty this," exclaim
the sweet voices.   And indeed, if they are to have a Saturnian
Kingdom, by appearance it will be on conditions only!

Anticipations there had been, that old unkindnesses against
the Crown-Prince, some of which were cruel enough, might be
remembered now: and certain people had their just fears, considering what account stood against them; others, *vice versâ*,
their hopes.   But neither the fears nor the hopes realized
themselves; especially the fears proved altogether ground-
less.   Derschau, who had voted Death in that Cöpenick Court-
Martial, upon the Crown-Prince, is continued in his functions,
in the light of his King's countenance, as if nothing such had
been.   Derschau, and all others so concerned; not the least
question was made of them, nor of what they had thought or
had done or said, on an occasion once so tragically vital to a
certain man.

Nor is reward much regulated by past services to the Crown-
Prince, or even by sufferings endured for him.   "Shocking in-
gratitude!" exclaim the sweet voices here too,—being of weak
judgment, many of them!   Poor Katte's Father, a faithful old
Soldier, not capable of being more, he does, rather conspicuously, make Feldmarschall, make Reichsgraf; happy, could
these honors be a consolation to the old man.   The Münchows
of Cüstrin,—readers remember their kindness in that sad
time; how the young boy went into petticoats again, and
came to the Crown-Prince's cell with all manner of furnish-

[1] Stenzel, iv. 41; Preuss, *Thronbesteigung*; &c.

ings, — the Münchows, father and sons, this young gentleman of the petticoats among them, he took immediate pains to reward by promotion : eldest son was advanced into the General Directorium ; two younger sons, to Majorship, to Captaincy, in their respective Regiments ; him of the petticoats " he had already taken altogether to himself," [1] and of him we shall see a glimpse at Wilhelmina's shortly, as a "milkbeard (*jeune morveux*) " in personal attendance on his Majesty. This was a notable exception. And in effect there came good public service, eminent some of it, from these Münchows in their various departments. And it was at length perceived to have been, in the main, because they were of visible faculty for doing work that they had got work to do ; and the exceptional case of the Münchows became confirmatory of the rule.

Lieutenant Keith, again, whom we once saw galloping from Wesel to save his life in that bad affair of the Crown-Prince's and his, was nothing like so fortunate. Lieutenant Keith, by speed on that Wesel occasion, and help of Chesterfield's Secretary, got across to England ; got into the Portuguese service ; and has there been soldiering, very silently, these ten years past, — skin and body safe, though his effigy was cut in four quarters and nailed to the gallows at Wesel ; — waiting a time that would come. Time being come, Lieutenant Keith hastened home ; appealed to his effigy on the gallows ; — and was made a Lieutenant-Colonel merely, with some slight appendages, as that of *Stallmeister* (Curator of the Stables) and something else ; income still straitened, though enough to live upon. [2] Small promotion, in comparison with hope, thought the poor Lieutenant ; but had to rest satisfied with it ; and struggle to understand that perhaps he was fit for nothing bigger, and that he must exert himself to do this small thing well. Hardness of heart in high places ! Friedrich, one is glad to see, had not forgotten the poor fellow, could he have done better with him. Some ten years hence, quite incidentally, there came to Keith, one morning, a fine purse of money from his Majesty, one pretty gift in Keith's experience ; — much the

---

[1] Preuss, i. 66.

[2] Preuss, *Friedrich mit seinen Verwandten und Freunden*, p. 281.

topic in Berlin, while a certain solemn English gentleman
happened to be passing that way (whom we mean to detain a
little by and by), who reports it for us with all the circumstances.[1]

Lieutenant Spaen too had got into trouble for the Crown-
Prince's sake, though we have forgotten him again; had
"admitted Katte to interviews," or we forget what;—had
sat his "year in Spandau" in consequence; been dismissed
the Prussian service, and had taken service with the Dutch.
Lieutenant Spaen either did not return at all, or disliked the
aspects when he did, and immediately withdrew to Holland
again. Which probably was wise of him. At a late period,
King Friedrich, then a great King, on one of his Cleve Journeys, fell in with Spaen; who had become a Dutch General of
rank, and was of good manners and style of conversation:
King Friedrich was charmed to see him; became his guest for
the night; conversed delightfully with him, about old Prussian matters and about new; and in the colloquy never once
alluded to that interesting passage in his young life and
Spaen's.[2] Hard as polished steel! thinks Spaen perhaps;
but, if candid, must ask himself withal, Are facts any softer,
or the Laws of Kingship to a man that holds it?—Keith
silently did his Lieutenant-Colonelcy with the appendages,
while life lasted: of the Page Keith, his Brother, who indeed
had blabbed upon the Prince, as we remember, and was not
entitled to be clamorous, I never heard that there was any notice taken; and figure him to myself as walking with shouldered firelock, a private Fusileer, all his life afterwards, with
many reflections on things bygone.[3]

Old friendship, it would seem, is without weight in public
appointments here: old friends are somewhat astonished to
find this friend of theirs a King every inch! To old com-

[1] Sir Jonas Hanway, *Travels,* &c. (London, 1753), ii. 202. Date of the Gift
is 1750.

[2] Nicolai, *Anekdoten,* vi. 178.

[3] These and the other Prussian Keiths are all of Scotch extraction; the
Prussians, in natural German fashion, pronounce their name *Kah-it* (English
"*Kite*" with nothing of the *y* in it), as may be worth remembering in a more
important instance.

rades, if they were useless, much more if they were worse than useless, how disappointing ! " One wretched Herr [name suppressed, but known at the time, and talked of, and whispered of], who had, like several others, hoping to rise that way, been industrious in encouraging the Crown-Prince's vices as to women, was so shocked at the return he now met, that in despair he hanged himself in Lobejün" (Löbegun, Magdeburg Country) : here is a case for the humane ! [1]

Friend Keyserling himself, " Cæsarion" that used to be, can get nothing, though we love him much; being an idle topsy-turvy fellow with revenues of his own. Jordan, with his fine-drawn wit, French logics, *Literary Travels*, thin exactitude ; what can be done for Jordan ? Him also his new Majesty loves much; and knows that, without some official living, poor Jordan has no resource. Jordan, after some waiting and survey, is made "Inspector of the Poor ; " — busy this Autumn looking out for vacant houses, and arrangements for the thousand spinning women; — continues to be employed in mixed literary services (hunting up of Formey, for Editor, was one instance), and to be in much real intimacy. That also was perhaps about the real amount of amiable Jordan. To get Jordan a living by planting him in some office which he could not do ; to warm Jordan by burning our royal bed for him : that had not entered into the mind of Jordan's royal friend. The Münchows he did promote; the Finks, sons of his Tutor Finkenstein : to these and other old comrades, in whom he had discovered fitness, it is no doubt abundantly grateful to him to recognize and employ it. As he notably does, in these and in other instances. But before all things he has decided to remember that he is King; that he must accept the severe laws of that trust, and do *it*, or not have done anything.

An inverse sign, pointing in the same way, is the passionate search he is making in Foreign Countries for such men as will suit him. In these same months, for example, he bethinks him of two Counts Schmettau, in the Austrian Service, with whom he had made acquaintance in the Rhine Campaign ; of a Count von Rothenburg, whom he saw in the French Camp

[1] Küster, *Characterzüge des &c. von Saldern* (Berlin, 1793), p. 63.

there; and is negotiating to have them if possible.   The
Schmettaus are Prussian by birth, though in Austrian Service; them he obtains under form of an Order home, with
good conditions under it; they came, and proved useful men
to him.   Rothenburg, a shining kind of figure in Diplomacy as
well as Soldiership, was Alsacian German, foreign to Prussia;
but him too Friedrich obtained, and made much of, as will be
notable by and by.   And in fact the soul of all these noble
tendencies in Friedrich, which surely are considerable, is even
this, That he loves men of merit, and does not love men of
none; that he has an endless appetite for men of merit, and
feels, consciously and otherwise, that they are the one thing
beautiful, the one thing needful to him.

This, which is the product of all fine tendencies, is likewise
their centre or focus out of which they start again, with some
chance of fulfilment; — and we may judge in how many directions Friedrich was willing to expand himself, by the multifarious kinds he was inviting, and negotiating for.   Academicians,
— and not Maupertuis only, but all manner of mathematical
geniuses (Euler whom he got, 's Gravesande, Muschenbroek
whom he failed of); and Literary geniuses innumerable, first
and last.   Academicians, Musicians, Players, Dancers even;
much more Soldiers and Civil-Service men: no man that carries any honest " Can do " about with him but may expect
some welcome here.   Which continued through Friedrich's
reign; and involved him in much petty trouble, not always
successful in the lower kinds of it.   For his Court was the
cynosure of ambitious creatures on the wing, or inclined for
taking wing: like a lantern kindled in the darkness of the
world; — and many owls impinged upon him; whom he had to
dismiss with brevity.

Perhaps it had been better to stand by mere Prussian or
German merit, native to the ground?   Or rather, undoubtedly
it had!   In some departments, as in the military, the administrative, diplomatic, Friedrich was himself among the best
of judges: but in various others he had mainly (mainly, by
no means blindly or solely) to accept noise of reputation as
evidence of merit; and in these, if we compute with rigor, his

success was intrinsically not considerable. The more honor
to him that he never wearied of trying. "A man that does
not care for merit," says the adage, "cannot himself have
any." But a King that does not care for merit, what shall
we say of such a King! —

Behavior to his Mother; to his Wife.

One other fine feature, significant of many, let us notice:
his affection for his Mother. When his Mother addressed
him as "Your Majesty," he answered, as the Books are careful to tell us: "Call me Son; that is the Title of all others
most agreeable to me!" Words which, there can be no doubt,
came from the heart. Fain would he shoot forth to greatness
in filial piety, as otherwise; fain solace himself in doing something kind to his Mother. Generously, lovingly; though again
with clear view of the limits. He decrees for her a Title
higher than had been customary, as well as more accordant
with his feelings; not "Queen Dowager," but "Her Majesty
the Queen Mother." He decides to build her a new Palace;
"under the Lindens" it is to be, and of due magnificence: in
a month or two, he had even got bits of the foundation dug,
and the Houses to be pulled down bought or bargained for;[1] —
which enterprise, however, was renounced, no doubt with consent, as the public aspects darkened. Nothing in the way of
honor, in the way of real affection heartily felt and demon-
strated, was wanting to Queen Sophie in her widowhood.
But, on the other hand, of public influence no vestige was
allowed, if any was ever claimed; and the good kind Mother
lived in her Monbijou, the centre and summit of Berlin
society; and restricted herself wisely to private matters. She
has her domesticities, family affections, readings, speculations;
gives evening parties at Monbijou. One glimpse of her in
1742 we get, that of a perfectly private royal Lady; which
though it has little meaning, yet as it is authentic, coming from
Büsching's hand, may serve as one little twinkle in that total
darkness, and shall be left to the reader and his fancy: —

[1] Rödenbeck, p. 15 (30th June–23d Aug. 1740); and correct Stenzel (iv. 44)

A Count Henkel, a Thuringian gentleman, of high speculation, high pietistic ways, extremely devout, and given even to
writing of religion, came to Berlin about some Silesian properties, — a man I should think of lofty melancholic aspect; and,
in severe type, somewhat of a lion, on account of his Book
called " *Death-bed Scenes,* in four Volumes." Came to Berlin;
and on the 15th August, 1742, towards evening (as the ever-
punctual Büsching looking into Henkel's Papers gives it),
" was presented to the Queen Mother; who retained him to
supper; supper not beginning till about ten o'clock. The
Queen Mother was extremely gracious to Henkel; but investigated him a good deal, and put a great many questions," not
quite easy to answer in that circle, " as, Why he did not play?
What he thought of comedies and operas? What Preachers
he was acquainted with in Berlin? Whether he too was a
Writer of Books? [covertly alluding to the *Death-bed Scenes,*
notes Büsching]. And abundance of other questioning. She
also recounted many fantastic anecdotes (*viel Abenteuerliches*)
about Count von Zinzendorf [Founder of *Hernnhuth,* far-
shining spiritual Paladin of that day, whom her Majesty
thinks rather a spiritual Quixote]; and declared that they were
strictly true." [1] Upon which, *exit* Henkel, borne by Büsching,
and our light is snuffed out.

This is one momentary glance I have met with of Queen
Sophie in her Dowager state. The rest, though there were
seventeen years of it in all, is silent to mankind and me; and
only her death, and her Son's great grief about it, so great as
to be surprising, is mentioned in the Books.

Actual painful sorrow about his Father, much more any
new outburst of weeping and lamenting, is not on record, after
that first morning. Time does its work; and in such a whirl
of occupations, sooner than elsewhere: and the loved Dead lie
silent in their mausoleum in our hearts, — serenely sad as
Eternity, not in loud sorrow as of Time. Friedrich was pious
as a Son, however he might be on other heads. To the last
years of his life, as from the first days of his reign, it was evident in what honor he held Friedrich Wilhelm's memory; and

[1] Büsching's *Beiträge,* iv. 27.

the words "my Father," when they turned up in discourse, had in that fine voice of his a tone which the observers noted. "To his Mother he failed no day, when in Berlin, however busy, to make his visit; and he never spoke to her, except hat in hand."

With his own Queen, Friedrich still consorts a good deal, in these first times; is with her at Charlottenburg, Berlin, Potsdam, Reinsberg, for a day or two, as occasion gives; sometimes at Reinsberg for weeks running, in the intervals of war and business: glad to be at rest amid his old pursuits, by the side of a kind innocent being familiar to him. So it lasts for a length of time. But these happy intervals, we can remark, grow rarer: whether the Lady's humor, as they became rarer, might not sink withal, and produce an acceleration in the rate of decline? She was thought to be capable of "pouting (*faire la fâchée*)," at one period! We are left to our guesses; there is not anywhere the smallest whisper to guide us. Deep silence reigns in all Prussian Books. — To feel or to suspect yourself neglected, and to become *more* amiable thereupon (in which course alone lies hope), is difficult for any Queen! Enough, we can observe these meetings, within two or three years, have become much rarer; and perhaps about the end of the third or fourth year, they altogether cease; and pass merely into the formal character. In which state they continued fixed, liable to no uncertainty; and were transacted, to the end of Friedrich's life, with inflexible regularity as the annual reviews were. This is a curious section of his life; which there will be other opportunities of noticing. But there is yet no thought of it anywhere, nor for years to come; though fables to the contrary were once current in Books.[1]

No Change in his Father's Methods or Ministries.

In the old mode of Administration, in the Ministries, Government Boards, he made no change. These administrative methods of his wise Father's are admirable to Friedrich, who knows them well; and they continue to be so. These men of

[1] Laveaux, &c.

FREDERICK THE GREAT AND HIS QUEEN.

Carlyle, Vol. Two, p. 474.

his Father's, them also Friedrich knows, and that they were well chosen. In methods or in men, he is inclined to make the minimum of alteration at present. One Finance Hofrath of a projecting turn, named Eckart, who had abused the last weak years of Friedrich Wilhelm, and much afflicted mankind by the favor he was in: this Eckart Friedrich appointed a commission to inquire into; found the public right in regard to Eckart, and dismissed him with ignominy, not with much other punishment. Minister Boden, on the contrary, high in the Finance Department, who had also been much grumbled at, Friedrich found to be a good man: and Friedrich not only retained Boden, but advanced him; and continued to make more and more use of him in time coming. His love of perfection in work done, his care of thrift, seemed almost greater than his late Father's had been, — to the disappointment of many. In the other Departments, Podewils, Thulmeyer and the rest went on as heretofore; — only in general with less to do, the young King doing more himself than had been usual. Valori, "*mon gros Valori* (my fat Valori)," French Minister here, whom we shall know better, writes home of the new King of Prussia: " He begins his government, as by all appearance he will carry it on, in a highly satisfactory way : everywhere traits of benevolence, sympathy for his subjects, respect shown to the memory of the Deceased,"[1] — no change made, where it evidently is not for the better.

Friedrich's "Three principal Secretaries of State," as we should designate them, are very remarkable. Three Clerks he found, or had known of, somewhere in the Public Offices; and now took, under some advanced title, to be specially his own Private Clerks : three vigorous long-headed young fellows, "Eichel, Schuhmacher, Lautensack" the obscure names of them;[2] out of whom, now and all along henceforth, he got immensities of work in that kind. They lasted all his life; and, of course, grew ever more expert at their function. Close,

---

[1] *Mémoires des Négociations du Marquis de Valori* (à Paris, 1820), i. 20 (" June 13th, 1740 "). A valuable Book, which we shall often have to quote: edited in a lamentably ignorant manner.

[2] Rödenbeck, 15th June, 1740.

silent; exact as machinery : ever ready, from the smallest
clear hint, marginal pencil-mark, almost from a glance of the
eye, to clothe the Royal Will in official form, with the due
rugged clearness and thrift of words. " Came punctually at
four in the morning in summer, five in winter; " did daily the
day's work; and kept their mouths well shut. A very notable
Trio of men; serving his Majesty and the Prussian Nation as
Principal Secretaries of State, on those cheap terms; — nay
almost as Houses of Parliament with Standing Committees
and appendages, so many *Acts* of Parliament admittedly rather
wise, being passed daily by his Majesty's help and theirs ! —
Friedrich paid them rather well; they saw no society; lived
wholly to their work, and to their own families. Eichel alone
of the three was mentioned at all by mankind, and that obscurely; an "abstruse, reserved, long-headed kind of man ; " and
" made a great deal of money in the end," insinuates Büsching,[1]
no friend of Friedrich's or his.

In superficial respects, again, Friedrich finds that the Prussian King ought to have a King's Establishment, and maintain
a decent splendor among his neighbors, — as is not quite the
case at present. In this respect he does make changes. A
certain quantity of new Pages, new Goldsticks; some considerable, not too considerable, new-furbishing of the Royal
Household, — as it were, a fair coat of new paint, with gilding
not profuse, — brought it to the right pitch for this King.
About "a hundred and fifty " new figures of the Page and
Goldstick kind, is the reckoning given.[2] So many of these;
and there is an increase of 16,000 to one's Army going on:
that is the proportion noticeable. In the facts as his Father
left them Friedrich persisted all his life; in the semblances or
outer vestures he changed, to this extent for the present. —
These are the Phenomena of Friedrich's Accession, noted
by us.

Readers see there is radiance enough, perhaps slightly in
excess, but of intrinsically good quality, in the Aurora of this
new Reign. A brilliant valiant young King; much splendor

[1] *Beiträge*, v. 238, &c.   [2] *Helden-Geschichte*, i. 353.

of what we could call a *golden* or soft nature (visible in those
"New-Era" doings of his, in those strong affections to his
Friends); and also, what we like almost better in him, something of a *steel-bright* or stellar splendor (meaning, clearness of
eyesight, intrepidity, severe loyalty to fact), — which is a fine
addition to the softer element, and will keep *it* and its philanthropies and magnanimities well under rule. Such a man is
rare in this world; how extremely rare such a man born King!
He is swift and he is persistent; sharply discerning, fearless to
resolve and perform; carries his great endowments lightly, as if
they were not heavy to him. He has known hard misery, been
taught by stripes; a light stoicism sits gracefully on him.

"What he will grow to?" Probably to something considerable. Very certainly to something far short of his aspirations; far different from his own hopes; and the world's concerning him. It is not we, it is Father Time that does the
controlling and fulfilling of our hopes; and strange work he
makes of them and us. For example, has not Friedrich's
grand "New Era," inaugurated by him in a week, with the
leading spirits all adoring, issued since in French Revolution
and a "world well suicided," — the leading spirits much
thrown out in consequence! New Era has gone to great
lengths since Friedrich's time; and the leading spirits do not
now adore it, but yawn over it, or worse! Which changes to
us the then aspect of Friedrich, and his epoch and his aspirations, a good deal. — On the whole, Friedrich will go his way,
Time and the leading spirits going theirs; and, like the rest
of us, will grow to what he can. His actual size is not great
among the Kingdoms: his outward resources are rather to be
called small. The Prussian Dominion at that date is, in extent, about four-fifths of an England Proper, and perhaps
not one-fifth so fertile: subject Population is well under Two
Millions and a Half; Revenue not much above One Million
Sterling,[1] — very small, were not thrift such a *vectigal*.

[1] The exact statistic cipher is, at Friedrich's Accession: *Prussian Territories*, 2,275 square miles German (56,875 English); *Population*, 2,240,000; *Annual Revenue*, 7,371,707 thalers 7 groschen (£1,105,756 without the pence).
See Preuss, *Buch für Jedermann*, i. 49; Stenzel, iii. 692; &c.

This young King is magnanimous; not much to be called ambitious, or not in the vulgar sense almost at all, — strange as it may sound to readers. His hopes at this time are many; — and among them, I perceive, there is not wanting secretly, in spite of his experiences, some hope that he himself may be a good deal "happier" than formerly. Nor is there any ascetic humor, on his part, to forbid trial. He is much determined to try. Probably enough, as we guess and gather, his agreeablest anticipations, at this time, were of Reinsberg: How, in the intervals of work well done, he would live there wholly to the Muses; have his chosen spirits round him, his colloquies, his suppers of the gods. Why not? There might be a King of Intellects conceivable withal; protecting, cherishing, practically guiding the chosen Illuminative Souls of this world. A new Charlemagne, the smallest new Charlemagne of Spiritual type, with *his* Paladins round him; how glorious, how salutary in the dim generations now. going! — These too were hopes which proved signally futile. Rigorous Time could not grant these at all; — granted, in his own hard way, other things instead. But, all along, the Life-element, the Epoch, though Friedrich took it kindly and never complained, was ungenial to such a man.

"Somewhat of a rotten Epoch, this into which Friedrich has been born, to shape himself and his activities royal and other!" — exclaims Smelfungus once: "In an older earnest Time, when the eternally awful meanings of this Universe had not yet sunk into dubieties to any one, much less into levities or into mendacities, into huge hypocrisies carefully regulated, — so luminous, vivid and ingenuous a young creature had not wanted divine manna in his Pilgrimage through Life. Nor, in that case, had he come out of it in so lean a condition. But the highest man of us is born brother to his Contemporaries; struggle as he may, there is no escaping the family likeness. By spasmodic indignant contradiction of them, by stupid compliance with them, — you will inversely resemble, if you do not directly; like the starling, you can't get out! — Most surely, if there do fall manna from Heaven, in the given Generation, and nourish in us reverence and genial nobleness day by day, it is blessed and well. Failing that, in regard to our poor spiritual interests, there is sure to be one of two results: mockery, contempt, disbelief, what we may call *short-diet* to the length of very famine (which was Friedrich's case); or else slow-poison, carefully elaborated and provided by way of daily nourishment.

"Unhappy souls, these same! The slow-poison has gone deep into them. Instead of manna, this long while back, they have been living on mouldy corrupt meats sweetened by sugar-of-lead; or perhaps, like Voltaire, a few individuals prefer hunger, as the cleaner alternative; and in contemptuous, barren, mocking humor, not yet got the length of geniality or indignation, snuff the east-wind by way of spiritual diet. Pilgriming along on such nourishment, the best human soul fails to become very ruddy! — Tidings about Heaven are fallen so uncertain, but the Earth and her joys are still interesting: 'Take to the Earth and her joys; — let your soul go out, since it must; let your five senses and their appetites be well alive.' That is a dreadful 'Sham-Christian Dispensation' to be born under! You wonder at the want of heroism in the Eighteenth Century. Wonder rather at the degree of heroism it had; wonder how many souls there still are to be met with in it of some effective capability, though dieting in that way, — nothing else to be had in the shops about. Carterets, Belleisles, Friedrichs, Voltaires; Chathams, Franklins, Choiseuls: there is an effective stroke of work, a fine fire of heroic pride, in this man and the other; not yet extinguished by spiritual famine or slow-poison; so robust is Nature the mighty Mother! —

"But in general, that sad Gospel, 'Souls extinct, Stomachs well alive!' is the credible one, not articulately preached, but practically believed by the abject generations, and acted on as it never was before. What immense sensualities there were, is known; and also (as some small offset, though that has not yet begun in 1740) what immense quantities of Physical Labor and contrivance were got out of mankind, in that Epoch and down to this day. As if, having lost its Heaven, it had struck desperately down into the Earth; as if it were a *beaver*-kind, and not a mankind any more. We had once a Barba-

rossa; and a world all grandly true. But from that to Karl VI.,
and *his* Holy Romish Reich in such a state of 'Holiness' — !"
I here cut short my abstruse Friend.

Readers are impatient to have done with these miscellaneous preludings, and to be once definitely under way, such
a Journey lying ahead. Yes, readers; a Journey indeed!
And, at this point, permit me to warn you that, where the
ground, where Dryasdust and the Destinies, yield anything
humanly illustrative of Friedrich and his Work, one will
have to linger, and carefully gather it, even as here. Large
tracts occur, bestrewn with mere pedantisms, diplomatic cobwebberies, learned marine-stores, and inhuman matter, over
which we shall have to skip empty-handed: this also was
among the sad conditions of our Enterprise, that it has to go
now too slow and again too fast; not in proportion to natural
importance of objects, but to several inferior considerations
withal. So busy has perverse Destiny been on it; perverse
Destiny, edacious Chance; — and the Dryasdusts, too, and
Nightmares, in Prussia as elsewhere, we know how strong
they are!

Friedrich's character in old age has doubtless its curious
affinities, its disguised identities, with these prognostic features and indications of his youth: and to our readers, — if
we do ever get them to the goal, of seeing Friedrich a little
with their own eyes and judgments, — there may be pleasant
contrasts and comparisons of that kind in store, one day.
But the far commoner experience (which also has been my
own), — here is Smelfungus's stern account of that: —

"My friend, you will be luckier than I, if, after ten years,
not to say, in a sense, twenty years, thirty years, of reading
and rummaging in those sad Prussian Books, ancient and new
(which often are laudably authentic, too, and exact as to details), you can gather any character whatever of Friedrich, in
any period of his life, or conceive him as a Human Entity
at all! It is strange, after such thousand-fold writing, but it
is true, his History is considerably unintelligible to mankind
at this hour; left chaotic, enigmatic, in a good many points, —
the military part of it alone being brought to clearness, and

rendered fairly conceivable and credible to those who will
study. And as to the Man himself, or what his real Physiognomy can have been — ! Well, it must be owned few men
were of such *rapidity* of face and aspect; so difficult to seize
the features of. In his action, too, there was such rapidity,
such secrecy, suddenness : a man that could not be read, even
by the candid, except as in flashes of lightning. And then
the anger of by-standers, *un*candid, who got hurt by him ; the
hasty malevolences, the stupidities, the opacities : enough, in
modern times, what is saying much, perhaps no man's motives,
intentions, and procedure have been more belied, misunder-
stood, misrepresented, during his life. Nor, I think, since
that, have many men fared worse, by the Limner or Bio-
graphic class, the favorable to him and the unfavorable ; or
been so smeared of and blotched of, and reduced to a mere
blur and dazzlement of cross-lights, incoherences, incredibili-
ties, in which nothing, not so much as a human nose, is clearly
discernible by way of feature !" — Courage, reader, nevertheless; on the above terms let us march according to promise.

CHAPTER II.

THE HOMAGINGS.

YOUNG Friedrich, as his Father had done, considers it un-
necessary to be crowned. Old Friedrich, first of the name,
and of the King series, we did see crowned, with a pinch
of snuff tempering the solemnities. That Coronation once
well done suffices all his descendants hitherto. Such an
expense of money, — of diluted mendacity too ! Such haranguing, gesturing, symbolic fugling, all grown half false : —
avoid lying, even with your eyes, or knees, or the coat upon
your back, so far as you easily can !

Nothing of Coronation : but it is thought needful to have
the *Huldigungen* (Homagings) done, the Fealties sworn; and

the young Majesty in due course goes about, or gives directions, now here now there, in his various Provinces, getting that accomplished. But even in that, Friedrich is by no means strait-laced or punctilious ; does it commonly by Deputy : only in three places, Königsberg, Berlin, Cleve, does he appear in person. Mainly by deputy ; and always with the minimum of fuss, and no haranguing that could be avoided. Nowhere are the old *Stände* (Provincial Parliaments) assembled, now or afterwards : sufficient for this and for every occasion are the " Permanent Committees of the *Stände ;*" nor is much speaking, unessential for despatch of business, used to these.

" *Stände* — of Ritterschaft mainly, of Gentry small and great — existed once in all those Countries, as elsewhere," says one Historian ; " and some of them, in Preussen, for example, used to be rather loud, and inclined to turbulence, till the curb, from a judicious bridle-hand, would admonish them. But, for a long while past, — especially since the Great Elector's time, who got an ' Excise Law ' passed, or the foundations of a good Excise Law laid ;[1] and, what with Excise, what with Domain-Farms, had a fixed Annual Budget, which he reckoned fair to both parties, — they have been dying out for want of work ; and, under Friedrich Wilhelm, may be said to have gone quite dead. What work was left for them ? Prussian Budget is fixed, many things are fixed : why talk of them farther ? The Prussian King, nothing of a fool like certain others," — which indeed is the cardinal point, though my Author does not say so, — " is respectfully aware of the facts round him ; and can listen to the rumors too, so far as he finds good. The King sees himself terribly interested to get into the right course in all things, and avoid the wrong one ! Probably he does, in his way, seek ' wise Advice concerning the arduous matters of the Kingdom ;' nay I believe he is diligent to have it of the wisest : — who knows if *Stände* would always give it wiser ; especially *Stände* in the haranguing condition ? " — Enough, they are not applied to. There is no Freedom in that Country. " No Freedom to

[1] Preuss, iv. 432 ; and *Thronbesteigung*, pp. 379–383.

speak of," continues he : " but I do a little envy them their
Fixed Budget, and some other things.   What pleasure there
can be in having your household arrangements tumbled into
disorder every new Year, by a new-contrived scale of expenses
for you, I never could ascertain ! " —

Friedrich is not the man to awaken Parliamentary sleeping-
dogs well settled by his Ancestors.   Once or twice, out of
Preussen, in Friedrich Wilhelm's time, there was heard some
whimper, which sounded like the beginning of a bark.   But
Friedrich Wilhelm was on the alert for it : Are you coming
in with your *Nie Pozwalam* (your *Liberum Veto*), then ? None
of your Polish vagaries here.   " *Tout le pays sera ruiné* (the
whole Country will be ruined)," say you ?   (Such had been
the poor Marshal or Provincial *Speaker's* Remonstrance on
one occasion) : "I don't believe a word of that.   But I do
believe the Government by *Junkers* [Country Squires] and
Nie Pozwalam will be ruined," — as it is fully meant to be !
" I am establishing the King's Sovereignty like a rock of
bronze (*Ich stabilire die Souverainetät wie einen Rocher von
Bronze*)," some extremely strong kind of rock ! [1] This was
one of Friedrich Wilhelm's marginalia in response to such a
thing ; and the mutinous whimper died out again.   Parliamentary Assemblages are sometimes Collective Wisdoms, but
by no means always so.   In Magdeburg we remember what
trouble Friedrich Wilhelm had with his unreasonable Ritters.
Ritters there, in their assembled capacity, had the Reich
behind them, and could not be dealt with like Preussen : but
Friedrich Wilhelm, by wise slow methods, managed Magdeburg too, and reduced it to silence, or to words necessary for
despatch of business.

In each Province, a Permanent Committee — chosen, I suppose, by King and Knights assenting ; chosen I know not how,
but admitted to be wisely chosen — represents the once Parliament or *Stände ;* and has its potency for doing good service
in regard to all Provincial matters, from roads and bridges
upwards, and is impotent to do the least harm.   Roads and

---

[1] Förster, b. iii. (*Urkundenbuch*, i. 50) ; Preuss, iv. 420 n.   " *Nie Pozwalam* "
(the formula of *Liberum Veto*) signifies " I Don't Permit ! "

bridges, Church matters, repartition of the Land-dues, Army matters, — in fact they are an effective non-haranguing Parliament, to the King's Deputy in every such Province; well calculated to illuminate and forward his subaltern *Amt*men and him. Nay, we observe it is oftenest in the way of gifts and solacements that the King articulately communicates with these Committees or their Ritterschafts. Projects for Draining of Bogs, for improved Highways, for better Husbandry; loans granted them, Loan-Banks established for the Province's behoof : — no need of parliamentary eloquence on such occasions, but of something far different.

It is from this quiescent, or busy but noiseless kind of *Stände* and Populations that Friedrich has his *Huldigung* to take ; — and the operation, whether done personally or by deputy, must be an abundantly simple one. He, for his part, is fortunate enough to find everywhere the Sovereignty *established ;* "rock of bronze" not the least shaken in his time. He will graciously undertake, by Written Act, which is read before the *Stände*, King or King's Deputy witnessing there, "To maintain the privileges" of his *Stände* and Populations ; the *Stände* answer, on oath, with lifted hand, and express invocation of Heaven, That they will obey him as true subjects; And so — doubtless with something of dining superadded, but no whisper of it put on record — the *Huldigung* will everywhere very quietly transact itself.

The *Huldigung* itself is nothing to us, even with Friedrich there, — as at Königsberg, Berlin, Cleve, the three exceptional places. To which, nevertheless, let us briefly attend him, for the sake of here and there some direct glimpse we may get of the then Friedrich's actual physiognomy and ways. Other direct view, or the chance of such, is not conceded us out of those sad Prussian Books; which are very full on this of the *Huldigung,* if silent on so many other points.[1]

---

[1] Preuss, *Thronbesteigung*, p 382.

Friedrich accepts the Homages, personally, in Three Places.

To Königsberg is his first excursion on this errand. Preussen has perhaps, or may be suspected of having, some remnants of sour humors left in it, and remembrances of *Stände* with haranguings and even mutinies: there if anywhere the King in person may do good on such an occasion. He left Berlin, July 7th, bound thitherward; here is Note of that first Royal Tour, — specimen of several hundreds such, which he had to do in the course of the next forty-five years.

"Friend Algarotti, charming talker, attended him; who else, official and non-official, ask not. The Journey is to be circuitous; to combine various businesses, and also to have its amusements. They went by Cüstrin; glancing at old known Country, which is at its greenest in this season. By Cüstrin, across the Neumark, into Pommern; after that by an intricate winding route; reviewing regiments, inspecting garrisons, now here now there; doing all manner of inspections; talking I know not what; oftenest lodging with favored Generals, if it suited. Distance to Königsberg, by the direct road, is about 500 miles; by this winding one, it must have been 800: Journey thither took nine days in all. Obliquely through Pommern, almost to the coast of the Baltic; their ultimatum there a place called Cöslin, where they reviewed with strictness, — omitting Colberg, a small Sea-Fortress not far rearward, time being short. Thence into West-Preussen, into Polish Territory, and swiftly across that; keeping Dantzig and its noises wide enough to the left: one night in Poland; and the next they are in Ost-Preussen, place called Liebstadt, — again on home-ground, and diligently reviewing there.

"The review at Liebstadt is remarkable in this, That the regiments, one regiment especially, not being what was fit, a certain Grenadier-Captain got cashiered on the spot; and the old Commandant himself was soon after pensioned, and more gently sent his ways. So strict is his Majesty. Contrariwise, he found Lieutenant-General von Katte's Garrison, at Angerburg, next day, in a very high perfection; and Colonel

Posadowsky's regiment specially so; with which latter gentleman he lodged that night, and made him farther happy by the
Order of Merit : Colonel Posadowsky, Garrison of Angerburg,
far off in East-Preussen, Chevalier of the Order of Merit henceforth, if we ever meet him again. To the good old Lieutenant-
General von Katte, who no doubt dined with them, his Majesty
handed, on the same occasion, a Patent of Feldmarschall; —
intends soon to make him Graf; and did it, as readers know.
Both Colonel and General attended him thenceforth, still by
a circuitous route, to Königsberg, to assist in the solemnities
there.   By Gumbinnen, by Trakehnen, — the Stud of Trakehnen : that also his Majesty saw, and made review of; not
without emotion, we can fancy, as the sleek colts were trotted
out on those new terms ! At Trakehnen, Katte and the Colonel
would be his Majesty's guests, for the night they stayed.
This is their extreme point eastward; Königsberg now lies a
good way west of them. But at Trakehnen they turn; and,
Saturday, 16th July, 1740, after another hundred miles or
so, along the pleasant valley of the Pregel, get to Königsberg:
ready to begin business on Monday morning, — on Sunday if
necessary." [1]

On Sunday there did a kind of memorability occur : The
Huldigungs-Predigt (Homage Sermon) by a reverend Herr
Quandt, chief Preacher there.   Which would not be worth
mentioning, except for this circumstance, that his Majesty
exceedingly admired Quandt, and thought him a most Demosthenic genius, and the best of all the Germans.   Quandt's
text was in these words : " *Thine are we, David, and on thy
side, thou Son of Jesse ; Peace, peace be unto thee, and peace be
to thine helpers ; for thy God helpeth thee.*" [2]   Quandt began,
in a sonorous voice, raising his face with respectful enthusiasm
to the King, " Thine are we, O Friedrich, and on thy side, thou
Son of Friedrich Wilhelm ; " and so went on : sermon brief,
sonorous, compact, and sticking close to its text.   Friedrich
stood immovable, gazing on the eloquent Demosthenic Quandt,
with admiration heightened by surprise ; — wrote of Quandt to

---

[1] From Preuss, *Thronbesteigung,* pp. 382, 385 ; Rödenbeck, p. 16 ; &c.
[2] *First Chronicles,* xii. 18.

Voltaire ; and, with sustained enthusiasm, to the Public long afterwards ; and to the end of his days was wont to make Quandt an exception, if perhaps almost the only one, from German barbarism, and disharmony of mind and tongue. So that poor Quandt cannot ever since get entirely forgotten, but needs always to be raked up again, for this reason when others have ceased : an almost melancholy adventure for poor Quandt and Another ! —

The *Huldigung* was rather grand ; Harangue and Counter-harangue permitted to the due length, and proper festivities following : but the *Stände* could not manage to get into vocal covenanting or deliberating at all ; Friedrich before leaving Berlin had answered their hint or request that way, in these words : " We are likewise graciously inclined to give to the said *Stände*, before their Homaging, the same assurance which they got from our Herr Father's Majesty, who is now with God,"— general assurance that their, and everybody's, " Rights shall be maintained [as we see they are], — with which, it is hoped (*hoffentlich*), they will be content, and get to peace upon this matter (*sich dabei beruhigen werden*)." [1] It will be best for them !

Friedrich gave away much corn here ; that is, opened his Corn-Granaries, on charitable terms, and took all manner of measures, here as in other places, for relief of the scarcity there was. Of the illuminations, never so grand, the reader shall hear nothing. A " Torch-Procession of the Students " turned out a pretty thing : — Students marching with torches, with fine wind-music, regulated enthusiasm, fine succinct address to his Majesty ; and all the world escorting, with its " Live Forever ! " Friedrich gave the Students " a *Trink-Gelag* (Banquet of Liquors)," how arranged I do not know : and to the Speaker of the Address, a likely young gentleman with *Von* to his name, he offered an Ensigncy of Foot (" in Camas's Fusileer Regiment," — Camas now gone to Paris, embassying), which was joyfully accepted. Joyfully accepted ; — and it turned out well for all parties ; the young gentleman having risen, where merit was the rule of rising, and become

[1] Preuss, *Thronbesteigung*, p. 380.

Graf and Lieutenant-General, in the course of the next fifty
years.[1]

Huldigung and Torch-Procession over, the Royal Party
dashed rapidly off, next morning (21st July), homewards by
the shortest route; and, in three days more, by Frankfurt-on-
Oder (where a glimpse of General Schwerin, a favorite General, was to be had), were safe in Berlin; received with acclamation, nay with "blessings and even tears" some say, after
this pleasant Fortnight's Tour.   General Schwerin, it is rumored, will be made Feldmarschall straightway, the Münchows
are getting so promoted as we said; edicts are coming out,
much business speeding forward, and the tongues of men keep
wagging.

Berlin *Huldigung* — and indeed, by Deputy, that of nearly
all the other Towns — was on Tuesday, August 2d.   At Berlin his Majesty was present in the matter : but, except the
gazing multitudes, and hussar regiments, ranked in the
Schloss-Platz and streets adjoining, there was little of notable in it; the upholstery arrangements thrifty in the extreme.
His Majesty is prone to thrift in this of the Huldigung, as
would appear; perhaps regarding the affair as scenic merely.
Here, besides this of Berlin, is another instance just occurring.   It appears, the Quedlinburg people, shut out from the
light of the actual Royal Countenance, cannot do their Homaging by Deputy, without at least a Portrait of the King and
of the Queen: How manage ? asks the Official Person.   "Have
a Couple of Daubs done in Berlin, three guineas apiece ; send
them these," answers the King![2]

Here in the Berlin Schloss, scene the Large Hall within doors,
there is a "platform raised three steps ; and on this, by way
of a kind of throne, an arm-chair covered with old black velvet ;" the whole surmounted by a canopy also of old black
velvet : not a sublime piece of upholstery ; but reckoned adequate.   Friedrich mounted the three steps ; stood before the

---

[1] Preuss, *Thronbesteigung*, p. 387.

[2] " *On doit faire barbouiller de mauvaises copies à Berlin, la pièce à 20 écus.* —
Fr." Preuss, ii. (*Urkundenbuch*, s. 222).

old chair, his Princes standing promiscuously behind it; his Ritters in quantity, in front and to right and left, on the floor. Some Minister of the Interior explains suitably, not at too great length, what they are met for; some junior Official, junior but of quality, responded briefly, for himself and his order, to the effect, "Yea, truly:" the *Huldigungs-Urkunde* (Deed of Homage) was then read by the proper Clerk, and the Ritters all swore; audibly, with lifted hands. This is the Ritter Huldigung.

His Majesty then steps out to the Balcony, for Oath and Homage of the general Population. General population gave its oath, and "three great shouts over and above." " *Es lebe der König!* " thrice, with all their throats. Upon which a shower of Medals, "Homage-Medals," gold and silver (quantity not mentioned) rained down upon them, in due succession; and were scrambled for, in the usual way. "His Majesty," they write, and this is perhaps the one point worth notice, "his Majesty, contrary to custom and to etiquette, remained on the Balcony, some time after the ceremony, perhaps a full half-hour;" — silent there, "with his look fixed attentively on the immeasurable multitude before the Schloss; and seemed sunk in deep reflection *(Betrachtung)* : " — an almost awfully eloquent though inarticulate phenomenon to his Majesty, that of those multitudes scrambling and huzzaing there![1]

These, with the Cleve one, are all the Homagings Friedrich was personally present at; the others he did by Deputy, all in one day (2d August); and without fuss. Scenic matters these; in which, except where he can, as in the Königsberg case, combine inspections and grave businesses with them, he takes no interest. However, he is now, for the sake chiefly of inspections and other real objects, bent on a Journey to Cleve; — the fellow of that to Königsberg: Königsberg, Preussen, the easternmost outlying wing of his long straggling Dominions; and then Cleve-Jülich, its counterpart on the southwestern side, — there also, with such contingencies hanging over Cleve-Jülich,

[1] Preuss, *Thronbesteigung*, p. 389.

it were proper to make some mustering of the Frontier garrisons and affairs.[1]   His Majesty so purposes : and we purpose again to accompany, — not for inspection and mustering, but for an unexpected reason.   The grave Journey to Cleve has an appendage, or comic side-piece, hanging to it ; more than one appendage ; which the reader must not miss ! — Before setting out, read these two Fractions, snatched from the Diplomatist Wastebag ; looking well, we gain there some momentary view of Friedrich on the business side.   Of Friedrich, and also of Another : —

Sunday, 14th August, 1740, Dickens, who has been reporting hitherto in a favorable, though in a languid exoteric manner, not being in any height of favor, England or he, — had express Audience of his Majesty ; being summoned out to Potsdam for that end : "Sunday evening, about 7 P.M." — Majesty intending to be off on the Cleve Journey to-morrow. Let us accompany Dickens.   Readers may remember, George II. has been at Hanover for some weeks past ; Bielfeld diligently grinning euphemisms and courtly graciosities to him ; Truchsess hinting, on opportunity, that there are perhaps weighty businesses in the rear ; which, however, on the Britannic side, seem loath to start.   Britannic Majesty is much at a loss about his Spanish War, so dangerous for kindling France and the whole world upon him.   In regard to which Prussia might be so important, for or against. — This, in compressed form, is what Dickens witnesses at Potsdam that Sunday evening from 7 P.M. : —

"Audience lasted above an hour : King turned directly upon business ; wishes to have 'Categorical Answers' as to Three Points already submitted to his Britannic Majesty's consideration.   Clear footing indispensable between us.   What you want of me ? say it, and be plain.   What I want of you is, These three things : —

" 1°. Guarantee for Jülich and Berg.   All the world knows *whose* these Duchies are.   Will his Britannic Majesty guaran-

---

[1] In regard to the Day of *Huldigung* at Cleve, which happily is not of the least moment to us, Preuss (*Thronbesteigung*, p. 390) and *Helden-Geschichte*, (i. 423) seem to be in flat contradiction.

tee me there ?   And if so, How, and to what lengths, will he proceed about it ?

"2°. Settlement about Ost-Friesland. Expectancy of Ost-Friesland, soon to fall heirless, which was granted *me* long since, though Hanover makes hagglings, counter-claimings : I must have some Settlement about that.

"3°. The like about those perplexities in Mecklenburg. No difficulty there if we try heartily, nor is there such pressing haste about it.

"These are my three claims on England; and I will try to serve England as far in return, if it will tell me how. 'Ah, beware of throwing yourself into the arms of France!' modestly suggests Dickens. — 'Well, if France will guarantee me those Duchies, and you will not do anything ?' answers his Majesty with a fine laugh : 'England I consider my most natural friend and ally; but I must know what there is to depend on there. Princes are ruled by their interest; cannot follow their feelings. Let me have an explicit answer; say, at Wesel, where I am to be on the 24th,'" ten days hence. Britannic Majesty is at Hanover, and can answer within that time. "This he twice told me, 'Wesel, 24th,' in the course of our interview. Permit me to recommend the matter to your Lordship," — my Lord Harrington, now attending the Britannic Majesty.

"During the whole audience," adds Dickens, "the King was in extreme good humor; and not only heard with attention all the considerations I offered, but was not the least offended at any objections I made to what he said. It is undoubtedly the best way to behave with frankness to him." These last are Dickens's own words; let them modestly be a memorandum to your Lordship. This King goes himself direct to the point; and straightforwardness, as a primary condition, will profit your Lordship with him.[1]

Most true advice, this; — and would perhaps be followed, were it quite easy! But things are very complicated. And the Britannic Majesty, much plagued with Spanish War and Parliamentary noises in that unquiet Island, is doubtless glad

[1] Dickens (in State-Paper Office, 17th August, 1740).

to get away to Hanover for a little; and would fain be on holiday in these fine rural months. Which is not well possible either. Jenkins's Ear, rising at last like a fiery portent, has kindled the London Fog over yonder, in a strange way, and the murky stagnancy is all getting on fire; the English intent, as seldom any Nation was, to give the Spaniards an effectual beating. Which they hope they can, — though unexpected difficulties will occur. And, in the mean while, what a riddle of potentialities for his poor Majesty to read, and pick his way from! —

Bielfeld, in spite of all this, would fain be full of admiration for the Britannic Majesty. Confesses he is below the middle size, in fact a tiny little creature, but then his shape is perfect; leg much to be commended, — which his Majesty knows, standing always with one leg slightly advanced, and the Order of the Garter on it, that mankind may take notice. Here is Bielfeld's description faithfully abridged: —

"Big blue eyes, perhaps rather of parboiled character, though proud enough; eyes flush with his face or more, rather *in relief* than on a level with it," — *à fleur de tête*, after the manner of a fish, if one might say so, and betokening such an intellect behind them! "Attitude constrained, leg advanced in that way; his courtiers call it majestic. Biggish mouth, strictly shut in the crescent or horse-shoe form (*fermée en croissant*); curly wig (*à nœuds*, reminding you of lamb's-wool, color not known); eyebrows, however, you can see are ashyblond; general tint is fundamentally livid; but when in good case, the royal skin will take tolerably bright colors (*prend d'assez belles couleurs*). As to the royal mind and understanding, what shall Bielfeld say? That his Majesty sometimes makes ingenious and just remarks, and is laudably serious at all times, and can majestically hold his tongue, and stand with advanced leg, and eyes rather more than flush. Sense of his dignity is high, as it ought to be; on great occasions you see pride and a kind of joy mantling in the royal countenance. Has been known to make explosions, and to be very furious to Prince Fred and others, when pricked into: — but, my friend, what mortal is exempt from failings? Majesty reads the Eng-

lish Newspapers every morning in bed, which are often biting.
Majesty has his Walmoden, a Hanoverian Improper Female,
Countess of Yarmouth so called; quiet, autumnal, fair com-
plexioned, stupid; who is much a comfort to him. She keeps
out of mischief, political or other; and gives Bielfeld a gra-
cious nod now and then." [1] Harrington is here too; — and
Britannic Majesty and he are busy governing the English
Nation on these terms. — We return now to the Prussian
Majesty.

About six weeks after that of Dickens, — Cleve Journey
and much else now ended, — Prætorius the Danish Envoy,
whom we slightly knew at Reinsberg once, gives this testimony; writing home to an Excellency at Copenhagen, whose
name we need not inquire into: —

"To give your Excellency a just idea of the new Government here, I must observe that hitherto the King of Prussia
does as it were everything himself; and that, excepting the
Finance Minister von Boden, who preaches frugality, and finds
for that doctrine uncommon acceptance, almost greater even
than in the former reign, his Majesty allows no counselling
from any Minister; so that Herr von Podewils, who is now the
working hand in the department of Foreign Affairs, has nothing given him to do but to expedite the orders he receives from
the Cabinet, his advice not being asked upon any matter; and
so it is with the other Ministers. People thought the loss of
Herr von Thulmeyer," veteran Foreign Minister whom we
have transiently heard of in the Double-Marriage time, and
perhaps have even seen at London or elsewhere, [2] "would be
irreparable; so expert was he, and a living archive in that
business : however, his post seems to have vanished with
himself. His salary is divided between Herr von Podewils,"
whom the reader will sometimes hear of again, "Kriegsrath
(Councillor of War) von Ilgen," son of the old gentleman we
used to know, "and Hofrath Sellentin who is *Rendant of the
Legations-Kasse*" (Ambassadors' Paymaster, we could guess,
Ambassador Body having specialty of cash assigned it, comparable with the specialty of value received from it, in this

---

[1] Bielfeld, i. 158.   [2] Died 4th August (Rödenbeck, p. 20).

strict frugal Country), — neither of which two latter names shall the reader be troubled with farther. "A good many resolutions, and responses by the King, I have seen: they combine laconic expression with an admirable business eye (*Geschäfts-blick*). Unhappily," — at least for us in the Diplomatic line, for your Excellency and me unhappily, — "there is nobody about the King who possesses his complete confidence, or whom we can make use of in regard to the necessary introductions and preliminary movements. Hereby it comes that, — as certain things can only be handled with cautious foresight and circumlocution, and in the way of beginning wide, — an Ambassador here is more thrown out of his course than in any other Court; and knows not, though his object were steadily in sight, what road to strike into for getting towards it." [1]

CHAPTER III.

FRIEDRICH MAKES AN EXCURSION, NOT OF DIRECT SORT, INTO THE CLEVE COUNTRIES.

King Friedrich did not quite keep his day at Wesel; indeed this 24th was not the first day, but the last of several, he had appointed to himself for finis to that Journey in the Cleve Countries; Journey rather complex to arrange. He has several businesses ahead in those parts; and, as usual, will group them with good judgment, and thrift of time. Not inspections merely, but amusements, meetings with friends, especially French friends: the question is, how to group them with skill, so that the necessary elements may converge at the right moment, and one shot kill three or four birds. This is Friedrich's fine way, perceptible in all these Journeys. The French friends, flying each on his own track, with his own load of impediments, Voltaire with his Madame for instance, are a difficult element in such problem; and there has been, and is, much scheming and corresponding about it, within the last month especially.

Voltaire is now at Brussels with his Du Châtelet, prosecuting that endless "lawsuit with the House of Honsbruck," — which he, and we, are both desirous to have done with. He is at the Hague, too, now and then ; printing, about to print, the *Anti-Machiavel ;* corresponding, to right and left, quarrelling with Van Duren the Printer ; lives, while there, in the *Vieille Cour,* in the vast dusky rooms with faded gilding, and grand old Bookshelves "with the biggest spider-webs in Europe." Brussels is his place for Law-Consultations, general family residence ; the Hague and that old spider-web Palace for correcting Proof-sheets ; doing one's own private studies, which we never quite neglect. Fain would Friedrich see him, fain he Friedrich ; but there is a divine Emilie, there is a Maupertuis, there are — In short, never were such difficulties, in the cooking of an egg with water boiling ; and much vain correspondence has already been on that subject, as on others equally extinct. Correspondence which is not pleasant reading at this time ; the rather as no reader can, without endless searching, even understand it. Correspondence left to us, not in the cosmic, elucidated or legible state ; left mainly as the Editorial rubbish-wagons chose to shoot it ; like a tumbled quarry, like the ruins of a sacked city ; — avoidable by readers who are not forced into it ![1] Take the following select bricks as sample, which are of some use ; the general Heading is,

King Friedrich to M. de Voltaire (at the Hague, or at Brussels).

" *Charlottenburg, 12th June,* 1740. — . . . My dear Voltaire, resist no longer the eagerness I have to see you. Do in my favor whatever your humanity allows. In the end of August I go to Wesel, and perhaps farther. Promise that you will

[1] Herr Preuss's edition (*Œuvres de Frédéric,* vols. xxi. xxii. xxiii.) has come out since the above was written : it is agreeably exceptional ; being, for the first time, correctly printed, and the editor himself having mostly understood it, — though the reader still cannot, on the terms there allowed.

come and join me; for I could not live happy, nor die tranquil, without having embraced you! Thousand compliments to the Marquise," divine Emilie. "I am busy with both hands [Corn-Magazines, Free Press, Abolition of Torture, and much else]; working at the Army with the one hand, at the People and the Fine Arts with the other."

"*Berlin, 5th August,* 1740. — . . . I will write to Madame du Châtelet, in compliance with your wish:" mark it, reader. "To speak to you frankly concerning her journey, it is Voltaire, it is you, it is my Friend that I desire to see; and the divine Emilie with all her divinity is only the Accessory of the Apollo Newtonized.

"I cannot yet say whether I shall travel [incognito into foreign parts a little] or not travel;" there have been rumors, perhaps private wishes; but — . . . "Adieu, dear friend; sublime spirit, first-born of thinking beings. Love me always sincerely, and be persuaded that none can love and esteem you more than I. *Vale.* Fédéric."

"*Berlin, 6th August* [which is next day]. — You will have received a Letter from me dated yesterday; this is the second I write to you from Berlin; I refer you to what was in the other. If it must be (*faut*) that Emilie accompany Apollo, I consent; but if I could see you alone, that is what I would prefer. I should be too much dazzled; I could not stand so much splendor all at once; it would overpower me. I should need the veil of Moses to temper the united radiance of your two divinities." . . . In short, don't bring her, if you please.

"*Remusberg* [poetic for *Reinsberg*], *8th August,* 1740. — . . . My dear Voltaire, I do believe Van Duren costs you more trouble and pains than you had with *Henri Quatre*. In versifying the Life of a Hero, you wrote the history of your own thoughts; but in coercing a scoundrel you fence with an enemy who is not worthy of you." To punish him, and cut short his profits, "*print,* then, as you wish [your own edition of the *Anti-Machiavel,* to go along with his, and trip the feet from it]. *Faites rouler la presse;* erase, change, correct; do as you see best; your judgment about it shall be mine." — "In eight days I leave for [where thinks the reader? *"Dantzig"* deliberately print all the Editors, careful Preuss among them; overturning the terrestrial azimuths for us, and making day night!] — for Leipzig, and reckon on being at Frankfurt on the 22d. In case you could be there, I expect, on my passage, to give you lodging! At Cleve or in Holland, I depend for certain on embracing you."[1]

Intrinsically the Friedrich correspondence at this time, with Voltaire especially, among many friends now on the wing towards Berlin and sending letters, has, — if you are forced into struggling for some understanding of it, and do get to read parts of it with the eyes of Friedrich and Voltaire, — has a certain amiability; and is nothing like so waste and dreary as it looks in the chaotic or sacked-city condition. Friedrich writes with brevity, oftenest on practicalities (the *Anti-Machiavel*, the coming Interview, and the like), evidently no time to spare; writes always with considerable sincerity; with friendliness, much admiration, and an ingenuous vivacity, to M. de Voltaire. Voltaire, at his leisure in Brussels or the Old-Palace and its spider-webs, writes much more expansively; not with insincerity, he either; — with endless airy graciosities, and ingenious twirls, and touches of flattering unction, which latter, he is aware, must not be laid on too thick. As thus: —

In regard to the *Anti-Machiavel*, — Sire, deign to give me your permissions as to the scoundrel of a Van Duren; well worth while, Sire, — *"it* is a monument for the latest posterity; the only Book worthy of a King for these fifteen hundred years."

This is a strongish trowelful, thrown on direct, with adroitness; and even this has a kind of sincerity. Safer, however, to do it in the oblique or reflex way, — by Ambassador *Camas*, for example: —

"I will tell you boldly, Sir [you M. de Camas], I put more value on this Book (*Anti-Machiavel*) than on the Emperor

[1] Preuss, *Œuvres de Frédéric*, xx. pp. 5, 19–21; Voltaire, *Œuvres*, lxxii. 226, &c. (not worth citing, in comparison).

Julian's *Cæsar*, or on the *Maxims* of Marcus Aurelius," — I do indeed, having a kind of property in it withal!¹

In fact, Voltaire too is beautiful, in this part of the Correspondence; but much in a twitter, — the Queen of Sheba, not the sedate Solomon, in prospect of what is coming. He plumes himself a little, we perceive, to his d'Argentals and French Correspondents, on this sublime intercourse he has got into with a Crowned Head, the cynosure of mankind: — Perhaps even you, my best friend, did not quite know me, and what merits I had! Plumes himself a little; but studies to be modest withal; has not much of the peacock, and of the turkey has nothing, to his old friends. All which is very naïve and transparent; natural and even pretty, on the part of M. de Voltaire as the weaker vessel. — For the rest, it is certain Maupertuis is getting under way at Paris towards the Cleve rendezvous. Brussels, too, is so near these Cleve Countries; within two days' good driving: — if only the times and routes would rightly intersect?

Friedrich's intention is by no means for a straight journey towards Cleve: he intends for Baireuth first, then back from Baireuth to Cleve, — making a huge southward *elbow* on the map, with Baireuth for apex or turning-point: — in this manner he will make the times suit, and have a convergence at Cleve. To Baireuth; — who knows if not farther? All summer there has gone fitfully a rumor, that he wished to see France; perhaps Paris itself incognito? The rumor, which was heard even at Petersburg,² is now sunk dead again; but privately, there is no doubt, a glimpse of the sublime French Nation would be welcome to Friedrich. He could never get to Travelling in his young time; missed his Grand Tour altogether, much as he wished it; and he is capable of pranks! — Enough, on Monday morning, 15th August, 1740,³ Friedrich and Suite leave Potsdam, early enough; go, by Leipzig, by the

---

¹ Voltaire, *Œuvres*, lxxii. 280 (to Camas, 18th October, 1740).

² Raumer's *Beiträge* (English Translation, London, 1837), p. 15 (Finch's Despatch, 24th June, 1740).

³ Rödenbeck, p. 15, slightly in error: see Dickens's Interview, suprà, p. 187.

route already known to readers, through Coburg and the Voigt-
land regions; Wilhelmina has got warning, sits eagerly expecting her Brother in the Hermitage at Baireuth, gladdest of
shrill sisters; and full of anxieties how her Brother would now
be.   The travelling party consisted, besides the King, of seven
persons: Prince August Wilhelm, King's next Brother, Heir-
apparent if there come no children, now a brisk youth of
eighteen; Leopold Prince of Anhalt-Dessau, Old Dessauer's
eldest, what we may call the "Young Dessauer;" Colonel von
Borck, whom we shall hear of again; Colonel von Stille,
already heard of (grave men of fifty, these two); milk-beard
Münchow, an Adjutant, youngest of the promoted Münchows;
Algarotti, indispensable for talk; and Fredersdorf, the House-
Steward and domestic Factotum, once Private in Schwerin's
Regiment, whom Bielfeld so admired at Reinsberg, foreseeing
what he would come to.   One of Friedrich's late acts was to
give Factotum Fredersdorf an Estate of Land (small enough,
I fancy, but with country-house on it) for solace to the
leisure of so useful a man, — studious of chemistry too, as I
have heard.   Seven in all, besides the King.[1]   Direct towards
Baireuth, incognito, and at the top of their speed.   Wednesday, 17th, they actually arrive.   Poor Wilhelmina, she finds
her Brother changed; become a King in fact, and sternly solitary; alone in soul, even as a King must be![2] —

"Algarotti, one of the first *beaux-esprits* of this age," as
Wilhelmina defines him, — Friend Algarotti, the young Venetian gentleman of elegance, in dusky skin, in very white linen
and frills, with his fervid black eyes, "does the expenses of
the conversation."   He is full of elegant logic, has speculations on the great world and the little, on Nature, Art, Papistry,
Anti-Papistry, and takes up the Opera in an earnest manner,
as capable of being a school of virtue and the moral sublime.
His respectable Books on the Opera and other topics are now
all forgotten, and crave not to be mentioned.   To me he is
not supremely beautiful, though much the gentleman in manners as in ruffles, and ingeniously logical: — rather yellow to

[1] Rödenbeck, p. 19 (and for Chamberlain Fredersdorf's estate, p. 15).
[2] Wilhelmina, ii. 322, 323.

me, in mind as in skin, and with a taint of obsolete Venetian
Macassar. But to Friedrich he is thrice-dear; who loves the
sharp faceted cut of the man, and does not object to his yellow or Extinct-Macassar qualities of mind. Thanks to that
wandering Baltimore for picking up such a jewel and carrying him Northward! Algarotti himself likes the North:
here in our hardy climates, — especially at Berlin, and were
his loved Friedrich *not* a King, — Algarotti could be very
happy in the liberty allowed. At London, where there is no
King, or none to speak of, and plenty of free Intelligences,
Carterets, Lytteltons, young Pitts and the like, he is also well,
were it not for the horrid smoke upon one's linen, and the
little or no French of those proud Islanders.

Wilhelmina seems to like him here; is glad, at any rate,
that he does the costs of conversation, better or worse. In
the rest is no hope. Stille, Borck are accomplished military
gentlemen; but of tacit nature, reflective, practical, rather
than discursive, and do not waste themselves by inconti-
nence of tongue. Stille, by his military Commentaries, which
are still known to soldiers that read, maintains some lasting
remembrance of himself: Borck we shall see engaged in a
small bit of business before long. As to Münchow, the *jeune
morveux* of an Adjutant, he, though his manners are well
enough, and he wears military plumes in his hat, is still an
unfledged young creature, "bill still yellow," so to speak; —
and marks himself chiefly by a visible hankering after that
troublesome creature Marwitz, who is always coquetting.
Friedrich's conversation, especially to me Wilhelmina, seems
"*guindé*, set on stilts," likewise there are frequent cuts of
banter in him; and it is painfully evident he distinguishes
my Sister of Anspach and her foolish Husband, whom he has
invited over hither in a most eager manner, beyond what a
poor Wilhelmina with her old love can pretend to. Patience,
my shrill Princess, Beauty of Baireuth and the world; let us
hope all will come right again! My shrill Princess — who
has a melodious strength like that of war-fifes, too — knows
how to be patient; and veils many things, though of a highly
unhypocritical nature.

These were Three great Days at Baireuth; Wilhelmina is to come soon, and return the visit at Berlin. To wait upon the King, known though incognito, " the Bishop of Bamberg " came driving over : [1] Schönborn, Austrian Kanzler, or who ? His old City we once saw (and plenty of hanged malefactors swinging round it, during that *Journey to the Reich*); — but the Bishop himself never to our knowledge, Bishop being absent then. I hope it is the same Bishop of Bamberg, whom a Friend of Büsching's, touring there about that same time, saw dining in a very extraordinary manner, with mediæval trumpeters, " with waiters in spurs and buff-belts; " [2] if it is not, I have not the slightest shadow of acquaintance with him, — there have been so many Bishops of Bamberg with whom one wishes to have none ! On the third day Friedrich and his company went away, towards Würzburg ; and Wilhelmina was left alone with her reflections. " I had had so much to say to him ; I had got nothing said at all: " alas, it is ever so. " The King was so changed, grown so much bigger (*grandi*), you could not have known him again ; " stands finely erect and at full breadth, every inch a King ; his very stature, you would say, increased. — Adieu, my Princess, pearl of Princesses ; all readers will expect your return-visit at Berlin, which is to be soon.

Friedrich strikes off to the left, and has a View of Strasburg for Two Days.

Through Würzburg, Frankfurt-on-Mayn, speeds Friedrich ; — Wilhelmina and mankind understand that it is homewards and to Cleve ; but at Frankfurt, in deepest privacy, there occurs a sudden whirl southward, — up the Rhine-Valley ; direct towards Strasburg, for a sight of France in that quarter ! So has Friedrich decided, — not quite suddenly, on new Letters here, or new computations about Cleve ; but by forethought taken at Baireuth, as rather appears. From Frankfurt to Strasburg, say 150 miles ; from Strasburg home, is not much farther than from Frankfurt home : it can be done, then ; husht !

---

[1] *Helden-Geschichte,* i. 419.

[2] Büsching's *Beiträge ;* — Schlosser (*History of the Eighteenth Century*) also quotes the scene.

The incognito is to be rigorous: Friedrich becomes *Comte Dufour;* a Prussian-French gentleman; Prince August Wilhelm is Graf von Schaffgotsch, Algarotti is Graf von Pfuhl, Germans these two; what Leopold, the Young Dessauer, called himself, — still less what the others, or whether the others were there at all, and not shoved on, direct towards Wesel, out of the way as is likelier, — can remain uncertain to readers and me. From Frankfurt, then, on Monday morning, 22d August, 1740, as I compute, through old known Philipsburg-Campaign country, and the lines of Ettlingen and Stollhofen; there the Royal Party speeds eagerly (weather very bad, as appears) : and it is certain they are at Kehl on Tuesday evening; looking across the long Rhine Bridge, Strasburg and its steeples now close at hand.

This looks to be a romantic fine passage in the History of the young King; — though in truth it is not, and proves but a feeble story either to him or us. Concerning which, however, the reader, especially if he should hear that there exists precise Account of it, Two Accounts indeed, one from the King's own hand, will not fail of a certain craving to become acquainted with details. This craving, foolish rather than wise, we consider it thriftiest to satisfy at once; and shall give the King's *Narrative* entire, though it is a jingling lean scraggy Piece, partly rhyme, "in the manner of Bachaumont and La Chapelle; " written at the gallop, a few days hence, and despatched to Voltaire : — "You," dear Voltaire, "wish to know what I have been about, since leaving Berlin; annexed you will find a description of it," writes Friedrich.[1] Out of Voltaire's and other people's waste-baskets, it has at length been fished up, patch by patch, and pasted together by victorious modern Editors; and here it is again entire. The other Narrative, which got into the Newspapers soon after, is likewise of authentic nature, — Fassmann, our poor old friend, confirming it, if that were needful, — and is happily in prose.[2]

---

[1] *Œuvres,* xxii. 25 (Wesel, 2d September, 1740).

[2] Given in *Helden-Geschichte,* i. 420–423 ; — see likewise Fassmann's *Merkwürdigster Regierungs-Antritt* (poor old Book on *Friedrich's Accession*); Preuss (*Thronbesteigung,* pp. 395–400) ; &c. &c.

Holding these two Pieces well together, and giving the King's
faithfully translated, in a complete state, it will be possible to
satisfy foolish cravings, and make this Strasburg Adventure
luminous enough.

King Friedrich to Voltaire (from Wesel, 2d September, 1740),
chiefly in Doggerel, concerning the Run to Strasburg.[1]

" I have just finished a Journey, intermingled with singular
adventures, sometimes pleasant, sometimes the reverse. You
know I had set out for Baireuth," — *Bruxelles* the beautiful
French Editor wrote, which makes Egyptian darkness of the
Piece ! — "to see a Sister whom I love no less than esteem.
On the road [thither or thence; or likeliest, *there*], Algarotti
and I consulted the map, to settle our route for returning
by Wesel. Frankfurt-on-Mayn comes always as a principal
stage ; — Strasburg was no great roundabout: we chose that
route in preference. The *incognito* was decided, names pitched
upon [Comte Dufour, and the others] ; story we were to tell :
in fine, all was arranged and concerted to a nicety as well as
possible. We fancied we should get to Strasburg in three
days [from Baireuth].

But Heaven, which disposes of all things,	*Mais le ciel, qui de tout dispose,*
Differently regulated this thing.	*Régla différemment la chose.*
With lank-sided coursers,	*Avec de coursiers efflanqués,*
Lineal descendants from Rosinante,	*En ligne droites issus de Rosinante,*
With ploughmen in the dress of postilions,	*Et des paysans en postillons masqués,*
Blockheads of impertinent nature ;	*Butors de race impertinente,*
Our carriages sticking fast a hundred times in the road,	*Notre carrosse en cent lieux accroché,*
We went along with gravity at a leisurely pace,	*Nous allions gravement, d'une allure indolente,*
Knocking against the crags.	*Gravitant contre les rochers.*

[1] Part of it, incorrect, in Voltaire, *Œuvres* (scandalous Piece now called
Mémoires, once *Vie Privée du Roi de Prusse*), ii. 24–26 ; finally, in Preuss,
Œuvres de Frédéric, xiv. 156–161, the real and complete affair, as fished up
by victorious Preuss and others.

The atmosphere in uproar with loud thunder,	*Les airs émus par le bruyant tonnerre,*
The rain-torrents streaming over the Earth	*Les torrents d'eau répandus sur la terre,*
Threatened mankind with the Day of Judgment [*very bad weather*],	*Du dernier jour menaçaient les humains ;*
And in spite of our impatience,	*Et malgré notre impatience,*
Four good days are, in penance,	*Quatre bons jours en pénitence*
Lost forever in these jumblings.	*Sont pour jamais perdus dans les charrains.*

" Had all our fatalities been limited to stoppages of speed on the journey, we should have taken patience ; but, after frightful roads, we found lodgings still frightfuler.

For greedy landlords	*Car des hôtes intéressés,*
Seeing us pressed by hunger	*De la faim nous voyant pressés,*
Did, in a more than frugal manner,	*D'une façon plus que frugale,*
In their infernal hovels,	*Dans une chaumière infernale,*
Poisoning instead of feeding,	*En nous empoisonnant,*
Steal from us our crowns.	*Nous volaient nos écus.*
O age different [in good cheer] from that of Lucullus !	*O siècle différent des temps de Lucullus !*

" Frightful roads ; short of victual, short of drink : nor was that all. We had to undergo a variety of accidents ; and certainly our equipage must have had a singular air, for in every new place we came to, they took us for something different.

Some took us for Kings,	*Les uns nous prenaient pour des rois,*
Some for pickpockets well disguised;	*D'autres pour des filous courtois,*
Others for old acquaintances.	*D'autres pour gens de connaissance;*
At times the people crowded out,	*Parfois le peuple s'attroupait,*
Looked us in the eyes,	*Entre les yeux nous regardait*
Like clowns impertinently curious.	*En badauds curieux, remplis d'impertinence.*
Our lively Italian [Algarotti] swore ;	*Notre vif Italien jurait,*
For myself I took patience ;	*Pour moi je prenais patience,*
The young Count [my gay younger Brother, eighteen at present] quizzed and frolicked ;	*Le jeune Comte folâtrait,*

The big Count [Heir-apparent of Dessau] silently swung his head,	*Le grand Comte se dandinait,*
Wishing this fine Journey to France,	*Et ce beau vogage de France*
In the bottom of his heart, most christianly at the Devil.	*Dans le fond de son cœur chré-tiennement damnait.*

"We failed not, however, to struggle gradually along; at last we arrived in that Stronghold, where [as preface to the War of 1734, known to some of us] —

Where the garrison, too supple,	*Où a garnison, troupe flasque,*
Surrendered so piteously	*Se rendit si piteusement*
After the first blurt of explosion	*Après la première bourasque*
From the cannon of the French.	*Du canon français foudroyant.*

You recognize Kehl in this description. It was in that fine Fortress, — where, by the way, the breaches are still lying unrepaired [Reich being a slow corpus in regard to such things], — that the Postmaster, a man of more foresight than we, asked If we had got passports ?

No, said I to him; of passports	*Non, lui dis-je, des passe-ports*
We never had the whim.	*Nous n'eûmes jamais la folie.*
Strong ones I believe it would need	*Il en faudrait, je crois, de forts*
To recall, to our side of the limit,	*Pour ressusciter à la vie*
Subjects of Pluto King of the Dead :	*De chez Pluton le roi des morts;*
But, from the Germanic Empire	*Mais de l'empire germanique*
Into the gallant and cynical abode	*Au séjour galant et cynique*
Of Messieurs your pretty Frenchmen, —	*De Messieurs vos jolis Français,*
A jolly and beaming air,	*Un air rebondissant et frais,*
Rubicund faces, not ignorant of wine,	*Une face rouge et bachique,*
These are the passports which, legible if you look on us,	*Sont les passe-ports qu'en nos traits*
Our troop produces to you for that end.	*Vous produit ici notre clique.*

"No, Messieurs, said the provident Master of Passports; no salvation without passport. Seeing then that Necessity had got us in the dilemma of either manufacturing passports ourselves or not entering Strasburg, we took the former branch of the alternative and manufactured one ; — in which feat the Prussian arms, which I had on my seal, were marvellously furthersome."

This is a fact, as the old Newspapers and confirmatory Fassmann more directly apprise us. "The Landlord [or Postmaster] at Kehl, having signified that there was no crossing without Passport," Friedrich, at first somewhat taken aback, bethought him of his watch-seal with the Royal Arms on it; and soon manufactured the necessary Passport, signeted in due form ; — which, however, gave a suspicion to the Innkeeper as to the quality of his Guest. After which, Tuesday evening, 23d August, "they at once got across to Strasburg," says my Newspaper Friend, "and put up at the *Sign of the Raven* there." Or in Friedrich's own jingle : —

"We arrived at Strasburg; and the Custom-house corsair, with his inspectors, seemed content with our evidences.

These scoundrels spied us,	*Ces scélérats nous épiaient,*
With one eye reading our passport,	*D'un œil le passe-port lisaient,*
With the other ogling our purse.	*De l'autre lorgnaient notre bourse.*
Gold, which was always a resource,	*L'or, qui toujours fut de ressource,*
Which brought Jove to the enjoyment	*Par lequel Jupin jouissait*
Of Danae whom he caressed ;	*De Danaé, qu'il caressait ;*
Gold, by which Cæsar governed	*L'or, par qui César gouvernait*
The world happy under his sway ;	*Le monde heureux sous son empire;*
Gold, more a divinity than Mars or Love;	*L'or, plus dieu que Mars et l'Amour,*
Wonder-working Gold introduced us,	*Le même or sut nous introduire,*
That evening, within the walls of Strasburg." [1]	*Le soir, dans les murs de Strasbourg.*

Sad doggerel; permissible perhaps as a sample of the Friedrich manufacture, surely not otherwise ! There remains yet

---

[1] Given thus far, with several slight errors, in Voltaire, ii. 24–26 ; — the remainder, long unknown, had to be fished up, patch by patch (Preuss, *Œuvres de Frédéric*, xiv. 159–161).

more than half of it; readers see what their foolish craving
has brought upon them! Doggerel out of which no clear story,
such story as there is, can be had; though, except the exaggeration and contortion, there is nothing of fiction in it. We fly
to the Newspaper, happily at least a prose composition, which
begins at this point; and shall use the Doggerel henceforth as
illustration only or as repetition in the Friedrich-mirror, of a
thing *otherwise* made clear to us: —

Having got into Strasburg and the *Raven Hotel;* Friedrich
now on French ground at last, or at least on Half-French,
German-French, is intent to make the most of circumstances.
The Landlord, with one of Friedrich's servants, is straightway
despatched into the proper coffee-houses to raise a supper-party
of Officers; politely asks any likely Officer, "If he will not
do a foreign Gentleman [seemingly of some distinction, signifies Boniface] the honor to sup with him at the Raven?" —
"No, by Jupiter!" answer the most, in their various dialects:
"who is he that we should sup with him?" Three, struck
by the singularity of the thing, undertake; and with these
we must be content. Friedrich — or call him M. le Comte
Dufour, with Pfuhl, Schaffgotsch and such escort as we see —
politely apologizes on the entrance of these officers: "Many
pardons, gentlemen, and many thanks. Knowing nobody;
desirous of acquaintance: — since you are so good, how
happy, by a little informality, to have brought brave Officers
to keep me company, whom I value beyond other kinds of
men!"

The Officers found their host a most engaging gentleman:
his supper was superb, plenty of wine, "and one red kind they
had never tasted before, and liked extremely;" — of which
he sent some bottles to their lodging next day. The conversation turned on military matters, and was enlivened with the
due sallies. This foreign Count speaks French wonderfully; a
brilliant man, whom the others rather fear: perhaps something
more than a Count? The Officers, loath to go, remembered
that their two battalions had to parade next morning, that
it was time to be in bed: "I will go to your review," said
the Stranger Count: the delighted Officers undertake to come

and fetch him, they settle with him time and method; how happy!

On the morrow, accordingly, they call and fetch him; he looks at the review; review done, they ask him to supper for this evening: "With pleasure!" and "walks with them about the Esplanade, to see the guard march by." Before parting, he takes their names, writes them in his tablets; says, with a smile, "He is too much obliged ever to forget them." This is Wednesday, the 24th of August, 1740; Field-Marshal Broglio is Commandant in Strasburg, and these obliging Officers are "of the regiment Piedmont," — their names on the King's tablets I never heard mentioned by anybody (or never till the King's Doggerel was fished up again). Field-Marshal Broglio my readers have transiently seen, afar off; — "galloping with only one boot," some say "almost in his shirt," at the Ford of Secchia, in those Italian campaigns, five years ago, the Austrians having stolen across upon him: — he had a furious gallop, with no end of ridicule, on that occasion; is now Commandant here; and we shall have a great deal more to do with him within the next year or two.

"This same day, 24th, while I [the Newspaper volunteer Reporter or Own Correspondent, seemingly a person of some standing, whose words carry credibility in the tone of them] was with Field-Marshal Broglio our Governor here, there came two gentlemen to be presented to him; 'German Cavaliers' they were called; who, I now find, must have been the Prince of Prussia and Algarotti. The Field-Marshal," — a rather high-stalking white-headed old military gentleman, bordering on seventy, of Piedmontese air and breed, apt to be sudden and make flounderings, but the soul of honor, "was very polite to the two Cavaliers, and kept them to dinner. After dinner there came a so-styled 'Silesian Nobleman,' who likewise was presented to the Field-Marshal, and affected not to know the other two: him I now find to have been the Prince of Anhalt."

Of his Majesty's supper with the Officers that Wednesday, we are left to think how brilliant it was: his Majesty, we hear farther, went to the Opera that night, — the Polichinello or whatever the "Italian *Comödie*" was; — "and a little girl

came to his box with two lottery-tickets fifteen pence each,
begging the foreign Gentleman for the love of Heaven to buy
them of her; which he did, tearing them up at once, and giving the poor creature four ducats," equivalent to two guineas,
or say in effect even five pounds of the present British currency.
The fame of this foreign Count and his party at The Raven
is becoming very loud over Strasburg, especially in military
circles. Our volunteer Own Correspondent proceeds (whom
we mean to contrast with the Royal Doggerel by and by) : —

"Next morning," Thursday, 25th August, "as the Marshal
with above two hundred Officers was out walking on the
Esplanade, there came a soldier of the Regiment Luxemburg,
who, after some stiff fugling motions, of the nature of salutation partly, and partly demand for privacy, intimated to the
Marshal surprising news : That the Stranger in The Raven
was the King of Prussia in person ; he, the soldier, at present
of the Regiment Luxemburg, had in other days, before he
deserted, been of the Prussian Crown-Prince's regiment; had
consequently seen him in Berlin, Potsdam and elsewhere a
thousand times and more, and even stood sentry where he
was : the fact is beyond dispute, your Excellency ! said this
soldier." — Whew !

Whereupon a certain Colonel, Marquis de Loigle, with or
without a hint from Broglio, makes off for The Raven ; introduces himself, as was easy ; contrives to get invited to stay
dinner, which also was easy. During dinner the foreign Gentleman expressed some wish to see their fortress. Colonel
Loigle sends word to Broglio ; Broglio despatches straightway
an Officer and fine carriage : "Will the foreign Gentleman do
me the honor ?" The foreign Gentleman, still struggling for
incognito, declines the uppermost seat of honor in the carriage ;
the two Officers, Loigle and this new one, insist on taking the
inferior place. Alas, the incognito is pretty much out. Calling at some coffee-house or the like on the road, a certain
female, "Madame de Fienne," named the foreign Gentleman
"Sire," — which so startled him that, though he utterly declined such title, the two Officers saw well how it was.

"After survey of the works, the two attendant Officers had

returned to the Field-Marshal; and about 4 P.M. the high Stranger made appearance there. But the thing had now got wind, 'King of Prussia here incognito!' The place was full of Officers, who came crowding about him: he escaped deftly into the Maréchal's own Cabinet; sat there, an hour, talking to the Maréchal [little admiring the Maréchal's talk, as we shall find], still insisting on the incognito," — to which Broglio, put out in his high paces by this sudden thing, and apt to flounder, as I have heard, was not polite enough to conform altogether. "What shall I do, in this sudden case?" poor Broglio is thinking to himself: "must write to Court; perhaps try to detain —?" Friedrich's chief thought naturally is, One cannot be away out of this too soon. "Sha'n't we go to the Play, then, Monsieur le Maréchal? Play-hour is come!" — Own Correspondent of the Newspaper proceeds: —

"The Maréchal then went to the Play, and all his Officers with him; thinking their royal prize was close at their heels. Maréchal and Officers fairly ahead, coast once clear, their royal prize hastened back to The Raven, paid his bill; hastily summoning Schaffgotsch and the others within hearing; shot off like lightning; and was seen in Strasburg no more. Algarotti, who was in the box with Broglio, heard the news in the house; regretful rumor among the Officers, 'He is gone!' In about a quarter of an hour Algarotti too slipped out; and vanished by extra post" — straight towards Wesel; but could not overtake the King (whose road, in the latter part of it, went zigzag, on business as is likely), nor see him again till they met in that Town.[1]

This is the Prose Truth of those fifty or eight-and-forty hours in Strasburg, which were so mythic and romantic at that time. Shall we now apply to the Royal Doggerel again, where we left off, and see the other side of the picture? Once settled in The Raven, within Strasburg's walls, the Doggerel continues: —

"You fancy well that there was now something to exercise my curiosity; and what desire I had to know the French Nation in France itself.

---

[1] From *Helden-Geschichte* (i. 420–424), &c.

There I saw at length those French, / Là je vis enfin ces Français
Of whom you have sung the glories; / Dont vous avez chanté la gloire ;
A people despised by the English, / Peuple méprisé des Anglais,
Whom their sad rationality fills with black bile ; / Que leur triste raison remplit de bile noire ;
Those French, whom our Germans Reckon all to be destitute of sense ; / Ces Français, que nos Allemands Pensent tous privés de bon sens ;
Those French, whose History consists of Love-stories, / Ces Français, dont l'amour pourrait dicter l'histoire,
I mean the wandering kind of Love, not the constant ; / Je dis l'amour volage, et non l'amour constant ;
Foolish this People, headlong, high-going, / Ce peuple fou, brusque et galant,
Which sings beyond endurance ; / Chansonnier insupportable,
Lofty in its good fortune, crawling in its bad ; / Superbe en sa fortune, en son malheur rampant,
Of an unpitying extent of babble, / D'un bavardage impitoyable,
To hide the vacancy of its ignorant mind. / Pour cacher le creux d'un esprit ignorant,
Of the Trifling it is a tender lover ; / Tendre amant de la bagatelle,
The Trifling alone takes possession of its brain. / Elle entre seule en sa cervelle ;
People flighty, indiscreet, imprudent, / Léger, indiscret, imprudent,
Turning like the weathercock to every wind. / Comme une girouette il revire à tout vent.
Of the ages of the Cæsars those of the Louises are the shadow ; / Des siècles des Césars ceux des Louis sont l'ombre ;
Paris is the ghost of Rome, take it how you will. / Rome efface Paris en tout sens, en tout point.
No, of those vile French you are not one : / Non, des vils Français vous n'êtes pas du nombre ;
You think ; they do not think at all. / Vous pensez, ils ne pensent point.

"Pardon, dear Voltaire, this definition of the French ; at worst, it is only of those in Strasburg I speak. To scrape acquaintance, I had to invite some Officers on our arrival, whom of course I did not know.

Three of them came at once, / Trois d'eux s'en vinrent à la fois,
Gayer, more content than Kings ; / Plus gais, plus contents que des rois,
Singing with rusty voice, / Chantant d'une voix enrouée,

In verse, their amorous exploits,	*En vers, leurs amoureux exploits,*
Set to a hornpipe.	*Ajustés sur une bourrée.*

"M. de la Crochardière and M. Malosa [two names from the tablets, third wanting] had just come from a dinner where the wine had not been spared.

Of their hot friendship I saw the flame grow,	*De leur chaude amitié je vis croître le flamme,*
The Universe would have taken us for perfect friends :	*L'univers nous eût pris pour des amis parfaits ;*
But the instant of good-night blew out the business ;	*Mais l'instant des adieux en détruisit la trame,*
Friendship disappeared without regrets,	*L'amitié disparut, sans causer des regrets,*
With the games, the wine, the table and the viands.	*Avec le jeu, le vin, et la table, et les mets.*

"Next day, Monsieur the Gouverneur of the Town and Province, Maréchal of France, Chevalier of the Orders of the King, &c. &c., — Maréchal Duc de Broglio, in fact," who was surprised at Secchia in the late War, —

This General always surprised.	*Ce général toujours surpris,*
Whom with regret young Louis [your King]	*Qu'à regret le jeune Louis*
Saw without breeches in Italy [1]	*Vit sans culottes en Italie,*
Galloping to hide away his life	*Courir pour dérober sa vie*
From the Germans, unpolite fighters ; —	*Aux Germains, guerriers impolis.*

this General wished to investigate your Comte Dufour, — foreign Count, who the instant he arrives sets about inviting people to supper that are perfect strangers. He took the poor Count for a sharper; and prudently advised M. de la Crochardière not to be duped by him. It was unluckily the good Maréchal that proved to be duped.

He was born for surprise.	*Il était né pour la surprise.*
His white hair, his gray beard,	*Ses cheveux blancs, sa barbe grise,*

---

[1] "With only one boot," was the milder rumor; which we adopted (supra, vol. vi. p. 472), but this sadder one, too, was current; and "Broglio's breeches," or the vain aspiration after them, like a vanished ghost of breeches, often enough turn up in the old Pamphlets.

Formed a reverend exterior.	*Formaient un sage extérieur.*
Outsides are often deceptive :	*Le dehors est souvent trompeur ;*
He that, by the binding, judges	*Qui juge par la reliure*
Of a Book and its Author	*D'un ouvrage et de son auteur*
May, after a page of reading,	*Dans une page de lecture*
Chance to recognize his mistake.	*Peut reconnaître son erreur.*

"That was my own experience; for of wisdom I could find nothing except in his gray hair and decrepit appearance. His first opening betrayed him; no great well of wit this Maréchal,

Who, drunk with his own grandeur,	*Qui, de sa grandeur enivré,*
Informs you of his name and his titles,	*Décline son nom et ses titres,*
And authority as good as unlimited.	*Et son pouvoir à rien borné.*
He cited to me all the records	*Il me cita tous les registres*
Where his name is registered,	*Où son nom est enregistré ;*
Babbled about his immense power,	*Bavard de son pouvoir immense,*
About his valor, his talents	*De sa valeur, de ces talents*
So salutary to France ; —	*Si salutaires à la France :*
He forgot that, three years ago [1]	*Il oubliait, passé trois ans,*
Men did not praise his prudence.	*Qu'on ne louait pas sa prudence.*

"Not satisfied with seeing the Maréchal, I saw guard mounted

By these Frenchmen, burning with glory,	*A ces Français brûlants de gloire,*
Who, on four sous a day,	*Dotés de quatre sous par jour,*
Will make of Kings and of Heroes the memory flourish :	*Qui des rois, des héros font fleurir la mémoire,*
Slaves crowned by the hands of Victory,	*Esclaves couronnés des mains de la victoire,*
Unlucky herds whom the Court	*Troupeaux malheureux que la cour*
Tinkles hither and thither by the sound of fife and drum.	*Dirige au seul bruit du tambour.*

"That was my fated term. A deserter from our troops got eye on me, recognized me and denounced me.

[1] Six to a nearness, — "15th September, 1734," if your Majesty will be exact.

This wretched gallows-bird got eye on me ;	*Ce malheureux pendard me vit,*
Such is the lot of all earthly things ;	*C'est le sort de toutes les choses ;*
And so of our fine mystery	*Ainsi de notre pot aux roses*
The whole secret came to light."	*Tout le secret se découvrit.*

Well; we must take this glimpse, such as it is, into the interior of the young man, — fine buoyant, pungent German spirit, roadways for it very bad, and universal rain-torrents falling, yet with coruscations from a higher quarter ; — and you can forget, if need be, the "Literature" of this young Majesty, as you would a staccato on the flute by him ! In after months, on new occasion rising, "there was no end to his gibings and bitter pleasantries on the ridiculous reception Broglio had given him at Strasburg," says Valori,[1] — of which this Doggerel itself offers specimen.

"Probably the weakest Piece I ever translated ? " exclaims one, who has translated several such. Nevertheless there is a straggle of pungent sense in it, — like the outskirts of lightning, seen in that dismally wet weather, which the Royal Party had. Its wit is very copious, but slashy, bantery, and proceeds mainly by exaggeration and turning topsy-turvy ; a rather barren species of wit. Of humor, in the fine poetic sense, no vestige. But there is surprising veracity, — truthfulness unimpeachable, if you will read well. What promptitude, too ; — what funds for conversation, when needed ! This scraggy Piece, which is better than the things people often talk to one another, was evidently written as fast as the pen could go. — "It is done, if such a Hand could have *done* it, in the manner of Bachaumont and La Chapelle," says Voltaire scornfully, in that scandalous *Vie Privée ;* — of which phrase this is the commentary, if readers need one : —

"Some seventy or eighty years before that date, a M. Bachaumont and a M. la Chapelle, his intimate, published, in Prose skipping off into dancings of Verse every now and then, ' a charming *Relation* of a certain *Voyage* or Home Tour' (whence

[1] *Mémoires,* i. 88.

or whither, or correctly when, this Editor forgets),[1] which they had made in partnership. ' *Relation* ' capable still of being read, if one were tolerably idle; — it was found then to be charming, by all the world; and gave rise to a new fashion in writing; which Voltaire often adopts, and is supremely good at; and in which Friedrich, who is also fond of it, by no means succeeds so well."

Enough, Friedrich got to Wesel, back to his business, in a day or two; and had done, as we forever have, with the Strasburg Escapade and its Doggerel.

Friedrich finds M. de Maupertuis; not yet M. de Voltaire.

Friedrich got to Wesel on the 29th; found Maupertuis waiting there, according to appointment: an elaborately polite, somewhat sublime scientific gentleman; ready to "engraft on the Berlin crab-tree," and produce real apples and Academics there, so soon as the King, the proprietor, may have leisure for such a thing. Algarotti has already the honor of some acquaintance with Maupertuis. Maupertuis has been at Brussels, on the road hither; saw Voltaire and even Madame, — which latter was rather a ticklish operation, owing to grudges and tiffs of quarrel that had risen, but it proved successful under the delicate guidance of Voltaire. Voltaire is up to oiling the wheels: "There you are, Monsieur, like the [don't name What, though profane Voltaire does, writing to Maupertuis a month ago] — Three Kings running after you!" A new Pension to you from France; Russia outbidding France to have you; and then that *Letter* of Friedrich's, which is in all the Newspapers: "Three Kings," — you plainly great man, Trismegistus of the Sciences called Pure! Madame honors you, has always done: one word of apology

---

[1] " First printed in 1665," say the Bibliographies; " but known to La Fontaine some time before." Good! — Bachaumont, practically an important and distinguished person, not literary by trade, or indeed otherwise than by ennui, was he that had given (some fifteen years before) the Nickname *Fronde* (Bickering of Schoolboys) to the wretched Historical Object which is still so designated in French annals.

to the high female mind, it will work wonders; — come
now![1]

No reader guesses in our time what a shining celestial body
the Maupertuis, who is now fallen so dim again, then was to
mankind. In cultivated French society there is no such lion
as M. Maupertuis since he returned from flattening the Earth
in the Arctic regions. "The Exact Sciences, what else is
there to depend on?" thinks French cultivated society: "and
has not Monsieur done a feat in that line?" Monsieur,
with fine ex-military manners, has a certain austere gravity,
reticent loftiness and polite dogmatism, which confirms that
opinion. A studious ex-military man, — was Captain of Dragoons once, but too fond of study, — who is conscious to himself, or who would fain be conscious, that he is, in all points,
mathematical, moral and other, the man. A difficult man to
live with in society. Comes really near the limit of what we
call genius, of originality, poetic greatness in thinking; — but
never once can get fairly over said limit, though always struggling dreadfully to do so. Think of it! A fatal kind of man;
especially if you have made a lion of him at any time. Of
his envies, deep-hidden splenetic discontents and rages, with
Voltaire's return for them, there will be enough to say in the
ulterior stages. He wears — at least ten years hence he
openly wears, though I hope it is not yet so flagrant — "a
red wig with yellow bottom (crinière jaune);" and as Flattener of the Earth, is, with his own flattish red countenance
and impregnable stony eyes, a man formidable to look upon,
though intent to be amiable if you do the proper homage. As
to the quarrel with Madame take this Note; which may prove
illustrative of some things by and by: —

Maupertuis is well known at Cirey; such a lion could not
fail there. All manner of Bernouillis, Clairauts, high mathematical people, are frequent guests at Cirey: reverenced by
Madame, — who indeed has had her own private Professor of
Mathematics; one König from Switzerland (recommended by
those Bernouillis), diligently teaching her the Pure Sciences

---

[1] Voltaire, Œuvres, lxxii. 217, 216, 230 (Hague, 21st July, 1740, and Brussels, 9th Aug. &c).

this good while back, not without effect; and has only just
parted with him, when she left on this Brussels expedition.
A *bon garçon*, Voltaire says; though otherwise, I think, a little
noisy on occasion. There has been no end of Madame's kindness to him, nay to his Brother and him, — sons of a Theological Professorial Syriac-Hebrew kind of man at Berne, who has
too many sons; — and I grieve to report that this heedless
König has produced an explosion in Madame's feelings, such
as little beseemed him. On the road to Paris, namely, as we
drove hitherward to the Honsbruck Lawsuit by way of Paris,
in Autumn last, there had fallen out some dispute, about the
monads, the *vis viva*, the infinitely little, between Madame
and König; dispute which rose *crescendo* in disharmonious
duet, and "ended," testifies M. de Voltaire, "in a scene *très-
désagréable*." Madame, with an effort, forgave the thoughtless fellow, who is still rather young, and is without malice.
But thoughtless König, strong in his opinion about the infinitely little, appealed to Maupertuis: "Am not I right, Monsieur?" "*He* is right beyond question!" wrote Maupertuis
to Madame; "somewhat dryly," thinks Voltaire: and the
result is, there is considerable rage in one celestial mind ever
since against another male one in red wig and yellow bottom;
and they are not on speaking terms, for a good many months
past. Voltaire has his heart sore ("*j'en ai le cœur percé*")
about it, needs to double-dose Maupertuis with flattery; and
in fact has used the utmost diplomacy to effect some varnish
of a reconcilement as Maupertuis passed on this occasion. As
for König, who had studied in some Dutch university, he went
by and by to be Librarian to the Prince of Orange; and we
shall not fail to hear of him again, — once more upon the
infinitely little.[1]

Voltaire too, in his way, is fond of these mathematical people; eager enough to fish for knowledge, here as in all elements, when he has the chance offered: this is much an
interest of his at present. And he does attain sound ideas,
outlines of ideas, in this province, — though privately defec-

[1] From *Œuvres de Voltaire*, ii. 126, lxxii. (20, 216, 230), lxiii. (229–239),
&c. &c.

tive in the due transcendency of admiration for it; — was
wont to discuss cheerily with König, about *vis viva*, monads,
gravitation and the infinitely little ; above all, bows to the
ground before the red-wigged Bashaw, Flattener of the Earth,
whom for Madame's sake and his own he is anxious to be well
with.   "Fall on your face nine times, ye esoteric of only Impure Science ! " — intimates Maupertuis to mankind.   "By all
means ! " answers M. de Voltaire, doing it with alacrity ; with
a kind of loyalty, one can perceive, and also with a hypoc-
risy grounded on love of peace.   If that is the nature of the
Bashaw, and one's sole mode of fishing knowledge from him,
why not ? thinks M. de Voltaire.   His patience with M. de
Maupertuis, first and last, was very great.   But we shall find
it explode at length, a dozen years hence, in a conspicuous
manner ! —

"Maupertuis had come to us to Cirey, with Jean Bernouilli,"
says Voltaire ; "and thenceforth Maupertuis, who was born
the most jealous of men, took me for the object of this passion, which has always been very dear to him." [1]   Husht,
Monsieur ! — Here is a poor rheumatic kind of Letter, which
illustrates the interim condition, after that varnish of reconcilement at Brussels : —

Voltaire to M. de Maupertuis (at Wesel, waiting for the King,
or with him rather).

"Brussels, 29th August (1740), *3d year since
the world flattened.*

"How the Devil, great Philosopher, would you have had
me write to you at Wesel ?   I fancied you gone from Wesel,
to seek the King of Sages on his Journey somewhere.   I had
understood, too, they were so delighted to have you in that
fortified lodge (*bouge fortifié*) that you must be taking pleasure
there, for he that gives pleasure gets it.

"You have already seen the jolly Ambassador of the amiablest Monarch in the world," — Camas, a fattish man, on his
road to Versailles (who called at Brussels here, with fine

[1] *Vie Privée.*

compliments, and a keg of Hungary Wine, as *you* may have
heard whispered). "No doubt M. de Camas is with you.   For
my own share, I think it is after you that he is running at
present.   But in truth, at the hour while I say this, you are
with the King;"—a lucky guess; King did return to Wesel
this very day.   "The Philosopher and the Prince perceive
already that they are made for each other.   You and M. Algarotti will say, *Faciamus hìc tria tabernacula:* as to me, I can
only make *duo tabernacula,*"—profane Voltaire!

"Without doubt I would be with you if I were not at Brussels; but my heart is with you all the same; and is the subject, all the same, of a King who is formed to reign over every
thinking and feeling being.   I do not despair that Madame du
Châtelet will find herself somewhere on your route: it will
be a scene in a fairy tale;—she will arrive with a *sufficient
reason* [as your Leibnitz says] and with *monads.*   She does
not love you the less though she now believes the universe a
plenum, and has renounced the notion of *void.*   Over her you
have an ascendant which you will never lose.   In fine, my
dear Monsieur, I wish as ardently as she to embrace you the
soonest possible.   I recommend myself to your friendship in
the Court, worthy of you, where you now are."—*Tout à vous,*
somewhat rheumatic![1]

Always an anxious almost tremulous desire to conciliate
this big glaring geometrical bully in red wig.   Through the
sensitive transparent being of M. de Voltaire, you may see
that feeling almost painfully busy in every Letter he writes
to the Flattener of the Earth.

[1] Voltaire, lxxii. p. 243.

CHAPTER IV.

VOLTAIRE'S FIRST INTERVIEW WITH FRIEDRICH.

At Wesel, in the rear of all this travelling and excitement, Friedrich falls unwell; breaks down there into an aguish feverish distemper, which, for several months after, impeded his movements, would he have yielded to it. He has much business on hand, too, — some of it of prickly nature just now; — but is intent as ever on seeing Voltaire, among the first things. Diligently reading in the Voltaire-Friedrich Correspondence (which is a sad jumble of misdates and opacities, in the common editions),[1] this of the aguish condition frequently turns up; "Quartan ague," it seems; occasionally very bad; but Friedrich struggles with it; will not be cheated of any of his purposes by it.

He had a busy fortnight here; busier than we yet imagine. Much employment there naturally is of the usual Inspection sort; which fails in no quarter of his Dominions, but which may be particularly important here, in these disputed Berg-Jülich Countries, when the time of decision falls. How he does his Inspections we know; — and there are still weightier matters afoot here, in a silent way, of which we shall have to speak before long, and all the world will speak. Business enough, parts of it grave and silent, going on, and the much that is public, miscellaneous, small: done, all of it, in a rapid punctual precise manner; — and always, after the crowded day, some passages of Supper with the Sages, to wind up with on melodious terms. A most alert and miscellaneously busy young King, in spite of the ague.

[1] Preuss (the recent latest Editor, and the only well-informed one, as we said) prints with accuracy; but cannot be read at all (in the sense of understood) without other light.

It was in these Cleve Countries, and now as probably as afterwards, that the light scene recorded in Laveaux's poor *History*, and in all the Anecdote-Books, transacted itself one day. Substance of the story is true; though the details of it go all at random, — somewhat to this effect : —

"Inspecting his Finance Affairs, and questioning the parties interested, Friedrich notices a certain Convent in Cleve, which appears to have, payable from the Forest-dues, considerable revenues bequeathed by the old Dukes, 'for masses to be said on their behalf.' He goes to look at the place; questions the Monks on this point, who are all drawn out in two rows, and have broken into *Te-Deum* at sight of him : 'Husht! You still say those Masses, then?' 'Certainly, your Majesty!' — 'And what good does anybody get of them?' 'Your Majesty, those old Sovereigns are to obtain Heavenly mercy by them, to be delivered out of Purgatory by them.' — 'Purgatory? It is a sore thing for the Forests, all this while! And they are not yet out, those poor souls, after so many hundred years of praying?' Monks have a fatal apprehension, No. 'When will they be out, and the thing complete?' Monks cannot say. 'Send me a courier whenever it *is* complete!' sneers the King, and leaves them to their *Te-Deum*." [1]

Mournful state of the Catholic Religion so called! How long must these wretched Monks go on doing their lazy thrice-deleterious torpid blasphemy; and a King, not histrionic but real, merely signify that he laughs at them and it? Meseems a heavier whip than that of satire might be in place here, your Majesty? The lighter whip is easier; — Ah yes, undoubtedly! cry many men. But horrible accounts are running up, enough to sink the world at last, while the heavier whip is lazily withheld, and lazy blasphemy, fallen torpid,

---

[1] C. Hildebrandt's Modern Edition of the (mostly dubious) *Anekdoten und Charakterzüge aus dem Leben Friedrichs des Grossen* (and a very ignorant and careless Edition it is ; 6 vols. 12mo, Halberstadt, 1829), ii. 160 ; Laveaux (whom we already cited), *Vie de Frédéric ;* &c. &c. Nicolai's *Anekdoten* alone, which are not included in this Hildebrandt Collection, are of sure authenticity ; the rest, occasionally true, and often with a kind of *mythic* truth in them worth attending to, are otherwise of all degrees of dubiety, down to the palpably false and absurd.

chronic, and quite unconscious of being blasphemous, insinuates itself into the very heart's-blood of mankind! Patience,
however; the heavy whip too is coming, — unless universal
death be coming. King Friedrich is not the man to wield
such whip. Quite other work is in store for King Friedrich;
and Nature will not, by any suggestion of that terrible task,
put him out in the one he has. He is nothing of a Luther,
of a Cromwell; can look upon fakirs praying by their rotatory calabash, as a ludicrous platitude; and grin delicately as
above, with the approval of his wiser contemporaries. Speed
to him on his own course!

What answer Friedrich found to his English proposals, —
answer due here on the 24th from Captain Dickens, — I do
not pointedly learn; but can judge of it by Harrington's reply
to that Despatch of Dickens's, which entreated candor and
open dealing towards his Prussian Majesty. Harrington is
at Herrenhausen, still with the Britannic Majesty there; both
of them much at a loss about their Spanish War, and the
French and other aspects upon it: "Suppose his Prussian
Majesty were to give himself to France against us!" We
will hope, not. Harrington's reply is to the effect, "Hum,
drum: — Berg and Jülich, say you? Impossible to answer;
minds not made up here: — What will his Prussian Majesty
do for *us?*" Not much, I should guess, till something more
categorical come from you! His Prussian Majesty is careful
not to spoil anything by over-haste; but will wait and try farther to the utmost, Whether England or France is the likelier
bargain for him.

Better still, the Prussian Majesty is intent to do something
for himself in that Berg-Jülich matter: we find him silently examining these Wesel localities for a proper "entrenched Camp,"
Camp say of 40,000, against a certain contingency that may be
looked for. Camp which will much occupy the Gazetteers when
they get eye on it. This is one of the concerns he silently
attends to, on occasion, while riding about in the Cleve Countries. Then there is another small item of business, important
to do well, which is now in silence diligently getting under
way at Wesel; which also is of remarkable nature, and will

astonish the Gazetteer and Diplomatic circles. This is the
affair with the Bishop of Liége, called also the Affair of Herstal, which his Majesty has had privately laid up in the corner
of his mind, as a thing to be done during this Excursion. Of
which the reader shall hear anon, to great lengths, — were a
certain small preliminary matter, Voltaire's Arrival in these
parts, once off our hands.

Friedrich's First Meeting with Voltaire! These other high
things were once loud in the Gazetteer and Diplomatic circles,
and had no doubt *they* were the World's History; and now
they are sunk wholly to the Nightmares, and all mortals have
forgotten them, — and it is such a task as seldom was to resuscitate the least memory of them, on just cause of a Friedrich
or the like, so impatient are men of what is putrid and extinct : — and a quite unnoticed thing, Voltaire's First Interview,
all readers are on the alert for it, and ready to demand of me
impossibilities about it! Patience, readers. You shall see it,
without and within, in such light as there was, and form some
actual notion of it, if you will co-operate. From the circumambient inanity of Old Newspapers, Historical shot-rubbish,
and unintelligible Correspondences, we sift out the following
particulars, of this First Meeting, or actual Osculation of the
Stars.

The Newspapers, though their eyes were not yet of the
Argus quality now familiar to us, have been intent on Friedrich during this Baireuth-Cleve Journey, especially since that
sudden eclipse of him at Strasburg lately; forming now one
scheme of route for him, now another; Newspapers, and even
private friends, being a good deal uncertain about his movements. Rumor now ran, since his reappearance in the Cleve
Countries, that Friedrich meant to have a look at Holland
before going home. And that had, in fact, been a notion or
intention of Friedrich's. "Holland? We could pass through
Brussels on the way, and see Voltaire!" thought he.

In Brussels this was, of course, the rumor of rumors. As
Voltaire's Letters, visibly in a twitter, still testify to us.
King of Prussia coming! Madame du Châtelet, the "Princess

Tour " (that is, Tour-and-Taxis), all manner of high Dames are
on the tiptoe.   Princess Tour hopes she shall lodge this unparalleled Prince in her Palace: " You, Madame ? " answers
the Du Châtelet, privately, with a toss of her head : " His Majesty, I hope, belongs more to M. de Voltaire and me : he shall
lodge here, please Heaven ! " Voltaire, I can observe, has sublime hostelry arrangements chalked out for his Majesty, in
case he go to Paris ; which he does n't, as we know.   Voltaire
is all on the alert, awake to the great contingencies far and
near ; the Châtelet-Voltaire breakfast-table, — fancy it on those
interesting mornings, while the post comes round ! [1]

Alas, in the first days of September, — Friedrich's Letter is
dated " Wesel, 2d " (and has the *Strasburg Doggerel* enclosed
in it), — the Brussels Postman delivers far other intelligence
at one's door ; very mortifying to Madame : " That his Majesty
is fallen ill at Wesel ; has an aguish fever hanging on him, and
only hopes to come : " *Voilà,* Madame ! — Next Letter, Wesel,
Monday, 5th September, is to the effect : " Do still much hope
to come ; to-morrow is my trembling day ; if that prove to be
off ! " — Out upon it, that proves not to be off ; that is on :
next Letter, Tuesday, September 6th, which comes by express
(Courier dashing up with it, say on the Thursday following)
is, — alas, Madame ! — here it is : —

King Friedrich to M. de Voltaire at Brussels.

" WESEL, 6th September, 1740.

" MY DEAR VOLTAIRE, — In spite of myself, I have to yield
to the Quartan Fever, which is more tenacious than a Jansenist ;
and whatever desire I had of going to Antwerp and Brussels,
I find myself not in a condition to undertake such a journey
without risk.   I would ask of you, then, if the road from
Brussels to Cleve would not to *you* seem too long for a meeting ; it is the one means of seeing you which remains to me.
Confess that I am unlucky ; for now when I could dispose of
my person, and nothing hinders me from seeing you, the fever

---

[1] Voltaire, xxii. 238–256 (Letters 22d August–22d September, 1740).

gets its hand into the business, and seems to intend disputing me that satisfaction.

"Let us deceive the fever, my dear Voltaire ; and let me at least have the pleasure of embracing you. Make my best excuses [polite, rather than sincere] to Madame the *Marquise*, that I cannot have the satisfaction of seeing her at Brussels. All that are about me know the intention I was in ; which certainly nothing but the fever could have made me change.

"Sunday next I shall be at a little Place near Cleve," — Schloss of Moyland, which, and the route to which, this Courier can tell you of ; — "where I shall be able to possess you at my ease. If the sight of you don't cure me, I will send for a Confessor at once. Adieu; you know my sentiments and my heart.[1]   FÉDÉRIC."

After which the Correspondence suddenly extinguishes itself ; ceases for about a fortnight, — in the bad *mis*dated Editions even does worse ; — and we are left to thick darkness, to our own poor shifts ; Dryasdust being grandly silent on this small interest of ours.   What is to be done ?

Particulars of First Interview, on severe Scrutiny.

Here, from a painful Predecessor whose Papers I inherit, are some old documents and Studies on the subject, — sorrowful collection, in fact, of what poor sparks of certainty were to be found hovering in that dark element ; — which do at last (so luminous are *certainties* always, or " sparks " that will shine *steady*) coalesce into some feeble general twilight, feeble but indubitable ; and even show the sympathetic reader *how* they were searched out and brought together.   We number and label these poor Patches of Evidence on so small a matter ; and leave them to the curious : —

No. 1. *Date of the First Interview.* It is certain Voltaire did arrive at the little Schloss of Moyland, September 11th, Sunday night, — which is the " Sunday " just specified in Friedrich's Letter.   Voltaire had at once decided on complying, —

1 Preuss, *Œuvres de Frédéric*, xxii. 27.

what else ? — and lost no time in packing himself : King's
Courier on Thursday late; Voltaire on the road on Saturday
early, or the night before.   With Madame's shrill blessing
(not the most musical in this vexing case), and plenty of fuss.
" Was wont to travel in considerable style," I am told ; "the
innkeepers calling him " Your Lordship (*M. le Comte*)."   Arrives, sure enough, Sunday night ; old Schloss of Moyland, six
miles from Cleve; "moonlight," I find, — the Harvest Moon.
Visit lasted three days.[1]

No. 2. Voltaire's Drive thither.   Schloss Moyland : How far
from Brussels, and by what route ?   By Louvain, Tillemont,
Tongres to Maestricht; then from Maestricht up the Maas
(left bank) to Venlo, where cross ; through Geldern and Goch
to Cleve : between the Maas and Rhine this last portion.   Flat
damp country ; tolerably under tillage; original constituents
bog and sand.   Distances I guess to be : To Tongres 60 miles
and odd ; to Maestricht 12 or 15, from Maestricht 75 ; in all
150 miles English.   Two days' driving ?   There is equinoctial
moon, and still above twelve hours of sunlight for " M. le
Comte."

No. 3. Of the Place Where.   Voltaire, who should have
known, calls it *" petit Château de Meuse ; "* which is a Castle
existing nowhere but in Dreams.   Other French Biographers
are still more imaginary.   The little Schloss of Moyland —
by no means " Meuse," nor even *Mörs*, which Voltaire probably
means in saying *Château de Meuse* — was, as the least inquiry
settles beyond question, the place where Voltaire and Friedrich first met.   Friedrich Wilhelm used often to lodge there
in his Cleve journeys : he made thither for shelter, in the sickness that overtook him in friend Ginkel's house, coming home
from the Rhine Campaign in 1734; lay there for several weeks
after quitting Ginkel's.   Any other light I can get upon it, is
darkness visible.   Büsching pointedly informs me,[2] " It is a
Parish [or patch of country under one priest], and Till *and* it
are a Jurisdiction " (pair of patches under one court of justice) : — which does not much illuminate the inquiring mind.

---

[1] Rödenbeck, p. 21 ; Preuss, &c. &c.
[2] *Erdbeschreibung*, v. 659, 677.

Small patch, this of Moyland, size not given ; " was bought,"
says he, "in 1695, by Friedrich afterwards First King, from
the Family of Spaen," — we once knew a Lieutenant Spaen,
of those Dutch regions, — " and was named a Royal Mansion
ever thereafter." Who lived in it; what kind of thing was it,
is it ? *Altum silentium*, from Büsching and mankind. Belonged to the Spaens, fifty years ago ; — some shadow of our
poor banished friend the Lieutenant resting on it ? Dim
enough old Mansion, with "court" to it, with modicum of
equipment ; lying there in the moonlight ; — did not look sublime to Voltaire on stepping out. So that all our knowledge
reduces itself to this one point : of finding Moyland in the
Map, with *date*, with *reminiscence* to us, hanging by it henceforth ! Good.[1]

Mörs — which is near the Town of Ruhrort, about midway
between Wesel and Düsseldorf — must be some forty miles
from Moyland, forty-five from Cleve; southward of both. So
that the place, "*à deux lieues de Clèves*," is, even by Voltaire's
showing, this Moyland ; were there otherwise any doubt
upon it. "Château de *Meuse*" — hanging out a prospect of
Mörs to us — is bad usage to readers. Of an intelligent man,
not to say a Trismegistus of men, one expects he will know in
what town he is, after three days' experience, as here. But he
does not always ; he hangs out a mere " shadow of Mörs by
moonlight," till we learn better. Duvernet, his Biographer,
even calls it " *Sleus-Meuse ;* " some wonderful idea of Sluices
and a River attached to it, in Duvernet's head ![2]

What Voltaire thought of the Interview Twenty Years afterwards.

Of the Interview itself, with general bird's-eye view of the
Visit combined (in a very incorrect state), there is direct testi-

[1] Stieler's *Deutschland* (excellent Map in 25 Pieces), Piece 12. — Till is a
mile or two northeast from Moyland ; Moyland about 5 or 6 southeast from
Cleve.

[2] Duvernet (2d *form* of him, — that is, *Vie de Voltaire* par T. J. D. V.),
p. 117.

mony by Voltaire himself. Voltaire himself, twenty years
after, in far other humor, all jarred into angry sarcasm, for
causes we shall see by and by, — Voltaire, at the request of
friends, writes down, as his Friedrich Reminiscences, that
scandalous *Vie Privée* above spoken of, a most sad Document;
and this is the passage referring to "the little Place in the
neighborhood of Cleve," where Friedrich now waited for him :
errors corrected by our laborious Friend. After quoting something of that Strasburg Doggerel, the whole of which is now
too well known to us, Voltaire proceeds : —

"From Strasburg he," King Friedrich, "went to see his
Lower German Provinces ; he said he would come and see me
incognito at Brussels. We prepared a fine house for him," —
were ready to prepare such hired house as we had for him,
with many apologies for its slight degree of perfection (*error
first*), — "but having fallen ill in the little Mansion-Royal of
Meuse (*Château de Meuse*), a couple of leagues from Cleve," —
fell ill at Wesel; and there is no Château de *Meuse* in the
world (*errors 2d and 3d*), — "he wrote to me that he expected
I would make the advances. I went, accordingly, to present my profound homages. Maupertuis, who already had his
views, and was possessed with the rage of being President to
an Academy, had of his own accord," — no, being invited, and
at my suggestion (*error 4th*), — "presented himself there; and
was lodged with Algarotti and Keyserling [which latter, I
suppose, had come from Berlin, not being of the Strasburg
party, he] in a garret of this Palace.

"At the door of the court, I found, by way of guard, one
soldier. Privy-Councillor Rambonet, Minister of State —
[very subaltern man; never heard of him except in the Herstal
Business, and here] was walking in the court; blowing in
his fingers to keep them warm." Sunday night, 11th September, 1740; world all bathed in moonshine ; and mortals mostly
shrunk into their huts, out of the raw air. "He" Rambonet
"wore big linen ruffles at his wrists, very dirty [visibly so in
the moonlight ? *Error 5th* extends *ad libitum* over all the
following details]; a holed hat; an old official periwig," —
ruined into a totally unsymmetric state, as would seem, —

"one side of which hung down into one of his pockets, and the other scarcely crossed his shoulder. I was told, this man was now intrusted with an affair of importance here; and that proved true," — the Herstal Affair.

"I was led into his Majesty's apartment. Nothing but four bare walls there. By the light of a candle, I perceived, in a closet, a little truckle-bed two feet and a half broad, on which lay a little man muffled up in a dressing-gown of coarse blue duffel: this was the King, sweating and shivering under a wretched blanket there, in a violent fit of fever. I made my reverence, and began the acquaintance by feeling his pulse, as if I had been his chief physician. The fit over, he dressed himself, and took his place at table. Algarotti, Keyserling, Maupertuis, and the King's Envoy to the States-General" — one Räsfeld (skilled in *Herstal* matters, I could guess), — "we were of this supper, and discussed, naturally in a profound manner, the Immortality of the Soul, Liberty, Fate, the Androgynes of Plato [the *Androgynoi,* or Men-Women, in Plato's *Convivium ;* by no means the finest symbolic fancy of the divine Plato], — and other small topics of that nature." [1]

This is Voltaire's account of the Visit, — which included *three* "Suppers," all huddled into one by him here ; — and he says nothing more of it ; launching off now into new errors, about *Herstal,* the *Anti-Machiavel,* and so forth : new and uglier errors, with much more of mendacity and serious malice in them, than in this harmless half-dozen now put on the score against him.

Of this Supper-Party, I know by face four of the guests : Maupertuis, Voltaire, Algarotti, Keyserling ; — Räsfeld, Rambonet can sit as simulacra or mute accompaniment. Voltaire arrived on Sunday evening ; stayed till Wednesday. Wednesday morning, 14th of the month, the Party broke up : Voltaire rolling off to left hand, towards Brussels, or the Hague ; King to right, on inspection business, and circuitously homewards. Three Suppers there had been, two busy Days intervening ; discussions about Fate and the Androgynoi of Plato by no means the one thing done by Voltaire and the rest, on this occa-

[1] Voltaire, *Œuvres* (Piece once called *Vie Privée*), ii. 26, 27.

sion. We shall find elsewhere, "he declaimed his *Mahomet*" (sublime new Tragedy, not yet come out), in the course of these three evenings, to the "speechless admiration" of his Royal Host, for one; and, in the daytime, that he even drew his pen about the Herstal Business, which is now getting to its crisis, and wrote one of the Manifestoes, still discoverable. And we need not doubt, in spite of his now sneering tone, that things ran high and grand here, in this paltry little Schloss of Moyland; and that those three were actually Suppers of the Gods, for the time being.

"Councillor Rambonet," with the holed hat and unsymmetric wig, continues Voltaire in the satirical vein, "had meanwhile mounted a hired hack (*cheval de louage;*" mischievous Voltaire, I have no doubt he went on wheels, probably of his own): "he rode all night; and next morning arrived at the gates of Liége; where he took Act in the name of the King his Master, whilst 2,000 men of the Wesel Troops laid Liége under contribution. The pretext of this fine Marching of Troops," — not a pretext at all, but the assertion, correct in all points, of just claims long trodden down, and now made good with more spirit than had been expected, — "was certain rights which the King pretended to, over a suburb of Liége. He even charged me to work at a Manifesto; and I made one, good or bad; not doubting but a King with whom I supped, and who called me his friend, must be in the right. The affair soon settled itself by means of a million of ducats," — nothing like the sum, as we shall see, — "which he exacted by weight, to clear the costs of the Tour to Strasburg, which, according to his complaint in that Poetic Letter [Doggerel above given], were so heavy."

That is Voltaire's view; grown very corrosive after Twenty Years. He admits, with all the satire : "I naturally felt myself attached to him; for he had wit, graces; and moreover he was a King, which always forms a potent seduction, so weak is human nature. Usually it is we of the writing sort that flatter Kings: but this King praised me from head to foot, while the Abbé Desfontaines and other scoundrels (*grédins*) were busy defaming me in Paris at least once a week."

What Voltaire thought of the Interview at the Time.

But let us take the contemporary account, which also we
have at first hand; which is almost pathetic to read; such a
contrast between ruddy morning and the storms of the afternoon! Here are two Letters from Voltaire; fine transparent
human Letters, as his generally are: the first of them written
directly on getting back to the Hague, and to the feeling of
his eclipsed condition.

Voltaire to M. de Maupertuis (with the King).

"THE HAGUE, 18th September, 1740.

"I serve you, Monsieur, sooner than I promised; and that
is the way you ought to be served. I send you the answer
of M. Smith," — probably some German or Dutch *Schmidt*,
spelt here in English, connected with the Sciences, say with
water-carriage, the typographies, or one need not know what;
"you will see where the question stands.

"When we both left Cleve," — 14th of the month, Wednes-
day last; 18th is Sunday, in this old cobwebby Palace, where
I am correcting *Anti-Machiavel*, — "and you took to the right,"
— King, homewards, got to *Ham* that evening, — "I could
have thought I was at the Last Judgment, where the Bon
Dieu separates the elect from the damned. *Divus Fredericus*
said to you, 'Sit down at my right hand in the Paradise of
Berlin;' and to me, 'Depart, thou accursed, into Holland.'

"Here I am accordingly in this phlegmatic place of punishment, far from the divine fire which animates the Friedrichs,
the Maupertuis, the Algarottis. For God's love, do me the
charity of some sparks in these stagnant waters where I am,"
— stiffening, cooling, — "stupefying to death. Instruct me of
your pleasures, of your designs. You will doubtless see M. de
Valori," — readers know de Valori; his Book has been published; edited, as too usual, by a Human Nightmare, ignorant
of his subject and indeed of almost all other things, and liable
to mistakes in every page; yet partly readable, if you carry
lanterns, and love "*mon gros Valori:*" — "offer him, I pray

you, my respects.   If I do not write to him, the reason is, I have no news to send : I should be as exact as I am devoted, if my correspondence could be useful or agreeable to him.

"Won't you have me send you some Books ?   If I be still in Holland when your orders come, I will obey in a moment. I pray you do not forget me to M. de Keyserling," — Cæsarion whom we once had at Cirey ; a headlong dusky little man of wit (library turned topsy-turvy, as Wilhelmina called him), whom we have seen.

"Tell me, I beg, if the enormous monad of Volfius — [Wolf, would the reader like to hear about him ?   If so, he has only to speak !] is arguing at Marburg, at Berlin, or at Hall [*Halle,* which is a very different place].

"Adieu, Monsieur : you can address your orders to me 'At the Hague :' they will be forwarded wherever I am ; and I shall be, anywhere on earth, — Yours forever (*à vous pour jamais*)." [1]

Letter Second, of which a fragment may be given, is to one Cideville, a month later ; all the more genuine as there was no chance of the King's hearing about this one.   Cideville, some kind of literary Advocate at Rouen (who is wearisomely known to the reader of Voltaire's Letters), had done, what is rather an endemical disorder at this time, some Verses for the King of Prussia, which he wished to be presented to his Majesty. The presentation, owing to accidents, did not take place ; hear how Voltaire, from his cobweb Palace at the Hague, busy with *Anti-Machiavel,* Van Duren and many other things, — 18th October, 1740, on which day we find him writing many Letters, — explains the sad accident : —

Voltaire to M. de Cideville (at Rouen).

"AT THE HAGUE, KING OF PRUSSIA'S PALACE,
18th October, 1740.

". . . This is my case, dear Cideville.   When you sent me, enclosed in your Letter, those Verses (among which there are some of charming and inimitable turn) for our Marcus Aurelius

[1] Voltaire, lxxii. 252.

of the North, I did well design to pay my court to him with them. He was at that time to have come to Brussels incognito: we expected him there; but the Quartan Fever, which unhappily he still has, deranged all his projects. He sent me a courier to Brussels," — mark that point, my Cideville; — " and so I set out to find him in the neighborhood of Cleve.

"It was there I saw one of the amiablest men in the world, who forms the charm of society, who would be everywhere sought after if he were not King; a philosopher without austerity; full of sweetness, complaisance and obliging ways (*agré-mens*); not remembering that he is King when he meets his friends; indeed so completely forgetting it that he made me too almost forget it, and I needed an effort of memory to recollect that I here saw sitting at the foot of my bed a Sovereign who had an Army of 100,000 men. That was the moment to have read your amiable Verses to him : " — yes; but then ?— " Madame du Châtelet, who was to have sent them to me, did not, *ne l'a pas fait.*" Alas, no, they are still at Brussels, those charming Verses; and I, for a month past, am here in my cobweb Palace ! But I swear to you, the instant I return to Brussels, I, &c. &c.[1]

Finally, here is what Friedrich thought of it, ten days after parting with Voltaire. We will read this also (though otherwise ahead of us as yet) ; to be certified on all sides, and sated for the rest of our lives, concerning the Friedrich-Voltaire First Interview.

King Friedrich to M. Jordan (at Berlin).

POTSDAM, 24th September, 1740.

"Most respectable Inspector of the poor, the invalids, orphans, crazy people and Bedlams, — I have read with mature meditation the very profound Jordanic Letter which was waiting here ; " — and do accept your learned proposal.

"I have seen that Voltaire whom I was so curious to know ; but I saw him with the Quartan hanging on me, and my mind

[1] Voltaire, lxxii. 282.

as unstrung as my body.   With men of his kind one ought not
to be sick ; one ought even to be specially well, and in better
health than common, if one could.

"He has the eloquence of Cicero, the mildness of Pliny, the
wisdom of Agrippa ; he combines, in short, what is to be collected of virtues and talents from the three greatest men of
Antiquity.   His intellect is at work incessantly ; every drop
of ink is a trait of wit from his pen.   He declaimed his *Mahomet* to us, an admirable Tragedy which he has done," —
which the Official people smelling heresies in it (" toleration,"
" horrors of fanaticism," and the like) will not let him act, as
readers too well know : — " he transported us out of ourselves ;
I could only admire and hold my tongue.   The Du Châtelet
is lucky to have him : for of the good things he flings out at
random, a person who had no faculty but memory might make
a brilliant Book.   That Minerva has just published her Work
on *Physics :* not wholly bad.   It was König " — whom we
know, and whose late tempest in a certain teapot — " that
dictated the theme to her : she has adjusted, ornamented here
and there with some touch picked from Voltaire at her Suppers.
The Chapter on Space is pitiable ; the " — in short, she is still
raw in the Pure Sciences, and should have waited. . . .

"Adieu, most learned, most scientific, most profound Jordan, — or rather most gallant, most amiable, most jovial
Jordan ; — I salute thee, with assurance of all those old feelings which thou hast the art of inspiring in every one that
knows thee.   *Vale.*

" I write the moment of my arrival : be obliged to me, friend ;
for I have been working, I am going to work still, like a Turk,
or like a Jordan." [1]

This is hastily thrown off for Friend Jordan, the instant
after his Majesty's circuitous return home.   Readers cannot
yet attend his Majesty there, till they have brought the Affair
of Herstal, and other remainders of the Cleve Journey, along
with them.

[1] *Œuvres de Frédéric,* xvii. 71.

CHAPTER V.

AFFAIR OF HERSTAL.

THIS Rambonet, whom Voltaire found walking in the court of the old Castle of Moyland, is an official gentleman, otherwise unknown to History, who has lately been engaged in a Public Affair; and is now off again about it, "on a hired hack" or otherwise, — with very good instructions in his head. Affair which, though in itself but small, is now beginning to make great noise in the world, as Friedrich wends homewards out of his Cleve Journey. He has set it fairly alight, Voltaire and he, before quitting Moyland; and now it will go of itself. The Affair of Herstal, or of the Bishop of Liége; Friedrich's first appearance on the stage of politics. Concerning which some very brief notice, if intelligible, will suffice readers of the present day.

Heristal, now called Herstal, was once a Castle known to all mankind; King Pipin's Castle, who styled himself "Pipin of Heristal," before he became King of the Franks and begot Charlemagne. It lies on the Maas, in that fruitful Spa Country; left bank of the Maas, a little to the north of Liége; and probably began existence as a grander place than Liége (*Lüttich*), which was, at first, some Monastery dependent on secular Herstal and its grandeurs: — think only how the race has gone between these two entities; spiritual Liége now a big City, black with the smoke of forges and steam-mills; Herstal an insignificant Village, accidentally talked of for a few weeks in 1740, and no chance ever to be mentioned again by men.

Herstal, in the confused vicissitudes of a thousand years, had passed through various fortunes, and undergone change of owners often enough. Fifty years ago it was in the hands of the Nassau-Orange House; Dutch William, our English Protestant King, who probably scarce knew of his possessing it, was Lord of Herstal till his death.   Dutch William had no children to inherit Herstal: he was of kinship to the Prussian House, as readers are aware; and from that circumstance, not without a great deal of discussion, and difficult "Division of the Orange Heritage," this Herstal had, at the long last, fallen to Friedrich Wilhelm's share; it and Neuchâtel, and the Cobweb Palace, and some other places and pertinents.

For Dutch William was of kin, we say; Friedrich I. of Prussia, by his Mother the noble Wife of the Great Elector, was full cousin to Dutch William: and the Marriage Contracts were express, — though the High Mightinesses made difficulties, and the collateral Orange branches were abundantly reluctant, when it came to the fulfilling point.   For indeed the matter was intricate.   Orange itself, for example, what was to be done with the Principality of Orange?   Clearly Prussia's; but it lies imbedded deep in the belly of France; that will be a Cæsarean-Operation for you!   Had not Neuchâtel happened just then to fall home to France (or in some measure to France) and be heirless, Prussia's Heritage of Orange would have done little for Prussia!   Principality of Orange was, by this chance, long since, mainly in the First King's time, got settled:[1] but there needed many years more of good waiting, and of good pushing, on Friedrich Wilhelm's part; and it was not till 1732 that Friedrich Wilhelm got the Dutch Heritages finally brought to the square: Neuchâtel and Valengin, as aforesaid, in lieu of Orange; and now furthermore, the Old Palace at Loo (that *Vieille Cour* and biggest cobwebs), with pertinents, with Garden of Honslardik; and a string of items, bigger and less, not worth enumerating.   Of the items, this Herstal was one; — and truly, so far as this went, Friedrich Wilhelm often thought he had better never have seen it, so much trouble did it bring him.

---

[1] Neuchâtel, 3d November, 1707, to Friedrich I., natives preferring him to "Fifteen other Claimants;" Louis XIV. loudly protesting : not till Treaty of Utrecht (14th March 1713, first month of Friedrich Wilhelm's reign) would Louis XIV., on cession of Orange, consent and sanction.

How the Herstallers had behaved to Friedrich Wilhelm.

The Herstal people, knowing the Prussian recruiting-system and other rigors, were extremely unwilling to come under Friedrich Wilhelm's sway, could they have helped it. They refused fealty, swore they never would swear: nor did they, till the appearance, or indubitable foreshine, of Friedrich Wilhelm's bayonets advancing on them from the East, brought compliance. And always after, spite of such quasi-fealty, they showed a pig-like obstinacy of humor; a certain insignificant, and as it were impertinent, deep-rooted desire to thwart, irritate and contradict the said Friedrich Wilhelm. Especially in any recruiting matter that might arise, knowing that to be the weak side of his Prussian Majesty. All this would have amounted to nothing, had it not been that their neighbor, the Prince Bishop of Liége, who imagined himself to have some obscure claims of sovereignty over Herstal, and thought the present a good opportunity for asserting these, was diligent to aid and abet the Herstal people in such their mutinous acts. Obscure claims; of which this is the summary, should the reader not prefer to skip it: —

"The Bishop of Liége's claims on Herstal (which lie wrapt from mankind in the extensive jungle of his law-pleadings, like a Bedlam happily fallen extinct) seem to me to have grown mainly from two facts more or less radical.

"*Fact first.* In Kaiser Barbarossa's time, year 1171, Herstal had been given in pawn to the Church of Liége, for a loan, by the then proprietor, Duke of Lorraine and Brabant. Loan was repaid, I do not learn when, and the Pawn given back; to the satisfaction of said Duke, or Duke's Heirs; never quite to the satisfaction of the Church, which had been in possession, and was loath to quit, after hoping to continue. 'Give us back Herstal; it ought to be ours!' Unappeasable sigh or grumble to this effect is heard thenceforth, at intervals, in the Chapter of Liége, and has not ceased in Friedrich's time. But as the world, in its loud thoroughfares, seldom or never heard, or could hear, such sighing in the Chapter, nothing had come of it, — till —

"*Fact second.* In Kaiser Karl V.'s time, the Prince Bishop

of Liége happened to be a Natural Son of old Kaiser Max's ; — and had friends at headquarters, of a very choice nature. Had, namely, in this sort, Kaiser Karl for Nephew or Half-Nephew ; and what perhaps was still better, as nearer hand, had Karl's Aunt, Maria Queen of Hungary, then Governess of the Netherlands, for Half-Sister.   Liége, in these choice circumstances, and by other good chances that turned up, again got temporary clutch or half-clutch of Herstal, for a couple of years (date 1546–1548, the Prince of Orange, real proprietor, whose Ancestor had bought it for money down, being then a minor) ; once, and perhaps a second time in like circumstance ; but had always to renounce it again, when the Prince of Orange came to maturity.   And ever since, the Chapter of Liége sighs as before, 'Herstal is perhaps in a sense ours.   We had once some kind of right to it!' — sigh inaudible in the loud public thoroughfares.   That is the Bishop's claim.   The name of him, if anybody care for it, is 'Georg Ludwig, titular *Count of Berg*,' now a very old man : Bishop of Liége, he, and has been snatching at Herstal again, very eagerly by any skirt or tagrag that might happen to fly loose, these eight years past, in a rash and provoking manner ;[1] — age eighty-two at present ; poor old fool, he had better have sat quiet.   There lies a rod in pickle for him, during these late months ; and will be surprisingly laid on, were the time come ! "

" I have Law Authority over Herstal, and power of judging there in the last appeal," said this Bishop : — "You ! " thought Friedrich Wilhelm, who was far off, and had little time to waste. — "Any Prussian recruiter that behaves ill, bring him to me ! " said the Bishop, who was on the spot. And accordingly it had been done ; one notable instance two years ago : a Prussian Lieutenant locked in the Liége jail, on complaint of riotous Herstal ; thereupon a Prussian Officer of rank (Colonel Kreutzen, worthy old Malplaquet gentleman) coming as Royal Messenger, not admitted to audience, nay laid hold of by the Liége bailiff instead ; and other unheard-of procedures.[2]   So that Friedrich Wilhelm had nothing but

[1] *Délices du Pais de Liége* (Liége, 1738) ; *Helden-Geschichte*, ii. 57–62.
[2] *Helden-Geschichte*, ii. 63–73.

trouble with this petty Herstal, and must have thought his neighbor Bishop a very contentious high-flying gentleman, who took great liberties with the Lion's whiskers, when he had the big animal at an advantage.

The episcopal procedures, eight years ago, about the First Homaging of Herstal, had been of similar complexion; nor had other such failed in the interim, though this last outrage exceeded them all. This last began in the end of 1738; and span itself out through 1739, when Friedrich Wilhelm lay in his final sickness, less able to deal with it than formerly. Being a peaceable man, unwilling to awaken conflagrations for a small matter, Friedrich Wilhelm had offered, through Kreutzen on this occasion, to part with Herstal altogether; to sell it, for 100,000 thalers, say £16,000, to the high-flying Bishop, and honestly wash his hands of it. But the high-flying Bishop did not consent, gave no definite answer; and so the matter lay, — like an unsettled extremely irritating paltry little matter, — at the time Friedrich Wilhelm died.

The Gazetteers and public knew little about these particulars, or had forgotten them again; but at the Prussian Court they were in lively remembrance. What the young Friedrich's opinion about them had been we gather from this succinct notice of the thing, written seven or eight years afterwards, exact in all points, and still carrying a breath of the old humor in it. "A miserable Bishop of Liége thought it a proud thing to insult the late King. Some subjects of Herstal, which belongs to Prussia, had revolted; the Bishop gave them his protection. Colonel Kreutzen was sent to Liége, to compose the thing by treaty; credentials with him, full power, and all in order. Imagine it, the Bishop would not receive him! Three days, day after day, he saw this Envoy apply at his Palace, and always denied him entrance. These things had grown past endurance."[1] And Friedrich had taken note of Herstal along with him, on this Cleve Journey; privately intending to put Herstal and the high-flying Bishop on a suitabler footing, before his return from those countries.

For indeed, on Friedrich's Accession, matters had grown

[1] Preuss, *Œuvres* (*Mémoires de Brandebourg*), ii. 53.

worse, not better. Of course there was Fealty to be sworn;
but the Herstal people, abetted by the high-flying Bishop,
have declined swearing it. Apology for the past, prospect of
amendment for the future, there is less than ever. What is
the young King to do with this paltry little Hamlet of Herstal? He could, in theory, go into some Reichs-Hofrath, some
Reichs-Kammergericht (kind of treble and tenfold English
Court-of-Chancery, which has lawsuits 280 years old), — if he
were a theoretic German King. He can plead in the Diets,
and the Wetzlar Reichs-Kammergericht without end : " All
German Sovereigns have power to send their Ambassador
thither, who is like a mastiff chained in the back-yard [ob-
serves Friedrich elsewhere] with privilege of barking at the
Moon," — unrestricted privilege of barking at the Moon, if
that will avail a practical man, or King's Ambassador. Or
perhaps the Bishop of Liége will bethink him, at last, what
considerable liberty he is taking with some people's whiskers ?
Four months are gone; Bishop of Liége has not in the least
bethought him : we are in the neighborhood in person, with
note of the thing in our memory.

Friedrich takes the Rod out of Pickle.

Accordingly the Rath Rambonet, whom Voltaire found at
Moyland that Sunday night, had been over at Liége; went
exactly a week before ; with this message of very peremptory
tenor from his Majesty : —

To the Prince Bishop of Liége.

"Wesel, 4th September, 1740.

"My Cousin, — Knowing all the assaults (atteintes) made
by you upon my indisputable rights over my free Barony of
Herstal; and how the seditious ringleaders there, for several
years past, have been countenanced (bestärket) by you in their
detestable acts of disobedience against me, — I have commanded my Privy Councillor Rambonet to repair to your
presence, and in my name to require from you, within two
days, a distinct and categorical answer to this question :

Whether you are still minded to assert your pretended sovereignty over Herstal; and whether you will protect the
rebels at Herstal, in their disorders and abominable disobedience ?

"In case you refuse, or delay beyond the term, the Answer
which I hereby of right demand, you will render yourself
alone responsible, before the world, for the consequences
which infallibly will follow. I am, with much consideration, — My Cousin, —

"Your very affectionate Cousin,

"FRIEDRICH. "[1]

Rambonet had started straightway for Liége, with this missive; and had duly presented it there, I guess on the 7th, —
with notice that he would wait forty-eight hours, and then
return with what answer or no-answer there might be. Getting no written answer, or distinct verbal one; getting only
some vague mumblement as good as none, Rambonet had disappeared from Liége on the 9th; and was home at Moyland
when Voltaire arrived that Sunday evening, — just walking
about to come to heat again, after reporting progress to the
above effect.

Rambonet, I judge, enjoyed only one of those divine Suppers at Moyland; and dashed off again, "on hired hack" or
otherwise, the very next morning; that contingency of No-
answer having been the anticipated one, and all things put
in perfect readiness for it. Rambonet's new errand was to
"take act," as Voltaire calls it, "at the Gates of Liége," — to
deliver at Liége a succinct Manifesto, Pair of Manifestoes, both
in Print (ready beforehand), and bearing date that same Sunday, "Wesel, 11th September; " much calculated to amaze
his Reverence at Liége. Succinct good Manifestoes, said to
be of Friedrich's own writing; the essential of the two is
this : —

[1] *Helden-Geschichte*, ii. 75, 111.

Exposition of the Reasons which have induced his Majesty the King of Prussia to make just Reprisals on the Prince Bishop of Liége.

"His Majesty the King of Prussia, being driven beyond bounds by the rude proceedings of the Prince Bishop of Liége, has with regret seen himself forced to recur to the Method of Arms, in order to repress the violence and affront which the Bishop has attempted to put upon him. This resolution has cost his Majesty much pain; the rather as he is, by principle and disposition, far remote from whatever could have the least relation to rigor and severity.

"But seeing himself compelled by the Bishop of Liége to take new methods, he had no other course but to maintain the justice of his rights (*la justice de ses droits*), and demand reparation for the indignity done upon his Minister Von Kreuzen, as well as for the contempt with which the Bishop of Liége has neglected even to answer the Letter of the King.

"As too much rigor borders upon cruelty, so too much patience resembles weakness. Thus, although the King would willingly have sacrificed his interests to the public peace and tranquillity, it was not possible to do so in reference to his honor; and that is the chief motive which has determined him to this resolution, so contrary to his intentions.

"In vain has it been attempted, by methods of mildness, to come to a friendly agreement: it has been found, on the contrary, that the King's moderation only increased the Prince's arrogance; that mildness of conduct on one side only furnished resources to pride on the other; and that, in fine, instead of gaining by soft procedure, one was insensibly becoming an object of vexation and disdain.

"There being no means to have justice but in doing it for oneself, and the King being Sovereign enough for such a duty, — he intends to make the Prince of Liége feel how far he was in the wrong to abuse such moderation so unworthily. But in spite of so much unhandsome behavior on the part of

this Prince, the King will not be inflexible; satisfied with
having shown the said Prince that he can punish him, and
too just to overwhelm him.　　　　　　　　　FRÉDÉRIC.[1]

"WESEL, September 11th, 1740."

Whether Rambonet insinuated his Paper-Packet into the
Palace of Seraing, left it at the Gate of Liége (fixed by nail,
if he saw good), or in what manner he "took act," I never
knew; and indeed Rambonet vanishes from human History
at this point: it is certain only that he did his Formality,
say two days hence; — and that the Fact foreshadowed by
it is likewise in the same hours, hour after hour, getting
steadily done.

For the Manifestoes printed beforehand, dated Wesel, 11th
September, were not the only thing ready at Wesel; waiting,
as on the slip, for the contingency of No-answer. Major-
General Borck, with the due Battalions, squadrons and equipments, was also ready. Major-General Borck, the same who
was with us at Baireuth lately, had just returned from that
journey, when he got orders to collect 2,000 men, horse and
foot, with the due proportion of artillery, from the Prussian
Garrisons in these parts; and to be ready for marching with
them, the instant the contingency of No-answer arrives, —
Sunday, 11th, as can be foreseen. Borck knows his route:
To Maaseyk, a respectable Town of the Bishop's, the handiest
for Wesel; to occupy Maaseyk and the adjoining "Counties
of Lotz and Horn;" and lie there at the Bishop's charge till
his Reverence's mind alter.

Borck is ready, to the last pontoon, the last munition-loaf;
and no sooner is signal given of the No-answer come, than
Borck, that same "Sunday, 11th," gets under way; marches,
steady as clock-work, towards Maaseyk (fifty miles southwest
of him, distance now lessening every hour); crosses the Maas,
by help of his pontoons; is now in the Bishop's Territory, and
enters Maaseyk, evening of "Wednesday, 14th," — that very
day Voltaire and his Majesty had parted, going different ways

---

[1] *Helden-Geschichte*, ii. 77. Said to be by Friedrich himself (Stenzel, iv. 59).

from Moyland; and probably about the same hour while Rambonet was "taking act at the Gate of Liége," by nail-hammer or otherwise. All goes punctual, swift, cog hitting pinion far and near, in this small Herstal Business; and there is no mistake made, and a minimum of time spent.

Borck's management was throughout good: punctual, quietly exact, polite, mildly inflexible. Fain would the Maaseyk Town-Raths have shut their gates on him; desperately conjuring him, "Respite for a few hours, till we send to Liége for instructions!" But it was to no purpose. "Unbolt, *ihr Herren;* swift, or the petard will have to do it!" Borck publishes his Proclamation, a mild-spoken rigorous Piece; signifies to the Maaseyk Authorities, That he has to exact a Contribution of 20,000 thalers (£3,000) here, Contribution payable in three days; that he furthermore, while he continues in these parts, will need such and such rations, accommodations, allowances, — "fifty *louis* (say guineas) daily for his own private expenses," one item; — and, in mild rhadamanthine language, waves aside all remonstrance, refusal or delay, as superfluous considerations: Unless said Contribution and required supplies come in, it will be his painful duty to bring them in.[1]

The high-flying Bishop, much astonished, does now eagerly answer his Prussian Majesty, "Was from home, was ill, thought he had answered; is the most ill-used of Bishops;" and other things of a hysteric character.[2] And there came forth, as natural to the situation, multitudinous complainings, manifestoings, applications to the Kaiser, to the French, to the Dutch, of a very shrieky character on the Bishop of Liége's part; sparingly, if at all noticed on Friedrich's: the whole of which we shall consider ourselves free to leave undisturbed in the rubbish-abysses, as henceforth conceivable to the reader. "*Sed spem stupende fefellit eventus,*" shrieks the poor old Bishop, making moan to the Kaiser: "*ecce enim, præmissâ duntaxat unâ Literâ,* one Letter," and little more, "the said King of Borussia has, with about 2,000 horse and foot, and warlike engines, in this month of September, entered the Ter-

ritory of Liége; "[1] which is an undeniable truth, but an unavailing.   Borck is there, and " 2,000 good arguments with
him," as Voltaire defines the phenomenon.   Friedrich, except
to explain pertinently what my readers already know, does
not write or speak farther on the subject; and readers and he
may consider the Herstal Affair, thus set agoing under Borck's
auspices, as in effect finished; and that his Majesty has left it
on a satisfactory footing, and may safely turn his back on it,
to wait the sure issue at Berlin before long.

What Voltaire thought of Herstal.

Voltaire told us he himself "did one Manifesto, good or
bad," on this Herstal business:—where is that Piece, then,
what has become of it?   Dig well in the realms of Chaos,
rectifying stupidities more or less enormous, the Piece itself
is still discoverable; and, were pieces by Voltaire much a
rarity instead of the reverse, might be resuscitated by a good
Editor, and printed in his *Works*.   Lies buried in the lonesome rubbish-mountains of that *Helden-Geschichte*, — let a
Siste Viator, scratched on the surface, mark where.[2]   Apparently that is the Piece by Voltaire?   Yes, on reading that,
it has every internal evidence; distinguishes itself from the
surrounding pieces, like a slab of compact polished stone, in a
floor rammed together out of ruinous old bricks, broken bottles
and mortar-dust; — agrees, too, if you examine by the micro-
scope, with the external indications, which are sure and at
last clear, though infinitesimally small; and is beyond doubt
Voltaire's, if it were now good for much.

It is not properly a Manifesto, but an anonymous memoir
published in the Newspapers, explaining to impartial mankind, in a legible brief manner, what the old and recent History of Herstal, and the Troubles of Herstal, have been, and
how chimerical and "null to the extreme of nullity (*nulles de
toute nullité*)" this poor Bishop's pretensions upon it are.   Voltaire expressly piques himself on this Piece;[3] brags also how

---

[1] *Helden-Geschichte*, ii. 88.   [2] Ib. ii. 93–98.
[3] Letter to Friedrich: dateless, datable "soon after 17th September;"
which the rash dark Editors have by guess misdated "August;" or, what

he settled "M. de Fénelon [French Ambassador at the Hague],
who came to me the day before yesterday," much out of square
upon the Herstal Business, till I pulled him straight.   And it
is evident (beautifully so, your Majesty) how Voltaire busied
himself in the Gazettes and Diplomatic circles, setting Friedrich's case right; Voltaire very loyal to Friedrich and his
Liége Cause at that time ; — and the contrast between what
his contemporary Letters say on the subject, and what his
ulterior Pasquil called *Vie Privée* says, is again great.

The dull stagnant world, shaken awake by this Liége adventure, gives voice variously ; and in the Gazetteer and Diplomatic circles it is much criticised, by no means everywhere in
the favorable tone at this first blush of the business.   "He
had written an *Anti*-Machiavel," says the Abbé St. Pierre,
and even says Voltaire (in the *Pasquil*, not the contemporary
Letters), "and he acts thus ! "   Truly he does, Monsieur de
Voltaire ; and all men, with light upon the subject, or even
with the reverse upon it, must make their criticisms.   For the
rest, Borck's "2,000 arguments " are there ; which Borck han-
dles well, with polite calm rigor : by degrees the dust will fall,
and facts everywhere be seen for what they are.

As to the high-flying Bishop, finding that hysterics are but
wasted on Friedrich and Borck, and produce no effect with
their 2,000 validities, he flies next to the Kaiser, to the Imperial Diet, in shrill-sounding Latin obtestations, of which we
already gave a flying snatch: "Your *humilissimus* and *fide-
lissimus Vassallus,* and most obsequient Servant, Georgius
Ludovicus ; meek, modest, and unspeakably in the right:
was ever Member of the Holy Roman Empire so snubbed,
and grasped by the windpipe, before ?   Oh, help him, great
Kaiser, bid the iron gripe loosen itself ! "[1]   The Kaiser does
so, in heavy Latin rescripts, in German *Dehortatoriums* more
than one, of a sulky, imperative, and indeed very lofty tenor ;
"Let Georgius Ludovicus go, foolish rash young Dilection

was safer for them, omitted it altogether.   *Œuvres de Voltaire* (Paris, 1818,
40 vols.) gives the Letter, xxxix. 442 (see also ibid. 453, 463) ; later Editors,
and even Preuss, take the safer course.

[1] *Helden-Geschichte,* ii. 86–116.

(*Liebden*, not *Majesty*, we ourselves being the only Majesty),
and I will judge between you; otherwise — ! " said the Kaiser, ponderously shaking his Olympian wig, and lifting his
gilt cane, or sceptre of mankind, in an Olympian manner.
Here are some touches of his second sublimest *Dehortatorium*
addressed to Friedrich, in a very compressed state : [1] —

We Karl the Sixth, Kaiser of (*Titles enough*), . . . " Considering these, in the Holy Roman Reich, almost unheard-of
violent Doings (*Thätlichkeiten*), which We, in Our Supreme-
Judge Office, cannot altogether justify, nor will endure . . .
We have the trust that you yourself will magnanimously see
How evil counsellors have misled your Dilection to commence
your Reign, not by showing example of Obedience to the Laws
appointed for all members of the Reich, for the weak and for
the strong alike, but by such Doings (*Thathandlungen*) as in
all quarters must cause a great surprise.

" We give your Dilection to know, therefore, That you must
straightway withdraw those troops which have broken into the
Liége Territory; make speedy restitution of all that has been
extorted; — especially General von Borck to give back at once
those 50 louis d'or daily drawn by him, to renounce his demand of the 20,000 thalers, to make good all damage done,
and retire with his whole military force (*Militz*) over the
Liége boundaries; — and in brief, that you will, by law or
arbitration, manage to agree with the Prince Bishop of Liége,
who wishes it very much. These things We expect from your
Dilection, as Kurfürst of Brandenburg, within the space of
Two Months from the Issuing of this; and remain," — Yours
as you shall demean yourself, — KARL.

" Given at Wien, 4th of October, 1740." — The last Dehortatorium ever signed by Karl VI. In two weeks after he ate
too many mushrooms, — and immense results followed!

Dehortatoriums had their interest, at Berlin and elsewhere,
for the Diplomatic circles; but did not produce the least
effect on Borck or Friedrich; though Friedrich noted the
Kaiser's manner in these things, and thought privately to

[1] *Helden-Geschichte*, ii. 127; a *first* and milder (ibid. 73).

himself, as was evident to the discerning, "What an amount
of wig on that old gentleman!" A notable Kaiser's Ambassador, Herr Botta, who had come with some Accession compliments, in these weeks, was treated slightingly by Friedrich;
hardly admitted to Audience; and Friedrich's public reply to
the last Dehortatorium had almost something of sarcasm in
it: Evil counsellors yourself, Most Dread Kaiser! It is you
that are "misled by counsellors, who might chance to set
Germany on fire, were others as unwise as they!" Which
latter phrase was remarkable to mankind. — There is a long
account already run up between that old gentleman, with his
Seckendorfs, Grumkows, with his dull insolencies, wiggeries,
and this young gentleman, who has nearly had his heart
broken and his Father's house driven mad by them! Borck
remains at his post; rations duly delivered, and fifty louis a
day for his own private expenses; and there is no answer to
the Kaiser, or in sharp brief terms (about "chances of setting
Germany on fire"), rather worse than none.

Readers see, as well as Friedrich did, what the upshot of
this affair must be;— we will now finish it off, and wash our
hands of it, before following his Majesty to Berlin. The
poor Bishop had applied, shrieking, to the French for help;—
and there came some colloquial passages between Voltaire and
Fénelon, if that were a result. He had shrieked in like manner to the Dutch, but without result of any kind traceable in
that quarter: nowhere, except from the Kaiser, is so much as
a *Dehortatorium* to be got. Whereupon the once high-flying,
now vainly shrieking Bishop discerns clearly that there is but
one course left,— the course which has lain wide open for
some years past, had not his flight gone too high for seeing
it. Before three weeks are over, seeing how Dehortatoriums
go, he sends his Ambassadors to Berlin, his apologies, proposals:[1] "Would not your Majesty perhaps consent to sell
this Herstal, as your Father of glorious memory was pleased
to be willing once?" —

Friedrich answers straightway to the effect: "Certainly!

[1] Ambassadors arrived 28th September; last Dehortatorium not yet out.
Business was completed 20th October (Rödenbeck, *in diebus*).

Pay me the price it was once already offered for: 100,000 thalers, *plus* the expenses since incurred. That will be 180,000 thalers, besides what you have spent already on General Borck's days' wages. To which we will add that wretched little fraction of Old Debt, clear as noon, but never paid nor any part of it; 60,000 thalers, due by the See of Liége ever since the Treaty of Utrecht; 60,000, for which we will charge no interest: that will make 240,000 thalers, — £36,000, instead of the old sum you might have had it at. Produce that cash; and take Herstal, and all the dust that has risen out of it, well home with you."[1] The Bishop thankfully complies in all points; negotiation speedily done (" 20th Oct." the final date): Bishop has not, I think, quite so much cash on hand; but will pay all he has, and 4 per centum interest till the whole be liquidated. His Ambassadors " get gold snuffboxes ; " and return mildly glad !

And thus, in some six weeks after Borck's arrival in those parts, Borck's function is well done. The noise of Gazettes and Diplomatic circles lays itself again ; and Herstal, famous once for King Pipin, and famous again for King Friedrich, lapses at length into obscurity, which we hope will never end. Hope ; —though who can say ? *Roucoux*, quite close upon it, becomes a Battle-ground in some few years ; and memorabilities go much at random in this world !

CHAPTER VI.

RETURNS BY HANOVER ; DOES NOT CALL ON HIS ROYAL UNCLE THERE.

FRIEDRICH spent ten days on his circuitous journey home; considerable inspection to be done, in Minden, Magdeburg, not to speak of other businesses he had. The old Newspapers are still more intent upon him, now that the Herstal Affair has broken into flame : especially the English Newspapers ; who

[1] Stenzel, iv. 60, who counts in gulden, and is not distinct.

guess that there are passages of courtship going on between great George their King and him. Here is one fact, correct in every point, for the old London Public: "Letters from Hanover say, that the King of Prussia passed within a small distance of that City the 16th inst. N.s., on his return to Berlin, but did not stop at Herrenhausen;"—about which there has been such hoping and speculating among us lately.[1] A fact which the extinct Editor seems to meditate for a day or two; after which he says (partly in *italics*), opening his lips the second time, like a Friar Bacon's Head significant to the Public: "Letters from Hanover tell us that the Interview, which it was said his Majesty was to have with the King of Prussia, did not take place, for certain *private reasons,* which our Correspondent leaves us to guess at!"

It is well known Friedrich did not love his little Uncle, then or thenceforth; still less his little Uncle him: "What is this Prussia, rising alongside of us, higher and higher, as if it would reach our own sublime level!" thinks the little Uncle to himself. At present there is no quarrel between them; on the contrary, as we have seen, there is a mutual capability of helping one another, which both recognize; but will an interview tend to forward that useful result? Friedrich, in the intervals of an ague, with Herstal just broken out, may have wisely decided, No. "Our sublime little Uncle, of the waxy complexion, with the proudly staring fish-eyes,—no wit in him, not much sense, and a great deal of pride,—stands dreadfully erect, 'plumb and more,' with the Garter-leg advanced, when one goes to see him; and his remarks are not of an entertaining nature. Leave him standing there: to him let Truchsess and Bielfeld suffice, in these hurries, in this ague that is still upon us." Upon which the dull old Newspapers, Owls of Minerva that then were, endeavor to draw inferences. The noticeable fact is, Friedrich did, on this occasion, pass within a mile or two of his royal Uncle, without seeing him; and had not, through life, another opportunity; never saw the sublime little man at all, nor was again so near him.

[1] *Daily Post,* 22d September, 1740; other London Newspapers from July 31st downwards.

I believe Friedrich little knows the thick-coming difficulties of his Britannic Majesty at this juncture; and is too impatient of these laggard procedures on the part of a man with eyes *à fleur-de-tête.* Modern readers too have forgotten Jenkins's Ear; it is not till after long study and survey that one begins to perceive the anomalous profundities of that phenomenon to the poor English Nation and its poor George II.

The English sent off, last year, a scanty Expedition, " six ships of the line," only six, under Vernon, a fiery Admiral, a little given to be fiery in Parliamentary talk withal; and these did proceed to Porto-Bello on the Spanish Main of South America; did hurl out on Porto-Bello such a fiery destructive deluge, of gunnery and bayonet-work, as quickly reduced the poor place to the verge of ruin, and forced it to surrender with whatever navy, garrison, goods and resources were in it, to the discretion of fiery Vernon, — who does not prove implacable, he or his, to a petitioning enemy. Yes, humble the insolent, but then be merciful to them, say the admiring Gazetteers. " The actual monster," how cheering to think, " who tore off Mr. Jenkins's Ear, was got hold of [actual monster, or even three or four different monsters who each did it, the " hold got " being *mythical,* as readers see], and naturally thought he would be slit to ribbons; but our people magnanimously pardoned him, magnanimously flung him aside out of sight; " [1] impossible to shoot a dog in cold blood.

Whereupon Vernon returned home triumphant; and there burst forth such a jubilation, over the day of small things, as is now astonishing to think of. Had the Termagant's own Thalamus and Treasury been bombarded suddenly one night by red-hot balls, Madrid City laid in ashes, or Baby Carlos's Apanage extinguished from Creation, there could hardly have been greater English joy (witness the " Porto-Bellos " they still have, new Towns so named); so flamy is the murky element growing on that head. And indeed had the cipher of tar-barrels burnt, and of ale-barrels drunk, and the general account of wick and tallow spent in illuminations and in alder-

---

[1] *Gentleman's Magazine,* x. 124, 145 (date of the Event is 3d December N.S., 1739).

manic exertions on the matter, been accurately taken, one doubts
if Porto-Bello sold, without shot fired, to the highest bidder,
at its floweriest, would have covered such a sum. For they are
a singular Nation, if stirred up from their stagnancy; and are
much in earnest about this Spanish War.

It is said there is now another far grander Expedition on
the stocks: military this time as well as naval, intended for
the Spanish Main; — but of that, for the present, we will
defer speaking. Enough, the Spanish War is a most serious
and most furious business to those old English; and, to us, after
forced study of it, shines out like far-off conflagration, with a
certain lurid significance in the then night of things. Night
otherwise fallen dark and somniferous to modern mankind.
As Britannic Majesty and his Walpoles have, from the first,
been dead against this Spanish War, the problem is all the
more ominous, and the dreadful corollaries that may hang by
it the more distressing to the royal mind.

For example, there is known, or as good as known, to be
virtually some Family Compact, or covenanted Brotherhood of
Bourbonism, French and Spanish: political people quake to
ask themselves, "How will the French keep out of this War,
if it continue any length of time? And in that case, how will
Austria, Europe at large? Jenkins's Ear will have kindled
the Universe, not the Spanish Main only, and we shall be at
a fine pass!" The Britannic Majesty reflects that if France
take to fighting him, the first stab given will probably be in the
accessiblest quarter and the intensely most sensitive, — our
own Electoral Dominions where no Parliament plagues us, our
dear native country, Hanover. Extremely interesting to know
what Friedrich of Prussia will do in such contingency?

Well, truly it might have been King George's best bargain
to close with Friedrich; to guarantee Jülich and Berg, and
get Fredrich to stand between the French and Hanover; while
George, with an England behind him, in such humor, went
wholly into that Spanish Business, the one thing needful to
them at present. Truly; but then again, there are considerations: "What *is* this Friedrich, just come out upon the world?
What real fighting power has he, after all that ridiculous drill-

ing and recruiting Friedrich Wilhelm made ? Will he be faithful in bargain; is not, perhaps, from of old, his bias always toward France rather ?   And the Kaiser, what will the Kaiser say to it ? " These are questions for a Britannic Majesty ! Seldom was seen such an insoluble imbroglio of potentialities ; dangerous to touch, dangerous to leave lying ; — and his Britannic Majesty's procedures upon it are of a very slow intricate sort ; and will grow still more so, year after year, in the new intricacies that are coming, and be a weariness to my readers and me. For observe the simultaneous fact. All this while, Robinson at Vienna is dunning the Imperial Majesty to remember old Marlborough days and the Laws of Nature; and declare for us against France, in case of the worst. What an attempt ! Imperial Majesty has no money ; Imperial Majesty remembers recent days rather, and his own last quarrel with France (on the Polish-Election score), in which you Sea-Powers cruelly stood neuter !   One comfort, and pretty much one only, is left to a nearly bankrupt Imperial heart ; that France does at any rate ratify Pragmatic Sanction, and instead of enemy to that inestimable Document has become friend, — if only she be well let alone.   " Let well alone," says the sad Kaiser, bankrupt of heart as well as purse : " I have saved the Pragmatic, got Fleury to guarantee it ; I will hunt wild swine and not shadows any more : ask me not ! " And now this Herstal business ; the Imperial Dehortatoriums, perhaps of a high nature, that are like to come ? More hopeless proposition the Britannic Majesty never made than this to the Kaiser. But he persists in it, orders Robinson to persist ; knocks at the Austrian door with one hand, at the Prussian or Anti-Austrian with the other ; and gazes, with those proud fish-eyes, into perils and potentialities and a sea of troubles. Wearisome to think of, were not one bound to it ! Here, from a singular *Constitutional History of England,* not yet got into print, are two Excerpts ; which I will request the reader to try if he can take along with him, in view of much that is coming : —

1. *A just War.* — " This War, which posterity scoffs at as the *War for Jenkins's Ear,* was, if we examine it, a quite indis-

pensable one; the dim much-bewildered English, driven into
it by their deepest instincts, were, in a chaotic inarticulate
way, right and not wrong in taking it as the Commandment of
Heaven. For such, in a sense, it was; as shall by and by
appear. Not perhaps since the grand Reformation Controversy, under Oliver Cromwell and Elizabeth, had there, to this
poor English People (who are essentially dumb, *in*articulate,
from the weight of meaning they have, notwithstanding the
palaver one hears from them in certain epochs), been a more
authentic cause of War. And, what was the fatal and yet
foolish circumstance, their Constitutional Captains, especially
their King, would never and could never regard it as such;
but had to be forced into it by the public rage, there being no
other method left in the case.

"I say, a most necessary War, though of a most stupid
appearance; such the fatality of it: — begun, carried on,
ended, as if by a People in a state of somnambulism! More
confused operation never was. A solid placid People, heavily
asleep (and *snoring* much, shall we say, and inarticulately
grunting and struggling under indigestions, Constitutional and
other? Do but listen to the hum of those extinct Pamphlets
and Parliamentary Oratories of theirs!), — yet an honestly
intending People; and keenly alive to any commandment from
Heaven, that could pierce through the thick skin of them into
their big obstinate heart. Such a commandment, then and
there, was that monition about Jenkins's Ear. Upon which,
so pungent was it to them, they started violently out of bed,
into painful sleep-walking; and went, for twenty years and
more, clambering and sprawling about, far and wide, on the
giddy edge of precipices, over house-tops and frightful cornices
and parapets; in a dim fulfilment of the said Heaven's command. I reckon that this War, though there were intervals,
Treaties of Peace more than one, and the War had various
names, — did not end till 1763. And then, by degrees, the poor
English Nation found that (at, say, a thousand times the necessary expense, and with imminent peril to its poor head, and all
the bones of its body) it had actually succeeded, — by dreadful
exertions in its sleep! This will be more apparent by and by;

and may be a kind of comfort to the sad English reader, drearily surveying such somnambulisms on the part of his poor ancestors."

2. *Two Difficulties.* — "There are Two grand Difficulties in this Farce-Tragedy of a war; of which only one, and that not the worst of the Pair, is in the least surmised by the English hitherto. Difficulty First, which is even worse than the other, and will surprisingly attend the English in all their Wars now coming, is : That their fighting-apparatus, though made of excellent material, cannot fight, — being in disorganic condition ; one branch of it, especially the 'Military' one as they are pleased to call it, being as good as totally chaotic, and this in a quiet habitual manner, this long while back. With the Naval branch it is otherwise; which also is habitual there. The English almost as if by nature can sail, and fight, in ships; cannot well help doing it. Sailors innumerable are bred to them ; they are planted in the Ocean, opulent stormy Neptune clipping them in all his moods forever : and then by nature, being a dumb, much-enduring, much-reflecting, stout, veracious and valiant kind of People, they shine in that way of life, which specially requires such. Without much forethought, they have sailors innumerable, and of the best quality. The English have among them also, strange as it may seem to the cursory observer, a great gift of organizing; witness their Arkwrights and others : and this gift they may often, in matters Naval more than elsewhere, get the chance of exercising. For a Ship's Crew, or even a Fleet, unlike a land Army, is of itself a unity, its fortunes disjoined, dependent on its own management ; and it falls, moreover, as no land army can, to the undivided guidance of one man, — who (by hypothesis, being English) has now and then, from of old, chanced to be an organizing man; and who is always much interested to know and practise what *has* been well organized. For you are in contact with verities, to an unexampled degree, when you get upon the Ocean, with intent to sail on it, much more to fight on it ; — bottomless destruction raging beneath you and on all hands of you, if you neglect, for any reason, the methods of keeping *it* down, and making it float you to your aim !

The English Navy is in tolerable order at that period. But as to the English Army, — we may say it is, in a wrong sense, the wonder of the world, and continues so throughout the whole of this History and farther! Never before, among the rational sons of Adam, were Armies sent out on such terms, — namely without a General, or with no General understanding the least of his business. The English have a notion that Generalship is not wanted; that War is not an Art, as playing Chess is, as finding the Longitude, and doing the Differential Calculus are (and a much deeper Art than any of these); that War is taught by Nature, as eating is; that courageous soldiers, led on by a courageous Wooden Pole with Cocked-hat on it, will do very well. In the world I have not found opacity of platitude go deeper among any People. This is Difficulty First, not yet suspected by an English People, capable of great opacity on some subjects.

"Difficulty Second is, That their Ministry, whom they had to force into this War, perhaps do not go zealously upon it. And perhaps even, in the above circumstances, they totally want knowledge how to go upon it, were they never so zealous; Difficulty Second might be much helped, were it not for Difficulty First. But the administering of War is a thing also that does not come to a man like eating. — This Second Difficulty, suspicion that Walpole and perhaps still higher heads want zeal, gives his Britannic Majesty infinite trouble; and " —
— And so, in short, he stands there, with the Garter-leg advanced, looking loftily into a considerable sea of troubles, — that day when Friedrich drove past him, Friday, 16th September, 1740, and never came so near him again.

The next business for Friedrich was a Visit at Brunswick, to the Affinities and Kindred, in passing; where also was an important little act to be done: Betrothal of the young Prince, August Wilhelm, Heir-Presumptive whom we saw in Strasburg, to a Princess of that House, Louisa Amelia, younger Sister of Friedrich's own Queen. A modest promising arrangement; which turned out well enough, — though the

young Prince, Father to the Kings that since are, was not
supremely fortunate otherwise.[1] After which, the review at
Magdeburg; and home on the 24th, there to "be busy as a
Turk or as a M. Jordan," — according to what we read long
since.

CHAPTER VII.

WITHDRAWS TO REINSBERG, HOPING A PEACEABLE WINTER.

By this Herstal token, which is now blazing abroad, now
and for a month to come, it can be judged that the young
King of Prussia intends to stand on his own footing, quite
peremptorily if need be ; and will by no means have himself
led about in Imperial harness, as his late Father was. So that
a dull Public (Herrenhausen very specially), and Gazetteer
Owls of Minerva everywhere, may expect events. All the
more indubitably, when that spade-work comes to light in the
Wesel Country. It is privately certain (the Gazetteers not
yet sure about it, till they see the actual spades going), this
new King does fully intend to assert his rights on Berg-Jülich ;
and will appear there with his iron ramrods, the instant old
Kur-Pfalz shall decease, let France and the Kaiser say No to
it or say Yes. There are, in fact, at a fit place, "Büderich
in the neighborhood of Wesel," certain rampart-works, begin-
nings as of an Entrenched Camp, going on ; — "for Review
purposes merely," say the Gazetteers, *in italics.* Here, it
privately is Friedrich's resolution, shall a Prussian Army, of
the due strength (could be well-nigh 100,000 strong if needful), make its appearance, directly on old Kur-Pfalz's decease,
if one live to see such event.[2] France and the Kaiser will
probably take good survey of that Büderich phenomenon
before meddling.

[1] Betrothal was 20th September, 1740; Marriage, 5th January, 1742 (Buchholz, i. 207).
[2] Stenzel, iv. 61.

To do his work like a King, and shun no peril and no toil in the course of what his work may be, is Friedrich's rule and intention.   Nevertheless it is clear he expects to approve himself magnanimous rather in the Peaceable operations than in the Warlike ; and his outlooks are, of all places and pursuits, towards Reinsberg and the Fine Arts, for the time being. His Public activity meanwhile they describe as "prodigious," though the ague still clings to him ; such building, instituting, managing : Opera-House, French Theatre, Palace for his Mother ; — day by day, many things to be recorded by Editor Formey, though the rule about them here is silence except on cause.

No doubt the ague is itself privately a point of moment. Such a vexatious paltry little thing, in this bright whirl of Activities, Public and other, which he continues managing in spite of it; impatient to be rid of it.   But it will not go : there *it* reappears always, punctual to its "fourth day," — like a snarling street-dog, in the high Ball-room and Work-room.   "He is drinking Pyrmont water;" has himself proposed Quinquina, a remedy just come up, but the Doctors shook their heads ; has tried snatches of Reinsberg, too short ; he intends soon to be out there for a right spell of country, there to be "happy," and get quit of his ague.   The ague went, — and by a remedy which surprised the whole world, as will be seen !

Wilhelmina's Return-Visit.

Monday, 17th October, came the Baireuth Visitors ; Wilhelmina all in a flutter, and tremor of joy and sorrow, to see her Brother again, her old kindred and the altered scene of things. Poor Lady, she is perceptibly more tremulous than usual ; and her Narrative, not in dates only, but in more memorable points, dances about at a sad rate ; interior agitations and tremulous shrill feelings shivering her this way and that, and throwing things topsy-turvy in one's recollection.   Like the magnetic needle, shaky but steadfast (*agitée mais constante*). Truer nothing can be, points forever to the Pole ; but also

what obliquities it makes; will shiver aside in mad escapades,
if you hold the paltriest bit of old iron near it, — paltriest
clack of gossip about this loved Brother of mine! Brother,
we will hope, silently continues to be Pole, so that the needle
always comes back again; otherwise all would go to wreck.
Here, in abridged and partly rectified form, are the phenomena
witnessed : —

"We arrived at Berlin the end of October [Monday, 17th, as
above said]. My younger Brothers, followed by the Princes
of the Blood and by all the Court, received us at the bottom
of the stairs. I was led to my apartment, where I found the
Reigning Queen, my Sisters [Ulrique, Amelia], and the Princesses [of the Blood, as above, Schwedt and the rest]. I
learned with much chagrin that the King was ill of tertian
ague [quartan; but that is no matter]. He sent me word that,
being in his fit, he could not see me; but that he depended on
having that pleasure to-morrow. The Queen Mother, to whom
I went without delay, was in a dark condition; rooms all hung
with their lugubrious drapery; everything yet in the depth
of mourning for my Father. What a scene for me! Nature
has her rights; I can say with truth, I have almost never in
my life been so moved as on this occasion." Interview with
Mamma — we can fancy it — "was of the most touching."
Wilhelmina had been absent eight years. She scarcely knows
the young ones again, all so grown; — finds change on change :
and that Time, as he always is, has been busy. That night the
Supper-Party was exclusively a Family one.

Her Brother's welcome to her on the morrow, though ardent
enough, she found deficient in sincerity, deficient in several
points; as indeed a Brother up to the neck in business, and
just come out of an ague-fit, does not appear to the best advantage. Wilhelmina noticed how ill he looked, so lean and
broken-down (*maigre et défait*) within the last two months;
but seems to have taken no account of it farther, in striking
her balances with Friedrich. And indeed in her Narrative of
this Visit, not, we will hope, in the Visit itself, she must have
been in a high state of magnetic deflection, — pretty nearly
her maximum of such, discoverable in those famous *Memoirs*, —

such a tumult is there in her statements, all gone to ground-and-lofty tumbling in this place; so discrepant are the still ascertainable facts from this topsy-turvy picture of them, sketched by her four years hence (in 1744). The truest of magnetic needles; but so sensitive, if you bring foreign iron near it!

Wilhelmina was loaded with honors by an impartial Berlin Public, that is, Court Public; "but, all being in mourning, the Court was not brilliant. The Queen Mother saw little company, and was sunk in sorrow; — had not the least influence in affairs, so jealous was the new King of his Authority, — to the Queen Mother's surprise," says Wilhelmina. For the rest, here is a King "becoming truly unpopular [or, we fancy so, in our deflected state, and judging by the rumor of cliques]; a general discontent reigning in the Country, love of his subjects pretty much gone; people speaking of him in no measured terms [in certain cliques]. Cares nothing about those who helped him as Prince Royal, say some; others complain of his avarice [meaning steady vigilance in outlay] as surpassing the late King's; this one complained of his violences of temper (*emportemens*); that one of his suspicions, of his distrust, his haughtinesses, his dissimulation" (meaning polite impenetrability when he saw good). Several circumstances, known to Wilhelmina's own experience, compel Wilhelmina's assent on those points. "I would have spoken to him about them, if my Brother of Prussia [young August Wilhelm, betrothed the other day] and the Queen Regnant had not dissuaded me. Farther on I will give the explanation of all this," — never did it anywhere. "I beg those who may one day read these *Memoirs*, to suspend their judgment on the character of this great Prince till I have developed it." [1] O my Princess, you are true and bright, but you are shrill; and I admire the effect of atmospheric electricity, not to say, of any neighboring marine-store shop, or miserable bit of broken pan, on one of the finest magnetic needles ever made and set trembling!

Wilhelmina is incapable of deliberate falsehood; and this

[1] Wilhelmina, ii. 326.

her impression or reminiscence, with all its exaggeration, is entitled to be heard in evidence so far. From this, and from other sources, readers will assure themselves that discontents were not wanting; that King Friedrich was not amiable to everybody at this time, — which indeed he never grew to be at any other time. He had to be a King; that was the trade he followed, not the quite different one of being amiable all round. Amiability is good, my Princess; but the question rises, "To whom? — for example, to the young gentleman who shot himself in Löbegun?" There are young gentlemen and old sometimes in considerable quantities, to whom, if you were in your duty, as a King of men (or even as a "King of one man and his affairs," if that is all your kingdom), you should have been hateful instead of amiable! That is a stern truth; too much forgotten by Wilhelmina and others. Again, what a deadening and killing circumstance is it in the career of amiability, that you are bound *not* to be communicative of your inner man, but perpetually and strictly the reverse! It may be doubted if a good King can be amiable; certainly he cannot in any but the noblest ages, and then only to a select few. I should guess Friedrich was at no time fairly loved, not by those nearest to him. He was rapid, decisive; of wiry compact nature; had nothing of his Father's amplitudes, simplicities; nothing to sport with and fondle, far from it. Tremulous sensibilities, ardent affections; these we clearly discover in him, in extraordinary vivacity; but he wears them under his polished panoply, and is outwardly a radiant but metallic object to mankind. Let us carry this along with us in studying him; and thank Wilhelmina for giving us hint of it in her oblique way. — Wilhelmina's love for her Brother rose to quite heroic pitch in coming years, and was at its highest when she died. That continuation of her *Memoirs* in which she is to develop her Brother's character, was never written: it has been sought for in modern times; and a few insignificant pages, with evidence that there is not, and was not, any more, are all that has turned up.[1]

---

[1] Pertz, *Ueber die Denkwürdigkeiten der Markgräfin von Bayreuth* (Paper read in the *Akademie der Wissenschaften*, Berlin, 25th April, 1850).

Incapable of falsity prepense, we say; but the known facts, which stand abundantly on record if you care to search them out, are merely as follows : Friedrich, with such sincerity as there might be, did welcome Wilhelmina on the morrow of her arrival; spoke of Reinsberg, and of air and rest, and how pleasant it would be; rolled off next morning, having at last gathered up his businesses, and got them well in hand, to Reinsberg accordingly; whither Wilhelmina, with the Queen Regnant and others of agreeable quality, followed in two days; intending a long and pleasant spell of country out there. Which hope was tolerably fulfilled, even for Wilhelmina, though there did come unexpected interruptions, not of Friedrich's bringing.

Unexpected News at Reinsberg.

Friedrich's pursuits and intended conquests, for the present, are of peaceable and even gay nature. French Theatre, Italian Opera-House, these are among the immediate outlooks. Voltaire, skilled in French acting, if anybody ever were, is multifariously negotiating for a Company of that kind, — let him be swift, be successful.[1] An Italian Opera there shall be; the House is still to be built : Captain Knobelsdorf, who built Reinsberg, whom we have known, is to do it. Knobelsdorf has gone to Italy on that errand; "went by Dresden, carefully examining the Opera-House there, and all the famed Opera-Houses on his road." Graun, one of the best judges living, is likewise off to Italy, gathering singers. Our Opera too shall be a successful thing, and we hope, a speedy. Such are Friedrich's outlooks at this time.

A miscellaneous pleasant company is here; Truchsess and Bielfeld, home from Hanover, among them; Wilhelmina is here; — Voltaire himself perhaps coming again. Friedrich drinks his Pyrmont waters; works at his public businesses all day, which are now well in hand, and manageable by couriers; at evening he appears in company, and is the astonishment of everybody; brilliant, like a new-risen sun, as if he

---

[1] Letters of Voltaire (*passim,* in these months).

knew of no illness, knew of no business, but lived for amusement only. "He intends Private Theatricals withal, and is
getting ready Voltaire's *Mort de César*." [1] These were pretty
days at Reinsberg. This kind of life lasted seven or eight
weeks, — in spite of interruptions of subterranean volcanic
nature, some of which were surely considerable. Here, in the
very first week, coming almost volcanically, is one, which
indeed is the sum of them all.

Tuesday forenoon, 25th October, 1740, Express arrives at
Reinsberg; direct from Vienna five days ago; finds Friedrich under eclipse, hidden in the interior, laboring under his
ague-fit: question rises, Shall the Express be introduced, or
be held back? The news he brings is huge, unexpected, transcendent, and may agitate the sick King. Six or seven heads
go wagging on this point, — who by accident are namable,
if readers care: "Prince August Wilhelm," lately betrothed;
"Graf Truchsess," home from Hanover; "Colonel Graf von
Finkenstein," old Tutor's Son, a familiar from boyhood upwards; "Baron Pöllnitz" kind of chief Goldstick now, or
Master of the Ceremonies, not too witty, but the cause of wit;
"Jordan, Bielfeld," known to us; and lastly, "Fredersdorf,"
Major-domo and Factotum, who is grown from Valet to be
Purse-Keeper, confidential Manager, and almost friend, — a
notable personage in Friedrich's History. They decide, "Bet-
ter wait!"

They wait accordingly; and then, after about an hour, the
trembling-fit being over, and Fredersdorf having cautiously
preluded a little, and prepared the way, the Despatch is delivered, and the King left with his immense piece of news.
News that his Imperial Majesty Karl VI. died, after short
illness, on Thursday, the 20th last. Kaiser dead: House of
Hapsburg, and its Five Centuries of tough wrestling, and
uneasy Dominancy in this world, ended, gone to the distaff: — the counter-wrestling Ambitions and Cupidities not
dead; and nothing but Pragmatic Sanction left between the
fallen House and them! Friedrich kept silence; showed

[1] Preuss, *Thronbesteigung*, p. 415.

no sign how transfixed he was to hear such tidings; which, he foresaw, would have immeasurable consequences in the world.

One of the first was, that it cured Friedrich of his ague. It braced him (it, and perhaps "a little quinquina which he now insisted on") into such a tensity of spirit as drove out his ague like a mere hiccough; quite gone in the course of next week; and we hear no more of that importunate annoyance. He summoned Secretary Eichel, "Be ready in so many minutes hence;" rose from his bed, dressed himself;[1] — and then, by Eichel's help, sent off expresses for Schwerin his chief General, and Podewils his chief Minister. A resolution, which is rising or has risen in the Royal mind, will be ready for communicating to these Two by the time they arrive, on the second day hence. This done, Friedrich, I believe, joined his company in the evening; and was as light and brilliant as if nothing had happened.

CHAPTER VIII.

THE KAISER'S DEATH.

THE Kaiser's death came upon the Public unexpectedly; though not quite so upon observant persons closer at hand. He was not yet fifty-six out; a firm-built man; had been of sound constitution, of active, not intemperate habits: but in the last six years, there had come such torrents of ill luck rolling down on him, he had suffered immensely, far beyond what the world knew of; and to those near him, and anxious for him, his strength seemed much undermined. Five years ago, in summer 1735, Robinson reported, from a sure hand: "Nothing can equal the Emperor's agitation under these disasters [brought upon him by Fleury and the Spaniards,

[1] Preuss, *Thronbesteigung*, p. 416.

as after-clap to his Polish-Election feat]. His good Empress
is terrified, many times, he will die in the course of the night,
when singly with her he gives a loose to his affliction, confusion and despair." Sea-Powers will not help; Fleury and
mere ruin will engulf! "What augments this agitation is his
distrust in every one of his own Ministers, except perhaps
Bartenstein," [1]—who is not much of a support either, though
a gnarled weighty old stick in his way ("Professor at Strasburg once"): not interesting to us here. The rest his Imperial Majesty considers to be of sublimated blockhead type,
it appears. Prince Eugene had died lately, and with Eugene
all good fortune.

And then, close following, the miseries of that Turk War,
crashing down upon a man! They say, Duke Franz, Maria
Theresa's Husband, nominal Commander in those Campaigns,
with the Seckendorfs and Wallises under him going such a
road, was privately eager to have done with the Business,
on any terms, lest the Kaiser should die first, and leave it
weltering. No wonder the poor Kaiser felt broken, disgusted
with the long Shadow-Hunt of Life; and took to practical
field-sports rather. An Army that cannot fight, War-Generals
good only to be locked in Fortresses, an Exchequer that has
no money; after such wagging of the wigs, and such Privy-
Councilling and such War-Councilling:—let us hunt wild
swine, and not think of it! That, thank Heaven, we still
have; that, and Pragmatic Sanction well engrossed, and
generally sworn to by mankind, after much effort!—

The outer Public of that time, and Voltaire among them
more deliberately afterwards, spoke of "mushrooms," an
"indigestion of mushrooms;" and it is probable there was
something of mushrooms concerned in the event. Another
subsequent Frenchman, still more irreverent, adds to this of
the "excess of mushrooms," that the Kaiser made light of
it. "When the Doctors told him he had few hours to live, he
would not believe it; and bantered his Physicians on the
sad news. 'Look me in the eyes,' said he; 'have I the air

[1] Robinson to Lord Harrington, 5th July, 1735 (in State-Paper Office).

of one dying? When you see my sight growing dim, then
let the sacraments be administered, whether I order or not.'"
Doctors insisting, the Kaiser replied: "'Since you are foolish
fellows, who know neither the cause nor the state of my
disorder, I command that, once I am dead, you open my body,
to know what the matter was; you can then come and let
me know!'"[1]—in which also there is perhaps a glimmering
of distorted truth, though, as Monsieur mistakes even the
day ("18th October," says he, not 20th), one can only accept
it as rumor from the outside.

Here, by an extremely sombre domestic Gentleman of great
punctuality and great dulness, are the authentic particulars,
such as it was good to mention in Vienna circles.[2] An extremely dull Gentleman, but to appearance an authentic; and
so little defective in reverence that he delicately expresses
some astonishment at Death's audacity this year, in killing
so many Crowned Heads. "This year 1740," says he, "though
the weather throughout Europe had been extraordinarily fine,"
or fine for a cold year, "had already witnessed several Deaths
of Sovereigns: Pope Clement XII., Friedrich Wilhelm of
Prussia, the Queen Dowager of Spain [Termagant's old step-
mother, not Termagant's self by a great way]. But that was
not enough: unfathomable Destiny ventured now on Imperial
Heads (*wagte sich auch an Kaiser-kronen*): Karl VI., namely,
and Russia's great Monarchess;"—an audacity to be remarked. Of Russia's great Monarchess (Czarina Anne, with
the big cheek) we will say nothing at present; but of Karl VI.
only,—abridging much, and studying arrangement.

"Thursday, October 13th, returning from Halbthurn, a
Hunting Seat of his," over in Hungary some fifty miles, "to
the Palace Favorita at Vienna, his Imperial Majesty felt
slightly indisposed,"—indigestion of mushrooms or whatever
it was: had begun *at* Halbthurn the night before, we rather
understand, and was the occasion of his leaving. "The Doctors called it cold on the stomach, and thought it of no

---

[1] *Anecdotes Germaniques* (Paris, 1769), p. 692.

[2] (Anonymous) *Des &c. Römischen Kaisers Carl VI. Leben und Thaten*
(Frankfurt und Leipzig, 1741), pp. 220–227.

consequence. In the night of Saturday, it became alarming;"
inflammation, thought the Doctors, inflammation of the liver,
and used their potent appliances, which only made the danger
come and go; "and on the Tuesday, all day, the Doctors did
not doubt his Imperial Majesty was dying. ["Look me in
the eyes; pack of fools; you will have to dissect me, you
will then know:" Any truth in all that? No matter.]

"At noon of that Tuesday he took the Sacrament, the
Pope's Nuncio administering. His Majesty showed uncommonly great composure of soul, and resignation to the Divine
Will;" being indeed "certain," — so he expressed it to "a
principal Official Person sunk in grief" (Bartenstein, shall we
guess?), who stood by him — "certain of his cause," not afraid
in contemplating that dread Judgment now near: "Look at
me! A man that is certain of his cause can enter on such
a Journey with good courage and a composed mind (*mit gutem
und gelassenem Muth*)." To the Doctors, dubitating what the
disease was, he said, "If Gazelli," my late worthy Doctor,
"were still here, you would soon know; but as it is, you will
learn it when you dissect me;" — and once asked to be shown
the Cup where his heart would lie after that operation.

"Sacrament being over," Tuesday afternoon, "he sent for
his Family, to bless them each separately. He had a long
conversation with Grand Duke Franz," titular of Lorraine,
actual of Tuscany, "who had assiduously attended him, and
continued to do so, during the whole illness." The Grand
Duke's Spouse, — Maria Theresa, the noble-hearted and the
overwhelmed; who is now in an interesting state again
withal; a little Kaiserkin (Joseph II.) coming in five months;
first child, a little girl, is now two years old; — "had been
obliged to take to bed three days ago; laid up of grief and
terror (*vor Schmerzen und Schrecken*), ever since Sunday the
16th. Nor would his Imperial Majesty permit her to enter
this death-room, on account of her condition, so important
to the world; but his Majesty, turning towards that side
where her apartment was, raised his right hand, and commanded her Husband, and the Archduchess her younger
Sister, to tell his Theresa, That he blessed her herewith, not-

withstanding her absence." Poor Kaiser, poor Theresa! "Most
distressing of all was the scene with the Kaiserin. The night
before, on getting knowledge of the sad certainty, she had
fainted utterly away (*starke Ohnmacht*), and had to be carried
into the Grand Duchess's [Maria Theresa's] room. Being
summoned now with her Children, for the last blessing, she
cried as in despair, 'Do not leave me, Your Dilection, do not
(*Ach Euer Liebden verlassen mich doch nicht*)!'" Poor good
souls! "Her Imperial Majesty would not quit the room
again, but remained to the last.

"Wednesday, 19th, all day, anxiety, mournful suspense;"
poor weeping Kaiserin and all the world waiting; the Inevitable visibly struggling on. "And in the night of that day
[night of 19th–20th Oct., 1740], between one and two in the
morning, Death snatched away this most invaluable Monarch
(*den preiswürdigsten Monarchen*) in the 56th year of his life;"
and Kaiser Karl VI., and the House of Hapsburg and its Five
tough Centuries of good and evil in this world had ended.
The poor Kaiserin "closed the eyes" that could now no more
behold her; "kissed his hands, and was carried out more dead
than alive." [1]

A good affectionate Kaiserin, I do believe; honorable, truth-
ful, though unwitty of speech, and converted by Grandpapa in
a peculiar manner. For her Kaiser too, after all, I have a
kind of love. Of brilliant articulate intellect there is nothing; nor of inarticulate (as in Friedrich Wilhelm's case) anything considerable: in fact his Shadow-Hunting, and Duelling

---

[1] Anonymous, *ut suprà*, pp. 220–227. — Adelung, *Pragmatische Staatsgeschichte* (Gotha, 1762–1767), ii. 120. *Johann Christoph* Adelung; the same who
did the *Dictionary* and many other deserving Books; here is the precise Title:
"*Pragmatische Staatsgeschichte Europens*," that is, "Documentary History of
Europe, from Kaiser Karl's Death, 1740, till Peace of Paris, 1763." A solid,
laborious and meritorious Work, of its kind; extremely extensive (9 vols. 4to,
some of which are double and even treble), mostly in the undigested, sometimes in the quite uncooked or raw condition; perhaps about a fifth part of it
consists of "Documents" proper, which are skippable. It cannot help being
dull, waste, dreary, but is everywhere intelligible (excellent Indexes too), —
and offers an unhappy reader by far the best resource attainable for survey of
that sad Period.

with the Termagant, seemed the reverse of wise. But there was something of a high proud heart in it, too, if we examine; and even the Pragmatic Sanction, though in practice not worth one regiment of iron ramrods, indicates a profoundly fixed determination, partly of loyal nature, such as the gods more or less reward. "He had been a great builder," say the Histories; "was a great musician, fit to lead orchestras, and had composed an Opera," — poor Kaiser. There came out large traits of him, in Maria Theresa again, under an improved form, which were much admired by the world. He looks, in his Portraits, intensely serious; a handsome man, stoically grave; much the gentleman, much the Kaiser or Supreme Gentleman. As, in life and fact, he was; "something solemn in him, even when he laughs," the people used to say. A man honestly doing his very best with his poor Kaisership, and dying of chagrin by it. "On opening the body, the liver-region proved to be entirely deranged; in the place where the gall-bladder should have been, a stone of the size of a pigeon's egg was found grown into the liver, and no gall-bladder now there."

That same morning, with earliest daylight, "Thursday, 20th, six A.M.," Maria Theresa is proclaimed by her Heralds over Vienna: "According to Pragmatic Sanction, Inheritress of all the," &c. &c.; — Sovereign Archduchess of Austria, Queen of Hungary and Bohemia, for chief items. "At seven her Majesty took the Oath from the Generals and Presidents of Tribunals, — said, through her tears, 'All was to stand on the old footing, each in his post,'" — and the other needful words. Couriers shoot forth towards all Countries; — one express courier to Regensburg, and the enchanted Wiggeries there, to say That a new Kaiser will be needed; *Reichs*-Vicar or Vicars (Kur-Sachsen and whoever more, for they are sometimes disagreed about it) will have to administer in the interim.

A second courier we saw arrive at Reinsberg; he likewise may be important. The Bavarian Minister, Karl Albert Kur-Baiern's man, shot off his express, like the others; answer is; by

return of courier, or even earlier (for a messenger was already
on the road), Make protest! "We Kur-Baiern solemnly protest against Pragmatic Sanction, and the assumption of such
Titles by the Daughter of the late Kaiser. King of Bohemia,
and in good part even of Austria, it is not you, Madam, but
of right *we ;* as, by Heaven's help, it is our fixed resolution to
make good!" Protest was presented, accordingly, with all
the solemnities, without loss of a moment. To which Bartenstein and the Authorities answered "Pooh-pooh," as if it were
nothing. It is the first ripple of an immeasurable tide or
deluge in that kind, threatening to submerge the new Majesty
of Hungary; — as had been foreseen at Reinsberg; though
Bartenstein and the Authorities made light of it, answering
"Pooh-pooh," or almost "Ha-ha," for the present.

Her Hungarian Majesty's chief Generals, Seckendorf, Wallis,
Neipperg, sit in their respective prison-wards at this time (from
which she soon liberates them): Kur-Baiern has lodged protest; at Reinsberg there will be an important resolution ready:
— and in the Austrian Treasury (which employs 40,000 persons, big and little) there is of cash or available resource,
100,000 florins, that is to say, £10,000 net.[1] And unless Pragmatic sheepskin hold tighter than some persons expect, the
affairs of Austria and of this young Archduchess are in a
threatening way.

His Britannic Majesty was on the road home, about Hel-
voetsluys or on the sea for Harwich, that night the Kaiser
died; of whose illness he had heard nothing. At London, ten
days after, the sudden news struck dismally upon his Majesty
and the Political Circles there: "No help, then, from that
quarter, in our Spanish War; perhaps far other than help!"
— Nay, certain Gazetteers were afraid the grand new Anti-
Spanish Expedition itself, which was now, at the long last,
after such confusions and delays, lying ready, in great strength,
Naval and Military, would be countermanded, — on Pragmatic-
Sanction considerations, and the crisis probably imminent.[2]

[1] Mailath, *Geschichte des Oestreichischen Kaiserstaats* (Hamburg, 1850), v. 8.
[2] London Newspapers (31st Oct.–6th Nov., 1740).

But it was not countermanded; it sailed all the same, "November 6th" (seventh day after the bad news); and made towards — Shall we tell the reader, what is Officially a dead secret, though by this time well guessed at by the Public, English and also Spanish? — towards Carthagena, to reinforce fiery Vernon, in the tropical latitudes; and overset Spanish America, beginning with that important Town!

Commodore Anson, he also, after long fatal delays, is off, several weeks ago;[1] round Cape Horn; hoping (or perhaps already not hoping) to co-operate from the Other Ocean, and be simultaneous with Vernon, — on these loose principles of keeping time! Commodore Anson does, in effect, make a Voyage which is beautiful, and to mankind memorable; but as to keeping tryst with Vernon, the very gods could not do it on those terms!

CHAPTER IX.

RESOLUTION FORMED AT REINSBERG IN CONSEQUENCE.

Thursday, 27th October, two days after the Expresses went for them, Schwerin and Podewils punctually arrived at Reinsberg. They were carried into the interior privacies, "to long conferences with his Majesty that day, and for the next four days; Majesty and they even dining privately together;" grave business of state, none guesses how grave, evidently going on. The resolution Friedrich laid before them, fruit of these two days since the news from Vienna, was probably the most important ever formed in Prussia, or in Europe during that Century: Resolution to make good our Rights on Silesia, by this great opportunity, the best that will ever offer. Resolution which had sprung, I find, and got to sudden fixity in the head of the young King himself; and which met with little save opposition from all the other sons of Adam, at the first blush and for long afterwards. And, indeed, the making

[1] 29th (18th) September, 1740.

of it good (of it, and of the immense results that hung by it) was the main business of this young King's Life henceforth; and cost him Labors like those of Hercules, and was in the highest degree momentous to existing and not yet existing millions of mankind, — to the readers of this History especially.

It is almost touching to reflect how unexpectedly, like a bolt out of the blue, all this had come upon Friedrich; and how it overset his fine program for the winter at Reinsberg, and for his Life generally. Not the Peaceable magnanimities, but the Warlike, are the thing appointed Friedrich this winter, and mainly henceforth. Those "*golden* or soft radiances" which we saw in him, admirable to Voltaire and to Friedrich, and to an esurient philanthropic world, — it is not those, it is "the *steel-bright* or stellar kind," that are to become predominant in Friedrich's existence: grim hail-storms, thunders and tornado for an existence to him, instead of the opulent genialities and halcyon weather, anticipated by himself and others! Indisputably enough to us, if not yet to Friedrich, "Reinsberg and Life to the Muses" are done. On a sudden, from the opposite side of the horizon, see, miraculous Opportunity, rushing hitherward, — swift, terrible, clothed with lightning like a courser of the gods: dare you clutch *him* by the thunder-mane, and fling yourself upon him, and make for the Empyrean by that course rather? Be immediate about it, then; the time is now, or else never! — No fair judge can blame the young man that he laid hold of the flaming Opportunity in this manner, and obeyed the new omen. To seize such an opportunity, and perilously mount upon it, was the part of a young magnanimous King, less sensible to the perils, and more to the other considerations, than one older would have been.

Schwerin and Podewils were, no doubt, astonished to learn what the Royal purpose was; and could not want for commonplace objections many and strong, had this been the scene for dwelling on them, or dressing them out at eloquent length. But they knew well this was not the scene for doing more than, with eloquent modesty, hint them; that the Resolution, being already taken, would not alter for commonplace; and

that the question now lying for honorable members was, How
to execute it? It is on this, as I collect, that Schwerin and
Podewils in the King's company did, with extreme intensity,
consult during those four days; and were, most probably, of
considerable use to the King, though some of their modifica-
tions adopted by him turned out, not as they had predicted,
but as he. On all the Military details and outlines, and on
all the Diplomacies of this business, here are two Oracles
extremely worth consulting by the young King.

To seize Silesia is easy: a Country open on all but the south
side; open especially on our side, where a battalion of foot
might force it; the three or four fortresses, of which only
two, Glogau and Neisse, can be reckoned strong, are provided
with nothing as they ought to be; not above 3,000 fighting
men in the whole Province, and these little expecting fight.
Silesia can be seized: but the maintaining of it? — We must
try to maintain it, thinks Friedrich.

At Reinsberg it is not yet known that Kur-Baiern has protested; but it is well guessed he means to do so, and that
France is at his back in some sort. Kur-Baiern, probably
Kur-Sachsen, and plenty more, France being secretly at their
back. What low condition Austria stands in, all its ready
resources run to the lees, is known; and that France, getting
lively at present with its Belleisles and adventurous spirits
not restrainable by Fleury, is always on the watch to bring
Austria lower; capable, in spite of Pragmatic Sanction, to
snatch the golden moment, and spring hunter-like on a moribund Austria, were the hunting-dogs once out and in cry. To
Friedrich it seems unlikely the Pragmatic Sanction will be
a Law of Nature to mankind, in these circumstances. His
opinion is, "the old political system has expired with the
Kaiser." Here is Europe, burning in one corner of it by
Jenkins's Ear, and such a smoulder of combustible material
awakening nearer hand: will not Europe, probably, blaze
into general War; Pragmatic Sanction going to waste sheepskin, and universal scramble ensuing? In which he who
has 100,000 good soldiers, and can handle them, may be an

important figure in urging claims, and keeping what he has got hold of! —

Friedrich's mind, as to the fact, is fixed: seize Silesia we will: but as to the manner of doing it, Schwerin and Podewils modify him. Their counsel is: "Do not step out in hostile attitude at the very first, saying, 'These Duchies, Liegnitz, Brieg, Wohlau, Jägerndorf, are mine, and I will fight for them;' say only, 'Having, as is well known, interests of various kinds in this Silesia, I venture to take charge of it in the perilous times now come, and will keep it safe for the real owner.' Silesia seized in this fashion," continue they, "nego-tiate with the Queen of Hungary; offer her help, large help in men and money, against her other enemies; perhaps she will consent to do us right?" — "She never will consent," is Friedrich's opinion. "But it is worth trying?" urge the Ministers. — "Well," answers Friedrich, "be it in that form; that is the soft-spoken cautious form: any form will do, if the fact be there." That is understood to have been the figure of the deliberation in this conclave at Reinsberg, during the four days.[1] And now it remains only to fix the Military details, to be ready in a minimum of time; and to keep our prepara-tions and intentions in impenetrable darkness from all men, in the interim. Adieu, Messieurs.

And so, on the 1st of November, fifth morning since they came, Schwerin and Podewils, a world of new business silently ahead of them, return to Berlin, intent to begin the same. All the Kings will have to take their resolution on this matter; wisely, or else unwisely. King Friedrich's, let it prove the wisest or not, is notably the rapidest, — complete, and fairly entering upon action, on November 1st. At London the news of the Kaiser's death had arrived the day before; Britannic Majesty and Ministry, thrown much into the dumps by it, much into the vague, are nothing like so prompt with their resolution on it. Somewhat sorrowfully in the vague. In fact, they will go jumbling hither and thither for about three years to come, before making up their minds to a resolution:

[1] Stenzel (from what sources he does not clearly say, no doubt from sources of some authenticity) gives this as summary of it, iv. 61–65.

so intricate is the affair to the English Nation and them!
Intricate indeed; and even imaginary, — definable mainly as
a bottomless abyss of nightmare dreams to the English Nation and them! Productive of strong somnambulisms, as my
friend has it! —

*Mystery in Berlin, for Seven Weeks, while the Prepara-
tions go on; Voltaire visits Friedrich to decipher it, but
cannot.*

Podewils and Schwerin gone, King Friedrich, though still
very busy in working-hours, returns to his society and its
gayeties and brilliancies; apparently with increased appetite
after these four days of abstinence. Still busy in his working-
hours, as a King must be; couriers coming and going, hundreds of businesses despatched each day; and in the evening
what a relish for society, — Prætorius is quite astonished at
it. Music, dancing, play-acting, suppers of the gods, "not
done till four in the morning sometimes," these are the accounts Prætorius hears at Berlin. "From all persons who
return from Reinsberg," writes he, "the unanimous report is,
That the King works, the whole day through, with an assiduity
that is unique; and then, in the evening, gives himself to the
pleasures of society, with a vivacity of mirth and sprightly
humor which makes those Evening-Parties charming."[1] So it
had to last, with frequent short journeys on Friedrich's part,
and at last with change to Berlin as head-quarters, for about
seven weeks to come, — till the beginning of December, and
the day of action, namely. A notable little Interim in Friedrich's History and that of Europe.

Friedrich's secret, till almost the very end, remained impenetrable; though, by degrees, his movements excited much
guessing in the Gazetteer and Diplomatic world everywhere.
Military matters do seem to be getting brisk in Prussia; arse-
nals much astir; troops are seen mustering, marching, plainly
to a singular degree. Marching towards the Austrian side,
towards Silesia, some note. Yes; but also towards Cleve,

[1] Excerpt, in Preuss, *Thronbesteigung*, p. 418.

certain detachments of troops are marching, — do not men
see? And the Intrenchment at Büderich in those parts, that
is getting forward withal, — though privately there is not the
least prospect of using it, in these altered circumstances.
Friedrich already guesses that if he could get Silesia, so invaluable on the one skirt of him, he will probably have to give
up his Berg-Jülich claims on the other; I fancy he is getting
ready to do so, should the time come for such alternative. But
he labors at Büderich, all the same, and "improves the roads
in that quarter," — which at least may help to keep an inquisitive public at bay. These are seven busy weeks on Friedrich's
part, and on the world's : constant realities of preparation, on
the one part, industriously veiled; on the other part, such
shadows, guessings, spyings, spectral movements above ground
and below; Diplomatic shadows fencing, Gazetteer shadows
rumoring ; — dreams of a world as if near awakening to something great ! "All Officers on furlough have been ordered to
their posts," writes Bielfeld, on those vague terms of his : "On
arriving at Berlin, you notice a great agitation in all departments of the State. The regiments are ordered to prepare their
equipages, and to hold themselves in readiness for marching.
There are magazines being formed at Frankfurt-on-Oder and at
Crossen," — handy for Silesia, you would say ? "There are considerable trains of Artillery getting ready, and the King has
frequent conferences with his Generals." [1] The authentic fact
is : "By the middle of November, Troops, to the extent of
30,000 and more, had got orders to be ready for marching in
three weeks hence ; their public motions very visible ever since,
their actual purpose a mystery to all mortals except three.

Towards the end of November, it becomes the prevailing
guess that the business is immediate, not prospective ; that
Silesia may be in the wind, not Jülich and Berg. Which infinitely quickens the shadowy rumorings and Diplomatic fenc-
ings of mankind. The French have their special Ambassador
here ; a Marquis de Beauvau, observant military gentleman,
who came with the Accession Compliment some time ago, and

---

[1] Bielfeld, i. 165 (Berlin, 30th November, is the date he puts to it).

keeps his eyes well open, but cannot see through mill-stones. Fleury is intensely desirous to know Friedrich's secret; but would fain keep his own (if he yet have one), and is himself quite tacit and reserved. To Fleury's Marquis de Beauvau Friedrich is very gracious; but in regard to secrets, is for a reciprocal procedure. Could not Voltaire go and try? It is thought Fleury had let fall some hint to that effect, carried by a bird of the air. Sure enough Voltaire does go; is actually on visit to his royal Friend; "six days with him at Reinsberg;" perhaps near a fortnight in all (20 November–2 December or so), hanging about those Berlin regions, on the survey. Here is an unexpected pleasure to the parties; — but in regard to penetrating of secrets, an unproductive one!

Voltaire's ostensible errand was, To report progress about the *Anti-Machiavel*, the Van Duren nonsense; and, at any rate, to settle the Money-accounts on these and other scores; and to discourse Philosophies, for a day or two, with the First of Men. The real errand, it is pretty clear, was as above. Voltaire has always a wistful eye towards political employment, and would fain make himself useful in high quarters. Fleury and he have their touches of direct Correspondence now and then; and obliquely there are always intermediates and channels. Small hint, the slightest twinkle of Fleury's eyelashes, would be duly speeded to Voltaire, and set him going. We shall see him expressly missioned hither, on similar errand, by and by; though with as bad success as at present.

Of this his First Visit to Berlin, his Second to Friedrich, Voltaire in the *Vie Privée* says nothing. But in his *Siècle de Louis XV.* he drops, with proud modesty, a little foot-note upon it: "The Author was with the King of Prussia at that time; and can affirm that Cardinal de Fleury was totally astray in regard to the Prince he had now to do with." To which a *date* slightly wrong is added; the rest being perfectly correct.[1] No other details are to be got anywhere, if they were of importance; the very dates of it in the best Prussian Books are all slightly awry. Here, by accident, are two poor flint-sparks caught from the dust whirlwind, which yield a certain sufficing

[1] *Œuvres* (Siècle de Louis XV., c. 6), xxviii. 74.

twilight, when put in their place; and show us both sides of the matter, the smooth side and the seamy : —

1. *Friedrich to Algarotti, at Berlin.*   From " Reinsberg, 21st Nov.," showing the smooth side.

" MY DEAR SWAN OF PADUA, — Voltaire has arrived; all sparkling with new beauties, and far more sociable than at Cleve. He is in very good humor; and makes less complaining about his ailments than usual. Nothing can be more frivolous than our occupations here : " mere verse-making, dancing, philosophizing, then card-playing, dining, flirting; merry as birds on the bough (and Silesia *in*visible, except to oneself and two others).[1]

2. *Friedrich to Jordan, at Berlin.*

" RUPPIN, 28th November.

" . . . Thy Miser [Voltaire, now gone to Berlin, of whom Jordan is to send news, as of all things else], thy Miser shall drink to the lees of his insatiable desire (*sic*) to enrich himself: he shall have the 3,000 thalers (£450). He was with me six days : that will be at the rate of 500 thalers (£75) a day. That is paying dear for one's merry-andrew (*c'est bien payer un fou*) ; never had court-fool such wages before." [2]

Which latter, also at first hand, shows us the seamy side. And here, finally, with date happily appended, is a poetic snatch, in Voltaire's exquisite style, which with the response gives us the medium view : —

VOLTAIRE'S ADIEU (" *Billet de Congé*, 2 December, 1740 ").

" Non, malgré vos vertus, non, malgré vos appas,
    Mon âme n'est point satisfaite ;
    Non, vous n'êtes qu'une coquette,
    Qui subjuguez les cœurs, et ne vous donnez pas."

[1] *Œuvres de Frédéric*, xviii. 25.
[2] Ib. xvii. 72.   Particulars of the money-payment (travelling expenses chiefly, rather exorbitant, and *this* journey added to the list ; and no whisper of the considerable Van-Duren moneys, and copyright of *Anti-Machiavel*, in abatement) are in Rödenbeck, i. 27.   Exact sum paid is 3,300 thalers ; 2,000 a good while ago, 1,300 at this time, which settles the greedy bill.

FRIEDRICH'S RESPONSE.

" Mon âme sent le prix de vos divins appas ;
Mais ne présumez point qu'elle soit satisfaite.
Traître, vous me quittez pour suivre une coquette ;
Moi je ne vous quitterais pas." [1]

— Meaning, perhaps, in brief English : *V.* "Ah, you are but
a beautiful coquette ; you charm away our hearts, and do
not give your own [won't tell me your secret at all] ! " *F.*
"Treacherous Lothario, it is you that quit me for a coquette
[your divine Emilie ; and won't stay here, and be of my Acad-
emy] ; but however — ! " Friedrich looked hopingly on the
French, but could not give his secret except by degrees and
with reciprocity. Some days hence he said to Marquis de
Beauvau, in the Audience of leave, a word which was remembered.

View of Friedrich behind the Veil.

As to Friedrich himself, since about the middle of November his plans seem to have been definitely shaped out
in all points ; Troops so many, when to be on march, and
how ; no important detail uncertain since then. November 17th, he jots down a little Note, which is to go to Vienna,
were the due hour come, by a special Ambassador, one Count
Gotter, acquainted with the ground there ; and explain to her
Hungarian Majesty, what his exact demands are, and what
the exact services he will render. Of which important little
Paper readers shall hear again. Gotter's demands are at first
to be high : Our Four Duchies, due by law so long ; these and
even more, considering the important services we propose ;
this is to be his first word ; — but, it appears, he is privately
prepared to put up with Two Duchies, if he can have them
peaceably : Duchies of Sagan and Glogau, which are not of
the Four at all, but which lie nearest us, and are far below the
value of the Four, to Austria especially. This intricate point
Friedrich has already settled in his mind. And indeed it is
notably the habit of this young King to settle matters with
himself in good time : and in regard to all manner of points,

---

[1] *Œuvres de Frédéric* (**xiv.** 167) ; *Œuvres de Voltaire ;* &c. &c.

he will be found, on the day of bargaining about them, to have
his own resolution formed and definitely fixed; — much to his
advantage over conflicting parties, who have theirs still flying
loose.

Another thing of much concernment is, To secure himself
from danger of Russian interference. To this end he despatches Major Winterfeld to Russia, a man well known to
him; — day of Winterfeld's departure is not given; day of
his arrival in Petersburg is "19th December" just coming.
Russia, at present, is rather in a staggering condition; hopeful for Winterfeld's object. On the 28th of October last,
only eight days after the Kaiser, Czarina Anne of Russia,
she with the big cheek, once of Courland, had died; "audacious Death," as our poor friend had it, "venturing upon
another Crowned Head" there. Bieren her dear Courlander,
once little better than a Horse-groom, now Duke of Courland,
Quasi-Husband to the late Big Cheek, and thereby sovereign
of Russia, this long while past, is left Official Head in Russia. Poor little Anton Ulrich and his august Spouse, well
enough known to us, have indeed produced a Czar Iwan, some
months ago, to the joy of mankind: but Czar Iwan is in his
cradle: Father and Mother's function is little other than to
rock the cradle of Iwan; Bieren to be Regent and Autocrat
over him and them in the interim. To their chagrin, to that
of Feldmarschall Münnich and many others: the upshot of
which will be visible before long. Czarina Anne's death had
seemed to Friedrich the opportune removal of a dangerous
neighbor, known to be in the pay of Austria: here now are
new mutually hostile parties springing up; chance, surely, of
a bargain with some of them? He despatches Winterfeld
on this errand; — probably the fittest man in Prussia for it.
How soon and perfectly Winterfeld succeeded, and what Winterfeld was, and something of what a Russia he found it, we
propose to mention by and by.

These, and all points of importance, Friedrich has settled
with himself some time ago. What his own private thoughts
on the Silesian Adventure are, readers will wish to know,
since they can at first hand. Hear Friedrich himself, whose

veracity is unquestionable to such as know anything of him . —

"This Silesian Project fulfilled all his (the King's) political views," — summed them all well up into one head. "It was a means of acquiring reputation; of increasing the power of the State; and of terminating what concerned that long-litigated question of the Berg-Jülich Succession;" — can be sure of getting that, at lowest; intends to give that up, if necessary.

"Meanwhile, before entirely determining, the King weighed the risks there were in undertaking such a War, and the advantages that were to be hoped from it. On one side, presented itself the potent House of Austria, not likely to want resources with so many vast Provinces under it; an Emperor's Daughter attacked, who would naturally find allies in the King of England, in the Dutch Republic, and so many Princes of the Empire who had signed the Pragmatic Sanction." Russia was — or had been, and might again be — in the pay of Vienna. Saxony might have some clippings from Bohemia thrown to it, and so be gained over. Scanty Harvest, 1740, threatened difficulties as to provisioning of troops. "The risks were great. One had to apprehend the vicissitudes of war. A single battle lost might be decisive. The King had no allies; and his troops, hitherto without experience, would have to front old Austrian soldiers, grown gray in harness, and trained to war by so many campaigns.

"On the other side were hopeful considerations," — four in number: *First*, Weak condition of the Austrian Court, Treasury empty, War-Apparatus broken in pieces; inexperienced young Princess to defend a disputed succession, on those terms. *Second*, There *will* be allies; France and England always in rivalry, both meddling in these matters, King is sure to get either the one or the other. *Third*, Silesian War lies handy to us, and is the only kind of Offensive War that does; Country bordering on our frontier, and with the Oder running through it as a sure high-road for everything. *Fourth*, "What suddenly turned the balance," or at least what kept it steady in that posture, — "news of the Czarina's death arrives:"

Russia has ceased to count against us; and become a manageable quantity.   On, therefore!—

"Add to these reasons," says the King, with a candor which
has not been well treated in the History Books, "Add to these
reasons, an Army ready for acting; Funds, Supplies all found
[lying barrelled in the Schloss at Berlin];—and perhaps the
desire of making oneself a name," from which few of mortals able to achieve it are exempt in their young time:
"all this was cause of the War which the King now entered
upon." [1]

"Desire to make himself a name; how shocking!" exclaim
several Historians.   "Candor of confession that he may have
had some such desire; how honest!" is what they do not exclaim.   As to the justice of his Silesian Claims, or even to his
own belief about their justice, Friedrich affords not the least
light which can be new to readers here.   He speaks, when
business requires it, of "those known rights" of his, and with
the air of a man who expects to be believed on his word; but
it is cursorily, and in the business way only; and there is not
here or elsewhere the least pleading:—a man, you would say,
considerably indifferent to our belief on that head; his eyes
set on the practical merely.   "Just Rights?   What are rights,
never so just, which you cannot make valid?   The world is
full of such.   If you have rights and can assert them into
facts, do it; that is worth doing!"—

We must add two Notes, two small absinthine drops, bitter
but wholesome, administered by him to the Old Dessauer,
whose gloomy wonder over all this military whirl of Prussian
things, and discontent that he, lately the head authority, has
never once been spoken to on it, have been great.   Guessing,
at last, that it was meant for Austria, a Power rather dear to
Leopold, he can suppress himself no longer; but breaks out
into Cassandra prophesyings, which have piqued the young
King, and provoke this return:—

1.   "*Reinsberg, 24th November,* 1740.—I have received your
Letter, and seen with what inquietude you view the approach-

[1] *Œuvres de Frédéric* (Histoire de mon Temps), i. 128.

ing march of my Troops. I hope you will set your mind at
ease on that score; and wait with patience what I intend with
them and you. I have made all my dispositions; and Your
Serenity will learn, time enough, what my orders are, without
disquieting yourself about them, as nothing has been forgotten
or delayed." — FRIEDRICH.

Old Dessauer, cut to the bone, perceives he will have to quit
that method and never resume it; writes next how painful it
is to an old General to see himself neglected, as if good for
nothing, while his scholars are allowed to gather laurels.
Friedrich's answer is of soothing character : —

2. " *Berlin, 2d December*, 1740. — You may be assured I
honor your merits and capacity as a young Officer ought to
honor an old one, who has given the world so many proofs of
his talent (*Dexterität*) ; nor will I neglect Your Serenity on
any occasion when you can help me by your good counsel and
co-operation." But it is a mere " bagatelle " this that I am
now upon; though, next year, it may become serious.
For the rest, Saxony being a neighbor whose intentions one
does not know, I have privately purposed Your Serenity should
keep an outlook that way, in my absence. Plenty of employment coming for Your Serenity. "But as to this present Expedition, I reserve it for myself alone; that the world may
not think the King of Prussia marches with a Tutor to the
Field." — FRIEDRICH.[1]

And therewith Leopold, eagerly complying, has to rest satisfied; and beware of too much freedom with this young King
again.
" Berlin, December 2d," is the date of that last Note to the
Dessauer ; date also of Voltaire's *Adieu* with the *Response* ; —
on which same day, " Friday, December 2d," as I find from the
Old Books, his Majesty, quitting the Reinsberg sojourn, " had
arrived in Berlin about 2 P.M. ; accompanied by Prince August
Wilhelm [betrothed at Brunswick lately]; such a crowd on

[1] Orlich, *Geschichte der Schlesischen Kriege* (Berlin, 1841), i. 38, 39.

the streets as if they had never seen him before." He continued at Berlin or in the neighborhood thenceforth. Busy
days these; and Berlin a much whispering City, as Regiment
after Regiment marches away. King soon to follow, as is
thought, — "who himself sometimes deigns to take the Regiments into highest own eyeshine, *höchst-eigenen Augenschein*"
(that is, to review them), say the reverential Editors. December 6th — But let us follow the strict sequence of Phenomena
at Berlin.

Excellency Botta has Audience; then Excellency Dickens, and others: December 6th, the Mystery is out.

Of course her Hungarian Majesty, and her Bartensteins and
Ministries, heard enough of those Prussian rumors, interior
Military activities, and enigmatic movements; but they seem
strangely supine on the matter; indeed, they seem strangely
supine on such matters; and lean at ease upon the Sea-Powers,
upon Pragmatic Sanction and other Laws of Nature. But at
length even they become painfully interested as to Friedrich's
intentions; and despatch an Envoy to sift him a little: an expert Marchese di Botta, Genoese by birth, skilful in the Russian and other intricacies; who was here at Berlin lately, doing
the Accession Compliment (rather ill received at that time),
and is fit for the job. Perhaps Botta will penetrate him?
That is becoming desirable, in spite of the gay Private Theatricals at Reinsberg, and the Berlin Carnival Balls he is so
occupied with.

England is not less interested, and the diligent Sir Guy is
doing his best; but can make out nothing satisfactory; — much
the reverse indeed; and falls into angry black anticipations.
"Nobody here, great or small," says his Excellency, "dares
make any representation to this young Prince against the
measures he is pursuing; though all are sensible of the confusion which must follow. A Prince who had the least regard
to honor, truth and justice, could not act the part he is going
to do." Alas, no, Excellency Dickens! "But it is plain his
only view was, to deceive us all, and conceal for a while his

ambitious and mischievous designs." [1] "Never was such dissimulation!" exclaims the Diplomatic world everywhere, being angered at it, as if it were a vice on the part of a King
about to invade Silesia. Dissimulation, if that mean mendacity, is not the name of the thing; it is the art of wearing a polite cloak of darkness, and the King is little disturbed
what name they call it.

Botta did not get to Berlin till December 1st, had no Audience till the 5th; — by which time it is becoming evident to
Excellency Dickens, and to everybody, that Silesia is the
thing meant. Botta hints as much in that first Audience,
December 5th : "Terrible roads, those Silesian ones, your Majesty !" says Botta, as if historically merely, but with a glance
of the eye. "Hm," answers his Majesty in the same tone,
"the worst that comes of them is a little mud !" — Next day,
Dickens had express Audience, "Berlin, Tuesday 6th :" a
smartish, somewhat flurried Colloquy with the King; which,
well abridged, may stand as follows : —

Dickens. . . . "Indivisibility of the Austrian Monarchy,
Sire !" — *King.* "Indivisibility? What do you mean?" —
Dickens. "The maintenance of the Pragmatic Sanction." —
King. "Do you intend to support it? I hope not; for such
is not my intention." (There is for you!) . . .

Dickens. "England and Holland will much wonder at the
measures your Majesty was taking, at the moment when your
Majesty proposed to join with them, and were making friendly
proposals !" (Has been a deceitful man, Sir Guy, at least an
impenetrable; — but this latter is rather strong on your part !)
"What shall I write to England?" ("When I mentioned
this," says Dickens, "the King grew red in the face," eyes
considerably flashing, I should think.)

King. "You can have no instructions to ask that question!
And if you had, I have an answer ready for you. England
has no right to inquire into my designs. Your great Sea-
Armaments, did I ask you any questions about them? No;
I was and am silent on that head; only wishing you good luck,

[1] Despatch, 29th November–3d December, 1740: Raumer, p. 58.

and that you may not get beaten by the Spaniards." (Dickens
hastily draws in his rash horns again ; after a pass or two,
King's natural color returns.) . . .

King. " Austria as a Power is necessary against the Turks.
But in Germany, what need of Austria being so superlative ?
Why should not, say, Three Electors united be able to oppose
her ? . . . Monsieur, I find it is your notion in England, as
well as theirs in France, to bring other Sovereigns under your
tutorage, and lead them about. Understand that I will not
be led by either. . . . Tush, *you* are like the Athenians, who,
when Philip of Macedon was ready to invade them, spent their
time in haranguing ! "

Dickens. . . . " Berg and Jülich, if we were to guarantee
them ? " — *King.* " Hm. Don't so much mind that Rhine
Country : difficulties there, — Dutch always jealous of one.
But, on the other Frontier, neither England nor Holland could
take umbrage," — points clearly to Silesia, then, your Excellency Dickens ? [1]

Alas, yes ! Troops and military equipments are, for days
past, evidently wending towards Frankfurt, towards Crossen,
and even the Newspapers now hint that something is on hand
in that quarter. Nay, this same day, *Tuesday, 6th December,*
there has come out brief Official Announcement, to all the
Foreign Ministers at Berlin, Excellency Dickens among them,
" That his Royal Majesty, our most all-gracious Herr, has
taken the resolution to advance a Body of Troops into Schlesien," — rather out of friendly views towards Austria (much
business lying between us about Schlesien), not out of hostile
views by any means, as all Excellencies shall assure their
respective Courts.[2] Announcement which had thrown the
Excellency Dickens into such a frame of mind, before he got
his Audience to-day ! —

Saturday following, which was December 10th, Marquis
de Beauvau had his Audience of leave ; intending for Paris
shortly : Audience very gracious ; covertly hinting, on both

[1] Raumer, (from State-Paper Office), pp. 63, 64.
[2] Copy of the Paper in *Helden-Geschichte,* i. 447.

sides, more than it said; ending in these words, on the King's
side, which have become famous: "Adieu, then, M. le Marquis. I believe I am going to play your game; if the aces
fall to me, we will share (*Je vais, je crois, jouer votre jeu: si
les as me viennent, nous partagerons*)!" [1]

To. Botta, all this while, Friedrich strove to be specially
civil; took him out to Charlottenburg, that same Saturday,
with the Queen and other guests; but Botta, and all the
world, being now certain about Silesia, and that no amount of
mud, or other terror on the roads, would be regarded, Botta's
thoughts in this evening party are not of cheerful nature.
Next day, Sunday, December 11th, he too gets his Audience of
leave; and cannot help bursting out, when the King plainly
tells him what is now afoot, and that the Prussian Ambassador has got instructions what to offer upon it at Vienna.
"Sire, you are going to ruin the House of Austria," cried
Botta, "and to plunge yourself into destruction (*vous abîmer*)
at the same time!" — "Depends on the Queen," said Friedrich, "to accept the Offers I have made her." Botta sank
silent, seemed to reflect, but gathering himself again, added
with an ironical air and tone of voice, "They are fine Troops,
those of yours, Sire. Ours have not the same splendor of appearance; but they have looked the wolf in the face. Think,
I conjure you, what you are getting into!" Friedrich answered with vivacity, a little nettled at the ironical tone of
Botta, and his mixed sympathy and menace: "You find my
troops are beautiful; perhaps I shall convince you they are
good too." Yes, Excellency Botta, goodish troops; and very
capable "to look the wolf in the face," — or perhaps in the
tail too, before all end! "Botta urged and entreated that at
least there should be some delay in executing this project.
But the King gave him to understand that it was now too
late, and that the Rubicon was passed." [2]

The secret is now out, therefore; Invasion of Silesia certain and close at hand. "A day or two before marching,"
may have been this very day when Botta got his audience, the

[1] Voltaire, *Œuvres* (Siècle de Louis XV., c. 6), xxviii. 74.
[2] Friedrich's own Account (*Œuvres*, ii. 57).

King assembled his Chief Generals, all things ready out in the Frankfurt-Crossen region yonder; and spoke to them as follows; briefly and to the point : —

"Gentlemen, I am undertaking a War, in which I have no allies but your valor and your good-will. My cause is just; my resources are what we ourselves can do; and the issue lies in Fortune. Remember continually the glory which your Ancestors acquired in the plains of Warsaw, at Fehrbellin, and in the Expedition to Preussen [across the Frische Haf on ice, that time]. Your lot is in your own hands : distinctions and rewards wait upon your fine actions which shall merit them.

"But what need have I to excite you to glory ? It is the one thing you keep before your eyes; the sole object worthy of your labors. We are going to front troops who, under Prince Eugene, had the highest reputation. Though Prince Eugene is gone, we shall have to measure our strength against brave soldiers : the greater will be the honor if we can conquer. Adieu, go forth. I will follow you straightway, to the rendez-vous of glory which awaits us." [1]

Masked Ball, at Berlin, 12th–13th December.

On the evening of Monday, 12th, there was, as usual, Masked (or Half-Masked) Ball, at the Palace. As usual; but this time it has become mentionable in World-History. Bielfeld, personally interested, gives us a vivid glance into it; — which, though pretending to be real and contemporaneous, is unfortunately *mythical* only, and done at a great interval of years (dates, and even slight circumstances of fact, refusing to conform); — which, however, for the truth there is in it, we will give, as better than nothing. Bielfeld's pretended date is, "Berlin, 15th December;" should have been 14th, — wrong by a day, after one's best effort!

"*Berlin, 15th December*, 1740. As for me, dear Sister, I am like a shuttlecock whom the Kings of Prussia and of England hit with their rackets, and knock to and fro. The night be-

[1] *Œuvres de Frédéric*, ii, 58.

fore last, I was at the Palace Evening Party (*Assemblée*);
which is a sort of Ball, where you go in domino, but without
mask on the face. The Queen was there, and all the Court.
About eight o'clock the King also made his appearance. His
Majesty, noticing M. de G—— [that is *de Guidiken*, or Guy
Dickens], English Minister, addressed him; led him into the
embrasure of a window, and talked alone with him for more
than an hour [uncertain, probably apocryphal this]. I threw,
from time to time, a stolen glance at this dialogue, which appeared to me to be very lively. A moment after, being just
dancing with Madame the Countess de — *Three-Asterisks*, —
I felt myself twitched by the domino; and turning, was much
surprised to see that it was the King; who took me aside, and
said, 'Are your boots oiled (*Vos bottes sont-elles graissées*, Are
you ready for a journey)?' I replied, 'Sire, they will always
be so for your Majesty's service.' — 'Well, then, Truchsess
and you are for England; the day after to-morrow you go.
Speak to M. de Podewils!' — This was said like a flash of
lightning. His Majesty passed into another apartment; and
I, I went to finish my minuet with the Lady; who had been
not less astonished to see me disappear from her eyes, in the
middle of the dance, than I was at what the King said to
me."[1] Next morning, I —

The fact is, next morning, Truchsess and I began preparation for the Court of London, — and we did there, for many
months afterwards, strive our best to keep the Britannic
Majesty in some kind of tune, amid the prevailing discord
of events; — fact interesting to some. And the other fact,
interesting to everybody, though Bielfeld has not mentioned
it, is, That King Friedrich, the same next morning, punctually
"at the stroke of 9," rolled away Frankfurt-ward, — into the
First Silesian War! Tuesday, "13th December, this morning, the King, privately quitting the Ball, has gone [after
some little snatch of sleep, we will hope] for Frankfurt, to
put himself at the head of his Troops."[2] Bellona his com-

[1] Bielfeld, i. 167, 168.
[2] Dickens (in State-Paper Office), 13th December, 1740; see also *Helden-
Geschichte*, i. 452; &c. &c.

panion for long years henceforth, instead of Minerva and the
Muses, as he had been anticipating.

Hereby is like to be fulfilled (except that Friedrich himself
is perhaps this "little stone") what Friedrich prophesied to
his Voltaire, the day after hearing of the Kaiser's death : " I
believe there will, by June next, be more talk of cannon, soldiers, trenches, than of actresses, and dancers for the ballet.
This small Event changes the entire system of Europe.   It
is the little stone which Nebuchadnezzar saw, in his dream,
loosening itself, and rolling down on the Image made of Four
Metals, which it shivers to ruin." [1]

[1] Friedrich to Voltaire, busy gathering actors at that time, 26th October,
1740 (*Œuvres de Frédéric*, xxii. 49).

BOOK XII.

FIRST SILESIAN WAR, AWAKENING A GENERAL EUROPEAN ONE, BEGINS.

December, 1740–May, 1741.

———◆———

CHAPTER I.

OF SCHLESIEN, OR SILESIA.

SCHLESIEN, what we call Silesia, lies in elliptic shape, spread on the top of Europe, partly girt with mountains, like the crown or crest to that part of the Earth; — highest table-land of Germany or of the Cisalpine Countries; and sending rivers into all the seas. The summit or highest level of it is in the southwest; longest diameter is from northwest to southeast. From Crossen, whither Friedrich is now driving, to the Jablunka Pass, which issues upon Hungary, is above 250 miles; the *axis*, therefore, or longest diameter, of our Ellipse we may call 250 English miles; — its shortest or conjugate diameter, from Friedland in Bohemia (Wallenstein's old Friedland), by Breslau across the Oder to the Polish Frontier, is about 100. The total area of Schlesien is counted to be some 20,000 square miles, nearly the third of England Proper.

Schlesien — will the reader learn to call it by that name, on occasion? for in these sad Manuscripts of ours the names alternate — is a fine, fertile, useful and beautiful Country. It leans sloping, as we hinted, to the East and to the North; a long curved buttress of Mountains (" *Riesengebirge,* Giant Mountains," is their best-known name in foreign countries) holding it up on the South and West sides. This Giant-

Mountain Range, — which is a kind of continuation of the
Saxon-Bohemian "Metal Mountains (*Erzgebirge*)" and of the
straggling Lausitz Mountains, to westward of these, — shapes
itself like a bill-hook (or elliptically, as was said): handle and
hook together may be some 200 miles in length. The pre-
cipitous side of this is, in general, turned outwards, towards
Böhmen, Mähren, Ungarn (Bohemia, Moravia, Hungary, in
our dialects); and Schlesien lies inside, irregularly sloping
down, towards the Baltic and towards the utmost East. From
the Bohemian side of these Mountains there rise two Rivers:
Elbe, tending for the West; Morawa for the South; — Morawa,
crossing Moravia, gets into the Donau, and thence into the
Black-Sea; while Elbe, after intricate adventures among the
mountains, and then prosperously across the plains, is out,
with its many ships, into the Atlantic. Two rivers, we say,
from the Bohemian or steep side: and again, from the Silesian side, there rise other two, the Oder and the Weichsel
(*Vistula*); which start pretty near one another in the Southeast, and, after wide windings, get both into the Baltic, at a
good distance apart.

For the first thirty, or in parts, fifty miles from the Mountains, Silesia slopes somewhat rapidly; and is still to be called
a Hill-country, rugged extensive elevations diversifying it: but
after that, the slope is gentle, and at length insensible, or
noticeable only by the way the waters run. From the central
part of it, Schlesien pictures itself to you as a plain; growing
ever flatter, ever sandier, as it abuts on the monotonous endless sand-flats of Poland, and the Brandenburg territories;
nothing but Boundary Stones with their brass inscriptions
marking where the transition is; and only some Fortified
Town, not far off, keeping the door of the Country secure in
that quarter.

On the other hand, the Mountain part of Schlesien is very
picturesque; not of Alpine height anywhere (the Schnee-
Koppe itself is under 5,000 feet), so that verdure and forest
wood fail almost nowhere among the Mountains; and multiplex industry, besung by rushing torrents and the swift
young rivers, nestles itself high up; and from wheat hus-

bandry, madder and maize husbandry, to damask-weaving,
metallurgy, charcoal-burning, tar-distillery, Schlesien has many
trades, and has long been expert and busy at them to a high
degree. A very pretty Ellipsis, or irregular Oval, on the summit of the European Continent; — "like the palm of a left
hand well stretched out, with the Riesengebirge for thumb!"
said a certain Herr to me, stretching out his arm in that
fashion towards the northwest. Palm, well stretched out,
measuring 250 miles; and the crossway 100. There are still
beavers in Schlesien; the Katzbach River has gold grains in
it, a kind of Pactolus not now worth working; and in the
scraggy lonesome pine-woods, grimy individuals, with kindled
mounds of pine-branches and smoke carefully kept down by
sods, are sweating out a substance which they inform you is
to be tar.

Historical Epochs of Schlesien; — after the Quads and Marchmen.

Who first lived in Schlesien, or lived long since in it, there
is no use in asking, nor in telling if one knew. "The *Quadi*
and the Lygii," says Dryasdust, in a groping manner : Quadi
and consorts, in the fifth or sixth Century, continues he with
more confidence, shifted Rome-ward, following the general
track of contemporaneous mankind; weak remnant of Quadi
was thereupon overpowered by Slavic populations, and their
Country became Polish, which the eastern rim of it still essentially is. That was the end of the Quadi in those parts, says
History. But they cannot speak nor appeal for themselves;
History has them much at discretion. Rude burial urns, with
a handful of ashes in them, have been dug up in different
places; these are all the Archives and Histories the Quadi
now have. It appears their name signifies *Wicked*. They are
those poor Quadi (*Wicked People*) who always go along with
the Marcomanni (*Marchmen*), in the bead-roll Histories one
reads; and I almost guess they must have been of the same
stock : "Wickeds and Borderers;" considered, on both sides
of the Border, to belong to the Dangerous Classes in those

times. Two things are certain: First, *quad* and its deriva-
tives have, to this day, in the speech of rustic Germans, something of that meaning, — "nefarious," at least "injurious,"
"hateful, and to be avoided:" for example, *quad*del, "a net-
tle-burn;" *quet*schen, "to smash" (say, your thumb while
hammering); &c. &c. And then a second thing: The Polish
equivalent word is *Zle* (Büsching says *Zlezi*); hence *Zle*zien,
*Schle*sien, meaning merely *Bad*land, *Quad*land, what we might
called *Damag*itia, or Country where you get into Trouble.
That is the etymology, or what passes for such. As to the
History of Schlesien, hitherwards of these burial urns dug
up in different places, I notice, as not yet entirely buriable,
Three Epochs.

First Epoch; Christianity: A.D. 966. Introduction of Christianity; to the length of founding a Bishopric that year, so
hopeful were the aspects; "Bishopric of Schmoger" (Sch*mag*-
ram, dim little Village still discoverable on the Polish frontier, not far from the Town of Namslau); Bishopric which,
after one removal farther inward, got across the Oder, to
"*Wratislav*," which we now call Breslau; and sticks there,
as Bishopric of Breslau, to this day. Year 966: it was in
Adalbert, our Prussian Saint and Missionary's younger time.
Preaching, by zealous Polacks, must have been going on, while
Adalbert, Bright in Nobleness, was studying at Magdeburg,
and ripening for high things in the general estimation. This
was a new gift from the Polacks, this of Christianity; an infinitely more important one than that nickname of "*Zlezien*,"
or "*Damag*itia," stuck upon the poor Country, had been.

Second Epoch; Get gradually cut loose from Poland: A.D.
1139-1159. Twenty years of great trouble in Poland, which
were of lasting benefit to Schlesien. In 1139 the Polack King,
a very potent Majesty whom we could name but do not, died;
and left his Dominions shared by punctual bequest among his
five sons. Punctual bequest did avail: but the eldest Son
(who was King, and had Schlesien with much else to his share)
began to encroach, to grasp; upon which the others rose upon
him, flung him out into exile; redivided; and hoped now they
might have quiet. Hoped, but were disappointed; and could

come to no sure bargain for the next twenty years, — not till
"the eldest brother," first author of these strifes, "died an
exile in Holstein," or was just about dying, and had agreed
to take Schlesien for all claims, and be quiet thenceforth.

His, this eldest's, three Sons did accordingly, in 1159,
get Schlesien instead of him; their uncles proving honorable.
Schlesien thereby was happy enough to get cut loose from
Poland, and to continue loose; steering a course of its own; —
parting farther and farther from Poland and its habits and
fortunes. These three Sons, of the late Polish Majesty who
died in exile in Holstein, are the "Piast Dukes," much talked
of in Silesian Histories: of whose merits I specify this only,
That they so soon as possible strove to be German. They
were Progenitors of all the "Piast Dukes," Proprietors of
Schlesien thenceforth, till the last of them died out in 1675,
— and a certain *Erbverbrüderung* they had entered into could
not take effect at that time. Their merits as Sovereign Dukes
seem to have been considerable; a certain piety, wisdom and
nobleness of mind not rare among them; and no doubt it was
partly their merit, if partly also their good luck, that they
took to Germany, and leant thitherward; steering looser and
looser from Poland, in their new circumstances. They themselves by degrees became altogether German; their Countries,
by silent immigration, introduction of the arts, the composures
and sobrieties, became essentially so. On the eastern rim
there is still a Polack remnant, its territories very sandy, its
condition very bad; remnant which surely ought to cease its
Polack jargon, and learn some dialect of intelligible Teutsch,
as the first condition of improvement. In all other parts
Teutsch reigns; and Schlesien is a green abundant Country;
full of metallurgy, damask-weaving, grain-husbandry, — instead
of gasconade, gilt anarchy, rags, dirt, and *Nie Pozwalam*.

A.D. 1327; *Get completely cut loose.* The Piast Dukes, who
soon ceased to be Polish, and hung rather upon Bohemia, and
thereby upon Germany, made a great step in that direction,
when King Johann, old *Ich-Dien* whom we ought to recollect,
persuaded most of them, all of them but two, "*pretio ac prece*,"
to become Feudatories (Quasi-Feudatories, but of a sovereign

sort) to his Crown of Bohemia. The two who stood out, resisting prayer and price, were the Duke of Jauer and the Duke
of Schweidnitz, — lofty-minded gentlemen, perhaps a thought
too lofty. But these also Johann's son, little Kaiser Karl IV.,
" marrying their heiress," contrived to bring in; — one fruitful adventure of little Karl's, among the many wasteful he
made, in the German Reich. Schlesien is henceforth a bit of
the Kingdom of Bohemia; indissolubly hooked to Germany;
and its progress in the arts and composures, under wise Piasts
with immigrating Germans, we guess to have become doubly
rapid.[1]

Third Epoch ; Adopt the Reformation : A. D. 1414–1517.
Schlesien, hanging to Bohemia in this manner, extensively
adopted Huss's doctrines; still more extensively Luther's;
and that was a difficult element in its lot, though, I believe,
an unspeakably precious one. It cost above a Century of sad
tumults, Zisca Wars; nay above two Centuries, including the
sad Thirty-Years War; — which miseries, in Bohemia Proper,
were sometimes very sad and even horrible. But Schlesien,
the outlying Country, did, in all this, suffer less than Bohemia
Proper; and did *not* lose its Evangelical Doctrine in result, as
unfortunate Bohemia did, and sink into sluttish "fanatical
torpor, and big Crucifixes of japanned Tin by the wayside,"
though in the course of subsequent years, named of Peace, it
was near doing so. Here are the steps, or unavailing counter-
steps, in that latter direction : —

A.D. 1537. Occurred, as we know, the *Erbverbrüderung ;*
Duke of Liegnitz, and of other extensive heritages, making
Deed of Brotherhood with Kur-Brandenburg; — Deed forbidden, and so far as might be, rubbed out and annihilated by
the then King of Bohemia, subsequently Kaiser Ferdinand I.,
Karl V.'s Brother. Duke of Liegnitz had to give up his
parchments, and become zero in that matter: Kur-Brandenburg entirely refused to do so; kept his parchments, to
see if they would not turn to something.

A.D. 1624. Schlesien, especially the then Duke of Liegnitz
(great-grandson of the *Erbverbrüderung* one), and poor Johann

---

[1] Büsching, *Erdbeschreibung*, viii. 725 ; Hübner, t. 94.

George, Duke of Jägerndorf, cadet of the then Kur-Brandenburg, went warmly ahead into the Winter-King project, first fire of the Thirty-Years War; sufferings from Papal encroachment, in high quarters, being really extreme. Warmly ahead; and had to smart sharply for it; — poor Johann George with forfeiture of Jägerndorf, with *Reiches-Acht* (Ban of the Empire), and total ruin; fighting against which he soon died. Act of Ban and Forfeiture was done tyrannously, said most men; and it was persisted in equally so, till men ceased speaking of it; — Jägerndorf Duchy, fruit of the Act, was held by Austria, ever after, in defiance of the Laws of the Reich. Religious Oppression lay heavy on Protestant Schlesien thenceforth; and many lukewarm individualities were brought back to Orthodoxy by that method, successful in the diligent skilled hands of Jesuit Reverend Fathers, with fiscals and soldiers in the rear of them.

A.D. 1648. Treaty of Westphalia mended much of this, and set fair limits to Papist encroachment; — had said Treaty been kept: but how could it? By Orthodox Authority, anxious to recover lost souls, or at least to have loyal subjects, it was publicly kept in name; and tacitly, in substance, it was violated more and more. Of the "Blossoming of Silesian Literature," spoken of in Books; of the Poet Opitz, Poets Logau, Hoffmannswaldau, who burst into a kind of Song better or worse at this Period, we will remember nothing; but request the reader to remember it, if he is tunefully given, or thinks it a good symptom of Schlesien.

A.D. 1707. Treaty of Altranstadt: between Kaiser Joseph I. and Karl XII. Swedish Karl, marching through those parts, — out of Poland, in chase of August the Physically Strong, towards Saxony, there to beat him soft, — was waited upon by Silesian Deputations of a lamentable nature; was entreated, for the love of Christ and His Evangel, to "Protect us poor Protestants, and get the Treaty of Westphalia observed on our behalf, and fair-play shown!" Which Karl did; Kaiser Joseph, with such weight of French War lying on him, being much struck with the tone of that dangerous Swede. The Pope rebuked Kaiser Joseph for such compliance in the

Silesian matter : " Holy Father," answered this Kaiser (not
of distinguished orthodoxy in the House), " I am too glad he
did not ask me to become Lutheran ; I know not how I should
have helped myself ! " [1]

These are the Three Epochs ; — most things, in respect of
this Third or Reformation Epoch, stepping steadily downward
hitherto. As to the Fourth Epoch, dating " 13th Dec. 1740,"
which continues, up to our day and farther, and is the final
and crowning Epoch of Silesian History, — read in the
following Chapters.

CHAPTER II.

FRIEDRICH MARCHES ON GLOGAU.

At what hour Friedrich ceased dancing on that famous
Ball-night of Bielfeld's, and how long he slept after, or
whether at all, no Bielfeld even mythically says : but next
morning, as is patent to all the world, Tuesday, 13th December, 1740, at the stroke of nine, he steps into his carriage ;
and with small escort rolls away towards Frankfurt-on-Oder ; [2]
out upon an Enterprise which will have results for himself and
others.

Two youngish military men, Adjutant-Generals both, were
with him, Wartensleben, Borck ; both once fellow Captains
in the Potsdam Giants, and much in his intimacy ever since.
Wartensleben we once saw at Brunswick, on a Masonic
occasion ; Borck, whom we here see for the first time, is not
the Colonel Borck (properly Major-General) who did the

---

[1] Pauli, *Allgemeine Preussische Staats-Geschichte* (viii. 298–592) ; Büsching,
Erdbeschreibung (viii. 700–739) ; &c. — Heinrich Wuttke, *Friedrichs des Grossen
Besitzergreifung von Schlesien* (Seizure of Silesia by Friedrich, 2 vols. Leipzig,
1843), I mention only lest ingenuous readers should be tempted by the Title
to buy it. Wuttke begins at the Creation of the World ; and having, in two
heavy volumes, at last struggled down close *to* the *Besitzergreifung* or Seizure
in question, calls halt ; and stands (at ease, we will hope) immovably there
for the seventeen years since.

[2] *Helden-Geschichte*, i. 452 ; Preuss, *Thronbesteigung*, p. 456.

Herstal Operation lately; still less is he the venerable old Minister, Marlborough Veteran, and now Field-Marshal Borck, whom Hotham treated with, on a certain occasion. There are numerous Borcks always in the King's service; nor are these three, except by loose cousinry, related to one another. The Borcks all come from Stettin quarter; a brave kindred, and old enough, — " Old as the Devil, *Das ist so old als de Borcken und de Düwel,*" says the Pomeranian Proverb; — the Adjutant-General, a junior member of the clan, chances to be the notablest of them at this moment. Wartensleben, Borck, and a certain Colonel von der Golz, whom also the King much esteems, these are his company on this drive. For escort, or guard of honor out of Berlin to the next stages, there is a small body of Hussars, Life-guard and other Cavalry, " perhaps 500 horse in all."

They drive rapidly, through the gray winter; reach Frankfurt-on-Oder, sixty miles or more; where no doubt there is military business waiting. They are forward, on the morrow, for dinner, forty miles farther, at a small Town called Crossen, which looks over into Silesia; and is, for the present, headquarters to a Prussian Army, standing ready there and in the environs. Standing ready, or hourly marching in, and rendezvousing; now about 28,000 strong, horse and foot. A Rearguard of Ten or Twelve Thousand will march from Berlin in two days, pause hereabouts, and follow according to circumstances: Prussian Army will then be some 40,000 in all. Schwerin has been Commander, manager and mainspring of the business hitherto: henceforth it is to be the King; but Schwerin under him will still have a Division of his own.

Among the Regiments, we notice "Schulenburg Horse-Grenadiers," — come along from Landsberg hither, these Horse-Grenadiers, with little Schulenburg at the head of them; — "Dragoon Regiment Bayreuth," "Lifeguard Carbineers," " Derschau of Foot;" and other Regiments and figures slightly known to us, or that will be better known.[1] Rearguard, just getting under way at Berlin, has for leaders the

---

[1] List in *Helden-Geschichte,* i. 453.

Prince of Holstein-Beck ("Holstein-*Vaisselle*," say wags, since the Principality went all to *Silver-Plate*) and the Hereditary Prince of Anhalt-Dessau, whom we called the Young Dessauer, on the Strasburg Journey lately: Rearguard, we say, is of 12,000; main Army is 28,000; Horse and Foot are in the proportion of about 1 to 3. Artillery "consists of 20 three-pounders; 4 twelve-pounders; 4 howitzers (*Haubitzen*); 4 big mortars, calibre fifty pounds; and of Artillerymen 166 in all."

With this Force the young King has, on his own basis (pretty much in spite of all the world, as we find now and afterwards), determined to invade Silesia, and lay hold of the Property he has long had there;—not computing, for none can compute, the sleeping whirlwinds he may chance to awaken thereby. Thus lightly does a man enter upon Enterprises which prove unexpectedly momentous, and shape the whole remainder of his days for him; crossing the Rubicon as it were in his sleep. In Life, as on Railways at certain points,—whether you know it or not, there is but an inch, this way or that, into what tram you are shunted; but try to get out of it again! "The man is mad, *cet homme-là est fol!*" said Louis XV. when he heard it.[1]

Friedrich at Crossen, and still in his own Territory, 14th–16th December;—steps into Schlesien.

At all events, the man means to try;—and is here dining at Crossen, noon of Wednesday, the 14th; certain important persons,—especially two Silesian Gentlemen, deputed from Grünberg, the nearest Silesian Town, who have come across the border on business,—having the honor to dine with him. To whom his manner is lively and affable; lively in mood, as if there lay no load upon his spirits. The business of these two Silesian Gentlemen, a Baron von Hocke one of them, a Baron von Kestlitz the other, was To present, on the part of the Town and Amt of Grünberg, a solemn Protest against this

---

[1] Raumer, *Beiträge* (English Translation, called *Frederick II. and his Times; from British Museum and State-Paper Office;*—a very indistinct poor Book, in comparison with what it might have been), p. 73 (24th Dec. 1740)

meditated entrance on the Territory of Schlesien ; Government
itself, from Breslau, ordering them to do so. Protest was
duly presented ; Friedrich, as his manner is, and continues to
be on his march, glances politely into or at the Protest ; hands
it, in silence, to some page or secretary to deposit in the
due pigeon-hole or waste-basket ; and invites the two Silesian
Gentlemen to dine with him ; as, we see, they have the honor
to do. " He (*Er*) lives near Grünberg, then, Mein Herr von
Hocke ? " " Close to it, *Ihro Majestät.* My poor mansion,
Schloss of Deutsch-Kessel, is some fifteen miles hence ; how
infinitely at your Majesty's service, should the march prove
inevitable, and go that way ! " — " Well, perhaps ! " I find
Friedrich did dine, the second day hence, with one of these
Gentlemen ; and lodged with the other. Government at Breslau has ordered such Protest, on the part of the Frontier populations and Official persons : and this is all that comes of it.

During these hours, it chanced that the big Bell of Crossen
dropped from its steeple, — fulness of time, or entire rotten-
ness of axle-tree, being at last completed, at this fateful moment. Perhaps an ominous thing ? Friedrich, as Cæsar and
others have done, cheerfully interprets the omen to his own
advantage : " Sign that the High is to be brought low ! "
says Friedrich. Were the march-routes, wagon-trains, and
multifarious adjustments perfect to the last item here at
Crossen, he will with much cheerfulness step into Silesia,
independent of all Grünberg Protests and fallen Bells.

On the second day he does actually cross ; " the regiments
marching in, at different points ; some reaching as far as 25 miles
in." It is Friday, 16th December, 1740 ; there has a game
begun which will last long ! They went through the Village
of Läsgen ; that was the first point of Silesian ground (" Circle of Schwiebus," our old friend, is on the left near by) ; and
" Schwerin's Regiment was the foremost." Others cross more
to the left or right ; " marching through the Village of Lessen,"
and other dim Villages and little Towns, round and beyond
Grünberg ; all regiments and divisions bearing upon Grünberg
and the Great Road ; but artistically portioned out, — several
miles in breadth (for the sake of quarters), and, as is generally

the rule, about a day's march in length. This evening nearly
the whole Army was on Silesian ground.

Printed "Patent" or Proclamation, briefly assuring all Silesians, of whatever rank, condition or religion, "That we
have come as friends to them, and will protect all persons in
their privileges, and molest no peaceable mortal," is posted on
Church-doors, and extensively distributed by hand. Soldiers
are forbidden, "under penalty of the rods," Officers under that
of "cassation with infamy," to take anything, without first
bargaining and paying ready money for it. On these terms the
Silesian villages cheerfully enough accept their new guests,
interesting to the rural mind; and though the billeting was
rather heavy, "as many as 24 soldiers to a common Farmer
(*Gärtner*)," no complaints were made. In one Schloss, where
the owners had fled, and no human response was to be had
by the wayworn soldiery, there did occur some breakages and
impatient kickings about; which it grieved his Majesty to
hear of, next morning; — in one, not in more.

Official persons, we perceive, study to be absolutely passive.
This was the Bürgermeister's course at Grünberg to-night;
Grünberg, first Town on the Frontier, sets an example of passivity which cannot be surpassed. Prussian troops being at the
Gate of Grünberg, Bürgermeister and adjuncts sitting in a tacit
expectant condition in their Town-hall, there arrives a Prussian Lieutenant requiring of the Bürgermeister the Key of
said Gate. "To deliver such Key? Would to God I durst,
Mein Herr Lieutenant; but how dare I! There is the Key
lying: but to *give* it — You are not the Queen of Hungary's
Officer, I doubt?" — The Prussian Lieutenant has to put out
hand, and take the Key; which he readily does. And on the
morrow, in returning it, when the march recommences, there
are the same phenomena: Bürgermeister or assistants dare not
for the life of them touch that Key: It lay on the table; and
may again, in the course of Providence, come to lie!— The
Prussian Lieutenant lays it down accordingly, and hurries out,
with a grin on his face. There was much small laughter over
this transaction; Majesty himself laughing well at it. Higher
perfection of passivity no Bürgermeister could show.

The march, as readers understand, is towards Glogau; a strongish Garrison Town, now some 40 miles ahead; the key of Northern Schlesien. Grünberg (where my readers once slept for the night, in the late King's time, though they have forgotten it) is the first and only considerable Town on the hither side of Glogau. On to Glogau, I rather perceive, the Army is in good part provisioned before starting: after Glogau, — we must see. Bread-wagons, Baggage-wagons, Ammunition-and-Artillery wagons, all is in order; Army artistically portioned out. That is the form of march; with Glogau ahead. King, as we said above, dines with his Baron von Hocke, at the Schloss of Deutsch-Kessel, short way beyond Grünberg, this first day: but he by no means loiters there; — cuts across, a dozen miles westward, through a country where his vanguard on its various lines of march ought to be arriving; — and goes to lodge, at the Schloss of Schweinitz, with his other Baron, the Von Kestlitz of Wednesday at Crossen.[1] This is Friday, 16th December, his first night on Silesian ground.

What Glogau, and the Government at Breslau, did upon it.

Silesia, in the way of resistance, is not in the least prepared for him. A month ago, there were not above 3,000 Austrian Foot and 600 Horse in the whole Province: neither the military Governor Count Wallis, nor the Imperial Court, nor any Official Person near or far, had the least anticipation of such a Visit. Count Wallis, who commands in Glogau, did in person, nine or ten days ago, as the rumors rose ever higher, run over to Crossen; saw with his eyes the undeniable there; and has been zealously endeavoring ever since, what *he* could, to take measures. Wallis is now shut in Glogau; his second, the now Acting Governor, General Browne, a still more reflective man, is doing likewise his utmost; but on forlorn terms, and without the least guidance from Court. Browne has, by violent industry, raked together, from Mähren and the neighboring countries, certain fractions which raise his Force to 7,000 Foot: these he throws, in small parties, into the defensible

[1] *Helden-Geschichte,* i. 459.

points; or, in larger, into the Chief Garrisons. New Cavalry
he cannot get; the old 600 Horse he keeps for himself, all the
marching Army he has.[1]

Fain would he get possession of Breslau, and throw in some
garrison there; but cannot. Neither he nor Wallis could compass that. Breslau is a City divided against itself, on this
matter; full of emotions, of expectations, apprehensions for
and against. There is a Supreme Silesian Government (*Ober-
Amt*, "Head-Office," kind of Austrian Vice-Royalty) in Breslau; and there is, on Breslau's own score, a Town-Rath;
strictly Catholic both these, Vienna the breath of their nostrils.
But then also there are forty-four Incorporated Trades; Oppressed Protestant in Majority; to whom Vienna is not breath,
but rather the want of it. Lastly, the City calls itself Free;
and has crabbed privileges still valid; a "*jus præsidii*" (or right
to be one's own garrison) one of them, and the most inconvenient just now. Breslau is a *Reichs-Stadt;* in theory, sovereign member of the Reich, and supreme over its own affairs,
even as Austria itself: — and the truth is, old Theory and new
Fact, resolved not to quarrel, have lapsed into one another's
arms in a quite inextricable way, in Breslau as elsewhere!
With a Head Government which can get no orders from
Vienna, the very Town-Rath has little alacrity, inclines rather
to passivity like Grünberg; and a silent population threatens
to become vocal if you press upon it.

Breslau, that is to say the *Ober-Amt* there, has sent courier
on courier to Vienna for weeks past: not even an answer; —
what can Vienna answer, with Kur-Baiern and others threatening war on it, and only £10,000 in its National Purse?
Answer at last is, "Don't bother! Danger is not so near.
Why spend money on couriers, and get into such a taking?"
General Wallis came to Breslau, after what he had seen at
Crossen; and urged strongly, in the name of self-preservation,
first law of Nature, to get an Austrian real Garrison introduced; wished much (horrible to think of!) "the suburbs
should be burnt, and better ramparts raised:" but could not

---

[1] Particulars in *Helden-Geschichte*, i. 465; total of Austrian Force seems to
be 7,800 horse and foot.

succeed in any of these points, nor even mention some of them in a public manner. "You shall have a Protestant for commandant," suggested Wallis; "there is Count von Roth, Silesian-Lutheran, an excellent Soldier!" — "Thanks," answered they, "we can defend ourselves; we had rather not have any!" And the Breslau Burghers have, accordingly, set to drill themselves; are bringing out old cannon in quantity; repairing breaches; very strict in sentry-work: "Perfectly able to defend our City, — so far as we see good!" — Tuesday last, December 13th (the very day Friedrich left Berlin), as this matter of the Garrison, long urged by the Ober-Amt, had at last been got agreed to by the Town-Rath, "on proviso of consulting the Incorporated Trades," or at least consulting their Guild-Masters, who are usually a silent folk, — the Guild-Masters suddenly became in part vocal; and their forty-four Guilds unusually so: — and there was tumult in Breslau, in the Salz-Ring (big central Square or market-place, which they call Ring) such as had not been; idle population, and guild-brethren of suspicious humor, gathering in multitudes into and round the fine old Town-hall there; questioning, answering, in louder and louder key; at last bellowing quite in alt; and on the edge of flaming into one knew not what: [1] — till the matter of Austrian Garrison (much more, of burning the suburbs!) had to be dropt; settled in what way we see.

Head Government (Ober-Amt) has, through its Northern official people, sent Protest, strict order to the Silesian Population to look sour on the Prussians: — and we saw, in consequence, the two Silesian Gentlemen did dine with Friedrich, and he has returned their visits; and the Mayor of Grünberg would not touch his keys. Head Government is now redacting a "Patent," or still more solemn Protest of its own; which likewise it will affix in the Salz-Ring here, and present to King Friedrich: and this — except "despatching by boat down the river a great deal of meal to Glogau," which was an important quiet thing, of Wallis's enforcing — is pretty much all it can do. No Austrian Garrison can be got in ("Perfectly able to defend ourselves!") — let Govern-

[1] *Helden-Geschichte*, i. 469.

ment and Wallis or Browne contrive as they may. And as to
burning the suburbs, better not whisper of that again. Breslau feels, or would fain feel itself " perfectly able ; " — has at
any rate no wish to be bombarded; and contains privately a
great deal of Protestant humor. Of all which, Friedrich, it is
not doubted, has notice more or less distinct; and quickens
his march the more.

General Browne is at present in the Southern parts ; an able
active man and soldier ; but with such a force what can he attempt to do ? There are three strong places in the Country,
Glogau, then Brieg, both on the Oder river ; lastly Neisse, on
the Neisse river, a branch of the Oder (one of the *four* Neisse
rivers there are in Germany, mostly in Silesia, — not handy to
the accurate reader of German Books). Browne is in Neisse ;
and will start into a strange stare when the flying post reaches
him : Prussians actually on march ! Debate with them, if debate there is to be, Browne himself must contrive to do ; from
Breslau, from Vienna, no Government Supreme or Subordinate
can yield his 8,000 and him the least help.

Glogau, as we saw, means to defend itself ; at least, General
Wallis the Commandant does, in spite of the Glogau public ;
and is, with his whole might, digging, palisading, getting in
meal, salt meat and other provender ; — likewise burning
suburbs, uncontrollable he, in the small place ; and clearing
down the outside edifices and shelters, at a diligent rate.
Yesterday, 15th December, he burnt down the " three Oder-
Mills, which lie outside the big suburban Tavern, also the
Ziegel-Scheune (Tile-Manufactory)," and other valuable buildings, careless of public lamentation, — fire catching the Town
itself, and needing to be quenched again.[1] Nay, he was clear
for burning down, or blowing up, the Protestant Church, indispensable sacred edifice which stands outside the walls : " Prussians will make a block-house of it ! " said Wallis. A chief
Protestant, Baron von Something, begged passionately for only
twelve hours of respite, — to lay the case before his Prussian
Majesty. Respite conceded, he and another chief Protestant

[1] *Helden-Geschichte,* i. 473–475.

had posted off accordingly; and did the next morning (Friday, 16th), short way from Crossen, meet his Majesty's carriage; who graciously pulled up for a few instants, and listened to their story. "*Meine Herren*, you are the first that ask a favor of me on Silesian ground; it shall be done you!" said the King; and straightway despatched, in polite style, his written request to Wallis, engaging to make no military use whatever of said Church, "but to attack by the other side, if attack were necessary." Thus his Majesty saved the Church of Glogau; which of course was a popular act. Getting to see this Church himself a few days hence, he said, "Why, it must come down at any rate, and be rebuilt; so ugly a thing!"

Wallis is making strenuous preparation; forces the inhabitants, even the upper kinds of them, to labor day and night by relays, in his rampartings, palisadings; is for burning all the adjacent Villages, — and would have done it, had not the peasants themselves turned out in a dangerous state of mind. He has got together about 1,000 men. His powder, they say, is fifty years old; but he has eatable provender from Breslau, and means to hold out to the utmost. Readers must admit that the Austrian military, Graf von Wallis to begin with, — still more, General Browne, who is a younger man and has now the head charge, — behave well in their present forsaken condition. Wallis (Graf *Franz Wenzel* this one, not to be confounded with an older Wallis heard of in the late Turk War) is of Scotch descent, — as all these Wallises are; "came to Austria long generations ago; *Reichsgrafs* since 1612:" — Browne is of Irish; age now thirty-five, ten years younger than Wallis. Read this Note on the distinguished Browne: —

" A German-Irish Gentleman, this General (ultimately Field-marshal) Graf von Browne; one of those sad exiled Irish Jacobites, or sons of Jacobites, who are fighting in foreign armies; able and notable men several of them, and this Browne considerably the most so. We shall meet him repeatedly within the next eighteen years. Maximilian-Ulysses Graf von Browne: I said he was born German; Basel his birthplace (23d October, 1705), Father also a soldier: he must not be confounded with a contemporary Cousin of his, who is also 'Fieldmarshal

Browne,' but serves in Russia, Governor of Riga for a long
time in the coming years. This Austrian General, Field-
marshal Browne, will by and by concern us somewhat; and
the reader may take note of him.

"Who the Irish Brothers Browne, the Fathers of these
Marshals Browne, were? I have looked in what Irish Peerages
and printed Records there were, but without the least result.
One big dropsical Book, of languid quality, called *King James's
Irish Army-List*, has multitudes of Brownes and others, in an
indistinct form; but the one Browne wanted, the one Lacy,
almost the one Lally, like the part of *Hamlet*, are omitted.
There are so many Irish in the like case with these Brownes.
A Lacy we once slightly saw or heard of; busy in the Polish-
Election time, — besieging Dantzig (investing Dantzig, that
Münnich might besiege it); — that Lacy, 'Governor of Riga,'
whom the *Russian* Browne will succeed, is also Irish: a conspicuous Russian man; and will have a Son Lacy, conspicuous
among the Austrians. Maguires, Ogilvies (of the Irish stock),
Lieutenants 'Fitzgeral;' very many Irish; and there is not
the least distinct account to be had of any of them." [1]

Let us attend his Majesty on the next few marches towards
Glogau, to see the manner of the thing a little; after which
it will behoove us to be much more summary, and stick by the
main incidents.

---

[1] For *Browne* see "Anonymous of Hamburg" (so I have had to label a
J. F. S. *Geschichte des &c.* — in fact, History of Seven-Years War, in successive volumes, done chiefly by the scissors; Leipzig and Frankfurt, 1759, et
seqq.), i. 123–131 n.: elaborate Note of eight pages there; intimating withal
that he, J. F. S., wrote the "*Life of Browne*," a Book I had in vain sought
for; and can now guess to consist of those same elaborate eight pages, *plus*
water and lathering to the due amount. Anonymous "of Hamburg" I call
my J. F. S., — having fished him out of the dust-abysses in that City: a very
poor take; yet worth citing sometimes, being authentic, as even the darkest
Germans generally are. — For a glimpse of *Lacy* (the Elder Lacy) see Büsching, *Beiträge*, vi. 162. — For *Wallis* (tombstone Note on Wallis) see (among
others who are copious in that kind of article, and keep large *sacks* of it, in
admired disorder) Anonymous Seyfarth, *Geschichte Friedrichs des Andern*
(Leipzig, 1784–1788), i. 112 n.; and Anonymous, *Leben der &c. Marie Theresie*
(Leipzig, 1781), 27 n.: laboriously authentic Books both; essentially *Diction-
aries*, — stuffed as into a row of blind *sacks*.

*March to Weichau (Saturday, 17th, and stay Sunday there);
to Milkau (Monday, 19th); get to Herrendorf, within
sight of Glogau, December 22d.*

Friedrich's march proceeds with speed and regularity. Strict
discipline is maintained; all things paid for, damage carefully
avoided: "We come, not as invasive enemies of you or of the
Queen of Hungary, but as protective friends of Silesia and of
her Majesty's rights there; — her Majesty once allowing us
(as it is presumable she will) our own rights in this Province,
no man shall meddle with hers, while we continue here." To
that effect runs the little "Patent," or initiatory Proclamation,
extensively handed out, and posted in public places, as was
said above; and the practice is conformable.

To all men, coming with Protests or otherwise, we perceive,
the young King is politeness itself; giving clear answer, and
promise which will be kept, on the above principle. Nothing
angers him except that gentlemen should disbelieve, and run
away. That a mansion be found deserted by its owners, is
the one evil omen for such mansion. Thus, at the Schloss of
Weichau (which is still discoverable on the Map, across the
"Black Ochel" and the "White," muddy streams which saunter
eastward towards the Oder there, nothing yet running westward for the Bober, our other limitary river), next night after
Schweinitz, second night in Silesia, there was no Owner to be
met with; and the look of his Majesty grew *finster* (dark); remembering what had passed yesternight, in like case, at that
other Schloss from which the owner with his best portable
furniture had vanished. At which Schloss, as above noticed,
some disorders were committed by angry parties of the march;
— doors burst open (doors standing impudently dumb to the
rational proposals made them!), inferior remainders of furniture smashed into firewood, and the like, — no doubt to his
Majesty's vexation. Here at Weichau stricter measures were
taken: and yet difficulties, risks were not wanting; and the
Amtmann (Steward of the place) got pulled about, and once
even a stroke or two. Happily the young Herr of Weichau

appeared in person on the morrow, hearing his Majesty was
still there: " Papa is old; lives at another Schloss; could
not wait upon your Majesty; nor, till now, could I have that
honor." — " Well; lucky that you have come: stay dinner!"
Which the young Count did, and drove home in the evening
to reassure Papa; his Majesty continuing there another night,
and the risk over.[1]

This day, Sunday, 18th, the Army rests; their first Sunday
in Silesia, while the young Count pays his devoir: and here
in Weichau, as elsewhere, it is in the Church, Catholic nearly
always, that the Heretic Army does its devotions, safe from
weather at least: such the Royal Order, they say; which is
taken note of, by the Heterodox and by the Orthodox. And
ever henceforth, this is the example followed; and in all
places where there is no Protestant Church and the Catholics
have one, the Prussian Army-Chaplain assembles his buff-
belted audience in the latter: " No offence, Reverend Fathers,
but there are hours for us, and hours for you; and such is the
King's Order." There is regular divine-service in this Prussian Army; and even a good deal of inarticulate religion, as
one may see on examining.

Country Gentlemen, Town Mayors and other civic Authorities, soon learn that on these terms they are safe with his
Majesty; march after march he has interviews with such, to
regulate the supplies, the necessities and accidents of the
quartering of his Troops. Clear, frank, open to reasonable
representation, correct to his promise; in fact, industriously
conciliatory and pacificatory: such is Friedrich to all Silesian
men. Provincial Authorities, who can get no instructions
from Head-quarters; Vienna saying nothing, Breslau nothing,
and Deputy-Governor Browne being far south in Neisse, — are
naturally in difficulties: How shall they act? Best not to
act at all, if one can help it; and follow the Mayor of Grünberg's unsurpassable pattern! —

" These Silesians," says an Excerpt I have made, " are still
in majority Protestant; especially in this Northern portion of
the Province; they have had to suffer much on that and other

[1] *Helden-Geschichte*, i. 459.

scores; and are secretly or openly in favor of the Prussians. Official persons, all of the Catholic creed, have leant heavy, not always conscious of doing it, against Protestant rights. The Jesuits, consciously enough, have been and are busy with them; intent to recall a Heretic Population by all methods, fair and unfair. We heard of Charles XII.'s interference, three-and-thirty years ago; and how the Kaiser, hard bested at that time, had to profess repentance and engage for complete amendment. Amendment did, for the moment, accordingly take place. Treaty of Westphalia in all its stipulations, with precautionary improvements, was re-enacted as Treaty of Altranstadt; with faithful intention of keeping it too, on Kaiser Joseph's part, who was not a superstitious man: 'Holy Father, I was too glad he did not demand my own conversion to the Protestant Heresy, bested as I am, — with Louis Quatorze and Company upon the neck of me!' Some improvement of performance, very marked at first, did ensue upon this Altranstadt Treaty. But the sternly accurate Karl of Sweden soon disappeared from the scene; Kaiser Joseph of Austria soon disappeared; and his Brother, Karl VI., was a much more orthodox person.

" The Austrian Government, and Kaiser Karl's in particular, is not to be called an intentionally unjust one; the contrary, I rather find; but it is, beyond others, ponderous; based broad on such multiplex formalities, old habitudes; and *gravitation* has a great power over it. In brief, Official human nature, with the best of Kaisers atop, flagitated continually by Jesuit Confessors, does throw its weight on a certain side:— the sad fact is, in a few years the brightness of that Altranstadt improvement began to wax dim; and now, under long Jesuit manipulation, Silesian things are nearly at their old pass; and the patience of men is heavily laden. To see your Chapel made a Soldiers' Barrack, your Protestant School become a Jesuit one, — Men did not then think of revolting under injuries; but the poor Silesian weaver, trudging twenty miles for his Sunday sermon; and perceiving that, unless their Mother could teach the art of reading, his boys, except under soul's peril, would now never learn it: such a Silesian could not want for reflections. Voiceless, hopeless, but heavy; and dwelling secretly, as under nightmare, in a million hearts. Austrian Officiality, wilfully unjust, or not wilfully so, is admitted to be in a most heavy-footed condition; can administer nothing well. Good Government in any kind is not known here : Possibly the Prussian will be better ; who can say ?

"The secret joy of these populations, as Friedrich advances among them, becomes more and more a manifest one. Catholic Officials do not venture on any definite hope, or definite balance of hope and fear ; but adopt the Mayor of Grünberg's course, and study to be passive and silent. The Jesuit-Priest kind are clear in their minds for Austria ; but think, Perhaps Prussia itself will not prove very tyrannous ? At all events, be silent ; it is unsafe to stir. We notice generally, it is only in the Southern or Mountain regions of Silesia, where the Catholics are in majority, that the population is not ardently on the Prussian side. Passive, if they are on the other side ; accurately passive at lowest, this it is prescribed all prudent men to be."

On the 18th, while divine service went on at Weichau, there was at Breslau another phenomenon observable. Provincial Government in Breslau had, at length, after intense study, and across such difficulties as we have no idea of, got its "Patent," or carefully worded Protestation against Prussia, brought to paper ; and does, this day, with considerable solemnity, affix it to the Rathhaus door there, for the perusal of mankind ; despatching a Copy for his Prussian Majesty withal, by two Messengers of dignity. It has needed courage screwed to the sticking-place to venture on such a step, without instruction from Head-quarters ; and the utmost powers of the Official mind have been taxed to couch this Document in language politely ambiguous, and yet strong enough ; — too strong, some of us now think it. In any case, here it now is ; Provincial Government's bolt, so to speak, is shot. The affixing took place under dark weather-symptoms ; actual outburst of thunder and rain at the moment, not to speak of the other surer omens. So that, to the common mind at Breslau, it did not seem there would much fruit come of this difficult performance. Breslau is secretly a much-agitated City; and Prussian Hussar Parties, shooting forth to great distances ahead, were, this day for the first time, observed within sight of it.

And on the same Sunday we remark farther, what is still more important: Herr von Gotter, Friedrich's special Envoy to Vienna, has his first interview with the Queen of Hungary, or with Grand-Duke Franz the Queen's Husband and Co-Regent; and presents there, from Friedrich's own hand, written we remember when, brief distinct Note of his Prussian Majesty's actual Proposals and real meaning in regard to this Silesian Affair. Proposals anxiously conciliatory in tone, but the heavy purport of which is known to us: Gotter had been despatched, time enough, with these Proposals (written above a month ago); but was instructed not to arrive with them, till after the actual entrance into Silesia. And now the response to them is — ? As good as nothing; perhaps worse. Let that suffice us at present. Readers, on march for Glogau, would grudge to pause over State-papers, though we shall have to read this of Friedrich's at some freer moment.

Monday, 19th, before daybreak, the Army is astir again, simultaneously wending forward; spread over wide areas, like a vast cloud (potential thunder in it) steadily advancing on the winds. Length of the Army, artistically portioned out, may be ten or fifteen miles, breadth already more, and growing more; Schwerin always on the right or western wing, close by the Bober River as yet, through Naumburg and the Towns on that side, — Liegnitz and other important Towns lying ahead for Schwerin, still farther apart from the main Body, were Glogau once settled.

So that the march is in two Columns; Schwerin, with the westernmost small column, intending towards Liegnitz, and thence ever farther southward, with his right leaning on the high lands which rise more and more into mountains as you advance. Friedrich himself commands the other column, has his left upon the Oder, in a country mounting continually towards the South, but with less irregularity of level, and generally flat as yet. From beginning to end, the entire field of march lies between the Oder and its tributary the Bober; climbing slowly towards the sources of both. Which two rivers, as the reader may observe, form here a rectangular or trapezoidal space, ever widening as we go southward. Both rivers, coming from the Giant Mountains, hasten directly north; but Oder, bulging out easterly in his sandy course, is obliged to turn fairly westward again; and at Glogau, and a good space farther, flows in that direction; — till once Bober strikes in, almost at right angles, carrying Oder with *him*, though he is but a branch, straight northward again. Northward, but ever slower, to the swollen Pommern regions, and sluggish exit into the Baltic there.

One of the worst features is the state of the weather. On Sunday, at Breslau, we noticed thunder bursting out on an important occasion; "ominous," some men thought; — omen, for one thing, that the weather was breaking. At Weichau, that same day, rain began, — the young Herr of Weichau, driving home to Papa from dinner with Majesty, would get his share of it; — and on Monday, 19th, there was such a pour of rain as kept most wayfarers, though it could not the Prussian Army, within doors. Rain in plunges, fallen and falling, through that blessed day; making roads into mere rivers of mud. The Prussian hosts marched on, all the same. Head-quarters, with the van of the wet Army, that night, were at Milkau; — from which place we have a Note of Friedrich's for Friend Jordan, perhaps producible by and by. His Majesty lodged in some opulent Jesuit Establishment there. And indeed he continued there, not idle, under shelter, for a couple of days. The Jesuits, by their two head men, had welcomed him with their choicest smiles; to whom the King was very gracious, asking the two to dinner as usual, and styling them "Your Reverence." Willing to ingratiate himself with persons of interest in this Country; and likes talk, even with Jesuits of discernment.

On the morrow (20th), came to him, here at Milkau, — probably from some near stage, for the rain was pouring worse than ever, — that Breslau "Patent," or strongish Protestation, by its two Messengers of dignity. The King looked over it "without visible anger" or change of countenance; "handed it," we expressly see, "to a Page to reposit" in the proper waste-basket; — spoke politely to the two gentlemen; asked each or one of them, "Are you of the Ober-Amt at Breslau, then?" — using the style of *Er* (He). — "No, your Majesty; we are only of the Land-Stände" (Provincial Parliament, such as it is). "Upon which [do you mark!] his Majesty became still more polite; asked them to dinner, and used the style of *Sie*." For their *Patent*, now lying safe in its waste-basket, he gave them signed receipt; no other answer.

Rain still heavier, rain as of Noah, continued through this Tuesday, and for days afterwards: but the Prussian hosts, hastening towards Glogau, marched still on. This Tuesday's march, for the rearward of the Army, 10,000 foot and 2,000 horse; march of ten hours long, from Weichau to the hamlet Milkau (where his Majesty sits busy and affable), — is thought to be the wettest on record. Waters all out, bridges down, the Country one wild lake of eddying mud. Up to the knee for many miles together; up to the middle for long spaces; sometimes even up to the chin or deeper, where your bridge was washed away. The Prussians marched through it, as if they had been slate or iron. Rank and file, nobody quitted his rank, nobody looked sour in the face; they took the pouring of the skies, and the red seas of terrestrial liquid, as matters that must be; cheered one another with jocosities, with choral snatches (tobacco, I consider, would not burn); and swashed unweariedly forward. Ten hours some of them were out, their march being twenty or twenty-five miles; ten to fifteen was the average distance come. Nor, singular to say, did any loss occur; except of *almost* one poor Army-Chaplain, and altogether of one poor Soldier's Wife; — sank dangerously both of them, beyond redemption she, taking the wrong side of some bridge-parapet. Poor Soldier's Wife, she is not named to me at all; and has no history save this, and that "she was of the regiment Bredow." But I perceive she washed herself away in a World-Transaction; and there was one rough Bre-

dower, who probably sat sad that night on getting to quarters.
His Majesty surveyed the damp battalions on the morrow
(21st), not without sympathy, not without satisfaction ; allowed them a rest-day here at Milkau, to get dry and bright
again; and gave them "fifteen thalers a company," which is
about ninepence apiece, with some words of praise.[1]

Next day, Thursday, 22d, his Majesty and they marched
on to Herrendorf; which is only five miles from Glogau, and
near enough for Head-quarters, in the now humor of the place.
Wallis has his messenger at Herrendorf, "Sorry to warn your
Majesty, That if there be the least hostility committed, I shall
have to resist it to the utmost." Head-quarters continue six
days at Herrendorf, Army (main body, or left Column, of the
Army) cantoned all round, till we consider what to do.

As to the right Column, or Schwerin's Division, that, after
a rest-day or two, gathers itself into more complete separation
here, tucking in its eastern skirts; and gets on march again,
by its own route. Steadily southward ; — and from Liegnitz,
and the upland Countries, there will be news of Schwerin and
it before long. Rain ending, there ensued a ringing frost ; —
not favorable for Siege-operations on Glogau : — and Silesia
became all of flinty glass, with white peaks to the Southwest,
whither Schwerin is gone.

CHAPTER III.

PROBLEM OF GLOGAU.

FRIEDRICH was over from Herrendorf with the first daylight, "reconnoitring Glogau, and rode up to the very glacis;"
scanning it on all sides.[2] Since Wallis is so resolute, here is
an intricate little problem for Friedrich, with plenty of corollaries and conditions hanging to it. Shall we besiege Glogau, then ? We have no siege-cannon here. Time presses,
Breslau and all things in such crisis ; and it will take time.

1 *Helden-Geschichte*, i. 482.   2 Ib. i. 484.

By what methods *could* Glogau be besieged ? — Readers can
consider what a blind many-threaded coil of things, heaping
itself here in wide welters round Glogau, and straggling to
the world's end, Friedrich has on hand : probably those six
days, of Head-quarters at Herrendorf, were the busiest he had
yet had.

One thing is evident, there ought to be siege-cannon got
straightway; and, still more immediate, the right posts and
battering-places should be ready against its coming. — " Let
the Young Dessauer with that Rearguard, or Reserve of
10,000, which is now at Crossen, come up and assist here,"
orders Friedrich; "and let him be swift, for the hours are
pregnant !"   On farther reflection, perhaps on new rumors
from Breslau, Friedrich perceives that there can be no besieging of Glogau at this point of time; that the Reserve, Half of
the Reserve, must be left to "mask" it; to hold it in strict
blockade, with starvation daily advancing as an ally to us, and
with capture by bombarding possible when we like.   That is
the ultimate decision; — arrived at through a welter of dubieties, counterpoisings and perilous considerations, which we
now take no account of.   A most busy week; Friedrich incessantly in motion, now here now there; and a great deal of
heavy work got well and rapidly done.   The details of which,
in these exuberant Manuscripts, would but weary the reader.
Choosing of the proper posts and battering-places (post "on
the other side of the River," "on this side of it," "on the
Island in the middle of it "), and obstinate intrenching and
preparing of the same in spite of frost; "wooden bridge built"
farther up; with "regulation of the river-boats, the Polish
Ferry," and much else: all this we omit; and will glance only
at one pregnant point, by way of sample : —

. . . "Most indispensable of all, the King has to provide
Subsistences : — and enters now upon the new plan, which will
have to be followed henceforth.   The Provincial Chief-men
(*Landes-Æltesten*, Land's-*Eldests*, their title) are summoned,
from nine or ten Circles which are likely to be interested :
they appear punctually, and in numbers, — lest contumacy
worsen the inevitable.   King dines them, to start with; as

many as 'ninety-five covers,' — day not given, but probably
one of the first in Herrendorf : not Christmas itself, one
hopes !

"Dinner done, the ninety-five Land's-Eldest are instructed
by proper parties, What the Infantry's ration is, in meat, in
bread, exact to the ounce ; what the Cavalry's is, and that
of the Cavalry's Horse. Tabular statement, succinct, correct,
clear to the simplest capacity, shows what quotities of men on
foot, and of men on horseback, or men with draught-cattle,
will march through their respective Circles ; Land's-Eldests
conclude what amount of meal and butcher's-meat it will be
indispensable to have in readiness ; — what Land's-Eldest can
deny the fact ? These Papers still exist, at least the long-
winded Summary of them does : and I own the reading of it
far less insupportable than that of the mountains of Proclama-
tory, Manifesto and Diplomatic matter. Nay it leaves a certain wholesome impression on the mind, as of business thoroughly well done ; and a matter, capable, if left in the chaotic
state, of running to all manner of depths and heights, com-
pendiously forced to become cosmic in this manner.

"These Land's-Eldest undertake, in a mildly resigned or
even hopeful humor. They will manage as required, in their
own Circles ; will communicate with the Circles farther on ;
and everywhere the due proviants, prestations, furtherances,
shall be got together by fair apportionment on the Silesian
Community, and be punctually ready as the Army advances.
Book-keeping there is to be, legible record of everything ; on
all hands 'quittance' for everything furnished ; and a time
is coming, when such quittance, presented by any Silesian
man, will be counted money paid by him, and remitted at the
next tax-day, or otherwise made good. Which promise also
was accurately kept, the hoped-for time having come. It
must be owned the Prussian Army understands business ;
and, with brevity, reduces to a minimum its own trouble, and
that of other people, non-fighters, who have to do with it.
Non-fighters, I say ; to fighters we hope it will give a respectable maximum of trouble when applied to ! " [1]

[1] *Helden-Geschichte*, i. 492–499.

The Gotter Negotiation at Vienna, which we saw begin there that wet Sunday, is now fast ending, as good as ended; without result except of a negative kind. Gotter's Proposals,— would the reader wish to hear these Proposals, which were so intensely interesting at one time? They are fivefold; given with great brevity by Friedrich, by us with still greater : —

1°. "Will fling myself heartily into the Austrian scale, and endeavor for the interest of Austria in this Pragmatic matter, with my whole strength against every comer.

2°. "Will make treaty with Vienna, with Russia and the Sea-Powers, to that effect.

3°. "Will help by vote, and with whole amount of interest will endeavor, to have Grand-Duke Franz, the Queen's Husband, chosen Kaiser; and to maintain such choice against all and sundry. Feel myself strong enough to accomplish this result; and may, without exaggeration, venture to say it shall be done.

4°. "To help the Court of Vienna in getting its affairs into good order and fencible condition, — will present to it, on the shortest notice, Two Million Gulden (£200,000) ready money." — Infinitely welcome this Fourth Proposition; and indeed all the other Three are welcome : but they are saddled with a final condition, which pulls down all again. This, which is studiously worded, politely evasive in phrase, and would fain keep old controversies asleep, though in substance it is so fatally distinct, — we give in the King's own words :

5°. "For such essential services as those to which I bind myself by the above very onerous conditions, I naturally require a proportionate recompense; some suitable assurance, as indemnity for all the dangers I risk, and for the part (*rôle*) I am ready to play : in short, I require hereby the entire and complete cession of all Silesia, as reward for my labors and dangers which I take upon myself in this course now to be entered upon for the preservation and renown of the House of Austria;" — Silesia all and whole; and we say nothing of our "rights" to it; politely evasive to her Hungarian Majesty, though in substance we are so fatally distinct.[1]

[1] Preuss, *Thronbesteigung*, p. 451; "from Olenschlager, *Geschichte des Inter regni* [Frankfurt, 1746], i. 134."

These were Friedrich's Proposals; written down with his own hand at Reinsberg, five or six weeks ago (November 17th is the date of it); in what mood, and how wrought upon by Schwerin and Podewils, we saw above. Gotter has fulfilled his instructions in regard to this important little Document; and now the effect of it is — ? Gotter can report no good effect whatever. "Be cautious," Friedrich instructs him farther; "modify that Fifth Proposal; I will take less than the whole, 'if attention is paid to my just claims on Schlesien.'" To that effect writes Friedrich once or twice. But it is to no purpose; nor can Gotter, with all his industry, report other than worse and worse. Nay, he reports before long, not refusal only, but refusal with mockery: "How strange that his Prussian Majesty, whose official post in Germany, as Kur-Brandenburg and Kaiser's Chamberlain, has been to present ewer and towel to the House of Austria, should now set up for prescribing rules to it!" A piece of wit, which could not but provoke Friedrich; and warn him that negotiation on this matter might as well terminate. Such had been his own thought, from the first; but in compliance with Schwerin and Podewils he was willing to try.

Better for Maria Theresa, and for all the world how much better, could she have accepted this Fifth Proposition! But how could she, — the high Imperial Lady, keystone of Europe, though by accident with only a few pounds of ready money at present? Twenty years of bitter fighting, and agony to herself and all the world, were necessary first; a new Fact of Nature having turned up, a new European Kingdom with real King to it; *not* recognizable as such, by the young Queen of Hungary or by any other person, till it do its proofs.

What Berlin is saying; what Friedrich is thinking.

What Friedrich's own humor is, what Friedrich's own inner man is saying to him, while all the world so babbles about his Silesian Adventure? Of this too there are, though in diluted state, some glimmerings to be had, — chiefly in the Correspondence with Jordan.

Ingenious Jordan, Inspector of the Poor at Berlin, — his thousand old women at their wheels humming pleasantly in the background of our imaginations, though he says nothing of that, — writes twice a week to his Majesty: pleasant gossipy Letters, with an easy respectfulness not going into sycophancy anywhere; which keep the campaigning King well abreast of the Berlin news and rumors: something like the essence of an Old Newspaper; not without worth in our present Enterprise. One specimen, if we had room!

Jordan to the King (successively from Berlin, — somewhat abridged).

No. 1. "*Berlin, 14th December,* 1740 [day after his Majesty left]. Everybody here is on tiptoe for the Event; of which both origin and end are a riddle to the most. I am charmed to see a part of your Majesty's Dominions in a state of Pyrrhonism; the disease is epidemical here at present. Those who, in the style of theologians, consider themselves entitled to be certain, maintain That your Majesty is expected with religious impatience by the Protestants, and that the Catholics hope to see themselves delivered from a multitude of imposts which cruelly tear up the beautiful bosom of their Church. You cannot but succeed in your valiant and stoical Enterprise, since both religion and worldly interest rank themselves under your flag.

"Wallis," Austrian Commandant in Glogau, "they say, has punished a Silesian Heretic of enthusiastic turn, as blasphemer, for announcing that a new Messiah is just coming. I have a taste for that kind of martyrdom. Critical persons consider the present step as directly opposed to certain maxims in the *Anti-Machiavel.*

"The word *Manifesto* — [your Majesty's little *Patent* on entering Silesia, which no reader shall be troubled with at present] — is the burden of every conversation. Rumor goes, there is a short Piece of the kind to come out to-day, by way of preface to a large complete exposition, which a certain Jurisconsult is now busy with. People crowd to the Book-

shops for it, as if looking out for a celestial phenomenon that
had been predicted. — This is the beginning of my Gazette;
can only come out twice a week, owing to the arrangement of
the Posts.   Friday, the day your Majesty crosses into Silesia,
I shall spend in prayer and devotional exercises : Astronomers
pretend that Mars will that day enter " — no matter what.

Note, The above Manifesto rumor is correct ; Jurisconsult
is ponderous Herr Ludwig, Kanzler (Chancellor) of Halle
University, monster of law-learning, — who has money also,
and had to help once with a House in Berlin for one Nüssler,
a son-in-law of his, transiently known to us ; — ponderous
Ludwig, matchless or difficult to match in learning of this
kind, will write ample enough Deductions (which lie in print
still, to the extent of tons' weight), and explain the *Erbverbrüderung* and violence done upon it, so that he who runs
may read.   Postpone him to a calmer time.

No. 2. *" Berlin, Saturday, 17th December.* Manifesto has
appeared," — can be seen, under thick strata of cobwebs, in
many Books ;[1] is not worth reading now : Incontestable
rights which our House has for ages had on Schlesien, and
which doubtless the Hungarian Majesty will recognize; not
the slightest injury intended, far indeed from that; and so
on ! — " people are surprised at its brevity ; and, studying
it as theologians do a passage of Scripture, can make almost
nothing of it.   Clear as crystal, says one ; dexterously obscure
by design, says another.

" Rumor that the Grand-Duke of Lorraine," Maria Theresa's
Husband, " was at Reinsberg incognito lately," Grand-Duke
a concerting party, think people looking into the thing with
strong spectacles on their nose !   " M. de Beauvau [French
Ambassador Extraordinary, to whom the aces were promised
if they came] said one thing that surprised me : ' What put
the King on taking this step, I do not know; but perhaps
it is not such a bad one.'   Surprising news that the Elector
of Saxony, King of Poland, is fallen into inconsolable remorse

---

[1] In *Helden-Geschichte,* i. 448, 453 (what Jordan now alludes to) ; *ib.* 559-
592 (" Deduction " itself, Ludwig in all his strength, some three weeks hence;
in *Olenschlager* (doubtless) ; in &c. &c.

for changing his religion [to Papistry, on Papa's hest, many long years ago] and that it is not to the Pope, but to the King of Prussia, that he opens his heart to steady his stagger-ing orthodoxy." Very astonishing to Jordan. "One thing is certain, all Paris rings with your Majesty's change of re-ligion" (over to Catholicism, say those astonishing people, first conjurers of the universe)!

No. 3. "*Berlin, 20th December.* M. de Beauvau," French Ambassador, "is gone. Ended, yesterday, his survey of the Cabinet of Medals ; charmed with the same : charmed too, as the public is, with the rich present he has got from said Cabinet [coronation medal or medals in gold, I could guess]: people say the King of France's Medal given to our M. de Camas is nothing to it.

"Rumor of alliance between your Majesty and France with Sweden," — premature rumor. Item, "Queen of Hungary dead in child-birth ; " — ditto with still more emphasis ! "The day before yesterday, in all churches, was prayer to Heaven for success to your Majesty's arms ; interest of the Protestant religion being the one cause of the War, or the only one assigned by the reverend gentlemen. At sound of these words, the zeal of the people kindles : 'Bless God for raising such a Defender ! Who dared suspect our King's indifference to Protestantism ? ' "

A right clever thing this last (*O le beau coup d'état*) ! exclaims Jordan, — though it is not clever or the contrary, not being dramatically prearranged, as Jordan exults to think. Jordan, though there are dregs of old devotion lying asleep in him, which will start into new activity when stirred again, is for the present a very unbelieving little gentleman, I can perceive. — This is the substance of public rumor at Berlin for one week. Friedrich answers : —

"To M. Jordan, at Berlin.

"*Quarter at Milkau, towards Glogau, 19th December,* **1740** [comfortable Jesuit-Establishment at Milkau, Friedrich just got in, out of the rain]. — Seigneur Jordan, thy Letter has

given me a deal of pleasure in regard to all these talkings thou
reportest. To-morrow [not to-morrow, nor next day; wet troops
need a rest] I arrive at our last station this side Glogau, which
place I hope to get in a few days. All favors my designs:
and I hope to return to Berlin, after executing them gloriously
and in a way to be content with. Let the ignorant and the
envious talk; it is not they that shall ever serve as loadstar to
my designs; not they, but Glory [*la Gloire;* Fame, depending
not on them]: with the love of that I am penetrated more
than ever; my troops have their hearts big with it, and I
answer to thee for success. Adieu, dear Jordan. Write me
all the ill that the public says of thy Friend, and be persuaded
that I love and will esteem thee always." — F.

Jordan to the King.

No. 4. " *Berlin,* 24th *December.* Your Majesty's Letter fills
me with joy and contentment. The Town declared your Majesty to be already in Breslau; founding on some Letter to
a Merchant here. Ever since they think of your Majesty acting for Protestantism, they make you step along with strides
of Achilles to the ends of Silesia. — Foreign Courts are all
rating their Ambassadors here for not finding you out.

"Wolf," his negotiations concluded at last, "has entered
Halle almost like the triumphant Entry to Jerusalem. A con-
course of pedants escorted him to his house. Lange [his old
enemy, who accused him of Atheism and other things] has
called to see him, and loaded him with civilities, to the astonishment of the old Orthodox." There let him rest, well buttoned in gaiters, and avoiding to mount stairs. . . . " Madame
de Roucoulles has sent me the three objects adjoined, for your
Majesty's behoof," — woollen achievements, done by the needle,
good against the winter weather for one she nursed. The good
old soul. Enough now of Jordan.[1]

Voltaire, who left Berlin 2d or 3d December, seems to have
been stopt by overflow of rivers about Cleve, then to have
taken boat; and is, about this very time, writing to Friedrich

---

[1] *Œuvres de Frédéric,* xvii. 75-78.

"from a vessel on the Coasts of Zealand, where I am driven mad." (Intends, privately, for Paris before long, to get his *Mahomet* acted, if possible.) To Voltaire, here is a Note coming:

King to M. de Voltaire (at Brussels, if once got thither).

"QUARTER OF HERRENDORF IN SILESIA,
23d December, 1740.

"MY DEAR VOLTAIRE, — I have received two of your Letters; but could not answer sooner; I am like Charles Twelfth's Chess-King, who was always kept on the move. For a fortnight past, we have been continually afoot and under way, in such weather as you never saw.

"I am too tired to reply to your charming Verses; and shivering too much with cold to taste all the charm of them : but that will come round again. Do not ask poetry from a man who is actually doing the work of a wagoner, and sometimes even of a wagoner stuck in the mud. Would you like to know my way of life ? We march from seven in the morning till four in the afternoon. I dine then; afterwards I work, I receive tiresome visits ; with these comes a detail of insipid matters of business. 'T is wrong-headed men, · punctiliously difficult, who are to be set right; heads too hot which must be restrained, idle fellows that must be urged, impatient men that must be rendered docile, plunderers to restrain within the bounds of equity, babblers to hear babbling, dumb people to keep in talk : in fine, one has to drink with those that like it, to eat with those that are hungry ; one has to become a Jew with Jews, a Pagan with Pagans.

"Such are my occupations; — which I would willingly make over to another, if the Phantom they call Fame (*Gloire*) did not rise on me too often. In truth, it is a great folly, but a folly difficult to cast away when once you are smitten by it. [Phantom of *Gloire* somewhat rampant in those first weeks ; let us see whether it will not lay itself again, forevermore, before long !]

"Adieu, my dear Voltaire ; may Heaven preserve from misfortune the man I should so like to sup with at night, after fighting in the morning ! The Swan of Padua [Algarotti, with his big hook-nose and dusky solemnly greedy countenance] is going, I think, to Paris, to profit by my absence; the Philosopher Geometer [big Maupertuis, in red wig and yellow frizzles, vainest of human kind] is squaring curves; poor little Jordan [with the kindly hazel eyes, and pen that pleasantly gossips to us] is doing nothing, or probably something near it. Adieu once more, dear Voltaire; do not forget the absent who love you.   Fédéric." [1]

Schwerin at Liegnitz; Friedrich hushes up the Glogau Problem, and starts with his best speed for Breslau.

Meanwhile, on the Western road, and along the foot of the snowy peaks over yonder, Schwerin with the small Right column is going prosperously forwards. Two columns always, as the reader recollects, — two parallel military currents, flowing steadily on, shooting out estafettes, or horse-parties, on the right and left; steadily submerging all Silesia as they flow forward. Left column or current is in slight pause at Glogau here; but will directly be abreast again. On Tuesday, 27th, Schwerin is within wind of Liegnitz; on Wednesday morning, while the fires are hardly lighted, or the smoke of Liegnitz risen among the Hills, Schwerin has done his feat with the usual deftness: Prussian grenadiers came softly on the sentry, softly as a dream; but with sudden levelling of bayonets, sudden beckoning, "To your Guard-house!" — and there, turn the key upon his poor company and him. Whereupon the whole Prussian column marches in; tramp tramp, without music, through the streets: in the Market-place they fold themselves into a ranked mass, and explode into wind-harmony and rolling of drums. Liegnitz, mostly in nightcap, looks cautiously out of window: it is a deed done, *ihr Herren;* Liegnitz ours, better late than never; and after so many years, the King has his own again. Schwerin is sumptuously lodged in the Jesuits' Palace: Liegnitz, essentially a Protestant Town, has many thoughts upon this event, but as yet will be stingy of speaking them.

---

[1] *Œuvres de Frédéric,* xxii. 57.

Thus is Liegnitz managed. A pleasant Town, amid pleasant hills on the rocky Katzbach; of which swift stream, and other towns and passes on it, we shall yet hear more. Population, silently industrious in weaving and otherwise, is now above 14,000; was then perhaps about half that number. Patiently inarticulate, by no means bright in speech or sentiment; a much-enduring, steady-going, frugal, pious and very desirable people.

The situation of Breslau, all this while, is very critical. Much bottled emotion in the place; no Austrian Garrison admissible; Authorities dare not again propose such a thing, though Browne is turning every stone for it, — lest the emotion burst bottle, and take fire. I have dim account that Browne has been there, has got 300 Austrian dragoons into the Dom Insel (*Cathedral Island;* "Not in the City, you perceive!" says General Browne: "no, separated by the Oder, on both sides, from the rest of the City; that stately mass of edifices, and good military post"); — and had hoped to get the suburbs burnt, after all. But the bottled emotion was too dangerous. For, underground, there are *Anti*-Brownes: one especially; a certain busy Deblin, Shoemaker by craft, whom Friedrich speaks of, but gives no name to; this zealous Cordwainer, Deblin, and he is not the only individual of like humor, operates on the guild-brothers and lower populations: [1] things seem to be looking worse and worse for the Authorities, in spite of General Browne and his activities and dragoons.

What the issue will be? Judge if Friedrich wished the Young Dessauer come! Friedrich's Hussar parties (or Schwerin's, instructed by Friedrich) go to look if the Breslau suburbs are burnt. Far from it, if Friedrich knew; — the suburbs merely sit quaking at such a proposal, and wish the Prussians were here. "But there is time ahead of us," said everybody at Breslau; "Glogau will take some sieging!" Browne, in the course of a day or two, — guessing, I almost think, that Glogau was not to be besieged, — ranked his 300 Austrian dragoons, and rode away; sending the Austrian State-Papers,

[1] Preuss, *Thronbesteigung,* p. 469; *Œuvres de Frédéric,* ii. 61.

in half a score of wagons, ahead of him. "Archives of Breslau !" cried the general population, at sight of these wagons;
and largely turned out, with emotion again like to unbottle
itself. "Mere Tax-Ledgers, and records of the Government
Offices ; come and convince yourselves ! " answered the Authorities. And the ten wagons went on ; calling at Ohlau and
Brieg, for farther lading of the like kind. Which wagons
the Prussian light-horse chased, but could not catch. On to
Mähren went these Archive-wagons ; to Brünn, far over the
Giant Mountains ; — did not come back for a long while, nor
to their former Proprietor at all.

Tuesday, 27th, Leopold the Young Dessauer does finally
arrive, with his Reserve, at Glogau : never man more welcome;
such a fermentation going on at Breslau, — known to Friedrich, and what it will issue in, if he delay, not known. With
despatch, Leopold is put into his charge; posts all yielded to
him ; orders given, — blockade to be strictness itself, but no
fighting if avoidable ; "starvation will soon do it, two months
at most," hopes Friedrich, too sanguine as it proved : — and
with earliest daylight on the 28th, Friedrich's Army, Friedrich himself in the van as usual, is on march again ; at its best
speed for Breslau. Read this Note for Jordan : —

Friedrich to M. Jordan, at Berlin.

                                "HERRENDORF, 27th Dec. 1740.

"SIEUR JORDAN, — I march to-morrow for Breslau; and
shall be there in four days [three, it happened ; there rising,
as would seem, new reason for haste]. You Berliners [of
the 24th last] have a spirit of prophecy, which goes beyond
me. In fine, I go my road ; and thou wilt shortly see Silesia
ranked in the list of our Provinces. Adieu; this is all I have
time to tell thee. Religion [Silesian Protestantism, and Breslau's Cordwainer], religion and our brave soldiers will do the
rest.

"Tell Maupertuis I grant those Pensions he proposes for
his Academicians; and that I hope to find good subjects for
that dignity in the Country where I am, withal. Give him my
compliments.   FÉDÉRIC."

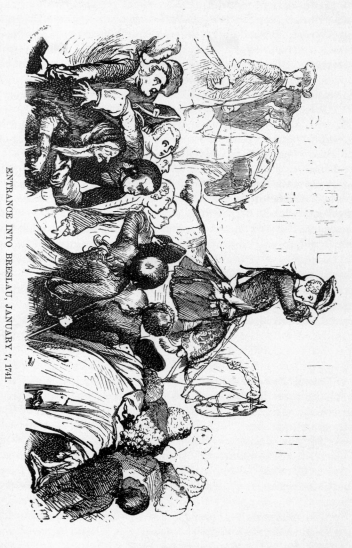

ENTRANCE INTO BRESLAU, JANUARY 7, 1741.

Carlyle, Vol. Two, p. 688.

The march was of the swiftest, — swifter even than had
been expected ; — which, as Silesia is all ringing glass, becomes
more achievable than lately.   But certain regiments outdid
themselves in marching ; " in three marches, near upon seventy miles,'[2] with their baggage jingling in due proximity.
Through Gläsersdorf, thence through Parchwitz, Neumarkt,
Lissa, places that will be better known to us; — on Saturday,
last night of the Year, his Majesty lodged at a Schloss called
Pilsnitz, five miles to west of Breslau ; and van-ward regiments, a good few, quartered in the Western and Southern
suburbs of Breslau itself ; suburbs decidedly glad to see them,
and escape conflagration.   The Town-gates are hermetically
shut ; — plenty of emotion bottled in the 100,000 hearts within.
The sentries on the walls presented arms ; nay, it is affirmed,
some could not help exclaiming, " *Wilkommen, Ihr lieben Herren*
(Welcome, dear Sirs) ! " [1]

Colonel Posadowsky (active Horse Colonel whom we have
seen before, who perhaps has been in Breslau before) left
orders " at the Scultet Garden-House," that all must be ready
and the rooms warmed, his Majesty intending to arrive here
early on the morrow.   Which happened accordingly ; Majesty
alighting duly at said Garden-House, near by the Schweidnitz
Gate, — I fancy almost before break of day.

CHAPTER IV.

BRESLAU UNDER SOFT PRESSURE.

THE issue of this Breslau transaction is known, or could be
stated in few words ; nor is the manner of it such as would,
for Breslau's sake, deserve many.   But we are looking into
Friedrich, wish to know his manners and aspects : and here,
ready to our hand, a Paper turns up, compiled by an exact
person with better leisure than ours, minutely detailing every

[1] *Helden-Geschichte*, i. 534.

part of the affair. This Paper, after the question, Burn or
insert ? is to have the lot of appearing here, with what abridg-
ments are possible : —

"*Sunday*, 1*st January*, 1741. The King having established
himself in Herrn Scultet's Garden-House, not far from the
Schweidnitz Gate, there began a delicate and great operation.
The Prussians, in a soft cautious manner, in the gray of the
morning, push out their sentries towards the three Gates on
this side of the Oder ; seize any 'Excise House,' or the like,
that may be fit for a post ; and softly put 'twenty grenadiers'
in it. All this before sunrise. Breslau is rigidly shut ; Breslau
thought always it could stand upon its guard, if attacked ; — is
now, in Official quarters, dismally uncertain if it can ; general
population becoming certain that it cannot, and waiting anxious
on the development of this grand drama.

"About 7 A.M. a Prussian subaltern advancing within cry
of the Schweidnitz Gate, requests of the Town-guard there, To
send him out a Town-Officer. Town-Officer appears ; is informed, 'That Colonels Posadowsky and Borck, Commission-
ers or plenipotentiary Messengers from his Prussian Majesty,
desire admittance to the Chief Magistrate of Breslau, for the
purpose of signifying what his Prussian Majesty's instructions
are.' Town-Officer bows, and goes upon his errand. Town
Officer is some considerable time before he can return ; City
Authorities being, as we know, various, partly Imperial, partly
Civic ; elderly ; and some of them gone to church, — for matins,
or to be out of the way. However, he does at last return ;
admits the two Colonels, and escorts them honorably, to the
Chief *Raths-Syndic* (Lord-Mayor) old Herr von Gutzmar's ;
where the poor old "President of the *Ober Amt*" (Von Schaffgotsch the name of this latter) is likewise in attendance.

"Prussian Majesty's proposals are of the mildest sort :
'Nothing demanded of Breslau but the plainly indispensable
and indisputable, That Prussia be in it what Austria has been.
In all else, *status quo*. Strict neutrality to Breslau, respect
for its privileges as a Free City of the Reich ; protection to
all its rights and privileges whatsoever. Shall be guarded by
its own Garrison ; no Prussian soldier to enter except with

side-arms; only 30 guards for the King's person, who will
visit the City for a few days; — intends to form a Magazine,
with guard of 1,000 men, but only outside the City: no requi-
sitions; ready money for everything. Chief Syndic Gutzmar
and President Schaffgotsch shall consider these points.'[1]
Syndic and President answer, Surely! Cannot, however,
decide till they have assembled the Town-Rath; the two
Herren Colonels will please to be guests of Breslau, and
lodge in the City till then.

"And they lodged, accordingly, in the '*Grosse Ring*' (called
also *Salz-Ring*, big Central Square, where the Rathhaus is);
and they made and received visits, — visited especially the
Chief President's Office, the Ober-Amt, and signified there,
that his Prussian Majesty's expectation was, They would give
some account of that rather high Proclamation or 'Patent'
they had published against him the other day, amid thunder
and lightning here, and what they now thought would be
expedient upon it? All in grave official terms, but of such a
purport as was not exhilarating to everybody in those Ober-
Amt localities.

"*Monday morning, 2d January.* The Rath is assembled;
and consults, — consults at great length. *Rath*-House and
Syndic Gutzmar, in such crisis, would fain have advice from
Amt-House or President Schaffgotsch; but can get none: considerable coming and going between them: at length, about
3 in the afternoon, the Treaty is got drawn up; is signed by
the due Breslau hands, and by the two Prussian Colonels, —
which latter ride out with it, about 4 of the clock; victorious
after thirty hours. Straight towards the Scultet Garden ride
they; Town-guard presenting Arms, at the Schweidnitz Gate;
nay Town-band breaking out into music, which is never done
but to Ambassadors and high people. By thirty hours of
steady soft pressure, they have brought it thus far.

"Friedrich had waited patiently all Sunday, keeping steady
guard at the Gates; but on Monday, naturally, the thirty hours
began to hang heavy: at all events, he perceived that it would

[1] *Helden-Geschichte,* i. 537.

be well to facilitate conclusions a little from without. Breslau stands on the West, more strictly speaking, on the South
side of the Oder, which makes an elbow here, and thus bounds
it, or mostly bounds it, on two sides. The big drab-colored
River spreads out into Islands, of a confused sort, as it passes;
which are partly built upon, and constitute suburbs of the
Town, — stretching over, here and there, into straggles of
farther suburb beyond the River, where a road with its bridge
happens to cross for the Eastern parts. The principal of
these Islands is the *Dom Insel*," — known to General Browne
and us, — " on which is the Cathedral, and the *Close* with rich
Canons and their edifices; Island filled with strong high architecture; and a superior military post.

"Friedrich has already as good as possessed himself of the
three landward Gates, which look to the south and to the
west; the riverward gates, or those on the north and the east,
he perceives that it were good now also to have; these, and
even perhaps something more? 'Gather all the river-boats,
make a bridge of them across the Oder; push across 400 men:'
this is done on Monday morning, under the King's own eye.
This done, 'March up to that riverward Gate, and also to that
other, in a mild but dangerous-looking manner; hew the beams
of said Gate in two; start the big locks; fling wide open said
Gate and Gates:' this too is done; Town-guard looking mournfully on. This done, 'March forward swiftly, in two halves,
without beat of drum, — whitherward you know!'

"Those three hundred Austrian Dragoons, we saw them
leave the Dom Island, three days ago; there are at present
only Six Men, of the Bishop's Guard, walking under arms
there, — at the end of the chief bridge, on the Townward side
of their Dom Island. See, Prussian caps and muskets, ye six
men under arms! The six men clutch at their drawbridge,
and hastily set about hoisting:— alas, another Prussian corps,
which has come privately by the eastern (or Country-ward)
Bridge, King himself with it, taps them on the shoulder at
this instant; mildly constrains the six into their guard-house:
the drawbridge falls; 400 Prussian grenadiers take quiet possession of the Dom Island: King may return to the Scultet

Garden, having quickened the lazy hours in this manner. To such of the Canons as he came upon, his Majesty was most polite; they most submiss. The six soldiers of the draw-bridge, having spoken a little loud, — still more a too zealous beef-eater of old Schaffgotsch's found here, who had been very loud, — were put under arrest; but more for form's sake; and were let go, in a day or two."

Nothing could be gentler on Friedrich's part, and on that of his two Colonels, than this delicate operation throughout: — and at 4 P.M., after thirty hours of waiting, it is done, and nobody's skin scratched. Old Syndic Gutzmar, and the Town-Rath, urged by perils and a Town Population who are Protes-tant, have signed the Surrender with good-will, at least with resignation, and a feeling of relief. The Ober-Amt Officials have likewise had to sign; full of all the silent spleen and despondency which is natural to the situation: spleen which, in the case of old Schaffgotsch, weak with age, becomes pas-sionately audible here and there. He will have to give account of that injurious Proclamation, or Queen's "Patent," to this King that has now come.

*King enters Breslau; stays there, gracious and vigilant,
Four Days* (Jan. 2d–6th, 1741).

In the Royal Entrance which took place next day, note these points. Syndic Gutzmar and the Authorities came out, in grand coaches, at 8 in the morning; had to wait awhile; the King, having ridden away to look after his manifold affairs, did not get back till 10. Town Guard and Garrison are all drawn out; Gates all flung open, Prussian sentries withdrawn from them, and from the Excise-houses they had seized: King's Kitchen-and-Proviant Carriages (four mules to each, with bells, with uncommonly rich housings): King's Body-Coach very grand indeed, and grandly escorted, the Thirty Body-guards riding ahead; but nothing in it, only a most superfine cloak "lined wholly with ermine" flung upon the seat. Other Coaches, more or less grandly escorted; Head Cup-bearers, Seneschals, Princes, Margraves: — but where is

the King? King had ridden away, a second time, with chief
Generals, taking survey of the Town Walls, round as far as
the *Ziegel-Thor* (Tile-Gate, extreme southeast, by the river-
edge): he has thus made the whole circuit of Breslau; — un-
wearied in picking up useful knowledge, "though it was very
cold," while that Procession of Coaches went on.

At noon, his Majesty, thrifty of time, did enter: on horseback, Schwerin riding with him; behind him miscellaneous
chief Officers; Borck and Posadowsky among others; some
miscellany of Page-people following. With this natural escort, he rode in; Town-Major (Commandant of Town-guard),
with drawn sword going ahead; — King wore his usual Cocked
Hat, and practical Blue Cloak, both a little dimmed by service:
but his gray horse was admirable; and four scarlet Footmen,
grand as galloon and silver fringe could make them, did the
due magnificence in dress. He was very gracious; saluting
to this side and to that, where he noticed people of condition
in the windows. "Along Schweidnitz Street, across the Great
Ring, down Albrecht Street." He alighted, to lodge, at the
Count-Schlegenberg House; which used to be the Austrian
Cardinal von Sinzendorf Primate of Silesia's hired lodging, —
Sinzendorf's furniture is put gently aside, on this new occasion. King came on the balcony; and stood there for some
minutes, that everybody might see him. The "immense shout-
ings," Dryasdust assures me, have been exaggerated; and I am
warned not to believe the *Kriegs-Fama* such and such a Number, except after comparing it with him. — That day there was
dinner of more than thirty covers, Chief Syndic Gutzmar and
other such guests; but as to the viands, says my friend, these,
owing to the haste, were nothing to speak of.[1]

Dinner, better and better ordered, King more and more gracious, so it continued all the four days of his Majesty's stay:
— on the second day he had to rise suddenly from table, and
leave his guests with an apology; something having gone
awry, at one of the Gates. Awry there, between the Town
Authorities and a General Jeetz of his, — who is on march
across the River at this moment (on what errand we shall

[1] *Helden-Geschichte*, i. 545-548.

hear), and a little mistakes the terms. His Majesty puts
Jeetz right; and even waits, till he sees his Brigade and him
clear across. A junior Schaffgotsch,[1] not the inconsolable
Schaffgotsch senior, but his Nephew, was one of the guests
this second day; an ecclesiastic, but of witty fashionable type,
and I think a very worthless fellow, though of a family important in the Province. Dinner falls about noon; does not
last above two hours or three, so that there is space for a ride
("to the Dom," the first afternoon, "four runners" always),
and for much indoor work, before the supper-hour.

As the Austrian Authorities sat silent in their place, and
gave no explanation of that "Patent," affixed amid thunder
and lightning, — they got orders from his Majesty to go their
ways next day; and went. In behalf of old President von
Schaffgotsch, a chief of the Silesian Nobility, and man much
loved, the Breslau people, and men from every guild and rank
of society, made petition That he should be allowed to continue in his Town House here. Which "first request of
yours" his Majesty, with much grace, is sorry to be obliged
to refuse. The suppressed, and insuppressible, weak indignation of old Schaffgotsch is visible on the occasion; nor, I think,
does Friedrich take it ill; only sends him out of the way with
it, for the time. The Austrian Ober-Amt vanished bodily
from Breslau in this manner; and never returned. Proper
"War-Commission (Feld-Kriegs-Commissariat)," with Münchow, one of those skilful Cüstrin Münchows, at the top of it,
organized itself instead; which, almost of necessity, became
Supreme Government in a City ungoverned otherwise: — and
truly there was little regret of the Ober-Amt, in Breslau; and
ever less, to a marked extent, as the years went on.

On the 5th of January (fourth and last night here), his
Majesty gave a grand Ball. Had hired, or Colonel Posadowsky
instead of him had hired, the Assembly Rooms (Redouten-Saal)
for the purpose: "Invite all the Nobility high and low;" —
expense by estimate is a ducat (half-guinea) each; do it
well, and his Majesty will pay. About 6 in the evening, his
Majesty in person did us the honor to drive over; opened the

[1] Helden-Geschichte, ii. 159.

Ball with Madam the Countess von Schlegenberg (I should guess, a Dowager Lady), in whose house he lodges. I am not aware that his Majesty danced much farther; but he was very condescending, and spoke and smiled up and down;—till, about 10 P.M., an Officer came in with a Letter. Which Letter his Majesty having read, and seemingly asked a question or two in regard to, put silently in his pocket, as if it were a finished thing. Nevertheless, after a few minutes, his Majesty was found to have silently withdrawn; and did not return, not even to supper. Perceiving which, all the Prussian official people gradually withdrew; though the dancing and supping continued not the less, to a late hour.[1]

"Open the Austrian Mail-bag (*Felleisen*); see a little what they are saying over there!" Such order had evidently been given, this night. In consequence of which, people wrote by Dresden, and not the direct way, in future; wishing to avoid that openable *Felleisen*. Next morning, January 6th, his Majesty had left for Ohlau,—early, I suppose; though there proved to be nothing dangerous ahead there, after all.

CHAPTER V.

FRIEDRICH PUSHES FORWARD TOWARDS BRIEG AND NEISSE.

OHLAU is a pleasant little Town, two marches southeast of Breslau; with the Ohlau River on one side, and the Oder on the other; capable of some defence, were there a garrison. Brieg the important Fortress, still on the Oder, is some fifteen miles beyond Ohlau; after which, bending straight south and quitting Oder, Neisse the still more important may be thirty miles:—from Breslau to Neisse, by this route (which is *bow*, not *string*), sixty-five or seventy miles. One of my Topographers yields this Note, if readers care for it:—

---

[1] *Helden-Geschichte*, i. 557.

"Ohlau River, an insignificant drab-colored stream, rises
well south of Breslau, about Strehlen; makes, at first, direct
eastward towards the Oder; and then, when almost close upon
it, breaks off to north, and saunters along, irregularly parallel
to Oder, for twenty miles farther, before it can fall fairly in.
To this circumstance both Breslau and a Town of Ohlau owe
their existence; Towns, both of them, 'between the waters,'
and otherwise well seated; Ohlau sheltering itself in the
attempted outfall of its little river; Breslau clustering itself
about the actual outfall: both very defensible places in the
old rude time, and good for trade in all times. Both Oder
and Ohlau Rivers have split and spread themselves into
islands and deltas a good deal, at their place of meeting; and
even have changed their courses, and cut out new channels for
themselves, in the sandy country; making a very intricate
watery network of a site for Breslau: and indeed the Ohlau
River here, for centuries back, has been compelled into wide
meanderings, mere filling of rampart-ditches, so that it issues
quite obscurely, and in an artificial engineered condition, at
Breslau."

Ohlau had been expected to make some defence; General
Browne having thrown 300 men into it, and done what he
could for the works. And Ohlau did at first threaten to make
some; but thought better of it overnight, and in effect made
none; but was got (morning of January 9th) on the common
terms, by merely marching up to it in minatory posture.
"Prisoners of War, if you make resistance; Free Withdrawal
[Liberty to march away, arms shouldered, and not serve against
us for a year], if you have made none:" this is the common
course, where there are Austrian Soldiers at all; the course where
none are, and only a few Syndics sit, with their Town-Key laid
on the table, a prey to the stronger hand, we have already seen.

From Ohlau, proper Detachment, under General Kleist,
is pushed forward to summon Brieg; Jeetz from the other
side of the river (whom we saw crossing at Breslau the
other day, interrupting his Majesty's dinner) is to co-operate
with Kleist in that enterprise, — were the Country once cleared
on his, Jeetz's, east side of Oder; especially were Namslau

once had, a small Town and Castle over there, which commands the Polish and Hungarian road. Friedrich's hopes are buoyant; Schwerin is swiftly rolling forward to rightward, nothing resisting him; Detachment is gone from Schwerin, over the Hills, to Glatz (the *Grafschaft*, or County Glatz, an Appendage to Schlesien), under excellent guidance; under guidance, namely, of Colonel Camas, who has just come home from his Parisian Embassy, and got launched among the wintry mountains, on a new operation, — which, however, proves of non-effect for the present.[1]

Indeed, it is observable that southward of Breslau, the dispute, what dispute there can be, properly begins; and that General Browne is there, and shows himself a shining man in this difficult position. It must be owned, no General could have made his small means go farther. Effective garrisons, 1,600 each, put into Brieg and Neisse; works repaired, magazines collected, there and elsewhere; the rest of his poor 7,000 thriftily sprinkled about, in what good posts there are, and "capable of being got together in six hours:" a superior soldier, this Browne, though with a very bad task; and seems to have inspired everybody with something of his own temper. So that there is marching, detaching, miscellaneous difficulty for Friedrich in this quarter, more than had been expected. If the fate of Brieg and Neisse be inevitable, Browne does wonders to delay it.

Of the Prussian marches in these parts, recorded by intricate Dryasdust, there was no point so notable to me as this unrecorded one: the Stone Pillar which, I see, the Kleist Detachment was sure to find, just now, on the march from Ohlau to Brieg; last portion of that march, between the village of Briesen and Brieg. The Oder, flowing on your left hand, is hereabouts agreeably clothed with woods: the country, originally a swamp, has been drained, and given to the plough, in an agreeable manner; and there is an excellent road paved with solid whinstone, — quarried in Strehlen,

---

[1] *Helden-Geschichte*, i. 678; Orlich, *Geschichte der beiden Schlesischen Kriege*, i. 49.

twenty miles away, among the Hills to the right yonder, as you may guess; — road very visible to the Prussian soldier, though he does not ask where quarried. These beautiful improvements, beautiful humanities, — were done by whom? "Done in 1584," say the records, by "George the Pious;" Duke of Liegnitz, Brieg and Wohlau; 156 years ago. "Pious" his contemporaries called this George; — he was son of the *Erbverbrüderung* Duke, who is so important to us; he was grandfather's grandfather of the last Duke of all; after whom it was we that should have got these fine Territories; they should all have fallen to the Great Elector, had not the Austrian strong hand provided otherwise. George did these plantations, recoveries to the plough; made this perennial whinstone road across the swamps; upon which, notable to the roughest Prussian (being "twelve feet high by eight feet square"), rises a Hewn Mass with this Inscription on it, — not of the name or date of George; but of a thought of his, which is not without a pious beauty to me: —

> *Straverunt alii nobis, nos Posteritati;*
> *Omnibus at Christus stravit ad astra viam.*

> Others have made roads for us; we make them for still others: Christ made a road to the stars for us all.[1]

I know not how many Brandenburgers of General Kleist's Detachment, or whether any, read this Stone; but they do all rustle past it there, claiming the Heritage of this Pious George; and their mute dim interview with him, in this manner, is a thing slightly more memorable than orders of the day, at this date.

It was on the 11th, two days after Ohlau, that General Kleist summoned Brieg; and Brieg answered resolutely, No. There is a garrison of 1,600 here, and a proper magazine: nothing for it but to "mask" Brieg too; Kleist on this side the River, Jeetz on that, — had Jeetz once done with Namslau, which he has not by any means. Namslau's answer was likewise stiffly in the negative; and Jeetz cannot do Namslau, at least not the Castle, all at once; having no siege-cannon.

---

[1] Zöllner, *Briefe über Schlesien*, i. 175; Hübner, i. t. 101.

Seeing such stiffness everywhere, Friedrich writes to Glogau, to the Young Dessauer, " Siege-artillery hither ! Swift, by the Oder; you don't need it where you are !" and wishes it were arrived, for behoof of Neisse and these stiff humors.

Friedrich comes across to Ottmachau; sits there, in survey of Neisse, till his Cannon come.

The Prussians met with serious resistance, for the first time (9th January, same day when Ohlau yielded), at a place called Ottmachau ; a considerable little Town and Castle on the Neisse River, not far west of Neisse Town, almost at the very south of Silesia. It lay on the route of Schwerin's Column ; long distances ahead of Liegnitz, — say, by straight highway a hundred miles ; — during which, to right and to left, there had been nothing but submission hitherto. No resistance was expected here either, for there was not hope in any ; only that Browne had been here ; industrious to create delay till Neisse were got fully ready. He is, by every means, girding up the loins of Neisse for a tight defence ; has put 1,600 men into it, with proper stores for them, with a resolute skilful Captain at the top of them : assiduous Browne had been at Ottmachau, as the outpost of Neisse, a day or two before ; and, they say, had admonished them " Not to yield on any terms, for he would certainly come to their relief." Which doubtless he would have done, had it been in his power ; but how, except by miracle, could it be ? On the 9th of January, when Schwerin comes up, Browne is again waiting hereabouts. Again in defensive posture, but without force to undertake anything ; stands on the Southern Uplands, with Böhmen and Mähren and the Giant Mountains at his back ; — stands, so to speak, defensive at his own House-door, in this manner ; and will have, after *seeing* Ottmachau's fate and Neisse's, to duck in with a slam ! At any rate, he had left these Towns in the above firm humor, screwed to the sticking-place ; and had then galloped else-whither to screw and prepare.

And so the Ottmachau Austrians, " 260 picked grenadiers " (400 dragoons there also at first were, who, after flourishing

about on the outskirts as if for fighting, rode away), fire
"*desperat*," says my intricate friend;[1] entirely refusing terms
from Schwerin; kill twelve of his people (Major de Rège, distinguished Engineer Major, one of them): so that Schwerin
has to bring petards upon them, four cannon upon them; and
burst in their Town Gate, almost their Castle Gate, and pretty
much their Castle itself; — wasting three days of his time
upon this paltry matter. Upon which they do signify a will-
ingness for "Free Withdrawal." "No, *ihr Herren*," answers
Schwerin; "not now; after such mad explosion. His Majesty
will have to settle it." Majesty, who is by this time not far
off, comes over to Ottmachau (January 12th); gives words of
rebuke, rebuke not very inexorable; and admits them Prisoners of War. "The officers were sent to Cüstrin, common men
to Berlin;" the usual arrangement in such case. Ottmachau
Town belongs to the Right Reverend von Sinzendorf, Bishop
of Breslau, and Primate; whose especial Palace is in Neisse;
though he "commonly sends his refractory Priests to do their
penance in the Schloss at Ottmachau here," — and, I should
say, had better himself make terms, and come out hitherward,
under present aspects.

Friedrich continues at Ottmachau; head-quarters there
thenceforth, till he see Neisse settled. On the morrow, 13th,
he learns that the Siege Artillery is at Grotkau; well forward
towards Neisse; half-way between Brieg and it. Same day,
Colonel Camas returns to him out of Glatz; five of his men
lost; and reports That Browne has had the roads torn up
that Glatz is mere ice and obstruction, and that nothing can
be made of it at this season. Good news alternating with not
so good.

The truth is, Friedrich has got no Strong Place in Schlesien;
all strengths make unexpected defence; paltry little Namslau
itself cannot be quite taken, Castle cannot, till Jeetz gets his
siege-artillery, — which does not come along so fast as that to
Neisse does. Here is an Excerpt from my Dryasdust, exact
though abridged, concerning Jeetz : —

---

[1] *Helden-Geschichte*, i. 672–677; Orlich, i. 50.

"*January 24th*, 1741. Prussians, masters of the Town for a couple of weeks back, have got into the Church at Namslau, into the Cloister; are preparing plank floors for batteries, cutting loop-holes; diligent as possible, — siege-guns now at last just coming. The Castle fires fiercely on them, makes furious sallies, steals six of our oxen, — makes insolent gestures from the walls; at least one soldier does, this day. 'Sir, may I give that fellow a shot?' asks the Prussian sentry. 'Do, then,' answers his Major: 'too insolent that one!' And the sentry explodes on him; brings him plunging down, head foremost (*herunter pürzelte*); the too insolent mortal, silent enough thenceforth." [1] — Jeetz did get his cannon, though not till now, this very day I think; and then, in a couple of days more, Jeetz finished off Namslau ("officers to Cüstrin, common men to Berlin"); and thereupon blockades the Eastern side of Brieg, joining hands with Kleist on the Western: whereby Brieg, like Glogau, is completely masked, — till the season mend.

Friedrich, now that his artillery is come, expects no difficulty with Neisse. A "paltry hamlet (*bicoque*)" he playfully calls it; and, except this, Silesia is now his. Neisse got (which would be the desirable thing), or put under "mask" as Glogau is, and as Brieg is being, Austria possesses not an inch of land within these borders. Here are some Epistolary snatches; still in the light style, not to say the flimsy and uplifted; but worth giving, so transparent are they; off-hand, like words we had heard his Majesty *speak*, in his high mood: —

King to M. Jordan, at Berlin (two successive Letters).

1°. "*Ottmachau, 14th January*, 1741 [second day after our arrival there]. My dear Monsieur Jordan, my sweet Monsieur Jordan, my quiet Monsieur Jordan, my good, my benign, my pacific, my humanest Monsieur Jordan, — I announce to Thy Serenity the conquest of Silesia; I warn thee of the bombardment of Neisse [just getting ready], and I prepare thee for still more important projects; and instruct thee of the happiest successes that the womb of Fortune ever bore.

[1] *Helden-Geschichte*, i. 703.

" This ought to suffice thee. Be my Cicero as to the justice of my cause, and I will be thy Cæsar as to the execution. Adieu: thou knowest whether I am not, with the most cordial regard, thy faithful friend. — F."

2°. " *Ottmachau*, 17*th January*, 1741. I have the honor to inform your Humanity that we are christianly preparing to bombard Neisse; and that if the place will not surrender of good-will, needs must that it be beaten to powder (*nécessité sera de l'abîmer*). For the rest, our affairs go the best in the world; and soon thou wilt hear nothing more of us. For in ten days it will all be over; and I shall have the pleasure of seeing you and hearing you, in about a fortnight.

" I have seen neither my Brother [August Wilhelm, not long ago at Strasburg with us, and betrothed since then] nor Keyserling: I left them at Breslau, not to expose them to the dangers of war. They perhaps will be a little angry; but what can I do? — The rather as, on this occasion, one cannot share in the glory, unless one is a mortar!

" Adieu, M. le Conseiller [Poor's-*Rath*, so styled]. Go and amuse yourself with Horace, study Pausanias, and be gay over Anacreon. As to me, who for amusement have nothing but merlons, fascines and gabions,[1] I pray God to grant me soon a pleasanter and peacefuler occupation, and you health, satisfaction and whatever your heart desires. — F." [2]

King Friedrich to M. le Comte Algarotti (gone on a journey).

" *Ottmachau*, 17*th January*, 1741 [same day as the above to Jordan]. I have begun to settle the Figure of Prussia: the outline will not be altogether regular; for the whole of Silesia is taken, except one miserable hamlet (*bicoque*), which perhaps I shall have to keep blockaded till next spring.

" Up to this time, the whole conquest has cost only Twenty

---

[1] Merlons are mounds of earth placed behind the solid or blind parts of the parapet (that is, between the embrasures) of a Fortification; fascines are bundles of brushwood for filling up a ditch; gabions, baskets filled with earth, to be ranged in defence till you get trenches dug.

[2] *Œuvres de Frédéric*, xvii. 84.

Men, and Two Officers, one of whom is the poor De Rège,
whom you have seen at Berlin," — De Rège, Engineer Major,
killed here at Ottmachau, in Schwerin's late tussle.

" You are greatly wanting to me here. So soon as you have
talked that business over, write to me about it. [What is the
business ? Whither is the dusky Swan of Padua gone ?] In
all these three hundred miles I have found no human creature
comparable to the Swan of Padua. I would willingly give ten
cubic leagues of ground for a genius similar to yours. But I
perceive I was about entreating you to return fast, and join
me again, — while you are not yet arrived where your errand
was. Make haste to arrive, then ; to execute your commission,
and fly back to me. I wish you had a Fortunatus Hat ; it is
the only thing defective in your outfit.

" Adieu, dear Swan of Padua : think, I pray you, sometimes
of those who are getting themselves cut in slices [*échiner*,
chined] for the sake of glory here, and above all do not forget
your friends who think a thousand times of you.

" FÉDÉRIC." [1]

The object of the dear Swan's journey, or even the where-
abouts of it, cannot be discovered without difficulty ; and is not
much worth discovering. " Gone to Turin," we at last make
out, " with secret commissions : " [2] desirable to sound the Sardinian Majesty a little, who is Doorkeeper of the Alps, between
France and Austria, and opens to the best bidder ? No great
things of a meaning in this mission, we can guess, or Algarotti
had not gone upon it, — though he is handy, at least, for keeping it unnoticed by the Gazetteer species. Nor was the Swan
successful, it would seem ; the more the pity for our Swan !
However, he comes back safe ; attends Friedrich in Silesia ;
and in the course of next month readers will see him, if any
reader wished it.

[1] *Œuvres de Frédéric*, xviii. 28.
[2] Denina, *La Prusse Littéraire* (Berlin, 1790), i. 198. A poor vague Book;
only worth consulting in case of extremity.

CHAPTER VI.

NEISSE IS BOMBARDED.

NEISSE, which Friedrich calls a paltry hamlet (*bicoque*) is a pleasant strongly fortified Town, then of perhaps 6 or 8,000 inhabitants, now of double that number; stands on the right or south bank of the Neisse, — at this day, on both banks. Pleasant broad streets, high strong houses, mostly of stone. Pleasantly encircled by green Hills, northward buttresses of the Giant Mountains; itself standing low and level, on rich ground much inclined to be swampy. A lesser river, Biele, or Bielau, coming from the South, flows leisurely enough into the Neisse, — filling all the Fortress ditches, by the road. Orchard-growth and meadow-growth are lordly (*herrlich*); a land rich in fruit, and flowing with milk and honey. Much given to weaving, brewing, stocking-making; and, moreover, trades greatly in these articles, and above all in Wine. Yearly on St. Agnes Day, "21st January, if not a Sunday," there is a Wine-fair here; Hungarian, of every quality from Tokay down-ward, is gathered here for distribution into Germany and all the Western Countries. While you drink your Tokay, know that it comes through Neisse. St. Agnes Day falls but unhandily this year; and I think the Fair will, as they say, *ausbleiben*, or not be held.

Neisse is a Nest of Priests (*Pfaffen-Nest*), says Friedrich once; which came in this way. About 600 years ago, an ill-conditioned Heir-Apparent of the Liegnitz Sovereign to whom it then belonged, quarrelled with his Father, quarrelled slightly with the Universe; and, after moping about for some time, went into the Church. Having Neisse for an apanage already his own, he gave it to the Bishop of Breslau; whose, in spite of the old Father's protestings, it continued, and continues.

Bishops of Breslau are made very grand by it; Bishops of Breslau have had their own difficulties here. Thus once (in our
Perkin-Warbeck time, A.D. 1497), a Duke of Oppeln, sitting in
some Official Conclave or meeting of magnates here, — zealous
for country privilege, and feeling himself insufferably put upon,
— started up, openly defiant of Official men; glaring wrath-
fully into Duke Casimir of Teschen (Bohemian-Austrian Captain of Silesia), and into the Bishop of Breslau himself; nay
at last, flashed out his sword upon those sublime dignitaries.
For which, by and by, he had to lay his head on the block, in
the great square here; and died penitent, we hope.

The place, my Dryasdust informs me, had many accidents
by floodage and by fire; was seized and re-seized in the Thirty-
Years War especially, at a great rate: Saxon Arnheim, Austrian Holk, Swedish Torstenson; no end to the battering and
burning poor Neisse had, to the big ransoms "in new Reichs-
thalers and 300 casks of wine." But it always rebuilt itself,
and began business again. How happy when it could get
under some effectual Protector, of the Liegnitz line, of the
Austrian-Bohemian line, and this or the other battering, just
suffered, was to be the last for some time! — Here again is
a battering coming on it; the first of a series that are now
imminent.

The reader is requested to look at Neisse; for besides the
Tokay wine, there will things arrive there. — Neisse River, let
us again mention, is one of four bearing that name, and all
belonging to the Oder: — could not they be labelled, then, or
numbered, in some way? This Neisse, which we could call
Neisse the *First* (and which careful readers may as well make
acquaintance with on their Map, where too they will find
Neisse the *Second*, "the *Wüthende* or Roaring Neisse," and
two others which concern us less), rises in the "Western
Snow-Mountains (*Schneegebirge*)," Southwestern or Glatz district of the Giant Mountains; drains Glatz County and grows
big there; washes the Town of Glatz; then eastward by
Ottmachau, by Neisse Town; whence turning rather abruptly
north or northeast, it gets into the Oder not far south of
Brieg.

Neisse as a Place of Arms, the chief Fortress of Silesia and
the nearest to Austria, is extremely desirable for Friedrich;
but there is no hope of it without some kind of Siege; and
Friedrich determines to try in that way. From Ottmachau,
accordingly, and from the other sides, the Siege-Artillery being
now at hand, due force gathers itself round Neisse, Schwerin
taking charge; and for above a week there is demonstrating
and posting, summoning and parleying; and then, for three
days, with pauses intervening, there is extremely furious bombardment, red-hot at times: " Will you yield, then ? " — with
steady negative from Neisse. Friedrich's quarter is at Ottmachau, twelve miles off; from which he can ride over, to see
and superintend. The fury of his bombardment, which naturally grieved him, testifies the intensity of his wish. But it
was to no purpose. The Commandant, Colonel von Roth (the
same who was proposed for Breslau lately, a wise head and a
stout, famed in defences) had " poured water on his ramparts,"
after well repairing them, — made his ramparts all ice and
glass; — and done much else. Would the reader care to look
for a moment ? Here, from our waste Paper-masses, is abundance, requiring only to be abridged : —

"*January*, 1741: *Monday, 9th–Wednesday, 11th.* Monday,
9th, day when that sputter at Ottmachau began, — Prussian
light-troops appeared transiently on the heights about Neisse,
for the first time. Directly on sight of whom, Commandant
Roth assembled the Burghers of the place; took a new Oath
of Fidelity from one and all; admonished them to do their utmost, as they should see him do. The able-bodied and likeliest
of them (say about 400) he has had arranged into Militia
Companies, with what drill there could be in the interim;
and since his coming, has employed every moment in making
ready. Wednesday, 11th, he locks all the Gates, and stands
strictly on his guard. The inhabitants are mostly Catholic;
with sumptuous Bishops of Breslau, with *Kreuzherren* (imaginary Teutsch or other Ritters with some reality of money), with
Jesuit Dignitaries, Church and Quasi-Church Officialities, resident among them : population, high and low, is inclined by
creed to the Queen of Hungary. Commandant Roth has only

1,200 regular soldiers; at the outside 1,600 men under arms :
but he has gunpowder, he has meal ; experience also and
courage ; and hopes these may suffice him for a time. One
of the most determined Commandants ; expert in the defence of strong places. A born Silesian (not Saxon, as some
think), — and is of the Augsburg Confession ; but that circumstance is not important here, though at Breslau Browne
thought it was.

" *Thursday*, 12*th*. The Prussians, in regular force, appear
on the Kaninchen Berg (Cony Hill, so called from its rabbits),
south of the River, evidently taking post there. Roth fires a
signal shot ; the Southern Suburbs of Neisse, as preappointed,
go up in flame ; crackle high and far ; in a lamentable manner
(*erbärmlich*), through the grim winter air." This is the day
Friedrich came over to Ottmachau, and settled the sputter
there.

" Next day, and next again, the same phenomena at Neisse ;
the Prussians edging ever nearer, building their batteries, preparing to open their cannonade. Whereupon Roth burns the
remaining Suburbs, with lamentable crackle ; on all sides now
are mere ashes. Bishop's Mill, Franciscan Cloister, Bishop's
Pleasure-garden, with its summer-houses ; Bishop's Hospital,
and several Churches : Roth can spare none of these things,
with the Prussians nestling there. Surely the Bishop himself,
respectable Cardinal Graf von Sinzendorf, had better get out
of these localities while time yet is ? "   " Saturday, 14th,"
that was the day Friedrich, at Ottmachau, wrote as above to
Jordan (Letter No. 1), while the Neisse Suburbs crackled
lamentably, twelve miles off, " Schwerin gets order to break
up, in person, from Ottmachau to-morrow, and begin actual
business on the Kaninchen Hill yonder.

" *Sunday*, 15*th*. Schwerin does ; marches across the River ;
takes post on the south side of Neisse : notable to the Sunday rustics. Nothing but burnt villages and black walls for
Schwerin, in that Cony-Hill quarter, and all round ; and Roth
salutes him with one twenty-four pounder, which did no hurt.
And so the cannonade begins, Sunday, 15th ; and intermittently, on both sides of the River, continues, always bursting

out again at intervals, till Wednesday; a mere preliminary cannonade on Schwerin's part; making noise, doing little hurt: intended more to terrify, but without effect that way on Roth or the Townsfolk. The poor Bishop did, on the second day of it, come out, and make application to Schwerin; was kindly conducted to his Majesty, who happened to be over there; was kept to dinner; and easily had leave to retire to Freywalde, a Country-House he has, in the safe distance.[1] There let him be quiet, well out of these confused batterings and burnings of property.

"His Majesty's Head-quarter is at Ottmachau, but in two hours he can be here any day; and looks into everything; sorry that the cannonade does not yet answer. And remnants of suburbs are still crackling into flame; high Country-Houses of Kreuzherren, of Jesuits; a fanatic people seemingly all set against us. 'If Neisse will not yield of good-will, needs is it must be beaten to powder,' wrote his Majesty to Jordan in these circumstances, as we read above. Roth is sorry to observe, the Prussians have still one good Bishop's-mansion, in a place called the Karlau (Karl-Meadow), with the Bishop's winter fuel all ready stacked there; but strives to take order about the same.

"*Wednesday,* 18*th.* This day two provocations happened. First, in the morning by his Majesty's order, Colonel Borck (the same we saw at Herstal) had gone with a Trumpeter towards Roth; intending to inform Roth how mild the terms would be, how terrible the penalty of not accepting them. But Roth or Roth's people singularly disregard Borck and his Parley Trumpet; answer its blasts by musketry; fire upon it, nay again fire worse when it advances a step farther; on these terms Borck and Trumpet had to return. Which much angered his Majesty at Ottmachau that evening; as was natural. Same evening, our fine quarters in the Karlau crackled up in flame, the Bishop's winter firewood all along with it: this was provocation second. Roth had taken order with the Karlau; and got a resolute Butcher to do the feat, under pretext of bringing us beef. It is piercing cold; only blackened walls for us

---

[1] *Helden-Geschichte,* i. 683.

now in the Karlau or elsewhere. His Majesty, naturally much
angered, orders for the morrow a dose of bomb-shells and red-
hot balls. Plant a few mortars on the North side too, orders
his Majesty.

"*Thursday*, 19*th*. Accordingly, by 8 of the clock, cannon
batteries reawaken with a mighty noise, and red-hot balls are
noticeable; and at 10 the actual bombarding bursts out, terrible
to hear and see; — first shell falling in Haubitz the Clothier's
shop, but being happily got under. Roth has his City Militia
companies, organized with water-hose for quenching of the
red-hot balls : in which they became expert. So that though
the fire caught many houses, they always put it out. Late in
the night, hearing no word from Roth, the Prussians went to
bed.

"*Friday*, 20*th*. Still no word; on which, about 4 P.M., the
Prussian batteries awaken again : volcanic torrent of red-hot
shot and shells, for seven hours; still no word from Roth.
About 11 at night his Majesty again sends a Drum (Parley
Trumpet or whatever it is) to the Gate; formally summons
Roth; asks him, 'If he has well considered what this can lead
to? Especially what he, Roth, meant by firing on our first
Trumpet on Wednesday last?' Roth answered, 'That as to
the Trumpet, he had not heard of it before. On the other hand,
that this mode of sieging by red-hot balls seems a little unusual; for the rest, that he has himself no order or intention
but that of resisting to the last.' Some say the Drum hereupon
by order talked of 'pounding Neisse into powder, mere child's-
play hitherto;' to which Roth answered only by respectful
dumb-show.

"*Saturday*, 21*st*–*Monday*, 23*d*. Midnight of Friday–Saturday, on this answer coming, the fire-volcanoes open again;
— nine hours long; shells, and red-hot material, in terrible
abundance. Which hit mostly the churches, Jesuits' Semi-
nariums and Collegiums; but produced no change in Roth.
From 9 A.M. the batteries are silent. Silent still, next morning : Divine Service may proceed, if it like. But at 4 of the
afternoon, the batteries awaken worse than ever; from seven
to nine bombs going at once. Universal rage, of noise and

horrid glare, making night hideous, till 10 of the clock; Roth continuing inflexible. This is the last night of the Siege."

Friedrich perceived that Roth would not yield; that the utter smashing-down of Neisse might more concern Friedrich than Roth; — that, in fine, it would be better to desist till the weather altered. Next day, "Monday, 23d, between noon and 1 o'clock," the Prussians drew back; — converted the siege into a blockade. Neisse to be masked, like Brieg and Glogau (Brieg only half done yet, Jeetz without cannon till to-morrow, 24th, and little Namslau still gesticulating): "The only thing one could try upon it was bombardment. A Nest of Priests (*Pfaffen-Nest*); not many troops in it: but it cannot well be forced at present. If spring were here, it will cost a fortnight's work." [1]

A noisy business; "King's high person much exposed: a bombardier and then a sergeant were killed close by him, though in all he lost only five men." [2]

Browne vanishes in a slight Flash of Fire.

Browne all this while has hung on the Mountain-side, witnessing these things; sending stores towards Glatz southwestward, and "ruining the ways" behind them; waiting what would become of Neisse. Neisse done, Schwerin is upon him; Browne makes off Southeastward, across the Mountains, for Moravia and home; Schwerin following hard. At a little place called Grätz,[3] on the Moravian border, Browne faced round, tried to defend the Bridge of the Oppa, sharply though without effect; and there came (January 25th) a hot sputter

---

[1] *Friedrich to the Old Dessauer:* Fraction of Letter (Ottmachau, 16th–21st January, 1741) cited by Orlich, i. 51; — from the Dessau Archives, where Herr Orlich has industriously been. To all but strictly military people these pieces of Letters are the valuable feature of Orlich's Book; and a general reader laments that it does not all consist of such, properly elucidated and labelled into accessibility.

[2] *Helden-Geschichte*, i. 680–690.

[3] The name, in old Slavic speech, signifies *Town;* and there are many *Grätzes: Königin*grätz (*Queen's*, which for brevity is now generally called *Königs*grätz, in Bohemia); Grätz in Styria; *Windisch*grätz (Wendish-town); &c.

between them for a few minutes : — after which Browne vanished into the interior, and we hear, in these parts, comparatively little more of him during this War. Friend and foe
must admit that he has neglected nothing; and fairly made
the best of a bad business here. He is but an interim General, too; his Successor just coming; and the Vienna Board of
War is frequently troublesome, — to whose windy speculations
Browne replies with sagacious scepticism, and here and there
a touch of veiled sarcasm, which was not likely to conciliate
in high places. Had her Hungarian Majesty been able to
retain Browne in his post, instead of poor Neipperg who was
sent instead, there might have been a considerably different
account to give of the sequel. But Neipperg was Tutor (War-
Tutor) to the Grand-Duke; Browne is still of young standing
(age only thirty-five), with a touch of veiled sarcasm ; and
things must go their course.

In Schlesien, Schwerin is now to command in chief; the
King going off to Berlin for a little, naturally with plenty of
errand there. The Prussian Troops go into Winter-quarters;
spread themselves wide ; beset the good points, especially
the Passes of the Hills, — from Jägerndorf, eastward to the
Jablunka leading towards Hungary ; — nay they can, and before
long do, spread into the Moravian Territories, on the other side ;
and levy contributions, the Queen proving unreasonable.

It was Monday, 23d, when the Siege of Neisse was aban-
doned : on Wednesday, Friedrich himself turns homeward ;
looks into Schweidnitz, looks into Liegnitz; and arrives at
Berlin as the week ends, — much acclamation greeting him
from the multitude. Except those three masked Fortresses,
capable of no defence to speak of, were Winter over, Silesia
is now all Friedrich's, — has fallen wholly to him in the space
of about Seven Weeks. The seizure has been easy; but the
retaining of it, perhaps he himself begins to see more clearly,
will have difficulties ! From this point, the talk about *gloire*
nearly ceases in his Correspondence. In those seven weeks he
has, with *gloire* or otherwise, cut out for himself such a life of
labor as no man of his Century had.